A Poet's Craft

BOOKS BY ANNIE FINCH

Poetry

The Encyclopedia of Scotland
Eve
Calendars
Among the Goddesses
Spells

Prose

The Ghost of Meter
The Body of Poetry
A Poet's Craft/A Poet's Ear

Translation

The Complete Poetry of Louise Labé

Editor

Villanelles (with Marie-Elizabeth Mali)
Multiformalisms (with Susan M. Schultz)
Lofty Dogmas: Poets on Poetics (with Deborah Brown and Maxine Kumin)
Carolyn Kizer: Perspectives (with Johanna Keller and Candace McClelland)
An Exaltation of Forms (with Kathrine Varnes)
After New Formalism
A Formal Feeling Comes: Poems in Form by Contemporary Women

A Poet's Craft

A COMPREHENSIVE GUIDE TO MAKING AND SHARING YOUR POETRY

Annie Finch

THE UNIVERSITY OF MICHIGAN PRESS

ANN ARBOR

Published in the United States of America by
The University of Michigan Press
Manufactured in the United States of America
♾ Printed on acid-free paper

2016 2015 2014 2013 5 4 3 2

A CIP catalog record for this book is available from the British Library.

Library of Congress Cataloging-in-Publication Data

Finch, Annie, 1956–
A poet's craft : a comprehensive guide to making and sharing your poetry / Annie Finch.
p. cm.
ISBN 978-0-472-11693-5 (cloth : acid-free paper) — ISBN 978-0-472-03364-5 (pbk. : acid-free paper)
1. Poetry—Authorship. I. Title.
PN1059.A9F56 2011
808.1—dc23 2011020876

Poetry must be as new as foam, and as old as the rock.

—EMERSON

Preface: Using *A Poet's Craft*

This book distills into a few hundred pages a lifetime of hearing, memorizing, reciting, reading, imagining, conceiving, scribbling, dictating, dreaming in, writing, typing, word-processing, revising, proofreading, publishing, perusing, discussing, parsing, analyzing, criticizing, scanning, editing, teaching, reviewing, translating, and loving poetry. I credit its insights to being raised in a family with a love for poetry generations deep on both sides, to a fine education focused on poetry from high school through the PhD, and to writing poetry for almost fifty years and teaching it for over twenty—but also to the good fortune of knowing and learning from a wonderful variety of other poets and lovers of poetry across the country and abroad. In gratitude and tribute to this rich and eclectic tapestry of poetics, I hope to pass on some of what I have learned, in a book that aims to be at once stimulatingly idiosyncratic and usefully comprehensive.

What's Different about This Book?

As a general guide to writing poetry that also includes a discussion of writing in form so thorough that it would otherwise be available only in a separate book, *A Poet's Craft* aims to combine the best of all other poetry-writing guides in one volume. Like poetry textbooks, it includes poetry-writing exercises, discusses classic and contemporary poems as examples, and provides a complete overview of the elements of poetry. Like creative writing guides, it aims for a lively and mature tone suitable for independent and adult students as well as undergraduates and graduates, and includes such sections as journaling and inspiration, revision, publishing, and how to put together a book. However, *A Poet's Craft* also offers a thorough and detailed discussion of what is commonly acknowledged to be the most difficult aspect of poetry to teach and learn—writing in meter and form—and, more than most existing form guides, takes a stimulating and culturally inclusive view of formal poetics, from sonnets and sapphics, epics and dactyls to rap, blues, pantoums, and avant-garde procedural techniques (for those interested only in building their knowledge of poetic form, this section of the book is also published separately, under the title *A Poet's Ear*).

A Poet's Craft can be used as the basis for an intermediate or advanced poetry-writing workshop, either undergraduate or graduate; a beginning undergraduate poetry workshop or a workshop with a focus predominantly on free verse; a "form" class; or an introduction-to-poetry class for literature students. Any of these approaches could also be used by independent readers and poets in workshops outside the academy.

Poems Included and Companion Texts

The poems included in this book represent a great range of aesthetics and origins—from classic to contemporary, traditional to experimental—and many backgrounds and cultures. They reflect my own eclectic choices and discoveries over decades of reading and teaching a wide spectrum of poetry. However, the comprehensive nature of this book makes it impossible to include all the poems I hope readers will use to accompany it; ideally, readers will also have at hand a standard anthology of poetry such as *The Norton Anthology of Poetry.*

While numerous classic poems and poets of all centuries are represented here, from "O Western Wind" to Shakespeare to Herbert to Marvell to Keats to Dickinson to Whitman to Browning to Yeats to Hughes to Frost to Bishop to Walcott, when in doubt, I have somewhat favored eclectic poems that readers would be unlikely to stumble over on their own. My reasoning has been that it is most useful to provide fresh poems with a greater aesthetic and cultural range to complement the familiar chestnuts readers can find in a standard poetry anthology or download from the Web. Still, *A Poet's Craft* is a self-contained text, in which I have tried to strike a balance that at once honors and delights in the canon and shares my excitement over my own poetic discoveries. It is my hope that this book, the product of so many years' work, will prove useful to readers looking for thorough, serious, and enjoyable guidance through the mysteries of the art that has guided and inspired my own life.

Structure, Organization, and a Note on Free Verse

I would like to assure those teachers who teach primarily free verse that, although this book does include more comprehensive information on poetic form than will be found in most formal poetry guides, the chapters on inspiration, reading, diction, etymology, metaphor, imagery, poetic modes, stanzas, revision, and performing your work, and of course the chapter on free verse itself, are germane to a workshop focused entirely on free verse.

However, I would also encourage such teachers to consider making use of this book's resources on form. In many years of teaching, I have consistently found that, while students with a knack for writing and a strong imagination can come up with good free verse and experimental poems with little help, most contemporary students need a few weeks of guidance and moral support to learn the skill of writing in form. Though writing in meter can be taught in a few weeks, it is rare for contemporary students to pick it up on their own. This book provides everything necessary to teach the skill of meter in chapters 11–14, and a teacher who commits to teaching it will be giving students a gift they may never have the chance to receive again.

Acknowledgments

With love and thanks to all my teachers, especially my mother Margaret Rockwell Finch—my first and best teacher of poetry—and to all my students, especially those in the Stonecoast MFA program, with whom I have learned so much.

For thoughts on the manuscripts of *A Poet's Craft* and *A Poet's Ear,* for ideas for poems, exercises, and topics, and for various other kinds of knowledge, encouragement, and inspiration, I would like to offer my thanks to Kelli Russell Agodon, Charles Alexander, Michael Alexander, Kazim Ali, Tanya Allen, Amy Alvarez, Cathleen Bailey, Charles Bernstein, Robert Bly, Marie Borroff, Anne Bowman, Glen Brand, Julian Brand, Stephen Burt, Marci Buschner, Tom Cable, Janine Canan, Julie Carr, Caroline Casey, Kathleen Ceveny, Mike Chasar, Fred Courtright, Joel Davis, Josh Davis, Solana D'Lamont, Francesca deGrandis, Leigh DiAngelo, Camille Dungy, Jilly Dybka, Martin Earl, Moira Egan, Jill Essbaum, Patricia Fargnoli, Marta Rijn Finch, Althea Finch-Brand, Ann Fisher-Worth, Gary B. Fitzgerald, Kathleen Flenniken, Ruth Foley, Soyini Ford, Diane Gage, Dana Gioia, David Graham, Vince Gotera, Arielle Greenberg, Cindy Guttierrez, R. S. Gwynn, Marilyn Hacker, Patricia Hagge, Alyssa Harad, Joy Harjo, Charles Hartman, Mary Harwood, Farideh Hasanzadeh, Terrance Hayes, Kate Hibbard, Tanya Higgins, Holly Hinkle, Richard Hoffman, John Hollander, Gray Jacobik, Kathleen Jesme, Judy Jones, Julie Kane, Robin Kemp, Diane Kendig, Penelope Laurans, Andrea Levin, Emily Lloyd, Rosemary Lloyd, Diane Lockward, Julia Manship, Ken Markee, Charles Martin, Bernadette Mayer, Janet McCann, Cynthia MacDonald, Shanna Miller McNair, Mark Melnicove, Diane Middlebrook, Peggy Miller, Christina Mock, Ellen Moody, Indigo Moor, Richard Mullen, Ross Murfin, Rochelle Namaroff, C. J. Sage, Ann Silsbee, Laurel Snyder, Jeff Oaks, D. G. Nanouk Okpik, Alexandra Oliver, Jena Osman, Alicia Ostriker, Kathleen Ossip, Christina Pacosz, Danielle Pafunda, Janet Passehl, Michael Peich, Jessica Piazza, Stanley Plumly, Fran Quinn, Christina Rau, Tad Richards, Adrian Richwell, Elizabeth Robinson, Fred Robinson, Sonia Sanchez, Susan M. Schultz, Ntozake Shange, Don Share, John Shaw, Ron Silliman, Beth Simon, John Oliver Simon, Evie Shockley, Patricia Smith, Tracy K. Smith, Laurel Snyder, Kevin St. Jarre, A. E. Stallings, Sue Standing, Lisa Storie, Chris Strofolino, Cheryl Boyce Taylor, Susan Tichy, John Tranter, Sina Queyras, Colin Ward, Karrie Waarala, Baron Wormser, Ingrid Wendt, Anne Witty, Wynn Yarbrough, and Lady Zen. My grateful appreciation also goes to all the others who are not listed here but should be.

Special thanks to Ruth Gundle of Eighth Mountain Press for her moral support and extensive hands-on editing help in the very earliest stages of this book, which even now includes some of her words and phrases; to Kathleen Clancy, for useful suggestions on the drafts of several chapters; to Daniel Tobin, for going far beyond the call of duty as a manuscript reader; to my talented graduate research assistant Teal Gardella for her invaluable work on the final round of corrections; to Ellen Bauerle and Marcia LaBrenz at the University of Michigan Press for their patience and care; to my supportive family, especially my daughter, Althea, for crucial photocopying; and to my sister, Marta Rijn Finch, who donated her extraordinary poetic and scholarly knowledge and her copyediting skills with such dedication and generosity.

Contents

Introduction: Technology and Inspiration

Poetry combines meaning and magic in a way that no other art can do. Poems offer a balance between the logical, verbal left side of the brain and the musical, spatial right side of the brain. Poetry originated in pre-literate cultures, often as the core of religious ritual and magical incantation. For millennia, the gods spoke in poetry—and some poets still literally "hear" their poems spoken by an internal voice. Yet poetry uses the same words we all use every day. The alchemy of poetry transmutes the intimate chatter of our lives into something deeper and more powerful.

How does poetry do this? And how can those who write poems learn to tap more effectively into this unique power of our art? That's what *A Poet's Craft* is about.

While good poetry uses the devices common to all effective language—meaning, sound, connotation, tone, and more—poets can also transform language in their own special way. Just as a painter makes pattern out of color and shape, a dancer makes pattern out of movement and gesture, and a singer makes pattern out of the tonality of voice, poets uses craft to make pattern out of language. They shape and mold certain physical aspects of language—rhythm, sound, and breath—to render poetic language more powerful than its meanings alone, powerful and palpable in a different way than the most expressive, well-written prose.

By "palpable," I mean that in a good poem, language has a physical presence, an indisputable "here-ness," a three-dimensionality, like a kind of hologram. And after having pondered the cause of this quality for twenty years, I have decided that it is formed by a simple but mysterious process: repetition. The special force at work, when we are writing a poem, is the structuring power of repetition. This is true for any poem, whether a sonnet, a nursery rhyme, a rap poem, a language experiment, or *Paradise Lost.* Repetition, in all its infinite and complex shapes, makes language something more than the sum of its parts. And the repetitions of poetry—meter, rhyme, refrain, the free-verse line break—also communicate with the rhythms of our hearts and breath and the repeating motions of our work, love, and play.

Repetition is one of the oldest and most universal cultural strategies on the planet. Long before writing developed, the tools of poetic repetition were developed in every tribal society. Repetition is useful; it allowed poets to memorize traditional stories and chant. It takes several days for 75-year-old Jussi Huovinen, the last living singer of the Finnish epic *The Kalevala,* to recite from memory the poem that was handed down to him from memory by previous poets. He sings certain repeating phrases as a base, and the whole memorized poem is grounded in a meter based on the hypnotic motion of rowing, preserving for the living the voices of long-dead ancestors.

In every culture, variations on the basic tool of repetition give superhuman power to words that are used to heal, to invoke, to bless, and to remember ancestors and events, as in this poem:

Song for Bringing a Child Into the World

You day-sun, circling around,
You daylight, circling around,
You night-sun, circling around,
You poor body, circling around,
You spotted with gray, circling around,
You wrinkled skin, circling around.

—ANONYMOUS, SEMINOLE (trans. Frances Densmore)

Contemporary poets use the same fundamental tools of repetition that have always made poetry a powerful force in human societies. And they still work to connect us with our deepest minds. This is why, even with all the other media available in the twenty-first century, people continue to turn to poetry—both as writers and readers—in times of personal emotion and meditation, social, religious, and political intensity, and communal celebration. For those willing to make the effort to learn the craft of shaping words in the playful, strengthening, comforting, challenging, inspiring ways of poetry, the rewards are both timeless and timely.

A Poet's Craft takes you step by step through the basic elements of poetry. Each chapter adds to the one before so that by the end of the book, you will have learned the essential skills for making and shaping poems. This is the "grammar" of poetry. But the point is not for you simply to learn a lot of terminology. Related to roots of the word "grammar" is the word "glamour": mystery, sacred magic, power. The "Muse" attends the idea of poetic inspiration as it does no other art. Dancers have no Mount Parnassus to climb, composers no Pegasus to ride. Painters and sculptors have no myth of Helicon, the divine spring whose water brings inspiration. Why does poetry hold such a unique place among the arts in Western tradition? Like the drumbeat of a shaman, poetic repetition not only makes a poem easy to remember; it can lull the logical part of the brain, hypnotize a listener, transport a reader into a new state of mind, speak directly to the physical, irrational part of our brains.

In a famous story told by Robert Frost, he had stopped work after staying up all night to craft a long poem and was standing in a doorway, watching the sun rise, when "Stopping by Woods on a Snowy Evening" came to him suddenly, without any effort. That is the paradox of poetic technology. Far from being something laid on top of pure inspiration, something wholly unrelated, the work of poetic craft, if done in a skilled and attentive way, will bring you full circle back into the realm of inspiration.

The view of poetry now prevalent in our culture tends to ignore the importance of craft, focusing instead on a paradoxical pair of stereotypes: the mundane assumption that "true" poetry is natural, unschooled self-expression, and the mystical sense that "true" poetry is impossible for mere mortals to reach. The word "poetic" is applied so indiscriminately that I've found it used in popular journalism to describe a film sequence, the movements of a dancer, a work of architecture, a sublime landscape, and a delicious dessert. This usage creates a bit of a problem: if "poetry" or "poetic" can apply to just about anything lyrical or graceful or inspired, that implies that just about anything lyrical or graceful or inspired can be poetry, and by the same token, that there is really no way to learn to write poetry except to try to become inspired.

The Romantic belief that poetry is not simply a certain way of writing but no less than, in Shelley's words, "the record of the best and happiest moments of the best minds" can put a lot of pressure on someone who is simply trying to do their best to learn how to write a poem. Some beginning poets are afraid to read poems by anyone else, fearing to damage the purity of their inspiration. Others are hesitant to revise and improve their poems, because they feel that only their first drafts have been sanctified by direct contact with the Muse. Taken to its extreme, the fetishization of poetic inspiration can lead to a romantic machismo of self-destructive behavior, ranging from Rimbaud's "systematic derangement of the senses" to the suicidal madness of Berryman, Crane, and Lowell described in Eileen Simpson's memoir *Poets in Their Youth.*

A Poet's Craft was written to help you steer a way between the two extremes of poetry as mere self-expression and poetry as holy writ, to help demystify some of the unique skills and techniques by which poetry works its glamorous, grammarish magic. This book is for everyone who wants to expand their knowledge of the craft of poetry in order to go deeper into a poem than cleverness or gracefulness or wild and gorgeous language can take you, to become skilled enough in the art of poetry that you can reach the place where writing allows the poet and the poem simply to be. That is the goal of the ancient alchemy of this unique art.

A Poet's Craft is designed to be used by a writer alone or in a writing group or class. Each chapter includes exercises for practice, questions for thought, poems for study, and often quotations for contemplation. I've included the full texts of most of the poems I mention, but where only a title is referred to, I urge you to go to the library or your local bookstore, find it, and consider reading the whole book while you're at it. Poets have always learned best by apprenticing themselves to the poets before them.

The poems included in this book go back to the seventh century BC. All the poems written before 1950, and some of those written after 1950, are dated. Where there's no date, you'll know the poem was first published after 1950.

To help you develop trust in your rhythmical ear, most scansions of poems are located in a key at the back of the book. I suggest you read a line or passage over to yourself several times, either literally aloud or aloud inside your mind, before you check the written scansion.

PART 1

Invoking Poems: Inspirations and Materials

"Poetry is not a luxury."

—AUDRE LORDE

CHAPTER 1

Inspiration: The Wood between the Worlds

> Come, come, whoever you are.
> Wonderer, worshipper, lover of leaving.
> It doesn't matter.
> Ours is not a caravan of despair.
> Come, even if you have broken your vow
> a thousand times
> Come, yet again, come, come.
>
> —JALAL AL-DIN MUHAMMMED RUMI

In the fairy tale *The Magician's Nephew,* one of the *Narnia Chronicles,* C. S. Lewis describes a magic place called "the wood between the worlds," a strangely quiet forest filled with small pools. If you jump into any of the pools, you will enter another world. That powerful wood is like the place where I return continually to focus myself as I am writing a poem.

Each pool holds a different creative tool. Which one is the right one for this particular moment in a poem? The right pool could be focusing on a memory or sensation. It could be meditating on a particular word or rhythm. It could be figuring out the next logical step. It could be playing randomly until something catches. It could be looking for the serendipity of an image, a sound, a meaning, or a feeling in our immediate surroundings. It could be writing out a prose version of the poem first, the way Yeats used to do, and then translating it into poetry. It could be lining up rhymes in advance, the way Shelley used to do, or hanging the poem on a wall with a blank space where something needs filling in, and leaving it there for months or even years, Elizabeth Bishop's habit.

Some poems, the données (from the French for "gift"), appear whole after one freezing jump into a pool and leave us gasping in gratitude. More often, the first pool makes it clear that a poem wants to be written, and provides a phrase, a rhythm, or a guiding feeling. When I was writing an elegy to my father, I kept the tangible emotion of one moment from his deathbed in my mind as a touchstone. I felt it as a physical sensation, hard to pinpoint exactly but very clear when I didn't try too hard to look at it directly. It lasted without fading during the weeks it took me to write the first version of the poem. These core feelings can be elusive and mysterious or as vivid as a smell or a taste. They can involve not just one sense but a confluence of different sensations, as evoked in this poem by Judith Barrington:

"*The Poem*"

It hides in my heart, waiting as if
in the small circle at the middle
of the labyrinth. I walk towards it

but the path turns away by a purple foxglove
and I must follow the windings that will
in the end lead me to the center.

It smells of cedars and honey'd skin,
capuccino with grated chocolate,
the brine of its own body's betrayal.

Like a chestnut horse, it hides in shadow,
one white sock and the moist gleam of an eye
announcing its steady presence.

It has lodged in my heart like a stone in the shoe:
each time the great muscle contracts
I feel it rubbing the same tender spot:

there is no avoiding it—no limping or hopping,
no shaking it to a more comfortable place,
no stillness that can ease the bruise

except the stillness of a motionless heart.
It is the door behind which somebody stands
waiting to kiss and be kissed.

Often it seems that poems come "from the unconscious." And they may. But what should we do with this fact, if it is true? Rilke was famously afraid to be psychoanalyzed because he was afraid he would lose the demons that made him write. But poems are exciting when they feel as if they are tapping into emotions far beyond individual memory, as does Rilke's own poem about his approach to the art:

"I Praise," Rainer Maria Rilke (1905) (trans. Denise Levertov)

O, tell us, poet, what you do?
I praise.
But the deadly and the violent days,
how do you undergo them, take them in?
I praise.
But the namelessness—how do you raise
that, invoke the unnameable?
I praise.
What right have you, through every phase,
in every mask, to remain true?
I praise.
—and that both stillness and the wild affray
know you, like star and storm?
Because I praise.

This poem is a beautiful example of an *ars poetica*, or a poem about what poetry means or does. *Ars poeticae*—to use the correct Latin form of the plural—can act as touchstones for a poet, as ways of reconnecting us with the point of it all. For more discussion of *ars poeticae*, please see the Questions and Poetry Practices sections at the end of this chapter.

Poets have also found anchors for creativity in the physical paraphernalia of our art. The brilliant Russian poet Marina Tsvetaeva wrote a long tribute to her desk which is all the more poignant because she ended up committing suicide, exiled far from home and, presumably, from her desk:

From "Desk" (1933–35)

My desk, most loyal friend
thank you. You've been with me on
every road I've taken.
My scar and my protection.

My loaded writing mule.
Your tough legs have endured
the weight of all my dreams, and
burdens of piled-up thoughts.

Thank you for toughening me.
No worldly joy could pass
your severe looking-glass . . .
(TRANS. ELAINE FEINSTEIN)

Contemporary poet Brenda Hillman meditates on her pencil:

Brenda Hillman, "Before My Pencil"

It took quiet
It took stone

Where the feeling left intensity
It saluted

The mannerism of the curve

Warm saprophyte
Its halo vest

Notched something's antic math

Draw your planet
Enigma
Come back when you have one

Then it crawled among syllables

Then it touched the white fact

And Seamus Heaney on his pen:

"Digging," Seamus Heaney

Between my finger and my thumb
The squat pen rests; as snug as a gun.

Under my window, a clean rasping sound
When the spade sinks into gravelly ground:
My father, digging. I look down

Till his straining rump among the flowerbeds
Bends low, comes up twenty years away
Stooping in rhythm through potato drills
Where he was digging.

The coarse boot nestled on the lug, the shaft
Against the inside knee was levered firmly.
He rooted out tall tops, buried the bright edge deep
To scatter new potatoes that we picked
Loving their cool hardness in our hands.

By God, the old man could handle a spade.
Just like his old man.

My grandfather cut more turf in a day
Than any other man on Toner's bog.
Once I carried him milk in a bottle
Corked sloppily with paper. He straightened up
To drink it, then fell to right away
Nicking and slicing neatly, heaving sods
Over his shoulder, going down and down
For the good turf. Digging.

The cold smell of potato mold, the squelch and slap
Of soggy peat, the curt cuts of an edge
Through living roots awaken in my head.
But I've no spade to follow men like them.

Between my finger and my thumb
The squat pen rests.
I'll dig with it.

Often, history or some internal or external event in your own life will provide you with the occasion or spur for a poem. To make such a poem work, a poet has to resonate with a specific physical or emotional quality of the event. Perhaps the capacity to feel that kind of inspiration is, in part, the habit of simply holding a feeling in your awareness without needing to solve or do something about it. It's like a kind of waiting. It may be related to the quality, commonly referred to as *negative capability,* that John Keats described in a letter about literary genius: the capacity for "being in uncertainties, Mysteries, doubts without any irritable reaching after fact & reason."

Poets, at home with the world of trope and allusion and imagination, have found all kinds of ways to conceive of poetic inspiration and the act of creating poems. Some, perhaps most famously Anne Bradstreet, have thought of writing poems as giving birth:

"The Author to Her Book," Anne Bradstreet (1659)

Thou ill-form'd offspring of my feeble brain,
Who after birth did'st by my side remain,
Till snatcht from thence by friends, less wise than true,
Who thee abroad expos'd to publick view,
Made thee in rags, halting to th' press to trudge,
Where errors were not lessened (all may judge).
At thy return my blushing was not small,
My rambling brat (in print) should mother call.
I cast thee by as one unfit for light,
Thy Visage was so irksome in my sight;
Yet being mine own, at length affection would
Thy blemishes amend, if so I could:

I wash'd thy face, but more defects I saw,
And rubbing off a spot, still made a flaw.
I stretcht thy joints to make thee even feet,
Yet still thou run'st more hobling than is meet;
In better dress to trim thee was my mind,
But nought save home-spun Cloth, i' th' house I find.
In this array, 'mongst Vulgars mayst thou roam.
In Criticks' hands, beware thou dost not come,
And take thy way where yet thou art not known.
If for thy Father askt, say, thou hadst none;
And for thy Mother, she alas is poor,
Which caus'd her thus to send thee out of door.

Two hundred years later a male poet, John Berryman, was inspired by Bradstreet to write a book of "imitations" called *Homage to Mistress Bradstreet,* where he also compared the creation of poetry to giving birth:

From "Two Organs," John Berryman

I remind myself at that time of Plato's uterus . . .
an animal passionately longing for children
. . . For "children" read: big fat fresh original & characteristic poems
My longing yes was a woman's

The Muse

Many poets over the centuries have imagined a **Muse,** a kind of poetry goddess who helped inspire poets as they "mused." The ancient Greeks envisioned nine Muses, one for each of nine kinds of art (see Box on page 14). Sappho, in this poem addressed to her daughter, conveys the feeling of living a life dedicated to the Muses:

"No Room for Grief," Sappho, 600 B.C. (trans. Josephine Balmer)

There is no room for grief, Cleis,
in a house that serves the Muses.
Our own is no exception.

Not only is Sappho's household dedicated to the Muses in the sense that she and her friends and students are devoted to Poetry; they are also aware of the Muses as a part of daily life that has an effect even on a child's tears.

The Nine Muses

ERATO, Muse of erotic poetry
CLIO, Muse of history
EUTERPE, Muse of music
THALIA, Muse of comic poetry
TERPSICHORE, Muse of dance
URANIA, Muse of astronomy
MELPOMENE, Muse of lyric poetry
CALLIOPE, Muse of epic poetry
POLYHYMNIA, Muse of sacred poetry

Poets' special relationship with the Muses is a thread that links poetry back to the most ancient cultures. Some poets (myself included) still often "hear" the words of poems quite physically in their minds, either before or as they write. If contemporary poets have this experience, how much more vivid it may have been for the Greeks of Homer's time, who were living in an oral-based culture where *all* literature was experienced in the mind without the mediation of the page. Julian Jaynes hypothesizes that ancient people heard the gods' voices physically in their minds, guiding them through life on a daily basis. In such a culture, the Muse would be a natural companion for poets.

Homer, who frequently describes mortals being told what to do by the gods, opens the *Iliad* with a simple invocation that has echoed down the centuries since: "Sing, Muse, of the wrath of Achilles." But Edmund Spenser, "the poet's poet," seems almost contemporary by contrast as, with elaborate self-consciousness, he begins his beautiful epic *The Faerie Queene* (1596) with a request to Clio, the Muse of history and "chief" of the nine muses, to help him, a poet whose Muse "whilome" (before) wore humble "weeds" (clothes), to write about the lofty adventures of "Faerie Knight":

Lo I the man, whose Muse whilome did maske,
As time her taught, in lowly Shepheards weeds,
Am now enforst a far unfitter taske,

For trumpets sterne to chaunge mine Oaten reeds,
And sing of Knights and Ladies gentle deeds;
Whose praises having slept in silence long,
Me, all too meane, the sacred Muse areeds
To blazon broad emongst her learned throng:
Fierce warres and faithfull loves shall moralize my song.

Helpe then, O holy Virgin chiefe of nine,
Thy weaker Novice to performe thy will,
Lay forth out of thine everlasting scryne
The antique rolles, which there lye hidden still,
Of Faerie knights and fairest *Tanaquill,*
Whom that most noble Briton Prince so long
Sought through the world, and suffered so much ill,
That I must rue his undeserved wrong:
O helpe thou my weake wit, and sharpen my dull tong.

Every poet who would like a muse deserves to have one. An exercise at the end of this chapter invites you to encounter your own idea of the muse. Your muse can be any gender, form, or species, animate or inanimate. One good place to start looking for your muse is among the nine Muses of Greek legend (see page 14). My own writing studio is full of figurines or reminders of inspiring Muses of various cultures, from Pegasus to the Celtic poetry goddess Brigid to Sarasvati, Hindu goddess of poetry and music. You may want to create an invocation or altar for your Muse. While there is a long tradition of envisioning the Muse as female among poets of both genders, some muses are male or androgynous, as is the owner of the powerful, delicate hand in the following poem:

"Solitude," Anna Akhmatova (1914) (trans. Judith Hemschemeyer)

So many stones have been thrown at me,
That I'm not frightened of them any more,
And the pit has become a solid tower,
Tall among tall towers.
I thank the builders,
May care and sadness pass them by.
From here I'll see the sunrise earlier,
Here the sun's last ray rejoices.

And into the windows of my room
The Northern breezes often fly.
And from my hand a dove eats grains of wheat . . .
As for my unfinished page,
The Muse's tawny hand, divinely calm
And delicate, will finish it.

But Philip Sidney may have had the most practical and realistic idea of the Muse's true function:

"Loving in Truth," Sir Philip Sidney (1591)

Loving in truth, and fain in verse my love to show,
That she, dear she, might take some pleasure of my pain,
Pleasure might cause her read, reading might make her know,
Knowledge might pity win, and pity grace obtain,
I sought fit words to paint the blackest face of woe;
Studying inventions fine, her wits to entertain,
Oft turning others' leaves to see if thence would flow
Some fresh and fruitful showers upon my sunburn'd brain.
But words came halting forth, wanting Invention's stay;
Invention, Nature's child, fled step dame Study's blows;
And others' feet still seemed but strangers in my way.
Thus, great with child to speak, and helpless in my throes,
Biting my truant pen, beating myself for spite:
"Fool," said my Muse to me, "look in thy heart and write!"

Whether you are interested in the idea of a muse or simply want to look in your own heart, any time you write poetry you find a way to experience inspiration (literally, a "breathing in"). Maybe you will find your inspiration in occasions, shared events. Such events are often public (from Milton's "On the Late Massacre in Piedmont" to the flood of 9/11 poems), but private events can be occasions too, whether recent or long ago, as in this poem:

"Ravelings," Linda Hogan

I still hear sounds
in quiet thoughts

like treadles clacking
at the base of mother's loom,

just as when I sat still
and though small

watched the whoosh
from shuttle sliding

across the warp; color
bumping up against color

and changing with each clack,
changing summer into fall.

In October the abundant
field comes undone;

no longer wild yellow from butter
cups or golden rod. There are only gray

and rust threads not quite holding
together in wind. Very fine snow

will gather heaviness and crack
the straw eventually. Thaw water

moves down with its bits
of passing years. Blue Jays snap

at the feeder and I remember
the way the warp was fed through

the loom's harness where the lengths
of fiber hung waiting for a unity

her hair woven with my blonde, her
patterns, our rhythms. I still tap my foot.

Though much contemporary poetry comes from private experience, the pool of shared occasions continues to inspire strong poems: elegies, wedding poems, valentines, graduation poems, devotional and ritual poems, and poems for the unveiling of a public building are all meant to be shared with others in a ritual situation. Political poems, like the thousands of "poems against the war" presented to Congress at the beginning of the Iraq war, are also occasional poems. Here is a poem on a political occasion:

From "Shine, Perishing Republic," Robinson Jeffers (1924)

While this America settles in the mold of its vulgarity, heavily thickening
    to empire,
And protest, only a bubble in the molten mass, pops and sighs out, and
    the mass hardens,
I sadly smiling remember that the flower fades to make fruit, the fruit rots
    to make earth
Out of the mother, and through the spring exultance, ripeness and
    decadence, and home to the mother.

Of course, a great range of poetry is "political." As Adrienne Rich records in her elegy for Anne Sexton, Sexton read a poem about her daughter, "Little Girl, My Stringbee, My Lovely Woman," when asked to read an anti-war poem at a rally. Some poets find enough inspiration in the art of poetry itself to approach a myriad of subjects. A metaphor, a poem by another poet, or a structural metaphor, whether a form invented for one poem or a rediscovery of an old form, can catch a poet's imagination. Joan Retallack's experimental poem for an AIDS victim, in the chapter "Exploratory Poetry," is driven by its invented form, which drops certain letters of the alphabet from each new stanza. Nellie Wong's "Grandmother's Song" in the chapter "Repeating Poems" is full of the passion and excitement of writing a pantoum about the ancestors. The experience of writing a poem in the same form as a favorite poem can inspire a poet as much as any other encounter.

Stories and myths, collective or personal, inhabit many pools in the wood between the worlds. Myths show us new ways to be human, which is why they have appealed to poets from the Beowulf poet and Spenser to Anne Sexton and Carolyn Kizer, from Ovid, Keats, Eliot, and H. D. to Alice Notley, Audre Lorde, and Anne Carson. Other pools might hold language games or found text for a poet like Heather McHugh or Harryette Mullen, or stories and personalities for a poet like Stephen Dunn or Ai. Poet Lee Ann Brown writes, "My advice to poets is constantly to look around you in all spheres of influence, from the most daily to the most worldly to the most cosmic for material and methodology for poetry. Try to think of a discipline, cultural practice, subculture, slang or way of thinking that is most far away from what you think of as poetry. Mine these forms, languages, modes of thinking and write that poem." Each poet has their own wood between the worlds, with an infinite number of pools.

Sometimes learning about the lives of other poets can provide what we need to persist. When I was growing as a poet, I took inspiration from a sentence in Pablo Neruda's autobiography: "We poets have a right to be happy, as long as we care about the people of our country and are involved in the struggle for their happiness." Some of us will find we need to have a political voice about our times if we are going to be able to keep that promise.

"In Dark Times," Bertolt Brecht (1937)

They won't say: when the walnut tree shook in the wind
But: when the house-painter crushed the workers.
They won't say: when the child skimmed a flat stone across
        the rapids
But: when the great wars were being prepared for.
They won't say; when the woman came into the room
But: when the great powers joined forces against the workers.
However, they won't say: the times were dark
Rather: why were their poets silent?

Each of us will find our own way to experience the wood between the worlds, and to me that is the real work. It might seem as if a poet would need the greatest artistic faith and skill during the actual process of opening to the mysterious and sometimes scary water. But what happens inside those pools depends on the focus, the strength of heart, and the self-awareness that we develop during every day of our lives as human beings; beyond that, inspiration is largely a simple matter of surrender. Between the worlds, we have the task of learning to recognize and maneuver between pools, and to have faith to keep going in the dry peaceful forest so we can return continually, unafraid and focused, to the poem's center.

QUESTIONS FOR MEDITATION OR DISCUSSION

Make a map of your own "wood between the worlds." If you already write poems, think of the things that inspire you: sounds of words? feelings? stories? ideas for shapes of poems? smells? overheard phrases? If you haven't written poems yet, think of the kinds of things that give you an excited or "inspired" feeling. Often you can recognize this feeling by physical sensations: butterflies in your stomach, a sudden quietness in your chest, or a racing heart.

The greatest accolade a poet can win—the traditional laurel wreath alluded to by the term "poet laureate"—traces its roots to a victory and a defeat. The story goes that Apollo, Greek god of poetry, music, and healing, was chasing the nymph Daphne to molest her. To escape him, she turned into a laurel tree. Defeated, he took the leaves as his crown in order to remember her. What can this story tell us about poetry's aims? What can it tell us about how a poem succeeds or fails?

In the preface to *Lyrical Ballads* (1797), the book of poems he published with Samuel Coleridge which is often considered the launch of the Romantic movement in poetry, William Wordsworth famously defined poetry as "the spontaneous overflow of powerful feelings from emotions recollected in tranquility." What do you think is the distinction he is making between feelings and emotions? Does this definition feel accurate to your own experience of writing poems?

What would your own "ars poetica" look like? While considering the question, look through some of the ars poetica excerpted in this book: the original *Ars Poetica* by the Latin poet Horace, Marianne Moore's "Poetry," and Archibald MacLeish's "Ars Poetica." In addition, you might want to look at "On Imagination" by Phillis Wheatley, "Tell all the Truth but tell it Slant" by Emily Dickinson, "Adam's Curse" by William Butler Yeats, "Digging" by Seamus Heaney, or my own "Encounter." And here are two very brief *ars poeticae* by contemporary poets, one logically coherent and one more experimental in approach:

"Ars Poetica," Dan Waber

You don't go looking for poetry finds.
You go, looking, for poetry finds.

"Dinosaur Meat," Elizabeth Treadwell

shy gifty, I felt snubbed.

poetry's like a small dried sponge seeped in time,
tongued at leisure (in peril) at safety (in chains)

we press ourselves to the earth

QUOTES

The "idea" for a poem may come as an image thrown against memory, as a sound of words that sets off a traveling of sound and meaning, as a curve of emotion (a form) plotted by certain crises of events or image or sound, or as a title which evokes a sense of inner relations.

—Muriel Rukeyser

In the beginning we have no choice but to accept what has come to us, hoping that the cinders some forest spirit saw fit to bestow may turn to gold when we have carried them back to the hearth.

—Lewis Hyde

Artistic growth is, more than it is anything else, a refining of the sense of truthfulness.

—Willa Cather, *The Song of the Lark*

Poetry is the record of the best and happiest moments of the best minds.

—Percy Bysshe Shelley

Write secretly . . . so you can actually be free to say anything you want.

—Allen Ginsberg

The delights of the poet, as I jotted them down, turned out to be light, solitude, the natural world, love, time, creation itself.

—May Swenson

Sunshine cannot bleach the snow,
Nor time unmake what poets know.
—Ralph Waldo Emerson

There is no one among men that has not a special failing:
and my failing consists in writing verses.
—Po Chu'i

Poetic creation still remains an act of perfect spiritual freedom. . . . The purest poetic act seems to re-create language from an inner experience that, like the ecstasy or the religious inspiration of "primitives," reveals the essence of things.
—Mircea Eliade

The figure a poem makes. It begins in delight and ends in wisdom. The figure is the same as for love.
—Robert Frost

Our deepest secret in our heart of hearts is that we are writing because we love the world.
—Natalie Goldberg

From "Requium," Anna Akhmatova (trans. Milton Ehre)

In the terrible years of Yezhov's terror I spent seventeen months in the prison lines of Leningrad. Once someone somehow "recognized" me. Then a woman standing behind me, lips blue from cold, who of course never had heard my name, woke from the stupor we all were in and whispered in my ear (we all spoke in whispers there):

"Could you describe this?"

"Yes" was my answer.

Then something like a smile slid across what was once her face.

From "The Cemetery by the Sea," Paul Valéry
(trans. Charles Guenther) (1942)

O for me, to me and within this me,
close to the heart, the source of poetry,

between the void and the absolute event,
I await my inner greatness' echoing knell
out of this bitter, dark, sonorous well . . .

"Dismission," I. A. Richards (1958)

Farewell, young Muse! you've teased me long enough,
Promising lines and rimes you didn't furnish.
You claimed you had some public's ear as well.
You've pestered me to clip and file and burnish
But rust adorns, I find, and dust's the stuff.

You've lectured me on What and How and Why
Until there's not a theme I care to touch.
Artful and heartless, innocent and sly
Go decorate some other poet's couch
Now all is almost over. Here! Goodbye!

Go wrench his sense and regulate his voice,
Tell him there's nothing left for verse to say
Though only you can find the way to say it.
Give him my greeting with your rates of pay
And never let him know he has no choice.

From "The Albatross," Charles Baudelaire (1859) (trans. George Dillon)

The Poet is like that wild inheritor of the cloud,
A rider of storms, above the range of arrows and slings;
Exiled on earth, at bay amid the jeering crowd,
He cannot walk for his unmanageable wings.

POETRY PRACTICES

An Audience with a Muse. Pick one of the nine Greek muses (Euterpe, Calliope, Urania, Thalia, Clio, Erato, Melpomene, Polyhymnia, or Terpsichore) and research as much as you can about her. Then write a poem addressed to her.

New Muse. Devise your own idea of a muse and write a poem about or addressed to him/her/it. The muse can be human, animal, inanimate, a force of nature, or any combination of these. Give your muse a name and some characteristics. Be as detailed as you like. Your poem can be, but does not have to be, an invocation asking for your muse's help in writing your poetry. Feel free to illustrate your poem with pictures, photos, collages, sample items of the muse's clothing, or whatever else you would like to add.

Ars Poetica. Write a poem that conveys your ideas about writing poetry. It doesn't have to be explicit; metaphors are fine. First, look at the examples included throughout this book.

Occasional Poem. Write a poem based on or in honor of or to be part of an actual occasion (wedding, birth, etc.) in the life of someone you know. It can be designed for you to read aloud, for someone else to perform, or to be presented in written or visual form.

CHAPTER 2

Poetry as Nourishment: How to Read Like a Poet

Poets as Readers

Giving a poetry reading years ago at a nursing home, I met Sally, a vibrant woman in her early nineties who loved literature. Her eyes were bad and she could no longer read, but she was such a delightful person that people gladly read aloud to her. However, no one in that pre-Internet time had been able to find a copy of what she most wanted to hear: a once-famous poem about a seashell, "The Chambered Nautilus" by Oliver Wendell Holmes.

As a schoolchild in the Midwest at the very beginning of the twentieth century, Sally had been required to memorize this poem along with many others. Now, approaching the end of her life, she remembered enough of "The Chambered Nautilus" to know that she needed to hear that poem again before she died. She asked if I would track down the poem and tape myself reading it, along with any other poems I thought she would enjoy. I will never forget the sheer hunger, the deep need, in her face as she asked me this favor.

The story goes that when Edmund Spenser, author of the epic poem *The Faerie Queene,* whose invocation you read in the last chapter, was buried in the "Poets' Corner" of Westminster Abbey in London in 1599, poets came to throw roses into his grave. Though the Renaissance was a time when the bonds among poets were particularly lively and essential, the story has survived because it captures something about Spenser: like John Keats, Gwendolyn Brooks, and Elizabeth Bishop, he is known as "a poet's poet." There are not many poets' poets, and they are prized like the fabled alchemical "quintessence": the essence of essences.

Only other poets can decide who are the poets' poets. The term implies that poets know best about poetry, and that they read poetry somewhat differently from other people. This chapter will focus on how, in the process of deciding who are *your* "poet's poets," you will become a better poet yourself. But it is always important to remember, at the same time, how crucial it is for poetry to have readers like Sally who are not poets at all. These pure readers, as I like to call them, play a role in poetry that is just as profound as the poets' role. Pure readers are essential to keep poetry a gift.

In my teens and twenties, doubtless like many young poets, I spent tormented hours reflecting that a poet's path is thankless and, even worse, seemed self-indulgent. What is the use of poetry, after all? The book that finally began to bring me peace of mind was anthropologist Lewis Hyde's cult classic *The Gift,* a brilliant exploration of the role of art in the world. Hyde reminds us that poetry provides value outside of the usual economy of usefulness and exchange, and that this freedom in itself is an essential human function that creates space for meaning in our lives.

To read "The Chambered Nautilus" for Sally, knowing how much it would mean to her and that she would carry it into death, as she was to do just a few months later, was a gift to myself as much as to her. She helped remind me that poetry does matter, to paraphrase the title of a book by Dana Gioia. The last stanza of the poem that Sally remembered after all those years provides a moving way to close, or to lead, a life.

From "The Chambered Nautilus," Oliver Wendell Holmes (1858)

Build thee more stately mansions, O my soul,
    As the swift seasons roll!
    Leave thy low-vaulted past!
Let each new temple, nobler than the last,
Shut thee from heaven with a dome more vast,
    Till thou at length art free,
Leaving thine outgrown shell by life's unresting sea!

Letting a Poem Read You

A question and answer session usually follows my readings at colleges and high schools. There is one question that usually gets asked early on, after a few questions about inspiration or writing habits. A particularly earnest hand waves in the air, and its owner asks: "What advice do you have for aspiring poets?"

There are all kinds of useful tips to offer, from finding a steady day job to keeping a flashlight and notebook by the bed. But the advice I give most often is so simple that a beginning poet might be tempted to ignore it—and so crucial that it is worth all the rest of the advice put together. *Read poetry. And then read more poetry.*

Not only read it, but get so good at reading it that you stop reading it the way you read other kinds of words, and instead begin to savor it like chocolate or wine. Not only read poetry you like, but also read poetry you hate, poetry that bores you, poetry so difficult it drives you crazy, poetry so easy it irritates you, poetry that makes you furious, poetry in languages you don't know, poetry written by the kindergartener down the block, self-published poetry, Pulitzer Prize–winning poetry, rapper poetry, "Immortal Poetry" in classroom anthologies, and long-forgotten poetry in cracked leather bindings on lower shelves in back rooms of junk shops.

Read so much of it that you learn to smell the different varieties of it through the cover of a closed book. Not only read it, but let it read you: read it with the other side of your brain, so that instead of knowing what it means, you will feel how it means; allow its words to unroll at their own pace (not your pace), and to occupy their own space (not your space). Not only read it, but become the dirt its roots can spread out in, the pool table where its balls can ricochet, the room its incense can perfume, the lyre its wind can play the way it plays the branches of a forest (if you recognize the poem from which I borrowed that last metaphor, you're well on your way).

But it's not just the quantity and scope of your reading that matters; "the quality of the attention," to paraphrase Ezra Pound, matters too. Let's say you take this advice seriously, and you've picked up some anthologies of poetry and individual books of poetry, borrowed lots more books of poetry from the library, browsed through the poetry in literary magazines in bookstores, subscribed to one or more of those literary magazines, surfed the innumerable poetry sites on the Web (did you know "poetry" is one of the top five terms people search on the Web?), printed out some of the thousands of poems there, and are well supplied with both classic and contemporary poetry. Now you are sitting there with all this poetry around you, ready to let it play you like a lyre. How do you begin to let a poem echo with its own voice? How do you not simply *read it,* but *let it read you?*

Let's start with the simplest of poems:

"Little Miss Muffet," Mother Goose (seventeenth century)

Little Miss Muffet
Sat on a tuffet
Eating her curds and whey.

Along came a spider
And sat down beside her
And frightened Miss Muffet away.

If you were simply going to read this little verse, you would give your attention to the meanings of the words. You would read it the way you are reading this paragraph of prose, in order to gather the information the words contain. Once you understood the information, you would experience a "been there, done that," feeling, a feeling of "Okay, I've read that. Now what?" You'd feel empty and anxious for something else to do, read, entertain yourself with.

Just as an experiment, read the poem that way. Read it straight through as if you were reading the cooking instructions on a package of spaghetti. Whew! Are you finished? Does your head hurt a little bit? Did you find the poem calling to you the way the seductive Sirens called to Ulysses, when he chained himself to the mast of his ship so he could resist their temptations in *The Odyssey*? If so, you have had a taste of the difference between poetry and prose.

The aspects of this modest poem that were calling you to slow down and enjoy its pleasures, as you dutifully plowed straight through its meaning, are the reason it has survived for hundreds of years. These aspects all involve circling back, entering a space beyond time and outside of time.

When you read a poem with its timeless aspects in mind, you are being far from dutiful. Instead, you are like, let's say, a toddler being taken on a walk by a parent. As you leave the house, your parent is planning to walk to the park, swing you on the swings, go home and make dinner, give you a bath, put you to bed, and answer email. A parent in full parent mode may even be mentally home before you've left the house. You, on the other hand, want to ring the doorbell a few dozen times on the way out, sit down on the bottom step to play with the ants crawling in and out of the little hole where the concrete is broken at the edge, and once you are cajoled into walking again, investigate the acorns scattered a hundred feet up the sidewalk . . . and so on.

The basic difference between toddler mode and parent mode involves time:

the toddler, unlike the parent, is living fully in the present, in a perpetually timeless state of mind. Children respond well to music, and to repetition, so hopefully our hypothetical parent knows that a walking song with a good refrain is one way to finally get moving toward the park. Kids love the repetitions of poetry because its structures are in tune with the timeless part of our minds.

The way to let a poem read you is to respond to it with that timeless part of your mind. Let's try reading Miss Muffet as if you are toddling through its two stanzas. Read the poem either out loud or letting yourself "hear" the words inside your mind. Take as long as you want, and let yourself stop whenever you feel like it. This reading aloud is crucial for appreciating poetry.

Little Miss Muffet
Sat on a tuffet
eating her curds and whey.

Along came a spider
and sat down beside her
and frightened Miss Muffet away.

"Muffet" and "tuffet" may be the first thing you notice. It was what made my little daughter laugh when I told her the poem. Before you get to the other rhymes, such as "spider" and "beside her," since you are in toddler mode, you might see how the third line sticks out farther than the first two on the page, and feel how the *t* in "sat" points the way to the *t*'s in "tuffet," which point the way toward the *t* in "eating," and even how the *t* in "eating" and the *d* in "curds" feel similar on your tongue when you say them.

You might also have enjoyed the way the ideas are put together, the way the verb "eating" is separated from the person doing the eating by a line with a funny word in it. By the time you have slowed down enough to unconsciously register all these things about the way the story is told, paradoxically, you might find the images of Miss Muffet, the curds and whey, and the spider have become a lot more vivid to you. One secret of the power of poetry is that, when sounds and patterns have slowed you down to timelessness, meanings can come through even more strongly (this vulnerability of timeless minds to impressions is why toddlers can be so strongly affected by movies and other experiences).

The influential scholar Walter Ong describes how, in cultures where poems, stories, and knowledge are passed on orally instead of in writing, people's lives have a sense of immediacy and directness very different than in our culture. By providing us access into the timeless state of mind, a well-structured poem like "Little Miss Muffet" allows us to experience life in this unmediated way. As literate people, we are used to being the ones who do the "reading" of everything we encounter in our lives: texts, other people, situations. We are used to being the ones who call the shots, set the pace, draw the conclusions—in short, the ones who provide structure to shapeless, raw experience. A poem, on the other hand, is all about structure. A good poem is structured with more richness and complexity than our own experience of the moment we are reading it could probably ever muster. By comparison with such a poem, then, *our* experience is what is shapeless and raw.

Therefore, when we encounter a good poem, we have the opportunity to feel what it is like for once to be not the reader, but the thing read: to have our own experience, as we are reading, shaped and interpreted by the complexities and meanings and interpenetrations of the poem. This is not only an amazing, worthwhile experience in itself: it is key for anyone who is serious about writing poetry and learning to provide such timeless experiences for other readers—because the more we open ourselves to being read by poems, the more sensitive we become to poetry, *even when it is our own words that we are allowing to read us as we write.*

Throughout this book you will be learning skills to help you develop this sensitivity to poetry, so that you will be better able to let poetry, including your own poems, read you. But the three most important steps of the process are not contained in any of the chapters you will read, because they come before any poem you will encounter. Here they are: 1. Slow down. 2. Breathe deeply and clear your mind. 3. Give the poem space to echo in.

If you have read this far, you will know that this process is not at all the same thing as worrying about what the poem means. But if you are in danger of forgetting the difference, you may find this poem helpful:

"Introduction to Poetry," Billy Collins

I ask them to take a poem
and hold it up to the light
like a color slide

or press an ear against its hive.

I say drop a mouse into a poem
and watch him probe his way out,

or walk inside the poem's room
and feel the walls for a light switch.

I want them to waterski
across the surface of a poem
waving at the author's name on the shore.

But all they want to do
is tie the poem to a chair with rope
and torture a confession out of it.

They begin beating it with a hose
to find out what it really means.

Needless to say, while "reading like a poet" may help you to notice all kinds of things you never noticed before about a poem, it is not going to involve you in torturing poetry. If anything, it will take you away from analysis and meaning, at least temporarily, and back into your most direct responses.

Poetry Compost and the Poet's Notebook

Even the most mundane life has poetry in it. If you are now reading this book, you have a rich history of poetic language within you, and part of learning to read as a poet is to wake up that history and let it resonate within your own poems now. When you were such a young child that you were always living in timeless mind, what words did you let echo within you? What phrases did you repeat over and over to yourself, even if you didn't know what they meant? What names, of places, family members, celebrities, or playmates, did you find yourself wanting to hear again and again?

As you grew older, what were the magic spells of words that you carried around with you, the words that you felt had "glamour"? What song lyrics, what sentences from the textbook or blackboard, what fragments of phrases from TV commercials, did you bring into yourself as a link back to timeless mind, and allow to echo within you as you walked home from school or before you went to sleep at night? And when you were reading, what texts, from poetry or other books, had this same quality for you?

As you connect with these memories of language, you will add them to the memories of poems you have read, and eventually to the memories of poems you have written. And as all these layers of linguistic matter decay on the floor of your internal forest or in your internal garden's compost pile, the result, if the ingredients are carefully chosen and full of authentic poetic energy, will be a very rich individualized compost that will provide excellent nourishment for your own growing poems. As with any compost pile, while you can certainly write poems based on all this language, you don't really have to "do" anything with it for it to be useful. All you need to do is give the memories some space to decay, and keep them nearby as you write.

The best place to keep your compost pile is in a poet's notebook. Many poets have used notebooks to compose their poems; one of the best known is Theodore Roethke, who left 277 spiral notebooks at his death, including quotes from reading, overheard phrases, thoughts, words, and drafts of poems. Roethke referred to his notebooks frequently and returned to revise things in them for years after they were full. The editor of Roethke's notebooks estimates that a third of his published poetry was based on these notebook entries.

In our day of computers, a notebook is an especially valuable tool for poets for several reasons. It keeps your body and your imagination connected by keeping you in direct physical contact with your handwriting; it holds versions that could otherwise be erased with the delete key; it can go with you anywhere, particularly into nature; and it is timeless, allowing you to flip between pages written months apart and make the creative links across which poetry can leap.

Touchstones

When you begin to let poetry read you on a regular basis, you will discover that certain poems are better at reading you than others are. And this is as it should be; not every poem can stand up to the powerful sensitivity of this kind of reading. The Victorian poet and critic Matthew Arnold wrote that certain lines of poetry are "touchstones" of excellence that remind us how great poetry can be. By creating a space where poems can echo, you will begin to develop your own repertoire of personal "touchstone" poems that will remind you what *you* value in poetry, and what you want to create in your own poems. This is how you will begin to develop the capacity of discrimination that is crucial to any art. One reason it is important to read not just acknowledged "good" poetry but poetry of all kinds—even poetry from junk shops, poetry in advertisements, and poetry by your neighbors—is that this way you will discover that touchstones are not the property of award-winners but can be found absolutely everywhere. Keeping alert for them, even in unlikely places, will teach you to develop and trust your own discrimination and to build the confidence in your own taste that is essential to being a good writer.

Memorization

Some of the most powerful material your notebook helps you remember may be words that you have never written down before, but which have stayed with you nonetheless. Poems, especially poems written in regular rhythm, are designed to be memorized easily. Since memorized words become, in a sense, a part of your personality and your life, by choosing to memorize poems, you can consciously choose to shape yourself and your life in certain directions. If you want more robustness in your life, you might memorize Kipling or Lucille Clifton; if you want to appreciate nature more, you might memorize some Hopkins or Wendell Berry; for more tenderness, Sara Teasdale or D. H. Lawrence; for more spirituality, George Herbert or the Sufi poet Rumi; for more humor and energy, Langston Hughes or Frank O'Hara or Eileen Myles; to slow down and appreciate life more, early H.D. or Frost or Luci Tapahonso or Li Young Lee; for more detachment and balance, Constantin Cavafy or Dickinson or A. E. Stallings; for more passionate feelings, Dylan Thomas or Hart Crane; for more assertiveness, Walt Whitman or Yeats or Sonia Sanchez.

The more you memorize, the easier it is to do, at any stage of life. Your brain gets used to it, and you'll find that you become more confident. You will probably develop your own habits. Some people like to write poems on index cards and memorize while running, working out, driving, knitting, or riding the bus or subway. My usual way is to start at the beginning of a poem and quote as far as I can, gradually increasing the amount I can recite until I get to the end. It's like combing hair: start at the top and remove more of the tangles (unmemorized places) each time you go down through the poem. That way you don't forget the beginning while you are memorizing the middle.

One of the most interesting pieces of advice I have heard about memorization came from an actor who had memorized hundreds of lines of Shakespeare. He said to break a poem into sections and to associate each section with a gesture, change of posture or position, or other physical movement. That way, your body will do the remembering for you. You might also try this when performing your own poems (see chapter 21).

As with many new challenges, you may find it is easier to memorize if you do it with other people. You could dare or challenge each other to see what poems you can memorize, and schedule a performance or "slam" to share afterwards. The longest poem I know is one I memorized decades ago, when I was separated for a summer from someone I loved. We each memorized the same poem as a way to feel we were in touch with each other.

Reading through Writing: Glosa, Parody, Imitation, Translation, and Response

There is another way that poets read: by writing. Our ideas about what a "poem" is, and how to write one, don't come out of nowhere; they are formed by the kind of poems we have read. Read widely, if you want to write interesting poems. If you read only what is provided for you in school or in current anthologies, you are more likely to end up sounding like everyone else than if you explore off the beaten path. That is what T. S. Eliot was getting at in his essay "Tradition and the Individual Talent." The critic Harold Bloom argues that every poem is written either under the influence of an earlier poem or in a struggle to escape the influence of an earlier poem; the strongest poets are those who choose to interact with the strongest precursor poems.

While the kinds of influences Eliot and Bloom are talking about can be subtle and hard to trace, there is one form of poetry that invites poets to engage directly with a poem that has inspired us. The **glosa,** a form invented in Spain during the Renaissance, takes a quatrain from another poet's poem as its inspiration and starting point. This form has been used with great richness in English, in particular by the Canadian poet P. K. Page. It consists of the *cabeza*—a line or short stanza taken from the work of another poet and credited to that poet—followed by a stanza for each line of the cabeza. The lines of these stanzas can be of any length; the point is that each stanza elaborates or explains one of the four lines in the cabeza, and incorporates it (sometimes as the final line, like a refrain). In the most traditional version of the glosa, the cabeza is always four lines long, and the sixth and ninth lines of each of the ten-line stanzas rhyme with the "borrowed" tenth line:

"Autumn," P. K. Page

Whoever has no house now will never have one.
Whoever is alone will stay alone
Will sit, read, write long letters through the evening
And wander on the boulevards, up and down . . .
—"Autumn Day," Rainer Maria Rilke

Its stain is everywhere.
The sharpening air
of late afternoon
is now the colour of tea.
Once-glycerined green leaves
burned by a summer sun
are brittle and ochre.
Night enters day like a thief.
And children fear that the beautiful daylight has gone.
Whoever has no house now will never have one.

It is the best and the worst time.
Around a fire, everyone laughing,
brocaded curtains drawn,
nowhere—anywhere—is more safe than here.
The whole world is a cup
one could hold in one's hand like a stone
warmed by that same summer sun.
But the dead or the near dead
are now all knucklebone.
Whoever is alone will stay alone.

Nothing to do. Nothing to really do.
Toast and tea are nothing.
Kettle boils dry.
Shut the night out or let it in,

it is a cat on the wrong side of the door
whichever side it is on. A black thing
with its implacable face.
To avoid it you
will tell yourself you are something,
will sit, read, write long letters through the evening.

Even though there is bounty, a full harvest
that sharp sweetness in the tea-stained air
is reserved for those who have made a straw
fine as a hair to suck it through—
fine as a golden hair.
Wearing a smile or a frown
God's face is always there.
It is up to you
if you take your wintry restlessness into the town
and wander on the boulevards, up and down.

This form concretely acknowledges the links between poets—the ways in which one poet's work can spring from another's. Page, who has published an entire book of glosas, has written, "I was introduced to the glosa through the ear. Its form, half hidden, powerfully sensed, like an iceberg at night, made me search for its outline as I listened. . . . I enjoyed the idea of constructing the poem backward—the final line of each stanza is, in effect, the starting line. . . . I liked being controlled by those three reining rhymes—or do I mean reigning?—and gently influenced by the rhythm of the original."

Another form that invites poets to interact directly with lines that inspire them is the Bop, a form invented by Afaa Michael Weaver for his students during a summer retreat of the African American poetry organization Cave Canem in 1997. The Bop is "a poetic argument" consisting of three stanzas, each stanza followed by a refrain line taken from a song. The first stanza (six lines long) states the problem. The second stanza (eight lines long) expands on the problem, and the final stanza (six lines) attempts or documents an attempt at resolution. The Bop can be in any meter or free verse.

For centuries, all the way until the early nineteenth century, the accepted way for beginning poets to learn to write was by direct imitation of the great poets of the past, usually the Classical poets. On the other hand, it seems that poets have also always attracted mocking imitation or parody—some more than others. Whether those poets who inspire more parodies do so because they are funnier or because they are more threatening is an intriguing question (Freud would say that they are funnier *because* they are more threatening). Walt Whitman inspired numerous parodies while his influence was on the rise, threatening the Victorian style of poetry he helped to destroy. The year 1923 saw the publication of an entire book's worth of parodies of Whitman, such as the four-page long parody from which this is excerpted:

Parody: an imitation that exaggerates the style of a previous poet or poem for comic effect.

Imitation: a poem that pays homage to, or draws creative inspiration from, an existing poet or poem; sometimes this term is used for a loose translation.

Forgery: a poem written exactly in the style of another poet, probably with the intent to deceive.

Response: A poem written explicitly in answer to a previous poem.

Translation: A rendering of a poem into another language.

From "After Walt Whitman," Richard Grant White (1884)

O eternal circles, O squares, O triangles, O hypotenuses, O centres,
circumferences, diameters, radiuses, arcs, sines, co-sines, tangents,
  parallelograms
and parallelopipedons! O pipes that are not parallel, furnace pipes, sewer
  pipes,
meerschaum pipes, briar-wood pipes, clay pipes! O matches, O fire, and
  coal-
scuttle, and shovel, and tongs, and fender, and ashes, and dust, and dirt! O
everything! O nothing!
O myself! O yourself!
O my eye!

Then there is Wendy Cope's takeoff of a nursery rhyme as it might have been written by T. S. Eliot:

A Nursery Rhyme
as it might have been written by T.S. Eliot

Because time will not run backwards
Because time
Because time will not run
Hickory dickory

In the last minute of the first hour
I saw the mouse ascend the ancient timepiece,
Claws whispering like wind in dry hyacinths.

One o'clock,
The street lamp said,
'Remark the mouse that races toward the carpet.'

And the unstilled wheel still turning
Hickory dickory
Hickory dickory

dock

For a more recent parody, see Carolyn Kizer's parody of *Hiawatha,* in the "Metrical Palette" chapter.

Ever since the famous Renaissance poetic exchange excerpted here, and probably long before, the reply poem has been a respected way to engage directly with a previous poem:

From "The Passionate Shepherd to His Love," Christopher Marlowe (1599)

Come live with me and be my love,
And we will all the pleasures prove,
That valleys, groves, hills, and fields,
Woods, or steepy mountain yields.

From "The Nymph's Reply to the Shepherd," Sir Walter Raleigh (1600)

If all the world and love were young,
And truth in every shepherd's tongue,

These pretty pleasures might me move
To live with thee and be thy love . . .

Raleigh, like Whitman's mocker, maintains the form, meter, and tone of the original poem. If you are going to write either a parody or a reply, you will find it helpful to do the same. In addition, it will strengthen your poem if you focus consciously on one central aspect of the original in your takeoff or reply. White's parody works because he focuses on the mundane and exhaustively detailed subject matter of Whitman's catalogs; Raleigh's reply works because he focuses on the naïveté of the shepherd. Other aspects of the originals could have been brought in, but they would have diluted the effect. It is just as important to stay aware of your central point in a parody or reply as it is when you are writing any other kind of poem.

Translation is another common way that poets deeply read and become influenced by other poets. Some poets publish numerous volumes of poetry in translation. The poet Robert Bly, translator of Neruda, Vallejo, Rumi, Hafiz, and many other poets into English, has advised, "When translating, don't pick a bad poet to translate. Pick one who is full of sugar, so you can steal some. That's why I feel so good: I've been stealing sugar for years."

QUESTIONS FOR MEDITATION OR DISCUSSION

"Good Poem Scouting Expedition." Visit at least three places where there is poetry: a library, a bookstore, the Internet, your own and your neighbors' bookshelves, your memory. Read through at least 30 poems with as great an aesthetic variety as possible (guideline to ensure variety: choose them from at least 10 different "books" including no more than four different websites and no more than two different memories or audio sources). Choose one poem from among the 30 that you think is a Good Poem—that does what a poem should. The other 29 poems are your "rejected poems." Think about why you made the choices you did. Optional: Write a five- to six-page page paper explanation of why you chose your Good Poem, including a brief description of what was lacking in at least five of the poems you rejected. Attach a list of the titles of the 29 rejected poems and where you found them.

"Let a Poem Read You." Sit down with your Good Poem, or another poem that appeals to you, and let it "read" you. Give yourself plenty of time, and don't forget to follow the three first steps: 1. Slow down. 2. Breathe deeply and clear your mind. 3. Give the poem space to echo in. What do you notice about the poem?

What is the experience like? Write about it in your poet's notebook.

Some beginning poets are afraid to read poetry by others for fear of losing their "own voice." Have you ever had such a fear? Where does one's "own voice" come from in the first place?

Do you think that a skillful and exact forgery of another poet's style could be considered as a "serious" poem? Why or why not?

What is the relation of the following poem by Brenda Hillman to Keats' "Ode to a Grecian Urn"?

STYROFOAM CUP

thou still unravished   thou
thou,   thou bride

thou unstill,
thou unravished   unbride

unthou   unbride

QUOTES

In all the disquisitions you have heard concerning the Happiness of Life, has it ever been recommended to you to read poetry? To one who has a Taste, the Poets serve to fill up Time which would otherwise pass in Idleness, Languor or Vice. You will never be alone with a Poet in your pocket.

—John Adams

What was learned by rote is remembered by heart.

—Eric Griffiths

Make me thy lyre, even as the forest is . . .

—Percy Bysshe Shelley

When we read poetry privately, silently, it rings; it sounds in our ears. It comes alive; it breathes in us. We meet it in some way.

—Anne Waldman

Poetry does not necessarily have to be beautiful to stick in the depths of our memory.

—Colette

Poetry is not a luxury.

—Audre Lorde

So, naturalists observe, the flea
hath smaller fleas that on him prey;
and these have smaller fleas to bite 'em
and so proceed *an infinitum.*
Thus every poet, in his kind,
is bit by him that comes behind.

—Jonathan Swift

In fact, it is as difficult to appropriate the thoughts of others as it is to invent.

—Ralph Waldo Emerson

The Chinese-American poet must reclaim lost voices, simultaneously debunking and reconstructing the past to reflect her own mirror image.

—Marilyn Chin

If there be nothing new, but that which is
Hath been before, how are our brains beguil'd,
Which, labouring for invention, bear amiss
The second burden of a former child!

—William Shakespeare

Tradition is not a public building. It is a love affair.

—Dana Gioia

Art is our chief means of breaking bread with the dead.

—W. H. Auden

Do not follow in the footsteps of the old masters, but seek what they sought.
—Bashō

POETRY PRACTICES

Notebook. Obtain or designate a notebook as your poetry notebook. A bound or spiral notebook is probably more compact and safer for this purpose than a looseleaf whose pages can be easily lost, but it's up to you. Consider if you want it to lie flat on its own, if you want it to be portable, what size page you like writing on, and if you want it lined or unlined. I know poets who write in all kinds of notebooks, from a large looseleaf notebook carried around full of drafts in various stages, to a tiny spiral notebook easy to write in bed in, to an unlined bound sketchbook. Your notebook is a good place to do all the writing exercises in this book, as well as to keep observations, freewriting, prewriting, dreamwriting, lists, wishes, words, phrases, outbursts, memories, and any other raw material that will help you to access your own personal sources of writing power.

Personal Language-Archaeology. In your notebook, write about the first experiences with language you remember. Think about words, phrases, or names you used to repeat or enjoy hearing. There may be song lyrics, phrases from books, or snatches of words from TV commercials that have stuck in your mind for a long time. Write down as many of these remembered bits of language as you can, even if they seem mundane or unpoetic or even ugly. As you write each one, jot down any memories or feelings that come along with it, and then look for patterns and connections between them. You might try these categories:

"***Personal Poetry-Archaeology***" Write down the titles and as much as you can remember of any poems, rhymes, or song lyrics that you remember from chilhood. These could even be jump-rope or playground rhymes.

Name-Archaeology. Write down the names of various people you have known in your life and whose names you happen to remember. These names are a unique personal litany of your life. How does it feel to read over these different names? Do any of them have an emotional charge? How does the sound of the name relate to the feeling they give you?

"***Title-Archaeology***" Write down the titles of all the books you can think of that you have always wanted to read someday.

Personal Poetry Anthology. Make a list of poems that have meant a lot to you in your life so far. Write, out, photocopy, or download as many of them as you can and make them into a book.

Poet's Archaeology Poem. If one or more of the exercises above inspires a poem for you, write the poem(s).

Touchstones. While you are working with *A Poet's Craft,* keep a "touchstone" section in your notebook to write down passages of poems that you especially like, and that seem to have some connection with the kind of poetry you want to write. Read these "touchstones" over frequently, and think about the connection between these poems and the language experiences you remember from childhood. Do you see any patterns connecting these different threads in your relationship with poetic language?

Poet's Reading Notebook. Less personal than "touchstones," this more general, but equally valuable, type of response consists of names of all or some of the poems you have been reading, and space for you to respond to them with your impressions, questions, judgments, imitations, parodies, attacks, critiques, meditations, or homages. Two principles to keep in mind in your choices and responses are variety and relevance. Variety: write on as wide a spectrum of styles, moods, genres, periods, and voices as you can possibly find. Relevance: write on poems that draw you in, perhaps for reasons you don't understand. Then, as you write, keep asking yourself how the work is relevant to your own projects and concerns.

Compass of Poetics. This is a complex undertaking that will take some time and may teach you a lot about your personal sense of poetry. Choose five pairs of poems, each pair written during a different century. At least half of the 10 poems should have been originally written in English. One of each pair should be a poem you love and/or admire as a model for your poetry, and the other a poem you dislike and/or are disinterested in as a model for your poetry. Date each poem at least approximately, and provide title and author. Accompany each pair of poems with written support for your choice (this could be either a developed paragraph or typed or handwritten notes including underlines and circling). Either alone or in a group, think about the patterns of similarities that unite your choices across the centuries. From looking at these choices, you should be able to delineate four or five pairs of qualities that are important to your own poetics. Then look at your own poems and meditate on how close they come to embodying your poetic ideals. Option: you can supplement/"illustrate" any of the poems in the compass with works of art from the same century in other aesthetic forms (images, etc.) accompanied by a brief explanation of how the image illuminates the same aspect of poetics you are focusing on in your contrast. Option: you can map out your pairs of qualities in terms of four directions and a center, with some of their traditional associations: East: mental; South: life-force/energy; West: emotional; North: physical/imagery; center: self/soul.

By Heart. Make a list of poems you would like to memorize. Then try memorizing some of them, perhaps starting with a short poem every week. How does this change you?

Translation from Another Language. If you know another language, even a little, pick a powerful poem in that language and translate it. You will probably want a dictionary nearby to help you if you get stuck. If you choose a well-known poem, it's fine to use previous translations as guides to meaning.

Translation from English. If you don't know another language, try translating a poem you really admire from English into English. You can try putting it into different line-lengths, form, or of diction, or simply into your own words.

Parody, Forgery, or Imitation. Write a poem in the style of a major poet who appeals to you, or irritates or confuses or threatens you. Any poet to whom you have a strong reaction is good for this exercise. Some poets with very distinctive voices you might want to try are e. e. cummings, Langston Hughes, Allen Ginsberg, Sylvia Plath, Robert Frost, Maya Angelou, Li-Young Lee, and Alexander Pope. See if you can either make your readers laugh (parody), or fool them into thinking it is actually written by your poet (forgery); test this out by showing them a poem by the poet alongside yours and see if they can tell which is the forgery. Or try a literary imitation (a poem in your own style that draws from, or is inspired by, another poet but doesn't mimic their style exactly).

A Poet's Bookshelf: For Further Reading

Accent

Attridge, Derek. *The Rhythms of English Verse*
Berry, Francis. *Poetry and the Physical Voice*
Carper, Thomas. *Meter and Meaning: An Introduction to Rhythm in Poetry*

Ballad

Fowler, David. *A Literary History of the Popular Ballad*
Lyle, Emily. *Scottish Ballads*
Quiller-Couch, Arthur, ed. *The Oxford Book of Ballads*

Etymology

Barney, Stephen. *Word-Hoard: Anglo-Saxon Words*
Baugh, Albert C., and Thomas Cable. *History of the English Language*
Byrne, Josefa. *Mrs. Byrne's Dictionary of Unusual and Preposterous Words*
Dictionary of Americanisms
Lewis, C. S. *Studies in Words*
Origins of English Words
Oxford Dictionary of English Etymology

Exploratory Forms

Beach, Christopher. *Artifice and Indeterminacy: An Anthology of New Poetics*
Dworkin, Craig. *Reading the Illegible*
Hinton, Laura, and Cynthia Hogue. *We Who Love to Be Astonished*
Hoover, Paul. *Postmodern American Poetry*
Kuszai, Joel, ed. *Poetics@*
Perelman, Bob. *The Marginalization of Poetry*
Retallack, Joan. "What Is Experimental Poetry and Why Do We Need It?" Jacket.com
Silliman, Ron. *In the American Tree*
Sloan, Mary Margaret. *Innovative Poetry by Women*

Found Poems

Porter, Bern. *Found Poems*, ed. Mark Melnicove

Free Verse

Beyers, Chris. *A History of Free Verse*
Dobyns, Stephen. *Best Words, Best Order*
Fenellosa, Ernest, ed. Ezra Pound. *The Chinese Written Character as a Medium for Poetry*
Hartman, Charles O. *Free Verse: An Essay on Prosody*
Justice, Donald. "The Free-Verse Line in Stevens," in *Platonic Scripts*
Lake, Paul. "Verse That Print Bred." In Finch, *After New Formalism*
Longenbach, James. *The Art of the Poetic Line*
Perloff, Marjorie. "After Free Verse: The New Non-linear Poetries." In Bernstein, *Close Listening*
Scully, James. *Line Break*

Handbooks and Introductions to Poetry

Boisseau, Michelle, and Robert Wallace. *Writing Poetry*
Brogan, T.V. F. *Princeton Encyclopedia of Poetry and Poetics*
Deutsch, Babette. *Poetry Handbook*
Drury, John. *A Poet's Dictionary*
Kinzie, Mary. *A Poet's Guide to Poetry*
Padgett, Ron. *Handbook of Poetic Forms*

Inspiration

Brown, Deborah, Annie Finch, and Maxine Kumin. *Lofty Dogmas: Poets on Poetics*
Behn, Robin, and Chase Twichell, eds. *The Practice of Poetry: Writing Exercises from Poets Who Teach*
Bender, Sheila. *Writing Personal Poetry: Creating Poems From your Life Experiences*
Cameron, Julia. *The Artist's Way*
Cameron, Julia. *The Vein of Gold: A Journey to Your Creative Heart*
Dunning, Stephen, and William Stafford. *Getting the Knack: 20 Poetry Writing Exercises.*
Gioa, Dana. *Can Poetry Matter?*
Goldberg, Natalie. *Writing Down the Bones*
Hyde, Lewis. *The Gift: Imagination and the Erotic Life of Property*
Jaynes, Julian. *The Origin of Consciousness in the Breakdown of the Bicameral Mind*
Keats, John. *The Letters of John Keats*
Newman, Leslea. *Write from the Heart: Exercises for Women Who Want to Write*
Smith, Michael C. *Writing Dangerous Poetry*
Rilke, Rainer Maria. *Letters to a Young Poet*
Weissman, Judith. *Of Two Minds: Poets Who Hear Voices*

Meter and Form (General Writing Guides)

Baer, William. *Writing Metrical Poetry*
Boland, Eavan, and Mark Strand. *The Making of a Poem*
Finch, Annie, and Kathrine Varnes. *An Exaltation of Forms*
Fry, Stephen. *The Ode Less-Travelled*
Hollander, John. *Rhyme's Reason*
Oliver, Mary. *Rules for the Dance*
Pinsky, Robert. *The Sounds of Poetry: A Brief Guide*
Shapiro, Karl, and Robert Beum. *A Prosody Handbook*

Turco, Lewis. *The New Book of Forms*
Williams, Miller. *Patterns of Poetry*

Meter and Form (Iambic Pentameter)

Shaw, Robert B. *Blank Verse: A Guide to its History and Use*
Steele, Timothy. *All the Fun's In How You Say a Thing*

Meter and Form (The Metrical Palette)

Finch, Annie. "Metrical Subversions: Prosody, Poetry and My Affair With the Amphibrach." *The Body of Poetry*
Hornsby, Roger. *Reading Latin Poetry*
Nims, John Frederick. "Maverick Meters" in Finch and Varnes, *An Exaltation of Forms: Contempoary Poets Celebrate the Diversity of Their Art*
Skelton, Robin. *The Shapes of Our Singing: A Comprehensive Guide to Verse Forms and Metres from Around the World*

Modes of Poetry

Dryden, John. *"An Essay of Dramatic Poesy" and Other Critical Essays*
Eliot, T. S. "The Possibility of a Poetic Drama" in *The Sacred Wood*
Lord, Alfred. *The Singer and the Tale*
Ong, Walter. *Orality and Literacy*
Walsh, Andrew. *Roots of Lyric*

Prosody (Theory and History)

Attridge, Derek. *Poetic Rhythm: An Introduction*
Baker, David, ed. *Meter in English: A Symposium*
Finch, Annie. *The Ghost of Meter: Culture and Prosody in American Free Verse*
Fussell, Paul. *Poetic Meter and Poetic Form*
Gross, Harvey. *The Sound of Poetry*
MacAuley, James. *Versification*
Nabokov, Vladimir. *Notes on Prosody*
O'Donnell, Brendan. *The Passion of Meter: A Study of Wordsworth's Metrical Art*
Pate, Alexs. *In the Heart of the Beat: The Poetry of Rap*
Saintsbury, George. *A History of English Prosody*

Publication and Readings

Associated Writing Programs. *Directory of Creative Writing Programs*
Bernstein, Charles. *Close Listening: Poetry and the Performed Word*
Berry, Francis. *Poetry and the Physical Voice*
CLMP Directory of Literary Magazines and Presses
Dustbooks. *Directory of Poetry Publishers*
Grimm, Susan, ed. *Ordering the Storm: How to Put Together a Book of Poems*
Jordan, June. *Poetry for the People*
Poets and Writers. *Directory of American Poets and Fiction Writers*
Rasula, Jed. *The American Poetry Wax Museum*
Shulevitz, Judith, "Sing, Muse . . . or Maybe Not," *New York Times* (online)
Writers Digest Books. *The Poets' Market*

Repeating Forms

Ali, Agha Shahid. *Ravishing DisUnities: Real Ghazals in English.*
Cummins, James. *The Perry Mason Sestinas*
Finch, Annie, and Marie-Elizabeth Mali. *Villanelles*
Frost, Helen. *Keesha's House: A Novel in Verse*
Welford, Theresa. *The Paradelle: An Anthology*

Revision

Cherry, Laura, and Robert Hartwell Fiske, eds. *Poem, Revised: 54 Poems, Revisions, Discussions*
Eliot, T. S. *The Waste Land, with notes by Ezra Pound*
Lehman, David. *Ecstatic Occasions, Expedient Forms*
Smith, Barbara Herrnstein. *Poetic Closure*
Thomas, Dylan, ed. Ralph Maud. *The Notebooks of Dylan Thomas*
Van Dyne, Susan R. *Revising Life: Sylvia Plath's Ariel Poems*
Wallenstein, Barry, and Robert Barr. *Visions and Revisions: The Poet's Process*
Yeats, W. B., ed. Curtis B. Bradley. *Yeats at Work*

Rhyme

Corn, Alfred. *The Poem's Heartbeat*
Espy, Willard. *Words to Rhyme With*
Jones, John. *Pope's Couplet Art*

Jonson, Ben. "A Fit of Rhyme Against Rhyme"
The Oxford Rhyming Dictionary
Piper, William Bowman. *The Heroic Couplet*
Wimsatt, W. K. *The Verbal Icon: Studies in the Meaning of Poetry*

Shaped Poetry

Higgins, Dick. *Pattern Poetry: Guide to an Unknown Literature*

Sonnet

Chiasson, Matthew, and Janine Rogers. *Beauty Bare: The Sonnet Form, Geometry, and Aesthetics*
Colie, Rosemary. *The Resources of Kind: Genre Theory in the Renaissance*
Doczi, Georgi. *The Power of Limits*
Hilson, Jeff, ed. *The Reality Street Book of Sonnets* (experimental sonnets)
Levin, Phillis, ed. *The Penguin Book of the Sonnet*
Oppenheimer, Paul. *The Origin of the Sonnet*
Wells, Zach. *Jailbreaks: 99 Canadian Sonnets*

Syntax and Rhetoric

Theune, Michael. *Structure and Surprise*

Tropes

Buckholz, William. *Understand Rap: Explanations of Confusing Rap Lyrics You and Your Grandma Can Understand*
Hedley, Jane. *Power in Verse: Metaphor and Metonymy in the Renaissance Lyric*
Lakoff, George, and Charles Johnson. *Metaphors We Live By*

Word-Music

Adams, Percy G. *Graces of Harmony: Alliteration, Assonance and Consonance in Eighteenth-Century British Poetry*
Karr, Mary. "Against Decoration" in *Viper Rum*
Wooldridge, Susan Goldsmith. *Poemcrazy: Freeing your Life with Words*

Writer's Notebook

Kuusisto, Stephen, Deborah Tall, and David Weiss, eds. *The Poet's Notebook: Excerpts from the Notebooks of Contemporary American Poets*

Mansfield, Katherine, ed. John Middleton Murray, *The Journals of Katherine Mansfield*

Roethke, Theodore, ed. David Wagoner. *Straw for the Fire: The Notebooks of Theodore Roethke*

Note: Because website URLs change often and can be found through search engines, this book does not include information on website resources. However, a great many up-to-date links to poetry resources may be found at the author's website, www.anniefinch.com.

CHAPTER 3

Thirty-Nine Ways to Make a Poem: A Generative Resource

There are as many ways to make a poem as there are poems, but sometimes the fact that there are so many options can make it hard to get started. Especially when you are just beginning to write poems, you may find yourself looking for an idea of what to write about.

This chapter will be helpful when you simply want to write but feel stuck, or if, while using this book, you need to write a poem based on imagery, or a poem using word-music, or a poem in trochaic meter, and you simply don't have an idea what to write it about at that moment.

Walkabout. Open your mind and your notebook and walk for at least a half hour in a place full of life. I have seen this exercise work equally well in a deserted natural spot or in a busy urban market. As you walk, let yourself be drawn from one inhabitant of this place—tree, animal, puddle, rock, bug, group of twigs, or lamppost, person, dog, mango, curbstone, truck—to the next. Stop and write, then walk until something else catches your attention. Stop and write, then walk till something else catches your attention. At each stop, write a brief reaction to what has drawn you there. Keep in mind the rhythms and length of the haiku. Stay specific in your images. Your poem may end up resembling a string of beads, or a map. As you revise your walkabout you may choose to expand on one or more of these brief moments. (An expanded description of this exercise appears in the "Imagery" chapter.)

Researched Piece. Research something you haven't known about before but have always wanted to know about in any field—history, rock climbing, dentistry, space engineering, politics, scuba diving, quilting, movies, beekeeping, anthropology, violin making, and so on. Incorporate your research into a poem, including at least five specialized terms, two facts, and an anecdote.

Synesthesia. Arthur Rimbaud is famous for his poem "Vowels," where he gave colors to each of the vowel sounds. Such crossing of the senses, a common experience to certain people, is called "synesthesia." Write a poem describing one sense in terms of other senses. You may want to imagine that you are describing what that sense is like to someone who lacks it: using sound to describe a particular sight to a blind friend, using touch to describe what hearing a symphony is like to someone who is deaf. You could write about taste in terms of touch, about sound in terms of smell, about smell in terms of sight.

Talking Toy. Write a poem in the voice of your favorite childhood stuffed animal or other toy. You might want to imagine you have asked the toy a question, and write the poem as a letter giving you advice about what to do now in your life.

Number Shuffle. Think of a topic you'd like to write about (an object, memory, or desire would work well). Write a list of at least nine numbers in random order. Then go down the list and next to each number, write an idea, thought, or image about your topic. Reshuffle the ideas in the correct order of the numbers, and add what you need to tie the poem together. Revise, cutting out items that don't work.

Homesickness. Write a poem expressing homesickness, either for someplace you remember and wish you could return to, or for someplace you have never been, but wish you could go.

Zoom. Wherever you are, look around you and become a camera that zooms in tight on a certain object. Imagine that you are making a movie and that a close-up of this object opens the movie. Write down the plot of the movie and turn it into a narrative poem.

Animal Words. Write a piece in the imagined voice of an animal, bird, insect, fish, or other creature. Do not include any people in your piece, and write as best you can from a perspective that is *not* human-centered. (Tips: do not use any recognizable human idioms [phrases like "saving for a rainy day" or "How's it going?"] in your piece. Try to keep the language free of too much abstraction and "meaning"—stick to direct images as much as possible.)

Protest. Write a poem of outrage on a political topic, something that makes you furious. Use the form of an invective or a lament. Feel free to assume a public voice and to use the political "we," meaning "the people."

Dialogue. Write an imaginary conversation between two members of your family or circle of friends, about a conflict over something either extremely important or ridiculously unimportant.

Photographic Quantities. I once heard a photographer say that the difference between a professional photographer and an amateur is that the professional takes a lot more pictures and throws almost all of them out. Try this technique with poetry. Write as many poems as you can, without stopping, in the time you have available. Give yourself permission to write as badly as possible; just don't stop writing. When you are done, pick the best poem and throw out all the others. Don't revise.

Element Words. Write a piece in the imagined voice of an element: earth (rock, dirt, gemstone, etc.), water (rain, stream, ocean, etc.), fire (candle, lightning, campfire, etc.), or air (tornado, breeze, breath, etc.). Follow directions for animal words.

Q?! Write a poem designed to communicate something new about something in the world. Write the poem with no pronouns. Use three beats in each line (see chapter 11 on accent). Include, in key places, at least four words that begin with the letter *Q*.

Headline. Poet Nancy Willard is fond of writing poems with titles taken from newspaper headlines. She is especially fond of the sports pages, making literal flights of imagination out of images such as Cardinals Mangle Giants; Cubs Trip Pirates; Tigers Slip Past Yankees. Look at a newspaper with this kind of literal-minded wonder, and write a poem based on one of the headlines.

Nature Preserve. Research a natural phenomenon or creature, and write a poem using the vocabulary you have found: the names of butterflies, fish, trees, mushrooms, clouds, and so on. Use as few other words as you can.

Guided Tour. Using the language of a guidebook, write a guided tour of a place familiar to you. For inspiration, you might want to look at Elizabeth Bishop's poem "12 O'Clock News," which describes a typewriter, for example, in these words: "What endless labor those / small, peculiarly shaped terraces represent! And / yet, on them the welfare of this tiny principality / depends."

Blason. Write a love poem, or a hate poem, consisting entirely of comparisons, in the manner of the poetic tradition known as the "blason": "His eyes are as bright as stars, his lips as sweet as raspberries," etc.

Mini Field Trip. Walk around in a place you enjoy or a place you hate. Find eight one-word topics. The topic is your title. Write a poem of no more than three lines about each topic.

Ritual Chant. Write a chantlike poem for use in the services of a religion, either a real religion or one you have made up.

Ekphrastic Poem. Write a poem describing, or based on, a work of visual art. For examples, look at W. H. Auden's "Musee des Beaux Arts," W. C. Williams's "The Kermess," or Elizabeth Bishop's "Large Bad Picture." Here is a suggested strategy: (1) Walk through an art exhibit in a museum (pictures in a book will do if necessary, but real art tends to be much more powerful). Pay close attention to your reactions to the art. These reactions may be subtly physical (racing pulse, stomach butterflies, lightness or excitement in upper chest) as well as intellectual or emotional. (2) Choose the two pieces of art that gave you the strongest reactions or that interest you the most. (3) Stand or sit in front of the first piece and observe and write down four surprising things about it. Remember that images can appeal to any of the senses, not only sight but also touch, taste, smell, and sound. Imagining the smell, sound, and so on the art would have is fine, as long as you gather four concrete, specific, detailed images. If you have trouble thinking of anything, wait quietly until something comes to you. If nothing comes to you, just write down the first four things you notice or imagine. (4) Do the same for the second piece. (5) Look over your eight observations and notice any pattern or possible meaning they share, or notice something that strikes your imagination about them. (6) Write a poem based on your observations. It can be a poem about the artwork(s) or it can be a poem about something else that the art suggested to you. In either case, be sure to incorporate as many of your surprising, specific images into your poem as you can. (7) Check over your line breaks to see if they work to emphasize the impression you want to create, remembering that words at the beginning or end of a line get extra attention.

Sappho's Cousin. Make up a poem by an imaginary poet who lived centuries ago, and whose poems have been fragmented and destroyed over the years as Sappho's poems were. You can write a full poem and destroy it yourself (get it wet, step on it, tear it, burn it), or write it in a fragmentary style to begin with. For inspiration, you can look at the Sappho translations by Stanley Lombardo, which show only the fragments that have survived with no attempt to fill in the blanks.

Fabric Pattern. Pick a small section of a piece of fabric whose pattern you know well and like. It can be plaid, flowered, or polka dotted, embroidered or woven or silk-screened. Write a poem that somehow follows the same design. One approach would be to assign parts of speech to different design elements: a verb ending in *-ing* for each green stripe in the plaid, a noun for each flower on the quilt with an adjective added for each flower with a stem. Copy or paste the fabric on the page. Or you could use the same rhythm, or a word beginning with the same letter of the alphabet, each time a color repeats.

Character Poem. Go to a place where you can observe strangers. Pick one person who intrigues you and use your imagination to write a character description in your notebook. Include numerous specific details to make the person believable: both things you can observe such as dress, speech, hygiene, gestures, posture, and friends, and things you might need to imagine, such as hobbies, religion, personal history, taste in food, art, or movies, and current problems and desires. Let your imagination go as wild as you want. Use your notes to write a poem about this person.

House Plant. Imagine a house plant you have encountered sometime in your life, in a home or office. Write a poem in its voice. It can be a narrative in third person, or a first person lyric.

Home Lore. Choose one expression common in your family, or a story that has been frequently told. Write a poem based on it. Experiment with different narrators / points of view.

Cross-Outs. Write down all the words and phrases you can think of. Leave the paper for a few minutes while you take a break. Come back and cross out all the words you want to cross out. Then write another group of words and phrases. Take a break, come back, and cross out as many as you want. Take another break. Combine and edit the two groups of remaining words into a poem.

Elegy. Write an elegy for a person you loved, a place that has been destroyed, a species that is extinct. You might look at elegies such as William Dunbar's "Lament for the Makers," Ben Jonson's "On My First Sonne," Milton's "Lycidas," Walt Whitman's "O Captain, My Captain," Tennyson's "In Memoriam," Auden's "In Memory of W.B. Yeats," Edna St. Vincent Millay's "Sonnets from an Ungrafted Tree," Theodore Roethke's "For My Student Jane, Thrown by a Horse," Frank O'Hara's "The Day Lady Died," Lucille Clifton's "The Abortion," my own "Elegy for My Father," or Marilyn Hacker's "Winter Numbers."

Serious Limerick. Using the form of a limerick as a stanza, see if you can write a serious poem of at least three limerick stanzas. Or, see if you can write some truly funny limericks.

Interactive Ritual. Write a piece to be performed over the next few weeks by yourself and/or as many other people as you like. The ritual should be interactive and should aim to create a result, whether in action, feeling, or awareness. You can bring any objects you need and you can specify where, when, and how it should be performed.

Dream Conversation. Pick a scene from a dream you remember. Describe the scene with concrete detail; or write a conversation between yourself and a character from the dream. Feel free to embellish or edit.

Architecture. Write a poem consisting of directions to make a building you would like to see exist. It can be a writing retreat, a palace, a school, a news kiosk, a museum, and so on. Make it exactly the way you want in terms of color, size, materials, location, and special features. Or write a poem that is guiding a visitor through the building after it is finished.

Gratitudes. Name at least five things you are grateful for. Use concrete imagery and metaphor to describe them and what makes you grateful for them. Revise into a poem.

Interdisciplinary Collaboration. Find a person who works in another art form: music, painting, dance, theater, film, video, and so forth. Work out a collaboration with that person to perform or present. You may also collaborate with yourself.

Obsessing. Think of something that obsesses you. In a magazine such as *Harper's* or *The New Yorker,* choose an article about something which does not interest you, or about something you are unfamiliar with. Select 20 words from that article. Then write about your obsession incorporating those 20 words (exercise from Christian Barter).

Activist Poem. Write a poem that raises consciousness, or even better, that inspires, encourages, incites, or necessitates a particular action, regarding a global or national issue that you feel affects you personally, such as domestic violence or global climate change. *Variation:* do so entirely through concrete images.

Paper Clip. According to Audre Lorde's student and mine, Cheryl Boyce Taylor, Lorde used to ask her students to write 100 words about a paper clip. Write a poem of 100 words about a paper clip, your fingernail, your kitchen table, or another innocuous object.

Truth-Telling. Write a poem consisting entirely of things you'd like to say, but never would, to a parent, lover, sibling, child, teacher, roommate, best friend, mayor, president, corporate CEO (thanks to Charles Bernstein and Bernadette Mayer).

Found Dialogue. Go somewhere where you can easily overhear strangers talking—a restaurant, bus or bus stop, bathroom, checkout line, and so forth. Listen until you hear a passage of dialogue that strikes you as intriguing, funny, strange, or compelling. Through memorization and/or discreet notetaking, get it down on paper, word for word. Choose some of it to reassemble into a poem. You may want to write a poem that is entirely dialogue, using all or some of your found dialogue.

Hated Person Poem. Write a poem from the point of view of a person you absolutely despise, someone who appalls and revolts you. It could be a person you are scared of, or who has hurt you very much, or someone you wish you could hurt. Get completely inside the character of the person; make sure they are a real three-dimensional character with a complex personality, not a stereotype or stick figure.

QUESTIONS FOR MEDITATION OR DISCUSSION

William Stafford, who had a habit of writing a poem every day no matter what, used to say that the key to writer's block is simply to lower one's standards. What do you think of this idea? What kind of writing practices do you tend to be following, at the times when you feel best about your writing?

What exercises in this chapter, and throughout this book, appeal to you the most? You might want to put marks next to those that sound interesting to you. Do you see a pattern among them? Can you think of other exercises that are similar that might also be useful for you to try? Why do you think you like this type of writing exercise? Is it familiar, or does it fit your usual personality style (for example, emotion-based versus technique-based)? What if you were to try a type of exercise completely different from the kind you usually choose? Does the idea frighten you? Do you think it would be fruitful for you to try?

Among poets, there is a great range of approaches to the idea of "writer's block." Some poets are tormented by it and tear their hair out over their empty pages. Some accept periods when writing doesn't come easily as necessary fallow periods when their creativity is recharging or, as Carolyn Kizer once told me, "the tide is out." Some try to trick themselves out of a block by using prompts and exercises. Some think the whole idea of writer's block is a myth, and that all you need to do is put your pen to the paper and get going so you will have something to revise. Where does your approach to writer's block fall along this spectrum of attitudes?

QUOTES

Few will dare or deign to dispute that the prime object of composing poetry is to keep any two poems from sounding alike. . . . my poems make so many different sounds—I don't write them all the same day. I have to keep them well separated so they'll have different sounds.

—Robert Frost

It is from longing my making proceeds.

—Robert Duncan

Candor . . . is the only wile.

—Emily Dickinson

Write about what burns in you, what you can't forget.

—Muriel Rukeyser

[Poetry is] the art in which one being calls out to, whispers to, sings to, one other being, in the most intimate way. Our species needs it, perhaps, to survive.

—Sharon Olds

The best craftsman always leaves holes and gaps in the works of the poem so that something that is not in the poem can creep, crawl, flash, or thunder in. The joy and function of poetry is, and was, the celebration of man, which is also the celebration of God.

—Dylan Thomas, "Poetic Manifesto"

It is the job of poetry to clean up our word-clogged reality by creating silences around things.

—Stéphane Mallarmé

With a great poet the sense of Beauty overcomes every other consideration, or rather obliterates all consideration.

—John Keats

Keep the pen moving.

—Natalie Goldberg

Poetry never has any kindness at all.

—Stevie Smith

POETRY PRACTICES

(Group) Secrets. This exercise is Garrett Hongo's contribution to Behn and Twichell's *The Practice of Poetry.* Each person writes down a secret—either a real one, or a made-up one, or a borrowed one. The teacher or facilitator redistributes the secrets, and each person writes a poem in the voice of the owner of the secret they have received.

(Group) Weaving. Do a timed freewriting, with everyone starting with the same word or group of words. People read them out loud. Then do another timed writing where people take phrases or words or images from what they heard the first time around and work them into their own writing. Do this for a few rounds, and notice how words, images, and ideas are recycled and transformed. (Thanks to Julie Carr for this exercise.)

Exercises to help you find your voice from Solana D'Lamont:

1. Be outrageous! The more freedom you feel, the more willing you will be to release your voice.
2. Write in the dark or with your eyes closed.
3. Dress all in one color and write.
4. Activate odors that move your spirit. Try cinnamon, pine, vanilla.
5. Write outdoors.

6. Surround yourself with special, evocative objects as you write.
7. Play music as you write. Change the music and see what happens.
8. Draw pictures with finger paints. Lose yourself in colors and shapes.
9. Write with the opposite hand.
10. Write fragments–dialogue, description, poetry. Don't worry about how everything will fit together.

Note: Every chapter in this book also includes further ideas for generating poems. You may find particularly fertile and open-ended ideas at the ends of the chapters on words and their roots (chap. 4), tropes (chap. 7), and exploratory poetics (chap. 10).

CHAPTER 4

The Raw Material: Words and Their Roots

The Many Languages of English

One of my sisters used to amuse me, when I was little, by singing this song:

Show me the way to go home,
I'm tired and I want to go to bed.
I had a little drink about an hour ago
and it went right to my head.
Wherever I may roam,
On land or sea or foam,
You can always hear me singing this song:
Show me the way to go home!

Indicate the way to my habitual abode,
I'm fatigued and I want to retire.
I had an alcoholic beverage 60 minutes ago
and it went right to my cerebellum.
Wherever I may perambulate,
On land or sea or atmospheric pressure,
You can always hear me chanting this melody:
Indicate the way to my habitual abode!

—IRVING KING, TWENTIETH CENTURY

Like much humor, the song calls attention to an uncomfortable truth. Most of the roots of English lie in two languages, and their relationship was established by war and oppression. The original root language of English, Germanic-based Anglo-Saxon, was native to Britain. But after the Norman Conquest in 1066—

when France, under William the Conqueror, invaded England—Anglo-Saxon became the despised language of the conquered people, who were reduced to the status of serfs, basically slaves to the land they farmed. Meanwhile, the conqueror's language, French, evolved into the language of government, law, wealth, and culture. In a famous scene in Sir Walter Scott's novel *Ivanhoe,* a group of Anglo-Saxons is tending pigs, cows, and sheep in the barn. One of them observes that these animals have English names when they are being fed and their stalls are being cleaned, but French names when they are prepared as pork (*porc*), beef (*boeuf*), and mutton (*mouton*) for the wealthy to eat.

The linguistic double-standard whereby French words are considered more cultured and refined than Anglo-Saxon words remains in English today. In fact, the richness and complexity of this double heritage is now a key source of English's strength as a poetic language. Though our most common words tend to be Anglo-Saxon, French has provided about 28 percent of English vocabulary, and there are two different ways—an Anglo-Saxon way and a French way—to say many things:

trip/voyage or journey
drink/imbibe
child/infant
answer/respond
tell/recount
want/desire
cooking/cuisine
house/mansion
guts/courage
bath/toilet

Then there is the mid-twentieth-century sexist remark, "Men sweat and women perspire." Irony aside, the status pattern is always the same. "We want you to be there" sounds very different than "We desire your presence." "Four-letter words" are all Anglo-Saxon, and scholars have posited that the reason these are considered obscene is not really because of the bodily functions they refer to—if you want to be polite, you can use the Latin words "defecate" and "fornicate"—but because of the political powerlessness of those who originally spoke them.

The "prestigious" sound of French words comes not only from this political context but also from the fact that French has its roots in Latin, the standard intellectual language of Western history and for centuries the official language of the most powerful institution in Europe, the Catholic Church. Because another large group of words (about another 28 percent of English) were derived or imported directly from Latin into English by priests, scholars, doctors, lawyers, scientists, and other professionals, we have pairs such as:

piss/urinate
spit/expectorate
chew/masticate
house/domicile
dress/attire
write/inscribe
light/illuminate
live/inhabit

This is the basis of the pleasure the fifth-graders in my neighborhood get from telling other kids, "Your epidermis is showing."

To complicate matters further there are three ways to say some very common things in our language: an Anglo-Saxon way, a French way, and a Latin way:

ask/inquire/interrogate
eat/dine/ingest
awake/alert/conscious
walk/stroll/perambulate
think/muse/cogitate
till/farm/cultivate
sleep/repose/rejuvenate
talk/converse/interlocute

Poets can, and frequently do, use the different vocabularies of English for poetic effects. The contrast between Anglo-Saxon and Latinate diction can be striking. A famous passage in which Macbeth says the same thing first in Latinate, and then in Anglo-Saxon words, illustrates this point:

diction: a particular type of vocabulary, distinguished from others by the etymology, level of formality, social context, or origin of the words.

Will all great Neptune's ocean wash this blood
Clean from my hand? No, this my hand will rather
The multitudinous seas incarnadine,
Making the green one red.
—FROM *MACBETH*, WILLIAM SHAKESPEARE (1605)

The word "incarnadine" means to redden, an idea repeated with Anglo-Saxon diction in the phrase that follows it. There is something chilling and, to my ear, quite insane-sounding in Macbeth's taking the time to restate this phrase in Anglo-Saxon words at such a crucial moment of the play.

It is not only Anglo-Saxon "swear" words that can sound shocking when you are not expecting them; any sudden Latinate word in the middle of an Anglo-Saxon poetic context can hit the reader with the intensity of entering a different part of the brain, as in this passage from Stevens:

From "The Emperor of Ice Cream," Wallace Stevens (1922)

Call the roller of big cigars,
The muscular one, and bid him whip
In kitchen cups concupiscent curds . . .

The following poem modulates between colloquial words and phrases ("the big strip tease") and a more Latinate, formal, educated diction ("exceptionally well," "annihilate," "vanish," "filaments").

"Lady Lazarus," Sylvia Plath

I have done it again.
One year in every ten
I manage it—

A sort of walking miracle, my skin
Bright as a Nazi lampshade,
My right foot

A paperweight,
My face a featureless, fine
Jew linen.

Peel off the napkin
O my enemy.
Do I terrify?—

The nose, the eye pits, the full set of teeth?
The sour breath
Will vanish in a day.

Soon, soon the flesh
The grave cave ate will be
At home on me

And I a smiling woman.
I am only thirty.
And like the cat I have nine times to die.

This is Number Three.
What a trash
To annihilate each decade.

What a million filaments.
The peanut-crunching crowd
Shoves in to see

Them unwrap me hand and foot—
The big strip tease.
Gentlemen, ladies,

These are my hands,
My knees.
I may be skin and bone,

Nevertheless, I am the same, identical woman.
The first time it happened I was ten.
It was an accident.

The second time I meant
To last it out and not come back at all.
I rocked shut

As a seashell.
They had to call and call
And pick the worms off me like sticky pearls.

Dying
Is an art, like everything else,
I do it exceptionally well.

I do it so it feels like hell.
I do it so it feels real.
I guess you could say I've a call.

It's easy enough to do it in a cell.
It's easy enough to do it and stay put.
It's the theatrical

Comeback in broad day
To the same place, the same face, the same brute
Amused shout:

"A miracle!"
That knocks me out.
There is a charge

For the eyeing of my scars, there is a charge,
For the hearing of my heart—
It really goes.

And there is a charge, a very large charge,
For a word or a touch
Or a bit of blood

Or a piece of my hair or my clothes.
So, so, Herr Doktor.
So, Herr Enemy.

I am your opus,
I am your valuable,
The pure gold baby

That melts to a shriek.
I turn and burn.
Do not think I underestimate your great concern.

Ash, ash—
You poke and stir.
Flesh, bone, there is nothing there—

A cake of soap,
A wedding ring,
A gold filling.

Herr God, Herr Lucifer
Beware
Beware.

Out of the ash
I rise with my red hair
And I eat men like air.

There are just enough Latinate words in this poem to lend the speaker's voice a dignified authority, but not enough to interfere with the intensity or the directness. In general, a little bit of Latinate diction goes a long way in poetry. Scholar and translator Marie Borroff has developed a "Latinate index" to measure how readers respond to language with different etymological roots. She has found that an index of 25 percent Latinate words creates a very "elevated" effect.

Greek and Latin words tend to consist of roots surrounded by prefixes and suffixes, which the reader needs to unpack in order to comprehend the word (the word "comprehend," for example, consists of the prefix *com-*, familiar from words such as "compress," and the root *prehendere,* familiar from words such as "prehensile," which add up to a word meaning "to grasp completely," which can then be changed with additional prefixes and suffixes into "comprehensive," "comprehension," "incomprehensible," etc.). Perhaps because of this complexity, a piece of writing with too many Latinate and Greek words sounds abstract and may feel dull, bureaucratic, and generic.

Anglo-Saxon words are more one of a kind (the word "kind," for example, is a self-contained word, and any prefixes or suffixes that can be attached are simple and self-evident: "kindred," "unkind," "kindly"). Passages with many Anglo-Saxon words tend to be more direct, immediate, and tangible, and to have a more vivid impact on the reader. Or, to put it another way, Anglo-Saxon words are stronger, closer, and easier to feel, and give the reader a better handle on the poem. The difference between these two sentences should make the point. Studies have shown that a "Latinate index" of 25 percent or more will make it hard for a reader to respond to a piece of writing. But as always, there are exceptions, so if you really feel like using Latinate diction and do so with full awareness for good reasons, then go for it.

Wallace Stevens is one poet who put Latinate words to good use; as with the word "concupiscent," they add richness and interest to his voice and are one of the hallmarks of his style:

From "The Comedian as the Letter C," Wallace Stevens (1922)

Nota: man is the intelligence of his soil,
The sovereign ghost. As such, the Socrates
Of snails, musician of pears, principium
And lex. Sed quaeritur: is this same wig
Of things, this nincompated pedagogue,
Preceptor to the sea? Crispin at sea
Created, in his day, a touch of doubt.
An eye most apt in gelatines and jupes,
Berries of villages, a barber's eye,
An eye of land, of simple salad-beds,
Of honest quilts, the eye of Crispin, hung
On porpoises, instead of apricots,
And on silentious porpoises, whose snouts
Dibbled in waves that were mustachios,
Inscrutable hair in an inscrutable world.

One eats one paté, even of salt, quotha.
It was not so much the lost terrestrial,

The snug hibernal from that sea and salt,
That century of wind in a single puff.
What counted was mythology of self,
Blotched out beyond unblotching. Crispin,
The lutanist of fleas, the knave, the thane,
The ribboned stick, the bellowing breeches, cloak
Of China, cap of Spain, imperative haw
Of hum, inquisitorial botanist,
And general lexicographer of mute
And maidenly greenhorns, now beheld himself,
A skinny sailor peering in the sea-glass.
What word split up in clickering syllables
And storming under multitudinous tones
Was name for this short-shanks in all that brunt?
Crispin was washed away by magnitude.
The whole of life that still remained in him
Dwindled to one sound strumming in his ear,
Ubiquitous concussion, slap and sigh,
Polyphony beyond his baton's thrust.

The extravagant use of Latinate (and some Latin) words in this poem emphasizes the artifice of Stevens's poet, creating a distance between the human world of imagination and the natural world.

The most reliable way to tell which words in your poems are Latinate is to look up their histories in the dictionary. But there are some shortcuts that you will learn or may find you already know; for example, any word that ends with a suffix such as *-ate* (negotiate, inculcate), *-ion* (nation, substantiation), or *-ize* (naturalize, customize) is a Latinate word. Words ending in the suffixes *-logy* or *-logic* (pedagogy, geologic) or *-meter* or *-metry* (pentameter, trigonometry) are Greek-derived words, also imported into English for learned or scientific purposes.

Of course, not all our words are derived from Anglo-Saxon, French, Greek, or Latin. English includes words from more than 120 different languages, possibly more than any other language. Some of my own favorite imports are jasmine, algebra, shawl; moose, skunk, squirrel; guitar, banana, mosquito; shampoo, dungarees, pajamas. Can you guess which language each of these groups of three words comes from? Any good dictionary that includes etymologies can tell you. Then there are more obvious borrowed words, such as boondocks, coffee, agitprop, tea, kayak, poncho, safari, bazaar, and brat (origins are at the end of the chapter). By using words with different origins in your poems, you can create a uniquely interesting verbal texture.

Poems such as Julia Alvarez's "Bilingual Sestina," Tamam Kahn's "Ghazal for Marakesh," and many of Harryette Mullen's poems mix words from two or more different languages into their poems. This poem uses an artful mix of languages:

"Freeway 280," Lorna Dee Cervantes

Las casitas near the gray cannery,
nestled amid wild abrazos of climbing roses
and man-high red geraniums
are gone now. The freeway conceals it
all beneath a raised scar.

But under the fake windsounds of the open lanes,
in the abandoned lots below, new grasses sprout,
wild mustard remembers, old gardens
come back stronger than they were,
trees have been left standing in their yards.
Albaricoqueros, cerezos, nogales . . .
Viejitas come here with paper bags to gather greens.
Espinaca, verdolagas, yerbabuena . . .

I scramble over the wire fence
that would have kept me out.
Once, I wanted out, wanted the rigid lanes
to take me to a place without sun,
without the smell of tomatoes burning
on swing shift in the greasy summer air.

Maybe it's here
en los campos extraños de esta ciudad
where I'll find it, that part of me
mown under
like a corpse
or a loose seed.

Cervantes introduces Spanish vocabulary into the poem with a single noun in the first line, followed by other nouns. It is only in the last stanza that she builds up to a full, complex phrase. The meaning of the phrase is no coincidence.

Such a practice can add great beauty and richness to a poem, for speakers of both languages and monolingual speakers of English alike. To come across words in another language can raise readers' consciousness about the importance to our culture of languages other than English, and can give monolingual readers the experience of learning to understand unfamiliar words in context. This contemporary Hawaiian poem incorporates the pidgin language used by many natives of Hawaii, using a pun on the word "pidgin" to make a statement in actual pidgin:

From "Da History of Pigeon," Joe Balaz

So nowadays get pigeon by da zoo—Get pigeon on
da beach—Get pigeon in town—Get pigeon in coops—
And no maddah wat anybody try do, dey kannot get rid of
pigeon—

I guess wit such a wide blue sky, everyting deserves to fly.

Levels of Diction

The Roman orator Cicero was the first to identify a distinction between "high" (formal), "middle" (everyday), and "low" (slang) diction that is still applicable today. "High" diction tends to be more highly Latinate than "low" diction; idiom and syntax also play a role in the different styles. This poem contrasts the high and low styles with great economy:

"I Know a Man," Robert Creeley

As I sd to my
friend, because I am
always talking,—John, I

sd, which was not his
name, the darkness sur-
rounds us, what

can we do against
it, or else, shall we &
why not, buy a goddamn big car,

drive, he sd, for
christ's sake, look
out where yr going.

The Latinate verb "surround" and the complex syntax of "what can we do against it" (even without the semicolon that should really precede that phrase!) provide just enough signals indicating "high" diction to contrast with the diction of the rest of the poem.

In the following short poem, the idiomatic grammar and spelling lend the poem an intimacy that paradoxically emphasizes the feeling of loneliness:

"Sometime," Ruth Forman

It don't matter who you are
Loneliness just come up n grab you
Like a best friend

Idiom: a figure of speech used in daily conversation, such as "let's not go there," "walking on air," "saw it out of the corner of your eye"

On the high end of the spectrum, Ray Gonzalez's "It Was a Turtle" uses formal diction (from Latinate words including "devour," "frightened," "transparent," and "emerges" to more subtly formal word choices such as "upon" and "becomes") to convey the significance of the turtle and the speaker's reverence:

"It was a Turtle," Ray Gonzalez

It was a turtle moving slowly toward the eyes
of an inaudible whisper—what we bring.

It was a turtle moving inside the arms as if skin
was transparent and could answer riddles,

devour secrets like tiny flies evaporating
in its snapping jaws—fumes from flowers,

digging nests for eggs touched
by wormlike fingers,

the husband crawling toward wrinkled layers
of the amphibian who let him out of his skin.

It was a turtle resembling the canoe moving up the arms,
crossing the vein in the elbow to shine on the lake.

How was it mistaken for a knot of thumbs?
Did it hiss when the foot pressed on its shell?

It was a turtle vibrating toward the cove
where claws are cleaned to breathe.

When the firefly streaked into the trees,
it sparked where nothing emerges,

flashed over the head of the turtle that resembles nightmares
where men are frightened into being themselves.

When waste surrounded the abandoned village, these men
found burned turtle shells in cold campfires.

One turtle escaped inside the moss of a horn.
It is the sound of a vowel and a place to see,

the turtle building upon silence that ends here.
When it moves, something floats in the air, then disappears.

Pictures of a turtle returning across the water.
The coin of misunderstanding finding its tracks in the mud.

When the retracted head becomes illusion, it is replaced.
When the shell is preserved, a head emerges with one stone syllable.

Allusion

Some poems use various kinds of "languages" derived from particular spheres of activity: bureaucratic language, the language of romance novels, sports, want ads, babytalk, and so on. Words that evoke another work of art, or a body of knowledge outside the poem, are called **allusions.** The following poem alludes to Charles Dickens's novel *Great Expectations.* Golos includes allusions to the novel and its character Miss Havisham:

> **An allusion is a special kind of word that evokes something outside the poem and brings it into the imagery of the poem.**

"South Carolina," Veronica Golos

What I remember about that morning was how the sky was corncob
    white,
and the sea spit up its smell, and filled the air with salt.
I never would have been standing there, watching,
but my car was rusting in a ditch along route 14,
titling its nose towards the highway—the highway
that passed through Virginia on its way
to more southern, more rural, North and South Carolina.

No one who came from South Carolina escaped the changelessness of
    that state;
while the rest of the country was kicking up Confederate dust
and marching on Montgomery jail houses or Mississippi schools,
or sitting at a lunch counter while a waitress worried over her wet mop,
South Carolina lay untouched, like Miss Havisham's wedding cake.
Dusty and mournful and old, the state kept its tremulous grasp
on the neck of its Black population, cured them like ham,
saturated the countryside with fear. South Carolina was fear,
and if you met a Black man or woman from those parts,

it was natural to nod a little, tip your hat, recognize
they were alive—alive in a way that was against all expectations,
great or small.

Golos's allusion is an ironic way to invoke the "high culture" of Dickens's novel. Henry Green's "The Naming of Parts," which uses military language, Gwendolyn Brooks's "We Real Cool," which uses teenage slang, and Josephine Miles's "Reason" are well-known poems that incorporate various special languages.

Diction and Difficulty

One of the peculiar pleasures of diction is that, more often than not, we can understand words in context without knowing exactly what they mean. Lewis Carroll's "Jabberwocky" is a case in point. It doesn't really matter what his invented words mean exactly; their sounds and their connotations, their pleasure in the mouth, are plenty meaningful:

"Jabberwocky," Lewis Carroll (1872)

'Twas brillig, and the slithy toves
Did gyre and gimble in the wabe:
All mimsy were the borogoves,
And the mome raths outgrabe.
"Beware the Jabberwock, my son!
The jaws that bite, the claws that catch!
Beware the Jubjub bird, and shun
The frumious Bandersnatch!"
He took his vorpal sword in hand;
Long time the manxome foe he sought—
So rested he by the tum-tum tree,
And stood awhile in thought.
And, as in uffish thought he stood,
The Jabberwock, with eyes of flame,
Came whiffling through the tulgey wood,
And burbled as it came!
One, two! One, two! And through and through
The vorpal blade went snicker-snack!

He left it dead, and with its head
He went galumphing back.
"And hast thou slain the Jabberwock?
Come to my arms, my beamish boy!
O frabjious day! Callooh! Callay!"
He chortled in his joy.
'Twas brillig, and the slithy toves
Did gyre and gimble in the wabe:
All mimsy were the borogoves,
And the mome raths outgrabe.

And there are plenty of real words that create an effect just as amazing. In W. H. Auden's poetry, for example, the words psychopompos, Mimas, watchet, hcpatoscopirts, catadoup, chafant, fabbling, sossing, mornes, gennel, cerebrotonic, soodling, hideola, sophrosyne, fioritura, fucoid, wambles, pinguid, and mdagation can be found, to name just a few.

If you are not used to including uncommon words in your own poems, you might find it surprisingly enjoyable to give them a try. It's easy to feel that it is pretentious or somehow embarrassing to use a word in a poem that you wouldn't use in speech, but from another point of view, you are giving your readers the gift of a word they wouldn't encounter in any other way. I used to avoid obscure words in my poems, until I entered a contest that offered a monetary prize for a poem using uncommon words. I found, as I wrote the poem, that to use words like "tintinnabular" and "cinnabar" deeply engaged my imagination, not to mention my ear—and afterward, people who heard the poem often told me specifically that they enjoyed those words.

Using a familiar word in a grammatically new way can be a subtly electrifying way to invent a new language in your poetry. The last stanza of this poem uses a verb as a noun:

From "Voyages: IV," Hart Crane

Whose counted smile of hours and days, suppose
I know as spectrum of the sea and pledge
Vastly now parting gulf on gulf of wings
Whose circles bridge, I know, (from palms to the severe
Chilled albatross's white immutability)
No stream of greater love advancing now

Than, singing, this mortality alone
Through clay aflow immortally to you.

All fragrance irrefragably, and claim
Madly meeting logically in this hour
And region that is ours to wreathe again,
Portending eyes and lips and making told
The chancel port and portion of our June—

Shall they not stem and close in our own steps
Bright staves of flowers and quills today as I
Must first be lost in fatal tides to tell?

In signature of the incarnate word
The harbor shoulders to resign in mingling
Mutual blood, transpiring as foreknown
And widening noon within your breast for gathering
All bright insinuations that my years have caught
For islands where must lead inviolably
Blue latitudes and levels of your eyes,—

In this expectant, still exclaim receive
The secret oar and petals of all love.

Crane is known (and celebrated by those like me who love his poetry) for his dense and difficult diction. But the end of this poem is, by contrast, shockingly direct. In combination with the use of the word "exclaim" as a noun, the effect is deeply moving. It is as if the alchemy of all the preceding difficulty has succeeded in turning one verb into a noun—and in the process, earned the quiet of clarity as a setting for the poem's offering of love.

If you can't find the perfect word for your poem, you can always invent a new word, or **neologism.** Lewis Carroll's "Jabberwocky" includes neologisms that Carroll called "portmanteau" words, invented through combination; for example, he created "chortle" by combining "chuckle" and "snort." Words are created all the time, and poets are especially suited to contribute to this process. In fact, it can be considered part of our job to help keep the language alive and responsive both seriously and playfully, or both, as in in the last stanza of the following poem:

From "Making Step Beautiful in Maine," Kate Sontag

. . . The origin of Step may be as one of them suggests
a parent one step removed from blood
or as the other offers
a parent who steps in to help like a stepladder

but for most of us the word has always

fallen like rotten summer apples
that linger and ferment in our backyards
intoxicating the yellow-jackets

bitten us like horseflies and blackflies
at the granite quarries
then smelled up the car like a wet dog

buzzed in our lamplit hair like Junebugs
on the deck after a dinner of
mussels gritty with pearls

loomed like the Milky Way's invisible black hole
over midnight harbors
as mosquitoes send us inside.

Today stepsails float magically on the horizon
a stepmoon offers translucence in the late afternoon sky
stepgrass holds our footprints in fading light
each stepshadow crosses the other
as stepbirds sing us into this starry stepnight
sweet note by sweet stepnote home.

Sontag's new words challenge and change our feeling about existing vocabulary and hence existing ideas. The following passage, from a poem about environmental devastation, uses made-up words to express emotions otherwise inexpressible:

"history," Dennis Lee

In cess, in dis-
ownmost, in ripture,
in slow-mo history cease,
in bio in haemo in necro-yet how
dumbfound, how
dazzled, how
mortally lucky to be.

Lee recombines familiar pieces of words in bizarre ways to give a sense of the unbelievable pollution and destruction of our world.

Here is a poem by one of the acknowledged experts in neologism:

"Hurrahing in Harvest," Gerard Manley Hopkins (first published 1918)

Summer ends now; now, barbarous in beauty, the stooks rise
Around; up above, what wind-walks! what lovely behaviour
Of silk-sack clouds! has wilder, wilful-wavier
Meal-drift moulded ever and melted across skies?

I walk, I lift up, I lift up heart, eyes,
Down all that glory in the heavens to glean our Saviour;
And, éyes, heárt, what looks, what lips yet gave you a
Rapturous love's greeting of realer, of rounder replies?

And the azurous hung hills are his world-wielding shoulder
Majestic—as a stallion stalwart, very-violet-sweet!—
These things, these things were here and but the beholder
Wanting; which two when they once meet,
The heart rears wings bold and bolder
And hurls for him, O half hurls earth for him off under his feet.

"Silk-sack," "meal-drift," and the other original terms seem invented out of sheer exuberance, clearly conveying the message that this poem is embodying awe and joy at the inexpressible.

The Power of Naming

By creating neologisms, poets claim one of our traditional greatest rights and responsibilities: that of naming. Naming has long been considered an extraordinarily powerful act in all cultures and societies. Think of the significance of addressing a teacher or respected elder by their first name for the first time; the secret name that T. S. Eliot claims, in *Ol'Possum's Book of Practical Cats,* is the source of a cat's dignity; the taboo on pronouncing the name of God in the Old Testament; the power the princess gains when she discovers the name of the dwarf Rumplestiltskin. Think of the importance for some African Americans, such as Amiri Baraka or Ntozake Shange, of changing their names to African-derived names during the Black Power movement of the 1960s and 1970s, and the importance for women of the decision of whether to change names when they marry. Think of the way a name in the Old West was called a "handle," and the political implications when an airport or a road is renamed in honor of a political leader. In a poem, names can be a particularly charged kind of word, combining the power of a general concept and the immediacy of a concrete particular:

"The Flower-Fed Buffaloes," Vachel Lindsay

The flower-fed buffaloes of the spring
In the days of long ago,
Ranged where the locomotives sing
And the prairie flowers lie low:—
The tossing, blooming, perfumed grass
Is swept away by wheat,
Wheels and wheels and wheels spin by
In the spring that still is sweet.
But the flower-fed buffaloes of the spring
Left us long ago.
They gore no more, they bellow no more:—
They trundle around the hills no more:
With the Blackfeet, lying low,
With the Pawnees, lying low,
Lying low.

Read the poem again, this time stopping after the phrase "hills no more." Notice the difference. The specific power of the beautiful names of two native American tribes transforms this poem from nice sentiment to a much more memorable invocation beloved by many readers. In the following poem, the poet imagines Adam naming the animals as the Bible's Book of Genesis narrates:

"Adam's Task," John Hollander

And Adam gave names to all cattle, and to the fowl of the air, and to every beast of the field . . . GEN. 2:20

Thou, paw-paw-paw; thou, glurd; thou, spotted
    Glurd; thou, whitestap, lurching through
The high-grown brush; thou, pliant-footed,
    Implex; thou, awagabu.

Every burrower, each flier
    Came for the name he had to give:
Gay, first work, ever to be prior,
    Not yet sunk to primitive.

Thou, verdle; thou, McFleery's pomma;
    Thou; thou; thou—three types of grawl;
Thou, flisket; thou, kabasch; thou, comma-
    Eared mashawk; thou, all; thou, all.

Were, in a fire of becoming,
    Laboring to be burned away,
Then work, half-measuring, half-humming,
    Would be as serious as play.

Thou, pambler; thou, rivarn; thou, greater
    Wherret, and thou, lesser one;
Thou, sproal; thou, zant; thou, lily-eater.
    Naming's over. Day is done.

Though Hollander makes affectionate fun of Adam here, the point is a powerful one. Poems create names. Because of a poem by Longfellow, for example, an incident in U.S. history is known as "Paul Revere's Ride." And a good poem can transform an existing name, as in this poem, where an African American poet uses repetition to change the entire feeling of the name of a state:

"Oregon," Bob Kaufman

You are with me Oregon,
Day and night, I feel you, Oregon.
I am Negro. I am Oregon.
Oregon is me, the planet
Oregon, the State Oregon, Oregon.
In the night, you come with bicycle wheels,
Oregon you come
With stars of fire. You come green.
Green eyes, hair, arms,
Head, face, legs, feet, toes
Green, nose green, your
Breast green, your cross
Green, your blood green.
Oregon winds blow around
Oregon. I am green, Oregon.
You are mine, Oregon. I am yours,
Oregon. I live in Oregon.
Oregon lives in me,
Oregon, you come and make
Me into a bird and fly me
To secret places day and night.
The secret places in Oregon,
I am standing on the steps
Of the holy church of Crispus
Attucks St. John the Baptist,
The holy brother of Christ,
I am talking to Lorca. We
Decide the Hart Crane trip, home to Oregon
Heaven flight from Gulf of
Mexico, the bridge is
Crossed, and the florid black found.

Mining Etymology

Emily Dickinson said that if she could have only one book with her, it would be a dictionary; if I were going to be shipwrecked on a desert island, I'd make sure to specify that my dictionary include **etymologies.** Etymologies, or the histories of words, are inexhaustibly inspiring for many of us. I know a poet who, when stuck writing a poem, looks up the etymology of the word she's stuck on, or the last word she wrote, as a way to get unstuck. Going to the root of the word can help you get down into the roots of your poem, making it easier to find out what is really going on, and decide where it is best to go next.

Finding out the etymology of words is like finding out where your friends grew up and what kind of families they had. It helps you get to know them in a deeper way, to understand their behavior better and get along with them more easily. Sometimes you find out things you'd rather not know: "pretty" used to mean silly; "handsome" used to mean generous. That reveals a lot about current gender roles.

The histories of some words are so beautiful or shocking or funny or rich with meaning that they are like poems in themselves. What about cereal, which comes from the goddess Ceres who made the crops grow? Or "supercilious," which originally meant raising an eyebrow? "Tree" and "true" come from the same root word in ancient German, because trees were sacred in the ancient Druid religion. Simple-looking words are often full of metaphoric as well as historical meaning: try looking up "believe," "berserk," "comfort," "disaster," "kind," "lord," "money," "month," "pervert," "planet," "read," "salary," "slave," and "university" to start; the dictionary is likely to seduce you into looking up other word-stories as you go.

When you cultivate an awareness of etymologies, even abstract language becomes vivid and uncannily alive, active with lives and moments lived long ago. Though etymologies rarely work their magic on the surface of a poem, ordinary-looking words can carry secrets that only you, as the poet, know. And the unconscious of your reader may well respond to the hidden lives of your words, and the choices that you make on the basis of etymology can enrich your poem many levels down, and give it the roots a strong, true poem needs.

Reading Etymologies: The gold standard for etymologies is the full multi-volume set of the *Oxford English Dictionary,* which most university libraries subscribe to as a database, though it is always worth a field trip to browse the hard copy in the library (some people own copies of the tiny-type *Shorter Oxford English Dictionary,* which comes with a little drawer

holding a magnifying glass). The best standard-sized dictionary for etymologies is *The American Heritage College Dictionary.* If you look up a word in a dictionary that includes etymologies, you will find the regular definition followed by the word's ancestor-words. Visually, these will be identified as coming from ME (Middle English), OE (Old English), ON (Old Norse), G (German), Gk (Greek), L (Latin), MF (Medieval French), ML (Medieval Latin), or IE (Indo-European, the most ancient language traced in Europe and parts of Asia). You can trace the root of a word through many different generations of languages; dictionaries usually start with the most recent language and go back in time. If one of the source words appears in capital letters or the dictionary directs you to another word, be sure to look that up as well, since at that point you are hot on the trail of the most resonant, ancient, concrete root meaning.

QUESTIONS FOR MEDITATION OR DISCUSSION

Notice how you feel when you hear someone speaking with heavily Latinate diction. What physical and emotional reactions do you have? What about when you are reading a passage that is more than 25 percent Latinate?

Try consciously to speak with more or less Latinate diction than usual. Try this in several different situations: talking to strangers, to elders or people you respect, to children. What is the experience like? Now look at how much Latinate diction you generally use in your poetry. How do you think it makes your readers feel?

The great activist poet Audre Lorde famously wrote, "The Master's tools can never dismantle the Master's house." She meant that the language that had been used to exert power over so many people needed to be remade in order to write poems that would help strengthen their liberation. In her essay "Owning the Masters," contemporary poet Marilyn Nelson argues the opposite point of view: "But why should we dismantle the house? Why toss the baby over the porch railing, with its bassinetteful of soapy water? Why instead don't we take possession of, why don't we own, the tradition?" What is your opinion on this question?

"Words," Sylvia Plath

Axes
After whose stroke the wood rings,
And the echoes!
Echoes traveling
Off from the center like horses.

The sap
Wells like tears, like the
Water striving
To re-establish its mirror
Over the rock

That drops and turns,
A white skull,
Eaten by weedy greens.
Years later I
Encounter them on the road—

Words dry and riderless,
The indefatigable hoof-taps.
While
From the bottom of the pool, fixed stars
Govern a life.

What is Plath's vision of words? What happens to the words by the end of the poem?

If you are bilingual, think about the experience of reading a poem that combines the two languages you know well. Does it satisfy you in a way that other poems don't? How can you bring some of that experience into the poems that you write? If you are not bilingual, what is it like to read a poem that includes words in a language you don't know?

Think about your name—first, middle, last—and about your nicknames. How do you feel about them? How have they affected your life? How do you use other people's names in your interactions with them? If you became more conscious of names, would you do anything differently in your life? In your poetry? Optional: read the section about Anthony Hecht's sestina "The Book of Yolek" in the chapter on repetition. What is Hecht's attitude toward Yolek's name?

QUOTES

this is the oppressor's language
yet I need it to talk to you
—Adrienne Rich, "The Burning of Paper Instead of Children"

The poets made all the words, and therefore language is the archives of history, and if we must say it, a sort of tomb of the muses. For, though the origin of most of our words is forgotten, each word was at first a stroke of genius, and obtained currency, because for the moment it symbolized the word to the first speaker and to the hearer. The etymologist finds the dead word to have been once a brilliant picture. Language is fossil poetry. As the limestone of the continent consists of infinite masses of the shells of animalcules, so language is made up of images, or tropes, which now, in their secondary use, have long ceased to remind us of their poetic origin.
—Ralph Waldo Emerson

The poet's job is to purify the words of the tribe.
—Stéphane Mallarmé

I wish our clever young poets would remember my homely definitions of prose and poetry: that is, prose—words in their best order; poetry—the best words in their best order.
—Samuel Taylor Coleridge

As when the forests, with the bending year,
First sheds the leaves which earliest appear,
So an old age of words maturely dies,
Others new-born in youth and vigour rise.
—Horace, *Ars Poetica* (trans. Ben Jonson)

Many words . . . don't have a strict meaning. But this is not a defect. To think it is would be like saying that the light of my reading lamp is no real light at all because it has no sharp boundary.

—Ludwig Wittgenstein

It would be one thing if poetry were made of words alone,
but it is not—no more than words themselves are.

—Paolo Freire

If I don't use these words, who the hell will?

—W. H. Auden

A writer inhabits his native language as if it were a foreign country.

—Proust

POETRY PRACTICES

(Group) Word Share. Each person picks out a favorite word and says a little bit about why they like it (sound, image, meaning, etc.). Someone writes each of the words on the board. Then, each person writes a poem that includes *all* the favorite words (or as many of them as they can manage). It is best to do this in a serious manner, not as a joke, though some of the poems will end up being funny. Then read them aloud and compare how different people handle different words, what choices they made, and so on. You will note characteristics of different writers based on how they do things, so it is a good getting-acquainted exercise. (This exercise comes from Elizabeth Robinson.)

(Group) Name Share. Write a poem using the name of someone else in the group. The poem can be an acrostic, where each letter of the name begins or ends a line; or the name can simply be included. Share it with the person and then with the group.

Who's Talking? Rewrite one of your poems in different diction, as if a completely different person were speaking it—a person with totally different education and background and manners.

Latinate Infusion. Write the same poem with 10 percent Latinate words and then with 50 percent Latinate words.

Vocabulary Fest. Write a poem using four words you don't already know the meanings of and have to look up in a dictionary.

Bilingual or Polyglot Poem. Write a poem using at least nine words from a language or languages other than English. It can be a language you know well, but it doesn't need to be.

"Shoptalk" Indulgence. Write a poem using at least eight words that come from a certain special subcategory of English with which you are familiar. It might be the language of computers, cooking, hockey, horseback riding, philosophy, film, sewing, religion, politics, music, skateboarding, law, or any other field that generates "shoptalk": its own unique words and expressions.

Root Canal. In a poem you are revising, look up the etymologies of a few of the words. Substitute other words whose etymology fits in better with what you want to convey in the poem.

Word-Family Reunion. Browse deeply in an etymological dictionary until you find a cluster of at least three words that are related to each other or from the same root. Write a poem centering on these words.

Source-languages of words listed:

jasmine, algebra, shawl, safari, bazaar: Arabic
moose, skunk, squirrel: Native American
guitar, banana, mosquito, poncho: Spanish
shampoo, dungarees, pajamas: Hindi
boondocks: Filipino
coffee: Turkish
agitprop: Russian
tea: Chinese
kayak: Inuit
brat: Irish

CHAPTER 5

Three Modes of Poetry: Lyric, Dramatic, and Narrative

When beginning students of creative writing are asked to define poetry, they often say something like, "Poetry is what you write when you want to express your feelings." And in fact, this is a pretty good definition of ***lyric poetry.*** But there are other poems you may know that this definition wouldn't really fit at all. What about Lewis Carroll's "Jabberwocky" or "The Night Before Christmas"? What about Poe's "The Raven," or "Casey at the Bat"? What about "To be or not to be," or "Ah, Romeo, Romeo, wherefore art thou Romeo?" Surely that is poetry too. But where does this kind of poetry fit in?

Twenty-three centuries ago, the philosopher Aristotle outlined three modes of poetry: lyric, dramatic, and narrative. His classification was rediscovered in the Renaissance, and poetry was written in English in all three modes for centuries.

> **Genres and Modes: "Modes" refers to the three sweeping poetic approaches of lyric, narrative, and dramatic outlined by Aristotle. "Genres" refers to more specific types of poetry, usually distinguished by subject matter as well as style, such as the elegy, ode, or love poem, or even narrower categories such as "the baseball poem," "the wedding lyric," or "the science fiction epic."**

At various times, each mode has had its own kind of presentation, a unique aesthetic role. In classical times, lyric poems were poems about the writer's state of heart or mind usually sung accompanied by a lute or other instrument, like the lyrics to songs today. Dramatic poems were plays, performed on the stage by actors. Narrative poems were usually long and usually in the third person, recited by storytellers, sometimes accompanied by a drum to keep the beat.

The lyric predominates in contemporary poetry, in part because of the rise of prose for dramatic and then for narrative literature. Plays began being written in prose for the first time in the seventeenth century, the prose novel blossomed in the nineteenth century, and the prose short story developed in the late nineteenth and twentieth centuries. Another reason is that the lyric mode, with its associative, nonlinear possibilities, seems for many to mesh best with the contemporary sensibility. Poet Gregory Orr remarked in an interview, "I know I can only write out of a lyrical mode . . . the lyric mode is what history, since the Romantics, has urged on us as the only really plausible choice we have." Orr's comment reflects the prevailing late-twentieth-century feeling (though it bears thinking that the greatest Romantic poets wrote numerous verse dramas and many long narrative poems, as did many modernist poets; it is we who have chosen not to read their dramatic and narrative poems, and to concentrate instead on their lyrics).

Interest in narrative and dramatic poetry has been on the rise again since the late twentieth century. And of course, there has always been overlap—lyrical passages in plays, stories included in lyrics, and so on. But contemporary poetry remains mostly lyrical, with some narrative and dramatic elements. To keep the three modes in mind remains a useful way to remind ourselves of the fuller range of poetry's powers. Thinking of poetry only as lyric makes it too easy to forget the wonderful things that can be accomplished by the use of persona, dialogue, and extended narrative in poems and to forgo the pleasures of working in longer and more ambitious modes of poetry, which are usually narrative or dramatic. (It is almost impossible to write a book-length lyric poem that reads as one poem, though Ginsberg's *Howl* and *Kaddish* show it can be done; even Whitman's *Leaves of Grass* breaks down into separate short sections). Furthermore, when we conflate all poetry with lyric, the definition of lyric itself tends to become confused. Then, we may forget to appreciate the special captivating nature and exacting requirements of lyric poetry in its purest sense.

The Lyric Poem

From Sappho in ancient Greece with her lyre (the instrument which gives lyric poetry its name) through Thomas Wyatt in Renaissance England with his lute, lyric poets were long expected to be proficient on a musical instrument that would accompany their performances of their poems. This tradition of self-performance may be why we now use the term "voice" to speak of a lyric poet's style, even when we have only encountered their voice on the printed page. In this Renaissance poem, Louise Labé shows how intimately she associates her poetic voice with her lute; she even blames the lute for turning all her poems about love into sad poems:

Sonnet 12, Louise Labé (1555) (trans. Annie Finch)

Lute, my companion in calamity,
irreproachable witness of my sighs,
faithful secretary of all my cries,
you have lamented so often with me
that my tears have driven you deep into pity.
Now, if a delicious sound starts to arise,
you turn it back to a sad lament, disguise
it with tones you've sung so much more frequently.
No matter how I try to force you the other way,
you struggle and loosed your strings and steal away
my song. Still, when you watch my tender sighing,
indulging me, listening again while I complain,
I know pleasure, I find an opposite in my pain;
and hope sweet suffering will lead me to sweet dying.

The modern lyric poem often maintains this original sense of a song. And in fact, with widespread recording technology, lyric poetry is returning more and more to its roots in performance. Lyric poetry suits performance because, to use Jonathan Culler's definition, lyric is at its root simply "memorable language—made memorable by its rhythmical shaping and phonological patterning." More generally, though, in poetry the term "lyric" tends to mean any poem focusing on the emotions of a first-person speaker. If you have felt your own emotions welling up into poetry as you read, don't feel alone. Since there are relatively few strong human emotions—longing, loneliness, contentment, bitterness, regret, anticipation, and so on—lyric poems can evoke emotions shared by different people over wide stretches of time and place, and can be remarkably timeless and placeless. This simple lyric poem of longing, for example, has lived for over 600 years:

"O Western Wind," Anonymous (fifteenth century)

O western wind, when wilt thou blow
that the small rain down can rain?

Christ, that my love were in my arms,
and I in my bed again!

What is this poem "about"? If you were to paraphrase it, who would care? Missing a lover is one of the oldest and most hackneyed feelings in the world. But just as love seems to be happening for the first time in history every single time we feel it, so a lyric poem can sometimes say the same old thing in a completely new way. That's what we aim for when we write one. When Robert Graves remarked that there were only three subjects for poetry, "love, death, and the changing of the seasons," he was probably thinking of lyric poetry. So don't worry about your feelings not being new if you are writing a lyric. The main thing is to find a new way of expressing them.

As an experiment, think of three ideas or images to express your own feelings of love toward someone. No doubt you thought of the most intense images you could find. Common characteristics of successful lyrics are compression and vivid intensity of image. Another common quality of lyric is musicality: even a poem that is abstract in its language and meaning can gain lyric intensity from a tight musical structure. The following lyric poem, most famous as the words to a lovely song, has both of these qualities of intense image and musical structure.

"My Love is Like a Red, Red Rose," Robert Burns (1794)

O my love's like a red, red rose
That's newly sprung in June:
O my love's like the melody
That's sweetly play'd in tune!

As fair art thou, my bonnie lass,
So deep in love am I,
That I will love you still, my dear
Till a' the seas gang dry.

Till a' the seas gang dry, my dear,
And the rocks melt wi' the sun,
I will love thee still, my dear
While the sands o' life shall run.

Burns uses the simple musical structure and the intensity of imagery to balance each other. The simplicity and familiarity of the images in the first stanza are somewhat lulling, as is the easy, predictable form of the poem. Because of this, the apocalyptic images of the second and third stanzas are even more intense, close to frightening, by contrast. They continue to startle, centuries later, with the originality and memorability of powerful lyric.

Edna St. Vincent Millay's "First Fig," like "O Western Wind," is a four-line poem with an iconic place in the history of poetry in English. Her lyric came to symbolize the wild lifestyle of the first generation of "liberated" women of the early twentieth century.

"First Fig," Edna St. Vincent Millay (1920)

My candle burns at both ends;
It will not last the night;
But ah, my foes, and oh, my friends,
It gives a lovely light!

Over a century after Robert Burns, with his roots in the country farming lifestyle and a centuries-old tradition of song and oral literature, the sophisticated Millay is clearly writing a lyric intended to be read on the page, not to be sung (although it would make a beautiful song, I have never heard a tune for it). Where Burns uses exact repetition, Millay is careful not to bore the book-reader by too much repeating and even takes pains to vary "oh" and "ah." She weaves a more complex pattern by rhyming two different sets of words in four lines, while Burns never rhymes more than one, leaving the first and third lines of each stanza unrhymed. (The repetition of "dear," technically called "identical rhyme," is cheating and doesn't count.)

A longer, more elaborate form of lyric poem is the ode, whether in the classical, meditative form (named after the Latin poet Horace) or the more irregular form called the Pindaric. This genre of poetry can take almost any form; its guiding principle is its elevated and meditative tone and its focus on celebrating something or someone (usually directly addressed by the poet, although this is not necessary), a tradition which inspired such great nineteenth-century poems as Shelley's "Ode to the West Wind," Wordsworth's "Ode: Intimations of Immortality," or Keats' "Ode to a Nightingale." Here is an ode on a more humble subject.

"Ode to the Onion," Pablo Neruda (trans. Ken Norris)

Onion,
luminous vial,
your beauty formed
layer by layer,
scales of crystal blossomed
as in the dark secretive earth
your belly of dew rounded.
Under the earth
a miracle happened,
and when your
awkward green shoots appeared,
and your leaves
blossomed like swords in the garden,
the earth gathered up her power,
revealing your transparent nakedness;
and, as that foreign sea,
swelling the breasts of Aphrodite,
duplicated the magnolia,
so the earth
made you,
onion,
illustrious as a planet
and destined
to shine,
a constant constellation,
a round watery rose
upon
the table
of the poor.

Onion, I celebrate all that exists,
but to me you are
more beautiful than a bird
with blinding plumage;
to my eyes you are
a celestial sphere, a platinum goblet,
the motionless dance

of snow-white anemones
and in your crystalline nature
dwells the fragrance of the earth.

"Pure" lyrics, such as Burns's and Millay's, directly expressing feelings with intensity and musical structure, became much less common by the late twentieth century. Almost as if to compensate for their narrowed aesthetic field, poets, who centuries earlier had dominated all three modes, recently have begun to bring many more elements of narrative and drama into their lyric poems. In Lucinda Roy's "The Curse," for example, historical narratives are evoked to express a contemporary poet's experience:

"The Curse," Lucinda Roy

As red as a tulip, smelling of pots and pans,
My blood announces itself with the clamor of sunrise.
It tells me what I've lost and who I am.
I don't know if those are the same.

In a primary remembrance of pain and intervals,
Women bled on slave ships onto the thighs
And cheeks of strangers. The few lucky ones
Who expelled their children from them
In fists of retribution felt
Their splintered backs pickled in feces and piss
And were glad for their good fortune.

I make these women up.
Except in toilet bowls or garbage,
In birth or times of illness and death,
I've never seen another woman's blood.
The skin of the egg comes down through me like clockwork.
It has the texture of patience.
I am a woman of color whose son was freely born.

I know nothing.

After describing the experience of the imagined women of the past, the poem circles back to the immediate experience. The feelings driving the poem are not directly expressed; even the direct statement in the last line is only a small part of the emotional story. Instead, the contrast between two narrative situations creates the emotional focus of this lyric poem.

The majority of the twentieth-century poems included in *A Poet's Craft,* as elsewhere, are lyric poems that make use of narrative elements. But rare as pure lyrics are now, some new kinds of "experimental" poetry that are not concerned with ordinary meanings have opened up new space for lyric that is largely free of narrative, such as this poem:

"Untitled," Lisa Jarnot

and at noon I will fall in love
and nothing will have meaning
except for the brownness of
the sky, and tradition, and water
and in the water off the railway
in New Haven all the lights
go on across the sun, and for
millennia those who kiss fall into
hospitals, riding trains, wearing
black shoes, pursued by those
they love, the Chinese in the armies
with the shiny sound of Johnny Cash,
and in my plan to be myself
I became someone else with
soft lips and a secret life,
and I left, from an airport,
in tradition of the water
on the plains, until the train
started moving and yesterday
it seemed true that suddenly
inside of the newspaper
there was a powerline and
my heart stopped, and everything
leaned down from the sky to kill me
and now the cattails sing.

Tess Gallagher has remarked, "The 'pure' lyric has been associated with the cry, the exclamation, the unanswerable voicing of states of being." Still, all kinds of poems, made with various mixtures of narrative, dramatic, and lyric elements, draw strength from the urgency of the lyric impulse, the need to sing out our feelings about experience.

Dramatic Poetry

A **dramatic poem** is a play in poetry. The idea might seem exotic to us, but for much of the history of Western literature all theater was in poetry. In fact, the names of many of our meters come from the ancient Greek plays, which were not only written in meter but performed on stage by dancers and choruses moving and chanting in time to the meter. At the height of English-language drama, such poets as Marlowe, Webster, Jonson, and of course Shakespeare achieved their heights as playwrights by writing dramatic poetry. In the eighteenth and into the nineteenth centuries, many plays were still written in verse, although the dominance of plodding rhymed couplets and the plethora of bawdy prose comedy began to dampen appreciation for dramatic poetry. Still, even in the nineteenth and twentieth centuries, poets continued to write dramatic verse, and many poets do so today. Keats, Shelley, Byron, and other Romantic poets wrote **closet dramas,** long plays that were intended to be read, not performed, and have little dramatic conflict. Finally, in the early twentieth century, modernist poets again began to write plays for performance. The most important modernist poets to do so were W. B. Yeats and then T. S. Eliot, who acknowledged Yeats as a pioneer of verse drama when he said, "Yeats had nobody. We had Yeats."

Yeats not only wrote plays; he founded and managed the Abbey Theater, an important part of the Irish Nationalist political movement because, by commissioning and producing plays about traditional mythology and other Irish-centered subjects, it built Irish self-awareness and unity. Here is an excerpt from Yeats's verse play about the death of the great Irish hero of mythology, Cuchulain, completed just before his own death:

From The Death of Cuchulain, *W. B. Yeats (1939)*

Cuchulain. I think that you know everything, Blind Man,
My mother or the nurse said that the blind
Know everything.

Blind Man. No, but they have good sense.
How could I have got twelve pennies for your head
If I had not good sense?

Cuchulain. There floats out there
The shape that I shall take when I am dead,
My soul's first shape, a soft feathery shape,
And is not that a strange shape for the soul
Of a great fighting man?

Blind Man. Your shoulder is there,
This is your neck. Ah! Ah! Are you ready, Cuchulain!

Cuchulain. I say it is about to sing.

[The stage darkens.]

Blind Man. Ah! Ah!
[Music of pipe and drum, the curtain falls. The music ceases as the curtain rises upon a bare stage. There is nobody upon the stage except a woman with a crow's head. She is the Morrigu. She stands towards the back. She holds a black parallelogram, the size of a man's head. There are six other parallelograms near the backcloth.]

The Morrigu. The dead can hear me, and to the dead I speak.
This head is great Cuchulain's, those other six
Gave him six mortal wounds . . .

Yeats wrote in his *Autobiography,* "No art can conquer the people alone—the people are conquered by an ideal of life upheld by authority. As this ideal is rediscovered, the arts, music and poetry, painting and literature, will draw closer together." His desire to "conquer" the Irish people to the cause of unity and independence drove his need to create the most powerfully effective art-form possible. Here at the climax of his last play, poetry works in synergy with music and with the vivid visual tableau of the crow-headed war goddess with severed head, to create a ritualistic effect that would not be possible in any other medium but dramatic verse.

Verse drama intended for the page, not the stage, can also create a distinctive dramatic effect. This dramatic poem, although realistic in its spoken language, is unlikely to be performed, in part because there is no action, only dialogue:

From "The Witch of Coos," Robert Frost

SON: You wouldn't want to tell him what we have
Up attic, mother?

MOTHER: Bones—a skeleton.

SON: But the headboard of mother's bed is pushed
Against the attic door: the door is nailed.
It's harmless. Mother hears it in the night
Halting perplexed behind the barrier
Of door and headboard. Where it wants to get
Is back into the cellar where it came from.

MOTHER: We'll never let them, will we, son! We'll
never !

SON: It left the cellar forty years ago
And carried itself like a pile of dishes
Up one flight from the cellar to the kitchen,
Another from the kitchen to the bedroom,
Another from the bedroom to the attic,
Right past both father and mother, and neither stopped
it . . .

On the other hand, this highly lyrical, nonreferential dramatic poem has been performed on the stage and is clearly intended for a performance situation:

From "Memory Play," Carla Harryman

The Miltonic Humiliator passes in the parade singing:
Maximize the whims
of men
in song

the master
gripe
shall be
song's guide
with "shall" the
license to provoke
and "be" the clumsy
notes that ring the wash
and rinse the tides
oh flood oh flood oh flood
oh flood oh flood oh flood

Reptile

A parade. I inflate. Midnight. Men wandering into floating labial fences. The sidelines are snoring, sniffling, wincing, evacuating old neighborhoods, forgetting. Dancing on ice blocks, ventriloquists have flooded the streets with nosegays. The spectator, I, a lady a gentleman, seats itself in the buzz waiting as the globs on gowns are fixed with metal links.

Instruction

All rise to "If I had needed them I could have eaten them!"

Fish passes in a float titled, "The World In A Fish Bowl."

It's hard to imagine that this piece would have such a quality of adventurous playfulness, nor, paradoxically, of lyricism, without the dramatic form.

In the vast majority of recent dramatic poems, the second character never speaks, though we know the other person is there. This tradition of the **dramatic monologue** poem has been strongly associated with one poet, Robert Browning, who wrote numerous dramatic monologues at a time when this genre was considered a daringly modern contrast to the Romantic "closet dramas." This famous poem tells an entire tale to an invisible listener, giving the reader cues about the setting:

"My Last Duchess," Robert Browning (1842)

That's my last Duchess painted on the wall,
Looking as if she were alive. I call

That piece a wonder, now: Fra Pandolf's hands
Worked busily a day, and there she stands.
Will't please you sit and look at her? I said
"Fra Pandolf" by design, for never read
Strangers like you that pictured countenance,
The depth and passion of its earnest glance,
But to myself they turned (since none puts by
The curtain I have drawn for you, but I)
And seemed as they would ask me, if they durst,
How such a glance came there; so, not the first
Are you to turn and ask thus. Sir, 'twas not
Her husband's presence only, called that spot
Of joy into the Duchess' cheek: perhaps
Fra Pandolf chanced to say "Her mantle laps
Over my lady's wrist too much," or "Paint
Must never hope to reproduce the faint
Half-flush that dies along her throat": such stuff
Was courtesy, she thought, and cause enough
For calling up that spot of joy. She had
A heart—how shall I say?—too soon made glad,
Too easily impressed; she liked whate'er
She looked on, and her looks went everywhere.
Sir, 'twas all one! My favor at her breast,
The dropping of the daylight in the West,
The bough of cherries some officious fool
Broke in the orchard for her, the white mule
She rode with round the terrace—all and each
Would draw from her alike the approving speech,
Or blush, at least. She thanked men—good! but thanked
Somehow—I know not how—as if she ranked
My gift of a nine-hundred-years-old name
With anybody's gift. Who'd stoop to blame
This sort of trifling? Even had you skill
In speech—which I have not—to make your will
Quite clear to such an one, and say, "Just this
Or that in you disgusts me; here you miss,
Or there exceed the mark"—and if she let
Herself be lessoned so, nor plainly set

Her wits to yours, forsooth, and made excuse
—E'en then would be some stooping; and I choose
Never to stoop. Oh sir, she smiled, no doubt,
Whene'er I passed her; but who passed without
Much the same smile? This grew; I gave commands;
Then all smiles stopped together. There she stands
As if alive. Will't please you rise? We'll meet
The company below, then. I repeat,
The Count your master's known munificence
Is ample warrant that no just pretense
Of mine for dowry will be disallowed;
Though his fair daughter's self as I avowed
At starting, is my object. Nay, we'll go
Together down, sir! Notice Neptune, though,
Taming a sea horse, thought a rarity,
Which Claus of Innsbruck cast in bronze for me!

It seems that the speaker and listener are walking through a grand house together. Who do you think the listener is? Why do you think the listener is there? Many readers have found this poem spine-chilling. Do you think it would be as effective if the listener also spoke?

Though Browning started a tradition of long dramatic monologues, they can be short as well, such as this poem in the voice of the Biblical Mary:

"holy night," Lucille Clifton

joseph, i afraid of stars,
their brilliant seeing.
so many eyes. such light.
joseph, i cannot still these limbs,
i hands keep moving toward i breasts,
so many stars. so bright.
joseph, is wind burning from east
joseph, i shine, oh joseph   oh
illuminated night.

Browning's and Clifton's poems address listeners, speechless characters who are, nonetheless, clearly there in the poems. Each also takes place in the middle of significant and important action. This makes them true dramatic monologues. Like Hamlet's famous soliloquy, "to be or not to be" (in which the second character is himself), it's easy to imagine either of these poems having been excerpted from a longer play.

The **persona poem** is a lyric poem in an imagined speaker's voice but not addressed to another character—only to the reader. In the following poem, for example, the person addressed could be a casual acquaintance or friend, but it could just as easily be the reader:

"The Man He Killed," Thomas Hardy (1914)

"Had he and I but met
    By some old ancient inn,
We should have sat us down to wet
    Right many a nipperkin!

    "But ranged as infantry,
    And staring face to face,
I shot at him as he at me,
    And killed him in his place.

    "I shot him dead because—
    Because he was my foe,
Just so; my foe of course he was;
    That's clear enough; although

    "He thought he'd 'list perhaps,
    Off-hand-like—just as I—
Was out of work—had sold his traps—
    No other reason why.

    "Yes; quaint and curious war is!
    You shoot a fellow down
You'd treat if met where any bar is,
    Or help to half-a-crown."

The poem is extraordinarily dramatic, capturing in the rhythms of speech the speaker's confusion, hesitation, and helplessness. But there is no hearer and no action—only the persona's thoughts, expressed in appropriate diction. To distinguish between a persona poem such as this and a true dramatic monologue helps us appreciate the strengths of each genre: the full presentation of character in the persona poem, and the dramatic suspense in the monologue.

When the implied second character is dead, the distinction between persona poem and dramatic monologue gets blurrier, as in this poem from a searing book about victims of rape and genocide in Bosnia:

From The Bosnia Elegies, *Adrian Oktenberg*

Darling, your face is turning white
becoming featureless   an untracked field of snow
Your eyes which once burned like blue sky
are flattening out memory fails us both
I curse my failing memory try to catch it
it disappears around a bend   another another
The exact timbre of your voice   the gesture
that moved me so the way your laughter began
deep in your chest   in your chest
three pieces of shrapnel   were buried
three years ago

This poem demonstrates eloquently the persona poem's capacity for inspiring empathy and for expressing strong emotion. Recalling Yeats's theory that a poet always needs to assume a "mask" to speak, Oktenberg has written: "I am shy, and I don't like the spotlight on myself. I like using dramatic monologues because they afford a measure of privacy. When expressing deep or extreme emotions like love, lust, or grief, I find it easier to shift away from my own voice into the voice of another, more clearly separate and fictive, self. S/he can then do or say whatever s/he needs to without the drag of my own usual fears, hesitations or evasions."

Writing a dramatic or persona poem can allow us to access secret parts of our personality helping to heal both poet and reader from the pain of hiding parts of ourselves. The psychologist C. G. Jung thought that people become whole and fulfilled by becoming aware of the qualities they have been taught to repress as bad (the "shadow" self) or inappropriate (such as a woman's supposedly male qualities, the "animus," or a man's supposedly female qualities, the "anima"). The poems of Ai, who writes in the voice of perpetrators of rape, murder, and child beating, are extreme example of poetry expressing the "shadow" self. In the following poem by a great Arabic poet, a male poet writes in a female voice, expressing his hidden "anima" self:

From "Two Stranger Birds in Our Feathers," Mahmoud Darwish (trans. Fady Joudah)

My sky is ashen. Scratch my back. And undo
Slowly, you stranger, my braids. And tell me
What's on your mind. Tell me what crossed
Youssef's mind. Tell me some simple
Talk . . . the talk a woman always desires
To be told. I don't want the phrase
Complete. Gesture is enough to scatter me in the rise
Of butterflies between springheads and the sun. Tell me
I am necessary for you like sleep, and not like nature
Filling up with water around you and me. And spread
Over me an endless blue wing . . .
My sky is ashen,
As a blackboard is ashen, before
Writing on it. So write with my blood's ink anything
That changes it: an utterance . . . two, without
Excessive aim at metaphor. And say we are
Two stranger birds in Egypt
And in Syria. Say we are two stranger birds
In our feathers. And write my name and yours
Beneath the phrase. What time is it now? What color
Are my face and yours in the mirrors?
I own nothing for anything to resemble me.
Did the water mistress love you more? Did she seduce you
By the sea rock? Confess now
That you have extended your wilderness twenty years
To stay prisoner in her hands. And tell me of what
You think when the sky is ashen . . .
My sky is ashen.

I resemble what no longer resembles me.
Do you want to return to your exile night
in a mermaid's hair? Or do you want to return
to your home figs? For no honey wounds a stranger
here or there. What time is it now?
What's the name of this place we're in? And what's
the difference between my sky and your land. Tell me
what Adam said in secret to himself. Was he emancipated
when he remembered. Tell me anything that changes the sky's
ashen color. Tell me some simple
talk, the talk a woman desires
to be told every now and then. Say
that two people, like you and me,
can carry all this resemblance between fog
and mirage, then safely return. My sky
is ashen, so what do you think of when the sky
is ashen?

In this poem a great rush of lyrical, associative energy seems to have been set free by the hidden persona of this already powerfully lyrical poet.

One simple way to tap into the dramatic potential of your poems is to write a response to the speaker of an existing poem, such as, for example, this one:

"To His Coy Mistress," Andrew Marvell (1650)

Had we but world enough, and time,
This coyness, Lady, were no crime.
We would sit down and think which way
To walk and pass our long love's day.
Thou by the Indian Ganges' side
Shouldst rubies find: I by the tide
Of Humber would complain. I would
Love you ten years before the Flood,
And you should, if you please, refuse
Till the conversion of the Jews.
My vegetable love should grow

Vaster than empires, and more slow;
An hundred years should go to praise
Thine eyes and on thy forehead gaze;
Two hundred to adore each breast:
But thirty thousand to the rest;
An age at least to every part,
And the last age should show your heart.
For, Lady, you deserve this state,
Nor would I love at lower rate.
    But at my back I always hear
Time's wingèd chariot hurrying near:
And yonder all before us lie
Deserts of vast eternity.
Thy beauty shall no more be found;
Nor, in thy marble vault, shall sound
My echoing song: then worms shall try
That long preserved virginity,
And your quaint honour turn to dust,
And into ashes all my lust:
The grave's a fine and private place,
But none, I think, do there embrace.
    Now therefore, while the youthful hue
Sits on thy skin like morning dew,
And while thy willing soul transpires
At every pore with instant fires,
Now let us sport us while we may;
And now, like amorous birds of prey,
Rather at once our Time devour,
Than languish in his slow-chapt power.
Let us roll all our strength and all
Our sweetness up into one ball,
And tear our pleasures with rough strife
Thorough the iron gates of life:
Thus, though we cannot make our Sun
Stand still, yet we will make him run.

Marvell uses classic rhetorical devices to make the age-old argument "carpe diem" ("seize the day"). When I was in college, a boyfriend read me this poem, which I had always admired, and I wrote an answer. When I look back at my poem "Coy Mistress" now, I see that what I felt the most need to do was not to respond to the ostensible subject of the poem—seduction—but instead to assert the importance of a female speaker writing poetry. This helped me feel more powerfully the silence of Marvell's lady; writing a reply is a wonderful way to understand a poem more deeply.

Another way to explore the possibilities of dramatic poetry is to write a series of persona poems spoken by interrelated characters. The most famous example of such a book is Edward Lee Masters's *Spoon River Anthology.* A number of contemporary poets have written book-length sequences of lyric poems in the voices of a group of characters; notable examples are Rita Dove's *Thomas and Beulah,* Natasha Tretheway's *Belloq's Ophelia,* and Daniel Hoffman's *Middens of the Tribe.*

If you want to write full-length verse drama, you will be in good company. The list of poets who have written verse drama includes not only Yeats and Eliot but also Wallace Stevens, Sylvia Plath, W. H. Auden, T. S. Eliot, Frank O'Hara, Ntozake Shange, Carla Harryman, and Derek Walcott. If you are serious about having your verse drama produced, here are some thoughts. It's a good idea to start thinking about the performance aspect as soon as you can. If you can manage it, connect with a theater company, like Shakespeare. There is nothing like seeing your work performed regularly to make you learn to do your best. Short of this, you can still imagine how the play will sound when performed by reading aloud frequently as you go, and hopefully organizing a few group "staged readings" along the way.

You may find a producer for your play, or you may need to become the driving force in getting your verse drama produced, at a theater, school, café, or bookstore. You may also find yourself joining the long line of poets who have directed their own verse plays. As one of them, I can tell you that it's a lot of fun, especially if you are willing to be flexible about your play and rewrite parts to suit the needs of the performance as it develops. There is nothing quite like writing dramatic poetry; it can feel like collaborating with a wonderful wild animal, the performance itself—with all its constituent parts, from actors to scenery to music.

Whether you write a monologue, persona poem, reply poem, or full-fledged verse play, you may discover what so many others have learned: The close connection between the first-person lyric voice and the dramatic voice, and the shared reliance on rhythm and pacing between poetry and plays, can make dramatic writing a natural medium for poets. Even in an age where verse drama does not occupy center stage, so to speak, it is still a vibrant art form where your talent and skill as a poet can discover a new audience and a unique set of challenges and aesthetic opportunities.

Narrative Poems

In a **narrative poem,** a narrator tells a story, typically from a third-person point of view but sometimes in the first person or even the second person. The story usually has a beginning, middle, and end. While the narrative poems that have historically had the most impact have tended to be long epic poems such as *The Odyssey,* narrative poems don't have to be long:

From The Black Riders, *Stephen Crane (1895)*

I saw a man pursuing the horizon;
Round and round they sped.
I was disturbed at this.
I accosted the man.
"It is futile," I said.
"You can never—"

"You lie," he cried,
And ran on.

This story follows a classic narrative pattern. The beginning sets up a scene (what the man was doing); the middle introduces the event or conflict (the accosting); and the ending shows the result or aftermath (the man's response).

Such a beginning, middle, and end is all you need for a narrative poem, though the line between a narrative and lyric poem often becomes quite complicated when the poem is being narrated by an "I" and we begin to find things out about the "I":

"A Red Palm," Gary Soto

You're in this dream of cotton plants.
You raise a hoe, swing, and the first weeds
Fall with a sigh. You take another step,
Chop, and the sigh comes again,
Until you yourself are breathing that way
With each step, a sigh that will follow you into town.

That's hours later. The sun is a red blister
Coming up in your palm. Your back is strong,
Young, not yet the broken chair
In an abandoned school of dry spiders.
Dust settles on your forehead, dirt
Smiles under each fingernail.
You chop, step, and by the end of the first row,
You can buy one splendid fish for wife
And three sons. Another row, another fish,
Until you have enough and move on to milk,
Bread, meat. Ten hours and the cupboards creak.
You can rest in the back yard under a tree.
Your hands twitch on your lap,
Not unlike the fish on a pier or the bottom
Of a boat. You drink iced tea. The minutes jerk
Like flies.

It's dusk, now night,
And the lights in your home are on.
That costs money, yellow light
In the kitchen. That's thirty steps,
You say to your hands,
Now shaped into binoculars.

You could raise them to your eyes:
You were a fool in school, now look at you.
You're a giant among cotton plants.
Now you see your oldest boy, also running.
Papa, he says, it's time to come in.
You pull him into your lap
And ask, What's forty times nine?
He knows as well as you, and you smile.
The wind makes peace with the trees,
The stars strike themselves in the dark.
You get up and walk with the sigh of cotton plants.
You go to sleep with a red sun on your palm,
The sore light you see when you first stir in bed.

The poet has disciplined this poem to the shape of a narrative, with one event following another, and yet there are many strongly lyrical moments, and the poem is also dramatic since it is basically a persona poem written in the second person. Each of these modes contributes to the effectiveness of the poem. The value in being able to untangle them, for you as a writer, is so that you will more consciously be able to use all of these modes in your own work.

Poets writing narratives can make good use of the fact that people are prone to make a narrative out of anything they read. To find some kind of story, some kind of meaning, in just about any sequence of events seems to be characteristic of human nature. In one experiment, a film audience was shown a bad car accident followed by a close-up shot of a woman's face. The same audience was then shown a cute baby and the same shot of the woman's face. The audience read her expression as horror the first time, and as delight the second time, even though they were both the exact same shot.

Whether we are reading or writing, we put the pieces together, even when reading poems that have nonlinear sense. And if we feel compelled to write some words that don't have a logical connection, we will probably read them over until we find some kind of connection taking shape. Encountering the lines, "The watchers of the civilized wastes / reverse their signals on our track," we eventually make a story out of our own reactions to the mysteries of Mina Loy's poem. Who are the watchers? What are civilized wastes? We come up with answers and then apply the answers to the next part of the poem, until we have constructed a story. In a way, when we respond to a poem like this, our own experience of reading and creating meaning becomes the poem's plot—and it may turn out to be a story as interesting as one the poet could have told us explicitly. This kind of nonlinear poetry is explored in more depth in chapter 10, on exploratory poetry.

To return to narrative poetry can enlarge the scope of a poem. The lyric "I" can be limiting, confining poets to their own experience or to the experiences they can imagine having in the first person. Telling a story about someone else, however, you may reveal parts of yourself of which you were not aware, or narrate stories you had no idea you could imagine. Many midlength narrative poems take on dreamlike or mythological subject matter. Keats's "Lamia" and Christina Rossetti's "Goblin Market," for example, tell stories about snake-women and goblins, and Tennyson's "Idylls of the King" goes back to the legends of King Arthur. Twentieth- and twenty-first-century narrative poems often keep ties to the world of dream-truths and unreal meanings; Galway Kinnell's "The Bear" has the character of a ritual story or a dream, and Carolyn Kizer's "Fanny" takes on a mythic character as it tells of Robert Louis Stevenson's wife, transplanted to the tropics, planting a garden that threatens to overtake her with its fecundity.

One of the best-known fantasy narratives is Coleridge's "Kubla Khan," a poem whose composition is now as famous a story as the poem itself:

"Kubla Khan," Samuel Taylor Coleridge (1797)

In Xanadu did Kubla Khan
A stately pleasure-dome decree:
Where Alph, the sacred river, ran
Through caverns measureless to man
Down to a sunless sea.

So twice five miles of fertile ground
With walls and towers were girdled round:
And there were gardens bright with sinuous rills,
Where blossom'd many an incense-bearing tree;
And here were forests ancient as the hills,
Enfolding sunny spots of greenery.

But oh! that deep romantic chasm which slanted
Down the green hill athwart a cedarn cover!
A savage place! as holy and enchanted
As e'er beneath a waning moon was haunted
By woman wailing for her demon-lover!
And from this chasm, with ceaseless turmoil seething,
As if this earth in fast thick pants were breathing,
A mighty fountain momently was forced;
Amid whose swift half-intermitted burst
Huge fragments vaulted like rebounding hail,
Or chaffy grain beneath the thresher's flail:
And 'mid these dancing rocks at once and ever
It flung up momently the sacred river.
Five miles meandering with a mazy motion
Through wood and dale the sacred river ran,
Then reached the caverns measureless to man,
And sank in tumult to a lifeless ocean:
And 'mid this tumult Kubla heard from far
Ancestral voices prophesying war!

The shadow of the dome of pleasure
Floated midway on the waves;
Where was heard the mingled measure
From the fountain and the caves.
It was a miracle of rare device,
A sunny pleasure-dome with caves of ice!

A damsel with a dulcimer
In a vision once I saw:
It was an Abyssinian maid,
And on her dulcimer she play'd,
Singing of Mount Abora.
Could I revive within me,
Her symphony and song,
To such a deep delight 'twould win me,
That with music loud and long,
I would build that dome in air,
That sunny dome! those caves of ice!

And all who heard should see them there,
And all should cry, Beware! Beware!
His flashing eyes, his floating hair!
Weave a circle round him thrice,
And close your eyes with holy dread,
For he on honey-dew hath fed,
And drunk the milk of Paradise.

"Kubla Khan" is a good example of how a narrative poem can partake of the lyric to gather its full impact—and this poem comes with a framing narrative, the story of how the poem was composed during "the Author's" dream: "On awakening he appeared to himself to have a distinct recollection of the whole, and taking his pen, ink, and paper, instantly and eagerly wrote down the lines that are here preserved. At this moment he was unfortunately called out by a person on business from Porlock, and detained by him above an hour, and on his return to his room, found, to his no small surprise and mortification, that though he still retained some vague and dim recollection of the general purport of the vision, yet, with the exception of some eight or ten scattered lines and images, all the rest had passed away like the images on the surface of a stream into which a stone has been cast, but, alas! without the after restoration of the latter." The poem opens with one narrative thread, but stories pile on until it is hard to trace the relation between them. And it doesn't matter; the lyric power of the imagery and evocative mood make it memorable enough.

No matter what the form or meter or free-verse form of a narrative poem, vivid narrative poems often rely on the contrast of scale, almost as if a camera zooms in on one object or moment. Such contrast is at work in this poem:

Poem 520, Emily Dickinson (c. 1862)

I started Early—Took my Dog—
And visited the Sea—
The Mermaids in the Basement
Came out to look at me—

And Frigates—in the Upper Floor
Extended Hempen Hands—
Presuming Me to be a Mouse—
Aground—upon the Sands—

But no Man moved Me—till the Tide
Went past my simple Shoe—
And past my Apron—and my Belt
And past my Bodice—too—

And made as He would eat me up—
As wholly as a Dew
Upon a Dandelion's Sleeve—
And then—I started—too—

And He—He followed—close behind—
I felt His Silver Heel
Upon my Ankle—Then my Shoes
Would overflow with Pearl—

Until We met the Solid Town—
No One He seemed to know
And bowing—with a Mighty look—
At me—The Sea withdrew—

The contrast between such specifics as the apron and the shoe, and the huge motion of the tide, is a major part of the narrative impact of the poem.

The great majority of narrative poetry in English has been written in two ancient forms: the **ballad** and the **epic.** The ballad is treated at length later in the book. The rest of this chapter will discuss the epic, a long narrative poem that reflects the values of a culture through the adventures of a heroic central character.

Traditional epics include *Beowulf* (England), the *Iliad* and *Odyssey* (Greece), the *Mahabharata* (India), *Gilgamesh* (Sumer), the *Kalevala* (Finland), the *Aeneid* (Rome), and Diane Wolkstein's assemblage of ancient poems about the Sumerian goddess Inanna, *The Descent of Inanna* (1983). Most of these epics seem to be either written versions of single poems that had been passed down orally for generations, or compilations of traditional legends and stories that had been passed down orally.

Epic poems are gripping, audience-tested poems with multiple plots and memorable, vivid characters. Traditional epic stories center on the heroic deeds of a heroic central figure, with special emphasis on a central episode called a "descent," such as Achilles' descent to the Underworld to visit the dead in the *Il-*

iad, and Beowulf's descent into the lake to battle a monster. Epics are written in regular meter, making them easier to recite and remember, and are sometimes characterized by long, extended comparisons called **epic similes,** such as this passage from Virgil's *Aeneid* where Aeneas sees the city of Carthage:

From The Aeneid, *Virgil (ca. 19 B.C.) (trans. John Dryden) (1697)*

The toiling Tyrians on each other call
To ply their labor: some extend the wall;
Some build the citadel; the brawny throng
Or dig, or push unwieldly stones along.
Some for their dwellings choose a spot of ground,
Which, first design'd, with ditches they surround.
Some laws ordain; and some attend the choice
Of holy senates, and elect by voice.
Here some design a mole, while others there
Lay deep foundations for a theater;
From marble quarries mighty columns hew,
For ornaments of scenes, and future view.
Such is their toil, and such their busy pains,
As exercise the bees in flow'ry plains,
When winter past, and summer scarce begun,
Invites them forth to labor in the sun;
Some lead their youth abroad, while some condense
Their liquid store, and some in cells dispense;
Some at the gate stand ready to receive
The golden burthen, and their friends relieve;
All with united force, combine to drive
The lazy drones from the laborious hive:
With envy stung, they view each other's deeds;
The fragrant work with diligence proceeds.

Epics such as *The Aeneid,* a central source of ancient Roman identity and pride, have played an important role in the stories of nations. This has been true even in recent centuries. The country of Finland, for example, might well not exist without the epic poem *The Kalevala,* which solidified Finnish culture and national identity at a key political moment and helped the country gain independence from Russia in 1917.

Not surprisingly, ever since the founding of the United States, American poets have felt at a disadvantage in not having a national epic of their own to look back to. Numbers of eighteenth-century poets tried to provide an epic for the United States; the best known is Joel Barlow, who looked to the story of Columbus for *The Columbiad* (1825). Lydia Sigourney used Native American characters and setting for her *Traits of the Aborigines of North America* (1822), and Longfellow researched Native American characters, language, and stories for the very popular *The Song of Hiawatha* (1855). But all of these attempts were forced. It may be that an authentic epic needs to arise out of oral tradition; as Longfellow realized, the best place to look for "the American epic" might be in the only oral tradition of storytelling ever to thrive on this continent, the Native American traditional stories. These (or possibly a pastiche of oral tales drawn also from many cultural groups who have emigrated to America) might be pieced together into a longer work, as the Finnish scholar Elias Lonnrot did in the nineteenth century, creating *The Kalevala* by weaving together remembered bits of oral narratives dictated to him. But in the meantime, the United States still awaits an epic that feels as if it belongs to everyone living here.

The most "successful" American epic to date in terms of audience, memorized by schoolchildren across the country in the nineteenth century, just as *The Kalevala* now is in Finland, was Henry Wadsworth Longfellow's *Evangeline* (1850). Interestingly, this epic does not concern war and struggle and conquest as did the classical epics Joel Barlow and his ilk were trying to emulate. Instead, its "heroine" is the young woman Evangeline, a French Acadian displaced by political oppression. During her "epic descent" she travels the country searching for her lost lover. The success of the poem (which still makes a very enjoyable read) may reflect the extent to which Longfellow did achieve the epic task of embodying the culture of a nation; after all, the geographical breadth of the story and its focus on a strong female character can both be seen as reflecting characteristic American qualities.

Modernist and postmodern poets who have produced epic poems have tended to use a fragmented collage form: W. C. Williams and Ezra Pound, whose *Paterson* and *The Cantos* use encyclopedic, nonnarrative pastiche to embody the scope of daily American life and world culture, respectively; Louis Zukofsky, whose gigantic work *A* incorporates sonnet sequences and stream of consciousness, politics, and culture; Hart Crane, whose *The Bridge* makes a lyrical attempt to celebrate the beauty of the United States in all its ugliness; Anne Waldman, whose *Jovis* is an ongoing lifelong project; and Alice Notley, whose *The Descent of Alette* returns hauntingly to the Goddess Inanna story brought to us by Diane Wolkstein. Other contemporary book-length poems or sequences of poems with epic implications include Cornelius Eady's *Brutal Imagination*, about white mother Susan Smith accusing a fictional black man of her murder of her own children; Derek Walcott's historical epic of the Caribbean, *Omeros;* Sharon Doubiago's journey epic *South America Mi Hija;* and George Keithley's grippingly tragic story *The Donner Party.*

As you can see from the amount of time I have spent discussing epics of the past, the epic has an imposing history which should not be invoked lightly. But it has been invoked lightly, particularly in Alexander Pope's *The Rape of the Lock* (1712), a satire that uses gods, heroes, and epic similes to tell a story about cutting a lock of a young woman's hair:

From The Rape of the Lock, *Alexander Pope (1712)*

The meeting Points that sacred Hair dissever
From the fair Head, for ever and for ever!
Then flash'd the living Lightnings from her Eyes,
And Screams of Horror rend th' affrighted Skies.
Not louder Shrieks to pitying Heav'n are cast,
When Husbands or when Lap-dogs breath their last,
Or when rich China Vessels, fal'n from high,
In glittring Dust and painted Fragments lie!

Let Wreaths of Triumph now my Temples twine,
(The Victor cry'd) the glorious Prize is mine!
While Fish in Streams, or Birds delight in Air,
Or in a Coach and Six the British Fair,
As long as Atalantis shall be read,
Or the small Pillow grace a Lady's Bed,
While Visits shall be paid on solemn Days,
When numerous Wax-lights in bright Order blaze,
While Nymphs take Treats, or Assignations give,
So long my Honour, Name, and Praise shall live!

What Time wou'd spare, from Steel receives its date,
And Monuments, like Men, submit to Fate!
Steel cou'd the Labour of the Gods destroy,
And strike to Dust th' Imperial Tow'rs of Troy.

Steel cou'd the Works of mortal Pride confound,
And hew Triumphal Arches to the Ground.
What Wonder then, fair Nymph! thy Hairs shou'd feel
The conqu'ring Force of unresisted Steel?

Pope reminds us, as do all the recent poets who have found ways to make epic strategies work in poetry, what it is timely to remember: there is no poetic tradition that is not available to us, if we can find a viable way to use it. Whether lyric, dramatic, or narrative epic, no poetic mode or potential is off limits. Awe in the face of the past can be debilitating, but with the global responsibilities facing all of us, it may be time for renewed attention to what the time-tested poetic modes can do.

QUESTIONS FOR MEDITATION OR DISCUSSION

Look through the other chapters in this book for poems in narrative, dramatic, and lyric modes. In addition to many examples of each, you will probably come across quite a few poems that combine two or even three modes. If possible, compare notes with others.

What kind of "I" do you usually use in your poems? The personal, autobiographical I? The public voice? The invisible narrator? An overheard speaker? Do you ever treat the "I" as something of a taboo? Have you ever experimented with another kind of "I"? Take a poem you have already written and alter the role of the "I." How does it change the poem?

Yeats wrote, "I think that all happiness depends on the energy to assume the mask of some other self; that all joyous or creative life is a re-birth as something not oneself, something which has no memory and is created in a moment and perpetually renewed." This description reminds me of the way children approach the world. How does this idea relate to Yeats's idea that in order to create a poem, a poet must always put on a mask of some kind? Do you think that the mask Yeats wore to create the character of Chuchulain is different from the mask he wore to create his lyric poems?

Takao Suzuki, in his book *Japan and the Japanese,* points out that the word "I" is taboo-related in Japanese. Unlike in Indo-European languages such as English, which have used the same word for "I" for thousands of years, in Japanese the word for "I" has changed often as the language changed, and people also use different terms for "I" at different stages in their lives and different situations. Suzuki says the concept of personal identity is a taboo in Japan and therefore personal pronouns are indirect and change often. Like teenage slang words for "good" (I've lived through "cool," "funky," "sweet," and "sick"), the words for a taboo concept must change frequently to avoid the embarrassment of referring too directly to the taboo quality. Does this model of the lyric self have implications for the lyric "I" in poetry? Yeats was especially fascinated with the Japanese Noh drama, and it played a big role in his own verse plays. How does the Japanese idea of the self as set out by Suzuki relate to Yeats's idea of the "mask"?

Why do you think that Adrian Oktenberg uses persona poems for her poems exploring the horrible consequences of war? How would her poem on page 104 be different if it were written in the third person? How would it be different if it were addressed to no-one, or to the reader, instead of to the loved one who has been killed?

Robert Creeley's "I Know a Man" (reprinted in chapter 4, on words and their roots) is a narrative poem including many dramatic elements (the setting and dramatic situation only become clear in the last stanza). Imagine this poem as pure narrative or as purely dramatic. What does the narrative element add to the poem? What does the dramatic element add?

Identify the beginning, middle, and end of this brief poem:

"Hide-and-Seek," Galway Kinnell

Once when we were playing
hide-and-seek and it was time
to go home, the rest gave up
on the game before it was done
and forgot I was still hiding.
I remained hidden as a matter
of honor until the moon rose.

Take the Stephen Crane poem that opens the narrative section. Revise it by adding more information about the "I." At what point does it begin to feel like a lyric poem? Does the distinction between narrative and lyric seem to depend more on the amount of information added, or on the type of information added?

QUOTES

When the so-called normal world is doing increasing environmental harm and eliminating species at a rapid rate, it is the poet's job not to sing normal, comforting ditties. The music of lyric poetry brings a voice from a wilderness we do not understand, to expose acts of false authority for the ways they are dismaying to human and other earthly life. Its mind is a counterculture.

—Brenda Hillman

Lyric is the foregrounding of language, in its material dimensions.

—Jonathan Culler

Possibly the majority of attempts to confect a poetic drama have begun at the wrong end; they have aimed at the small public which wants "poetry." . . . The Elizabethan drama was aimed at a public which wanted *entertainment* of a crude sort, but would *stand* a good deal of poetry; our problem should be to take a form of entertainment, and subject it to the process which would leave it a form of art.

—T. S. Eliot

If a chap can't compose an epic poem while he's weaving tapestry, he had better shut up; he'll never do any good at all.

—William Morris

If a story is in you it has got to come out.

—William Faulkner

POETRY PRACTICES

(Group) Live Performance. Write and perform a collaborative verse play, for two or more characters. Essentially you will be writing poems that are talking to each other. The play can be realistic, surreal, whimsical, or absurd.

(Group) Three Mode Collaboration. Divide into groups of three. Within each group of three, agree on a common topic or theme, the more specific the better. Each choose one mode to write a poem about this theme. Shuffle the poems so no one knows who wrote which. Read aloud all three poems and have the group guess which is in which mode. Optional follow-up: Provide feedback as a group and revise the poems to distinguish the three modes more clearly from each other. Then read them aloud for the larger group.

Three Modes in Action. Write a series of three poems, or three separate poems, or a poem in three sections, about the same incident or perception: one lyric, one dramatic, and one narrative.

Pure Lyric. Write a poem in the first person that is as purely a lyric poem as possible; express your feelings with as few narrative or dramatic elements as you can. Remember to pay attention to imagery and music. Imagine that you are going to perform it with a lyre or lute or guitar. You may want to focus on one of Graves's eternal themes: love, death, or the changing of the seasons.

All the Poem's a Stage. Write a dramatic monologue in the voice of one of the characters in a book or play who don't get to speak for themselves. Or, write a poem replying in the voice of the character addressed in a famous poem. Or, write a poem in two voices. Or, write a short scene of verse drama in which your characters talk in meter. If possible, perform your verse play.

Gossip and Talk. Invent a fictional town like Spoon River or another community. Write two or more poems in the voices of people who live in the town. If you can, have them write about each other or about an incident that they have experienced in common. Or write two or more poems in the voices of an actual group of people you know. (You don't have to show them the poems . . .)

Reply Poem. Write your own reply to the speaker of an existing poem. Notice how many poems you might have thought of as lyrics are actually quite dramatic.

Tale-telling. Write a narrative poem based on a story that is told in your family, or an incident from your life. Think about the structure of beginning, middle, and end. Move between specific details and larger descriptions of action.

Transposition. Pick a narrative poem you admire from another time or place and retell the same basic story, using characters and setting from your own time and place.

Episode. Write a poem telling a story from one of your favorite movies, TV episodes, or pieces of fiction. Use dialogue.

Fairy Tale. Write a fairy tale, classic or original, in poetic form.

PART 2

Making Poems: Sense and Sound

"I name all things in my room and they rehearse their names, gather in groups, form tesseracts, discussing their names among themselves."

—GWENDOLYN MACEWEN

CHAPTER 6

Making Senses: Imagery and Abstraction

How do you feel when you read this sentence: "I became extremely anxious"? If you're like most people, you might not feel much. But when you read this sentence, "I felt my heart stop and my stomach turn over," you'll feel anxiety more convincingly. The difference between these two ways of communicating can be summed up in the word "imagery." The word "image" in poetry doesn't refer only to the visual; an image in poetry means any information that is understood through the five senses: smell, taste, touch, sound, or sight. Since we experience and express emotion through our senses, it is often through the use of specific sensual images that literature can touch a reader's emotions most directly. This has been true of poetry at all times and in all cultures, since the Psalmist said, "God takes care of me" by writing, "He maketh me to lie down in green pastures"; since Robert Burns said, "I will love you forever" by writing, "I will love you until all the seas run dry, and the rocks melt in the sun"; since Alice Dunbar-Nelson said "I am confined to the domestic sphere" by writing "I sit and sew"; since W. B. Yeats said, "It is fall" by writing, "The trees are in their autumn beauty, the woodland paths are dry"; since Emma Lazarus said "immigrants to the United States" by writing "huddled masses yearning to breathe free."

What Is an Image?

An image is not an idea or a thought; it is sensory information. In the examples above it is the image, as opposed to the abstract idea, that engages us. Words such as pastures, sea, rock, sun, tree, woodland path, and breathe are concrete. Words such as anxious, care, love, forever, and immigrant are abstract. Ideas are, of course, essential to many good poems, but unless a poem has imagery, it is likely to leave the reader behind, without a real emotional connection. One of the best-known statements of this idea is a section of this poem, called "Ars Poetica" or "the art of poetry":

> **Imagery refers to the sensations produced in the mind by the language of touch (including kinesthetic sensations: awareness of muscle tension and movement), taste, smell, sound or sight.**

From "Ars Poetica," Archibald MacLeish

A poem should be palpable and mute
As a globed fruit

Dumb
As old medallions to the thumb

Silent as the sleeve-worn stone
Of casement ledges where the moss has grown—

A poem should be wordless
As the flight of birds

A poem should be motionless in time
As the moon climbs

Leaving, as the moon releases
Twig by twig the night-entangled trees,

Leaving, as the moon behind the winter leaves,
Memory by memory the mind—

A poem should be motionless in time
As the moon climbs

A poem should be equal to:
Not true

For all the history of grief
An empty doorway and a maple leaf

For love
The leaning grasses and two lights above the sea—

A poem should not mean
But be

Here is a poem that embodies the same idea purely through practice, by one of the most well-known proponents of the poetic image:

"Nantucket," William Carlos Williams

Flowers through the window
lavender and yellow

changed by white curtains—
Smell of cleanliness—

Sunshine of late afternoon—
On the glass tray

a glass pitcher, the tumbler
turned down, by which

a key is lying—And the
immaculate white bed

Contrasting the two poems, one might feel that MacLeish's poem would be improved if he took his own advice even more literally. Humans seem to be wired so that we feel and convey emotion through concrete details. We dream in images that evoke feelings. If a person is sense-deprived, the mind will start to hallucinate sensory experience. Emily Dickinson described her reaction to poetry in terms of its physical effect on her: "[I]f it makes my body so cold no fire can warm me I know *that* is poetry. If I feel physically as if the top of my head were taken off, I know *that* is poetry. These are the only ways I know it."

The following poem involves imagery of all the five senses to convey the reality of war. The poet knew that you can't see a war, but you can see an individual soldier; you can't hear a war, but you can hear a cough or the sound of a shell. The poem communicates with all the senses: there is the feeling of trudging through sludge, the sound of coughing and choking, the smothering smell of gas, the sight of the misty panes of the gas mask's window, the taste of sores in the young soldier's mouths. "Seeing is believing," as they say—and so are smelling, tasting, touching, and hearing.

"Dulce et Decorum Est," Wilfred Owen (1917)

Bent double, like old beggars under sacks,
Knock-kneed, coughing like hags, we cursed through sludge,
Till on the haunting flares we turned our backs
And towards our distant rest began to trudge.
Men marched asleep. Many had lost their boots
But limped on, blood-shod. All went lame; all blind;
Drunk with fatigue; deaf even to the hoots
Of disappointed shells that dropped behind.

GAS! Gas! Quick, boys!—An ecstasy of fumbling,
Fitting the clumsy helmets just in time;
But someone still was yelling out and stumbling
And flound'ring like a man in fire or lime . . .
Dim, through the misty panes and thick green light
As under a green sea, I saw him drowning.

In all my dreams, before my helpless sight,
He plunges at me, guttering, choking, drowning.

If in some smothering dreams you too could pace
Behind the wagon that we flung him in,
And watch the white eyes writhing in his face,
His hanging face, like a devil's sick of sin;
If you could hear, at every jolt, the blood
Come gargling from the froth-corrupted lungs,
Obscene as cancer, bitter as the cud
Of vile, incurable sores on innocent tongues,—
My friend, you would not tell with such high zest
To children ardent for some desperate glory,
The old Lie: Dulce et decorum est
Pro patria mori.

The specific truth we learn from Owen's appeals to our senses is pitted against the abstract statement he quotes in Latin at the end, that "it is sweet and right to die for one's country." The concrete details ring true, vivid against the grandly and cruelly shallow general statement.

In the following poem by Wendell Berry, however, a relatively abstract final statement is underlain by the powerful concrete images that precede it:

"The Peace of Wild Things," Wendell Berry

When despair for the world grows in me
and I wake in the night at the least sound
in fear of what my life and my children's lives may be,
I go and lie down where the wood drake
rests in his beauty on the water, and the great heron feeds.
I come into the peace of wild things
who do not tax their lives with forethought
of grief. I come into the presence of still water.
And I feel above me the day-blind stars
waiting with their light. For a time
I rest in the grace of the world, and am free.

In Berry's poem the rather old-fashioned diction and syntax, and the rhythm hovering around iambic pentameter, unite the images and the abstractions. This poem unites them with a different strategy:

"God's List of Liquids," Anne Carson

It was a November night of wind.
Leaves tore past the window.
God had the book of life open at PLEASURE

and was holding the pages down with one hand
because of the wind from the door.
For I made their flesh as a sieve

wrote God at the top of the page
and then listed in order:

Alcohol
Blood
Gratitude
Memory
Semen
Song
Tears
Time.

The character of God, the challenge of deciphering the allegory, and above all the narrative itself hold the imagery and the abstractions together, grounding the abstractions so they seem as necessary and specific as the images.

Writing with Imagery

One of the great values of imagery in our time is that it takes time. You are not likely to fill a poem with striking, moving images if you write it in harried haste, "out of your head." To notice imagery requires waiting: moving into the slowness of your senses and allowing sounds, smells, sights, touches, and tastes to well up in your awareness, to come to you. Poet Baron Wormser uses a simple mantra to remind his writing students of the importance of filling in details of imagery: "dwell, linger, stay." This is not a bad group of words to keep in your mind as you try to convey to a reader the vivid physical realities that seem so self-evident to you that they may not at first suggest themselves as words on the page.

The choice of which images to write about is a key aspect of writing with imagery. If you choose well, effective concrete details may flow easily. But if you are having trouble making a particular image come alive, it may be time to reconsider the image you chose in the first place. I was once in a workshop where a student had written that something was like "holding a delicate bird in my hands." The image seemed forced and needed detail. Finally someone asked, "Have you ever held a delicate bird in your hands?" On hearing the answer was no, they went on, "If you had, you might have more to say about it." This does not necessarily mean, though, to follow the old workshop cliché and *only* "write what you know." You may have very vivid knowledge, even if only imaginary knowledge, of experiences you have never actually had, and those images might flow beautifully. But if you are having trouble with making an image work well, the problem may be with the image itself, either because it is too unfamiliar for you to really experience it on the page, or simply because it does not stimulate your imagination.

Haiku, Focus, and Objective Correlative

Imagery is at the core of the Japanese poetic tradition of **haiku,** which influenced Ezra Pound and other early modernist poets. A haiku is a three-line syllabic poem. In the best-known form, invented by the poet Bashō, it is made of 17 syllables arranged in lines of 5, 7, and 5 syllables. Conventionally, a haiku takes place in nature during a specific season, and it consists almost entirely of a concrete description of objects, often connecting two things that seem unrelated. A haiku is traditionally meant to capture the essence of a moment of pure awareness of life:

Issa, "I look close and see" (ca. 1800) (translator unknown)

I look close and see
inside the dragonfly's eye
mountains behind me
—ISSA

Each line of a good haiku is traditionally self-contained and has a strong image or some new information that changes the reader's experience of the poem. Haiku emphasizes the feeling of immediacy, sometimes with a kind of "punch line" effect in the final line:

Bashō, "Inside the old pond" (ca. 1680) (translator unknown)

Inside the old pond
a sudden sound of splashing
where the frog jumped in
—BASHŌ

"Prelude to a Kiss," Tracie Morris

"Men must love your lips"
he said. Sure do. Long as I
ain't saying nothing.

Haiku can convey strong emotion, but this is always done largely or entirely through images, as in these poems (which are in the five-line form called *waka,* a precursor of haiku but in the same spirit):

Izumi Shikibu (ca. 1000), Lying Alone (trans. Jane Hirshfield)

Lying alone
My black hair tangled,
Uncombed,
I long for the one
Who touched it first

Ono no Komachi (ca. 900), This Autumn Night (trans. Jane Hirshfield)

This autumn night
Is long only in name—
We've done no more
Than gaze at each other
And it's already dawn.

Since a haiku is the spontaneous response to a certain moment, haiku poets normally produce many haiku and discard those that don't work, rather than revising one poem over and over. Like a koan, the riddle that a Zen master could use to startle a student into enlightenment, the haiku is designed to bypass our logical minds and bring us into a timeless state. The images in a haiku are a way to speak directly to our capacity for enlightenment, without intervening interpretations. This connection between haiku and enlightenment is clear in a dream that Bashō (a meditative poet, whose nickname arose from the "basho" or hut where he retreated for solitude) had in 1685. In the dream, he was caught in the rain and ran to a shrine for shelter. The priest told him he could only stay if he could create a suitable haiku. Bashō composed this haiku, which became one of his most famous, in that dream:

Bashō, "Temple Bells Die Out" (1685) (translator unknown)

Temple bells die out.
The fragrant blossoms remain.
A perfect evening!

It is in the balance between ending and new life, the temporary and the permanent, and the complete acceptance of this balance, that the power of the poem rests.

The intensity of a vivid image can create political as well as spiritual and emotional power. This poem, which Langston Hughes is said to have called "the most beautiful poem I know," uses images of Africa to make a distant place become a vivid and persuasive necessity:

From "Heritage," Countee Cullen (1925)

What is Africa to me:
Copper sun or scarlet sea,
Jungle star or jungle track,
Strong bronze men, or regal black
Women from whose loins I sprang
When the birds of Eden sang?
One three centuries removed
From the scenes his fathers loved,
Spicy grove, cinnamon tree,
What is Africa to me?

So I lie, who all day long
Want no sound except the song
Sung by wild barbaric birds
Goading massive jungle herds,
Juggernauts of flesh that pass
Trampling tall defiant grass
Where young forest lovers lie,
Plighting troth beneath the sky.
So I lie, who always hear,
Though I cram against my ear
Both my thumbs, and keep them there,
Great drums throbbing through the air.
So I lie, whose fount of pride,
Dear distress, and joy allied,
Is my somber flesh and skin,
With the dark blood dammed within
Like great pulsing tides of wine

That, I fear, must burst the fine
Channels of the chafing net
Where they surge and foam and fret.

The combination of the piling of specific images with the driving rhythm is relentlessly persuasive for Cullen's goal of building a historical awareness and solidarity among African Americans during the time of the Harlem Renaissance.

Like a close-up or zoom in film, an unexpected focus can add tremendous impact to images. In Sara Teasdale's "Gramercy Park," the iron gate becomes loaded with importance for a couple's tormented relationship:

"Gramercy Park," Sara Teasdale (1911)

The little park was filled with peace,
The walks were carpeted with snow,
But every iron gate was locked,
Lest if we entered, peace would go.

We circled it a dozen times,
The wind was blowing from the sea,
I only felt your restless eyes
Whose love was like a cloak for me.

Oh heavy gates that fate has locked
To bar the joy we can not win.
Peace would go out forever
If we should enter in.

The repetitions of the poem's basic idea, circling around the way the couple circles the gate, seem obsessive, perhaps a way for the speaker to try to accept the reality of the relationship. The image of the two trapped outside the gates would be called, in T. S. Eliot's terminology, an "objective correlative" for their inner state. As Eliot put it in his essay on *Hamlet,* "The only way of expressing emotion in the form of art is by finding an 'objective correlative'; in other words, a set of objects, a situation, a chain of events which shall be the formula of that particular emotion; such that when the external facts, which must terminate in sensory experience, are given, the emotion is immediately evoked."

This theory was the aesthetic credo of a poet who didn't believe in expressing personal emotions directly. But it also provides a useful way to think about poetic imagery in general; strong poetic imagery has the quality of inevitability that Eliot describes, and it can tell an entire emotional story perhaps more powerfully because the emotions are not stated:

"They Flee from Me," Thomas Wyatt (1503–1542)

They flee from me that sometime did me seek
With naked foot stalking in my chamber.
I have seen them gentle tame and meek
That now are wild and do not remember
That sometime they put themselves in danger
To take bread at my hand; and now they range
Busily seeking with a continual change.

Thanked be fortune, it hath been otherwise
Twenty times better; but once in special,
In thin array after a pleasant guise,
When her loose gown from her shoulders did fall,
And she me caught in her arms long and small;
And therewithal sweetly did me kiss,
And softly said, *Dear heart, how like you this?*

It was no dream, I lay broad waking.
But all is turned thorough my gentleness
Into a strange fashion of forsaking;
And I have leave to go of her goodness
And she also to use newfangleness.
But since that I so kindely am served,
I would fain know what she hath deserved.

The naked feet, the bread, the mysterious equation of the women with wild animals, and the arms, are all so vividly evoked that little needs to be said to describe the speaker's emotion directly. This recent poem uses description even more clearly to stand for the expression of emotion:

"Eating Together," Li-Young Lee

In the steamer is the trout
seasoned with slivers of ginger,
two sprigs of green onion, and sesame oil.
We shall eat it with rice for lunch,
brothers, sister, my mother who will
taste the sweetest meat of the head,
holding it between her fingers
deftly, the way my father did
weeks ago. Then he lay down
to sleep like a snow-covered road
winding through pines older than him,
without any travelers, and lonely for no one.

It is only after the poem is over that the reader realizes how much emotion was hiding in the opening scene. The balance between the disciplined objective imagery of the opening and the slightly shorter simile of the closing has proportions very similar to a sonnet; if the lengths or positions of the two sections were reversed, and the metaphor were to take more space than the concrete description, the poem would lose its control. This poem relies heavily on the human capacity for making meaning discussed in the section on narrative in chapter 5. Imagine a completely different ending, perhaps describing a happy scene of love; the same opening would work equally well.

When using imagery in a poem, be aware that if you draw upon too many different and/or conflicting kinds of imagery in a short space, your reader will probably experience a reading overload, if not a stomachache. If you draw on related image-clusters throughout a poem, each image takes power from the others and the result can be haunting:

"The Cat in the Kitchen," Robert Bly
(For Donald Hall)

Have you heard about the boy who walked by
The black water? I won't say much more.
Let's wait a few years. It wanted to be entered.
Sometimes a man walks by a pond, and a hand
Reaches out and pulls him in.

There was no
Intention, exactly. The pond was lonely, or needed
Calcium, bones would do. What happened then?

It was a little like the night wind, which is soft,
And moves slowly, sighing like an old woman
In her kitchen late at night, moving pans
About, lighting a fire, making some food for the cat.

The fairy-tale-like images of the pond, the hand, and the kitchen are not part of any story together; they are related only as part of the metaphor, perhaps a description of a mood or psychological state. But clustered together, they create a harmonious mood that permeates the reader's awareness and deepens the understanding. In some ways, the imagery structures the poem.

In Kathrine Varnes's sonnet below, the first in a "crown" of 48 sonnets called "His Next Ex-Wife," the loving attention to every detailed image of cooking conveys the disoriented reaction of the speaker (did you ever notice how at times of shock, mundane details can become extraordinarily clear?) and also adds a vivid, sensual dimension to the thread of an abstract conversation.

"Sonnet 1," Kathrine Varnes

"Hi, this is weird, but I'm Paul's second wife—"
"Nancy?" My mouth asks before I've time to think.
"Yes, are you busy? Do you mind that I called?"
"No" to both, I say, "I'm not busy at all"
and continue cubing the tofu with my knife,
slanting the board so the water runs in the sink,
"What's up?" I ask, as if she calls twice a week,
though actually I've never heard her voice before.
I cut halfway through the white flesh of a leek
and rinse out the sand by holding the layers apart.
"Paul moved out." "He did?" "About three weeks ago."
Suspended in shock, I tilt the tamari and pour
a tiny pool in my garlic paste. "Oh,"
I say as I stir, "I'm sorry—I didn't know."

Stirring tamari into garlic paste is the perfect objective correlative for the mood of the speaker. What other objective correlatives can you find in poems included in this book?

Unreal Imagery

Imagery does not have to be realistic. Surreal or dream imagery can be effective, as in the following poem:

"Jerusalem Song," Lisa Suhair Majaj

Jerusalem, fold me like a handkerchief
into your bosom. I am
one word in a lover's letter,

a chip of blue tile in your sky.
Even those who have never seen you
walk your streets at night.

We wipe your dust from our feet
each morning, rise from our beds wearied
by the long distances

we have traveled to reach you.
See how we save even the broken bits of pottery,
fitting fragments together

along jagged lines to remember you.
Jerusalem, we are fledglings
crying for a nest!

At first glance the poem does not seem particularly far-fetched or surreal. Yet on close reading many of the images prove to be impossible: a sky made of tile, the comparison of a person to a word in a letter or a folded handkerchief, a city with a bosom. Each of these deeply imaginative images adds to the poem a layer of experience that stretches beyond the realities of the speaker's situation. Their presence lends the emotions conveyed in the poem the quality of an almost magical strength of feeling. A different dynamic is at work in the following poem:

"Love After Love," Derek Walcott

The time will come
when, with elation
you will greet yourself arriving
at your own door, in your own mirror
and each will smile at the other's welcome,

and say, sit here. Eat.
You will love again the stranger who was your self.
Give wine. Give bread. Give back your heart
to itself, to the stranger who has loved you

all your life, whom you ignored
for another, who knows you by heart.
Take down the love letters from the bookshelf,

the photographs, the desperate notes,
peel your own image from the mirror.
Sit. Feast on your life.

Ordinary and mundane imagery—wine, bread, photographs—lend a quality of naturalness to the surreal scene of the encounter with the self, at the same time that they lead the reader carefully through the permutations of what such an encounter means, and how it feels.

Federico García Lorca was a powerful poet of surrealistic imagery, which he used with a simplicity and assuredness that lend it the quality of inevitability:

"La Guitarra," Federico García Lorca (ca. 1927)

Empieza el llanto
de la guitarra.
Se rompen las copas

de la madrugada.
Empieza el llanto
de la guitarra.
Es inútil
callarla.
Es imposible
callarla.
Llora monótona
comollora el agua,
comollora el viento
sobre la nevada.
Es imposible
callarla.
Llora por cosas
lejanas.
Arena del Sur caliente
que pide camellias blancas.
Llora flecha sin blanco,
la tarde sin mañana,
y el primer pájaro muerto
sobre la rama.
¡Oh guitarra!
Corazón malherido
por cinco espadas.

"The Guitar," Federico García Lorca (trans. Cindy Williams Gutiérrez)

The keening of the guitar
begins.
The goblets of dawn
are shattered.
The keening of the guitar
begins.
It is useless
to silence it.
Impossible
to silence it.

It weeps monotonously
the way water weeps
the way the wind weeps
over the snowdrift.
It is impossible
to silence it.
It weeps for distant
things.
Hot southern sands
begging for white camellias.
It weeps arrow without target
evening without morning
and the first dead bird
on the branch.
Oh guitar!
Heart fatally wounded
By five swords.

When describing something as impossible to describe as the effect of music, sometimes surreal imagery is, paradoxically, the most accurate resource a poet has.

Lyric and Narrative Imagery

It is natural to think of imagery as primarily lyrical, and, indeed, imagery can go a long way to express even an inexpressible feeling, as in Italian poet Maura Del Serra's remarkable lyric on Emily Dickinson:

"Emily Dickinson," Maura Del Serra (trans. Michael Palma)

Here in the heart's divine nowhere
is the sepulcher
of the bumblebee in sunlight,
a thimble fallen right
to the bottom of my well of words:
you'll find it if you fish in the morning there
for violets that bloom by night.

If you are familiar with Dickinson, you will recognize some of her imagery; other imagery is entirely Del Serra's own. What feeling about Dickinson do you get from this imagery? How is the form of the poem different from and similar to the form of Dickinson's poems?

Images can also tell a story on their own, even without illustrating an accompanying narrative. Simply to list imagery can create an inner story, as in this poem:

From "She Says," Venus Khoury-Ghata (trans. Marilyn Hacker)

Autumn preceded summer by one day
vigilant gardeners cut the passionflowers' damp lashes earlier than
    expected
and the clocks knit narrower nights

A yellow wind dyed the forests' facades
the trees stopped playing
and the swings full of little girls and robins stopped moving
with a great rustling of wings and petticoats

November had banished tears
compassionate angels licked the small scraped knees

The mood of this particular autumn, gentle but in some way menacing, would be difficult to create through paraphrase; and besides, mood is not really the point. The precise descriptions of the actions and the sequencing of the story are their own justification.

It goes without saying that ideas can be expressed solely through imagery. Just because there are no abstractions in a poem doesn't mean there are no ideas being expressed, as in the poem below:

"Motherhood," May Swenson (1967)

She sat on a shelf,
Her breasts two bellies
On her poked-out belly,
On which the navel looked
Like a sucked-in mouth—

Her knees bent and apart,
Her long left arm raised,
With the large hand knuckled
To a bar in the ceiling—
Her right hand clamping
The skinny infant to her chest—
Its round, pale, new
Soft muzzle hunting
In the brown hair for a nipple,
Its splayed, tiny hand picking
At her naked, dirty ear.
Twisting its little neck,
With tortured, ecstatic eyes
The size of lentils, it looked
Into her severe, close-set,
Solemn eyes, that beneath bald
Eyelids glared—dull lights
In sockets of leather.

She twitched some chin-hairs,
With pain or pleasure,
As the baby-mouth found and
Yanked at her nipple;
Its pink-nailed, jointless
Fingers, wandering her face,
Tangled in the tufts
Of her cliffy brows.
She brought her big
Hand down from the bar—
With pretended exasperation
Unfastened the little hand,
And locked it within her palm—
While her right hand,
With snag-nailed forefinger
And short, sharp thumb, raked
The new orange hair
Of the infant's skinny flank—
And found a louse

Which she lipped, and
Thoughtfully crisped
Between broad teeth.
She wrinkled appreciative
Nostrils which, without a nose,
Stood open—damp holes
Above the poke of her mouth.

She licked her lips, flicked
Her leather eyelids—
Then, suddenly flung
Up both arms and grabbed
The bars overhead.
The baby's scrabbly fingers
Instantly caught the hair—
As if there were metal rings there—
In her long, stretched armpits.
And, as she stately swung,
And then proudly, more swiftly
Flung herself from corner
To corner of her cell—
Arms longer than her round
Body, short knees bent—
Her little wild-haired,
Poke-mouthed infant hung,
Like some sort of trophy,
Or decoration, or shaggy medal—
Shaped like herself—but new,
Clean, soft and shining
On her chest.

When you started reading, how long did it take you to realize who the poem is about? Did the pronoun "she," so much less used in reference to animals than "he," influence your reading of the poem? Did the details give you a different understanding of the differences between humans and animals? Though Swenson starts the poem with the term "breasts," she ends it with "chest" and at the same time closes the poem with a description of the importance of the baby to its mother.

Though the following poem includes no tropes, no interpretation and hardly any stated feelings, just a straightforward account of facts through images, the organization of the images tells everything:

"Harvesting Wheat for the Public Share," Li Chu (trans. Kenneth Rexroth and Ling Chung)

It is a year of good harvest
The wheat is brought to the threshing yard.
The second sister crushes it.
The elder sister threshes it.
The third sister winnows it
Very carefully and throws away the husks.
The golden grain piles high in the yard.
Round, round wheat, better than pomegranate seeds.
Bite it with your teeth, it goes "go-pou!"
The first pile of wheat is really lovely.
After we have dried it in the sun,
And cleaned it,
We will turn it in as the public share.

The last line seems to balance the entire rest of the poem, in its understated weight. Which images in the poem contribute the most to the poem's effect?

In contrast to "Motherhood," this poem seems to need a little abstraction to bring the meanings of the imagery, startling and memorable as they are, into full importance:

"Design," Robert Frost (1936)

I found a dimpled spider, fat and white,
On a white heal-all, holding up a moth
Like a white piece of rigid satin cloth—
Assorted characters of death and blight
Mixed ready to begin the morning right,
Like the ingredients of a witches' broth—

A snow-drop spider, a flower like a froth
And dead wings carried like a paper kite

What had that flower to do with being white,
The wayside blue and innocent heal-all?
What brought the kindred spider to that height, . . .
Then steered the white moth thither in the night?
What but design of darkness to appall—
If design govern in a thing so small.

A Place for Abstraction

"No ideas but in things," admonished William Carlos Williams in the most famous statement on poetics of the twentieth century. This was also the credo of the Imagists, a group devoted to writing poems that centered on the "direct treatment of the thing" in simple, almost spartan language. In a reaction to what they saw as the eighteenth- and nineteenth-century tendency to draw on symbolism and abstraction rather than actual experience, poets of the early twentieth century made a great effort to, as Ezra Pound wrote, "go in fear of abstractions." As Marianne Moore famously put it in her poem called "Poetry," poems should be "imaginary gardens with real toads in them."

The modernists' obsession with image has had a healthy influence on poetry-writing; beginning writers are often prone to abstraction, and being forced to think about the sensual details of a remembered or imagined scene, or the specific realities that imply a general fact, has never hurt a poet. Great poetry of all eras almost always incorporates strong, vivid imagery.

Still, I think contemporary poetry is narrowed in scope and weakened in effect, nearly a hundred years later, by taking Williams's dictum too literally. The zeal to weed out all abstractions, a common characteristic of creative writing teachers, can be misplaced. Some poems get their strength from balancing specific imagery with abstraction. Sappho's "no room for grief" (see chapter 1) is largely an abstract statement, but the concrete metaphor of the house having no room for grief grounds the abstraction just enough to make it stick. Emily Dickinson's poetry is full of abstractions made vivid through metaphor:

Hope is the thing with feathers,
that perches in the soul
and sings the tune without the words . . .

The fact that hope has no words is part of the point; hope is an abstraction, as are beauty, truth, freedom, and many other things that poets sometimes like to write about. But without the powerful abstraction of hope, the whole impact of this poem would be lost. The following poem saves the abstraction for the end:

"Those Winter Sundays," Robert E. Hayden

Sundays too my father got up early
and put his clothes on in the blueblack cold,
then with cracked hands that ached
from labor in the weekday weather made
banked fires blaze. No one ever thanked him.

I'd wake and hear the cold splintering, breaking.
When the rooms were warm, he'd call,
and slowly I would rise and dress,
fearing the chronic angers of that house,

Speaking indifferently to him,
who had driven out the cold
and polished my good shoes as well.
What did I know, what did I know
of love's austere and lonely offices?

The movingly detailed descriptions of the father waking early and warming the house for his family would be incomplete without the powerful abstraction that sums up the poem: "love's austere and lonely offices."

Adrienne Rich's work is characterized by a balance between the far ends of the spectrum of abstract and specific:

"In Those Years," Adrienne Rich

In those years, people will say, we lost track
of the meaning of we, of you
we found ourselves
reduced to I
and the whole thing became
silly, ironic, terrible:

we were trying to live a personal life
and, yes, that was the only life
we could bear witness to

But the great dark birds of history screamed and plunged
into our personal weather
They were headed somewhere else but their beaks and pinions drove
along the shore, through rages of fog
where we stood, saying I

The pronoun "I" becomes equated, not only with the personal self but also, ironically, with the position of abstraction which opens the poem; the birds of history are specific and inescapable, and yet they stand for the biggest abstraction of all.

The following poem blends imagery and abstraction in the service of a visionary portrait of our condition:

From "Poem for Friends," Quincy Troupe

we flounder, we climb
we trip
we fall
we call upon dead prophets
to help us
yet

they do not answer

(we hear instead the singing in the leaves
the waves of oceans, pounding)

we see sheer cliffs
of mountains polished by storms
sculptured to god's perfection
we see the advancing age of technology
see soulless monsters
eating up nature's perfections
hear wails & screams

& sirens howling

but hear no human voices calling

we sit at the brink of chaos laughing
we idle away time
when there is no time
left us

Troupe uses quite a bit of imagery in the poem, but it is always a means of illustrating the ideas he does not hesitate to spell out clearly, even if that involves him in abstract ideas such as calling on prophets, the age of technology, and idling away time. Political poetry such as Rich's and Troupe's needs abstractions to make up the large statements that are vital to that kind of poetic vision. Blended with inspired imagery, abstractions can greatly move a reader.

It is no coincidence that the near-total privileging of imagery over abstraction entered poetry at the same time that free verse displaced meter as the medium of choice. Meter has long provided a way to render abstractions three-dimensional by anchoring them in its constant, driving physical energy. John Keats's very abstract lines, "beauty is truth, truth beauty; that is all / ye know on earth, and all ye need to know," are some of his most memorable and famous, as are Ella Wheeler Wilcox's "Laugh and the world laughs with you, / cry and you cry alone," W. B. Yeats's "How but in custom and in ceremony / are innocence and beauty born?" and Alexander Pope's "a little learning is a dangerous thing" and "to err is human; to forgive, divine."

In all these passages, the abstract ideas are rendered both memorable and poetic by the sound of the words: the assonance of "forgive" and "divine," "little" and "learning"; the musical repetition and criss-crossing structure in "beauty is truth, truth beauty"; the parallelism in "to err, to forgive"—and above all, the strong metrical drive in all these lines—is not abstract at all. These physical, musical effects help to make the abstractions feel concrete, so that they lodge in our minds the same way that images do.

QUESTIONS FOR MEDITATION OR DISCUSSION

Browse through a sizable group of poems by others and jot down all the images that strike you. Play with these images, arranging them in groups of abstractness and concreteness. What tendencies do they have in common? What does your attraction to these images teach you about your own tendencies as a poet? Now browse through a group of your own poems and do the same thing. Which kinds of poems of yours have your favorite images?

Some contemporary poets avoid abstract concepts or statements; others use them with some frequency. What is your own tolerance level for abstraction? Are there extenuating circumstances that will lead you to accept an abstraction? How about if there is only one of them, or if it comes at the end of a poem, or if it is in the title? How do you think the final abstraction works in this poem?

James Wright, "Lying in a Hammock at William Duffy's Farm"

Over my head, I see the bronze butterfly,
Asleep on the black trunk,
Blowing like a leaf in green shadow.
Down the ravine behind the empty house,
The cowbells follow one another
Into the distances of the afternoon.
To my right,
In a field of sunlight between two pines,
The droppings of last year's horses
Blaze up into golden stones.
I lean back, as the evening darkens and comes on.
A chicken hawk floats over, looking for home.
I have wasted my life.

Poem

Go to a place you like, close your eyes, and remember everything you can about the place. Write it down. Look around again. Repeat steps one to three more times. Use every sense: touch, smell, sight, sound, taste. What was this experience like for you?

Look through the poems in this book or elsewhere for images that appeal to each of the five senses. Which senses are most common? Do you see any patterns of imagery based on time period, gender, class, nationality or ethnicity, length of poem, subject matter, or form? Optional: try the same thing with your own poems. Which senses do your own images tend to invoke the most?

Take one of your existing poems and add three concrete and very specific images. Does the rest of the poem need to change? Is the poem improved? Try adding or taking away images from various poems included in this book. Which changes have the most impact?

QUOTES

Poetry is the deification of reality.
—Edith Sitwell

A poet cannot bring us any truth without introducing into his [*sic*] poetry the problematic, the painful, the ordinary.
—W. H. Auden

Seeing is of course very much a matter of verbalization. Unless I call my attention to what passes before my eyes, I simply won't see it.
—Annie Dillard

I tell the abstractions to wait at the door until I am ready to invite them into my poem.
—Baron Wormser

Trees and stones will teach you that which you can never learn from masters.
—St. Bernard

POETRY PRACTICES

(Group) Experience a Sense. Share an experience with others. Then write as immediately as possible about the experience or whatever memories arise. Possibilities: Pass out a raisin or a piece of fruit to each person; each person can take a full minute to finish eating it. Pass out herbs, spices, coffee, and other things with strong smells in small plastic bags. Pass around opaque "touching bags" containing objects of various textures (fur, sand, metal). Or everyone simply close their eyes (preferably outside), have someone spin you around or spin yourself, open your eyes and look at whatever is in front of you. Or sit in silence as a group for at least 10 minutes and listen to every sound, first closer, then moving further away.

(Group) Concrete Noun. As a group, name 10 concrete nouns (the leader chooses ones that are unusual in poems). Each person writes a love poem using those 10 words, and without using "love," "heart," "romance," or any words commonly associated with love poems. (This exercise comes from Marvin Bell.)

(Group) Palpable and Mute. Write a poem of pure description about any object. Don't name the object; see if the others in the group can guess what it is. Avoid all interpretative language; don't judge it or analyze it. Concentrate completely on description.

Concrete Mood. Perhaps using the previous practice as a basis, write a poem of at least 20 lines that conveys a mood entirely through concrete images. While all words have a degree of abstraction, your image poem should employ as few abstractions as you can possibly manage. Remember to include only information that you can see, touch, hear, smell, or feel, and to delete all interpretations, explanations, and generalizations.

Eyes of the Beholder (aka "Embodying the Objective Correlative"). Go to a place that is rich in detail and imagery (it is best not to do this exercise from memory, but to be in the place you are writing about). Choose two contrasting states of mind (peacefulness/anxiety; melancholy/elation; anticipation/regret, etc.). Write two poems, one for each mood, by describing the scene using only images that convey the mood. Check to make sure you haven't used any language that directly expresses the emotions; express them only through images. Read both poems aloud to someone and see if they can guess the emotions.

Haiku Sampler. Write at least eight haiku and choose your two favorites. Why do you like those best?

Walkabout. This exercise is designed to carry you along the thread of your own unique trail of images, the scent you follow as you move through your writing process. Choose a place you enjoy that is full of sensual detail. My students and I have enjoyed doing this exercise in a forest and in a farmers' market.

Step 1. Open your notebook and take out your pen.

Step 2. Walk with full awareness until you encounter an experience—a scene, smell, texture, configuration, or object—that draws you in some way. It may mystify, anger, inspire, amuse, or deeply please you.

Step 3. Stop, meditate, and then write in communion with this experience. Write until you feel you have captured the core of its appeal. Don't feel you need to write a lot. Think haiku.

Step 4. Move on until you come to another experience that appeals to you. Stop, meditate, write.

Step 5. Repeat until you have a chain of small poems or writings, at least six or eight experiences long.

Step 6. Revise as you see fit. Feel free to rearrange or omit as well as edit individual pieces. Think about common threads.

Optional addition: If you find yourself disturbed or perplexed by a particular object or scene you've written about, so that it's hard to let it go, try this: write a dialogue between yourself and that object or scene, or between two parts of that object or scene. Take both voices and keep the dialogue going until you reach some kind of resolution. (This part of the exercise comes from Shamanic teaching tradition.)

CHAPTER 7

Turn, Turn, Turn: Metaphors and Other Tropes

When my grandmother began teaching me to read at age three, she told me that the letter *A* looks like a tent. I don't think I would have remembered that moment for the rest of my life if she hadn't used a trope. **Trope** is a general term for describing one thing in terms of something else. As Marvin Bell has pointed out, tropes can be viewed as a form of repetition: "tent" repeats "A." Although tropes are a core part of all literature, they have, perhaps because of this repeating quality, a special place in poetry. A good trope can make the unfamiliar familiar and the abstract vivid; it combines the immediate impact of images with the surprise of a new idea.

Using tropes is not only a literary device; people always understand the world by relating new experiences to what we already know. For example, if we come across a tall brown branching item rooted in the ground, we pass the information along our brain circuits until we find something that resembles it. Then we are able to recognize its kinship with other trees we've known. Because of this inherent tendency, we are vulnerable to powerful comparisons, which can be counted on to inspire us with emotional responses: "You're breaking my heart," "They're filthy rich," "The lord is my shepherd," "We'll weather this storm." And we delight constantly in making more: "It's raining cats and dogs" (in Greece, they say "It's raining chairs"). "Once burned, twice shy." "Jammed up and jelly tight." "I'm walking on eggshells."

Like the smell of a familiar home-cooked meal, familiar tropes can transport us vividly to certain times and places. Each language, dialect, and subdialect is full of vivid and delicious tropes: "nuttier than a fruitcake," "you can't judge a book by its cover," "cut off your nose to spite your face," "your eyes are bigger than your stomach," "so hungry I could eat a polecat." Sometimes tropes become painfully memorable, as in this poem:

"Threats and Lamentations," Andrew Hudgins

I'll jerk a knot in your tail, boy.
Jack's staring at me. He's touching me.
Mom, George is breathing on my face.
What am I going to do with you?
Go shake the dew off your lily.
We won't be stopping every five yards
for you to pee. Don't try me, boy.
Shut up or I'll blister your behind.
I'll slap you silly. I'll tan your bottom.
No one can love you like I do.
Mom, Andrew spit in my Kool-Aid.
You'll be the death of me. If you
don't pull that pouty lip back in,
I'll knock it back in place for you,
young man. Just once I'd like to pee
without somebody yelling "Mom!"
Mom, Andrew's breathing on my pillow.
Each night I pray for you. You hush now.

Hudgins's poem follows a vein of tropes and expressions mined from the speech he heard as a child. What are some of the tropes you remember from your own background?

Fertile tropes can also come from the most unfamiliar places. Dictionaries of languages whose worldviews differ from our own, whether or not you understand the language, are a wonderful resource for making creative connections and thinking outside the usual patterns. My collection of dictionaries includes those for several languages I don't speak, and I love to browse in them. My Navajo dictionary tells me that in Navajo the same word, *banahoo'aah,* means both "there is usually room for them" and "time is usually set aside for them." On the next page, I learn that there is a specific word, *baazhnitq,* meaning "he gave it (a stiff, slender object) to him; he brought it to him." My Arabic dictionary tells me that in Arabic the word for knitting, knotting, tying, locking, is the same word for summoning people to a meeting and for finalizing a contract or agreement. To think about these meanings as linked puts my mind in a place to meet poetry.

Of course, our own language is a practically infinite source of fresh approaches to metaphorical thinking. For one thing, new areas of endeavor always generate new kinds of tropes, as do specialized fields of work or leisure. Think of nautical tropes: "three sheets to the wind," "shipshape," "on an even keel," "posh" (which originally stood for booking a cabin on the port side for the outgoing trip, on the starboard side for the homecoming trip), "smooth sailing," "the ship of state." Or sewing tropes: "invented out of whole cloth," "having a bias against something," "a stitch in time saves nine." What kinds of tropes are associated with special fields with which you are familiar, such as particular sports, arts, crafts, or technologies?

The etymology of the word "trope" leads us to the Greek word for "to turn"; we see this root word in "heliotrope" (turning toward the sun), "phototropism" (turning toward light), "zoetrope" (turning toward life). The two most common types of trope, simile and metaphor, each use one thing (the **vehicle**) to describe a different thing (the **tenor**).

Simile

Simile is the Latin word for "like." In a simile, the writer is explicit about the fact that comparing is going on. The writer says one thing is like another, as in this passage using geology to express the feeling of being at a transition in life:

From "Maria Nefele's Song," Odysseus Elytis (1978)

I haven't met joy
And I step on grief
Like an angel I turn
Over the ravine

In addition to "like," there are many other words a poet can use to make a comparison explicit, such as "as," "as if," and "than." The following poem uses the phrase "even so" to connect the poet's attitude toward death to the image of a nursing child:

"Gitanjali 95," Rabinodrath Tagore (1912)

I was not aware of the moment when I
first crossed the threshold of this life.

What was the power that made me open
out into this vast mystery like a bud in the
forest at midnight?

When in the morning I looked upon the
light I felt in a moment that I was no
stranger in this world, that the inscrutable
without name and form had taken me in
its arms in the form of my own mother.

Even so, in death the same unknown
will appear as ever known to me. And
because I love this life, I know I shall love
death as well.

The child cries out when from the right
breast the mother takes it away, in the
very next moment to find in the left one
its consolation.

The first stanza uses a conventional simile, "like a bud in the forest at midnight." The last two stanzas constitute a much longer simile introduced by the comparative phrase "even so"; the reader is able to inhabit the simile of the nursing child more extensively than if it were broken by repeated comparative words. By using a simile that makes the comparison explicit (rather than a metaphor where it would be implicit), Tagore gives the comparison a poignantly ceremonial, ritual quality, a respectful distance, as if the actualities of life and death are too profound to be taken for granted as part of a metaphor.

The exuberance of the following poem, by contrast, derives partly from its playful, casual, greedy, extravagant use of multiple different similes:

"A Birthday," Christina Rossetti (1857)

My heart is like a singing bird
Whose nest is in a watered shoot;
My heart is like an apple-tree
Whose boughs are bent with thick-set fruit;
My heart is like a rainbow shell

That paddles in a halcyon sea;
My heart is gladder than all these,
Because my love is come to me.

Raise me a dais of silk and down;
Hang it with vair and purple dyes;
Carve it in doves and pomegranates,
And peacocks with a hundred eyes;
Work it in gold and silver grapes,
In leaves and silver fleur-de-lys;
Because the birthday of my life
Is come, my love is come to me.

To imagine that one of these things is true, let alone all of them, creates a sense of the innumerable possibilities of joy. And yet, with one almost flippant phrase ("gladder than all these"), the poem rejects them all in favor of developing a sustained image. It is the balance between the contrasted strategies of the two stanzas that creates the sense of true inexpressibility within which the true communication of the poem rests. The similes are rejected, but without them the poem would not do its job.

The earliest literature is full of similes, whether in lyric, as in "The Song of Solomon," or in the epic simile, discussed in the section on narrative in chapter 5. But contemporary poetry seems to favor the imaginative boldness of the metaphor.

Metaphor, Implied Metaphor, and Double Entendre

Metaphor is from the Greek word for "transfer" (I've seen the word written on the sides of the buses in Athens). You could say a metaphor transfers meaning from one word to another, and it does so quite explicitly. Metaphors don't beat around the bush with terms like "like" or "as." Metaphors get right to the point. In those two metaphors, "beat around the bush" and "get right to the point," I didn't use any extra words to tell you that a comparison is being made; the comparisons speak for themselves.

Most comparisons could be made either as a simile or a metaphor; "her eyes were like daggers" or "her eyes were daggers." In a metaphor the *like* is implied. We know her eyes were not *real* daggers. But, perhaps because a metaphor takes us aback on an unconscious level and persuades us briefly that her eyes *were* daggers, a metaphor often has a stronger impact than a simile. Notice how Sylvia Plath's poem "Words" (at the end of chapter 4, "The Raw Material: Words and Their Roots"), begins with similes but ends in metaphors. How does this change affect the tone of the poem?

A metaphor can combine vehicle and tenor in many ways: you could say, "His eyes (tenor) were daggers (vehicle)," "He flashed his dagger (vehicle) eyes (tenor)," "When he looked (tenor) at me, I was pierced by daggers (vehicle)." On the other hand, though, the positions of vehicle and tenor are usually hard to exchange. You can't really say, "His dagger was like an eye" or "When he revealed his daggers, I saw eyes." A vehicle is often more vivid and specific than a tenor, which is why it casts light on the tenor and enables us to understand something new about it.

Here is a poem that uses metaphors in a number of different ways:

Maxine Kumin, "Morning Swim"

Into my empty head there come
a cotton beach, a dock wherefrom

I set out, oily and nude
through mist, in chilly solitude.

There was no line, no roof or floor
to tell the water from the air.

Night fog thick as terry cloth
closed me in its fuzzy growth.

I hung my bathrobe on two pegs.
I took the lake between my legs.

Invaded and invader, I
went overhand on that flat sky.

Fish twitched beneath me, quick and tame.
In their green zone they sang my name

and in the rhythm of the swim
I hummed a two-four-time slow hymn.

I hummed "Abide With Me." The beat
rose in the fine thrash of my feet,

rose in the bubbles I put out
slantwise, trailing through my mouth.

My bones drank water; water fell
through all my doors. I was the well

that fed the lake that met my sea
in which I sang "Abide With Me."

The vehicles in the early part of the poem are striking in their familiarity and specificity: the cotton beach, the terry cloth fog. But as the poem progresses, the tropes change. The mentioning of the possible metaphor (roof and floor) only to negate it in the third stanza begins to distance the experience from daily life. As the poem goes on and the experience becomes increasingly transformative, the vehicles (singing fish, drinking bones) become increasingly powerful themselves, distancing the speaker further from reality.

An **implied metaphor** can be even more powerful than a stated one, since the reader makes the comparisons, as in this epigraph which compresses several steps of metaphor into two brief sentences:

"Proverb II," William Blake (c. 1790)

Prisons are built with stones of Law,
Brothels with bricks of Religion.

Here is another example, just as powerful in translation as in the original Arabic:

The fog is darkness, thick white darkness,
peeled by an orange and a promising woman.
—MAHMOUD DARWISH (trans. Fady Joudah)

Implied metaphors can be evocative enough to build an entire poem on:

"Some Last Questions," W. S. Merwin

What is the head
    a. Ash
What are the eyes
    a. The wells have fallen in and have
    Inhabitants
What are the feet
    a. Thumbs left after the auction
No what are the feet
    a. Under them the impossible road is moving
    Down which the broken necked mice push
    Balls of blood with their noses
What is the tongue
    a. The black coat that fell off the wall
    With sleeves trying to say something
What are the hands
    a. Paid
No what are the hands
    a. Climbing back down the museum wall
    To their ancestors the extinct shrews that will
    Have left a message
What is the silence
    a. As though it had a right to more
Who are the compatriots
    a. They make the stars of bone

The great variety of images are tied together with a common sense of violence, mourning, and loss of identity. The surrealistic mode and simple but flexible structure of this poem links metaphysical to psychological to political concerns, evoking strong emotions within a simple framework.

The **double entendre** is an ancient and never-exhausted form of trope, usually involving a subtle metaphor of a sexual nature. Its effectiveness depends entirely on not making the comparison explicit. The following is an anonymous poem from the Middle Ages:

I have a gentle cock,
Croweth me day;
He doth me risen erly
My matins for to say.

I have a gentle cock,
Comen he is of great:
His comb is of red coral,
His tail is of jet.

I have a gentle cock,
Comen he is of kinde:
His comb is of red coral,
His tail is of inde.

His legges be of azure,
So gentle and so small;
His spurres are of silver white
Into the wortewale.

His eyen are of crystal,
Locked all in amber:
And every night he percheth him
In my lady's chamber.

As with any classic double entendre, the "gentle cock" can be read completely innocently, and yet something always seems missing from such a reading.

Kennings and Formulae

One of the most ancient kinds of metaphors, **kennings** are increasingly appreciated by contemporary poets. A kenning is a circumlocution, a riddle-like, concise metaphor that appears frequently in Old English and Old Norse poetry. Often, kennings developed because of various metrical requirements; if an Anglo-Saxon poet who was improvising a poem orally needed a way to say "sea" with two stressed syllables, he or she could use a kenning as a preexisting poetic phrase (also called a "formula"). Two-syllable kennings for "sea" would include "whale-road" or "swan-road." Mysterious, evocative, and beautiful, kennings pepper the poems of those cultures with phrases such as "bone-house" (body), "world-candle" (sun), and "spear-trees" (warriors). "Kenning" is related to the word "ken," meaning "awareness," and to the words "kin" and "kinship." It's hard to say whether the people who invented these kennings appreciated them as art or whether they were taken for granted as part of the language, like some of our own vivid expressions. This poem uses a number of invented kennings:

"Speech to the Young: Speech to the Progress-Toward," Gwendolyn Brooks

Say to them,
say to the down-keepers,
the sun-slappers,
the self-soilers,
the harmony-hushers,
"even if you are not ready for day
it cannot always be night."
You will be right.
For that is the hard home-run.

Live not for battles won.
Live not for the-end-of-the-song.
Live in the along.

Unlike the Anglo-Saxons, who tended to use mostly kennings that were already familiar to their listeners, Brooks's one-of-a-kind kennings are evocative and sometimes mysterious, with meanings not always evident on the surface. Can you think of a reason she would use a riddling tone when addressing the audience she is aiming for in this poem?

Extended Metaphor, Analogy, Allegory, and Symbol

An **extended metaphor** compares the tenor and vehicle in more than one area. While the brief kenning seems so natural and offhand that it can feel suggested inevitably by nature, the longer extended metaphor can sometimes seem consciously artificial, or at least intellectualized. Here, life is compared to a fire both when it burns and when it dies out:

"Finis," Walter Savage Landor (1850)

I strove with none, for none was worth my strife.
Nature I loved, and next to nature, art.
I warmed both hands before the fire of life;
It sinks, and I am ready to depart.

On the other hand, even a simple extended metaphor can function like a parable, providing room for a deeper understanding of the vehicle and hence of the tenor:

"Late Self-Portrait by Rembrandt," Jane Hirshfield

The dog, dead for years, keeps coming back in the dream.
We look at each other there with the old joy.
It was always her gift to bring me into the present—

Which sleeps, changes, awakens, dresses, leaves.

Happiness and unhappiness
differ as a bucket hammered from gold differs from one of pressed tin,
this painting proposes.

Each carries the same water, it says.

The "metaphysical poets" of the seventeenth century are renowned for their extended metaphors, such as the famous one at the end of this poem:

"A Valediction: forbidding Mourning," John Donne (1611)

As virtuous men pass mildly away,
And whisper to their souls, to go,
Whilst some of their sad friends do say,
"The breath goes now," and some say, "No."

So let us melt, and make no noise,
No tear-floods, nor sigh-tempests move;
'Twere profanation of our joys
To tell the laity our love.

Moving of th' earth brings harms and fears;
Men reckon what it did, and mean,
But trepidation of the spheres,
Though greater far, is innocent.

Dull sublunary lovers' love
(Whose soul is sense) cannot admit
Absence, because it doth remove
Those things which elemented it.

But we by a love, so much refined,
That our selves know not what it is,
Inter-assurèd of the mind,
Care less, eyes, lips and hands to miss.

Our two souls therefore, which are one,
Though I must go, endure not yet
A breach, but an expansion,
Like gold to aery thinness beat.

If they be two, they are two so
As stiff twin compasses are two,
Thy soul, the fix'd foot, makes no show
To move, but doth, if th' other do.

And though it in the centre sit,
Yet, when the other far doth roam,
It leans, and hearkens after it,
And grows erect, as that comes home.

Such wilt thou be to me, who must,
Like th' other foot, obliquely run;

Thy firmness makes my circle just,
And makes me end where I begun.

Donne, Herbert, and their peers felt that comparisons such as this one of the lovers to a compass underlined deeper philosophical similarities uniting different aspects of the physical world—hence their name "metaphysical" poets. This contemporary poem uses a list format to juxtapose separate aspects of the extended metaphor:

"Love Like Salt," Lisel Mueller

It lies in our hands in crystals
too intricate to decipher

It goes into the skillet
without being given a second thought

It spills on the floor so fine
we step all over it

We carry a pinch behind each eyeball

It breaks out on our foreheads

We store it inside our bodies
in secret wineskins

At supper, we pass it around the table
talking of holidays by the sea.

This poem, by contrast, weaves all the points of comparison together into one metaphor:

"Huswifery," Edward Taylor (1684)

Make me, O Lord, thy Spinning Wheele compleat;
  Thy Holy Worde my Distaff make for mee.

Make mine Affections thy Swift Flyers neate,
And make my Soule thy holy Spoole to bee.
My Conversation make to be thy Reele,
And reele the yarn thereon spun of thy Wheele.

Make me thy Loome then, knit therein this Twine:
And make thy Holy Spirit, Lord, winde quills:
Then weave the Web thyselfe. The yarn is fine.
Thine Ordinances make my Fulling Mills.
Then dy the same in Heavenly Colours Choice,
All pinkt with Varnish't Flowers of Paradise.

Then cloath therewith mine Understanding, Will,
Affections, Judgment, Conscience, Memory;
My Words and Actions, that their shine may fill
My wayes with glory and thee glorify.
Then mine apparell shall display before yee
That I am Cloathd in Holy robes for glory.

Finding certain points of comparison between the tenor himself and the vehicles of the spinning wheel and loom leads the poet to search for, or create, further points of comparison with the vehicles, which in turn illuminate new things about the tenor. This method seems appropriate for a religious poem because there is an element of faith at work, sometimes, in tropes; tropes can hark back to the medieval idea of "correspondences," the notion that everything on earth has a meaning that echoes a meaning in the spiritual world.

In the most successful extended metaphors, the metaphor acts as a force of discovery so that the tenor, originally intended to express what the poet already knows about the tenor, instead ends up teaching us, and presumably the poet, something new about the tenor. Perhaps it is the constant hope and possibility of this kind of discovery, this deeper understanding, that keeps metaphor so endlessly fascinating:

"Island," Langston Hughes (c. 1949)

Wave of sorrow,
Do not drown me now:

I see the island
Still ahead somehow.

I see the island
And its sands are fair:
Wave of sorrow,
Take me there.

This metaphor extends to several levels, perhaps at least one of them unconscious on the part of the poet: since one meaning of "fair" is "white," and since Hughes wrote so often about race, it is possible that the whiteness of the sand loops back to the sorrow of the beginning, along with the skillfully conveyed message of optimism and endurance that is surely the main message of the poem.

An extended metaphor that is fully developed to include actions as well as images, as in the poem below, is called an **analogy.**

"A Noiseless Patient Spider," Walt Whitman (1868)

A noiseless patient spider,
I mark'd where on a little promontory it stood isolated,
Mark'd how to explore the vacant vast surrounding,
It launch'd forth filament, filament, filament, out of itself,
Ever unreeling them, ever tirelessly speeding them.

And you O my soul where you stand,
Surrounded, detached, in measureless oceans of space,
Ceaselessly musing, venturing, throwing, seeking the spheres to connect
them,
Till the bridge you will need be form'd, till the ductile anchor hold,
Till the gossamer thread you fling catch somewhere, O my soul.

The analogy of the soul as a spider is implied, but the metaphor of the soul throwing out its threads into the world is stated. By analogy, the reader can figure out that the soul, like the spider, is tirelessly building a web, but the idea of the thread needing to catch somewhere comes with the force of a discovery.

An analogy doesn't have to be long. Here's an intense and compact one by Canadian poet Gwendolyn MacEwen: *"Something is eating away at me / with splendid teeth."*

An **allegory** is an extended analogy in many dimensions, an entire world of implied other meanings that often teaches a moral truth. Some allegories, such as the medieval religious poem "Pearl" and perhaps the most widely read allegory ever, the novel *Pilgrim's Progress,* have religious significance. Others, such as the Spenser's *Faerie Queene,* are secular but still concerned with teaching. Traditionally, allegorical figures have names that reveal their true meanings, as does the monster named "Error" in *The Faerie Queene:*

From The Faerie Queene, *Edmund Spenser (1590)*

And as she lay vpon the durtie ground,
Her huge long taile her den all ouerspred,
Yet was in knots and many boughtes vpwound,
Pointed with mortall sting. Of her there bred
A thousand yong ones, which she dayly fed,
Sucking vpon her poisonous dugs, eachone
Of sundry shapes, yet all ill fauored:
Soone as that vncouth light vpon them shone,
Into her mouth they crept, and suddain all were gone.

Their dam vpstart, out of her den effraide,
And rushed forth, hurling her hideous taile
About her cursed head, whose folds displaid
Were stretcht now forth at length without entraile.
She lookt about, and seeing one in mayle
Armed to point, sought backe to turne againe;
For light she hated as the deadly bale,
Ay wont in desert darknesse to remaine,
Where plaine none might her see, nor she see any plaine.

Which when the valiant Elfe perceiu'ed, he lept
As Lyon fierce vpon the flying pray,
And with his trenchand blade her boldly kept

From turning backe, and forced her to stay:
Therewith enrag'd she loudly gan to bray,
And turning fierce, her speckled taile aduaunst,
Threatning her angry sting, him to dismay:
Who nought aghast, his mightie hand enhaunst:
The stroke down from her head vnto her shoulder glaunst.

Much daunted with that dint, her sence was dazd,
Yet kindling rage, her selfe she gathered round,
And all attonce her beastly body raizd
With doubled forces high aboue the ground:
Tho wrapping vp her wrethed sterne arownd,
Lept fierce vpon his shield, and her huge traine
All suddenly about his body wound,
That hand or foot to stirre he stroue in vaine:
God helpe the man so wrapt in *Errours* endlesse traine.

His Lady sad to see his sore constraint,
Cride out, Now now Sir knight, shew what ye bee,
Add faith vnto your force, and be not faint:
Strangle her, else she sure will strangle thee.
That when he heard, in great perplexitie,
His gall did grate for griefe and high disdaine,
And knitting all his force got one hand free,
Wherewith he grypt her gorge with so great paine,
That soone to loose her wicked bands did her constraine.

Therewith she spewd out of her filthy maw
A floud of poyson horrible and blacke,
Full of great lumpes of flesh and gobbets raw,
Which stunck so vildly, that it forst him slacke
His grasping hold, and from her turne him backe:
Her vomit full of bookes and papers was,
With loathly frogs and toades, which eyes did lacke,
And creeping sought way in the weedy gras:
Her filthy parbreake all the place defiled has.

Allegories can stand on their own, but stories reinforce the symbolic meaning of each of their parts. *The Faerie Queene,* which is packed full of such tales, makes a rousing adventure story whether or not you pay attention to the allegory. If you notice that Error hates the light, spawns numerous offspring, and vomits books and papers, you gain another level of meaning from the poem. The end of E. A. Robinson's sonnet "New England" (1937) ends with a miniature allegory:

> Joy shivers in the corner where she knits
> And Conscience always has the rocking-chair,
> Cheerful as when she tortured into fits
> The first cat that was ever killed by Care.

It is a telling condemnation of New England's stereotypical faults that Joy is neglected and Conscience, who has tortured a cat, is privileged. The following poem offers a subtler allegory. Though it doesn't capitalize the names of qualities like "Joy" and "Care," its narrative of tropes about human nature conveys a concise insight:

> *"A Poison Tree," William Blake (1794)*
>
> I was angry with my friend:
> I told my wrath, my wrath did end.
> I was angry with my foe:
> I told it not, my wrath did grow.
>
> And I water'd it in fears,
> Night & morning with my tears:
> And I sunned it with smiles,
> And with soft deceitful wiles.
>
> And it grew both day and night,
> Till it bore an apple bright;
> And my foe beheld it shine,
> And he knew that it was mine,

And into my garden stole
When the night had veil'd the pole:
In the morning glad I see
My foe outstretch'd beneath the tree.

While many poets use trope on trope with wild abandon, others find tropes something to use sparingly if at all. The following stanza from a long poem by Adrienne Rich uses only one trope, which is much more powerful because of her restraint:

From "Waking in the Dark," Adrienne Rich

I walk the unconscious forest,
a woman dressed in old army fatigues
that have shrunk to fit her, I am lost
at moments, I feel dazed
by the sun pawing between the trees,
cold in the bog and lichen of the thicket.
Nothing will save this. I am alone,
kicking the last rotting logs
with their strange smell of life, not death,
wondering what on earth it all might have become.

The single word "pawing" is given a more frightening power, like a terrifying force half-glimpsed behind a tree, because of the absence of any other trope in the stanza.

In the Blake poem, some images have the additional resonance of a **symbol:** an object or action that carries a meaning far beyond itself. Some symbols are culture-specific; while Blake's apple would have a clear symbolic meaning to Christians or Jews familiar with the Old Testament story of the garden of Eden, it would not have that same meaning for Buddhists or Hindus or Wiccans. Some symbols appear culture-neutral and yet carry unacknowledged associations, as is pointed out in this poem:

"Black Poet, White Critic," Dudley Randall

A critic advises
not to write on controversial subjects

like freedom or murder,
but to treat universal themes
and timeless symbols
like the white unicorn.

A white unicorn?

Certain symbols, psychologist Carl Jung pointed out, do seem to be universal among people: sleep as a symbol for death, or life as a journey, a symbol evoked by Robert Frost's use of "the road less traveled" to stand for the narrator's choices in life. And some, such as Yeats's private image of spiraling gyres, which he carried from poem to poem, have meaning only as part of the work of one particular poet. If a symbol is used well in a poem, even a private meaning should become apparent on some level to the reader:

"Acquired Immune Deficiency Syndrome," Eduardo C. Corral

I approach a harp
abandoned
in a harvested field.
A deer
leaps out of the brush
and follows me

in the rain, a scarlet
snake wound
in its dark antlers.
My fingers
curled around a shard
of glass—

it's like holding the hand
of a child.
I'll cut the harp strings
for my mandolin,
use the frame as a window
in a chapel
yet to be built. I'll scrape

off its blue
lacquer, melt the flakes
down with
a candle and ladle
and paint
the inner curve
of my soup bowl.

The deer passes me.
I lower my head,
stick out my tongue
to taste
the honey smeared
on its hind leg.

In the field's center,
I crouch near
a boulder engraved
with a number
and stare at a gazelle's
blue ghost,
the rain falling through it.

Though the symbol of the harp here is quite idiosyncratic, it gains depth both from the images and narrative within this poem about confronting death from AIDS, as well as from the traditional cultural use of the harp as a symbol of grace and of heaven.

This ancient poem is addressed to Charon, the mythical Greek ferryman once believed to carry souls into the land of the dead. It shows how the delicate the lines and links between an image, a trope, and a symbol can be:

"Charon," Zonas (trans. Brooks Haxton) (first century B.C.)

You who pull the oars, who meet the dead,
who leave them at the other bank, and glide

alone across the reedy marsh, please take
my boy's hand as he climbs into the dark hull.
Look. The sandals trip him, and you see,
he is afraid to step there barefoot.

Whether or not one believes in the existence of Hades, the plea to help the child into the boat, with the detailed image of the sandals, serves as a vivid image embodying the parent's helpless and futile care for the child. At the same time, the bare feet are a metaphor for the child's vulnerability to death, embodied in relation to the culturally shared symbols of Hades, the boat, and Charon.

I usually know when I am writing a metaphor; often it is preceded by a kind of questioning, reaching feeling, as I wonder how best to put something—and then the metaphor is resolved by an "aha" feeling, a sense of having finished and moving on. A symbol, however, can be more unconscious. Like the symbols that come to us in dreams, symbols in poetry can seem to have their own lives and no real right meaning, and they can recur over and over again in a poet's work. Much of their appeal is in the mystery. As Charles Baudelaire wrote in "Correspondences," a poem that helped give the name "Symbolism" to an entire school of French poetry built on symbols,

Nature is a temple whose pillars live,
Sometimes emanating confused words.

Synesthesia, Synecdoche, Metonymy, Personification, and Antaclasis

Over all the centuries during which poets have used tropes, many particular kinds of trope have been developed. Here are a few of the best-known:

Synesthesia is interpreting one sense in terms of another, or understanding something nonphysical in terms of the senses. Some people are born with a strong sense of synesthesia and habitually perceive sense information in this way. Whether or not you are one of them, you can use synesthesia to add vividness to the images in your poems. You might say that your mother's skin feels like the sound of ocean waves, or that the smell of lentil soup cooking has the colors of a forest. The most famous example of synesthesia in poetry is the following sonnet:

"Vowels," Arthur Rimbaud (1871) (trans. Oliver Bernard)

A black, E white, I red, U green, O blue: vowels,
I shall tell, one day, of your mysterious origins:
A, black velvety jacket of brilliant flies
which buzz around cruel smells,
Gulfs of shadow; E, whiteness of vapours and of tents,
lances of proud glaciers, white kings, shivers of cow-parsley;
I, purples, spat blood, smile of beautiful lips
in anger or in the raptures of penitence;
U, waves, divine shudderings of viridian seas,
the peace of pastures dotted with animals, the peace of the furrows
which alchemy prints on broad studious foreheads;
O, sublime Trumpet full of strange piercing sounds,
silences crossed by [Worlds and by Angels]:
—O the Omega! the violet ray of [His] Eyes!

By describing vowels so clearly in visual terms, Rimbaud gives an abstraction three-dimensionality and adds great imaginative resonance to the poem.

Another kind of metaphor is **synecdoche,** the substitution of a part for the whole, as in referring to shelter as "a roof over your head," or in this description of the destruction of Troy:

From "Leda and the Swan," W. B. Yeats (1924)

The broken wall the burning roof and tower
And Agamemmnon, dead

Metonymy is referring to something by referring to something associated with it: "The White House announced today . . ." We use the metonymical "I" to stand for "my car" when we say, "I'm parked a block away." In this passage, the metonymy of "mouth" for "words" adds vividness and intimacy:

From "To the Diaspora," Gwendolyn Brooks

I could not have told you then that some sun
would come,

somewhere over the road,
would come evoking the diamonds
of you, the Black continent—
somewhere over the road.
You would not have believed my mouth.

Personification is referring to a nonhuman creature or thing in human terms, as this poem does with the sun and ocean:

From "Thanatopsis," William Cullen Bryant (1817)

Yet a few days, and thee
The all-beholding sun shall see no more
In all his course; nor yet in the cold ground,
Where thy pale form was laid, with many tears,
Nor in the embrace of ocean, shall exist
Thy image.

Personification is a time-honored device of Romantic poets and easy to use in a fusty way. But used freshly, it can still create a sense of recognition and surprise.

One subtle way to personify is through the use of apostrophe, or direct address. An apostrophe can be addressed to a person, creature, place, or thing—to anything that you could address in your imagination. The address to the wind in the following passage implies that the wind can understand words:

From "Ode to the West Wind," Percy Bysshe Shelley (1819)

O! lift me as a wave, a leaf, a cloud!
I fall upon the thorns of life! I bleed!

Another trope-like rhetorical device is **antaclasis,** the use of the same word or phrase with two different meanings:

If I didn't want so much
so much, why would I ever
say anything?
FROM "AFTER AWHILE," Tim Seibles

Sometimes a poem misleads us into perceiving an antaclasis momentarily:

> I guess being colored doesn't make me NOT like
> the same things other folks like who are other races.
>
> FROM "THEME FOR ENGLISH B," Langston Hughes (1951)

We may think the word "like" means "similar" in the first line, until we understand from the second line that, instead, it means "enjoy" just as the second "like" does. Like all kinds of wordplay, this device makes a reader more aware of our experience of language itself. Because it momentarily substitutes one meaning of a word for another, antaclasis also reminds us of the ways that all trope involves repetition.

Once you are aware of these many different kinds of tropes, you will find your imaginative vocabulary expanding. Hopefully, you will eventually be able to move between various kinds of tropes in your own poems.

Writing Tropes

The whole point of making a comparison is to bring a fresh insight or understanding or perception to the vehicle. Without this tension of the unfamiliar, most of the point of tropes is lost. Few things are duller in a poem than an overfamiliar trope. On the other hand, a trope that seems too random may be even worse; it can seem like a real insult to a reader. I. A. Richards, who thought so much about metaphors and invented the terms "vehicle" and "tenor" in 1938, points out that the more of a difference there is between the two things being compared, the more tension and power the trope will have—unless the comparison is stretched so far that it breaks.

Sometimes, it is a matter of opinion whether a trope goes too far. This poem is based on the Greek myth of the nymph Syrinx, turned to hollow reeds to avoid rape by the god Pan and becoming the first "pan-pipes." It provides a wry extended metaphor for a poet: a reed that has been cut and killed and had its heart removed so that it can make beautiful music:

From "A Musical Instrument," Elizabeth Barrett Browning (1860)

> He cut it short, did the great god Pan,
> (How tall it stood in the river!),

Then drew the pith, like the heart of a man,
Steadily from the outside ring,
And notched the poor dry empty thing
In holes, as he sat by the river.

"This is the way," laughed the great god Pan
(Laughed while he sat by the river),
"The only way, since gods began
To make sweet music, they could succeed."
Then, dropping his mouth to a hole in the reed,
He blew in power by the river.

Depending on your own experience of being a poet, you may find the trope of yourself as a hollowed-out reed an illuminating truth or far-fetched. To a large extent, the answer will depend on the skill with which the poet has developed the trope.

It is clear that as children we learn empathy through observing similarities between ourselves and others; the capacity to see likeness in unlike things is not only an exercise for ingenuity, but a spiritual exercise in finding commonality among many things in the world. One of the most wonderful things about tropes in general is that they are one of the surest ways to communicate to someone else an experience they have never had. This poem about speaking in one's own language, by an expatriate Romanian poet, describes an experience unfamiliar to most native speakers of English:

"Licentiousness," Nina Cassian (trans. Brenda Walker and Andrea Deletant)

Letters fall from my words
as teeth might fall from my mouth.
Lisping? Stammering? Mumbling?
Or the last silence?
Please God take pity
on the roof of my mouth,
on my tongue,
on my glottis,
on the clitoris in my throat
vibrating, sensitive, pulsating,
exploding in the orgasm that is Rumanian.

Cliché

A trope is the only way that one who has never had the experience of not being able to speak one's native tongue can get a sense of what it feels like not to speak it, and finally to be able to speak it again.

When thinking of tropes, keep in mind the principle of tension. Things that are too close to each other can sound too bland (the center of the daisy was as yellow as a daffodil). If they are too far from each other they can sound forced (his eyes shone like fire engines). Be extra careful of the most common pitfall, the "mixed metaphor," which can make a reader nauseous with conflicting meanings (she tiptoed around the subject with kid gloves on).

Another danger of troping is that a trope can become a **cliché** very quickly. The term "cliché" in French means a metal plate that is stamped with particular patterns or letters for printing purposes. A cliché in language is a phrase that has been overused and sounds generic, rigid and hard like metal. To say that someone's hands were "clammy with sweat," that the sun was "as bright as a new penny," or that something was "as soft as new-fallen snow" is deadening for a reader, and ends up being less vivid than using no tropes at all. On the other hand, the power of clichés can be used with great impact if both poet and reader are familiar with the tradition that is being changed. Here are four poems that use the same traditional kind of tropes, the **catalog** by a speaker of someone else's physical attributes.

From "Song of Solomon" (ca. 965 B.C.), King James Bible (1611)

His head is as the most fine gold, his locks are bushy, and black as a raven.
His eyes are as the eyes of doves by the rivers of waters, washed with milk,
 and fitly set.
His cheeks are as a bed of spices, as sweet flowers: his lips like lilies,
 dropping sweet smelling myrrh.
His hands are as gold rings set with the beryl: his belly is as bright ivory
 overlaid with sapphires.
His legs are as pillars of marble, set upon sockets of fine gold: his
 countenance is as Lebanon, excellent as the cedars.
His mouth is most sweet: yea, he is altogether lovely. This is my beloved,
 and this is my friend, O daughters of Jerusalem.

From Sonnet 292, Francesco Petrarch (ca. 1350) (trans. A. S. Kline)

The eyes I spoke about so warmly,
and the arms, the hands, the ankles, and the face
that left me so divided from myself,
and made me different from other men:

the crisp hair of pure shining gold
and the brightness of the angelic smile,
which used to make a paradise on earth,
are now a little dust, that feels no thing.

Sonnet 130, William Shakespeare (1600)

My mistress' eyes are nothing like the sun;
Coral is far more red than her lips' red;
If snow be white, why then her breasts are dun;
If hairs be wires, black wires grow on her head.
I have seen roses damask'd, red and white,
But no such roses see I in her cheeks;
And in some perfumes is there more delight
Than in the breath that from my mistress reeks.
I love to hear her speak, yet well I know
That music hath a far more pleasing sound;
I grant I never saw a goddess go;
My mistress, when she walks, treads on the ground:
And yet, by heaven, I think my love as rare
As any she belied with false compare.

"Portrait in Georgia," Jean Toomer (1923)

Hair-braided chestnut,
coiled like a lyncher's rope,
Eyes—fagots,
Lips—old scars, or the first red blisters,

Breath—the last sweet scent of cane,
And her slim body, white as ash
of black flesh after flame.

Though the speaker in the Old Testament passage is female, in the centuries since, the genders have gone the other way and numerous heterosexual male poets have cataloged their women's qualities in conventionalized tropes. A few hundred years after Petrarch, those kinds of tropes—the golden hair, the bright smile, and all the rest of the qualities lesser poets had repeated over and over—had become clichés, ripe for Shakespeare to mock in order to prove his originality. For Toomer, the same tropes are powerful reminders of the price paid to preserve this kind of beauty, and of the relation between sexism and racism. (The same issues are explored in Harryette Mullen's poem "Dim Lady," based on the same Shakespeare sonnet, in chapter 10, on exploratory poetry.)

One step beyond a cliché is a dead trope, one that has become such a common figure of speech, or idiom, that a reader won't even recognize it as a trope. Phrases such as "don't rock the boat," "sift the evidence," "see the point," or "I don't follow what you're saying," for example, fall in this category. If a trope is allowed to stick around long enough, through periods of historical change, it can become a permanent part of the language, working its power from deep in the hidden roots of a word, as you saw in chapter 4.

No matter what specific tricks you play with metaphor in your poems, the power of trope lies in the control the poet holds over the distance between vehicle and tenor. The following poem plays with this distance, teasing it like a cat with a mouse.

"Pineapple," Gabriela Mistral (trans. Ursula Le Guin)

Pick her up, don't be afraid
of the pineapple's swords.
Her mother gave her weapons
for life in the plantation.

My knife sings as it slices
the beheaded Amazon,
who lost her power
with her bundle of daggers.

Onto the plate comes tumbling
her skirt's full circle,
skirt of golden taffeta,
the Queen of Sheba's train.

Crush between your teeth
the poor tender mouthful of queen,
while juice runs down my arms
and down the silver knifeblade.

The first stanza eases us into the metaphor, playfully explaining why a pineapple might need swords. But by the time the last stanza begins there is no distance at all; horrifyingly, the pineapple has completely become the queen. Still, Mistral the poet has the last word. By using "juice" instead of "blood," she reminds us triumphantly that the horror is all just a metaphor, her own poetic creation.

QUESTIONS FOR MEDITATION OR DISCUSSION

Tropes, because they are indirect, are a useful way to refer to things that people are not free to talk about openly—taboos. For example, it is taboo to refer directly to bears (an animal traditionally reverenced worldwide) in both traditional Slavic societies and in Japanese. So each culture has developed a trope to refer to a bear: *oyaji,* "the old man," in Japanese, and *medved,* "honey eater," in Slavic languages. Takao Suzuki believes a similar taboo led to the English word for bear, which, like the German word for bear, originally meant simply *brown*—"the brown one." What tropes are used in our culture to refer to taboo subjects? If a trope is a way to refer to something too powerful for ordinary language, what does that mean about poetry, in which tropes play such an important role? How would you go about writing a poem about a subject you consider too taboo to refer to directly?

As mysterious and powerful as they are, tropes are a fertile area for discussion in the most complex and abstract literary theory. And even at the level of simpler thought, they can be mind-boggling. For example, Matthew Arnold's famously pessimistic poem "Dover Beach," often seen as foreshadowing all the violence and cruelty that the twentieth century was about to bring, ends with this stanza:

Ah, love, let us be true
To one another! for the world, which seems
To lie before us like a land of dreams,
So various, so beautiful, so new,
Hath really neither joy, nor love, nor light,
Nor certitude, nor peace, nor help for pain;
And we are here as on a darkling plain
Swept with confused alarms of struggle and flight,
Where ignorant armies clash by night.

What is reality and what is the trope here? At first, the illusory "land of dreams" seems contrasted with the sober truth of a world with "really" no joy, love, or light. Yet within the same sentence, the poem immediately veers off into another simile; the tiny word "as" reminds us that the world is not really a darkling plain, any more than it is a land of dreams. It is perhaps exactly this kind of slipperiness that causes some poets, such as Hayden Carruth and Mary Karr, to protest against metaphor and advocate a more objective presentation of reality. It is useful to remember that there are entire traditions of poetry, such as haiku, that do not involve metaphor at all, and many successful poems that do not use it (for example, "Harvesting Wheat for the Public Share" in chapter 6, on imagery). What is the place of metaphor in your own idea of poetry, your own poetics?

What do you think Shelley means by opening his "Ode to a Skylark" with these lines?

Hail to thee, blithe spirit!
Bird thou never wert—

QUOTES

It is absolutely necessary to acquire some knowledge of Chinese metaphors and idioms before one can hope to read Chinese newspapers with any degree of comprehension. . . . Chinese literature is regarded as being highly precise and pregnant with meaning. Its idioms give it this precise mode of expression. . . . Quoting these terms in speech or writing is like introducing gems into an otherwise undecorated and uninteresting pattern.

—Chiang Ker Chiu

Things admit of being used as symbols, because nature is a symbol, in the whole, and in every part. Every line we can draw in the sand, has expression; and there is no body without its spirit of genius.

—Ralph Waldo Emerson

A bricklayer falls from the roof, dies, no longer eats lunch.
Am I to innovate, then, the trope, the metaphor?

—Cesar Vallejo

Her metaphor is never a device but a meaningful disclosure.

—Robert Duncan, on Marianne Moore

POETRY PRACTICES

Mix and Match Similes (Group). Each person in the group invents a simile and writes it on a strip of paper. Read the similes aloud and discuss why they work—what connection the group finds between the two parts of the simile.

Then collect all the similes. Cut them in half. Mix them up. Tape them back together (color code them so you're sure you're not taping anyone's simile back together).

Pass the strips out again. Have each person read the new mix-and-matched simile aloud, and have the class discuss how this new simile works. The human mind is a connection-making machine. The people in the group will always find something, and they'll be opening up their minds to wider possibilities of image-making. (Thanks to Tad Richards for this exercise.)

Familiar Turnings. Write a poem using at least four tropes you used to hear in childhood, or a poem that is based, like Andrew Hudgins's "Threats and Lamentations," on a cluster of related tropes from common speech.

Fresh Proverbs. This passage from Paul Muldoon's "The Old Country" makes the most of some dour Irish idioms:

> Every start was a bad start . . .
> Every major road had major roadworks . . .
> Every resort was a last resort . . .
> Every lookout was a poor lookout . . .
> Every ditch was a last ditch . . .

Every boat was a burned boat . . .
Every cut was a cut to the quick . . .
Every hope was a forlorn hope . . .
Every slope was a slippery slope.

If you know, or have a book that includes, idioms or sayings from another culture, write a poem embodying one of them. If not, use an English saying, or borrow one of the Mandarin Chinese idioms below (from the book *Chinese Idioms,* by Chiang Ker Chiu) or one of the African proverbs (from the book *African Proverbs,* by Gerd De Lay). One possible approach is to write your poem as if the trope were literally true.

Chinese idioms:
"A person's life is like a sunbeam passing through a crevice"—life is fleeting: brevity of human life.
"A fuel and rice marriage"—a marriage of convenience
"Noise of people bubbling like a bubbling cauldron"—a hubbub; a tumult; a crowd of dissatisfied people
"Walking about at night in an embroidered robe"—the glory of a person who has acquired wealth and honor in a foreign land is unknown to his own people, if he does not return home.

African proverbs:
If the fight is tomorrow, why then clench your fist today?—Cameroon
Drink beer, think beer.—Zaire
The chief is like a rubbish heap; everything comes to him.—Myore
A woman gets her beauty from her husband.—Ashanti
The child hates the one who gives him all he wants.—Jabo
If you know the beginning well, the end will not trouble you.—Wolof
It's a low fire that warms the soup.—Shona

Extending Metaphors. Write a poem of three stanzas, in which each stanza consists of a different extended metaphor for the same thing.

Allegory. Write an allegorical poem illustrating a moral or spiritual story you know to be true.

O, Poem! Write a poem using personification and/or apostrophe.

Like What? Write a poem using at least two original examples each of metonymy or synecdoche.

CHAPTER 8

What If a Much of a Which of a Word-Music?

A poet's voice, more than anything else, keeps a reader coming back for more. Though images and ideas are much of the reason we read poetry, no poet ever lodged a poem in the world's internal ear without having a distinctive "voice." **Word-music,** or the sounds of the vowels and consonants in a poem, can look like decoration, but as often as not it shapes much of the essence of a poem's approach to the world. Who but Dylan Thomas, with his emotional bravado, could have woven together the *f*'s and *l*'s of "and wake the farm forever fled from the childless land?" Who but Lucille Clifton, with her unflinchingly open awareness, could have harnessed together the almost irritating short *i*'s, *s*'s and *t*'s of "I with my mother's itch / took it to breast / and named it / History"? Who but the defiantly playful e. e. cummings could have begun a poem, "what if a much of a which of a wind / gave the truth to the summer's lie?"

Most if not all memorable writing uses word-music to some extent. If you think of any piece of language you carry in your mind, the odds are good that it is in a strong rhythm and/or that it includes some kind of word-music, whether it is rhyme (fill in your favorite advertising jingle here), repetition ("when the going gets tough, the tough get going"; "I have a dream . . . I have a dream," "ask not what your country can do for you; ask what you can do for your country"); alliteration ("hot and heavy," "tried and true," "you go, girl!"); assonance ("free as a breeze," "once in a blue moon"); consonance ("old as the hills," "under the weather"), or a combination of consonance and assonance ("A stitch in time saves nine"; "fourscore and seven years ago, our forefathers. . ."). Poet Carolyn Kizer recounts that the first piece of language that ever fascinated her was a phrase from Gertrude Stein: "be cool inside the mule." She would recite it endlessly to herself, walking around with that internally rhyming piece of language fixed in her mind, fascinated, perhaps, by the way the rhyme words sounded the same but different, looked the same but different.

Alliteration, Assonance, Consonance, and Onomatopoeia

Word-music has been classified into a number of patterns of repeating sounds. The most common are assonance, consonance, and alliteration. While most skillfully musical passages of poetry involve all three of these, it is worth considering them separately to appreciate the unique qualities each brings to a poem.

Assonance involves the repetition of vowel sounds. Look for the interplay of the long "e" sound and the short "u" sound as you read this passage:

From "Sunday Morning," Wallace Stevens (1915)

Complacencies of the peignoir, and late
Coffee and oranges in a sunny chair,
And the green freedom of a cockatoo
Upon a rug mingle to dissipate
The holy hush of ancient sacrifice.
She dreams a little, and she feels the dark
Encroachment of that old catastrophe,
As a calm darkens among water-lights.
The pungent oranges and bright, green wings
Seem things in some procession of the dead,
Winding across wide water, without sound.
The day is like wide water, without sound,
Stilled for the passing of her dreaming feet
Over the seas, to silent Palestine,
Dominion of the blood and sepulchre.

II
Why should she give her bounty to the dead?
What is divinity if it can come
Only in silent shadows and in dreams?
Shall she not find in comforts of the sun,
In pungent fruit and bright, green wings, or else
In any balm or beauty of the earth,
Things to be cherished like the thought of heaven?
Divinity must live within herself:
Passions of rain, or moods in falling snow;

THE INTERNATIONAL PHONETIC ALPHABET (revised to 2005)

ONSONANTS (PULMONIC)

	Bilabial	Labiodental	Dental	Alveolar	Postalveolar	Retroflex	Palatal	Velar	Uvular	Pharyngeal	Glottal
osive	p b			t d		ʈ ɖ	c ɟ	k ɡ	q ɢ		ʔ
asal	m	ɱ		n		ɳ	ɲ	ŋ	ɴ		
ill	ʙ			r					ʀ		
ıp or Flap		ⱱ		ɾ		ɽ					
icative	ɸ β	f v	θ ð	s z	ʃ ʒ	ʂ ʐ	ç ʝ	x ɣ	χ ʁ	ħ ʕ	h ɦ
iteral icative				ɬ ɮ							
pproximant		ʋ		ɹ		ɻ	j	ɰ			
iteral proximant				l		ɭ	ʎ	ʟ			

Where symbols appear in pairs, the one to the right represents a voiced consonant. Shaded areas denote articulations judged impossible.

ONSONANTS (NON-PULMONIC)

Clicks		Voiced implosives		Ejectives	
ʘ	Bilabial	ɓ	Bilabial	ʼ	Examples:
ǀ	Dental	ɗ	Dental/alveolar	pʼ	Bilabial
ǃ	(Post)alveolar	ʄ	Palatal	tʼ	Dental/alveolar
ǂ	Palatoalveolar	ɠ	Velar	kʼ	Velar
ǁ	Alveolar lateral	ʛ	Uvular	sʼ	Alveolar fricative

VOWELS

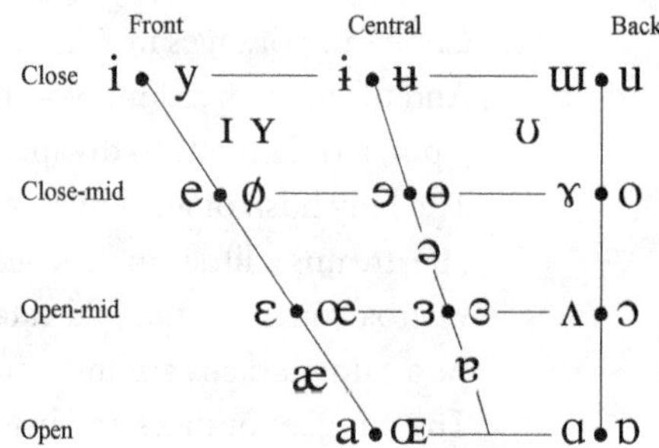

Where symbols appear in pairs, the one to the right represents a rounded vowel.

HER SYMBOLS

Voiceless labial-velar fricative

Voiced labial-velar approximant

Voiced labial-palatal approximant

Voiceless epiglottal fricative

Voiced epiglottal fricative

Epiglottal plosive

ɕ ʑ Alveolo-palatal fricatives

ɺ Voiced alveolar lateral flap

ɧ Simultaneous ʃ and x

Affricates and double articulations can be represented by two symbols joined by a tie bar if necessary. k͡p t͜s

SUPRASEGMENTALS

ˈ Primary stress

ˌ Secondary stress ˌfoʊnəˈtɪʃən

ː Long eː

ˑ Half-long eˑ

˘ Extra-short ĕ

| Minor (foot) group

‖ Major (intonation) group

. Syllable break ɹi.ækt

‿ Linking (absence of a break)

CRITICS Diacritics may be placed above a symbol with a descender, e.g. ŋ̊

Voiceless	n̥ d̥	Breathy voiced	b̤ a̤	Dental	t̪ d̪
Voiced	s̬ t̬	Creaky voiced	b̰ a̰	Apical	t̺ d̺
Aspirated	tʰ dʰ	Linguolabial	t̼ d̼	Laminal	t̻ d̻
More rounded	ɔ̹	Labialized	tʷ dʷ	Nasalized	ẽ
Less rounded	ɔ̜	Palatalized	tʲ dʲ	Nasal release	dⁿ
Advanced	u̟	Velarized	tˠ dˠ	Lateral release	dˡ
Retracted	e̠	Pharyngealized	tˤ dˤ	No audible release	d̚
Centralized	ë	Velarized or pharyngealized	ɫ		
Mid-centralized	e̽	Raised	e̝ (ɹ̝ = voiced alveolar fricative)		
Syllabic	n̩	Lowered	e̞ (β̞ = voiced bilabial approximant)		
Non-syllabic	e̯	Advanced Tongue Root	e̘		
Rhoticity	ɚ a˞	Retracted Tongue Root	e̙		

TONES AND WORD ACCENTS

LEVEL		CONTOUR	
e̋ or ˥	Extra high	ě or ˩˥	Rising
é ˦	High	ê ˥˩	Falling
ē ˧	Mid	e᷄ ˦˥	High rising
è ˨	Low	e᷅ ˩˨	Low rising
ȅ ˩	Extra low	e᷈ ˧˦˧	Rising-falling
↓	Downstep	↗	Global rise
↑	Upstep	↘	Global fall

Grievings in loneliness, or unsubdued
Elations when the forest blooms; gusty
Emotions on wet roads on autumn nights;
All pleasures and all pains, remembering
The bough of summer and the winter branch.
These are the measures destined for her soul.

The long "e" sound recurs strongly in the opening: "complacencIEs," "coffEE," "sunnY," and of course "The grEEn frEEdom" of the cockatoo. The "u" sound is also introduced early, by the end of the second line: "Upon," "rUg," and then "hUsh Of." As the poem continues, these two vowel sounds dance a kind of duet: "pUngent, grEEn," "drEAming, blOOd," "sEEm, sOme," "divinitY," "cOme." As the passage reaches its climax, the counterpoint becomes more frequent and pronounced: "divinitY mUst," 'UnsUbdued Elations," "gUstY EmotIOns," and then subsides into one final more distant pair: "sUmmer, ThEse." Of course, there are many other kinds of assonance and word-music going on in this passage at the same time; tracing this pair gives some idea of the thoroughness of the interweaving that makes a truly memorable poetic music.

"Word-music" means all the patterns made by the sounds of consonants and vowels together: assonance (repeated vowel sounds), consonance (repeated consonant sounds), alliteration (a special term for consonance or assonance at the beginnings of words), and rhyme (a combination of assonance and consonance in a stressed syllable at the end of a word).

Consonance is the repetition of consonant sounds. With all these repetitions, each poem builds up a certain kind of word texture that can be altered for contrast or emphasis, as in this poem:

"Days," Ralph Waldo Emerson (1857)

Daughters of Time, the hypocritic Days,
Muffled and dumb like barefoot dervishes,
And marching single in an endless file,
Bring diadems and fagots in their hands.
To each they offer gifts after his will,

Bread, kingdoms, stars, and sky that holds them all.
I, in my pleached garden, watched the pomp,
Forgot my morning wishes, hastily
Took a few herbs and apples, and the Day
Turned and departed silent. I, too late,
Under her solemn fillet saw the scorn.

Most of this poem is characterized by repetition of the kinds of phonemes that stop the air flowing in the vocal tract, called "stops"or "plosives": "d" and "b" and "p" and "t." If you speak these sounds, you will notice that they press your lips and/or tongue and palate together, giving a rich, full feeling in the mouth as they are spoken. In the middle of the next-to-the last line, however, Emerson changes the sound-texture, adding a greater proportion of more slippery and subtle sounds, the fricatives "s" and "l," just as the speaker is left with the realization of emptiness at the end of the day. Along with the meaning, meter, syntax, imagery, and other aspects of the poem, this change in sound-texture plays a significant role in the change of mood at the poem's end.

The most well-known kind of word-music, and the easiest to recognize, is a special kind of consonance that occurs at the beginnings of words: the repetition of initial sounds, called **alliterations.** Alliteration is a very common feature of our daily speech, from quotes and sayings ("O my Luve's like a red, red rose") to idioms ("short and sweet"). Generally, while consonants alliterate only with themselves, any two vowels are thought to alliterate together ("over and under").

This moving passage from a Renaissance poem is woven through with a texture of alliteration. It was written by Mary Herbert as an elegy for her brother, Sir Philip Sidney:

From "The Dolefull Lay of Clorinda," Mary Herbert (1595)

Breake now your gyrlonds, O ye shepheards lasses,
Sith the faire flowre, which them adornd, is gon:
The flowre, which them adornd, is gone to ashes,
Neuer againe let lasse put gyrlond on:
    In stead of gyrlond, weare sad Cypres nowe,
    And bitter Elder, broken from the bowe.

Ne euer sing the loue-layes which he made,
Who euer made such layes of loue as hee?

Ne euer read the riddles, which he sayd
Vnto your selues, to make you mery glee.
    Your mery glee is now laid all abed,
    Your mery maker now alasse is dead.

Death, the deuourer of all worlds delight,
Hath robbed you and reft from me my ioy:
Both you and me, and all the world he quight
Hath robd of ioyance, and left sad annoy.
    Ioy of the world, and shepheards pride was hee,
    Shepheards hope neuer like againe to see.

Onomatopoeia (from the Greek word for "name-making"): words that embody the sound of the thing they describe. Examples: buzz, snort, bubble, oomph, ping. What other examples can you think of?

Unlike the consonance in "Sunday Morning," the alliteration in this poem tends to be local, happening only in one phrase or line: "faire flowre," "bitter Elder, broken," "read the riddles," "death, the devourer." This creates a lighter, less dense effect throughout the poem and perhaps a feeling of greater simplicity and sincerity than a more intense texturing would make—a simplicity and sincerity appropriate for an intimate elegy.

Word-Music and Meaning

Like facial expressions, some aspects of word-music are deeply embedded in a poem's character, and others are more fleeting. On the deep level of a poem, word-music can clearly affect or even help create a poem's meaning:

"Fable for Blackboard," George Starbuck

Here is the grackle, people.
Here is the fox, folks.
The grackle sits in the bracken. The fox
hopes.

Here are the fronds, friends,
that cover the fox.
The fronds get in a frenzy. The grackle
looks.

Here are the ticks, tykes,
that live in the leaves, loves.
The fox is confounded,
        and God is above.

While conventional advice says never to let sound drive the meaning of a poem, this odd but stubbornly charming tale proves that there is no rule about writing poetry that can't be broken if it is broken well. It's hard to imagine that the bracken and the fronds didn't get there only because of their sound, and yet who wouldn't want them there?

Sometimes word-music patterns help create meaning through structure, as with the rhyme pattern of a sonnet or ballad, or the alliteration of an Anglo-Saxon poem. The following poem makes a very rare use of onomatopoeia to structure a poem, using the word "drum" to create a narrative of suspense that moves throughout the whole poem:

"Going to Hear My Child's Heartbeat for the First Time—
Part 2," Yona Harvey

it's the girl
in deep water
who will not drown

(drum)

come down

(drum)

come down

(drum)

zora's instrument
hidden in the belly

(drum)

carried
across the atlantic

(drum)

it's a mystery to master

(drum)

it don't stop

(drum)

don't stop

(drum)

gotta story to tell

(drum)

won't stop

(drum)

gold-black fish

(drum)

swimming

(drum)

an old one
come back

(drum)

blood

(drum)

breath

(drum)

memory

(drum)

ka-doom (drum)

ka-doom

(drum)

ka-doom (drum)

live (drum)

live (drum)

live

As the word-music takes over Harvey's poem, the sense of awe at the baby's new life leaves the speaker wordless.

Like the drone of Harvey's repeating word "drum," the sounds of our language have a physical as well as emotional effect on us. "S" sounds can create a kind of frightening hiss, "m" sounds a murmuring calm, "p" sounds a quick emptying. Think of the related meanings of the cluster of words that begin with *sn:* sneer, snoop, sneeze; or words that begin with *sl:* slither, slippery, slink. Expressive word-music is akin to onomatopoeia, as in the last two lines of Tennyson's "Come Down, O Maid" (1847):

> Sweeter thy voice, but every sound is sweet
> Myriads of rivulets, hurrying through the lawn,
> The moan of doves in immemorial elms,
> And murmuring of innumerable bees.

Often, the patterns of word-music do not structure an entire poem but simply make a particular line or phrase more expressive. Each consonant and vowel takes a different kind of physical motion to articulate, and our awareness of the pattern of the weight and tension of these motions is an important aspect of a poem's effect on us, even if we don't say the poem aloud. The phonetics chart in this chapter shows the relations between different kinds of sounds; for example, "t" and "d" are both alveolar plosives (articulated against the palate of the mouth, with force from the throat); the "t" is unvoiced and the "d" is voiced, but otherwise they are identical in the mouth, as are "p" and "b." Seeing these relationships adds a whole new layer to our awareness of alliteration, consonance, and assonance.

Word-music can help to convey, through such physical movements of the reader's ear and tongue, the mood at particular places in a poem. Read aloud these two lines from Keats's "Ode to a Nightingale" (1819) and listen to the difference between them:

> Thou wast not born for death, immortal bird!
> No hungry generations tread thee down.

The open vowels and light consonant clusters ("st" and "rn") of the first line make it feel as if your voice is flying; you fly over the momentary stop of the heavy consonant "d" in "death," and then continue again with the light mutter of the "im" and the trill of "rd." The second line is a different story. The heavy consonant cluster "ngr" is echoed in the "g" of "generations," the "r" in "generations" echoes in the "r" of "tread," and the heavy "d" of tread" picks up on the "d" of "death" in the previous line and echoes again in the final, overwhelming weight of the "d" in "down." During the course of the two lines, the "ow" sound of "thou" is transformed into an entirely different incarnation, the low-pitched "ow" of down, and the identity of the two sounds makes the transformation of death feel inescapable, inevitable, emphasizing the dying of the "hungry generations" with such eloquence that it adds a layer of complexity and ambivalence to what the lines actually say.

In **onomatopoeia,** however, the level of ambivalence and counterbalance that makes the lines about the nightingale so complex is often missing. Some poets have made fun of the whole idea of sound-symbolism, as this kind of expressive word-music is sometimes called, and it can certainly be carried too far. But if you find it inspiring, you will enjoy using the meanings of sounds to enrich your poems, as Jenny Factor does in "Song Beside a Sippy Cup":

In the never truly ever
truly dark dark night, ever
blinds-zipped, slat-cut,
dark-parked light,
you (late) touch my toes
with your broad flat own
horny-nailed cold toes.
Clock-tock, wake-shock.

In the ever truly never
truly long long night, our
little snoring-snarling
wild-child mild-child
starling-darling wakes every
two, three (you-sleep) hours,
in the never truly ever
truly lawn brawn fawn dawn.

As with any poetic device, the key to word-music is to use it in a way that is in harmony with other aspects of the poem. The excessiveness of Factor's word-music is amusingly appropriate, since the poem is in the voice of a sleep-deprived, disoriented parent. Onomatopoeia can let loose most freely in a pure lyric poem, such as the following poem by Thomas Nashe (a poem I treasure since reciting it at a festival with my young daughter performing the refrain):

"Spring," Thomas Nashe (1594)

Spring, the sweet Spring, is the year's pleasant king;
Then blooms each thing, then maids dance in a ring,
Cold doth not sting, the pretty birds do sing,
Cuckoo, jug-jug, pu-we, to-witta-woo!

The palm and may make country houses gay,
Lambs frisk and play, the shepherds pipe all day,
And we hear aye birds tune this merry lay,
Cuckoo, jug-jug, pu-we, to-witta-woo!

The fields breathe sweet, the daisies kiss our feet,
Young lovers meet, old wives a-sunning sit,
In every street these tunes our ears do greet,
Cuckoo, jug-jug, pu-we, to-witta-woo!

Spring! The sweet Spring!

Nearly 500 years ago, long before widespread habitat destruction and climate change, Nashe's town must have rung with a richness of birdsong we could barely imagine without this unabashedly celebratory poem to share it with us.

Word-Music as Experimentation

As I discovered hearing Nashe's bird sounds in the voice of a six-year-old, word-music has the capacity to carry a reader or listener away. The most extreme lover of word-music may have been William Morris, the "pre-Raphaelite" designer, carpenter, and writer of the late nineteenth century. Morris started a movement called "Pure Poetry" which advocated poetry that wasn't concerned much with meaning, but wove a magic out of the sounds of words. If you take this idea to its conclusion, you lose meaning altogether, as in the following "sound poem" written in 1916 by Dadaist poet Hugo Ball:

Karawane, Hugo Ball (1916)

jolifanto bambla o falli bambla
großiga m'pfa habla horem
egiga goramen
higo bloiko russula huju
hollaka hollala
anlogo bung
blago bung blago bung
bosso fataka
ü üü ü
schampa wulla wussa olobo
hej tatta gorem
eschige zunbada
wulubu ssubudu uluwu ssubudu
tumba ba-umf
kusa gauma
ba—umf
ugo

Ball wrote, "In these phonetic poems we want to abandon a language ravaged and laid barren by journalism. We must return to the deepest alchemy of the Word, and leave even that behind us, in order to keep safe for poetry its holiest sanctuary."

But you don't have to give up meaning entirely to weave a powerful web of word-music. This poem balances a narrative with a kind of word-music-heavy invocation at the end:

"Nightmare Boogie," Langston Hughes (1950)

I had a dream
and I could see
a million faces
black as me!
A nightmare dream:
Quicker than light
All them faces

Turned dead white!
Boogie-woogie,
Rolling bass,
Whirling treble
of cat-gut lace.

The poem can be seen as divided into three sections of four lines each: the preface, the dream itself, and the description of the music, whose sound functions like a kind of exorcism, a way to cleanse the memory of the dream by embodying the sheer physical power of African American music. The meaningful meaninglessness of the ending is an integral part of the poem, but obviously does not overshadow it. Marilyn Hacker's "Rune of the Finland Women" also strikes a balance between sense and sound, woven together as if to do exactly what the poem describes:

"Rune of the Finland Woman," Marilyn Hacker

For Sára Karig

"You are so wise," the reindeer said, "you can bind the winds of the world in a single strand."—H. C. Andersen, "The Snow Queen"

She could bind the world's winds in a single strand.
She could find the world's words in a singing wind.
She could lend a weird will to a mottled hand.
She could wind a willed word from a muddled mind.

She could wend the wild woods on a saddled hind.
She could sound a wellspring with a rowan wand.
She could bind the wolf's wounds in a swaddling band.
She could bind a banned book in a silken skin.

She could spend a world war on invaded land.
She could pound the dry roots to a kind of bread.
She could feed a road gang on invented food.
She could find the spare parts of the severed dead.

She could find the stone limbs in a waste of sand.

She could stand the pit cold with a withered lung.
She could handle bad puns in the slang she learned.
She could dandle foundlings in their mother tongue.

She could plait a child's hair with a fishbone comb.
She could tend a coal fire in the Arctic wind.
She could mend an engine with a sewing pin.
She could warm the dark feet of a dying man.

She could drink the stone soup from a doubtful well.
She could breathe the green stink of a trench latrine.
She could drink a queen's share of important wine.
She could think a few things she would never tell.

She could learn the hand code of the deaf and blind.
She could earn the iron keys of the frozen queen.
She could wander uphill with a drunken friend.
She could bind the world's winds in a single strand.

The complex texture of woven sounds in this poem incorporates not only consonance (look at "Arctic" and "coal," "learn" and "blind"), assonance ("earn" and "iron," "breathe" and "green"), but also alliteration and off-rhyme (you can find more examples in the poem).

In this contemporary chant, a Native American poet uses the repetitions of the traditional chant form as a basis for syntactic experimentation:

"Indian Chant," Diane Glancy

Hunted and sung
unhunted / unsung

clump of
loghouse / chaxed hill

unuttered / unstrung

clistered bow
hunted and unsung

hunted / strung
hunted / sung.

Word music holds the poem together, making audible, organic sense out of connections that might otherwise seem forced. The poem's journey from "unhunted/unsung" at the beginning to "hunted/sung" at the end happens through an accretion of sounds. The poem may not seem to make logical sense, but if you meditate on the clusters of words and sounds, you may find a palpable, coherent presence starting to take shape in your mind, just as the repetitions of a traditional chant create a palpably different state of mind in its hearers.

Rhyme: Definitions

Technically, a **rhyme** is when two words have the same vowel sound in the last stressed syllable as well as the same sounds for everything that follows the last stressed syllable: "fly" and "spy," and also "flying" and "spying."

When marking rhyme patterns, we repeat a lowercase letter to mark rhyming sounds, starting from *a* with each poem, with *x* for unrhymed sounds. Capital letters starting with *A* are used for any words that are repeated exactly.

> **Rhyme: Technically, the repetition of the same vowel sound on a stressed syllable as well as on all the syllables that come after the stressed syllable.**

Rhyme's Roots

While classical and medieval verse did not rhyme, two factors led rhyme to become firmly established throughout European poetry by the Renaissance. The first was a change in the pronunciation of vowels so that Latin became pronounced as an accented language; rhyme helps emphasize the patterns of accent, so rhyme and accent usually go together. The second factor was the influence of the complex and beautiful rhyme patterns of Persian (Iranian) poetry. Persian poetry influenced English by way of the Moors (Arabs) and then through the Troubadour poets of Provence, in southern France and Spain.

This influence was so prevalent that by 1589, George Puttenham wrote, "All nations now use rhyme." But rhyme in English has remained controversial: poets and critics from Thomas Campion (who called rhyme "vulgar, artificial, easy, rude, barborous, shifting, and fat") to Milton (who said he had freed *Paradise Lost* from "the troublesome and modern bondage of rhyming") to Ezra Pound (who famously called Edgar Allan Poe a "jingle man" because of his intense rhymes) and T. S. Eliot have claimed to find it vulgar and degrading. Many believe that, because English has a greater variety of word endings than Romance languages, rhyming is harder in English. Still, as A. E. Stallings points out, "English has a richness in rhymes across different parts of speech, whereas in many other languages, rhyme is often merely a coincident jingle of accidence." Whatever the reason, for hundreds of years rhyme has been so crucial to poetry in English that it is now synonymous with it. Just as, in the eighteenth century, verse was called "numbers," now it is often called "rhyme" and poems are called "rhymes," as in, "come and listen to my rhymes!"

Here's a story that may help remind us why rhyme persists in spite of it all. Not long ago, Scott Adams, the creator of the *Dilbert* cartoons, developed a condition called Spasmodic Dysphonia, where the part of the brain that controls speech stops functioning. There is no known cure for the condition. But as he wrote on his blog,

> The part of my brain responsible for normal speech was still intact, but for some reason had become disconnected from the neural pathways to my vocal cords. . . . [But then] while helping on a homework assignment, I noticed I could speak perfectly in rhyme:
>
> Jack be nimble, Jack be quick.
> Jack jump over the candlestick.
>
> I repeated it dozens of times, partly because I could. It was effortless, even though it was similar to regular speech . . . Then something happened.
>
> My brain remapped.
>
> My speech returned.

> . . . A few times I felt my voice slipping away, so I repeated the nursery rhyme and tuned it back in. By the following night my voice was almost completely normal.

Amazing and mysterious, and borne out by modern studies showing that rhythmical language is processed in a different part of the brain from prose and normal speech, this story (which presumably involves the accentual meter of the poem as much as the rhyme) reminds us of the power long believed to be held by rhymed words—the reason, for example, that witches' spells always rhyme. Poets who bring rhyme into their poems, and with it the power of symmetry and pattern, are harnessing a potentially mighty force.

Kinds of Rhyme

There are many different types of rhyme, and two overarching ways to classify them: by the kind of rhyme sound, and by the rhyme's location in the line. Here is a list of types of rhyme, with discussion at greater length of some of the most important.

Types of Rhyme Classified by Kind of Rhyme Sound

Perfect, exact, true, or pure rhyme: the words begin differently, then have identical stressed vowel sounds, with any other following sounds also being identical: sigh, high, vye, underlie; sowing, flowing, hoeing, ongoing. There are two types of perfect rhyme: **rising, single, one-syllable, or masculine rhyme** (cat, sat); and **falling, double, two-syllable, or feminine rhyme** (seven, heaven). Occasionally there are even triple or three-syllable rhymes (visible, risible).

Light rhyme: rhyming a one-syllable with a two-syllable rhyme (arise, prize; falling, ring):

From "Blown Apart by Loss," Rita Dove

Winter came early and still
She frequented the path by the river until . . .

Slant rhyme (also called off-rhyme, half rhyme, near rhyme, imperfect rhyme, and approximate rhyme): Rhyme that is not perfect. There are two kinds of slant rhyme. In the first type, **consonant rhyme,** the stressed vowel sounds are different, but the consonants or whatever else comes after them is the same:

From "The Calm," John Donne (1597)

earth's hollownesses, which the world's lungs are,
have no more wind than the upper vault of air.

Here are some other examples: come, tomb; taut, knit; nation, attention; gone, moan; heaven, given. The following poem is entirely written with consonant rhyme:

"Futility," Wilfred Owen (1917)

Move him into the sun—
Gently its touch awoke him once,
At home, whispering of fields unsown.
Always it woke him, even in France,
Until this morning and this snow.
If anything might rouse him now
The kind old sun will know.

Think how it wakes the seeds,—
Woke, once, the clays of a cold star.
Are limbs, so dear-achieved, are sides,
Full-nerved,—still warm,—too hard to stir?
Was it for this the clay grew tall?
—O what made fatuous sunbeams toil
To break earth's sleep at all?

In the second type of slant rhyme, **assonant rhyme,** the stressed vowel sounds are the same and a consonant that comes after them is different:

When he came to the king's gate,
he sought a drink for Hind Horn's sake.
—ANONYMOUS BALLAD

From "The Poet Reflects on Her Solitary Fate," Sandra Cisneros

They have left her
To her own device.
Her nightmares and pianos.
She owns a lead pipe.

Emily Dickinson's poems are famous for their consonantal slant rhymes, which sometimes push the rhyme so far that it approaches wrenched rhyme, which is discussed later in this chapter. Note that the rhyme scheme is xaxa, so only the alternating lines rhyme:

Poem 1078, Emily Dickinson (1866)

The Bustle in a House
The Morning after Death
Is solemnest of Industries
Enacted upon Earth—

The Sweeping up the Heart
And putting Love away
We shall not want to use again
Until Eternity.

Slant rhyme, like meter or any other poetic device, has no inherent "meaning" or effect; it can truly be used for a range of purposes. In Dickinson's poems, the use of slant rhyme tends to add a feeling of energy and independence of spirit. In the following contemporary poem, slant rhyme achieves a very different effect, seeming the perfect expression for a mood of jaded, cynical weariness:

"Blues for Dante Alighieri," Kim Addonizio

> . . . without hope we live on in desire. . . .
> *Inferno* IV

Our room was too small, the sheets scratchy and hot—
Our room was a kind of hell, we thought,
and killed a half-liter of Drambuie we'd bought.

We walked over the Arno and back across.
We walked all day, and in the evening, lost,
argued and wandered in circles. At last

we found our hotel. The next day we left for Rome.
We found the Intercontinental, and a church full of bones,
and ate takeout Chinese in our suite, alone.

It wasn't a great journey, only a side trip.
It wasn't love for eternity, or any such crap;
it was just something that happened. . . .

We packed suitcases, returned the rental car.
We packed souvenirs, and repaired to the airport bar
and talked about pornography, and movie stars.

In this passage from the Russian-born poet Joseph Brodsky, both the consonants and the vowels are slightly off.

From "December in Florence," Joseph Brodsky

There are always six bridges spanning the sluggish river.
There are places where lips touched lips for the first time ever,
or pen pressed paper with real fervor.
There are arcades, colonnades, iron idols that blur your lens.
There the streetcar's multitudes, jostling, dense,
speak in the tongue of a man who's departed thence.

As if to underscore the impossibility of exact rhyme, it is not only single consonant sounds that are off-rhymed, but syllables and consonant clusters. The effect is one of poignant dissonance and pain.

Compound rhyme: rhymes two groups of words (of her, love her)

Broken rhyme: divides a word at the end of a line by hyphenating it, so it will rhyme with the end of the next line (I know you are read- / y for anything, I said)

Apocopate rhyme: the last syllable is dropped in one rhyming word: gain, painless

Mosaic rhyme: rhymes one word with a group (justice, trust is). Often this kind of rhyme is used for humorous effects, by writers such as Ogden Nash and Gilbert and Sullivan, or in this famous limerick by a newspaper editor:

"The Pelican," Dixon Lanier Merritt (1910)

A wonderful bird is the pelican,
His mouth can hold more than his belly can,
He can hold in his beak,
Enough food for a week!
I'm damned if I know how the hell he can!

This poem uses the device more seriously:

From "Church Going," Philip Larkin

A serious house on serious earth it is,
In whose blent air all our compulsions meet,
Are recognised, and robed as destinies.
And that much never can be obsolete,
Since someone will forever be surprising
A hunger in himself to be more serious,
And gravitating with it to this ground,
Which, he once heard, was proper to grow wise in,
If only that so many dead lie round.

Larkin saves the only mosaic rhyme till the very end of this seven-stanza poem. It is an impressive rhyme, both because of its difficulty and cleverness, and because of the way the easier words to rhyme come in the second position (see "Advice on Rhyming" at the end of this chapter). When the reader encounters the phrase "grow wise in," it functions as a kind of climax, as the speaker's initial suspicion and cynicism toward the church modulates into reluctant respect.

Rime rich: the rhyme includes the preceding consonants, so the words sound identical. There are two kinds of rich rhyme:

Homographic (words have different meanings but are spelled the same). Example: "I know you did not mean / that she was acting mean."

Homonymic (words look different but sound the same): time, thyme

Identical rhyme: repeating of the exact same word, with same meaning. Here is an example by the young Yeats:

"Aedh Wishes for the Cloths of Heaven," W. B. Yeats (1899)

Had I the heavens' embroidered cloths,
Enwrought with golden and silver light,
The blue and the dim and the dark cloths
Of night and light and the half-light,
I would spread the cloths under your feet:
But I, being poor, have only my dreams;
I have spread my dreams under your feet;
Tread softly because you tread on my dreams.

Wrenched rhyme: words that depend on exaggerated or distorted pronunciation or spelling to rhyme: Tulsa, ulcer (Ogden Nash); rhinestones, grindstones

Visual, sight, or eye rhyme: looks but does not sound the same: eight, sleight

Sometimes, eye rhyme can have the effect of slant rhyme even if it is not exact. This ingenious free verse poem uses a kind of rhyme I have never seen before, which we might call **anagram rhyme;** it has the effect of an eye rhyme combined with a slant rhyme:

"The Heron," Randall Mann

A pond the color of Oriental teas.
A heron refusing to look anywhere but east.

Mangroves flecked with a fire,
deep-set birches rife

with the wait for night. In stone,
the heron stares: the stoic tones

of the sky a storied procession of palms;
their red-tipped fronds, overhanging lamps.

Water-bird, it has been centuries since I felt
anything for you. You have been left:
look around. Why does the owl
rest on a goddess's shoulder while you wade so low?

Kinds of Rhyme Classified by Location

End rhyme: rhyme at the ends of lines
Head rhyme (or initial rhyme): some use this term for alliteration, others for rhyming initial words
Internal rhyme: the end of a line rhymes with the center of a line

There are four types of internal rhyme:

Leonine rhyme (or **medial rhyme**): an internal rhyme directly before the caesura of the same line. This type of internal rhyme is most common in popular poems in English, such as this famous poem in trochaic octometer:

From "The Raven," Edgar Allan Poe (1845)

Once upon a midnight dreary, while I pondered, weak and weary,
Over many a quaint and curious volume of forgotten lore . . .
While I nodded, nearly napping, suddenly there came a tapping,
As of some one gently rapping, rapping at my chamber door.
"'Tis some visitor," I muttered, "tapping at my chamber door—
Only this, and nothing more."

Ah, distinctly I remember it was in the bleak December,
And each separate dying ember wrought its ghost upon the floor.
Eagerly I wished the morrow;—vainly I had sought to borrow

From my books surcease of sorrow—sorrow for the lost Lenore—
For the rare and radiant maiden whom the angels name Lenore—
Nameless *here* for evermore.

And the silken, sad, uncertain rustling of each purple curtain
Thrilled me—filled me with fantastic terrors never felt before;
So that now, to still the beating of my heart, I stood repeating,
"'Tis some visitor entreating entrance at my chamber door—
Some late visitor entreating entrance at my chamber door;—
This it is, and nothing more."

Poe's poem uses internal rhyme to break up the long lines into smaller units, and to emphasize the hypnotic repetitions of the action in the poem's story. These types of internal rhyme are much subtler in their effects:

Cross-rhyme: the end of the line rhymes with the center of the adjacent line:

I know there is a summer tree
inside the freeing autumn gold

Interlaced rhyme: the center of the line rhymes with the center of the adjacent line:

the summer tree lives on inside
the living freedom of the gold

Linked rhyme: the end of a line rhymes with the first syllable of the following line:

I know there is a summer tree
freed by the autumn gold

While the various forms of internal rhyme are used most often for decoration in English-language poetry, cross-rhyme is a central element of form in some poetic traditions, including the Celtic. I used it for a poem dedicated to Brigid, the Celtic goddess of healing and poetry, in one of the only contemporary poems written in the ancient Celtic form called the **awdl gwyddyd,** which uses a combination of linked rhyme, internal rhyme, end rhyme, and cross-rhyme:

"Brigid," Annie Finch

Ring, ring, ring, ring! Hammers fall.
Your gold will all be beaten
over sudden flaming fire
moving from you, the pyre. Sweeten
your cauldron, until the sun
runs with one flame through the day
and the healing water will sing,
linger on tongues, burn away.

Enjambed rhyme: the first consonant of the next line completes the end rhyme:

He arose and I
descended to his side

Rimas dissolutas: a medieval French technique which can be used with any length of line or stanza. The first lines of each stanza rhyme with each other, the second lines of each stanza rhyme with each other, the third lines of each stanza rhyme with each other, and so on, as in these stanzas:

From "Black Rook in Rainy Weather," Sylvia Plath

Although, I admit, I desire,
Occasionally, some backtalk
From the mute sky, I can't honestly complain:
A certain minor light may still
Lean incandescent

Out of kitchen table or chair
As if a celestial burning took
Possession of the most obtuse objects now and then—
Thus hallowing an interval
Otherwise inconsequent

A more subtle technique of rhyming than most, here the *rima dissoluta* helps capture the dry alienation of the speaker's mood.

Unpatterned rhyme—random rhymes. These may be as unnatural-seeming as John Skelton's famous "Skeltonics," made more overbearing by the short lines, whose style is so distinctive that they have their own nickname:

From "Colin Clout," John Skelton (1521–22)

His head is so fat,
He wotteth never what
Nor whereof he speaketh;
He crieth and he creaketh,
He prieth and he peeketh,
He chides and he chatters,
He prates and he patters,
He clitters and he clatters,
He meddles and he smatters,
He gloses and he flatters;
Or if he speak plain,
Then he lacketh brain,
He is but a fool;
Let him go to school,
On a three footed stool
That he may down sit,
For he lacketh wit;
And if that he hit
The nail on the head
It standeth in no stead.

Or they may be as simple and speechlike in effect as in this poem:

"After Apple-Picking," Robert Frost (1914)

My long two-pointed ladder's sticking through a tree
Toward heaven still,
And there's a barrel that I didn't fill
Beside it, and there may be two or three

Apples I didn't pick upon some bough.
But I am done with apple-picking now.
Essence of winter sleep is on the night,
The scent of apples: I am drowsing off.
I cannot rub the strangeness from my sight
I got from looking through a pane of glass
I skimmed this morning from the drinking trough
And held against the world of hoary grass.
It melted, and I let it fall and break.
But I was well
Upon my way to sleep before it fell,
And I could tell
What form my dreaming was about to take.
Magnified apples appear and disappear,
Stem end and blossom end,
And every fleck of russet showing clear.
My instep arch not only keeps the ache,
It keeps the pressure of a ladder-round.
I feel the ladder sway as the boughs bend.

And I keep hearing from the cellar bin
The rumbling sound
Of load on load of apples coming in.
For I have had too much
Of apple-picking: I am overtired
Of the great harvest I myself desired.
There were ten thousand thousand fruit to touch,
Cherish in hand, lift down, and not let fall.
For all
That struck the earth,
No matter if not bruised or spiked with stubble,
Went surely to the cider-apple heap
As of no worth.
One can see what will trouble
This sleep of mine, whatever sleep it is.
Were he not gone,
The woodchuck could say whether it's like his

Long sleep, as I describe its coming on,
Or just some human sleep.

Rhyme and Emphasis

Rhyme emphasizes the rhyming words. This simple effect can be used in numerous ways by skilled poets. In the following poem, rhyme falls on the short, simple word "me":

"She Dwelt Among the Untrodden Ways," William Wordsworth (1799)

She dwelt among the untrodden ways
    Beside the springs of Dove,
A Maid whom there were none to praise
    And very few to love:

A violet by a mossy stone
    Half hidden from the eye!
Fair as a star, when only one
    Is shining in the sky.

She lived unknown, and few could know
    When Lucy ceased to be;
But she is in her grave, and, oh,
    The difference to me!

The rhyme on "me" surprisingly—almost shockingly—emphasizes the speaker's aloneness, and the subjective nature of the pain of grieving, at the very moment it introduces the speaker into the poem for the first time.

The emphasis, through rhyming, of strongly contrasting words can strengthen the effects of wit and satire. This is a favorite device of Alexander Pope, as in this couplet:

The hungry judges soon the sentence sign,
and wretches hang that jurymen may dine.

It is the rhyme that highlights the word and the intended effect; if the last line read, "wretches hang for the dinners of jurymen," the cutting sarcasm contrasting the profit of the juries to the fate of the punished poor would be far less effective. Sonia Sanchez explores this device in this stanza from "Song No. 2":

> i say, all you young girls molested at ten,
> i say, all you young girls giving it up again and again,
> i say, all you sisters hanging out in every den
> i say, all you sisters needing your own oxygen.

The angry contrast between the meanings of the lines ending in "ten" and oxygen" is heightened, and the irony deepened, because of the repeating of the rhyme sounds in the two words.

Rhyme is also traditionally used in many situations to highlight the endings of final lines, emphasizing a sense of closure. Shakespeare and other writers of blank verse use it to signal the end of an unrhymed passage, as in this passage from Macbeth:

From Macbeth, *William Shakespeare (1606)*

> . . . Thou sure and firm-set earth,
> Hear not my steps, which way they walk, for fear
> Thy very stones prate of my whereabout,
> And take the present horror from the time,
> Which now suits with it. Whiles I threat, he lives:
> Words to the heat of deeds too cold breath gives.

A rhymed tercet can add similar closure to a passage in rhymed couplets. And a rhymed couplet is built into the endings of such forms as the English sonnet or, as you will see, a stanza of rhyme royal, or a Spenserian stanza.

Rhyme and Meaning

When you rhyme words, you are linking them in the meaning dimension as well as in the sound dimension. If you take a rhymed poem you admire and read only the rhymed words together in a string, you will probably see that they make an intensely linked underpoem, which we experience unconsciously at the same time we are consciously reading the poem as a whole. You can see this in Sonnet 73 (1609), for example, where Shakespeare makes time pass viscerally by rhyming the present-tense verb "hang" with the past-tense verb "sang."

Sonnet 73, William Shakespeare (1609)

That time of year thou mayst in me behold
When yellow leaves, or none, or few, do hang
Upon those boughs which shake against the cold,
Bare ruin'd choirs, where late the sweet birds sang.
In me thou see'st the twilight of such day
As after sunset fadeth in the west;
Which by and by black night doth take away,
Death's second self, that seals up all in rest.
In me thou see'st the glowing of such fire,
That on the ashes of his youth doth lie,
As the death-bed whereon it must expire,
Consum'd with that which it was nourish'd by.
This thou perceiv'st, which makes thy love more strong,
To love that well which thou must leave ere long.

This is the underpoem: "Behold hang cold, sang day west away, rest fire lie expire, nourish'd by strong long." The rhyming words are so vivid that they create a story parallel to that of the poem as a whole. The same technique has heartbreaking effects in this brief dramatic monologue:

"Casualty," Langston Hughes (1950)

He was a soldier in the army,
But he doesn't walk like one.
He walks like his soldiering
Days are done.

Son! . . . Son!

Hughes is playing off the expected abab rhyme pattern of the ballad stanza. Just when we think the poem is over because the ballad stanza rhyme is completed, we are shocked with the clincher, the third rhyme on the same sound, which turns the entire poem from a general lament into a personal tragedy; the repetition of the word, with its implication that the son is too injured (deaf?) or too depressed or disoriented to respond, also turns the poem from the third-person to the second-person voice. The single word "son" could never have such a powerful effect if the ground hadn't been subtly laid for it by the preceding rhymes. When you write using rhyme, check your underpoem to make sure the rhyming words are intense and effective. Rhyme puts extra focus on words, and this is one way to make sure that your rhyme words are interesting enough to deserve the attention.

The underlying rhyme pattern becomes a surface structure of meaning in the following poem:

"Of Night," Molly Peacock

A city mouse darts from the paws of night.
A body drops from the jaws of night.
A woman denies the laws of night,
Awake and trapped in the was of night.
A young man turns in the gauze of night,
Unravelling the cause of night:
That days extend their claws at night
To re-enact old wars at night,
Though dreams can heal old sores at night
And Spring begins its thaw at night,
While worry bones are gnawed at night.
He sips her through a straw at night.
Verbs whisper in the clause of night.
A finger to her lips, the pause of night.

The internal rhyme creates patterns of meaning in the poem, linking the imagery into a narrative: paws, jaws, laws, was, gauze . . .

Peacock's poem uses **monorhyme,** the rhyming of many words on a single sound. The same technique, combined with trochees at the beginnings of lines and a powerful rush of images and syntax with no stanza breaks, creates great forward propulsion in this poem:

"Bereft," Robert Frost (1928)

Where had I heard this wind before
Change like this to a deeper roar?
What would it take my standing there for,
Holding open a restive door,
Looking downhill to a frothy shore?
Summer was past and day was past.
Somber clouds in the west were massed.
Out in the porch's sagging floor,
Leaves got up in a coil and hissed,
Blindly struck at my knee and missed.
Something sinister in the tone
Told me my secret must be known:
Word I was in the house alone
Somehow must have gotten abroad,
Word I was in my life alone,
Word I had no one left but God.

The partly random, hurried-seeming rhyme scheme piles on additional words as if the speaker is too nervous to look back over his shoulder and count them. The syntax adds new information in groups of two or three lines, always changing the pattern so there is no rest or security. The relentlessly monosyllabic rhymes are only altered slightly with the word "alone," which is repeated exactly as if in desperation or resignation.

The following poem uses the same rhyme sound to build an entire poem:

"The Outlier," Paul Muldoon

I
In Armagh or Tyrone
I fell between two stones.

In Armagh or Tyrone
on a morning in June
I fell between two stones.

In Armagh or Tyrone
on a morning in June
in 1951
I fell between two stones.

In Armagh or Tyrone
on a morning in June
in 1951
I fell between two stones
that raised me as their own.

II
I had one eye, just one,
they prised and propped open.
I had one eye, just one,
they prised and propped open
like a Fomorian's.

I had one eye, just one,
they prised and propped open
like a Fomorian's
with a fire-toughened pine.

I had one eye, just one,
they prised and propped open
like a Fomorian's
so all I looked upon
would itself turn to stone.

Because Muldoon's stanza structure (discussed further in chapter 16, "Stanzas") adds suspense and drama through the addition of new lines, the monorhyme seems anything but monotonous; it serves as a counterbalance to the constantly shifting ground of the stanza, even as it adds haunting bleakness to this terrible story of childhood's loss of self.

Of course, rhyme does not have to be so blatant to be effective. In the following poem, rhyme works subtly to counterbalance a rhetorical effect:

"The Painted Lady," Margaret Danner

The Painted Lady is a small African
butterfly, gayly toned orchid or peach
that seems as tremulous and delicately sheer

as the objects I treasure, yet, this cosmopolitan
can cross the sea at the icy time of the year
in the trail of the big boats, to France.

Mischance is as wide and somber grey as the lake here
in Chicago. Is there strength enough in my huge
peach paper rose, or lavender sea-laced fan?

Between stanzas 2 and 3, Danner makes a sudden rhetorical leap from the African butterfly's abilities to her own situation (a connection made more meaningful, though no less sudden, by the fact that she often wrote about African American themes). However, the suddenness of that leap is ingeniously counterpointed with the other ways that the stanzas of the poem are woven together: the complex original rhyme scheme, which moves the same three rhyme sounds (including the off-rhyme of "peach" and "year") from stanza to stanza, and the rhyme that links across stanzas, with a particularly powerful internal rhyme just at the moment of the rhetorical leap itself.

Rhyme can also work along with other sound effects to create new effects:

"The Night Piece," Thom Gunn

The fog drifts slowly down the hill,
And as I mount gets thicker still,
Closes me in, makes me its own
Like bedclothes on the paving stone.

Here are the last few streets to climb,
Galleries, run through veins of time,
Almost familiar, where I creep
Toward sleep like fog, through fog like sleep.

Here, as the couplet rhyme scheme begins to "mount," a sort of horror of paralysis mounts with it. When the word "fog" repeats for the second and third time in the last line, it is accompanied by an internal repetition of the rhyme word "sleep," so that, when the expected rhyme comes at the end, it is not just a couplet rhyme anymore but also the near-stupefying completion of a chiasmus (literally, a "crossing"—a rhetorical figure that makes a kind of X by switching the places of repeating words or ideas).

Sometimes rhyme has been mistakenly associated with old-fashioned or conservative poetry; of course that is not a necessary connection, as will be clear in chapter 10 on exploratory poetics. This poem by Aaron Shurin uses rhyme words from Shakespeare's sonnets:

If the judgment's cruel
that's a wake-up call: increase
energy, *attention.* These little pumpkins ornament
themselves with swells, die
pushing live volume packed spring-
form hard as a knock: Decease
and resist. Content
surges exactly as memory
closes its rear-guarding
eyes
—the world rushes *in* not *by*! just be
steady, receptors, measure is fuel:
whatever moves move with the
drift which moving never lies.

The 14-line poem uses a distorted sonnet-style rhyme scheme, with the couplet split between the first and third-to-last lines. A paean to the importance of paying attention to the solidity of the present moment without preconceptions, this poem about pumpkin pie, memory, and experience demonstrates that rhyme can help make language fresh and unfamiliar.

Advice on Rhyming

Though rhyme has important effects on structure, emphasis, and meaning, that is not its most important function in a poem. The fundamental reason that rhyme is so prevalent in poetry is that it sounds good; it provides stimulation to the outer or inner ear. Rhyme may sound artificial if you aren't used to it, but after reading poems in rhyme for a while, you will learn to slow down, allowing time for the rhymes to surround and surprise you until they do feel natural.

The repeated use of rhyme also accustoms the reader to the pleasure of like sounds coming together: a reader who expects rhyme to occur on a regular basis begins to desire it, and poetry makes use of this desire to keep the reader involved. A series of rhymed couplets makes use of the recurring desire for rhyme in the first line of each couplet, and the pleasure of satisfied desire in the second line of each couplet. Other, more complex rhyme patterns—moving from the abab to abba stanza, and to such stanzas as rhyme royal and ottava rima—provide increasingly complex forms of pleasure.

It is important to make this movement of desire and satisfaction work on your poem's behalf by keeping an element of unpredictability in your rhyming. Rhymes that are too expected rob the reader of the sensation of suspense and delay. For example, you can rhyme different parts of speech so the rhyme will have more significance for the reader: "lied" and "pride" is a more surprising and interesting rhyme than "lied" and "died." An occasional omitted rhyme, or a repeated or extra rhyme when you don't expect it, can provide a useful teasing or surprising effect.

The more organic a rhyme seems, the better; anything forced will distract the reader from the sweet moment of discovery. The three most common hazards of rhyming all have to do with unnaturalness: trite, overused rhymes; the forcing of extra words into a poem only for the rhyme; and unnatural or archaic inversions of speech for the sake of the rhyme.

One easy shortcut to help your rhymes sound more natural is to put the more commonplace word last in the rhyming sequence. A reader will get more satisfaction out of the second of these couplets than the first:

So I could simply be with you,
I found my way to Timbuktoo.

I found my way to Timbuktoo
so I could simply be with you.

Reading the first couplet, the reader may feel that the poet has gone to great lengths to find a word to rhyme with "you." Reading the second couplet, the reader may feel that the poet has cleverly come up with a simple, inevitable, and natural-sounding rhyme for "Timbuktoo." As long as you put the simpler word last, the reader will never know which one you actually thought of first. On the other hand, sometimes the more surprising word is more powerful at the end. Try reversing the second and fourth lines in the last stanza of this poem by Gwendolyn Brooks:

"Beverly Hills, Chicago," Gwendolyn Brooks

The dry brown coughing beneath their feet,
(Only a while, for the handyman is on his way)
These people walk their golden gardens.
We say ourselves fortunate to be driving by today.

That we may look at them, in their gardens where
The summer ripeness rots. But not raggedly.
Even the leaves fall down in lovelier patterns here.
And the refuse, the refuse is a neat brilliancy.

When they flow sweetly into their houses
With softness and slowness touched by that everlasting gold,
We know what they go to. To tea. But that does not mean
They will throw some little black dots into some water
And add sugar and the juice of the cheapest lemons
that are sold,

While downstairs that woman's vague phonograph bleats,
"Knock me a kiss."
And the living all to be made again in the sweatingest physical manner
Tomorrow . . . Not that anybody is saying that these people have no
 trouble.
Merely that it is trouble with a gold-flecked beautiful banner.

Nobody is saying that these people do not ultimately cease to be.
And sometimes their passings are even more painful than ours.
It is just that so often they live till their hair is white.
They make excellent corpses, among the expensive flowers . . .

Nobody is furious. Nobody hates these people.
At least, nobody driving by in this car.
It is only natural, however, that it should occur to us
How much more fortunate they are than we are.

It is only natural that we should look and look
At their wood and brick and stone
And think, while a breath of pine blows,
How different these are from our own.

We do not want them to have less.
But it is only natural that we should think we have not enough.
We drive on, we drive on.
When we speak to each other our voices are a little gruff.

Perhaps because the other stanzas generally do follow the principle of ending on the commonplace word ("sold" instead of "gold," "are" instead of "car," "own" instead of "stone"), "gruff" in the last line is shocking and effective, and conveys the forced resentment as if the rhyme itself were forced.

The best advice I've ever heard about how to make rhymes seem natural instead of forced is this, from Richard Wilbur, who got it in turn from Robert Frost: "Don't rhyme words, rhyme phrases." If you think in terms of entire phrases, it will be easier for the rhyming words to follow inevitably instead of needing to be tacked on.

QUESTIONS FOR MEDITATION OR DISCUSSION

What other meaning-related word clusters can you think of, besides the "s," "m," "p," "sn," and "sl" sounds mentioned in the text? Try to make up some words that other people will know the meaning of, just because of the way they sound. Imaging you are an advertising team, trying to invent new words to name a new arthritis medicine and a new sports car.

Identify the word-music at play in these common quotes and sayings: "the patter of little feet," "a stitch in time saves nine," "least said soonest mended," "a watched pot never boils." Think of other examples.

The consonance in the following poem can be seen as carrying its own story. How do you think the story goes?

"Whenas in Silks My Julia Goes," Robert Herrick (1647)

Whenas in silks my Julia goes,
Then, then (methinks), how sweetly flows
That liquefaction of her clothes!

Next, when I cast mine eyes and see
That brave vibration each way free;
O, how that glittering taketh me!

In the following two poems, how does the interplay of assonance, consonance, and word-music accentuate particular parts of the poem?

"Touch Me," Stanley Kunitz

Summer is late, my heart.
Words plucked out of the air
some forty years ago
when I was wild with love
and torn almost in two
scatter like leaves this night
of whistling wind and rain.
It is my heart that's late,
it is my song that's flown.
Outdoors all afternoon
under a gunmetal sky
staking my garden down,
I kneeled to the crickets trilling
underfoot as if about
to burst from their crusty shells;
and like a child again
marveled to hear so clear
and brave a music pour
from such a small machine.

What makes the engine go?
Desire, desire, desire.
The longing for the dance
stirs in the buried life.
One season only,
and it's done.
So let the battered old willow
thrash against the windowpanes
and the house timbers creak.
Darling, do you remember
the man you married? Touch me,
remind me who I am.

From "The Quaker Graveyard Off Nantucket," Robert Lowell (1946)

This is the end of the whaleroad and the whale
Who spewed Nantucket bones on the thrashed swell
And stirred the troubled waters to whirlpools
To send the Pequod packing off to hell:
This is the end of them, three-quarters fools,
Snatching at straws to sail
Seaward and seaward on the turntail whale,
Spouting out blood and water as it rolls,

Sick as a dog to these Atlantic shoals:
Clamavimus, O depths. Let the sea-gulls wail

For water, for the deep where the high tide
Mutters to its hurt self, mutters and ebbs.
Waves wallow in their wash, go out and out,
Leave only the death-rattle of the crabs,
The beach increasing, its enormous snout
Sucking the ocean's side.
This is the end of running on the waves;
We are poured out like water. Who will dance
The mast-lashed master of Leviathans
Up from this field of Quakers in their unstoned graves?

Poems throughout this book use rhyme. Look through the other chapters with rhyme in mind. Which four poems in the book do you think use rhyme to the best effect? Why?

What does it mean if rhyme words can convey the entire story of a poem? Do you agree that this happens in Shakespeare's Sonnet 73? I recall my college teacher John Hollander making the same claim about the end words of Robert Frost's poem "The Most of It":

> He thought he kept the universe alone;
> For all the voice in answer he could wake
> Was but the mocking echo of his own
> From some tree-hidden cliff across the lake.
> Some morning from the boulder-broken beach
> He would cry out on life, that what it wants
> Is not its own love back in copy speech,
> But counter-love, original response.
> And nothing ever came of what he cried
> Unless it was the embodiment that crashed
> In the cliff's talus on the other side,
> And then in the far-distant water splashed,
> But after a time allowed for it to swim,
> Instead of proving human when it neared
> And someone else additional to him,
> As a great buck it powerfully appeared,
> Pushing the crumpled water up ahead,
> And landed pouring like a waterfall,
> And stumbled through the rocks with horny tread,
> And forced the underbrush—and that was all.

Do you agree? Try this question on other poems in the book, and with poems of your own.

What do you think the poet means by the word "rhyme" in the phrase "hope and history rhyme" in the last line of the poem below? Do you think the rhyming of hope and history is an accurate metaphor for justice?

History says, Don't hope
On this side of the grave.
But then, once in a lifetime
The longed-for tidal wave
Of justice can rise up
And hope and history rhyme.
—Seamus Heaney

QUOTES

Sound was my doorway into poems and I believe you taste sounds. You chew on them. And they are delicious. When I read poems, just sitting silently here in my chair, I can feel the muscles of my throat working.

—Donald Hall

I put a premium on rhymes—how could I
  Not living the times of the Supa
Emcees where styles are def, lyrics fly,
  Tight the way our minds move over
    Beats and grooves.
—Major Jackson

I wish to write such rhymes as shall not suggest a restraint, but contrariwise the wildest freedom.

—Ralph Waldo Emerson

Interviewer: "Mr. Frost, how do you get your ideas for poems?"
Robert Frost: "By searching for rhyme-words."

There are no tired rhymes. There are no forbidden rhymes. Rhymes are not predictable unless lines are. Death and breath, womb and tomb, love and of, moon, June, spoon, all still have great poems ahead of them.

—A. E. Stallings

In small towns, where one must spend close daily life with unchosen fellows, the major use of speech is to accommodate. A small-town reader-writer has an island of use-vocabulary, set in a vast sea of recognition vocabulary, which using rhyme forces him to embark upon. Words that he loves, but that do not readily come to mind for use, are found by rowing out after rhyme. Free verse, which draws from the island of speech, does not force this quest.

—Mona Van Duyn

The profit of rhyme is that it drops seeds of a sweeter and more luxuriant rhyme, and of uniformity that it conveys itself into its own roots in the ground out of sight.

—Walt Whitman

Rhyme has been said to contain in itself a constant appeal to Memory and Hope.

—Arthur Hallam

Rhyme becomes necessary in poetry as rhythm weakens.

—Louise Bogan

For slant-rhyme, I find that if I listen for the "weight" of the vowels, then balance vowel sounds of equivalent "weights," the poem . . . feels satisfying.

—Marilyn Nelson

Excessive devotion to rhyme has thickened the modern ear. Shifting away from rhyme might be a liberation of rhyme . . . freed from its exacting task . . . it could be applied with greater effect where most needed.

—T. S. Eliot

I'm always inadvertently using rhyme. I don't ever try; it comes out naturally. My ear has been tuned.

—Sandra Cisneros

Rhyme has the great advantage of infuriating the simple people who naively think there is something under the sun more important than a convention. They have an innocent belief that an idea may be "deeper," more durable than any convention. This is not the least of the charms of rhyme, nor thereby does it caress the ear less sweetly.

—Paul Valéry

Never too late to rhyme!

—Robert Creeley (unpublished letter to Chris Stroffolino)

POETRY PRACTICES

(Group) Sound Volleyball. Everyone sit in a circle. One person throws in a word to start (any word will do). The person to your left (or right) answers with a word that rhymes, off-rhymes, alliterates, or has assonance with the first. The idea is to keep the words going around the circle as long as possible. The response should be immediate; they who hesitate are lost. Keep going until one person is left, or until you get sick of it. Example: first/thirst/thrust/trust/tryst/cyst/crypt/crap/flap/flip/hip/chip/chirp/burp/bread/head et cetera.

Found Word-Music. Look for examples of alliteration and other word-music in the language around you. Often, familiar phrases such as clichés, popular phrases, advertisements, and mnemonic sayings are structured by word-music. Write a poem out of a group of these.

Onomatopoeia/Anti-onomatopoeia. Make a list of words whose sound seems to echo their sense. Then make a list of words whose sound seems to counteract their sense. This is quite subjective, so there are no wrong answers. Write a poem using all the first group in the first stanza, and the second group in the second stanza.

Word-Music Tone-up. Write a poem of your own that has a line you like the sound of. Experiment with allowing, expanding and emphasizing its word-music, repeating the sounds to extend into other lines.

Over the Top. Write a poem that plays shamelessly with word-music. Let yourself go. Read it aloud frequently as you write. Finally, perform it for others.

Four Objects, Sixteen Lines. Pick four objects in the room. For each object, write a four-line stanza in abab rhyme that ends with the name of the object.

Beginning the End. Choose a rhymed poem you enjoy and write a poem using the same end-words in the same order.

Crazy Rhyme Quilt. Write a poem that uses at least eight of the kinds of rhyme discussed in this chapter. Optional: trade these poems with a partner, and see if you can recognize all the kinds of rhyme in each other's poems.

Just Do It. Invent an original rhyme scheme.

CHAPTER 9

Syntax and Rhetorical Structure: Words in Order and Disorder

The sound of sense is as vital to a poem as the sense of sound.

Syntax is the part of grammar that is concerned with the way words or phrases are ordered to show the relationship of one part of a sentence to another. A good poem uses syntax, grammar, and punctuation fluently, just as it uses rhythm, connotation, and word sounds. While these elements of language are easy to take for granted, or to treat as invisible, the fact is that every time you write poetry, you make choices about sentence length, sentence complexity, word order, and punctuation that will deeply affect the impact of your poem.

Although in some languages, such as Latin, word order can change without changing meaning, in English, the majority of our sentences rely on word order to convey information. "Jane ate the bear" means something quite different than "The bear ate Jane." Syntax has its own rhythms that bring readers into a poet's way of meeting the world.

Of course, poems also make meaning on a much larger level than that of the individual sentence. The final section of this chapter will consider briefly some of the larger rhetorical choices that shape poems, including irony, rhetorical strategy, and point of view.

Simple and Complex Syntax

The grammar of some poems involves short sentences or clauses that are all pretty much equal to each other in importance. When many conjunctions are used in a row, the style is called *polysyndeton.* It is as old as the Hebrew Bible and as new as Gertrude Stein:

. . . and Judas begat Phares and Zara of Thamar; and Phares begat Esrom; and Esrom begat Aram; And Aram begat Aminadab; and Aminadab begat Naasson; and Naasson begat Salmon;

From *King James Bible,* Matthew 1:3

Not and is added added is and not added added is not and added added is and not added added added is not and added added not and is added added is and is added added and is not and added added and is not and added added is and is not added added is and not and added added is and not and added . . .

From *Patriarchal Poetry* by Gertrude Stein, 1927

Of course, these two examples of polysyndeton are extreme. Most poems fall somewhere along the middle of the continuum from simple to complex syntax. Here is a powerful old poem from near the simple end of the continuum:

"The Man of Double Deed," Anonymous

There was a man of double deed,
who sowed his garden full of seed.
When the seed began to grow,
'twas like a garden full of snow;
when the snow began to fall,
like birds it was upon the wall;
and when the birds began to fly,
'twas like a shipwreck in the sky;
and when the sky began to crack,
'twas like a stick upon my back;
and when my back began to smart,
'twas like a penknife in my heart;
and when my heart began to bleed,
then I was dead and dead indeed.

The same grammatical relationship is repeated over and over throughout the poem. This kind of syntax, in which the grammatical phrases and shapes repeat each other from sentence to sentence, is called **parallelism.** A simple technique, parallelism can still achieve subtle and sophisticated effects. Here, as the phrases with parallel syntactical structures follow each other, they create momentum and a sense of urgency. The growing violence of the poem's imagery has an especially wrenching effect against the unchanging grammatical background, lending immediacy and directness that give a sense of inevitability to the painful ending.

The central stanza of this poem is based on very clear grammatical parallelism:

"To a Dark Girl," Gwendolyn B. Bennett (1927)

I love you for your brownness
And the rounded darkness of your breast.
I love you for the breaking sadness in your voice
And shadows where your wayward eye-lids rest.

Something of old forgotten queens
Lurks in the lithe abandon of your walk
And something of the shackled slave
Sobs in the rhythm of your talk.

Oh, little brown girl, born for sorrow's mate,
Keep all you have of queenliness,
Forgetting that you once were slave,
And let your full lips laugh at Fate!

The middle stanza, with its balance of repeating phrases, acts as the fulcrum of the poem, balancing between the emotion of the first stanza and the blessing of the third stanza. Sometimes parallel phrases can become too flat or expected, too smooth, but in this second stanza, Bennett uses metrical imbalance (the pentameter in the second line and the tetrameter of the last line) to roughen the stanza. Though the first and third lines are so similar, the metrical difference underscores the sad shock when we get to the fourth line.

The following poem has subtler kinds of parallelism:

"Earth Poem," Mahmoud Darwish (trans. Abdullah Al-Udhari)

A dull evening in a run down village
Eyes half asleep
I recall thirty years

And five wars
I swear the future keeps
My ear of corn
And the singer croons
About a fire and some strangers
And the evening is just another evening
And the singer croons

And they asked him:
Why do you sing?
And he answered:
I sing because I sing

And they searched his chest
But could only find his heart
And they searched his heart
But could only find his people
And they searched his voice
But could only find his grief
And they searched his grief
But could only find his prison
And they searched his prison
But could only find themselves in chains

The archetypal, nursery-rhymish effect of this type of syntax can be especially powerful when used in an unexpected context, as in this political poem. Just as in the anonymous song above, here also the simplicity of the syntax frees the reader to focus on the growing complexity of the imagery, as the prisoner reveals his imprisoners to be the real prisoners.

A more complex kind of parallel syntax is called **chiasmus,** from the Greek letter chi or X. In chiasmus, the parallel elements are criss-crossed. A witty device and a favorite of Alexander Pope, it is so popular that it even has an extensive website devoted to it (www.chiasmus.com). When chiasmus is used well, it has the convincing ring of an inherent truth, as in this rueful remark by Shakespeare's King Richard II, "I wasted time, and now doth time waste me." Shakespeare chose a chiasmus for the last line of his last sonnet:

Sonnet 154, William Shakespeare (1609)

The little Love-god lying once asleep,
Laid by his side his heart-inflaming brand,
Whilst many nymphs that vow'd chaste life to keep
Came tripping by; but in her maiden hand
The fairest votary took up that fire
Which many legions of true hearts had warm'd;
And so the general of hot desire
Was, sleeping, by a virgin hand disarm'd.
This brand she quenched in a cool well by,
Which from Love's fire took heat perpetual,
Growing a bath and healthful remedy
For men diseas'd; but I, my mistress' thrall,
Came there for cure and this by that I prove,
Love's fire heats water, water cools not love.

When parallelism is used to contrast words or ideas it is called antithetical parallelism or antithesis, as in these quotes from poets of the eighteenth century, otherwise known as the "Age of Reason":

Charm strikes the sight, but merit wins the soul
—ALEXANDER POPE

Be cautioned then my Muse, and still retired;
Nor be despised, aiming to be admired.
—ANNE FINCH, COUNTESS OF WINCHELSEA

The parallelism of syntax points out the contrast between surface and reality in Pope's line, and makes the contrast between desire and actuality more striking in the couplet from Finch's "Introduction" to her work. A contemporary of Pope's, Finch was ironically reminding herself that a woman's poetry was unlikely to be admired, no matter how skillful.

At the other end of the poetic spectrum from simple syntax is **hypotaxis** or **complex syntax**—compound sentences with independent and dependent clauses joined by subordinating conjunctions (after, although, as, because, before, how, if, once, since, than, that, though, till, until, when, where, whether, while, etc.). Generally, complex syntax appeals more to the mind than to the emotions. Milton impressed and astonished his literary world by copying the convolutions of Latin syntax into English:

From Paradise Lost, John Milton (1667)

Since first this subject for heroick song
Pleas'd me, long choosing and beginning late,
Not sedulous by nature to indite
Wars, hitherto the only argument
Heroick deem'd, chief mastery to dissect
With long and tedious havock fabled knights
In battles feign'd (the better fortitude
Of patience and heroic martyrdom
Unsung) . . .

It might take some parsing to recognize that "long choosing" and "not sedulous" modify "me," that the clause beginning "hitherto" modifies "wars," which is also the object of "to dissect," and so on. The effect of this learned syntax on the readers of the time was to increase Milton's authority to write about biblical matters.

Hundreds of years later, after the Romantic movement had lent more inherent authority to the individual poet's experience, Hopkins used complex syntax to convey the authenticity of his tortured self-doubt:

"My Own Heart Let Me More Have Pity On," Gerard Manley Hopkins (1883)

My own heart let me more have pity on; let
Me live to my sad self hereafter kind,
Charitable; not live this tormented mind
With this tormented mind tormenting yet.
I cast for comfort I can no more get
By groping round my comfortless, than blind
Eyes in their dark can day or thirst can find
Thirst's all-in-all in all a world of wet.

Soul, self; come, poor Jackself, I do advise
You, jaded, let be; call off thoughts awhile
Elsewhere; leave comfort root-room; let joy size
At God knows when to God knows what; whose smile
's not wrung, see you; unforeseen times rather—as skies
Between pie mountains—lights a lovely mile.

Both complex and simple sentence structure have their place. Notice how "The Garden," below, makes use of both, and of the contrast between them:

From "The Garden," Andrew Marvell (ca. 1650)

Ripe apples drop about my head;
The luscious clusters of the vine
Upon my mouth do crush their wine;
The nectarine and curious peach,
Into my hands themselves do reach;
Stumbling on melons as I pass,
Ensnared with flowers, I fall on grass.

Meanwhile, the mind, from pleasure less,
Withdraws into its happiness:
The mind, that ocean where each kind
Does straight its own resemblance find;
Yet it creates, transcending these,
Far other worlds, and other seas;
Annihilating all that's made
To a green thought in a green shade.

These two stanzas occur one after the other in the middle of a long poem. The first stanza uses simple syntax to give the feeling of bodily reality; four separate sentences, each with a straightforward subject and object, pile on to each other replete with physical images and adjectives suggesting sensation. The second stanza quoted, however, uses the complex structures of hypotaxis to return the reader to the mental realm. There are only two sentences in the stanza, half as many as in the previous stanza. The first sentence introduces the mind, says what it does, and then in lines 3 and 4 returns to define the mind again with a lengthy appositive (a way of describing something again). The second sentence is also half an appositive. If you are rusty on grammar, get your handbooks ready if you want to fully appreciate Marvell's syntactic complexity in this sentence. It starts with a subject-verb phrase ("it creates"), modifies it with a subordinate clause ("transcending these"), then gives us the object ("far other worlds, and other seas"), and then gives us a two-line appositive, restating the idea of "creating other worlds" in a different way that, ironically, echoes the green imagery of the simpler stanza above. Marvell's complete control over both modes allows him to play them off of each other for the maximum good of the poem.

Syntax, like other aspects of English-language poetry, can present a different set of challenges and opportunities for speakers of English as a second language. This poem, by an American poet born in China, directly addresses the difference between Chinese and English syntax:

"Syntax," Wang Ping

She walks to a table
She walk to table

She is walking to a table
She walk to table now

What difference does it make
What difference it make

In Nature, no completeness
No sentence really complete thought

Language, like woman,
Look best when free, undressed.

Wang Ping uses the tension between the two kinds of syntax to render language fresh and unfamiliar. In an interview about this poem, she points out that "she walk to table" is a literal translation of how Chinese syntax works. Like Ernest Fenellosa, who had such an influence on modernist poetry through Ezra Pound, Wang feels that the Chinese language, because of the direct simplicity of its syntax, is especially close to poetry.

Punctuation

Even the voiceless part of grammar—punctuation—can attain new power in a poem. Before computers, when I used to revise my poems on a typewriter, I would have thought nothing of typing an entire poem over four times, just to change one punctuation mark from a comma to a period to a semicolon to a dash and see how it looked in a clean version each time. Each of these punctuation marks has its own tone, feeling, and look on the page, and in a poem those subtle distinctions can be wonderfully magnified. T. S. Eliot once said that he adored semicolons; no wonder! Look at this eloquent semicolon from the third of his *Four Quartets:*

> I do not know much about gods; but I think that the river
> Is a small brown god—sullen, untamed and intractable . . .

Emily Dickinson's dashes are famous—no one else could use them as she did:

> I reckon—when I count at all—
> First—Poets—then the Sun—
> (POEM 569)

Edmund Spenser's love sonnets, the *Amoretti,* use colons in an archaic way that lends an air of triumphant objectivity to the most personal effusions. In his Sonnet 81, written in 1595, "heares" means "hairs," "ye" means "you," "marke" means "notice," "barke" means "boat," "dight" means "decorated," and "spright" means "spirit":

> Fayre is my love, when her fayre golden heares
> With the loose wynd ye waving chance to marke:
> Fayre when the rose in her red cheekes appears,
> Or in her eyes the fyre of love does sparke.
> Fayre when her brest lyke a rich laden barke,
> With pretious merchandize she forth doth lay:
> Fayre when that cloud of pryde, which oft doth dark
> Her goodly light with smiles she drives away.
> But fayrest she, when so she doth display

The gate with pearles and rubyes richly dight:
Throgh which her words so wise do make their way
To beare the message of her gentle spright.
The rest be works of natures wonderment,
But this the worke of harts astonishment.

Punctuation marks, like words, can reveal new depths when you consider their origins. For example, the exclamation point comes from the Latin word *io,* meaning "joy." Written in the margins of dramas to remind actors how to perform certain passages, it took the shape of a capital *I* placed over a lowercase *o,* and eventually evolved into the mark we use today. Though the exclamation point is often snubbed nowadays as an unnecessary indulgence, some passages of poetry manage to use it in ways that evoke the aura of its root meaning:

From "Wedlock," D. H. Lawrence (1918)

But how lovely to be you! Creep closer in, that I am more.
I spread over you! How lovely, your round head, your arms,

Your breasts, your knees and feet! I feel that we
Are a bonfire of oneness, me flame flung leaping round you . . .

Even parentheses can become a powerful poetic device. Imagine e. e. cummings's famous poem without the parentheses:

"O sweet spontaneous," e. e. cummings (1923)

O sweet spontaneous
earth how often have
the
doting

fingers of
prurient philosophers pinched
and
poked

thee
, has the naughty thumb
of science prodded
thy

beauty . how
often have religions taken
thee upon their scraggy knees
squeezing and

buffeting thee that thou mightest conceive
gods
(but
true

to the incomparable
couch of death thy
rhythmic
lover

thou answerest

them only with

spring)

Without the parentheses, much of the humor, beauty, grace, and defiance of this poem would be lost. Among other things, the parentheses evoke the unspeaking quietness of nature; they create a symmetrical counterbalance between the energetic human efforts and the earth's simple, inherent power; and they visually create the image of the earth's fertility, its pregnancy. In this free verse poem, the parentheses are a structural element that repeats:

"Last Hill," Margaret Rockwell (2000)

My love, a last hill
Green,

Crowned with September roses
Where the bold bees linger
Fattening gold in the sun:

Perhaps knowing, perhaps not
(The green, the gold)

Perhaps knowing (perhaps not)
Of that approaching leveller
Called
Cold.

The first set of parentheses creates a symmetrical balance between the abstract pair of phrases "Perhaps knowing, perhaps not" and the concrete images of colors that are hidden in parentheses. If the poem is about the awareness of mortality, it might seem that death is held at bay in the abstract thinking process of "Perhaps knowing, perhaps not," but evident in the physical realities of the colors (which also evoke the first two lines of another poem about impermanence, the lines "Nature's first green is gold, / her hardest hue to hold" in Robert Frost's poem "nothing gold can stay"). In the last stanza, the interruption of the sentence by parentheses shows that the physical reality of death has seeped, like the colors, into the speaker's thoughts; the phrase "perhaps not" evokes death more strongly because it is haunted by the earlier parentheses.

Rhetorical Devices

Some syntactic maneuvers have been used so often in poetry and rhetoric that they have been given special names. Here are a small sampling of the many poetic devices based on rhetoric. They underscore the fact that a poem is a creation not only of words, sounds, and images, but also of thought.

Anadiplosis begins a new sentence or clause with the end of the previous sentence or clause. Sometimes called the "terrace pattern," it is common in classical Hebrew poetry, where it creates a unique mood of incantatory dignity:

I said
I'll never see *Yah*
Yah in the land of the living

In the poem below, it has a wittier effect:

From "Astrophel and Stella," Sir Philip Sidney (1580)

That she, dear she, might take some pleasure of my pain,—
Pleasure might cause her read, reading might make her know,
Knowledge might pity win, and pity grace obtain . . .

Aposiopesis ends a sentence abruptly, as if it has been interrupted, as happens at the end of several stanzas in the following excerpt:

From "Male Nipples," Brenda Hillman

When I first put
My tongue on his (having decided
He is not my mother)—

Oh, the bodies I loved were very tired.
I liked their skin. And
I was no sad animal no graveyard—

—and after you saw that desire
is hell, that the flower of hell
is not hell but a flower, well,

—So I told the little hairs
around his nipple: lie flat! And they did,
like a campfire, without the stories—

those of soldiers in the desert war and often
his left one tastes metallic as in
childhood, when I licked my brother's BB gun

Kept not finishing
        people I loved.
I tried, —but.

The top lip of a Corona beer
Is about the size
Of one of his—

    And after you saw that the flower
    Of hell is desire, the almost, well,
You still had desire—

What effect do the interruptions have on your experience of this passage? Do they give a sense of the difficulty of what is being said, or of the mood of the speaker?

Anacoluthon achieves a similar effect by changing the sentence structure in the middle of a sentence, as if the speaker has been irresistibly drawn away by a new thought:

From "pity this busy monster, manunkind," e. e. cummings (1944)

pity this busy monster, manunkind

not. Progress is a comfortable disease:
your victim (death and life safely beyond)

plays with the bigness of his littleness
—electrons deify one razorblade
into a mountainrange; lenses extend
unwish through curving wherewhen till unwish
returns on its unself.
A world of made
is not a world of born—pity poor flesh

and trees, poor stars and stones, but never this
fine specimen of hypermagical

ultraomnipotence. We doctors know

a hopeless case if—listen: there's a hell
of a good universe next door; let's go

The anacoluthon in the middle of the poem, after "world of born," gives the effect of the speaker being cut off at the beginning of a train of thought that might end up leading to the opposite conclusion, that the animals of the "born" world are better off than humans. This helps pave the way for the tragicomic anacoluthon at the end of the poem, where the speaker's true attitude cuts off the whole charade in midsentence.

Anastrophe is the inversion of usual word order for poetic effect; in this case, it underscores that Desdemona is white-skinned and Othello, the speaker, is not:

Yet I'll not shed her blood,
Nor scar that whiter skin of hers than snow.

As in Latin, changing the word order allows the poet to end a sentence with a particularly strong word or image. The same strategy is evident in the quote from Tim Seibles in the section on breaking syntax, below. In a contemporary poem, the effect of anastrophe is more innovative and daring than it would have been in Shakespeare's time, when word order was generally more flexible.

Syllepsis is the use of a word understood differently in relation to two or more other words which it modifies or governs:

From "The Rape of the Lock," Alexander Pope (1712)

This day, black Omens threat the brightest Fair,
That e'er deserv'd a watchful spirit's care;
Some dire disaster, or by force, or slight;
But what, or where, the fates have wrapt in night.
Whether the nymph shall break Diana's law,
Or some frail China jar receive a flaw;
Or stain her honour or her new brocade;
Forget her pray'rs, or miss a masquerade;
Or lose her heart, or necklace, at a ball;
Or whether Heav'n has doom'd that Shock must fall...

Syllepsis is the perfect device for this part of Pope's mock-epic about a huge Homeric style battle over the cutting of one lock of a woman's hair by an admirer. Each syllepsis exploits the parallel between the tragic and the trivial:

breaking Diana's law (of chastity, since Diana was a virgin goddess) or a vase, staining a dress or one's honor, losing a necklace or a heart.

In the following poem, syllepsis has a very different role:

"The Butcher's Wife," Louise Erdrich

1.
Once, my braids swung heavy as ropes.
Men feared them like the gallows.
Night fell
When I combed them out.
No one could see me in the dark.

Then I stood still
Too long and the braids took root.
I wept, so helpless
The braids tapped deep and flourished.

A man came by with an ox on his shoulder.
He yoked it to my apron
And pulled me from the ground.
From that time on I wound the braids around my head
So that my arms would be free to tend him.

2.
He could lift a grown man by the belt with his teeth.
In a contest, he'd press a whole hog, a side of beef.
He loved his highballs, his herring, and the attentions of women.
He died pounding his chest with no last word for anyone.

The gin vessels in his face broke and darkened. I traced them
Far from that room into Bremen on the Sea.
The narrow streets twisted down to the piers.
And far off, in the black, rocking water, the light of trawlers
Beckoned, like the heart's uncertain signals,
Faint, and final.

The simple syntax in this first section of this poem underscores the innocence and freedom of the girl and young woman. The second section moves almost immediately into syllepsis, in the second line and then at greater length in the third line. The most complex syntax so far in the poem, it helps this section contrast strongly with the first section and creates a sense of abstraction, a distance from the butcher husband so that his death in the following line feels very remote.

Syntax, like diction, is a key part of creating an elevated or colloquial, high or low, elegant or rude "tone" in a poem. In this tour de force of contrasts, Dorothy Parker uses the inverted syntax of eighteenth-century poetry to create the ridiculously "poetic" language that makes the poem work:

"Verse for a Certain Dog," Dorothy Parker (1926)

Such glorious faith as fills your limpid eyes,
Dear little friend of mine, I never knew.
All-innocent are you, and yet all-wise.
(For Heaven's sake, stop worrying that shoe!)
You look about, and all you see is fair;
This mighty globe was made for you alone.
Of all the thunderous ages, you're the heir.
(Get off the pillow with that dirty bone!)

A skeptic world you face with steady gaze;
High in young pride you hold your noble head;
Gayly you meet the rush of roaring days.
(Must you eat puppy biscuit on the bed?)
Lancelike your courage, gleaming swift and strong,
Yours the white rapture of a wingèd soul,
Yours is a spirit like a May-day song.
(God help you, if you break the goldfish bowl!)

"Whatever is, is good"—your gracious creed.
You wear your joy of living like a crown.
Love lights your simplest act, your every deed.
(Drop it, I tell you—put that kitten down!)
You are God's kindliest gift of all—a friend.

Your shining loyalty unflecked by doubt,
You ask but leave to follow to the end.
(Couldn't you wait until I took you out?)

The inverted syntax of such phrases as "all innocent are you," "lancelike your courage," and "high you hold" is a perfect way to create poetic irony. Why do you think that Parker starts to replace this syntax with more familiar syntax ("you wear," "love lights," "you ask") in the last stanza? Would the poem be as funny if she continued the inversions right through to the end?

Stretching and Breaking Language

Unlike ordinary language, poetry can get away with unorthodox syntax sometimes because poems outlast syntactic habits ("that the small rain down can rain"—anonymous, sixth century) and sometimes because poetry is allowed to experiment ("a rose is a rose is a rose"—Gertrude Stein). And we will see in the chapter on exploratory poetry (chapter 10) what breaking syntax completely can do.

One simple but powerful unorthodox syntactic technique, pioneered by Audre Lorde, is to use the same word as part of two different syntactic units. This technique, a more intense relative of anadiplosis, has also been used recently by the young poet Matthea Harvey, who calls it the **hinge** technique. Such poems have a distinct grammatical identity; while most poems would make sense if you took away the line breaks and typed them out as prose, poems that use this strategy would not:

"Letting Go," Audre Lorde

The first time he saw a bell do a full somersault
Against the sky everything afterwards felt too
Flat on his back during break he saw clouds
Regardless of whether his eyes were open or
Not the geese on the pond below nor the plants
Around it reflected his new perspective he expected
Them to swim at a slant or to detect a dizziness in
The daisies were partly covered by a late snow but
Their yellow centers shone through like bells in

Fog mutes the pealing but can't completely conceal
It made sense to him the first time he was told that
Bells were made loud so the Lord would listen
Because it did often seem like he wasn't paying any
Attention and discipline and a pair of leather gloves
Were required for beginners lessons in the tower
Later he went without and got rope burns to show for
This didn't hurt him what did was letting go when
He wanted to hang on and go clanging up into the sky

Lorde uses words and phrases including "flat," "not," "the daisies," "fog," and "attention" in two separate senses, making her syntax completely dependent on the line breaks in an unusual way. Each line has so much momentum that the initial dislocation is soon forgotten in the new rush of meaning, but the effect is that the reader is helplessly swung back and forth. The syntactic dizziness perfectly conveys the feeling of disorientation the bell-player feels, high in the tower with bottomless sky and the swinging of bells.

It's possible to stretch the meaning-making potential of syntactic structures without breaking them. Though "natural" word order says we need to always put the words in the order subject-verb-object (Jane ate the bear), in fact we are more used to hearing "unnatural syntax" than we may think we are. Familiar old poems and songs frequently invert (reverse) the expected word order: "My country 'tis of thee . . . of thee I sing"; "From this valley they say you are going" (from the song "Red River Valley"). Readers know how to understand unusual syntax when they want to, and conscious choices of word order can become a vibrant element of a poem's syntax. In the following passage, Tim Seibles does not violate syntax but rearranges the word order in a challenging way, so that a surprising image is postponed to the very end:

For all the world
What looked exactly like gold leaf,
The chef arranged on her sushi.

This strategy makes language seem odd and unfamiliar without violating the reader's trust in grammar. Robert Duncan used this technique to the point where the reader can feel pleasantly dizzy but not abandoned, as in this excerpt from *The Opening of the Field:*

She it is Queen Under The Hill
whose hosts are a disturbance of words within words
that is a field folded.

It is only a dream of the grass blowing
east against the source of the sun
in an hour before the sun's going down

whose secret we see in a children's game
of ring a round of roses told.

It is something of a truism of creative writing classes that syntax and word order should always be "natural," the way we normally speak. But variations in syntax have the potential to give words a lot of impact. A surprise can be prepared, a rhythm can be cultivated, an important word can be saved for the end. Every aspect of syntax is available for artistic use.

When syntax is preserved, while the meanings of the words themselves move to unexpected places, syntax itself becomes the most meaningful actor in the poem. Such a poem can create a shocking sense of x-raying the way we usually think:

From "Plasma," Barrett Watten

A paradox is eaten by the space around it.

I'll repeat what I said.

To make a city into a season is to wear sunglasses inside a volcano.

He never forgets his dreams.
The effect of the lack of effect.

He would live against sentences.
Trees here of leaf the several speakers.
Tiered objects of her talking and water below.
Trees of sound to broaden shadow.
Damp walls will quiet things.

Ron Silliman writes that this poem taught him "how to read within the sentence as a dynamic architecture": it allowed him to feel what sentences are like *as sentences,* without being distracted by what particular sentences are about.

e. e. cummings's famous passage on syntax, quoted later in this chapter, encapsulated the idea that logical patterns of syntax can interfere with the immediacy of experience, and foreshadowed developments in contemporary poetry. Playing with syntax can sometimes make poetry feel more directly accessible, bypassing the requirements of the logical mind. The current tendency to write poetry that is freer of traditional conventions of syntax and grammar may be a sign of the times; an article in the *New York Times* quoted a young blogger remarking with affectionate wonder, "I think it's nice how older people use grammar in their emails." But on the other hand, it is hard to imagine poetry forsaking entirely the strong grammatical bones that, though changing over time, have formed meaningful language as long as the language has existed and which, when followed respectfully, can lend such simple dignity and accessible beauty to poetry. This area, like so many others, is one where poets have aesthetic choices to make—choices that work best, for the sake of each individual poem, when we are educated about many possibilities.

Rhetorical Structure and Strategy

Every time you write a poem, and probably before you even begin, you make a myriad of even more fundamental choices about its rhetorical stance and structure. Many of these choices are unconscious, based on ideas of "what a poem is" that you have absorbed long before. To make these choices conscious, at least once in a while, can be refreshing and even eye-opening. For example:

Is your poem written from the first-, second-, or third-person point of view? If it is from the first- or second-person point of view, who is the poem addressing? From any point of view, who is the implied audience for the poem? Remember that the audience may be quite different from who is addressed.

What is the grammatical tense and time frame of the poem?

What is the rhetorical stance of the poem? How is it trying to engage the reader? For example, does it aim to move the reader emotionally, persuade the reader to action, or argue a cause and effect? Where does the tone of the poem fall along the spectrum from irony to sincerity?

And finally, what are the rhetorical turns taken in the poem? How does the poem shape itself so that, when one has finished reading, one feels the poem is over, that something has happened, something has changed? For example, Michael Theune's book *Structure and Surprise* describes nine kinds of rhetorical turns, the most important of which are the ironic turn, the dialectical turn, and the descriptive turn. In a poem using the ironic turn, the second part of the poem (which can be any length, from half the poem to just a line or two) undercuts or alters what has come before, like the punch line of a joke. In a poem using the dialectical turn, the first part of the poem sets up one voice or attitude, and the second offers a very different tone of voice or perspective (the "turn" in a sonnet is often of this type). In a poem using the descriptive turn, the speaker describes a scene, object, or memory, and then turns to meditate on its meaning.

QUESTIONS FOR MEDITATION OR DISCUSSION

Simply by juxtaposing elements in a certain order, a poem creates meaningful relationships between them. "Minimal poems," the specialty of contemporary poet Aram Saroyan, developed an entire poetics based on this fact. Here is a complete poem from his 1966 series "5 Poems":

> cat
> book
> city

How do you think syntax is at work in this poem?

If you usually break syntax, write a poem that respects it. If you usually respect it, write a poem that breaks it. How uncomfortable did this feel? Why do you think you normally make the choice you do? Are there ethical, political, or other deeper issues tied in with your attitude toward syntax?

Look through poems in this book for examples of the ironic turn, the dialectical turn, and the descriptive turn. Does every poem you encounter fit into one of these three categories?

QUOTES

The pull between sound and syntax creates a kind of musical tension in the language that interests me.

—Marilyn Hacker

Poetry . . . is a vocabulary based on the noun as prose is essentially and determinately and vigorously not based on the noun.
—Gertrude Stein

Since feeling is first,
Who pays any attention
To the syntax of things
Will never wholly kiss you
—e. e. cummings

You can be a little ungrammatical if you come from the right part of the country.
—Robert Frost

A cloud of philosophy can be condensed into a drop of grammar.
—Ludwig Wittgenstein

And the words slide into the slots ordained by syntax, and glitter as with atmospheric dust with those impurities which we call meaning.
—Anthony Burgess

Words of course there are some
hard as granite will break off
and leave a syntax open
and precarious as cliffwork
to the sea or air around
—Theodore Enslin

The poem, a prolonged hesitation between sound and sense.
—Paul Valéry

POETRY PRACTICES

(Group) Group Cut-Up. Everyone in the group writes a short poem on the same subject. Cut the lines apart and mix the strips of paper together. Now recombine the lines to create new poems.

(Group) Two-Tone Poems. Write two poems, at least 10 lines each, that say the same thing but in two different tones (for example, admiration and disgust, anger and acceptance). While both poems will "say" the same thing as much as possible, you will subtly change the poem's attitude, and hence its *real* "meaning," by using a variety of poetic techniques, such as different line-length, meter, imagery, word-music, tropes, syntax, idioms, and connotations. To make sure the tones are identifiable and clearly distinguishable from each other, test it out on someone else afterward.

Syntax Switch. Write a poem using mostly simple clauses on an equal footing with each other. Rewrite the same poem using mostly complex sentences with subordinate clauses. Or, write a poem using mostly complex sentences with subordinate clauses. Rewrite the same poem using mostly simple clauses on an equal footing with each other.

Playing Pope. Write a poem of at least 20 lines in rhymed couplets, using several of the rhetorical tricks that Pope used to structure his heroic couplets: chiasmus, parallelism, and antithesis.

Marking. Write a poem in which at least one punctuation mark, or as many as you like, is/are crucial to the experience of the poem.

Mix It Up. Write a poem that makes use either of Audre Lorde's "hinge" technique or of inverted word order.

CHAPTER 10

Stop Making Sense: Exploratory Poetics and Poetic Experiments

In all my years teaching poetry writing, I have found that the most common mistake beginners make is that they are inhibited when it comes to playing with language. Instead of enjoying the chance to write with originality and freshness, they slip into tired, predictable ways of putting things. One of the best cures for the cliché is to cast off your expectations of what language is supposed to do, and instead spend some time reading the kind of poetry often called "experimental" or "exploratory."

Making sense is not the point in exploratory poems. "It's not I doing it all, the buttering and alphabetizing." Meaning emanates from the words, but it is not the primary value; heightening the reader's experience of language is more important. "It takes leaning a long bicycle against a smudged wall and stumbling over a bent bicycle beside a sucking ditch to distinguish between against and beside." Language becomes heightened when words are liberated from the automatic habits of conventional usage. "The beginner feels skin and sees trail, the clouds shift and shadows crouch in the swing of opportunity, cynicism is out of place." In fact, trying to make logical sense as a reader will probably only distance you from an exploratory poem. You are meant to experience it, with all its ellipses or disjunctions, its mystery or obscurity, and, especially, its playfulness. "Plan with optimism, a new note, singing."

Maybe when you read these interspersed quotes from Lyn Hejinian's beautiful book *The Beginner,* you found that the words gained a kind of shimmering independence from their meanings. Meanings can be found in these sentences, but they don't get in the way of your experience of the words *as* words. You have no doubt had a similar experience reading the poetry of Shakespeare, or Audre Lorde, or another more conventional poet. Making language come alive is part of what all good poetry does. But exploratory poetry does it quite differently—by exploring language rather than using language according to the rules, by making language itself the subject.

Sometimes while listening to this kind of poetry, even though the poet may be reading quite fast, I find myself listening more and more slowly until, partway through the reading, I feel I have become so slowed down that I am able to do all my understanding of the poem not between sentences or phrases but between syllables. Listening to the following poem read by the poet, I felt the various meanings the sounds and words evoked flow through me without having to be compared to other meanings on the basis of sense:

From "Case in Point," John Wilkinson

Ingratiating sleep, sleep carrying out,
Thumbed its sandstone but its well-loved face
In piles, in barbs of millet—

Sleep-rolled buttons, bleeding heart
Vibrates for its limited best
Retention for to smooth, or if venturing down

Look the stonechats hull lickety-split—
Indigestible rosaries of
Pips annoy these dream scavengers, laid-back

Pioneers skid awake. Apply my hopeless pads
But wager none, give package flowers,
A stereo print of deep forest

Replicates as life-long or wherever sleep,
Either collapsed, either perfect,
Cahooting over the blocked hopper, stressful,

Wrecked on a cheek shore this mild Odysseus,
Holds of grain have burst,
Carpeting the way to a shed of caresses.

Shuffle their point ribcage! Dream
Dahlia-spread like one ribbed echographically
From birth. Husk smack.

This poem subverts our grammatical and syntactical expectations, and declines to provide a logically cohesive narrative, with the aim of exploring our own consciousness. As we read a phrase such as "cahooting over the blocked hopper," we feel how it plays with the sounds of language (the "o's" in "blocked hopper"), with the mechanics of word construction (making a verb out of "cahoots"), with the radically differing connotations evoked by the words "hopper" and "cahoots," and with imagery (the idea of a hopper blocked with corn or coal). These maneuvers allow the poet and the reader to pass from one sphere of language to an entirely different sphere and then another, motivated only by a sense of freedom and exploration.

Poems such as this one are rooted in the belief that a reader should be an active collaborator in the production of the poem's meaning and not just a passive consumer. The "difficulty" of exploratory poetry is part of the point.

Poetry and Meaning

"Exploratory poetry" is a term for poetry that takes playing with language seriously. Like most literary labels, it is a simplistic term for a complex group of poetic impulses and movements; many poets who are thought of as exploratory—"experimental," "avant-garde," or "Language" poets—would resist these labels. This kind of poetics has roots in surrealism and modernist experiments, such as the following prose poem:

"Dirt and Not Copper," Gertrude Stein (1914)

Dirt and not copper makes a color darker. It makes the shape so heavy and makes no melody harder.
It makes mercy and relaxation and even a strength to spread a table fuller. There are more places not empty. They see cover.

Stein's wordplay here links words that have little logical connection, creating, for example, a parallel between "color darker" and "no melody harder." Nevertheless, we experience something that feels like understanding as we imagine a color denser than the pattern of any melody; wild associative leaps take the place of more ordinary kinds of connections.

In the following poem, meaning is created almost entirely by connotation, sound, and imagery. It is more like the meaning of a sculpture than the meaning of referential language:

"Signatures of Doctrine," Rosemarie Waldrop

& approach be biblical
& couch existed existential
& days determined fainting & feared figs
& food for honey is like loss
& made nothing of one on other olives
& seizures set spells & table tea
& that that the the three

Though the syntax and thread of imagery is nonreferential, a constellation of related objects and words creates the unified sense of an archaic, Mediterranean, biblical space: "honey," "figs," "olives," as well as the words "biblical" and "doctrine." The column of ampersands evokes the genealogies in the early books of the Bible. The poem seems to tell of some kind of crisis of energy or possibly of faith, with the words "couch," "fainting," "loss," and "seizures." But the last line, with its repetitions, iambic meter, and couplet rhyme, as well as its evocation of the Trinity with the number three, seems to add a note of peace and resolution.

To analyze the poem in this way is not to "explain" it, any more than to analyze the effects in a more traditional poem is to explain it. Perhaps even more insistently than a referential poem, an exploratory poem insists on its own being, its own tangible existence apart from our interpretations of it. It may be unlikely that Waldrop thought about these meanings as she created the poem. But they can be found there, as a way of helping explain the effect of the poem on a reader, just as moving and strong undercurrents of meaning can be found under the surface in a referential poem. In fact, it can be argued that the most important part of a referential poem is usually what is unsaid—the deeper subtexts—and that a nonreferential poem makes it a bit easier to reach that deeper level of engagement with a poem.

Procedural, Nonce, Found, and Genre Forms

Experimental legend Jackson MacLow describes the process of writing poetry as "a dialectic between making and letting be." Some exploratory poems fall more heavily on the making side, and some more heavily on the side of letting be. In the latter category are **procedural poems,** poems that rely on chance operations to open language to the personal unconscious or even, some feel, to the collective unconscious we all share. Antonin Artaud's group game of "Exquisite Corpse" is one of the first and probably the most famous of these. Each person writes a line, then passes the poem to the next person, folding the page down to cover what they wrote. After everyone has written a line, someone reads the text aloud. The game can be played with chance slightly diminished by choosing a topic, a first or last word for each line, or a word that must be used.

In Tristan Tzara's classic procedure "Hat," a poet throws words from a source text (a poem, a newspaper article, the first chapter of a novel) into a hat and picks them out at random to generate a new text. More recent poets have developed such procedures in various directions, including **S + 7,** an amusing game in which you choose a source poem and substitute for each important word a word of the same part of speech chosen from seven words away in either direction in the dictionary.

Here is Harryette Mullen's prose poem version of a famous Shakespeare sonnet, which uses a technique of word substitution that works similarly to S + 7, though it doesn't follow such a rigid scheme:

"Dim Lady," Harryette Mullen

My honeybunch's peepers are nothing like neon. Today's special at Red Lobster is redder than her kisser. If Liquid paper is white, her racks are institutional beige. If her mop were Slinkys, dishwater Slinkys would grow on her noggin. I have seen tablecloths in Shakey's Pizza Parlors, red and white, but no such picnic colors do I see in her mug. And in some minty-fresh mouthwashes there is more sweetness than in the garlic breeze my main squeeze wheezes. I love to hear her rap, yet I'm aware that Muzak has a hipper beat. I don't know any Marilyn Monroes. My ball and chain is plain from head to toe. And yet, by gosh, my scrumptious Twinkie has as much sex appeal for me as any lanky model or platinum movie idol who's hyped beyond belief.

S + 7 was devised by members of Oulipo, a group of writers and mathematicians founded in Paris in 1960 which has had a strong influence on contemporary procedural poetry. The name stands for Ouvrior de Litterature Potentielle (Workshop of Potential Literature), and the focus of the group was to experiment with the effects of constraint on poetry. Oulipo inventions also included the lipogram, a text written without particular letters, such as Christian Bok's *Eunoia*, discussed later in this chapter. Some procedures are devised for one poem only: Joan Retallack's "AIDS/Disappearance" is an elegy for a friend who died of AIDS. It is based in part on a found text from the essay "The Atomic Theory and the Fundamental Principles underlying the Description of Nature" by physicist Niels Bohr, in *The Philosophical Writings of Niels Bohr.*

AID/I/SAPPEARANCE
for Stefan Fitterman

1. in contrast with the demand of continuity in the customary description
2. of nature the indivisibility of the quantum of action requires an essential
3. element of discontinuity especially apparent through the discussion of the
4. nature of light she said it's so odd to be dying and laughed still it's early
5. late the beauty of nature as the moon waxes turns to terror when it wanes
6. or during eclipse or when changing seasons change making certain things
7. disappear and there is no place to stand on and strangely we're glad

AIDS
for tefn Fttermn

1. n contrt wth the emn of contnuty n the cutomry ecrpton
2. of nture the nvblty of the quntum of cton requre n eentl
3. element of contnuty epeclly pprent through the cuon of the
4. nture of lght he t o o t be yng n lughe tll t erly
5. lte the beuty of nture the moon wxe turn to terror when t wne
6. or urng eclpe or when chngng eon chnge mkng certn thng
7. pper n there no plce to tn on n trngely we're gl

BHJCERT
fo fn Fmn

1. n on w mn of onnuy n uomy pon
2. of nu nvly of qunum of on qu n nl

3. lmn of onnuy plly ppn oug uon of
4. nu of lg o o yng n lug ll ly
5. l uy of nu moon wx un o o wn wn
6. o ung lp o wn ngng on ng mkng n ng
7. pp n no pl o n on n ngly w gl

F G K Q U

o n mn

1. no n w m no on ny no my pon
2. o n nvly o nm o on n nl
3. lm no onny plly pp no on o
4. no l o o yn nl ll ly
5. l y o n moon wx no own wn
6. o n l pow n n no n n mn n n
7. pp n no pl o no n n nly w l

L P V

o n mn

1. no n w m no on ny no my on
2. o n ny o nm o on n n
3. m no onny y no on o
4. no o o y n n y
5. y o n moon wx no own wn
6. o now n n no n n mn n n
7. n no o no n n n y w

M O W

n

1. n n n n n y n y n
2. n n y n n n n
3. n n n y y n n
4. n y n n y
5. y n n x n n n
6. n n n n n n n n n
7. n n n n n n y

N X

1. y y
2. y
3. y y
4. y y
5. y
6.
7. y

Y

1.
2.
3.
4.
5.
6.
7.

Retallack writes, "The disappearance moves through the letters of the alphabet (and the source text) in this way: Beginning with letters A I D S, it spreads to adjoining letters B H J C E R T, to F G K Q U, to L P V, to M O W, to N X, to Y." Of course, what this means is that after enough letters of the alphabet disappear, the only letters left are *o* and *y*. Finally these expressions of sadness disappear as well.

Many procedural forms look very similar to traditional forms, such as the chant or sestina (a sestina by Oulipo poet Harry Mathews is discussed in the section on repeating forms). Others have forms that are easily perceived:

"Call Me Ishmael," Jackson MacLow

Circulation. And long long
Mind every
Interest Some how mind and every long

Coffin about little little
Money especially
I shore, having money about especially little

Cato a little little
Me extreme
I sail have me an extreme little

Cherish and left, left,
Myself extremest
It see hypos myself and extremest left,

City a land. Land.
Mouth; east,
Is spleen, hand mouth; an east, land.

A kind of super-acrostic, this clever poem consists of a ritual spelling out of the famous opening sentence of Melville's *Moby Dick* (the poem's title), so that it enacts itself in each stanza without ever speaking itself. The decision to use one word to stand for each letter, and to maintain those words within each stanza but to change them from stanza to stanza, makes the poem into a series of unique permutations that may be seen as a comment on the way our identity is constantly constructed anew.

Some procedural poets' work is faithful to the computer-generated or pulled-out-of-a-hat gifts of chance or the collective unconscious; others use these procedures as the starting point for a poem and might take it a long way from where it began. This poem is from a long series of poems in the same invented form:

From "Isotopes," Dan Zimmerman

W A V E
O B I T
M O O R
B A L E

I owe, to a verbal mob,
a Babel movie or two

above a limbo tower
or below a movie bat.
I've a bramble to woo,
a bamboo tower, live
owl tier above a mob,
brow to a limbo eave.
move a wit, able boor,
rove a loom, bait a web:
we roil above a tomb;
we brim a love taboo.
be a boa, violet worm:
I leave a bomb or two.

Each line of the poem uses each letter of the wordsquare once. The result is a poem incorporating an uncanny overlap of sounds and feelings, a deep exploration of one corner of the language.

The reader is also well aware of the constraint operating in Christian Bok's tour de force of prose poetry, *Eunoia.* Bok's work here is influenced by two famous novels by George Perec, one missing the letter E and one missing all the other vowels. *Euonia* has a chapter for each vowel in the alphabet that includes *only* that vowel. Here are the openings of two chapters:

CHAPTER I for Dick Higgins

Writingis inhibiting. Sighing, I sit, scribbling in ink
this pidgin script. I sing with nihilistic witticism,
disciplining signs with trifling gimmicks—impish
hijinks which highlight stick sigils. Isn't it glib?
Isn't it chic? I fit chil writing shtick which might instill priggish misgiv-
ings in critics blind with hindsight. I dismiss nit-
picking criticism which flirts with philistinism. I
bitch; I kibitz—griping whilst criticizing dimwits,
sniping whilst indicting nitwits, dismissing simplistic thinking, in which phillipic wit is still illicit.

CHAPTER O for Yoko Ono

Loops on bold fonts now form lots of words for books.
Books form cocoons of comfort—tombs to hold book-

> worms. Profs from Oxford show frosh who do post-
> docs how to gloss works of Wordsworth. Dons who
> work for proctors or provosts do not fob off school to
> work in crosswords, nor do dons go off to dorm
> rooms to loll on cots. Dongs go crosstown to look for
> bookshops known to stock lots of topnotch goods:
> cookbooks, workbooks—room on room of how-to
> books for jocks (how to jog, how to box), books on
> pro sports, golf or polo. Old colophons . . .

Clearly there is great skill and ingenuity at work here, not to mention patience. (In his essay "How to Write Euonia," Bok lists as step 5, "Work on these stories everyday for seven years. Work only at night between the hours of 11:00 P.M. and 5:00 A.M . . .")

As Jena Osman explains, procedural poems "seem to diminish or completely eliminate authorial intention . . . [in the] belief that systems of 'constraint' . . . reveal something in language that our conventional usages might occlude." In this way, procedural poets have something in common with formalist poets generally: any poet who writes in "traditional" form would probably agree that one of the main appeals of writing in form is that something larger, or smaller, than your own individual voice is given a part in the poem's composition. Poets who write in form have all had experiences when the need to find a word that rhymes or fits a certain metrical pattern reveals an unexpected possibility that seems to come from outside our usual way of thinking.

Many of the forms invented by exploratory poets—from the Oulipo poets to Jackson MacLow—are surprisingly close in structure to traditional forms. Or maybe not so surprisingly. After all, as revolutionary as the philosophy and attitudes of procedural poetry may be, all poets are still limited to working with the same languages, the same words and sounds, the same mathematical possibilities of arrangement, and the same brain structures and body rhythms. While coediting *An Exaltation of Forms,* a book devoted to the variety of poetic forms, I conducted an active search among exploratory poets for innovative kinds of poetic forms. After several years of inquiries, most of what emerged involved innovative compositional methods rather than innovative kinds of form; perhaps there really are a limited number of possible ways of arranging words into poems.

Exploratory poems, with their unique ability to force writers and readers to focus on painful and alienating aspects of contemporary language, or on new ways of understanding poetry, have a strongly democratic, even revolutionary role to play. They can make us aware of oppressive language and stiflingly habitual thought patterns. If you are feeling stuck in a formal rut, inventing your own procedural technique or using one pioneered by an exploratory poet can show you a new way to relate to the formal potential of poetry. Exploratory poets tend to be passionate about poetry's potential to open people's minds to new ways of thinking; their emphasis on the importance of creative freedom has been both influential and salutary.

Nonce Forms

Many exploratory poems, such as Retallack's AIDS elegy, are written in **nonce forms.** A nonce form is simply a form that you, the poet, invent for a particular poem—"for the nonce," meaning, "for now"—and don't use again. Nonce forms don't have to be exploratory; they can be as simple as inventing a stanza form that rhymes in a certain pattern, or uses a certain order of line-lengths. Sometimes a nonce form can arise while you are in the process of working on a poem, and sometimes you can think it out ahead of time. Inventing your own form can be one of the most empowering and liberating activities for a poet who is just beginning to learn forms. Sonia Sanchez told me that she always asks her students to invent a nonce form, since it is the best way for them to feel as if the tools of poetic form are truly *theirs.*

Don't worry too much about pure originality in your nonce form. As discussed above, there are really only a limited number of formal materials available: meter, line length, rhyme, stanza length, refrain, and various other kinds of repetition. But the combinations of these elements with each other and with words are infinite. Concentrate on using the materials to create the effect you want, as if you were a painter working with different colors, or an architect using design elements to create a building.

I often find it helpful to think metaphorically when creating a nonce form for a particular poem. If I want the poem to be upbeat, I might think metaphorically and choose a rising and expansive rhythm. If the theme of a poem reminds me in some metaphorical way of baskets or weaving, I might think of using terza rima, which interweaves stanzas, overlapping different threads somewhat like a basket. This kind of metaphorical form can be evident on the surface—like the shape of the wreath commemorating the murdered teenager in Marilyn Nelson's crown of sonnets "A Wreath for Emmett Till"—or it can remain a secret, unspoken aspect of the poem, like the hidden name of Yolek in Anthony Hecht's sestina.

Some nonce forms are conceived with the poem; others develop during the process of rewriting, sometimes after multiple revisions. Either way, nonce forms can be so engrossing to work on that it is easy to forget they don't have an existence independent of you. Since, in this book, you have already learned a wide basic vocabulary of tools and strategies, you are in a good position to put the needs of a particular poem first as you create a nonce form.

Found and Genre Poems

A **found poem** is any poem that is made up of language found elsewhere. It can be language from a lecture, from overheard speech, from a classic or contemporary book, from a catalog, a medical textbook, a law brief, a child's story, a political speech, a newspaper, a sermon, etc. etc. etc. Much found poetry is not formal; two of the most well-known examples on the Internet are free verse poems made up of excerpts from speeches by, respectively, President George W. Bush and Secretary of Defense Donald Rumsfeld.

However, much found poetry does turn out to be formal (structured by repetition) because the very act of finding language often either borrows or imposes a form. An example of a poet borrowing a form is Charles Bernstein's poem consisting of a list of names of businesses taken from the yellow pages that all begin with the word "Bob's" ("Bob's Body Shop," "Bob's Car Wash," etc.). An example of a poet imposing a form is when Jen Bervin, following the procedure that poet Ronald Johnson did earlier with Milton's *Paradise Lost,* creatively erased most of Shakespeare's sonnets. Bervin's book *Nets* prints the sonnets in white ink; on a transparent oversheet, certain words she has chosen to catch in her **nets** are printed in black. Here is Shakespeare's Sonnet 15, with her version of it:

When I consider every thing that grows
Holds in perfection but a little moment,
That this huge stage presenteth nought but shows
Whereon **the stars** in secret influence comment;
When I perceive that men as plants increase,
Cheered and check'd even by **the self-same sky,**
Vaunt in their youthful sap, at height decrease,
And wear their brave state out of memory;
Then the conceit of this inconstant stay
Sets you most rich in youth before my sight,

Where wasteful Time debateth with Decay,
To change your day of youth to sullied night;
And all in war with Time **for love of you,**
As he takes from you, I engraft you new.

On the transparent oversheet, over the white text of the sonnet, appears an evocative minimalist poem that captures, as do many of the nets, some essence of the original:

Sonnet 15

the stars

the selfsame sky

for love of you

Because of the consistency with which Bevins repeats her procedure, I think of *Nets* as essentially a book of formal poetry. Whether or not her nets would stand on their own without Shakespeare is a moot point; they are perpetually wedded to the original sonnets, and if they borrow some of their formality from that fact, they are entitled to it by virtue of the marriage.

Found poems can be extremely fun to write. For one thing, they get you in the habit of thinking creatively during every moment of your daily life. Every construction sign, notice board, bit of graffiti, license plate, or other bit of language you pass during your day is a potential poem. After doing some found poetry exercises, you are likely to find that your mind is buzzing and the world seems packed with poetry. To discover or create a formal design as part of your found poems can add another layer of creative pleasure for you and your readers.

A more active way to create a found poem is to write an **echo poem,** built by a procedure akin to the Oulipo game S + 7, but with more freedom in the choice of words:

"Pledge: 1," Michael Magee

I plug elegance
two thief rag
off-Dionysus tastes of America
in tune theory public

four widgets hands
one day shun
on dirge odd
ring the busy bell
with lip hurting
and just this
for all

This poem is part of a series of 16 poems, all echoing the pledge in different ways. Like so many of the procedural forms that "operate" on language, the poem is both funny and somber, a chance to spoof and mock and take off on serious language that, at its most successful, also offers a serious critique of that language.

A more tangential relation to found language appears in the popular type of poem that I have called a **genre poem.** These poems borrow a form, and often a style, a tone, a physical layout, and even particular words and phrases, from a nonliterary genre, or kind, of language. Examples would be poems that look and act like letters, recipes, newspaper articles, wedding invitations, *TV Guide* reviews, catalogs, and so on. Genre poems are sometimes thought of as forms, and writing them can feel as if one is writing a form, because of the element of copying. However, while a genre may involve formal elements (for example, the listing of ingredients in a recipe), there is always much more to a successful genre poem than simply the structural repetition of form. Here is one, from a book of poems about the life of Sylvia Plath:

"Wedding Invitation III," Cathy Bowman

Mr. and Mrs. Naked and Bald
have the wind sneer of announcing
the opaque belly-scale
of their daughter
Dark Flesh, Dark Pairing
to
Easter Egg, the Ill-Starved Thing
on Sunday, the fish-tail of September
The Suck of the Sea, New Jersey

While the stanza form does have some visual formal elements, it is mostly the replication of the tone, syntax, and vocabulary that creates the relationship between this genre poem and the original model. The same would be true of most genre poems.

Primary Process

In ways ranging from found language to procedures to simple openness to the play of the individual unconscious, exploratory poetry tends to tap into, and connect with, the kind of dream state that Freud called "primary process," as does the following poem:

"Special Tales in Ten Lines," Margo Berdeshevsky

Rapunzel's hair goes gray. No horse riding a white knight—gallops.
Busy for a second coming, stung by wasps of dawn, sun will have bees in
 it.

Not milkwood or shine as mama's taffeta supper gown. In all of modern
 art
is there promise clean as the impressionist's window, or secret as a room of

caged autumn? In a fairy tale are bluebeards, bears & dragons & villains &
swords, gold & power, frogs & cookies, spinning wheels, death, slippers. In

a life—that & the repetitious yellow we cling to:mimosa, mimosa,
 mimosa.
I ask the blind, what is pretty? Stop counting the dust. Oh where is
the gazelle's

thin ankled canter? Where, my coach of mice to tempt me? Poor bleeding
 little
mouse, us. And another, climbing, enraging the leg it mistakes for mother.

Poet Kimiko Hahn has used a classical Japanese form called the **zuihitsu,** whose name translates "running brush," as in "following the impulse of the brush," to access her own stream of associations:

From "Wellfleet, Midsummer," Kimiko Hahn

0
At low tide, this marsh pools around the road, the vein from the illicit
cottage to the unfeeling world.

8
It is the heart-that-is-afraid-to-be-heard, this bridge over the salt marsh at
high tide. Still—it is passable.

3
He picks up a box-turtle in the middle of the road. He's fifty-two but
believes it will bring childhood back in a box.
12
From grasses fretting with oysters and crabs, the mud stutters and I can
tell you wait for another dusk to ask me. And I am not impatient.

14
At dawn, wading in the bay's shallows, I am pinched by something
sharp—I still feel beside myself.

The *zuihitsu* is a form originally cultivated by women, and Hahn associates the frequent complexities of women's multitasking lives with the form's capacious randomness, its capacity to absorb many and sometimes conflicting feelings and images. She writes, "I've always been interested in a sort of dialectic: where there's blurring and ambiguity, there's, finally, clarity. Where there's contradiction, there's clarity. Where there's intuition, there's reason. Fragmentation, wholeness. All these things can coexist."

Arielle Greenberg also thinks of poetry as a way of combining the apparently uncombinable. She describes her exploratory writing process as "winding": "for awhile, I called my poems 'winders,' for lack of a better term, because I often start with two or three very disparate ideas/bits of language and the goal, like in a game or puzzle, is for me to try to wind them together like the ribbons on a maypole, not so they blend together, but so that they complement and play off one another throughout the poem. At the center of that winding is the pole, some kind of honesty. While I try to let the language get the best of me, to let it take me places I had no idea I could go before beginning the poem, I try to stay mindful, to stay grounded in honesty, and in humor, which may be the same thing." You can read Greenberg's poem "The Meter of the Night Sky" in chapter 14, "The Metrical Palette."

When I was a child I used to love to repeat words over and over to myself until they sounded completely unfamiliar: "iron, iron, iron, iron, iron, iron, iron, iron, iron, iron, iron, iron, iron, iron, iron, iron, iron, iron." One of the strangest capacities of language is its disorienting quality, where words that we take for granted, as if they were solid ground, can so easily begin to move under our feet and reveal the size of the universe stretching underneath them. Simply to explore language for its own sake can be one of the most liberating approaches to writing a poem. Freed from their usual primary obligation to logical meaning, words become free to interrelate to one another in fresh and exciting ways, and you can take on a less controlling role, almost as if the language itself were doing the writing.

To become a reader of exploratory poetry and to learn from its fresh creative power, don't let yourself be intimidated by a poem's abandonment of ordinary language conventions. Let the words prod and poke you out of your habitual ways of seeing and thinking. At its best, an exploratory poem can function like a zen **koan,** one of the riddles that spiritual seekers ponder in order to free themselves from the desire for meaning. It can remind us what it is like to experience life without centering all meaning around our own ego, without expectations or demands.

QUESTIONS FOR MEDITATION OR DISCUSSION

Throughout this book, there are other "exploratory poems" illustrating other aspects of poetry. When you encountered those poems, did you respond differently than you did to the exploratory poems in this chapter? How did the context of having a label and an explanation affect your appreciation of the poems?

Prominent Language poet Charles Bernstein, in "Against National Poetry Month as Such," writes, "Promoting poetry as if it were an 'easy listening' station just reinforces the idea that poetry is culturally irrelevant . . . I want a poetry that's bad for you." No wonder exploratory poetry is one of the more controversial topics in poetry today. Does it arouse strong feelings in you? Why? How important is "making sense" to you as a poet and as a reader?

QUOTES

Poetry is language playing with itself.
—Harryette Mullen

There is no "direct treatment" of the thing possible, except the "things" of language.
—Bruce Andrews

I made incalculable efforts to put words together without sense and found it impossible.
—Gertrude Stein

Language is one of the principal forms our curiosity takes. It makes us restless. . . . Language itself is never in a state of rest.
—Lyn Hejinian

The greatest danger which besets modern art is that of slighting the "great audience" whose response alone can give it authority and volume, of magnifying the importance of a coterie. . . . Art is not an isolated phenomenon of genius, but the expression of a reciprocal relation between the artist and his public . . . nothing can stand alone, genius least of all.
—Harriet Monroe

I for one am happy to embrace the description of my work as ungainly solipsistic incoherence that has no meaning. No meaning at all.
—Charles Bernstein

Everything changes but the avant-garde.
—Paul Valéry

POETRY PRACTICES

Syntax Stranger. Take one of your existing poems and revise it to collapse or alter the syntax in surprising ways. Try to make every word feel fresh and strange.

S 7. Write a poem according to the procedure "S + 7."

Irksome Found Language. Think of some everyday language that really irks you: shameless political speeches, condescending bureaucratic jargon, consumerist magazine writing, etc. Write a poem, using the "cut-up" or any other procedure, that turns this kind of language against itself. Along with your poem include the original text with the words that you have incorporated into your poem circled.

Found Loved Language. Do the same with a kind of language you really enjoy, whether your favorite beach novel, a guidebook to your favorite city, an interview with a musician you love, a great literary work such as Bervin used with Shakespeare, or a favorite love letter.

Trance Poem. Move yourself into a dream-state through any method you like and write a poem in that state. Let your unconscious dictate the poem to you. Don't worry about it making sense. If you don't have a preferred method, try listening to repetitive music or a tape of drumming or chanting a simple phrase to yourself over and over. You can also try writing a poem in the "hypnogogic" state: just after you wake up or as you are drifting to sleep. When doing this, it may be best to write down the words that come into your mind without looking at the page. I recommend, based on tough personal experience, that you use a fine-tip felt pen so it will be sure to be dark and consistent enough to be legible, and use a big pile of paper so you can turn pages often and not have to worry about where you are on the page.

Bernstein's and Mayer's Experiments. Try a few of the poetic "experiments" below, adapted from a list developed by Charles Bernstein and Bernadette Mayer. You may want to use them to write a poem, to stimulate the idea for a poem or a line, or simply to practice loosening up your linguistic imagination. Let the experiment take you wherever it will; don't worry if the poem (if you end up with one) is exploratory or more conventional.

- Homophonic translation: Take a poem in a foreign language that you can pronounce but not necessarily understand and translate the sound of the poem into English (i.e., French *blanc* to "blank" or *toute* to "toot").
- Mad libs. Take a poem and put blanks in place of three or four words in each line, noting the part of speech under each blank. Fill in the blanks, being sure not to recall the original context.

- Find and replace. Systematically replace one word in a poem with another word or string of words. Perform this operation serially with the same poem, increasing the number of words in the replace string.
- Collaboration. Write a poem with one or more other people: alternating lines (chaining or renga), writing simultaneously and collaging, rewriting, editing, supplementing the previous version. This can be done in person, via email, or through "snail" mail.
- Write a poem consisting entirely of overheard conversation.
- Erasure: Take a poem of your own or someone else's, cross out most of the words, and retype what remains as your poem.
- Write a poem trying to transcribe as accurately as you can your thoughts while you are writing. Don't throw anything out. Write as fast as you can without planning what you are going to say.
- Write a new poem made up entirely of neologisms or nonsense fragments of words (cf. Lewis Carroll's "Jabberwocky," Khlebnikov's "zaum," P. Inman's "Platin," David Melnick's "Pcoet").

PART 3

Breathing Poems: Rhythm and Meter

"Inebriate of air am I"

—EMILY DICKINSON

CHAPTER 11

Hearing the Beat: Accent and Accentual Poetry

Hazrat Inayat Khan wrote that "motion is the significance of life, and the law of motion is rhythm." A metrical poem is a poem with a regular pattern of rhythm, and the heartbeat of rhythm underlies all patterns of regular poetic meter. Since accent is the basis of rhythm in English, accent forms the beat, the lifeblood of a metrical poem. As we have seen, even some of the best-known passages of free verse are written in accentual meter—in lines with a regular pattern of accents.

What is an accent? It is an essential part of language that we all use every day. Anyone can distinguish the identical-looking noun and verb in these two sentences: "If you love this old record, then record it." "A desert is a bad place to desert someone." If you understand English, you can easily understand the difference in accent between the words; moreover, you rely on those accents for meaning.

Accent (marked / in many dictionaries and when marking poems, and sometimes signified with capital letters) is a technical term for stress or emphasis. The way accents are placed on certain syllables and not others as we speak is central to our understanding of everyday English. Say THIS sentENCe with THE acCENTS in unusUal placES. If you put the accents on the wrong syllables when you speak, it will sound as if you are not familiar with the language, as if you have a foreign "accent."

Although pauses and the lengths of syllables play a part in rhythm, accent is the most pervasive and clearest aspect of rhythm in English. The pattern of accents in a word or phrase speaks to our body, not just our mind. You can test this idea by thinking about the accented and unaccented syllables of your name. Notice how intimate and familiar you are with your name's accentual pattern, how it feels when you say it. Try changing it on purpose; instead of "maHALia JACKson," say "MA-halia jackSON." Notice how strange it sounds and feels.

With the aid of computers, linguists have isolated three elements that go into making a syllable sound accented. Stop reading for a minute and guess what they might be. You may have guessed loudness. That's one of them. The second is the length of the syllable—how long it takes to pronounce it. If you stretch out the time it takes to say a syllable, you will emphasize it even if you don't say it any louder than the other syllables in the sentence; try it and see. The final element is pitch: how high or low the syllable sounds compared to other syllables in the word (for example, syllables containing the sound "ee" sound higher-pitched than syllables containing the sound "uh," so "beet" sounds more accented than "but" in the phrase "but I like beets!"). Accent can be created by any of these three factors—loudness, length, and pitch—or by any combination of them, depending on the speaker and the situation.

When you start listening to the accents in a sentence or line of poetry, you may notice that some accented syllables have bigger accents than others. After all, all syllables have some accent; if they didn't, we couldn't hear them. One trick for telling which syllable has the strongest accent is to hold the back of your hand under your chin while saying the word (it helps to say the word loudly). When your chin drops the lowest, that's the most strongly accented syllable.

How to Hear Accent

When you first become aware of hearing accents, it is easy to get nervous or confused about which syllable is actually carrying the accent. Here are some handy tricks to help figure out where an accent belongs. If you ever find yourself at a loss, try these, in this order:

1. **When confused by which syllable to accent in a word, use my method of "reverse exaggeration": say a two-syllable word aloud to yourself, whispering one syllable and practically shouting the other so that there is a strong contrast. Then try the other way. Which sounds right?**
2. **Try the "single-syllable shout method," developed by Jessica Piazza: "Imagine you are trying to convey a word to someone across a room, but are forbidden to shout more than ONE syllable of the word at a time. Which syllable would you shout? . . . For example, try it with the word 'meter.' When you must shout only one syllable, you get either 'MEEE-ter'—which sounds pretty good or 'me-TEEER' which sounds pretty awkward. You can see, in this case, that the first syllable is the stressed one. . . . If two syllables sound right, chances are they aren't**

next to each other, and both might hold a stress in the word. Trying the shout method on the word 'enemy,' for example, you'll find that shouting the first AND third syllables will both sound somewhat right—at least a whole lot better than shouting the second."

3. Insert the word or phrase into regular speech: if you are confused by the accent on "planet" in Keats's lines "Then felt I like some watcher of the skies / when a new planet swims into his ken," instead try saying, "I went to the planetarium to see a show about planets." (Thanks to Karrie Waarala for this idea.)
4. Get a few people to say the word aloud with you in unison. The group will exaggerate the difference between the stressed and unstressed syllables. If none of these works, try the reverse exaggeration or single-syllable shout method as a group! Look the word up in a dictionary to check your answer. The stressed syllable will have an accent mark.

Certain linguists mark every syllable in a line of poetry on a scale of 1 to 4. While it can help you appreciate the beauty of a line to notice so many levels of accent, it can also become confusing. Don't let yourself get too distracted. Sometimes I imagine a line of poetry as a riverbed full of rocks of different sizes. All of the syllables, like all of the rocks, have height, but some are higher than others. Once your ear decides where the water level is, you will know that any syllables that rise above that particular level are thought of as "accented," and those underwater are not. It doesn't mean they have no accent, but for our purposes, we can consider the smaller rocks that are hidden under the water as unaccented (and if you find that *all* the syllables in a line seem accented to you, just imagine that it rains for a while and the water rises till only the highest of them are showing). Generally, any word of two syllables will have one stressed syllable; words of four syllables will have two. Among one-syllable words, more important words—nouns, verbs, adjectives, or adverbs—tend to be stressed, as in "Jack and Jill went up the hill / to fetch a pail of water."

Accentual poetry is poetry that has a regular pattern of accents in every line. Much of the first poetry we learn as children is accentual: "Janey and Johnny, up in a tree,/ K-I-S-S-I-N-G./ First comes love, then comes marriage, / then comes Johnny with a baby carriage." "MY mother SAYS to PICK the VEry best ONE and YOU are NOT it." Sometimes your ear will tell you that a syllable in a line of poetry is accented or not accented, but your mind will try to talk you out of it.

You may find it hard to believe that a tiny part of a word, like the suffix *-ly*, or an insignificant word, like "and," can be accented. No matter what your mind says, always trust your ear. One way accentual poems work is by playing against our expectations of where the accent should fall. (The scholar of accentual poetry Derek Attridge uses the helpful terms "promotion" and "demotion" to describe what happens when a stress falls on an unexpected syllable, or doesn't fall on an expected syllable.) A helpful principle to keep in mind is that *stress is relative:* a stressed syllable is considered to be one with more emphasis than the syllables around it. For example, the word "and" is unstressed in George Herbert's line "my HAND was NEXT to THEM, and THEN my HEART," where it falls between two heavier syllables. But in Emily Dickinson's line "The ADmirAtions AND conTEMPTS of TIME, "and" is stressed, because it falls between two lighter syllables.

In poetry there are three ways that a syllable can be accented. *Lexical accent* is what is marked in the dictionary; every word of two syllables or more has a lexical accent that never changes. With words of one syllable, other factors come into play. *Phrasal accent* is created by a grammatical situation, where more important words (usually nouns and verbs) are accented more: "house" is stressed more than "to the" in the sentence: "I RUN to the HOUSE." *Performative accent* is created by the speaker's meaning and can override normal phrasal stress: "She lives in the GREEN house, not the blue one!" Because of performative accent, the same syllable can be accented if you mean one thing ("I SAID, get over here!") but not in others ("I said, get over HERE!"). As you'll see in later chapters, metrical poetry has the ability to control exactly how performative accent falls—a marvelous capacity unique to metrical poetry among all types of literature.

Accent and Emotion

If you heard someone saying, "I SAID, get over here!" and couldn't hear the words, your body might tense up anyway, simply from the physical recognition of anger in the accentual patterns. Because of this direct, emotional line of communication to our bodies, accentual patterns are one of poetry's most potentially powerful tools. Children and crowds, perhaps because they are not very interested in reason, are particularly attuned to this bodily aspect of poetry. Nursery rhymes, jump rope songs, teasing songs, and childhood poems are usually composed in a rhythm based on accents, as are the slogans chanted during political rallies. Though it is impossible to isolate accentual patterns entirely from the way a poem is performed, we can hear how different accentual patterns soothe, incite, or cause anxiety. The staccato rhythm of the antiwar chant "Hell, no! We won't go!" in which every single syllable is accented, raises defiant energy. The quick, frantic rhythm of "Baby, baby, stick your head in gravy" causes anxiety. The civil rights slogan "We shall overcome" has a "falling rhythm," progressing more slowly from accented to nonaccented syllables; even without its traditional rolling melody, this pattern of accents sounds both peaceful and persistent. Poems built on these powerful kinds of accent-based rhythm are known as accentual poems.

If we think of language as made up of syllables, some of them accented and some not, and we want to make countable, repeatable, easy-to-remember patterns out of these syllables as we turn them into lines of poetry, there are three choices. We could choose patterns based on the number of accents, the number of syllables, or a combination of the two. And in fact, these are the three basic systems of poetic lines, or meter, that can be found in English: accentual meter, syllabic meter, and accentual-syllabic meter. We'll take up accentual-syllabic poetry—it's the most common metered poetry in English—in the next few chapters, but first we will discuss the others.

Syllabic Poetry

Syllabic poetry is based on a consistent number of syllables in each line, without any regard to accent. This is the main organizing principle of poetry in French, Italian, and other Romance languages. But in English, no well-known poet has used this system predominantly except Marianne Moore:

"She Trimmed the Candles Like One Who Loves the Beautiful," Marianne Moore (1917)

It was right that such light
        As there was in the room should burn before her. She
Made me think of Diana—monkeys and penguins and white

Bears and herons: of wood
        Covered ravines cut by waterfalls, of mountains
With streaks of white smoke across them, of knife blades set in good

Syllabic poetry is poetry with lines that follow a repeating pattern of syllables.

African ivory
        Hafts: of white and blue foxes on the confines of
The icy sea." But when she spoke of externality

She flouted it and called
        Good looks, mortality decked out in circumstance:
She said: You speak of death and are respectfully appalled.

Things that one can suffer
        Without the appearance of a surface scratch, put
Dying far away. Death is not unique in character:

Always overrated,
        It is a needful happening like lighting these—
Or like reiterating to the deaf what has been said.

Moore's typical syllabic practice, which we can call "corresponding syllabics," matches up each stanza to the same template: there are a certain number of syllables in each of the first lines, a certain number in each of the second lines, and so on. The combination of syllabic consistency and regularly indented lines lends a ceremonial quality to this poem. Unlike an accentual pattern, evident primarily to the ear and transcribed onto the page as an afterthought, a syllabic pattern becomes evident during the process of reading on the page. Because its form is so dependent on the reader's interpretative process, corresponding syllabics conveys the cryptic quality of a secret language. This almost ironic, literary type of meter is well suited to Moore's refined musings on an object in a museum. On the other hand, poems like Dylan Thomas's "Fern Hill" and "Poem in October," also written in corresponding syllabics, are very much poems for the ear; in these poems, the syllabic pattern structures the strong rhythms and intense word-music while keeping it from becoming *too* lush and predictable.

"Fern Hill," Dylan Thomas (1946)

Now as I was young and easy under the apple boughs
About the lilting house and happy as the grass was green,
The night above the dingle starry,
Time let me hail and climb
Golden in the heydays of his eyes,
And honoured among wagons I was prince of the apple towns
And once below a time I lordly had the trees and leaves
Trail with daisies and barley
Down the rivers of the windfall light.

And as I was green and carefree, famous among the barns
About the happy yard and singing as the farm was home,
In the sun that is young once only,
Time let me play and be
Golden in the mercy of his means,
And green and golden I was huntsman and herdsman, the calves
Sang to my horn, the foxes on the hills barked clear and cold,
And the sabbath rang slowly
In the pebbles of the holy streams.

All the sun long it was running, it was lovely, the hay
Fields high as the house, the tunes from the chimneys, it was air
And playing, lovely and watery
And fire green as grass.
And nightly under the simple stars
As I rode to sleep the owls were bearing the farm away,
All the moon long I heard, blessed among stables, the nightjars
Flying with the ricks, and the horses
Flashing into the dark.

And then to awake, and the farm, like a wanderer white
With the dew, come back, the cock on his shoulder: it was all
Shining, it was Adam and maiden,
The sky gathered again
And the sun grew round that very day.

So it must have been after the birth of the simple light
In the first, spinning place, the spellbound horses walking warm
Out of the whinnying green stable
On to the fields of praise.

And honoured among foxes and pheasants by the gay house
Under the new made clouds and happy as the heart was long,
In the sun born over and over,
I ran my heedless ways,
My wishes raced through the house high hay
And nothing I cared, at my sky blue trades, that time allows
In all his tuneful turning so few and such morning songs
Before the children green and golden
Follow him out of grace.

Nothing I cared, in the lamb white days, that time would take me
Up to the swallow thronged loft by the shadow of my hand,
In the moon that is always rising,
Nor that riding to sleep
I should hear him fly with the high fields
And wake to the farm forever fled from the childless land.
Oh as I was young and easy in the mercy of his means,
Time held me green and dying
Though I sang in my chains like the sea.

Another type of syllabic poem uses the same number of syllables in every line:

"The Thin Man," Donald Justice

I indulge myself
In rich refusals.
Nothing suffices.
I hone myself to
This edge. Asleep, I
Am a horizon.

This appropriately thin poem about renunciation builds interest in part by renouncing any audible pattern (until the last line). Each line is different; only lines 2 and 6 have the same pattern of word lengths, and even that is counterbalanced by a difference in the stress patterns of the first two syllables (the accent on the second syllable of "in rich" and on the first syllable of "am a"). Though the rhythms until the end are deliberately prosy, the last line achieves closure in part by adhering to the well-known rhythm of the adonic line, described in chapter 16, "Stanzas."

The following poem uses syllabics to keep a narrative thrust going, the 11-syllable lines like half-noticed signposts as the story moves along past them:

"Zinc Fingers," Peter Meinke

Though scientists inform us that criminals
have insufficient zinc I've always believed
it's insufficient gold and silver that gets
them going. The man who slipped his hand into
my front pocket on the jammed Paris Metro
wasn't trying to make friends. His overcoat
smelled greasy and it was unpleasant holding
hands above my wallet pressed in on all sides
like stacked baguettes. There was no way to move or
take a swing. Still some action on my part seemed
to be called for. We stood nose to nose. I tried
to look in his eyes but he stared at my chin
shy on our first date so after a while as
we rattled along toward the Champs-Elysees

I lost concentration and began to think

of our scholarly daughter working at Yale
on a project called Zinc Fingers scanning a
protein with pseudopods each with a trace of
zinc that latch onto our DNA and help
determine what we become. This brought me back
to *mon ami* the pickpocket. I wondered
how he chose his hard line of work and if as
a boy he was good at cards for example
or sewing and for that matter what choice did
I have either so when we reached our stop and

he looked up from my chin at last I smiled at
him and his eyes flashed in fear or surprise and
I called *It's OK* as he scuttled away
Tout va bien! though I held tight to my wallet

Though every line has 11 syllables, this poem reads like free verse until you start counting the syllables. As a result, the poem achieves a subtler kind of control than the audible obviousness of accentual or accentual-syllabic meter would allow. The poet has written about the composition of this poem, "One advantage of syllabic poetry is that it's kind of a regulated free verse, giving some shape but still being pretty loose." Balancing between these two forces, syllabic verse can achieve an intriguing tension.

When writing syllabic verse, one of the most important things to keep in mind is to avoid falling into accentual-syllabic meter. For this reason, it is a good idea to use an irregular number of syllables in each line. If Meinke had used ten rather than eleven syllables, it would have been much harder for him to avoid distracting readers with accidental meter.

Accentual Poetry

While syllabic poetry in English is an arcane practice, carried out consciously by sophisticated poets in relatively recent times, accentual poems have been composed in English since the beginning of the spoken language. **Accentual poetry** is the most common form for folk poetry, popular poetry, and poetry meant to be heard not read. This makes sense, because the nature of each poetic meter is closely related to its language. Accent is an important feature of English, as it is of all Germanic-based languages.

An accentual poem can have any number of syllables per line, but it must have the same number of accents in each line. Unlike syllabic poetry, which can vary the number of syllables in each line of a stanza as long as it keeps to a pattern, accentual poetry works best if each line has a predictable number of accents. It would be confusing to have a "corresponding accentual" poem, because accent patterns are *alive* in a way that syllabic patterns are not; they can sound different in different contexts, and the pattern of one line influences the way we hear the next line. (That's why a lot of people emphasize the last syllable of "water" when they hear "Jack and Jill went up the hill / to fetch a pail of water.")

Legend says the poem below was written by comedian Gilda Radner for an early episode of *Saturday Night Live.* Childish and exaggerated, it is a perfect choice of theme for an accentual poem:

"Jeans," Roseanne Roseannadanna (Gilda Radner)

Jeans jeans the magical pants	(seven syllables)
the more they itch the more you dance	(eight syllables)
the more you dance the more people watch	(nine syllables)
to see how you scratch that itch in your crotch.	(ten syllables)

Can you hear the four strong accents in each line? Accents override the differences in the number of syllables. Maneuvering through this tension is part of the fun of hearing accentual poetry.

Accentual poems in English predate writing. In fact, accentual meter may be thought of as our earliest form of communicative technology, because it is designed, at least in part, to make it possible to remember poems that could take days to recite, such as the epic poem *Beowulf.* "The Seafarer," below, is another long accentual poem, first written down in A.D. 950 but probably composed earlier as an oral poem. Like *Beowulf* and much other Anglo-Saxon poetry, it was composed in **accentual alliterative verse.**

The term **alliteration** means that a sound or cluster of sounds is repeated at the beginning of two or more words of a line (track and true, sob and sea). So in accentual alliterative verse each line has the same number of accents, and alliteration links two or more of the stressed syllables. The alliteration may work along with the accentual pattern to make the poem easier to memorize. Although accentual alliterative poems can have any number of accents per line, the most common number is four, as in the poem below. The layout of the poem reflects the **medial pause** that divides each line of this kind of poem in half. Notice how the alliterations link the two halves in the Anglo-Saxon.

"The Seafarer" (ninth century AD), trans. Annie Finch

MÆG ic be me sylfum	soðgied wrecan
siþas secgan	hu ic geswincdagum
earfoðwile	oft þrowade
bitre breostceare	gebidan hæbbe
gecunnad in ceole	cearselda fela

atol yþa gewealc   þær mec oft bigeat
nearo nihtwaco   æt nacan stefnan
þonne he be clifan cnossað   calde geþrungen
wæron mine fet   forste gebunden
caldum clommum   þær þa ceare seofedun
hate ymb heortan   hungor innan slat
merewerges mod

From "The Seafarer" (ninth century A.D.) (trans. Annie Finch)

I keep the track   of a song true of me,
to tell of trials,   struggling times,
hard days,   how I endured.
I have carried   bitter cares,
had on ships   a house of cares;
terrible sea-waves   tossed when I kept
narrowed watches   on the stern at night
and the ship thrust at cliffs.   Thronged in cold
were my feet,   bound in frost,
with chains of cold,   while hunger cut
my ocean-weary mood.

The strength and simplicity of the accentual pattern gives the poem an air of inevitability and dignity. The fittingness of that feeling to the poem's themes, of loneliness and courage in exile, may be the reason this remains one of the most-loved poems of the Anglo-Saxon era.

Most more recent accentual poems rely on a regular accentual pattern, but without alliteration. Rap poetry is composed in an accentual pattern, often with some lines linked together by rhyme:

From "Respiration," Mos Def

This ain't no time where the usual is suitable
Tonight alive, let's describe the inscrutable
The indisputable, we New York the narcotic
Strength in metal and fiber optics
where mercenaries is paid to trade hot stock tips

for profits, thirsty criminals take pockets
Hard knuckles on the second hands of workin' class watches
Skyscrapers is colossus, the cost of living
is preposterous, stay alive, you play or die, no options
No Batman and Robin, can't tell between
the cops and the robbers, they both partners, they all heartless
With no conscience, back streets stay darkened
Where unbeliever hearts stay hardened
My eagle talons stay sharpened, like city lights stay throbbin'
You either make a way or stay sobbin', the Shiny Apple
is bruised but sweet and if you choose to eat
You could lose your teeth, many crews retreat
Nightly news repeat, who got shot down and locked down
Spotlight to savages, NASDAQ averages
My narrative, rose to explain this existence
Amidst the harbor lights which remain in the distance

So much on my mind that it can't recline
Blastin' holes in the night 'til she bled sunshine
Breathe in, inhale vapors from bright stars that shine
Breathe out, weed smoke retrace the skyline
Heard the bass ride out like an ancient mating call
I can't take it y'all, I can feel the city breathin'
Chest heavin', against the flesh of the evening
Sigh before we die like the last train leaving . . .

Almost all the lines have four beats, with a few exceptions for emphasis and variety. Since the lines vary in length from 9 syllables (STRENGTH in METal and FIBer optics) to 15 syllables (my EAGle talons stay SHARPened, like CITy lights stay THROBbing), it can take intense energy to rap out the beat on the longer lines. The more strong syllables, like "lights" or the "tal" in "talons," need to be overridden, the more tension the rapping voice needs to resolve. A rap poem is meant to be performed, and the performance helps to manifest the poem's form.

Rap is often improvised and uses some of the same composition techniques as ancient oral poetry, including the accentual beat, word-music such as alliteration to hold the poem tighter together, and a technique called a **formula,** which is a piece of language the poet has used before, one that already fits the poem's accentual pattern and can be inserted as necessary. Repetition of phrases allows improvisation to gather steam. Rhyme emphasizes the connections between lines and provides markers that remind your ear of the poem's overall progression. I have heard rap poets make up brilliant raps on the spur of the moment using these techniques.

When writing a rap or rap-influenced poem, it's important to keep in mind that sometimes what works in performance may not work well on the page—and vice versa. Poems that perform well generally keep a strong sense of the line breaks. Their language is direct and their emotional mood clear. They work especially well when they build to a particular dramatic point in the poem that allows you to really let loose as a climax to your performance. Reading aloud as you go will help you do a better job with writing *any* kind of poetry, but with rap and other performance poetry, of course, it is an absolute must. For a poem to work well on the page, it also needs a certain amount of subtlety and complexity. The best poems, like many in this book, have always worked well both on *and* off the page.

Dramatically effective free verse often gains some of its power from passages with a strong, regularly accented rhythm, basically identical to accentual poetry:

"The Moose," Elizabeth Bishop

For Grace Bulmer Bowers

From narrow provinces
of fish and bread and tea,
home of the long tides
where the bay leaves the sea
twice a day and takes
the herrings long rides,

where if the river
enters or retreats
in a wall of brown foam
depends on if it meets
the bay coming in,
the bay not at home;

where, silted red,
sometimes the sun sets
facing a red sea,
and others, veins the flats'
lavender, rich mud
in burning rivulets;

on red, gravelly roads,
down rows of sugar maples,
past clapboard farmhouses
and neat, clapboard churches,
bleached, ridged as clamshells,
past twin silver birches,

through late afternoon
a bus journeys west,
the windshield flashing pink,
pink glancing off of metal,
brushing the dented flank
of blue, beat-up enamel;

down hollows, up rises,
and waits, patient, while
a lone traveller gives
kisses and embraces
to seven relatives
and a collie supervises.

Goodbye to the elms,
to the farm, to the dog.
The bus starts. The light
grows richer; the fog,
shifting, salty, thin,
comes closing in.

Its cold, round crystals
form and slide and settle

in the white hens' feathers,
in gray glazed cabbages,
on the cabbage roses
and lupins like apostles;

the sweet peas cling
to their wet white string
on the whitewashed fences;
bumblebees creep
inside the foxgloves,
and evening commences.

One stop at Bass River.
Then the Economies—
Lower, Middle, Upper;
Five Islands, Five Houses,
where a woman shakes a tablecloth
out after supper.

A pale flickering. Gone.
The Tantramar marshes
and the smell of salt hay.
An iron bridge trembles
and a loose plank rattles
but doesn't give way.

On the left, a red light
swims through the dark:
a ship's port lantern.
Two rubber boots show,
illuminated, solemn.
A dog gives one bark.

A woman climbs in
with two market bags,
brisk, freckled, elderly.
"A grand night. Yes, sir,

all the way to Boston."
She regards us amicably.

Moonlight as we enter
the New Brunswick woods,
hairy, scratchy, splintery;
moonlight and mist
caught in them like lamb's wool
on bushes in a pasture.

The passengers lie back.
Snores. Some long sighs.
A dreamy divagation
begins in the night,
a gentle, auditory,
slow hallucination. . . .

In the creakings and noises,
an old conversation
—not concerning us,
but recognizable, somewhere,
back in the bus:
Grandparents' voices

uninterruptedly
talking, in Eternity:
names being mentioned,
things cleared up finally;
what he said, what she said,
who got pensioned;

deaths, deaths and sicknesses;
the year he remarried;
the year (something) happened.
She died in childbirth.
That was the son lost
when the schooner foundered.

He took to drink. Yes.
She went to the bad.
When Amos began to pray
even in the store and
finally the family had
to put him away.

"Yes . . ." that peculiar
affirmative. "Yes . . ."
A sharp, indrawn breath,
half groan, half acceptance,
that means "Life's like that.
We know *it* (also death)."

Talking the way they talked
in the old featherbed,
peacefully, on and on,
dim lamplight in the hall,
down in the kitchen, the dog
tucked in her shawl.

Now, it's all right now
even to fall asleep
just as on all those nights.
—Suddenly the bus driver
stops with a jolt,
turns off his lights.

A moose has come out of
the impenetrable wood
and stands there, looms, rather,
in the middle of the road.
It approaches; it sniffs at
the bus's hot hood.

Towering, antlerless,
high as a church,
homely as a house

(or, safe as houses).
A man's voice assures us
"Perfectly harmless. . . ."

Some of the passengers
exclaim in whispers,
childishly, softly,
"Sure are big creatures."
"It's awful plain."
"Look! It's a she!"

Taking her time,
she looks the bus over,
grand, otherworldly.
Why, why do we feel
(we all feel) this sweet
sensation of joy?

"Curious creatures,"
says our quiet driver,
rolling his r's.
"Look at that, would you."
Then he shifts gears.
For a moment longer,

by craning backward,
the moose can be seen
on the moonlit macadam;
then there's a dim
smell of moose, an acrid
smell of gasoline.

The long, thin jolt of the lines toward and away from their core of three accents reminds us of the jolt of the bus through the night. Much of the mystery of this poem comes from its rhythm, which creates an ongoing basic template of time and darkness along which the brief, illuminated described occurrences come and go.

While it's fun to focus on the hypnotic intensity of much accentual poetry, some poems use accentual prosody in a subtler way:

"Famine," Landis Everson

In the middle of the night at least twenty deer
Came out upon my pillow to graze,
Gazing down at me with sad, round eyes,
Their pointed hooves quilting my pillow.

And I thrashed gently in sleeplessness,
Moving not to disturb them, wondering
At the famine this year that forces so many
To roam to poor, unfamiliar pastures.

The moon through the window throws cold light
Upon their curved backs, making a forest
Of crossed antler shadows on sheets
That until now have been flawless and starved.

Rather than forcing the accent to fall in a certain place, this poem allows it to hover over the words. The poem is too prosodically delicate to commit to any meter, yet it is a formal poem, with the same number of accents in every line, and so it is accentual almost by default, without the rocking, forward drive that underlies most accentual poems.

By contrast, these two lines from a free-verse poem each have four strongly perceptible accents, though they have very different rhythmic patterns and numbers of syllables:

From "The Girlfriends," Elizabeth Woody

Filled with old lovers, in the clutch of the chair,
you are a bloom of uncombed hair.

As you read accentual poems, you may notice that sometimes the rhythm makes you not stress words you normally would stress (such as "old" in Woody's poem above) and stress words you normally wouldn't stress (such as "to" in the third line of the Yeats passage below). That is normal, and part of the power and fun of accentual poetry. You may also notice that you and others may not always agree on which syllables are stressed. That is also normal. Sometimes these disagreements arise from regional or generational differences in speech. Probably you will agree on the basic number of syllables per line, and on how most of the lines in the poem work. But hearing accents is not a completely exact science. That's okay. A disagreement here and there doesn't invalidate the entire system of meter; it just means that there are a few places where people hear things differently. When in doubt, just shrug, read aloud, don't think too much, trust your ear and your body, read aloud again, and remember to enjoy—after all, the point of understanding poetry's rhythms is to enjoy poetry more.

Scanning Exercises. Read the following passages aloud (reading aloud under your breath is ok if necessary). As you read, mark a little accent mark (´) with a pencil over the places where you notice an accent. When in doubt about a particular syllable, just write a quick question mark and move on, following your body's response to the words:

From "Easter 1916," W. B. Yeats (1916)

Hearts with one purpose alone
Through summer and winter seem
Enchanted to a stone
To trouble the living stream.
The horse that comes from the road,
The rider, the birds that range
From cloud to tumbling cloud,
Minute by minute they change;
A shadow of cloud on the stream
Changes minute by minute;
A horse-hoof slides on the brim,
And a horse plashes within it;
The long-legged moor-hens dive,
And hens to moor-cocks call;
Minute by minute they live:
The stone's in the midst of all.

Each of these lines has three accents. The number of syllables varies from six to eight; though the number doesn't vary as widely as in the rap poem, the order and pattern of accents and syllables still changes greatly from line to line. The result is a chant-like, mesmerizing feeling, as if the rhythmic pattern, like the stone, is so strong that it withstands any syllabic obstacles in its way.

QUESTIONS FOR MEDITATION OR DISCUSSION

Many of the most memorable accentual poems are written for children, and there is much that such poems can teach us about how accentual meter works. Mark the rhythmical pattern in the three children's poems below by putting an accent mark over each syllable you think is accented. Remember that *accent is relative.* The lines may have lots of stresses. You don't need to mark every stress; just mark the strongest ones. If you read the poem aloud, it will help you to "get in the groove." Then you can check your scansion against the ones in the back of the book.

"Up the Tallest Tree," Annie Finch and Althea Finch-Brand (on the model of the children's book Chicka Chicka Boom Boom!*)*

I told you and you told me,
I'll meet you at the top of the tallest tree.
So we climbed and we climbed till we could see
The highest mountain and the deepest sea.
Rat a tat a tat tat!
What do you think of that!

"From a Railway Carriage," Robert Louis Stevenson (1913)

Faster than fairies, faster than witches,
Bridges and houses, hedges and ditches;
And charging along like troops in a battle
All through the meadows the horses and cattle:
All of the sights of the hill and the plain
Fly as thick as driving rain;
And ever again, in the wink of an eye,
Painted stations whistle by.

Here is a child who clambers and scrambles,
All by himself and gathering brambles;
Here is a tramp who stands and gazes;
And here is the green for stringing the daisies!
Here is a cart runaway in the road
Lumping along with man and load;
And here is a mill, and there is a river:
Each a glimpse and gone forever!

Scottish proverb, Anonymous, ca. 1726

If wishes were horses, beggars would ride.
If turnips were watches, I would wear one by my side.
And if "ifs" and "an's" were pots and pans,
There'd be no work for tinkers' hands.

QUOTES

Limitations are a form of understanding, and we should not so easily treat them as stop signs. A limitation is often like the pivot point for a pole-vaulter. It is that place you hope to put down your pole, but only so that it will carry you up, much higher and farther than where the pole has stopped, so long as you have run fast and far enough to make this confrontation work.

—Alberto Rios

All is a procession,
The universe is a procession with measured and perfect motion.

—Walt Whitman

Words in themselves do not convey meaning . . . let us take the example of two people who are talking on the other side of a closed door whose voices can be heard but whose words cannot be distinguished. Even though the words do not carry, the sound of them does, and the listener can catch the meaning of the conversation.

—Robert Frost

A poem with a strong accentual meter . . . can be "heard" as a poem even if it is printed out as prose.

—Marilyn Hacker

POETRY PRACTICES

Group (Electropoetrygram). While one person reads aloud a text of prose or poetry, someone else graphs it on the board like an electrocardiogram, marking the "highs" of intensity and the "lows." (Based on Alan Zeigler, *The Writing Workshop.*)

Group (Power Marking). Read aloud a free-verse poem to a partner while they mark the accents they hear in each line. Switch places. Do you hear any regularly recurring accents? Solo variation: Make an audio recording of one of your free-verse poems. Play it back several times, listening for and marking the patterns of the accents.

Accentual Poem. Write a poem of at least 20 lines that has the same number of accents in each line. The poem should not fall into a regular, "singsong" meter; instead, the accents should dominate the syllables—as in a rap poem. In other words, the poem should not necessarily have the same number of syllables in each line the way a metrical poem does. Accentual poetry is basically an oral form. Try yours out by reading it aloud to a friend or roommate, and see if they can hear how many accents are in each line.

Shape-shifting: Syllabic to Accentual. Write a poem of at least 12 lines with the same number of syllables in each line. Then revise it into an accentual poem. How does your poem change?

Song Stanzas. Think of a song you know by heart that has a strong beat. Make up two new stanzas of your own for the song without writing them down until they're finished. Sing them to a friend.

Symbolic Syllables. Write a poem in corresponding syllabics in which each line has a number of syllables that is meaningful to you in some way. Maybe the numbers tell a story, like your birth month followed by the age you were when you moved, followed by your lucky number. See if you can weave awareness of these numbers into your lines.

Make Your Own Nursery Rhyme. Think of a short poem from the oral tradition (maybe a nursery rhyme or playground rhyme), preferably one you know by heart with a rhythm that you enjoy. Say it aloud several times in a row. (*a*) Use that rhythmic momentum to help you compose a new poem in the exact same pattern of accents and syllables. The words don't have to make any sense at all (it's fine to write nonsense like, "hats are green and make a tax, winter wakes us on our backs"); all that matters here is accentual sense. As with the song, try to compose two stanzas *before* you copy it down. If it rhymes, feel free to use the original rhyme pattern or discard it. (*b*) Check the accentual pattern by marking the accents and counting the syllables in both your poem and the original to see if they match up. (*c*) Write a few more "stanzas" in the same pattern. (*d*) Revise to make more sense, if you want to.

Being Beowulf. Write a poem in accentual-alliterative meter of at least 12 lines. Don't forget to include the medial pause and to link the half-lines with alliteration. Try to use the Anglo-Saxon mood evoked by the meter to your advantage: tell a heroic story, or evoke an archetypal setting.

You the Rapper. Write and perform a rap poem of at least 12 lines. Feel free to go way over the top in your performance.

CHAPTER 12

Meter: A Language for the Body

Whether in a single accentual poem or in its more complex, developed incarnation, meter remains the traditional transporting power, the intoxicant, hypnotic drumbeat of poetry. Meter can manifest the language of the body, the beating of the wings of Pegasus; it can become a direct channel to the blood beating through a reader's veins. Meter is, after all, the reason that poets have been compared to drunkards, priests, shamans, the reason that Shakespeare wrote, "The lunatic, the lover and the poet / are of imagination all compact." To write in meter for me can be an experience so intense that it feels like a joyful secret, at once physical and private and a publicly shared gift.

Writing in meter is the skill most unique to writing poetry. Novels, stories, and plays in prose all make use of images, metaphors, word-music, tone of voice, and story, and sometimes of metrical and rhythmic passages, but poetry is the only kind of literature that can be completely structured by meter.

Some kind of meter has been central to poetry, has defined poetry, for most of remembered time in every culture. In the twentieth century, after the typewriter made it possible for poets to control their spacing exactly, the free verse movement blossomed and led many to think that the time of meter was over. But meter persisted and has begun to appeal to younger poets more and more alongside free verse, as the novelty of free verse has worn off and the popularity of rap and slam poetry has brought poems back off the page and into the ear.

When babies are starting to learn a language, long before they understand the meanings of words, they wiggle and move in response to a language's physical contours; an adult talking to an infant will exaggerate the physical elements of the language that are meaningful: "You're so *cute*! Look at your little *toes*!!" Meter works in a similarly physical way. By organizing and emphasizing the English language's inherent accents, meter talks to the body in us, communicates in a way that can be understood prior to our understanding of the words' meanings.

The word **meter** comes literally from the Greek word for "measure." Its basic meaning is simple: it refers to any kind of repeating, countable pattern within lines of poetry. In the last chapter we discussed syllabic meter, patterns based on the number of syllables in a line, and accentual meter, patterns based on the number of accents in a line. In this chapter and the two that follow, we'll be looking at accentual-syllabic meter, patterns based on both accents and syllables. Accentual-syllabic meter is the heart of metrical poetry in English.

Slam poetry: poetry performed, usually from memory, at oral competitions called "poetry slams," where judges rank poets for the quality of their poems and performance.

Writing in accentual-syllabic meter, according to one of my students who composes music, is similar to the process of writing music. In both cases, "It is crucial to keep the structure (meter in poetry, time signatures in music) you are working with in the background. First hum or say the rhythm aloud to yourself a few times, then put it out of your mind" while you use your imagination to lay the foundation of the poem. Finally, "delve into" the meter and vary it to strengthen the poem.

Sometimes, I notice myself humming a tune at random—and then realize it's not random at all: the words of the tune connect with something that has just happened in my life. In the same way, a poem can arrive as a tune that has a certain physical wisdom to it. If you let the tune lead the way, it can take you to words you may not have realized you wanted to say. If you are conversant with the meters, or tunes, of poetry, you will know better how to dance with the rhythm and allow the words to follow.

Poems can be written according to various kinds of meter, as we have seen with syllabic and accentual meter. This is because various features of the language can be counted or made into patterns. Any system of such counted elements is called a **prosody.**

Prosody and History

A durable prosody is always based on key elements that are meaningful to ordinary speakers of the language. Accent is central to meaning in Germanic languages. Old English, being a Germanic language, had an accentual prosody: a line of Anglo-Saxon or Old English poetry was based on a certain number of accents. Accent is not as meaningful in French words, and it is not part of French prosody. Instead French has a syllabic prosody: a line of French poetry is based on a certain number of syllables. Chinese meter incorporates pitch and tone because, in Chinese, pitch and tone are meaningful elements that change the definitions of words. A meter based on pitch and tone would have no meaning to English speakers.

Prosody: a general term for the metrical structure of poetry. Theoretically, anything that can be repeated or counted—words, syllables, accented syllables, sentences, even line breaks—can be experimented with as an element in prosody.

The accentual-syllabic meter which is now the mainstay of English prosody came about through a historical event. England had a purely accentual prosody until the Norman Conquest in 1066, when the French conquered the Germanic-speaking tribes of England. Over centuries, with the addition of more and more French-derived words into the language, the four-beat bedrock line of accentual verse gradually evolved into an iambic tetrameter or iambic pentameter line in which there is a regular pattern of syllables in addition to accents, and the number of syllables in a line is almost (not quite!) as important as the number of accents. The fourteenth-century narrative poem "Sir Gawain and the Green Knight" gives a sense of this transition. Like the Anglo-Saxon poem "The Seafarer" in the last chapter, "Gawain" maintains four strong beats and the alliterative pattern; but it has much more regularity in terms of syllables, and the caesura in the middle of the line is less pronounced:

From "Sir Gawain and the Green Knight," The Gawain Poet
(fourteenth century AD)

From Þe lorde ful lowde with lote and laȝter myry,
When he seȝe Sir Gawayn, with solace he spekez;
Þe goude ladyez were geten, and gedered þe meyny,
He schewez hem þe scheldez, and schapes hem þe tale
Of þe largesse and þe lenþe, þe liþernez alse

Of þe were of þe wylde swyn in wod þer he fled.
Þat oþer kny3t ful comly comended his dedez,
And praysed hit as gret prys þat he proued hade,
For suche a brawne of a best, þe bolde burne sayde,
Ne such sydes of a swyn segh he neuer are.

From "Sir Gawain and the Green Knight" (trans. Marie Borroff)

The lord laughed aloud, with many a light word.
When he greeted Sir Gawain—with good cheer he speaks.
They fetch the fair dames and the folk of the house;
He brings forth the brawn, and begins the tale
Of the great length and girth, the grim rage as well,
Of the battle of the boar they beset in the wood.
The other man meetly commended his deeds
And praised well the prize of his princely sport,
For the brawn of that boar, the bold knight said,
And the sides of that swine surpassed all others.

Many of the four-beat accentual lines in the original (for example, each of the last four lines) could be scanned as iambic pentameter; you can try it after you've read the next chapter. From there it is not far to Chaucer's line, which is generally accepted as the earliest consistent iambic pentameter in English (a "gossip" means a woman's female friend):

From "The Wife of Bath's Tale," Geoffrey Chaucer (ca. 1390)

My fifthe housbonde, God his soule blesse,
Which that I took for love and no richesse,
He somtyme was a clerk of Oxenford,
And hadde left scole, and wente at hom to bord
With my gossib, dwellynge in oure toun,
God have hir soule! hir name was Alisoun.
She knew myn herte and eek my privetee
Bet than oure parisshe preest, as moot I thee.
To hir biwreyed I my conseil al,
For hadde myn housbonde pissed on a wal,

Or doon a thyng that sholde han cost his lyf,
To hir, and to another worthy wyf,
And to my nece, which that I loved weel,
I wolde han toold his conseil every deel.
And so I dide ful often, God it woot,
That made his face ful often reed and hoot
For verray shame, and blamed hym-self, for he
Had toold to me so greet a pryvetee.

From "The Wife of Bath's Tale" (trans. Sinan Kökbugur)

My fifth husband, may God his spirit bless!
Whom I took all for love, and not riches,
Had been sometime a student at Oxford,
And had left school and had come home to board
With my best gossip, dwelling in our town,
God save her soul! Her name was Alison.
She knew my heart and all my privity
Better than did our parish priest, s'help me!
To her confided I my secrets all.
For had my husband pissed against a wall,
Or done a thing that might have cost his life,
To her and to another worthy wife,
And to my niece whom I loved always well,
I would have told it—every bit I'd tell,
And did so, many and many a time, knows God,
Which made his face full often red and hot
For utter shame; he blamed himself that he
Had told me of so deep a privity.

Just as the two languages have combined (Chaucer uses French-based words such as "conseil" and "pryvetee"), the native, Germanic accentual system of prosody has combined with the conquerers' French syllabic system, producing a metrical system that takes into account both number of syllables and number of accents. The iambic tetrameter line remained important in English poetry, especially in Scotland, and accentual prosody never really lost its core relationship to English; Suzanne Wood claims that even the *Canterbury Tales* is based

Metrical feet

u/	iamb
/u	trochee
uu	pyrrhic
//	spondee
uu/	anapest
/uu	dactyl
u/u	amphibrach
/u/	cretic (also called amphimacer)
u//	bacchius
//u	antibacchius
uuu	tribrach
///	molossos
/uuuu	first paeon
u/uu	second paeon
uu/u	third paeon
uuu/	fourth paeon
uu//	double iamb (also called minor iambic)
//uu	major ionic
u//u	antispast
u/u/	diamb
u///	first epitrite
/u//	second epitrite
//u/	third epitrite
///u	fourth epitrite
/uu/	choriamb
uuuu	tetrabrach (also called proceleus or maticus)
////	dispondee

mostly in the older four-beat accentual line, and Derek Attridge's *Poetic Rhythm* uses a system based in scanning accentual verse to scan all poetry in English. But by the Renaissance, along with the evolution of the language into the English we speak today, the longer, iambic pentameter line evolved into the dominant position. English now is built on a base of about 25 percent Germanic (including Anglo-Saxon and some Old Norse words) words and 60 percent

Latinate (about half French and half Latin) words. Because of its hybrid nature, our accentual-syllabic system of prosody combines strength and fluidity; it is one of the unique and magnificent strengths of poetry in English.

This chapter introduces a few key terms of accentual-syllabic meter and the four most common metrical patterns. The important thing, at first, is to begin to hear these different patterns and to get a sense of how they change a poem's energy, how they affect readers, and especially how they affect you as a poet. I recommend that you read the passages in meter aloud slowly and with attention to any physical sensations you have as you read (heart racing, sense of excitement in stomach, heart slowing, relaxing of shoulders, sense of calm, etc.). Reading aloud, loudly if possible or under your breath if necessary, is important because meters are meant for your internal or external ear, not your brain. Enjoy them as much as you can. It's okay if you don't remember all the names and terms right away; they will be repeated in other chapters. But I hope you will stay with this chapter, rereading the poems and looking for others in the same meters throughout the book, until you have a solid sense of the four basic patterns.

Scansion Marks

The process of marking the metrical patterns in a poem is called **scansion.** (At the end of the last chapter, when you were asked to mark the rhythmical pattern of some accentual poems, you were scanning the poems as you marked the accents.)

In accentual-syllabic meter, we pay attention to both the number of accents *and* the number of syllables. Also, unlike in both accentual and syllabic poems, where it's simply the counting that matters, here we are noticing not only the number but also the recurring *pattern* of stressed and unstressed syllables—noticing it, and marking it. How can you mark such a pattern? There are many possible ways, from the numbers 1 to 4 to musical notation (quarter notes, half notes, and whole notes) to capital letters, which we have used occasionally in this book. But from now on, we will be using the symbols u, /, \, and |,which are the standard and most common scansion marks. Here is what they mean: u is used for an unstressed syllable or breve (from the Greek word for "short"); / is used for a stressed syllable or ictus (from the Greek word for "accent"). \ is optional and can be used for a lighter stress, or "half-stress"; | is used to mark the boundary between repeating units, called a "foot break." To refer to these symbols, rather than the arcane words "breve" and "ictus" or the unwieldy terms "accented syllable" and "unaccented syllable," we will use two terms that have proven useful in my own teaching because they are so visual and easy to remember: the **cup** (u) and the **wand** (/) Don't worry—by the end of the chapter these four symbols—cup, wand, half-accent, and foot boundary—should be quite familiar to you.

The Four Most Common Metrical Patterns

When we speak conversational English, an accent naturally falls every two or three syllables. The most common metrical patterns in poetry are ones where the accent happens every two syllables (**duple meter**) or every three syllables (**triple meter**).

In **trochaic** meter, the accent always comes first (/ u), so the pattern sounds as if it is **falling:** TUM ta TUM ta TUM ta TUM ta. Read the poem below aloud. We'll be coming back to it more closely, but this time, just read it aloud to feel the meter physically in your throat and/or your ear.

From The Song of Hiawatha, *Henry Wadsworth Longfellow (1855)*

/ ˘ / ˘ / ˘ / ˘
YE who LOVE the HAUNTS of NATure,
Love the sunshine of the meadow,
Love the shadow of the forest,
Love the wind among the branches,
And the rain-shower and the snow-storm,
And the rushing of great rivers
Through their palisades of pine-trees,
And the thunder in the mountains,
Whose innumerable echoes
Flap like eagles in their eyries;—
Listen to these wild traditions,
To this Song of Hiawatha!

Did you find yourself accenting "and" and "to" slightly? Longfellow chose this meter, which he had heard used in ancient Finnish epic poetry, because it reminded him of drumbeats and seemed appropriate to the stateliness and power he found in Native American culture. The meter is very regular, though sometimes there are variations, as in line 6, where he changes the rhythm to a **rising** font ("of great") instead of staying with the trochaic, falling pattern.

In **iambic** meter, the unstressed syllable comes before the accent (u /), so the pattern sounds as if it is rising: ta TUM ta TUM ta TUM ta TUM. Read this poem aloud and experience the meter:

From "To My Dearest and Loving Husband," Anne Bradstreet (1678)

˘ / ˘ / ˘ / ˘ / ˘ /
If EVer TWO were ONE, then SURElу WE.
If ever man were loved by wife, then thee;
If ever wife was happy in a man,
Compare with me ye women if you can.
I prize thy love more than whole mines of gold,
Or all the riches that the East doth hold.
My love is such that rivers cannot quench,
Nor ought but love from thee give recompense.
Thy love is such I can no way repay;
The heavens reward thee manifold, I pray.
Then while we live, in love let's so persever,
That when we live no more we may live ever.

One of the United States' first published poets, Bradstreet chose this dignified, rational-sounding meter to lend her words the authority of the British poetic tradition. The familiar metrical pattern echoes Shakespeare, Milton, and other powerful poets, and the rising rhythm's insistent regularity lends force to the argument about love's power and persistence. One of the most interesting aspects of the poem is the varying of the rising pattern with extra syllables at the end of the last two lines, a variation we will discuss in the next chapter.

The **anapestic** meter is a rising triple meter (u u /): ta ta TUM ta ta TUM ta ta TUM ta ta TUM. Here is the an excerpt from the most famous anapestic poem in English:

From "The Night Before Christmas," Henry Livingston Jr. (ca. 1822)

˘ ˘ / ˘ ˘ / ˘ ˘ / ˘ ˘ /
Twas the NIGHT before CHRISTmas, and ALL through the HOUSE,
not a creature was stirring, not even a mouse.
The stockings were hung by the chimney with care,
in hopes that St. Nicholas soon would be there.

The children were nestled all snug in their beds,
while visions of sugarplums danced in their heads,
and mamma in her 'kerchief, and I in my cap,
had just settled down for a long winter's nap,
when out on the lawn there arose such a clatter,
I sprang from the bed to see what was the matter.
Away to the window I flew like a flash,
tore open the shutters and threw up the sash.
The moon on the breast of the new-fallen snow
gave the lustre of mid-day to objects below . . .

The anapest is like an extended iamb with an extra unaccented syllable; anapests are often found in iambic lines and vice versa. Do you notice any places where Livingston varies the anapests with iambs? Notice especially the beginnings of lines. But the overall lilt of the triple pattern, each anapest skating over two syllables at a time on its way to the accent, lends speed and a light, whimsical touch to the poem.

In **dactylic** meter the accent comes before two unstressed syllables, making it a falling triple meter (/uu): TUM ta ta TUM ta ta TUM ta ta TUM ta ta, almost like an extended trochee with an extra unstressed syllable. The pattern resembles that of a waltz:

From Evangeline, *Henry Wadsworth Longfellow (1850)*

´ ˘ ˘ ´ ˘ ˘ ´ ˘ ˘ ´ ˘ ˘ ´ ˘ ˘
THIS is the FORest primEval. The MURmuring PINES and the
´ ˘
HEMlocks,
Bearded with moss, and in garments green, indistinct in the twilight,
Stand like Druids of eld, with voices sad and prophetic,
Stand like harpers hoar, with beards that rest on their bosoms.
Loud from its rocky caverns, the deep-voiced neighboring ocean
Speaks, and in accents disconsolate answers the wail of the forest.

This is the forest primeval; but where are the hearts that beneath it
Leaped like the roe, when he hears in the woodland the voice of the
huntsman?
Where is the thatch-roofed village, the home of Acadian farmers?

Men whose lives glided on like rivers that water the woodlands,
Darkened by shadows of earth, but reflecting an image of heaven?
Waste are those pleasant farms, and the farmers forever departed!
Scattered like dust and leaves, when the mighty blasts of October
Seize them, and whirl them aloft, and sprinkle them far o'er the ocean.
Naught but tradition remains of the beautiful village of Grand-Pré.

While dactyls, like any meter, can lend themselves to any mood, this falling triple meter is well suited for solemn, thoughtful passages such as the opening of Longfellow's epic poem *Evangeline,* once so famous it was memorized by schoolchildren throughout the United States. Longfellow's American epic is a story of love, not war, but he copied his lines of dactylic meter from the meter of classical epics, the *Iliad, Odyssey,* and *Aeneid.* Like classical dactylic meter, *Evangeline* intersperses many trochees (the two-syllable pattern used in *Hiawatha*) with the dactyls. Each line moves through a series of falling patterns, until at the end it seems to complete itself, resolving in a kind of meditative balance before the next line begins.

That's it. The four patterns you have just learned—two triple, two double, two falling, two rising—are the basis of almost all metrical poetry in English.

Practice: Go back over the four poems and scan them by marking with a wand (/) where you hear a strong accent. Remember to mark only the accents that are stronger than the syllables around them. If you hear an accent that is not as strong as the others, you may use a half-accent to mark it (\). Don't worry if the words don't match up exactly with the patterns. Later you will go back and finish your scansions.

Meter, Rhythm, and the Metrical Foot

We've discussed syllable and accent (sometimes called stress, beat, or strong syllable). The next key term you need to know is **foot.** A foot is the repeating pattern of accents and unaccented syllables that moves a line of meter along. It pays no attention to words, only syllables. Each iamb, trochee, anapest, or dactyl (along with other, less common feet we'll get to later) is called a foot. A straight vertical line, the **foot break,** is used to indicate where one foot stops and another starts. A foot break can happen between words or in the middle of a word.

Most metrical lines have either three feet, four feet, or five feet, but a line could have as many as nine feet.

1 foot monometer
2 feet dimeter
3 feet trimeter
4 feet tetrameter
5 feet pentameter
6 feet hexameter
7 feet heptameter
8 feet octameter
9 feet nonameter

Let's look at the first lines of each of the four poems above:

This line of trochaic meter has four feet, so it's trochaic tetrameter:
YE who I LOVE a I NAtion's I LEgends, /u I /u I / I /u

This line of iambic meter has five feet, so it's iambic pentameter:
If EVIer TWO I were ONE, I then SUREIly WE. u/ I u/ I u/ I u/ I u/

This line of anapestic meter has four feet, so it's anapestic tetrameter:
Twas the NIGHT I before CHRISTImas, and ALL I through the HOUSE,
uu/ I uu/ I uu/ I uu/

This line of dactylic meter has six feet, so it's dactylic hexameter:
THIS is the I FORest primIEval. The I MURmuring I PINES and the I HEMlocks,
/uu I /uu I /uu I /uu I /uu I /u

Notice that the last foot above, HEMlocks, is not the same as the others. In fact, go back and re-read the four poems above one more time. If you listen carefully, you'll see that none of them is perfectly regular. Each has some variations, such as an initial syllable of the first word of a line or the final syllable of the last word left off; some lines slip in another kind of foot besides the basic foot of the poem. When metrically accomplished poets write in meter, they almost always vary it. In fact, it's often this interplay between the basic foot, which the reader comes to expect, and the variations from it, that carries the tension and expression of the poem. We'll explore this further in the next chapters.

For now, it may help to understand that meter and **rhythm** are two different things. Meter is a predictable structure of stressed and unstressed syllables in a clear pattern. It's a scaffolding, a skeleton, like the framework of a house. Rhythm is an expressive movement of energy that can change. Rhythm, the underlying life-pulse of the poem, derives not only from patterns of stress and unstress but also from other elements including word length, word-music, line breaks in free verse, and syntax and phrasing.

I have a student who grew up reading "The Night Before Christmas" aloud expressively in family poetry-reading competitions. Because of the strong, predictable anapestic meter of the poem, she was able to read the poem in any rhythm she chose for dramatic effect: a racing galloping, or a long suspenseful hush after "not a creature was stirring." Whatever she did, it wouldn't change the underlying meter.

Meter is by definition predictable, and rhythm is not. That's why different poets, or poems, using the exact same meter can sound so very different in their pacing and overall effect. But meter is the most fundamental, powerful, conspicuous, and distinctive tool that poets have available to create, and break, rhythm, and to mark a poem with their own uniquely recognizable rhythmic pulse.

Meter in Contemporary Poetry

Beginning writers are often leery of meter, associating it with "old" poems and believing that forward-looking contemporary poetry is not concerned with it. This is far from the case. The following poems were all written during the last few years. Read them aloud, first just to enjoy them and then a second time to identify their meters. Listen for the predominant meter and notice with your ear any variations from it. How does the meter add to the effect of each poem? You'll note that in the Jarnot poem, the ends of the metrical feet may not correspond exactly with the ends of the lines. This is an unusual strategy, but it doesn't change the meter of the poem.

"Hound Pastoral," Lisa Jarnot

Of the hay in the barn
and the hound in the field

of the bay in the sound, of the
sound of the hound in the field

of the back of the field of the
bay and the front of the field

of the back of the hound and the
front of the hound and the sound
of the hound when he bays at
the sound in the field

with the baying of hounds in the
baying of arms in the field

of the hound on the page in the
sound of the hound in the field

of the hay that unrests near
the hound in the barn in the field

of the bend in the barn in the
sound of the hound in the bay
by the barn in the field.

From "Parable," Allison Joseph

Sweep the walk and cook the dinner,
have his babies but stay thinner.

Raise his children, feed them knowledge,
clean the house with spit and polish.

Wipe their noses, scrub their fingers,
do their laundry, tweeze their splinters,

buy the groceries, sew on patches,
while your hair falls out in thatches.

Chop the veggies, fry the bacon,
tell your girlfriends they're mistaken

when you see your husband straying,
though his hair is dull and graying.

Wash the windows, weed the garden,
feel yourself begin to harden

as your husband packs his suitcase,
shines his shoes then ties each shoelace . . .

"Nineveh Fallen," Rachel Loden

Kuyunjik, palace mound

Nineveh fallen. My
Ghostly battalion
Silver-bell ankle rings
Tatterdemalion

Babylon Cadillac. Black
Candle guttering
Nettle-leav'd bellflowers
Sweet-faced American

Elvis in Cuneiform
Black-winged deity
Fifteen-gate city of
Mooncalf & talisman

Nineveh fallen. My
Ghostly battalion
Daughters of Sargon
Be carried away

The Line in Free Verse and Metrical Poetry

Writing free verse can give us the habit of thinking of the line as something to "break," for cleverness's or surprise's sake or to build energy in the poem. But a line in metrical poetry needs to be treated with more respect; it has a stronger inherent identity than the line in free verse. As we will see in the chapter on free verse, free-verse poems tend to break the line based on visual effect, not on sound. But metrical poems use the line as a unit of sound, of voice.

When poets who are used to writing in free verse first begin writing in meter, sometimes they break lines in a visual manner, as if they were breaking lines of free verse. For example, a student in a beginning meter class opened an iambic pentameter poem with these lines: "He walks in late again and sits his little / girl on the tiny plastic chair. She starts / to cry . . ." These might be interesting free-verse line breaks, but in a metrical poem they tend to undermine the aural integrity of the line. She was happier with the opening of her poem after she had rewritten it to break the lines in accord with the natural sound of their phrasing: "He walks in late and sits his little girl / on the tiny plastic chair. She starts to cry. . ." As a basis for a metrical line, the habit of keeping phrases together is much more effective; if the poet did decide to break one line against the natural phrase-sounds for a special effect, the line break would be much more dramatic by contrast.

For those used to reading and writing free verse, here's something else to keep in mind: lines of metrical poetry should break in places where the syntax provides a natural break. This is not at all the case for most types of free verse (except for incantatory or accent-based free verse). But for metrical poetry, though you can vary this principle for expressive purposes, it should always be the general rule. Why? Because meter creates the same kind of kinetic surprise and energy throughout an entire poetic line that free verse creates at the line breaks; it's as if each foot break is a miniature line-break, with the same potential for syntactical surprise, enjambment into the next foot, and meaningful variation that line breaks provide in free verse. As a result, by the end of each line of a good metrical poem, a reader's rhythmic attention has already had quite a workout. If you break lines in metrical poetry with the freedom and casualness regarding syntax that you might use in free verse, your reader will become at best rhythmically confused, and at worst seasick.

How to Scan a Poem

Now go back through each group of poems, the old and the new, and scan them. It is important not to skip steps but to follow each step in turn (you have already done step 1 for the group of old poems). Follow this system until you know a particular meter inside out, and your foundation will remain accurate.

Step 1. Mark the accents: listen to where you hear an accent and mark it with a wand over the syllable, just as you did for accentual poetry in the last chapter. Use a reversed wand if you need to. Remember, your ear, not your brain, is the ultimate authority. It may help to read the poem aloud while emphasizing the strongest accents and reducing the emphasis on any secondary accents.

Step 2. The remaining syllables are unstressed. Mark them with cups over the syllables.

Step 3. Look for repeating patterns. Mark the foot breaks between repeating patterns with a vertical line (if the foot break falls in the middle of a word, put the foot break line right through the middle of the word). Sometimes there will be two correct ways to divide the feet, say, into anapestic tetrameter or iambic pentameter. If you have a choice, always choose the meter that gives the same number of feet as the other lines in poem.

Step 4. Some scanners like to mark "promoted" syllables—places where the meter creates a stress where there would not be one in speech—with a special mark: an accent over a cup. This makes you more aware of how the line works, and you can do this if you like.

As you go, savor how the process of scanning helps you appreciate each syllable of the poem and its particular, unique weight at this spot in the poem. Feel the delicious differences between lines that scan identically but have very different words. Feel the effects of any contrasts between your expectation and the actual pattern, as you move through the lines. This is the pleasure of scansion: it helps you to feel a poem's physical presence more attentively, more deeply.

Hints:

Look at the context of the poem for clues about the line length. In an iambic pentameter poem, every line will have five feet, even if the poet has used variation so that some of those feet are not iambs. As a good rule of thumb, remember that there is usually at least one accent per foot; so, if you know from the other lines that a poem is written in pentameter, your scansion of each line should have at least five accents in it.

While most lines scan quite straightforwardly, some lines are difficult to scan. There are even a few lines that critics have spent decades arguing over the correct way of scanning. So, if you get confused about a particular line, don't worry too much about it. The following advice will help with tricky lines:

1. When in doubt, read the poem aloud again in a relaxed manner. The stressed syllables may seem to "pop out" at you. Listen for the swing of the meter.
2. Go back and check your scansion to make sure that you marked the accents first, before bothering with cups and foot breaks, and that you marked the accents your ear was actually hearing. Many scansion problems come from trying to force a poem into a meter we *think* it should have, instead of *listening* to the actual rhythm.
3. Hear the line you have doubts about in the context of the rest of the poem.
4. Remind yourself that if other lines in the poem have a certain number of feet, your scansion of this line probably should have at least that number of accents (for example, in iambic pentameter, each line generally has at least five accents). Maybe you are missing a light accent that is actually supposed to be promoted (made stronger) by the meter. Or maybe there is a variation, such as a spondee (which we will discuss in the next chapter).
5. If a line has more accents than other lines in the poem, remember that though every syllable in speech is somewhat accented, you only need to mark the *strong* accents.
6. Get a friend or two (or a big group!) to say the poem aloud with you. Combined voices usually decide quite clearly where the accents should fall.
7. If you are still confused about whether a syllable is accented or not, consider using the half-accent, marked by the reverse wand (\), a symbol that has resolved many metrical arguments. For example, listen to the meter in the following lines from an iambic pentameter sonnet by Edna St. Vincent Millay:

Love is not all: it is not meat nor drink,
Nor slumber nor a roof against the rain.

Most people would be comfortable scanning the second "nor" in the second line as an accent (making the second foot an iamb), but others might hear it as so lightly stressed compared to "roof" that they would prefer to scan it with a cup (making the second foot a pyrrhic). For still others, neither of those would feel accurate; they could use a compromise symbol, the reversed wand. None of these is the "right" scansion of this foot—it's a matter of individual preference. Some other choices, such as, for example, scanning the first line as a footless dactylic tetrameter, would in fact be "wrong" scansions, since they would violate the metrical contract between the poet and reader that says the poem is in iambic pentameter and each line has five feet. But in the case of the scansion of "nor," any of the three choices would be reasonable and would preserve the metrical contract and maintain the poem's overall scansion as iambic pentameter.

One word of caution: I would advise you to use half-accents sparingly, as they are rarely necessary and can make scansions look like a confusing thicket—but if using one will allow you to move on and enjoy the sound of a poem instead of worrying over whether a syllable is accented or not, it is well worth it.

If you are very confused about how to scan a particular line, consider starting your scanning at the end of the line instead of at the beginning. I remember vividly that when I was a young poet and first met the formalist poet Dana Gioia, Dana showed me some notebooks that he kept solely to practice scansion in, filled with metrically tricky poems copied out in his extremely neat handwriting and then scanned. One line, which happened to be the opening of one of my favorite poems by Yeats, had given him particular trouble:

Suddenly I saw the cold and rook-delighting heaven

He explained that after repeated attempts, he had only figured out how to scan the line by starting at the end of the line. To do that, he had ignored the extra-syllable ending and then marked all the iambs, since he knew from the context of the rest of the poem that the line was iambic. That process had made it clear to him that the line was in iambic heptameter with the first syllable of the first iamb left off (such a "headless" line is not uncommon).

Don't get too focused on the idea of the meter. That will ruin your enjoyment and lead to mistakes. Your ear and/or your body are the final metrical authority. So, when in doubt, read aloud! Pleasure is the ultimate aim of scansion—to help you hear better where the rhythms of a poem lie, to distinguish between subtle degrees of emphasis that can poignantly affect meaning, and to appreciate and learn from the exquisite skill of a poet who may have spent decades perfecting the subtle art of metrical writing.

A Note on Scansion and Subjectivity: The 80/20 Rule

When people first learn how to scan, sometimes they are dismayed to discover the subjective component of meter and scansion. Two people in a group may disagree, for example, on whether a certain syllable in a poem should be stressed or not. Maybe one person has a different pronunciation of the word based on a regional dialect, or a different emotional interpretation of the line. It is not uncommon to feel frustrated at such moments, and perhaps even to be tempted to give up the entire effort. After all, prosody is sometimes dubbed a "science," and if you are going to go to all the trouble to learn it, shouldn't there be a guarantee of solid answers? If there's no clear answer to the simple question, "Is this syllable stressed or not?" does that mean there aren't any clear answers? Maybe the whole business of scanning a poem is subjective, so then who's to say that a line is iambic? Why not just call it dactylic? Who could stop me if I said that's how I hear it?

If you are having such thoughts, it may help to remember the 80/20 rule. As a rule, a group of people hearing a given poem will all agree on at least 80 percent of its scansion—and the proportion is usually higher. The area for disagreement will be 20 percent or less of syllables in the poem. Furthermore, even in those cases, it's likely the disagreement won't affect the overall scansion of the poem, but only the foot in question. For example, people who hear "fire" pronounced with two syllables will hear the second foot as an anapest in the line, "I fire the smoke and let the heat resound," while people who hear "fire" pronounced with one syllable will hear that foot as an iamb. But whether the second foot is an iamb or an anapest, both groups can still agree that the line is iambic pentameter. Or, in this line by Charles Martin, "Tired of earth, they dwindled on their hill," some will hear "tired" as one syllable and the first line as a headless iambic pentameter; others will hear the first foot as a trochee. But either way, the rest of the line is not affected.

The 80/20 rule assumes a shared basic level of knowledge about meter. You may occasionally encounter people who are so unfamiliar with a certain meter that they are physically unable to hear it; because of the long-reigning dominance of iambic meter in poetry, this sometimes happens with noniambic meters. As with any field of which someone is truly ignorant, in that case discussion may not be possible since even the 80 percent may not be shared. But in general, you can rest assured that the 20 percent or less of scansion that is subjective, while it allows for individual variations in linguistic background, speech patterns, personality, mood, and interpretation of the poem, does not make it necessary to throw the validity of the shared, objective 80 percent of scansion into question, nor to forgo the innumerable benefits of scansion.

Knowing how to scan puts you on an intimate basis with poems so that you can feel the ear and the body of the poets at work, not only in the choice of what meter they used but in how and why they varied it. In the Millay poem quoted above, for example, scanning the poem will remind you that the word "love" which opens the poem should not be accented at all, metrically speaking. The fact that Millay does accent the word, in the context of the poem's overall meaning, lends the opening of the poem a poignant and touching bravado. As you begin to hear such effects in other poets, your own metrical writing will become increasingly assured and effective. And in the process of becoming proficient at scanning, you will broaden the repertoire of meters that come naturally to you.

Why Bother?

Some poets who aren't used to writing in meter are afraid that it will be constricting. It is. It requires the sacrifice of infinite choices, and a possible commitment to spending extra time on a poem, to yield meter's benefits: increased rhythmical, musical, and performative control over your lines; surprising discoveries of words and phrases you would never have found on your own; the potential for powerful impact on the reader and for remarkable beauty. These fruits are more than worth the trouble to those poets willing to put in some metrical practice (usually only a month or two is sufficient to learn the basics). And once you've learned the basics, the skill will be with you forever. It's like playing music. As *The Jazz Piano Book* says: "When McCoy Tyner is playing a million notes a minute, he is not thinking, 'Left hand 3-5-7-9, 7th down a half step.' He's done that already, many years ago. He knows what the chord looks like and feels like when he plays it. Aim for the state of grace where you no longer have to think about theory. In order to reach that point, you'll have to think about theory a great deal."

QUESTIONS FOR MEDITATION OR DISCUSSION

Recently, scientists in Germany experimented with the effect of meter on heart rate. They found that reading aloud poetry in dactylic hexameter for 15 minutes was much better for synchronizing people's heart rate with their breath after a heart attack than either regular breathing or controlled breathing. Researchers have also found that reading aloud metrical poetry helps stroke victims and autistic people talk when nothing else can. Think about your own experience reading metrical poetry. Do you experience any physical effects?

For centuries there has been an ongoing discussion about whether certain meters are better suited for certain moods or subjects. What do you think? Experiment with different phrases and meanings and see if it is harder for you to express certain kinds of things in certain rhythms.

Derek Attridge's books *Rhythms of English Poetry* and *Poetic Rhythm* sparked something of a controversy in the world of prosody. Attridge, a linguist who has worked extensively with accentual poetry, proposes a system of scansion that does away with the foot altogether and concentrates on the relation between the expectation of a certain number of stresses in a line and the occurrence (or nonoccurrence) of those stresses.

By contrast, *A Poet's Craft* focuses on the traditional accentual-syllabic system of scansion for three reasons: it is still by far the most commonly known and accepted system; the terminology seems to me simpler and more graceful than Attridge's; and, most importantly, I find the foot indispensable to understanding the rhythms of poetry. The foot marks out a certain period of time, a kind of "waiting" place in which a stress can occur as expected, or occur unexpectedly lightly, or unexpectedly heavily, or occur not at all, in relation to the other feet in analogous places in other lines in the poem. For example, when we read the excerpt from Anne Bradstreet's poem above, the stress on the word "whole" at the beginning of the third foot strikes us intensely, if we are reading carefully, because unconsciously we are aware of the grid of the poem and are registering the fact that the previous three lines have not had a stress in the corresponding foot of the line. To me, the foot breaks are like the "warp" in weaving, a strong framework of parallel threads that the rest of the poem can be woven across, like a "weft" of lines ducking in and out through the warp-threads. Without the feet, awareness of that important spatial aspect of the poem's rhythmic tapestry is completely lost.

That said, Attridge's theories have passionate proponents who think the concept of the foot is unnecessary. A useful project for readers interested in prosody would be to read some of Attridge's work and come to their own conclusions.

QUOTES

Poetry is emotion put into measure. The emotion must come by nature, but the measure can be acquired by art.

—Thomas Hardy

I think that a poet who doesn't know anything about metrics, who hasn't really practiced the discipline of formal metrics is at a great loss. . . . You can be free in heroic couplets. In completely unconfined, unrestrained verse, one is a prisoner of infinity; that is the worst kind of bondage because there is no escape from it.

—Stanley Kunitz

True Ease in Writing comes from Art, not Chance,
As those move easiest who have learn'd to dance.

—Alexander Pope

However minute the employment may appear, and whatever ridicule may be incurred by a solemn deliberation upon accents and pauses, it is certain that without this petty knowledge no man [*sic*] can be a poet.

—Samuel Johnson

"Fighting Words," Dorothy Parker (1927)

Say my love is easy had,
Say I'm bitten raw with pride,
Say I am too often sad—
Still behold me at your side.

Say I'm neither brave nor young,
Say I woo and coddle care,
Say the devil touched my tongue—
Still you have my heart to wear.

But say my verses do not scan,
And I get me another man!

I approach a poem in just the same way a free-verse writer does. What matters is the subject and the words that are going to be found for conveying and exploring the subject. The only difference is that I include meters and rhymes in my free-verse proceeding.

—Richard Wilbur

Verse form literally embodies theme. If you think of form as the outside of an Inside, that's only half the truth. Verse form is also inside the Inside. It acts as a skeleton as well as a skin. It is a body.

—Molly Peacock

Jettison ornament gaily but keep shape.

—Basil Bunting

Poetry begins to atrophy when it gets too far from the music.

—Ezra Pound

On the matter of song: I believe there must be a return toward the musical structure of poetry, just as there must be, for certain people at least, a return to warmth within a relationship.

—Paul Blackburn

POETRY PRACTICES

(Group) Name Dance. Scan your names and those of your friends.

(Group) Dada Meter Hat. With a group of poets, or even alone, try my metrical version of the famous Dada hat game. It's a great way to bypass the compulsion to make sense, opening yourself to the sheer fun of meter. Each person writes down a dozen of their favorite words, cuts them apart, and puts the separated words in a communal basket. Individually or in small groups, pull out several words from the basket and arrange groups of words into lines of iambs, trochees, dactyls, and anapests. Share the lines with the rest of the group. If you write lines on a board, notice how all the lines in a certain meter can combine into surprising poems that are held together by their common metrical pattern. Also be sure to notice how any word, of any length and rhythm, can be used in a line of any meter; you may think at first, for example, that the word "beautiful" can only be used in a dactylic line, since it is a dactylic word, but if you play this game correctly you should find yourself using it in lines of all four meters: not only the dactylic "beautiful fun in the teeth of the infinite," but also the anapestic "in the teeth of the beautiful infinite fun," the iambic "in fun the teeth of beautiful the infinite," and the trochaic "beautiful the teeth in fun of infinite the" (nobody said these phrases had to make sense). This lesson is one of the most important things you can learn about meter.

(Group) Call and Response. One person reads a metrical line (regular or, later on, with variations) and everyone else needs to write down a line in the identical, syllable-by-syllable rhythm of accented and unaccented syllables. The response lines can be read aloud separately, or combined into one poem. This is a good method of ear training, since it makes you focus on every syllable.

(Group) Metrical Mad Libs. Pick a poem in a regular meter and cross out certain words. Solicit words in the same metrical pattern from the group, and fill in the blanks before you read the result aloud, as in Mad Libs.

(Group) Metrical Talking. Form conversational-size groups and practice talking in one meter of the four basic meters at a time. The rule is that you can only speak if you talk in the appropriate meter. You may want to rotate meters so each group has a chance to try all four. Then have a large group conversation with one of these variations: (*a*) conversation stays in one meter until someone calls "switch" or otherwise signals a change to another meter; (*b*) any meter is allowed, and each person says which meter the last sentence was before they say their own sentence; (*c*) any meter is allowed and everyone talks the best they can.

(Group or individual) Drumming on the Table. Drumming in different meters is an excellent way to become familiar with the patterns. Use your palms on the table or your feet on the floor, or even better, get a drum and use patterns of loud and soft drumming. See if you can identify meters someone taps out. Or accompany yourself or someone else reciting a metrical poem, like an Anglo-Saxon **scop.** The recitation should be slow enough that you can drum once per syllable. Practice at least a few times before performing.

Metrical Compass. (This exercise is recommended as a foundation in addition to any of the others.) Write nine unrhymed lines in trochaic tetrameter. (Tetrameter is a good line-length to start with because it is long enough to get momentum going but short enough to stay focused.) Don't worry about making any sense at first; just focus on the rhythm (if you want to write nonsense like "Sting the open roses happy, springing follicles rely," that's fine). Try using your ear to guide you. My advice is to read a poem in the same meter aloud before you start, to "entrain" the rhythm in your ear. A drum can have the same effect. Just absorb the rhythm through reading the poem or listening to the drum, and then keep going on your own ("entraining" is a term developed by my student Patricia Hagge, a yoga teacher, who has a strong sense of the physical reality of meter).

When you think you have done it, scan the lines following the three steps on page 322 to make sure the meter is exact. If you have trouble hearing the meter, it can help to ask someone else to read it aloud. First mark the stresses and then fill in the unstressed syllables. You can use the standard method, u and / on your keyboard, or write marks in by hand above the words, or use boldface or capital letters for stressed syllables. But whatever marks you use, *be sure to do the final step—after the syllables are marked, add foot breaks to show where the pattern repeats. Use pencil at first, until you get the hang of it.* Making decisions about foot breaks will force you to listen to the underlying heartbeat of the line—the norm from which variation occurs—and will deepen the quality of your attention: not only your awareness of the contrasts between varying lines, but also even of the way passages that look metrically identical are using the meter in different ways.

Don't worry if the process seems mechanical at first, and you find yourself exaggerating or counting on your fingers. You'll get beyond that soon enough. Keep scanning and rewriting until your words fit the pattern. Then use the same technique to write at least nine lines each in unrhymed anapestic tetrameter, iambic tetrameter, and dactylic tetrameter. Don't forget to scan each one, including foot breaks, to show the meter. Ideally, you will review the sections on each meter in this chapter, and in the "Metrical Palette" chapter up ahead if you like, noting common variations and so forth, before you engage with each of the four meters. Switching between meters can be tiring the first time or two, but the metrical flexibility that is your goal is well within reach.

After you have the basics of each point of the metrical compass down, you will learn in the next few chapters about how to vary the meter and aim for a more complex, natural sound.

Note: if you have any trouble with this exercise, or if you feel inhibited or stuck when you try to write in meter, please do the next exercise, "Meter Moving," first, and then return to the "Metrical Compass."

Meter Moving. Using a drum or your voice chanting to mark the rhythms, dance or move to the four different meters learned in this chapter. A simple way is to choose a line of your own, or one from another poem, that you like and that you know is in the correct meter. Recite the line aloud as many times as you like while dancing in a rhythmic way, perhaps moving in a circle. When you feel confident, stop saying the line and start making up new lines in the same meter and saying them aloud while you continue dancing. Lay a notebook open, and pause to write the lines down.

Advanced dancing: The ancient Greek choruses used to use special steps to dance parts of verse plays in various meters. I will never forget seeing poet and classicist A. E. Stallings dancing meters out in the ancient manner. She lowered her arms and took a long step for the long (stressed syllable), raised her arms and took short steps for the short (cupped) syllable. Try this method, or develop your own vocabulary of dance steps or hand gestures to dance out a favorite metrical passage.

CHAPTER 13

The Many Voices of Iambic Meter

Just as skilled saxophone players can make distinct and different voices sound through the same musical instrument, skilled poets can make distinct and different voices sound through the same metrical instrument. The basic iambic pentameter pattern, the most common iambic line-length, can encompass lines as simple as "I work all day, and get half-drunk at night" or as convoluted as "the sceptred terror of whose sessions rends"; as gentle as "How do I love thee? Let me count the ways" or as intense as "gusty emotions on wet roads on autumn nights"; as light as "I hold my honey and I store my bread" or as heavy as "rocks, caves, lakes, fens, bogs, dens, and shades of death"; as direct as "Shall I compare thee to a summer's day?" (or as the title of this chapter) or as arcane as "Dead locked with them, taking root as cradles rock." These lines (by Philip Larkin, Hart Crane, Elizabeth Barrett Browning, Wallace Stevens, Gwendolyn Brooks, John Milton, William Shakespeare, Alexander Pope, and Sylvia Plath), are all just simple 10-syllable iambic pentameters, most of them consisting of five iambs in a row. Even without any rhythmic variation, they are astonishingly different in voice. When you add in the numerous possibilities of metrical variation through substitution—the central subject of this chapter—the rhythmic options of iambic pentameter are inexhaustible. And even that is without the variation of actual words themselves, the way the lengths of syllables and play of vowels and consonants also change the rhythms of words.

Even after a century dominated by free verse, it is still true to say that the vast bulk of respected, literary poetry written in English over the last five hundred years has been written in iambic pentameter. This is one of the reasons the following poem is so wryly funny:

"Approaching a Significant Birthday, He Peruses The Norton Anthology of Poetry,*" R. S. Gwynn*

All human things are subject to decay.
Beauty is momentary in the mind.
The curfew tolls the knell of parting day.
If Winter comes, can Spring be far behind?
Forlorn! the very word is like a bell
And somewhat of a sad perplexity.
Here, take my picture, though I bid farewell,
In a dark time the eye begins to see
The woods decay, the woods decay and fall—
Bare ruined choirs where late the sweet birds sang.
What but design of darkness to appall?
An aged man is but a paltry thing.
If I should die, think only this of me:
Crass casualty obstructs the sun and rain
When I have fears that I may cease to be,
To cease upon the midnight with no pain
And hear the spectral singing of the moon
And strictly meditate the thankless muse.
The world is too much with us, late and soon.
It gathers to a greatness, like the ooze.
Do not go gentle into that good night.
Fame is no plant that grows on mortal soil.
Again he raised the jug up to the light:
Old age hath yet his honor and his toil.
Downward to darkness on extended wings,
Break, break, break, on thy cold gray stones, O sea,
And tell sad stories of the death of kings.
I do not think that they will sing to me.

Each of these lines is taken from a famous poem in iambic pentameter. Gwynn's clever use of their rhymes to link them across poets and centuries underscores their disarming rhythmic kinship. You can get a related effect by skimming the index of first lines in an older anthology such as the classic *Palgrave's Golden Treasury of Poetry.* Most of the index will be in iambic pentameter, and those lines that are not will be mostly in the runner-up meter, iambic tetrameter.

(Please note that this is not true of contemporary anthologies of formal verse such as the often-used *Strong Measures,* which include many poems that do *not* scan regularly.)

Louise Bogan called iambic pentameter "the large carrier of English poetry." Iambic pentameter is so common in English-language poetry, so familiar, that if people want to evoke the idea of meter in general, often they will murmur in this pattern: ta-TUM-ta-TUM-ta-TUM-ta-TUM-ta-TUM. Even with Dickinson, Whitman, and the major free verse poets of the twentieth century taken into account, the majority of the so far-acknowledged great poets of the English language wrote much or all of their poetry in iambic pentameter, among them Chaucer, Spenser, Shakespeare, Milton, Donne, Pope, Wordsworth, Coleridge, Keats, Shelley, Tennyson, both Brownings, and in the twentieth-century Yeats, Frost, Auden, Crane, Millay, Stevens, Hayden, Heaney, and Walcott.

Blank Iambic Verse, Enjambment, and Caesura

A note on terminology: The technical term for unrhymed poetry in meter is **blank verse.** You should be aware that, since such a huge majority of metrical poetry is in iambic pentameter, some books use the term blank verse to mean simply "unrhymed iambic pentameter." (Of course, iambic pentameter can also be combined into many kinds of rhyme patterns, from the basic "heroic couplet" of two rhymed lines on up to 10-line stanzas.) But in this book, which acknowledges the importance of noniambic meters, I will specify **blank iambic verse** when discussing unrhymed iambic pentameter specifically, to distinguish this prevalent meter of English poetry from **blank dactylic verse, blank trochaic verse,** and so on.

Much of the most influential iambic pentameter poetry, from Shakespeare's plays to *Paradise Lost,* is blank iambic verse. Unlike rhymed stanzas which tend to make a reader stop at the ends of lines, all blank verse is a fluid, flexible medium in which the sentences tend to roll over from line to line. Skillful blank verse poets manipulate not only the meter within each line but also the play of language over the lines. The poem below, according to family stories, was a favorite poem of my great-aunt Jessie Hughan—a brave woman who ran for office before U.S. women even had the vote. I feel I know more about her whenever I read this famous poem told in the voice of Ulysses, after the adventures of the *Odyssey* were over. The poem is designed to sound well aloud and to be enjoyable to read aloud; in those days before television, a favorite poem would be read aloud to friends and family often in the evenings. Read it aloud, and notice the variety of sentence lengths in the poem, beginning with the contrast between the first two sentences (and while you're at it, keep an eye out for the line that appears in Gwynn's parody above):

"Ulysses," Alfred, Lord Tennyson (1842)

It little profits that an idle king,
By this still hearth, among these barren crags,
Match'd with an aged wife, I mete and dole
Unequal laws unto a savage race,
That hoard, and sleep, and feed, and know not me.
I cannot rest from travel; I will drink
Life to the lees. All times I have enjoy'd
Greatly, have suffer'd greatly, both with those
That loved me, and alone; on shore, and when
Thro' scudding drifts the rainy Hyades
Vext the dim sea. I am become a name;
For always roaming with a hungry heart
Much have I seen and known:—cities of men
And manners, climates, councils, governments,
Myself not least, but honor'd of them all,—
And drunk delight of battle with my peers,
Far on the ringing plains of windy Troy.
I am a part of all that I have met;
Yet all experience is an arch wherethrough
Gleams that untravell'd world whose margin fades
For ever and for ever when I move.
How dull it is to pause, to make an end,
To rust unburnish'd, not to shine in use!
As tho' to breathe were life! Life piled on life
Were all too little, and of one to me
Little remains: but every hour is saved
From that eternal silence, something more,
A bringer of new things; and vile it were
For some three suns to store and hoard myself,
And this gray spirit yearning in desire

To follow knowledge like a sinking star,
Beyond the utmost bound of human thought.
This is my son, mine own Telemachus,
to whom I leave the sceptre and the isle—
Well-loved of me, discerning to fulfill
This labor, by slow prudence to make mild
A rugged people, and thro' soft degrees
Subdue them to the useful and the good.
Most blameless is he, centred in the sphere
Of common duties, decent not to fail
In offices of tenderness, and pay
Meet adoration to my household gods,
When I am gone. He works his work, I mine.
There lies the port; the vessel puffs her sail;
There gloom the dark, broad seas. My mariners,
Souls that have toil'd, and wrought, and thought with me,—
That ever with a frolic welcome took
The thunder and the sunshine, and opposed
Free hearts, free foreheads,—you and I are old;
Old age hath yet his honor and his toil.
Death closes all; but something ere the end,
Some work of noble note, may yet be done,
Not unbecoming men that strove with Gods.
The lights begin to twinkle from the rocks;
The long day wanes; the slow moon climbs; the deep
Moans round with many voices. Come, my friends.
'Tis not too late to seek a newer world.
Push off, and sitting well in order smite
The sounding furrows; for my purpose holds
To sail beyond the sunset, and the baths
Of all the western stars, until I die.
It may be that the gulfs will wash us down;
It may be we shall touch the Happy Isles,
And see the great Achilles, whom we knew.
Tho' much is taken, much abides; and tho'
We are not now that strength which in old days
Moved earth and heaven, that which we are, we are,—
One equal temper of heroic hearts,

Made weak by time and fate, but strong in will
To strive, to seek, to find, and not to yield.

One of the manifestations of Tennyson's considerable skill here is the variety of ways he uses **enjambment** (from the French for "jumping off," this refers to a sentence that jumps off the end of one line and continues in the next) to keep the lines from being monotonous: for example, one line ends between a verb and its object ("I will drink / Life to the lees"), another between the addressees and the address ("Come, my friends. / 'Tis not too late").

In addition to the variations in sentence length and enjambment, Tennyson also uses another subtle method of modulating the language across lines in this poem. Each line contains a **caesura,** or pause, created by grammatical phrases and/or punctuation. The caesura's position within the line changes constantly (Alexander Pope said it should never occur in the same place for three lines in a row), and creates a rhythm of phrases that counterpoints the metrical rhythm, adding still another layer of complexity on top of the natural speech rhythms.

If you read a poem aloud, you can hear the caesuras as the places where your voice naturally pauses. Most lines that are pentameter or longer have at least one caesura, and some have two—or sometimes even three or four. The caesura in line 2 of "Ulysses" is easy to spot, since it is created by a comma. In line 1, the caesura is subtler: it is the brief pause created by the end of the verb phrase "it little profits" (subject-adverb-verb)—in line 1. Line 3 has a caesura marked and accentuated by a comma. Line 4 has a caesura after the end of the noun phrase "unequal laws" (adjective-noun). Line 5 has three caesuras marked by punctuation, the last of them the strongest. Line 6 has one caesura at the semicolon. Read the poem again, noticing caesuras, and how Tennyson balances the strength of the caesuras against the strength of the line endings. If the caesuras were too strong in comparison to the line endings, the whole orientation of the poem would be skewed, undermining the foundation of the lines.

When scanning a poem, it is customary to mark the caesuras with a double vertical line (||-like a double foot-break). If you are scanning the poem, you will notice that some caesuras occur in the middle of a metrical foot, and some between metrical feet. Traditionally, the former is called a **feminine caesura** and the latter a **masculine caesura.** Look for at least two examples of each kind of caesura in "Ulysses." Do you find that they have different effects?

The Five Basic Metrical Variations in Iambic Pentameter

Like a kaleidoscope that shifts a few pieces of color into infinite patterns, a metrical line can create innumerable rhythmic patterns by means of only a few basic changes. Because iambic pentameter is by far the most commonly used meter, the possible variations in this meter are well understood. The rest of this chapter will explore the most common of those changes—the basic vocabulary of rhythmic variation in a line of iambic pentameter. Though you will recognize the names of some meters from the previous chapter, the information here only applies to when those feet appear as variations in iambic meter.

Anapests as Variations

You will remember anapestic meter from "The Night Before Christmas." In iambic pentameter, anapests are used to vary the rhythm. Adding an anapest in place of one of the iambs in an iambic line is often said to have the effect of speeding up the line, and lightening it. Since more syllables have to fit in the same space, or time, they seem to need to be read, or spoken, more quickly. For example, scan this passage of iambic pentameter from Charles Martin's "Breaking Old Ground," and notice how the anapest in the first foot of the last line gives a feeling of lightness and casualness:

It really seems to want to be our friend,
Returning, is it, out of sympathy
Or just to see how everything will end?
Waiting, in either case, for one like me
To show up some morning at the backyard fence.

In the following sonnet, Edna St. Vincent Millay uses only one anapest in the entire poem. Scan the poem and see if you can find it. The foot where it appears has a freedom and lightness that is eloquent in the context of the rest of the poem.

"Sonnet 30," Edna St. Vincent Millay (1923)

I shall go back again to the bleak shore,
And build a little shanty on the sand

In such a way that the extremest band
Of brittle seaweed will escape my door
But by a yard or two. And nevermore
Shall I return to take you by the hand.
I shall be gone to what I understand,
And happier than I ever was before.
The love that stood a moment in your eyes,
The words that lay a moment on your tongue,
Are one with all that in a moment dies,
A little undersaid and oversung.
But I shall find the sullen rocks and skies
Unchanged from what they were when I was young.

Of course, meter is just as complex as language, and metrical effects can't be labeled all that easily. Sometimes, the effect of an anapest is not of quickness or lightness, but of struggle where three syllables try to fit in the space of two, as in the fourth foot of this iambic pentameter line:

Your DY|ing WAS | a DIF|ficult EN|terPRISE

Please note that to hear the iambic pentameter pattern in this line, you need to recognize that though the accent on the last syllable of "enterprise" is softer than the accent on the first syllable, it is still accented. (Remember the principle of relative stress: it doesn't matter how accented an accented syllable is, only that it is more accented than the syllable[s] next to it.) The third syllable of "difficult," however, is not accented, because it is in the same anapest with the much stronger syllable *en* (some people might prefer to scan "cult" as a half-stress, and this is no problem, since it doesn't change the basic pattern of the line).

The anapest can also create an effect of bending, as our expectation of a two-syllable iamb in the second and third foot in this line bends to accept a three-syllable anapest instead:

And WHET|her she BENDS | or STRAIGHT|ens TO | each BUSH

or of slowness and peace, as a two-syllable foot relaxes to hold three syllables in the second and third foot of this line:

DesPAIR | of our DAYS | and the CALM | MILK-GIV|er WHO

In each of these cases, of course, the meter is not working alone to create the effect. Meaning plays a part, and other aspects of the words—such as the unstressed, suppressed second syllable of "whether" followed by the quick short word "bend" and the contrasting, strong high-pitched syllable "straight," or the two murmuring "m's" of "calm" and "milk" next to each other—have a role as well.

In the following poem, the anapests carry a lot of emotional weight:

"The Illiterate," William Meredith

Touching your goodness, I am like a man
Who turns a letter over in his hand
And you might think this was because the hand
Was unfamiliar but, truth is, the man
Has never had a letter from anyone;
And now he is both afraid of what it means
And ashamed because he has no other means
To find out what it says than to ask someone.

His uncle could have left the farm to him,
Or his parents died before he sent them word,
Or the dark girl changed and want him for beloved.
Afraid and letter-proud, he keeps it with him.
What would you call his feeling for the words
That keep him rich and orphaned and beloved?

There are many remarkable things about this sonnet, including the use of identical words for rhymes and the last syllable which perhaps answers the poem's question in a hidden way. Meredith spent his life as a closeted gay man, a situation which perhaps adds intensity to the hidden feelings of shame and elation conveyed so subtly and skillfully in this poem. The poem is equally remarkable on the metrical level (if you scan the poem and are confused by line 12, don't worry, we'll discuss it below). Every one of the four anapests in this poem adds to the meaning. The first one, in line 5, delays a stress and so forces us to give a stronger accent to the word "anyone," pronouncing it with the exact surprise that the man must have felt. This ability to force the reader to use performative stress of particular kinds is, to my mind, one of the most marvelous capacities of metrical poetry. After this first anapest, each one in the poem emphasizes the man's confused emotions at exactly the points of most heightened poignancy: his embarrassment at the thought of asking someone, his fear about his parents, and his elation over love. Not a single metrical variation is wasted.

As in the sonnets by Meredith and Millay, ideally any variation from the basic pattern of your own metrical poems should have a sense of inevitability. When you are writing meter well and are comfortable with it, you may not even notice that you are varying the meter as you write—but when you go back and revise your poems, the sense of inevitability is something you can look for. It is a high standard to uphold, but one that will repay your attention. In a way, the skillful use of variation gets at the essence, the point, of meter, which is to make it impossible to separate the rhythm from the words, the form from the function, or, to use a phrase of Yeats', the "dancer from the dance."

Trochees as Variations

When trochees are used to vary iambic pentameter, there is an additional factor to take into account. It's easy for an anapest to fit anywhere in an iambic line without undermining the rhythm, since anapests and iambs are both rising feet: when we read Elizabeth Bishop's iambic line "some realms I owned, two rivers, a continent," the anapest in the fourth foot doesn't disturb our momentum. But a trochee is a falling foot. Since it moves in the opposite direction from an iambic line, it can cause the line to stumble. If the iambic pentameter line were, "a deep river and realms and continents," the trochee in the second foot would confuse the meter as we read the line aloud, tempting a reader to pronounce "river" as "rivER" or to stop suddenly after "deep." (If you don't notice this happening, try reading Bishop's line directly after a completely regular iambic pentameter, such as Alexander Pope's maxim "A little learning is a dangerous thing," to accentuate the effect.)

Linguists have discovered that, probably for this reason, a trochee usually occurs in iambic poems only where there is time to brace yourself and catch your balance to get ready for it: when you've had a whole line break to prepare, as in the first foot of a line (the first line below is an example), or after a caesura, as in the third foot of the third line below:

From "Among School Children," W. B. Yeats (1928)

Labour is blossoming or dancing where
The body is not bruised to pleasure soul,
Nor beauty born out of its own despair.

A trochee in the first foot, as in the word "labour," is an extremely common variation, probably the most common in iambic poetry. Trochees in the middle of a line often occur after periods or commas; in the third line of this poem, though, the phrase "nor beauty born" is followed by a strong grammatical caesura that prepares us for the trochee "out of." Unlike my hypothetical trochee "river" above, this trochee does not disturb the rest of the line; though the rhythm of "out of" surprises our ears, because of the grammatical pause, we have no trouble hearing it almost as if it were the first foot of a line, which makes it easier to reestablish the meter and hear "its own despair" as two iambs.

Because of the trochee's tendency to catch you up short, one effect of a trochee in iambic pentameter, especially at the beginning of a line, can be a sense of immediacy or surprise:

From "I Wandered Lonely as a Cloud," William Wordsworth (1804)

I wander'd lonely as a cloud
That floats on high o'er vales and hills,
When all at once I saw a crowd,
A host of golden daffodils,
Beside the lake, beneath the trees,
Fluttering and dancing in the breeze!

Though the daffodils are described as appearing suddenly, it is not until the word "Fluttering" that we feel the immediacy of their effect on the poet, the sudden vividness of the sight. This trochee, cited by Paul Fussell in his classic book *Poetic Meter and Poetic Form,* is a good illustration of how much can be accomplished with just a little metrical variation. This single foot is the only variation from strict iambic pentameter in six lines of poetry, and yet the two syllables have such an impact that I doubt the poem would be half as famous without it.

Spondees and Pyrrhics as Variations

The **spondee** (//), a foot with two stresses, and the **pyrrhic** (uu), a foot with two light syllables, are two feet that are only used to vary other meters. Given the accentual nature of English, it would be impossible to write a poem all in pyrrhics or spondees. The closest I have ever seen are Gwendolyn Brooks's great poem that begins "We real cool" and George Peele's poem below; still, notice how the spondees tend to turn into trochees as you read:

"The Pool Players, Seven at the Golden Shovel," Gwendolyn Brooks

We real cool. We
Left school. We

Lurk late. We
Strike straight. We

Sing sin. We
Thin gin. We

Jazz June. We
Die soon.

"Bathsheba's Song," George Peele (1599)

Hot sun, cool fire, tempered with sweet air,
Black shade, fair nurse, shadow my white hair,
Shine, sun, burn, fire, breathe, air, and ease me,
Black shade, fair nurse, shroud me and please me;
Shadow, my sweet nurse, keep me from burning,
Make not my glad cause, cause of mourning.
    Let not my beauty's fire
    Inflame unstaid desire,
    Nor pierce any bright eye
    That wandereth lightly.

From this unusual and extreme example, you can see that spondees are *intense.* They leave no room for breathing. When we speak in spondees, we do so out of urgency: "*Stop that*!" So when Dylan Thomas wants to hold his father back from dying, he speaks in spondees instead of iambs for four out of the poem's first six feet:

Do not go gentle into that good night,
Rage, rage against the dying of the light.

Some people may hear "Do not" as a trochee, rather than a spondee. Others will feel that it is a spondee because the expected metrical stress on "not" (because it is the second syllable of an iamb) helps give the word as much stress as "do." Others may hear it as an iamb. It doesn't really matter; the scansion of monosyllables often varies in different readers' ears because of performative accent. If you are in a group and there is disagreement over scanning, you can always compromise and mark "do" or "not" with a reversed wand (\) to signify a half-accent, which will still convey the urgency of the phrase.

Once you have the sound of a regular meter deeply established in your ear, it is humbling how deeply you can be moved by just one variation in it. For 30 years I have had the same intense response to the spondee that opens the first line of Hart Crane's "To Brooklyn Bridge," the balance and shock of whose stresses moves me just as it did when I used to carry the old paperback edition of his book *The Bridge* with me on the subway to my first job in New York City, reading the line over and over as the train jostled:

How many dawns, chill from his rippling rest
The seagull's wings shall dip and pivot him,
Shedding white rings of tumult, building high
Over the chained bay waters Liberty—

This famous opening line of Crane's epic is enhanced not just by the spondee but also by the trochee that follows the caesura, "chill from." Imagine if the line read, "How many dawns that from his rippling rest." The impact of the word "how," with its urgent, poignant dipthong defiantly stressing the first syllable like a seagull balancing on a powerful air current, would be far weaker.

A spondee and pyrrhic frequently occur together in the same line, and very often the spondee immediately follows the pyrrhic. Since the pyrrhic loses an accent, and the spondee immediately replaces it, the combination has the effect of righting the rhythm almost immediately, so the ear expecting iambs is not confused for long. This is such a common pattern that it is sometimes called by its own name, the **double iamb.** It is a favorite and distinctive trick of Shakespeare's. Can you find one double iamb in each of these lines from his sonnets?

I summon up remembrance of things past

And beauty making beautiful old rhyme

If this be error and upon me proved

That I in your sweet thoughts would be forgot

In very metrically regular poems, a single substitution can have a large effect. The following poem has one spondee in the last line, which single-footedly elevates the subtlety and impact of the whole poem.

From "Some Girls," Suzanne Doyle

The risk is moral death each time we act,
And every act is whittled by the blade
Of history, pared down to brutal fact . . .
We are a different kind of tough; we hawk
Our epic violence in bleak bars, in bed, in art.

The spondee is "bleak bars," giving an additional intensity and urgency to the bleakness Doyle describes. (If you had trouble finding it, it may have been hard to find because Doyle uses a longer line, iambic hexameter instead of pentameter, for the last line of the poem.)

One of the following lines has two spondees; the others have one each. See if you can find them:

We crept in the tall grass and slept till noon

With his damned hoobla-hoobla-hoobla-how

There is a wide, wide wonder in it all

Slowly the poison the whole blood stream fills

Usually, the spondee has the effect of slowing down an iambic line by making it hold more accents (remember, one of the aspects of an accented syllable is length, so a line with more accented syllables will probably seem to last longer). Alexander Pope's famous passage about metrical effects shows how spondees and anapests can create the effects of slowness and speed, respectively:

From "Essay on Criticism," Alexander Pope (1711)

But when loud surges lash the sounding shore,
The hoarse, rough verse should like the torrent roar;
When Ajax strives some rock's vast weight to throw,
The line too labors, and the words move slow;
Not so, when swift Camilla scours the plain,
Flies o'er the unbending corn, and skims along the main.

Pope is actually making fun here of poets who use too much expressive variation. He makes it easy for us to notice the spondees and anapests by describing the line slowing down and the words moving slow in lines including the spondees "loud surge," "rough verse," "some rocks'" "vast weight," "too lab," and "move slow." The last line speeds up with the anapest "the unbend" as well as with an extra iamb.

Though a skillful poet can use a rhythm to create virtually any effect, still, the standard accepted "meanings" of the feet are valid enough, enough of the time, that it is worth repeating them one more time: spondee-slowness, anapest-quickness, trochee-surprise.

Headless and Extra-Syllable Lines

The two variations in iambic pentameter that remain for us to discuss are quite simple. One variation cuts off the first unstressed syllable from the line, and the other adds a final extra syllable. A line with a missing first syllable is given the gruesome name **headless pentameter** (a translation of the technical Greek term *akephalos,* meaning a "headless" line). Here are two examples from the first feet of two very famous iambic pentameter poems:

From "Those Winter Sundays, " Robert Hayden

Sundays too my father got up early

From "Prologue" to The Canterbury Tales, *Geoffrey Chaucer*

When that Aprille with his showres soote

This variation can look like an initial trochee, but the effect is different—because the first foot it is not a trochee but half of an iamb, this opening seems to catch the reader in midsentence, as if we are coming in on the middle of a conversation. To show what is happening, we scan the line by indicating the missing syllable in parentheses:

(u) /] u / | u / | u / | u / | (u)
Sundays too my father got up early

(u) /] u / | u / | u / | u / | (u)
When that Aprille with his showres soote

The line from Hayden is not only headless; it also has an extra syllable at the end. Parentheses are also used to indicate such an extra unstressed syllable at the end of the line, an effect that used to be called a "feminine ending" but is now more properly called an **extra-syllable ending.** It might seem that Hayden's line would scan more simply as a trochaic line, and one prosodist, James MacAuley, would in fact scan it that way. But most would agree that it is most important to recognize a poem's metrical consistency wherever possible, and that because all the rest of Hayden's poem is iambic, not trochaic, and this line can be scanned as iambic with two common variations, that is the correct scansion. Another well-known example of an extra-syllable ending occurs in this line from *Hamlet:*

/ | u / | u / | / u | u / | (u)
To be, or not to be, that is the question

The extra-syllable ending can create a lingering, falling, meditative effect and can be very beautiful, like a minor key in music. Again, we show the extra syllable in parentheses, to indicate that it is not part of the underlying metrical pattern of the line. Usually an extra-syllable ending involves a very unimportant syllable, like the last syllable of "question." There is a remarkable exception in "The Illiterate" by William Meredith above, where the man's secretive hiding of the letter is conveyed by the hiding of the important word "him" within an extra-syllable ending.

To recap, here are the most important basic variations in iambic pentameter:

1. The anapest, a metrical foot with a stress followed by two unaccented syllables (uu/) such as "on the way," can be substituted for an iamb anywhere in the line.
2. The trochee, a metrical foot with a stress followed by an unaccented syllable (/u) such as "open," can be substituted after a caesura in the line, or at the beginning of the line.
3. The pyrrhic, a metrical foot with two light syllables (uu) such as "in the," or the spondee, a metrical foot with two stressed syllables (//) such as "airplane," can be substituted for an iamb anywhere in the line, as long as the line as a whole keeps at least five accents.
4. An extra syllable can be added at the end, an effect simply referred to as an "extra-syllable ending."
5. The first, unstressed syllable can be dropped, making a "headless" line.

If you ever hear a definition of iambic pentameter as a 10-syllable line, ignore it. With four anapests and an extra-syllable ending, an iambic pentameter line could have as many as fourteen syllables. With a missing unstressed syllable (a rare variation sometimes called a *rest*), it could have as few as eight syllables. The nine-syllable line below has a rest or omitted unstressed syllable at the first syllable of the third foot, before "I," which adds force to the rest of the line:

From "To the Desert," Benjamin Alire Saenz

And keep me warm. I was born for you

Rarely, there is a two-syllable rest where a whole foot is missing, as happens in the extra-long caesura before the trochee in line 13 of Hamlet's soliloquy below:

Must give us pause: there's the respect

It is unlikely that Shakespeare would have paused this line for so long without such a self-conscious verbal warning!

Helpful Tip. While many lines of iambic pentameter do not have 10 syllables, it *is* true that almost all iambic pentameter lines will have at least five strong stresses. If you write a line of iambic pentameter and can hear only four strong stresses, it is likely that your line is not metrical.

Another Helpful Tip. The second foot of a line of iambic pentameter is especially sensitive and can upset the rhythm of a line. When in doubt about whether one of your lines scans, start by making sure the second foot is an iamb.

Scansion Exercise: Expressive Variation

Expressive variation is the term used to describe changes in the basic metrical pattern that are not random or at odds with the poem but work with the poem, emphasizing the feelings conveyed in the words. The amazing thing about expressive variation is that so many factors besides meter can be brought into play—including meaning, as in the line in the anapest section of this chapter about dying being difficult; imagery, as in the word "bend"; and word-music, as in the juxtaposition of "m's" in "calm milk-giver." As you will see in the chapter "The Metrical Palette," a skillful poet can literally make any meter create any effect, and still have it seem as if no other meter could have done the job. Nonetheless, meters do have strong tendencies. Anapestic speed and lightness, like spondaic slowness and intensity, are well-known effects for a good reason. When starting out writing in meter, it's a good idea to respect these commonly acknowledged metrical tendencies at first. It's too easy to write an unintentional joke if you choose a meter whose mood undermines the mood of your poem. Save your anapestic dirges until you have had more practice.

The poems below contain many exquisite examples of expressive variation, from the heaviness of the branches "loaded with ice a sunny winter morning" to the obsessive drivenness of "I might be driven to sell your love for peace." They show how natural and inevitable metrical variations seem when they connect seamlessly with the meaning of the line. At such points, it is impossible to tell whether the meter holds the meaning or the meaning holds the meter, and the old cliché of poetic form as a vessel or container into which the meaning of the poem is poured seems a very clumsy analogy. I prefer, instead, a paradoxical metaphor used by the Buddhist monk Thich Nhat Hanh: "Form is the wave, emptiness the water." Just as the water of the ocean can only come to us in the shape of the waves that embody and make it real, the emptiness of reality can only come to us in the shapes of the multiple forms we experience, which make it real. And just so, the meaning of lines of poetry can only come to us in the rhythms that embody and make them real. Though Thich Nhat Hanh was talking about the nature of our perception of reality, not about poetry, I have never found a closer approximation to my experience of the mystery of expressive variation.

Hamlet's soliloquy is one of the most famous iambic pentameter passages in our literature. Yet not one of the first five lines is a simple iambic pentameter made of five iambs. Read it aloud, enjoying and experiencing the meter, and noticing the variations.

From Hamlet, *William Shakespeare (1602)*

To be, or not to be: that is the question:
Whether 'tis nobler in the mind to suffer
The slings and arrows of outrageous fortune,
Or to take arms against a sea of troubles,
And by opposing end them? To die: to sleep;
No more; and by a sleep to say we end
The heart-ache and the thousand natural shocks
That flesh is heir to. 'Tis a consummation
Devoutly to be wish'd. To die, to sleep;
To sleep: perchance to dream: ay, there's the rub;
For in that sleep of death what dreams may come
When we have shuffled off this mortal coil,
Must give us pause: there's the respect
That makes calamity of so long life;
For who would bear the whips and scorns of time,
The oppressor's wrong, the proud man's contumely,
The pangs of despised love, the law's delay,
The insolence of office, and the spurns
That patient merit of the unworthy takes,
When he himself might his quietus make
With a bare bodkin? who would fardels bear,
To grunt and sweat under a weary life,
But that the dread of something after death,
The undiscover'd country from whose bourn

No traveller returns, puzzles the will
And makes us rather bear those ills we have
Than fly to others that we know not of?
Thus conscience does make cowards of us all;
And thus the native hue of resolution
Is sicklied o'er with the pale cast of thought.

Now scan the passage (if you want to see how I would scan it, look in the back of the book). Notice how the variations build in frequency as the mood of the passage intensifies. The interplay between the expected meter and the actual rhythm of the syllables is a powerful relationship. The memory or expectation of a metrical pattern becomes an active force in the line, adding its rueful or delicate or wry or enthusiastic twist to whatever is happening rhythmically in that line.

Read the following poem out loud, and notice how just a few variations can have dramatic impact in a poem that is so metrically regular.

Sonnet 30, Edna St. Vincent Millay (1931)

Love is not all: it is not meat nor drink
Nor slumber nor a roof against the rain;
Nor yet a floating spar to men that sink
And rise and sink and rise and sink again;
Love can not fill the thickened lung with breath,
Nor clean the blood, nor set the fractured bone;
Yet many a man is making friends with death
Even as I speak, for lack of love alone.
It well may be that in a difficult hour,
Pinned down by pain and moaning for release,
Or nagged by want past resolution's power,
I might be driven to sell your love for peace,
Or trade the memory of this night for food.
It well may be. I do not think I would.

Now scan it (again, to check your scanning against mine, look in the back). Notice the defiance in the spondee "Love can" and the pain in "pinned down." What is the effect on you of the extreme regularity of the meter in line 4? Notice how the anapests, increasing in frequency toward the end of the poem, interweave with certain consonant sounds that help them to echo anapests earlier in the poem.

"Chosen," Marilyn Nelson

Diverne wanted to die, that August night.
His face hung over hers, a sweating moon.
She wished so hard, she killed part of her heart.

If she had died, her one begotten son,
her life's one light, would never have been born.
Pomp Atwood might have been another man:

born with a single race, another name.
Diverne might not have known the starburst joy
her son would give her. And the man who came

out of a twelve-room house and ran to her
close shack across three yards that night, to leap
onto her cornshuck pallet. Pomp was their

share of the future. And it wasn't rape.
In spite of her raw terror. And his whip.

Only three spondees vary this historical poem, all involving the slave Diverne's son and his importance to her life: "Pomp At-," "born with," "burst joy." There are also three trochees expressing the excitement of Pomp's father: "out of," "onto," and "share of." There are no other substitutions, and no extra syllables. This sonnet, like Millay's, does a lot with very few variations.

By contrast, read aloud this passage from Frost's "Birches," and you will see how far a poem can move in the other direction—away from regularity—without crashing. Notice how Frost uses an occasional perfectly regular line to reestablish the rhythm after especially wild variations.

From "Birches," Robert Frost (1915)

When I see birches bend to left and right
Across the lines of straighter darker trees,

I like to think some boy's been swinging them.
But swinging doesn't bend them down to stay
As ice-storms do. Often you must have seen them
Loaded with ice a sunny winter morning
After a rain. They click upon themselves
As the breeze rises, and turn many-colored
As the stir cracks and crazes their enamel.
Soon the sun's warmth makes them shed crystal shells
Shattering and avalanching on the snow-crust—
Such heaps of broken glass to sweep away
You'd think the inner dome of heaven had fallen.
They are dragged to the withered bracken by the load,
And they seem not to break; though once they are bowed
So low for long, they never right themselves:
You may see their trunks arching in the woods
Years afterwards, trailing their leaves on the ground . . .

Now scan the poem and if you want to, check your scansion against mine in the back of the book. Notice how trochees enter the poem with the surprise of the ice-storm, how spondees can convey excitement (breeze rises, stir cracks) and also slowness, as in the three spondees in a row in line 10. Frost is good enough to break rules and make it work; not only does he use a stressed syllable for an extra-syllable ending; he manages to make anapests convey slowness in line 14 and pushes trochees almost to the brink of confusion in line 11, slightly over the brink in line 18.

Scanning poems written by poets skilled in variations on iambic meter can be challenging. It's easy to get disoriented. Don't forget your foot breaks! And one more thing: when scanning, bear in mind the simplicity principle. Like Occam's razor, the medieval philosophical idea that, all other things being equal, it's best to choose the simplest explanation, this principle reminds us always to stay as close to the basic metrical pattern as possible. In other words, where the base foot is iambic, keep as many iambic feet as you can. So it is better to scan Frost's line, "As the stir cracks and crazes their enamel," as pyrrhic | spondee | iamb | iamb | iamb | extra-syllable ending:

u u | / / | u /|u / | u /(u)
as the stir cracks and crazes their enamel

than as anapest-trochee-trochee-trochee-trochee:

u u / | / u | /u| / u|/ u
as the stir cracks and crazes their enamel

In this case, the simpler scansion gives you three iambs, manifesting both the line's underlying metrical expectation and its rhythmic kinship with other lines in the poem. The simplicity principle applies not only to the kind of feet but also to the number of feet. If you are scanning a poem you know is basically in iambic pentameter, first do your best to scan each line with five feet before you decide that a line is longer or shorter, as it is at the ending of "Some Girls." In a nutshell, here is the simplicity principle: *The simplest (accurate) scansion is always best!*

Expressive Variation and Keeping Your Balance

Like learning to ride a bicycle, writing in meter is a skill that gets better with a little practice. At first, you're so afraid of falling over that you ride only in a straight line and always keep your wheels straight up and down. But after a while, you get a sense of how far you can lean at an angle and still keep your balance. When you are starting to write iambic pentameter, it's fine to start with a very regular basic line, trying out new combinations of syllables one by one to see how you can change the rhythm through substitutions. After you are more comfortable with meter, you will be riding your bicycle with full control, able to veer around corners and hop over curbs without worrying about balance. You won't have to think about varying the rhythm; it will happen by itself as you write.

Just as a bicycle going around a curve is balancing between momentum and gravity, a metrical line moving through a poem is balancing between the metrical pattern and ordinary, nonmetrical speech. Which angle to strike between these two rhythms is, up to a point, a matter both of fashion and of individual taste. In the eighteenth century, metrical poetry had a steady regularity that would have sounded dull in the Renaissance or the late nineteenth century. The common eighteenth-century term for metrical verse was "numbers," and each line of iambic pentameter did keep to "numbers": each line had 10 syllables, after the French model, and to add extra syllables was a sign of poor taste or poor skill. To avoid extra syllables, poets used **elisions** such as "wand'ring" and "ev'ry," as in this poem:

"The Apology," Anne Finch, Countess of Winchilsea (1685)

'Tis true I write and tell me by what Rule
I am alone forbid to play the fool,
To follow through the Groves a wand'ring Muse
And fain'd Idea's for my pleasures chuse.
Why shou'd it in my Pen be held a fault
Whilst Mira paints her face, to paint a thought?
Whilst Lamia to the manly Bumper flys
And borrow'd Spiritts sparkle in her Eyes,
Why should it be in me a thing so vain
To heat with Poetry my colder Brain?
But I write ill and there-fore should forbear.
Does Flavia cease now at her fortieth year
In ev'ry Place to let that face be seen
Which all the Town rejected at fifteen?
Each Woman has her weaknesse; mine indeed
Is still to write tho' hopeless to succeed.
Nor to the Men is this so easy found;
Ev'n in most Works with which the Wits abound
(So weak are all since our first breach with Heav'n)
Ther's less to be Applauded then forgiven.

Some poets today continue to prefer to write very regular iambic pentameter that always stays close to the basic ta-TUM ta-TUM ta-TUM ta-TUM ta-TUM pattern. Sometimes known as the "plain style," this type of meter was championed by the poet-critic Yvor Winters and his students at Stanford University in the middle of the twentieth century, such as Timothy Steele and Thom Gunn. Other contemporary poets prefer a dense and rhythmically complex iambic pentameter line (we might call it the "clotted style"), full of spondees, anapests, and caesuras, that stretches the pattern as far as it will go, more like the style of John Donne. If you scan this poem, you will discover numerous trochees, spondees, and anapests that clot and slow and complicate the underlying iambic beat:

"Batter My Heart," John Donne (1635)

Batter my heart, three-person'd God; for you
As yet but knock, breathe, shine, and seek to mend;
That I may rise and stand, o'erthrow mee, and bend
Your force to break, blow, burn, and make me new.
I, like an usurp'd town to'another due,
Labor to'admit you, but Oh, to no end;
Reason, your viceroy in mee, mee should defend,
But is captiv'd, and proves weak or untrue.
Yet dearly I love you, and would be lov'd fain,
But am betroth'd unto your enemie;
Divorce mee, untie, or breake that knot again,
Take me to you, imprison mee, for I,
Except you'enthrall mee, never shall be free,
Nor ever chaste, except you ravish me.

Experimenting with stretching the basic pattern is fun, and it's one of my own favorite ways to write in meter. But if your variations end up undermining the rhythm instead of stretching it, you can involve your readers in a bike crash and lose their trust for the rest of the poem. If you read a lot of metrical poems, scanning lines that sound unusual so you can really understand their rhythms, you will begin to develop an ear for which variations threaten the iambic pentameter and which ones stretch or tease it.

How to Avoid a Metrical Crash

As you are developing your ear, here are two tricks that can be used for a quick metrical check of iambic pentameter:

1. **Make sure there are no trochees except at the beginnings of lines (and, if you are feeling confident, after punctuation or another strong caesura in the line).**
2. **Make sure the line has at least five strong accents.**

How much substitution should you use in your metrical poems? Three factors, at least, will come into play. The first is your own aesthetic taste combined with your own skill level (even if you are drawn to a style with lots of variation, it's probably best to try only a few simple substitutions until you really get the hang of keeping your balance). The second is the expressive need at any particular moment in the poem—which variations will express the feeling or idea or aesthetic effect you want to get across. The third factor, which in a way implies the others, is your overall "metrical contract" with the reader. In a nutshell, you should vary the meter when it will be expressive and when it won't confuse or betray the reader's ear.

Metrical contract is a term, coined by John Hollander, for the understanding that reader and poet share about a poem's meter. The reader comes to count on a certain meter in a particular poem; if the poem suddenly breaks the meter, it is a violation of this unspoken contract. The metrically literate reader may respond in different ways: by feeling betrayed, getting bored, getting distracted, or just deciding the poet doesn't know how to use meter. Poets who want to honor the metrical contract and reap the full benefits of meter have more or less leeway to stretch the meter depending on how far the reader's ability to keep the meter in mind has already been tried at that point in the poem. For example, if you scan the first six lines of the following poem, you will see that the opening is very irregular, but there is a certain point where the meter has been stretched to the breaking point and, just then, the poet brings it back to exact regularity again—almost as if to say, "See, I was only teasing!"—before adding one extra variation for good measure. (When you are done, check the scansion against the one at the back of the book.)

Sonnet 116, William Shakespeare (1609)

Let me not to the marriage of true minds
Admit impediments. Love is not love
Which alters when it alteration finds,
Or bends with the remover to remove:
O no! it is an ever-fixed mark
That looks on tempests and is never shaken;
It is the star to every wandering bark,
Whose worth's unknown, although his height be taken.
Love's not Time's fool, though rosy lips and cheeks
Within his bending sickle's compass come:

Love alters not with his brief hours and weeks,
But bears it out even to the edge of doom.
If this be error and upon me proved
I never writ, nor no man ever loved.

As you write in meter and especially as you read aloud in meter, you will begin to get a sense of when to push and play and when to reassure. Working creatively with your reader's metrical expectations (and of course, at the same time with your own!) is one of the deep satisfactions of writing in meter. This chapter sets out rules and conventions that are generally accepted today for maintaining the iambic meter and keeping the "metrical contract" with a reader. However, it is worth keeping in mind that, as we noted above, ideas of meter change over time, and the line between expressing one's personal aesthetic and breaking the metrical contract is not always clear-cut. In the eighteenth century, as we have seen, anapestic substitutions were considered to break the meter, so poets such as Anne Finch and Alexander Pope used elisions to avoid them, as Pope does in this couplet:

At ev'ry Trifle scorn to take Offence,
That always shows Great Pride, or Little Sense.

A century and a half later, poets began to use anapests in iambic pentameter again, haltingly—and now they are common. But like anything that changes as our society changes, prosody can be controversial. Donne's more prosodically conservative contemporary Ben Jonson, presumably not just taking offense at a trifle, wrote that "Donne for not keeping of accent deserved hanging." And every century since has had its own prosodic controversies.

Iambic Dimeter, Trimeter, Tetrameter, and Fourteeners

With all the attention to iambic pentameter, we shouldn't overlook the other common iambic meters. Iambic tetrameter is the next most common meter after iambic pentameter. This shorter line can create an effect of openness and directness, used for different purposes by Marvell in "Coy Mistress" (in the "Dramatic Poetry" section of chapter 5) and by Theodore Roethke, below:

From "Open House," Theodore Roethke (1941)

My secrets cry aloud.
I have no need for tongue.
My heart keeps open house,
My doors are widely swung.

Sometimes a line that could scan as iambic pentameter in an iambic pentameter poem needs to be scanned differently in iambic tetrameter. Scan this poem, paying particular attention to lines 3, 8, and 10:

"I Had a Dove," John Keats (1817)

I had a dove and the sweet dove died;
And I have thought it died of grieving:
O, what could it grieve for? Its feet were tied,
With a silken thread of my own hand's weaving;
Sweet little red feet! why should you die—
Why should you leave me, sweet bird! why?
You liv'd alone in the forest-tree,
Why, pretty thing! would you not live with me?
I kiss'd you oft and gave you white peas;
Why not live sweetly, as in the green trees?

There are many triple feet in the poem, contributing a casualness and innocence of tone, and also giving several lines in the poem 10 syllables. Each of lines 3, 8, and 10 could be scanned as iambic pentameter in another context. But Keats hurriedly skips over a syllable involving the bird directly ("it," "you," "live") in each of these lines, forcing it to fit the tetrameter pattern instead. The cumulative effect is chilling, as awareness of the bird's identity is repeatedly erased in order to keep the poem's almost flippant tone. This is a remarkably subtle example of creative use of the interplay between two possible scansions.

Iambic trimeter is not nearly as common as iambic tetrameter, but has been used for some memorable poems. This three-foot meter can have a strong waltzing effect, like the dance with a strong triple rhythm which was considered scandalous when it was first introduced in the nineteenth century. Here, the poet plays directly with the dance association:

"My Papa's Waltz," Theodore Roethke (1942)

The whiskey on your breath
Could make a small boy dizzy;
But I hung on like death:
Such waltzing was not easy.

We romped until the pans
Slid from the kitchen shelf;
My mother's countenance
Could not unfrown itself.

The hand that held my wrist
Was battered on one knuckle;
At every step you missed
My right ear scraped a buckle.

You beat time on my head
With a palm caked hard by dirt,
Then waltzed me off to bed
Still clinging to your shirt.

Roethke emphasizes the waltzing rhythm with strategically placed anapests and extra-syllable endings. By contrast, in the following poem, the speaker's determination to stand her ground feels even more dogged because the poem is successfully resisting the dancing tendency of the meter:

From "Under the Rose," Christina Rossetti (1866)

I think my mind is fixed
On one point and made up:
To accept my lot unmixed;
Never to drug the cup
But drink it by myself.
I'll not be wooed for pelf;
I'll not blot out my shame
With any man's good name;

But nameless as I stand,
My hand is my own hand,
And nameless as I came

I go to the dark land.

The single anapest in this passage (in the third line) is immediately balanced by a powerful trochee/iamb combination in the following line, and the rest of the lines never waver from iambic.

Even in a relatively short line, the contrast between irregularity and regularity can be used for strong effects. This four-line poem was the first one in a pamphlet Hughes put together to raise money for a legal defense fund:

"Justice," Langston Hughes (ca. 1931)

That Justice is a blind goddess
Is a thing to which we black are wise:
Her bandage hides two festering sores
That once perhaps were eyes.

Each line until the last has an irregularity in the iambic meter: A trochee ends the first line and a single anapest lightens each of the second and third lines. So the startling regularity of the last, shorter line, which brings the iambic meter into clear focus at the same time it brings the metaphor into focus, makes a strong contrast. Not a syllable of this poem is wasted.

Iambic poems also sometimes mix lines of different lengths, as George Herbert mixes pentameter and trimeter in this famous poem:

"Love (III)," George Herbert (1633)

Love bade me welcome; yet my soul drew back,
Guilty of dust and sin.
But quick-eyed Love, observing me grow slack
From my first entrance in,
Drew nearer to me, sweetly questioning
If I lacked anything.

"A guest," I answered "worthy to be here";
Love said, "You shall be he."
"I, the unkind, ungrateful? Ah, my dear,
I cannot look on Thee."
Love took my hand and smiling did reply,
"Who made the eyes but I?"

"Truth, Lord; but I have marr'd them: let my shame
Go where it doth deserve."
"And know you not," says Love, "who bore the blame?"
"My dear, then I will serve."
"You must sit down," says Love, "and taste my meat."
So I did sit and eat.

A minister who wrote poetry only about his complex relationship with God, Herbert skillfully uses the short line to draw the reader into the intimate spiritual space of the poem, with the alternating long and short lines capturing the approach and retreat, trust and mistrust, of this spiritual courtship.

The **ballad stanza,** discussed at length in another chapter, consists of alternating lines of iambic tetrameter and trimeter. It is the other central meter in English-language poetry besides iambic pentameter. A literary version is called **fourteeners**—a seven-foot line, once extremely popular, which simply combines two lines of ballad stanza into one line of seven iambs (iambic heptameter). The best-known poem ever written in fourteeners is Arthur Golding's translation of Ovid's *Metamorphoses* (1567), which includes the following description of Daphne being turned into a laurel tree to save herself from Apollo's pursuit. Since Apollo was the god of poetry in classical Greece, it also provides an explanation of why a laurel crown is the legendary ceremonial decoration worn by poets. Notice that you may have to pronounce some words in the old-fashioned way to keep the meter (e.g., "hanged" with two syllables in line 3, and "advised" with three syllables in line 7); the meter will guide you:

And as she ran the meeting windes hir garments backewarde blue,
So that hir naked skinne apearde behinde hir as she flue,
Hir goodly yellowe golden haire that hanged loose and slacke,
With every puffe of ayre did wave and tosse behinde hir backe.

Hir running made hir seeme more fayre, the youthfull God therefore
Coulde not abyde to waste his wordes in dalyance any more.
But as his love advysed him he gan to mende his pace,
And with the better foote before, the fleeing Nymph to chace.
And even as when the greedie Grewnde doth course the sielie Hare,
Amiddes the plaine and champion fielde without all covert bare, . . .
Both twaine of them doe straine themselves and lay on footemanship,
Who may best runne with all his force the tother to outstrip,
The t'one for safetie of his lyfe, the tother for his pray,
The Grewnde aye prest with open mouth to beare the Hare away,
Thrusts forth his snoute and gyrdeth out and at hir loynes doth snatch,
As though he would at everie stride betweene his teeth hir latch:
Againe in doubt of being caught the Hare aye shrinking slips
Upon the sodaine from his Jawes, and from betweene his lips:
So farde Apollo and the Mayde: hope made Apollo swift,
And feare did make the Mayden fleete devising how to shift. . . .
Howebeit he that did pursue of both the swifter went,
As furthred by the feathred wings that Cupid had him lent,
So that he would not let hir rest, but preased at hir heele
So neere that through hir scattred haire she might his breathing feele.
But when she sawe hir breath was gone and strength began to fayle,
The colour faded in hir cheekes, and ginning for to quayle,
Shee looked to Penaeus streame and sayde: Nowe Father dere,
And if yon streames have powre of Gods then help your daughter here.
O let the earth devour me quicke, on which I seeme too fayre,
Or else this shape which is my harme by chaunging straight appayre. . . .
This piteous prayer scarsly sed: hir sinewes waxed starke,
And therewithall about hir breast did grow a tender barke.
Hir haire was turned into leaves, hir armes in boughes did growe,
Hir feete that were ere while so swift, now rooted were as slowe.
Hir crowne became the toppe, and thus of that she earst had beene,
Remayned nothing in the worlde, but beautie fresh and greene.
Which when that Phoebus did beholde (affection did so move)
The tree to which his love was turnde he coulde no lesse but love,
And as he softly layde his hande upon the tender plant,
Within the barke newe overgrowne he felt hir heart yet pant. . . .
And in his armes embracing fast hir boughes and braunches lythe,

He proferde kisses to the tree, the tree did from him writhe.
Well (quoth Apollo) though my Feere and spouse thou can not bee,
Assuredly from this tyme forth yet shalt thou be my tree.
Thou shalt adorne my golden lockes, and eke my pleasant Harpe,
Thou shalt adorne my Quyver full of shaftes and arrowes sharpe.
Thou shalt adorne the valiant knyghts and royall Emperours:
When for their noble feates of armes like mightie conquerours,
Triumphantly with stately pompe up to the Capitoll,
They shall ascende with solemne traine that doe their deedes extoll. . . .
Before Augustus Pallace doore full duely shalt thou warde,
The Oke amid the Pallace yarde aye faythfully to garde,
And as my heade is never poulde nor never more without
A seemely bushe of youthfull haire that spreadeth rounde about,
Even so this honour give I thee continually to have
Thy braunches clad from time to tyme with leaves both fresh and brave.

Golding's skill with fourteeners is still famous after all these centuries because it is hard to equal; such long lines tend to break in the middle and sound clumsy. But Golding brings out their suppleness and their usefulness for telling stories and developing the dramatic situation; seven feet allow the momentum to build so that, for example, the reader's heart beats fast during the chase scene as Apollo closes in on his victim.

Iambic Pentameter in the Twenty-First Century

Because of the charged history of iambic pentameter during the twentieth century, it seems appropriate to pause and consider some of the implications of writing in this meter today. After all, Ezra Pound and the Imagists declared very early in the twentieth century that "to break the pentameter" was the "first heave" toward developing a new poetry. During much of the twentieth century, poets in the United States took their cue from this attitude, and to scoff at the artificiality or old-fashionedness of poets who wrote in meter eventually became fashionable. Meter seemed too mechanical, too easy, too expected a way to achieve that mysterious thing we call true poetry; "real" poetry, as opposed to mere verse, was bound to come in an original, unique, and unexpected shape and size.

In the innovation-weary twenty-first century, that attitude has been changing. Perhaps it is because technology is making it possible for audiences to experience regular rhythm through the ear again; or perhaps it is because, at a time when many of us are prone to feel helpless in the face of sobering realities, poets are rediscovering that this deeply grounded meter can give to a poem a satisfying solidity, a grace, and a strength and energy that can feel, at any rate, akin to power. And of course, in the wake of a full century of free verse, iambic pentameter no longer seems as constricting as it did. The great iconoclastic poet Robert Creeley's last book of poetry, which I heard him read from a few weeks before he died in 2005, was written largely in iambic pentameter couplets. He remarked to me that day that meter "had been there all along" for him. Now a younger generation of poets, even some of the most experimental stripe, are beginning to write iambic pentameter as well, whether plain style iambic like Karen Volkman, or a looser, more Donne-like iambic like Joshua Mehigan.

However, now that meter is beginning to seep back into contemporary poetry again, it is essential not to forget modernism's lessons. As Timothy Steele's book *Missing Measures* shows, the modernists did not mean to banish all meter permanently, but only to break down the dominance of iambic pentameter and to open the way for different kinds of metrical patterns. The centuries-long domination of meter by iambic pentameter proved stifling, and it's important to keep other metrical options available. Some noniambic meters are the subject of the next chapter.

QUESTIONS FOR MEDITATION OR DISCUSSION

Theodore Roethke wrote in his poem "Four for Sir John Davies,"

> I take this cadence from a man named Yeats;
> I take it, and I give it back again:
> For other tunes and other wanton beats
> Have tossed my heart and fiddled through my brain.
> Yes, I was dancing-mad, and how
> That came to be the bears and Yeats would know.

Read some poems by Yeats in this book and elsewhere. Is this passage really in the cadence of Yeats? If so, by what specific strategies do you think Roethke achieved this effect? Write your own iambic pentameter quatrain that attempts to capture another poet's cadence exactly.

How does it feel to read iambic pentameter? How does it feel to write it? Do you find that using this meter affects the "voice" in your poems? How?

Marilyn Nelson, in her essay "Owning the Masters," enters an ongoing conversation about the use of European-based meters by contemporary poets of color. Nelson writes, "Yes, writing in traditional form is taxing. But it is also liberating. . . . As we own the masters and learn to use more and more levels of this language we love, for whose continued evolution we share responsibility, the signifiers become ours." What do you think a contemporary writer gains or loses by engaging with poetic tradition?

When you read this line, you may have noticed a trochee in the middle of the line. Since trochees break the rhythm of iambic pentameter, why is this one here?

> /] u /| u / | / u | u / | (u)
> To be, or not to be, that is the question

Look for other examples, in the poems throughout this book, of iambic lines that include trochees. In each case, how does it affect the momentum of the iambic line? Is there a rhythmic factor (having to do with syntax, grammar, punctuation, speech emphasis, or word-music) that influences the effect? In each case, is there a relation between this rhythmic change and the meaning or emotion of the poem at that point?

Richard Hoffman points out that a single anapest moves through the iambic lines of Robert Frost's famous poem "The Road Not Taken." Trace this anapest through the poem and meditate on its meaning. If it is ever missing, can you find a place where it appears again, in counterbalance?

Timothy Steele writes, "English iambic versification has greatly benefited from the historical tendency towards monosyllabism in our language . . . monosyllabic words are wonderfully handy." Do you agree? Look for examples of iambic pentameter lines that use monosyllabic words to support your claim.

QUOTES

Iambic pentameter goes da dum da dum da dum da dum da dum. And it shouldn't do that too often.

—Howard Nemerov, via Charles Martin

Good blank verse does not sound like a series of identically measured lines. It sounds like a series of subtle variations on the same theme.

—James Fenton

Writing about the iambic pentameter is like writing a defense of breathing. When I was a child I had severe asthma. I would lie perfectly still and concentrate on the production of the next breath. So I have never since been able to take breathing for granted. It is both the most natural and the most concentrated activity I know. One breath and the pentameter line have the same duration.

—Carolyn Kizer

The more art is controlled, limited, worked over, the more it is free. . . . The more constraints one imposes, the more one frees oneself of the chains that shackle the spirit.

—Igor Stravinsky

POETRY PRACTICES

(Group) Variation Sampler. Each person writes 15 lines in iambic pentameter that include at least two spondees, two pyrrhics, two anapests, and two trochees, as well as one headless line and one extra-syllable ending. Either look at everyone's as a group, or trade in pairs, and scan the poems to spot each other's variations. Copy your favorite line from the poem you have been scanning on the blackboard.

(Group) Group Blank Iambics. Pass a piece of paper around the group (or a subgroup). Each person writes one line of iambic pentameter and folds the paper so the next person can't see the previous line. Option: the first person can leave a clue ("verb," "plural noun," etc.) for the beginning of the next line. Circulate, and share the finished product.

Blank Iambic Verse. Write a poem of 20 lines in blank iambic verse. Write it in at least three drafts. Draft 1: Say what you want to say. Draft 2: Deepen the meaning and/or sound, and add word-music. 3. Build and focus the emotional coherence. In each draft, try these strategies: move the caesura as much as you can from line to line to add variety, including feminine and masculine caesuras. Change from long to short sentences to play off sentence length against the line length. Experiment with long and short syllables. Use a variety of metrical variations to help express the mood you want. Use at least three spondees, three anapests, three trochees, and two extra-syllable endings in your poem.

Caesura Thread. Read Tennyson's "Ulysses," or another passage of blank iambic verse, slowly and mark the caesura in each line. You may find that some lines have one stronger caesura and also some weaker ones. It's okay to mark only the strongest caesuras. Connect the caesuras in one line down the poem to notice how the caesura changes position as the poem proceeds. If the caesura occurred in the same place in every line, we would be likely to find the poem terribly monotonous. The modulation of caesuras is an important aspect of writing any poem in lines, whether in meter or free verse.

Meter Mimicry. Choose a passage in iambic pentameter that you admire or even love, from the poems in this book or elsewhere. Write an exact metrical copy of the passage, in different words but with the same metrical variations, syllable by syllable. Don't forget the line beginnings and endings, and any other substitutions or changes. Once you know the line's rhythm well, you may want to go further and also reproduce the relative weight of the different accents in the line, as well as the caesuras (whether caused by punctuation or simply by the meanings of the phrases in the line).

Pentameter Pastiche. Along the model of R. S. Gwynn's "Approaching a Significant Birthday," choose lines in iambic pentameter from a number of poems in this book and combine them into one poem. (Optional: See if others in the group can recognize where the lines came from.) Advanced variation: use the rhymes to arrange them into heroic couplets or into a sonnet (you can include lines from poems outside the book if necessary).

Iambic Pentameter Dialogue. With one other poet, practice your metrical chops by taking turns telling each other a line of iambic pentameter with variations. The other poet has to imitate the rhythmic pattern exactly in their own line. This will probably go more quickly if you decide that making sense is optional. Experiment with writing the lines down as you hear them and with keeping it oral. Is there a difference in how easily you pick up the rhythm?

CHAPTER 14

The Metrical Palette: Beyond Iambic Pentameter

Just as music has other time signatures besides 4/4 time, and painting has other ranges of color besides greens and yellows, poetry has other meters besides iambic. Yet for hundreds of years, almost all serious poetry in English meter has been written in iambs. One of the most exciting aspects of being a poet today is our access to a fascinating and almost unexplored landscape of metrical possibilities: the "noniambic" meters. In teaching a variety of meters to my students, I have found that certain poets come alive in trochees, dactyls, or anapests, writing poems that they could never have written in iambic meter.

Iambic meter can seem inevitable, if only because of its pervasiveness. Poets and critics have sometimes quoted phrases like, "I'll have a shake, a burger and some fries" (quoted by Robert Hass) or "a glass of California chardonnay" (quoted by Marilyn Hacker) to prove that iambs are simply "natural" to English speech. But in fact, it turns out that all meters with stresses every two or three syllables are equally natural to English. I have learned from conversation with linguists that, since English has a stress every second or third syllable no matter what the syntax is doing, anapests, trochees, and dactyls are just as likely to arise in English as iambs. This thought was confirmed for me years ago, when I was returning from a conference where I had heard a talk asserting the naturalness and centrality of iambic meter. Just as I was thinking that other meters could be natural as well, we hit some choppy skies and my idea was confirmed by some flawless anapests that may be familiar to you as well: "Please return to your seats and make sure that your seatbelts are fastened securely."

And it's not just rising meters. We also talk in trochees: "Pass the salt and pepper, sweetie." "Did you see what she was wearing?" "Have I got a story for you!" And in dactyls: "After you buy it, you need to assemble it." "Do you have time? Take a look at your calendar!" "When did she tell you that I couldn't be there?" Any regular rhythmic pattern that involves a stress every two or three syllables will turn up routinely in the everyday modulations of English. While writing this chapter, I stepped out to the post office. I was waiting in line looking at the placards on the walls when I found myself idly reading not only a phrase in iambic pentameter (with one anapest, which by now you should be able to find)—"Wherever you see this symbol, you'll find stamps"—but also a trochaic pentameter followed by a dactylic tetrameter: "Are you shipping something liquid, fragile, / perishable or potentially dangerous?"

I was once taught by a poet who had little experience with scansion but felt confident in solemnly assuring her students that "English falls naturally into iambics" (a sentence which scans as perfect dactyls). Still, I'm convinced by now that the real reason so many poets find iambic the inevitable meter is not ignorance or stubbornness, but simply the force of collective habit. After reading and being taught to venerate so many thousands of cherished iambic lines from so many centuries, and rarely hearing any other meters, naturally our ears have become attuned to recognize and imitate iambic meter. And that is exactly why noniambic meters have such fresh, exciting expressive riches to offer, not only as patterns used for substitution in iambic meter, but as rhythmic patterns of their own. This chapter will explore a few of their possibilities, building on the basic introduction to meter in the chapter before last.

Trochaic Meter (/u)

Double, double, toil and trouble,
Fire burn and cauldron bubble . . .
Eye of newt, and toe of frog,
Wool of bat, and tongue of dog,
Adder's fork, and blind-worm's sting,
Lizard's leg and owlet's wing;
For a charm of powerful trouble,
Like a hell-broth boil and bubble.

It is no coincidence that Shakespeare chose trochaic meter to help the witches brew up their "charm of powerful trouble" in act 4 of *Macbeth.* For almost as long as iambic meter has been the meter of logic, reason, power, and civilization, trochaic meter has tended to be associated with the uncanny and subversive. The most well-known lyric poem in trochees evokes a powerful creature of the wilderness in such a way as to make it seem to call into question all the ideas about God that were prevalent in Blake's time:

"Tyger! Tyger!" William Blake (1794)

Tyger! Tyger! burning bright
In the forests of the night
What immortal hand or eye
Could frame thy fearful symmetry?

In what distant deeps or skies
Burnt the fire of thine eyes?
On what wings dare he aspire?
What the hand dare seize the fire?

And what shoulder, & what art,
Could twist the sinews of thy heart?
And when thy heart began to beat,
What dread hand? & what dread feet?

What the hammer? what the chain?
In what furnace was thy brain?
What the anvil? what dread grasp
Dare its deadly terrors clasp?

When the stars threw down their spears
And water'd heaven with their tears,
Did he smile his work to see?
Did he who made the Lamb make thee?

Tyger! Tyger! burning bright
In the forests of the night,
What immortal hand or eye
Dare frame thy fearful symmetry?

Though several of these lines are iambic, the overwhelming power of the trochaic meter is what lends this poem its compelling vitality and its rare memorability. The trochee's power is not limited to lyric poetry: one of the most popular narrative poems, Edgar Allan Poe's "The Raven," is trochaic. Like the witches' song and "The Tyger," "The Raven" also invokes spooky subject matter. The long-standing association of trochees with the uncanny is the reason that witches' spells in popular culture—in movies or on television shows such as *Sabrina* or *Buffy the Vampire Slayer*—are usually written in trochees.

But there's no need to restrict your trochees only to spooky subjects. The mysterious power of this meter can be used for many different moods. When Longfellow chose trochaic meter for *Hiawatha,* his inspiration was not Shakespeare's witches but a completely different source: the meter of ancient Finnish oral poetry, the captivating, push-pull rhythm I describe in the introduction to this book. This rhythm, with pulsating stronger and weaker stresses in alternating feet, seems to have developed to accompany the pull of oars through rivers and fjords of northern Finland, where perhaps the ancient stories collected in the *Kalevala,* like the Native American legends gathered by Longfellow, were recounted for hours on end to entertain the rowers. Even in its English version, the meter can convey the lulling motion of oars. Try reading this excerpt aloud:

From Hiawatha, *Henry Wadsworth Longfellow (1855)*

And Nokomis, the old woman,
Pointing with her finger westward,
Spake these words to Hiawatha:
"Yonder dwells the great Pearl-Feather,
Megissogwon, the Magician,
Manito of Wealth and Wampum,
Guarded by his fiery serpents,
Guarded by the black pitch-water.
You can see his fiery serpents,
The Kenabeek, the great serpents,
Coiling, playing in the water;
You can see the black pitch-water
Stretching far away beyond them,
To the purple clouds of sunset!
"He it was who slew my father,
By his wicked wiles and cunning,
When he from the moon descended,

When he came on earth to seek me.
He, the mightiest of Magicians,
Sends the fever from the marshes,
Sends the pestilential vapors,
Sends the poisonous exhalations,
Sends the white fog from the fen-lands,
Sends disease and death among us!
"Take your bow, O Hiawatha,
Take your arrows, jasper-headed,
Take your war-club, Puggawaugun,
And your mittens, Minjekahwun,
And your birch-canoe for sailing,
And the oil of Mishe-Nahma,
So to smear its sides, that swiftly
You may pass the black pitch-water;
Slay this merciless magician,
Save the people from the fever
That he breathes across the fen-lands,
And avenge my father's murder!"
Straightway then my Hiawatha
Armed himself with all his war-gear,
Launched his birch-canoe for sailing;
With his palm it sides he patted,
Said with glee, "Cheemaun, my darling,
O my Birch-canoe! leap forward,
Where you see the fiery serpents,
Where you see the black pitch-water!"
. . . Then he took the oil of Nahma,
And the bows and sides annointed,
Smeared them well with oil, that swiftly
He might pass the black pitch-water.
All night long he sailed upon it,
Sailed upon that sluggish water,
Covered with its mould of ages,
Black with rotting water-rushes,
Rank with flags and leaves of lilies,
Stagnant, lifeless, dreary, dismal,

Lighted by the shimmering moonlight,
And by will-o'-the-wisps illumined,
Fires by ghosts of dead men kindled,
In their weary night-encampments.
All the air was white with moonlight,
All the water black with shadow,
And around him the Suggema,
The mosquito, sang his war-song,
And the fire-flies, Wah-wah-taysee,
Waved their torches to mislead him;
And the bull-frog, the Dahinda,
Thrust his head into the moonlight,
Fixed his yellow eyes upon him,
Sobbed and sank beneath the surface;
And anon a thousand whistles,
Answered over all the fen-lands,
And the heron, the Shuh-shuh gah,
Far off on the reedy margin,
Heralded the hero's coming.

As you were reading this passage, did you find yourself unnaturally stressing certain syllables at the beginnings of lines, such as "and" at the beginning of line 8, or "in" at the beginning of line 10? Readers commonly read noniambic meters in this unnatural way, simply because we are not as used to their variations as we are to the variations in iambic meter. But to do a good passage of noniambic poetry justice, we should read it with the same respect for its variations from the base meter as we read iambic meter. An educated reader of metrical poetry would not pronounce Shakespeare's line "to BE, or NOT to BE, that IS the QUESTion." Nor should you pronounce Longfellow's line, "AND aROUND him THE sshuhSHUHgah." Instead, read the lines with natural word-emphasis, simply pausing for a split second at the end of each line, but otherwise accenting them as if each line were prose. The meter will take care of itself; just listen, and appreciate the way Longfellow creates beauty and interest by varying from the basic trochaic meter, just as Shakespeare varies from the basic iambic meter.

Of course, sometimes a poet wants to create a pounding, intense trochaic rhythm, as Sara Josepha Hale does in the middle of the following passage.

From "Iron," Sarah Josepha Hale (1823)

. . . Then a voice, from out the mountains,
As an earthquake shook the ground,
And like frightened fawns the fountains,
Leaping, fled before the sound;
And the Anak oaks bowed lowly,
Quivering, aspen-like, with fear—
While the deep response came slowly,
Or it must have crushed mine ear!
"Iron! Iron! Iron!" crashing,
Like the battle-axe and shield;
Or the sword on helmet clashing,
Through a bloody battle-field:
"Iron! Iron! Iron!" rolling,
Like the far-off cannon's boom;
Or the death-knell, slowly tolling,
Through a dungeon's charnel gloom!
"Iron! Iron! Iron!" swinging,
Like the summer winds at play;
Or as bells of Time were ringing
In the blest Millennial Day!

Hale, who was not only the author of "Mary Had a Little Lamb" but also the person who spearheaded the movement to make Thanksgiving a national holiday, understood the value of public language and rhetoric. She starts this passage by building the trochaic rhythm slowly, interspersing clearly trochaic feet like "earthquake" and "frightened" after pyrrhics ("and the") or even iambs ("and like"). Because of this subtle buildup, when the poem reaches its climax with the word "Iron," the release of pent-up energy is dramatic and energetic, a movement similar to that in Claude McKay's "If We Must Die," which will be discussed in the chapter on the sonnet. (Locate Hale's entire poem online for the full effect.)

A skilled writer of noniambic meter, like a skilled writer of iambic meter, will develop a sense of the "metrical contract" with the reader and be sure not to push the variations too far. One fascinating example of how this works in trochaic meter is William Blake's revision of the beginning of stanza 2 of "The Tyger." An earlier version of the stanza began,

Burnt in distant deeps or skies
The cruel fire of thine eyes?

But Blake revised it to read,

In what distant deeps or skies
Burnt the fire of thine eyes?

The new version saves the powerful word "Burnt" for later in the sentence, giving the reader a chance to prepare for it and appreciate it. It also moves the trochaic phrase "burnt the" to a place where the grammar strengthens the emphasis on "burnt" even further, reconfirming the trochaic meter. In the first version, the second line starts with a strong iamb, continuing the iambs that began the last lines of the first stanza. In the new version, both lines start with trochees, the second with an extremely strong one. This reconfirmed trochaic meter resounds through the entire poem, making the sound of the meter indisputable at just the point where it might have been about to weaken.

These lines are a good reminder that the trochaic line is not simply the opposite of an iambic line. You will remember that it is common for a trochee to appear as the first foot of an iambic line, but the opposite is not true, because an iamb in the first foot of a trochaic line is harder to recover from. When writing trochees, it's a good idea to keep a trochee in the first foot whenever possible, unless you have a very good reason to vary it. This moving little poem does have a good reason; it would sound mechanical were it not for the variation at the beginning of the last line:

"Upon A Child," Robert Herrick (1648)

Here a pretty baby lies
Sung asleep with lullabies:
Pray be silent, and not stir
Th'easy earth that covers her.

Partly because iambs are so unusual at the beginnings of trochaic lines, this half-iamb surprises us, slows the line, makes us literally gasp a bit, just on the brink of realizing the true theme of the poem. (I say "half-iamb" because of the apostrophe, which would make most readers slur the first syllable and pronounce it very lightly.) This bone-chillingly casual effect is accomplished entirely through this single, subtle substitution in the trochaic meter.

You may have noticed that many of the lines in these trochaic poems—including every other line of "Iron" and all the lines of "The Tyger"—seem to be missing the final unstressed syllable. In lines of "falling meter"—trochees and dactyls—it is a common variation to leave off one or both of the last two unstressed syllables. I call such lines **footless** when leaving off one syllable, and **double footless** when leaving off two syllables. Correspondingly, just as the end of a line in falling meter can commonly lose syllables, the beginning of a line in falling meter can commonly add syllables; I call this the **running start.** These are the inverse variations to the common conventions for iambic and anapestic meter, where it's the end of the line that commonly adds unstressed syllables (the extra-syllable ending) and the beginning that loses them (the "headless" line).

The way to scan a "footless" trochaic line is, as with the headless iambic line, to mark the missing unstressed syllables in parentheses:

´ ˘ | ´ ˘ | ´ ˘ | ´ (˘)
Tyger, Tyger, burning bright

In "The Tyger," the missing final unstressed syllables are a key part of the beating rhythm which helps create this poem's physical and emotional impact. The meter is intertwined with the imagery of the forge, anvil, and hammer that builds gradually through the poem and is fully expressed in the fourth stanza.

When you are writing in a falling meter, remaining aware of running starts and footless lines can help reconcile your ear and your eye. For example, if you write,

I will write a lot of meter
Because it makes my poems sweeter,

your ear may say the lines sound fine together, but your eye may think there is a problem. In fact, the first syllable of "because" is part of a running start; readers won't hear it as interfering with the line. You'd scan the second line with parentheses around the extra-syllable beginning, like this:

(u) | / u | / u | / u | / u
be cause it makes my poems sweeter

Notice how the parentheses make it very clear exactly how this line matches up with the line before it, and also how they differ. Such awareness of sameness and difference is one of the basic aims of scansion.

The subtle variations possible in a meter are among its delights and glories. Still, when you are starting out in any new meter, be careful not to overdo the variations. Too many running starts will turn your trochees into iambs and your dactyls into anapests. So start out by sticking very closely to the basic pattern. After you've read, and written, a lot of poems in a certain meter, you'll gain a surer sense of how much variation will work in a given spot without tipping things over the edge. A good rule of thumb, as in anything involving writing poetry, is: don't do something just because you can do it; do it only when other aspects of the poem demand it.

In addition to varying the meter with dactyls, footless lines, and perhaps an occasional running start, when writing trochees, keep the following two guidelines in mind to help you modulate the meter in subtle ways:

1. Vary the placement of the caesura
2. Not all stresses are equal; contrast light and strong stresses within your lines.

The word "trochee" (/u) comes from the Greek word for "running," and sometimes trochees, especially when they use the final unstressed syllables consistently, can have a very light, playful quality, as in this peddler's call from Shakespeare's *A Winter's Tale:*

Gloves as sweet as damask roses;
Masks for faces and for noses;
Bugle bracelet, necklace amber,
Perfume for a lady's chamber . . .

Or even funnier, as in Carolyn Kizer's wonderful parody of *Hiawatha,* "Mud Soup":

From "Mud Soup," Carolyn Kizer

Dice the pork and chop the celery,
Chop the onions, chop the carrots,
Chop the tender index finger.
Put the kettle on the burner,
Drop the lentils into kettle:
Two quarts water, two cups lentils.
Afternoon is wearing on . . .

So it is important to remember that trochees do not always have to be intense or heavy. Like any meter, they can really be used for any mood or subject. Still, awareness of the history and connotations of trochees as a clear alternative to the dominant meter of iambics can help you use them well. It is especially interesting to note that, as mentioned in the sonnet chapter, trochees have developed a tradition among African American poets in the twentieth century, including two important, ambitious, and self-consciously African American poems, Gwendolyn Brooks's epic *The Anniad* and Countee Cullen's lyric "Heritage." Here is a passage from the opening of *The Anniad:*

From The Anniad, *Gwendolyn Brooks (1949)*

Think of sweet and chocolate,
Left to folly or to fate,
Whom the higher gods forgot,
Whom the lower gods berate;
Physical and underfed
Fancying on the featherbed
What was never and is not . . .

In addition to the common footless line, FEATHerBED, Brooks also uses variations such as the substitution of a dactyl for a trochee, both at the end of a line (SWEET and CHOColate) and in the middle (FANCYing ON the). Occasionally an iamb can be substituted, such as "and is" in the last line (WHAT was NEVer and IS NOT); just like substituting a trochee in an iambic line, this usually happens after a caesura or pause in the grammar, in this case the grammatical pause after "never." Read the last line aloud. The momentum of the line might tempt you to read the line in an unnaturally accented way and pronounce "and is" as a trochee: "WHAT was NEVer AND is NOT," but I would urge you to resist this temptation. In fact, "and is" is most definitely an iamb, since "is" is a much more important monosyllable than "and" and would get more stress in any context. The correct way to read this line aloud, as with any line of metrical poetry, is to find a balance between the expected stress and the actual stress, so that you simultaneously remind your hearers of the underlying pattern and let them enjoy the pleasure of the variation from it. I would probably read the line with a half-stress on "is," less of a stress than on "not" but still more perceptible than on "and."

At a time when even iambic meter is mysterious to most poets, noniambic meters have been truly flying under the conscious radar of poetics. For example, I have not seen recent discussion of the common variations in noniambic meter outside of my own writings. Nor have I ever seen any mention in writing of such issues as the importance of trochaic meter in twentieth-century African American poetry. Yet for poets whose internal ears are fully attuned to meter, a meter such as trochees speaks a distinct language available to anyone who cares to notice it. Like Poe's purloined letter, meter is a secret left out in plain sight:

"Lullaby," W. H. Auden (1940)

Lay your sleeping head, my love,
Human on my faithless arm;
Time and fevers burn away
Individual beauty from
Thoughtful children, and the grave
Proves the child ephemeral:
But in my arms till break of day
Let the living creature lie,
Mortal, guilty, but to me
The entirely beautiful.

Soul and body have no bounds:
To lovers as they lie upon
Her tolerant enchanted slope
In their ordinary swoon,
Grave the vision Venus sends

Of supernatural sympathy,
Universal love and hope;
While an abstract insight wakes
Among the glaciers and the rocks
The hermit's sensual ecstasy.

Certainty, fidelity
On the stroke of midnight pass
Like vibrations of a bell
And fashionable madmen raise
Their pedantic boring cry:
Every farthing of the cost,
All the dreaded cards foretell,
Shall be paid, but from this night
Not a whisper, not a thought,
Not a kiss nor look be lost.

Beauty, midnight, vision dies:
Let the winds of dawn that blow
Softly round your dreaming head
Such a day of sweetness show
Eye and knocking heart may bless,
Find the mortal world enough;
Noons of dryness see you fed
By the involuntary powers,
Nights of insult let you pass
Watched by every human love.

We may be moved by this poem simply as a love poem. If we know that Auden was gay, the description of the suffering at the end, from which the speaker wants to protect his lover, takes on a much deeper meaning. And if we know that "Lullaby" is written in trochaic meter and have some awareness of the subversive and revolutionary meanings that have been carried by that metrical tradition, the rhythmic body of the poem can speak to us as eloquently as do its history, its words, and its images.

Anapestic Meter (uu/)

"Questions and Answers," Cirilo F. Bautista (trans. José Edmundo Ocampo Reyes)

Don't you know that a mountain is nothing but smoke?
Don't you know that a thought is nothing but foam?
Don't you know that sackfuls of rice will go bad
when they're hidden deep down in the breast of a poem?

Make a dragon swoop down from a mountain of smoke
that your thoughts made of foam may be put to the test;
make a throne out of rice that's been kept in a nook
that a God may be wrought from the poem in your breast.

This poem, originally written in Tagalog by a Filipino poet, has been translated into anapests to approximate the rhythm of the original. An exhortation for the openness of imagination and of courage, it shows that, like trochees, anapests can have chantlike power. But the effect is more expansive than that of a trochaic chant—more of a sweeping rhythm, like the beating of wings, than like a heartbeat.

The origin of the word anapestic is a Greek word meaning "to strike up," an easy way to remember this pattern which rises at the end of the foot (uu/). When reading or writing anapestic meter, it may be useful to remember that the variations for anapestic meter are similar to those for iambic meter (since both are rising meters).

"I Would Live in Your Love," Sara Teasdale (1911)

I would live in your love as the sea-grasses live in the sea,
Borne up by each wave as it passes, drawn down by each wave that
 recedes;
I would empty my soul of the dreams that have gathered in me,
I would beat with your heart as it beats, I would follow your soul as it
 leads.

In this poem, variations include the cretic (GRAses LIVE) and the bacchius (es DRAWN DOWN), (by EACH WAVE). Anapestic poems frequently use "headless" lines, leaving off an initial unstressed syllable. The two-syllable feet that begin headless anapestic lines are often iambs; here it is a spondee that substitutes for the initial anapest (BORNE UP). Occasionally, anapestic lines also end with an extra syllable, as with the extra-syllable ending in iambic meter.

Like every meter, and every person, anapests have a great range of potential moods. And yet, like every meter, and every person, they have a distinctive flavor all their own as well. There is something deeply familiar about anapests, a quality that can feel gentle and homey, reassuring and even lulling. This is, after all, the meter of *The Cat in the Hat* and "The Night Before Christmas" and of some well-known favorites by "the Fireside poets," a group of five New England poets in the nineteenth century (Whittier, Longfellow, Holmes, Lowell, and Bryant) whose poetry was considered especially good for reading aloud around a fire.

Anapestic meter lends itself to reading aloud at length, particularly to narrative poetry. It engages the forward-stepping pace of the other rising meter, iambic, while also allowing extra space for details. The three syllables in each foot provide the potential for extra relaxation or the opposite, pounding momentum. Read these passages, including passages by two of the Fireside poets *aloud,* either physically aloud or aloud inside your mind, since that is how all metrical poetry is intended to be read. Notice how it feels. Note that in order not to lose pace with the meter, you will have to pause in places like after "climbed" in the first line quoted, after "and" in the third line from the end of the first stanza, and after "on" in the second line from the end.

From "Paul Revere's Ride," Henry Wadsworth Longfellow (1860)

. . . Then he climbed the tower of the Old North Church,
By the wooden stairs, with stealthy tread,
To the belfry-chamber overhead,
And startled the pigeons from their perch
On the sombre rafters, that round him made
Masses and moving shapes of shade,–
By the trembling ladder, steep and tall,
To the highest window in the wall,
Where he paused to listen and look down
A moment on the roofs of the town
And the moonlight flowing over all.

Beneath, in the churchyard, lay the dead,
In their night-encampment on the hill,
Wrapped in silence so deep and still
That he could hear, like a sentinel's tread,
The watchful night-wind, as it went
Creeping along from tent to tent,
And seeming to whisper, "All is well!"
A moment only he feels the spell
Of the place and the hour, and the secret dread
Of the lonely belfry and the dead . . .

A hurry of hoofs in a village street,
A shape in the moonlight, a bulk in the dark,
And beneath, from the pebbles, in passing, a spark
Struck out by a steed flying fearless and fleet;
That was all! And yet, through the gloom and the light,
The fate of a nation was riding that night.

The last passage quoted, the climax of the poem, demonstrates total command of pacing. Longfellow uses repeated caesuras to break up the lines and create a momentum that is forced to gather tension to override the pauses. When the first real pause happens, with the exclamation point, the person reading aloud experiences a tangible combination of relief and exhilaration. In the ensuing pause, like a hush, the next line and a half build a sense of extreme seriousness, sobered further by a counterpointing dactylic rhythm: "fate of a nation was."

With all its potential for narrative and dramatic action, the anapestic meter can be extremely conversational and natural, especially if there are strong caesuras in some of the lines. This stanza occurs near the end of a passionate poem about religious tolerance; it is a moment of lull in the poem's energy. Read the stanza aloud and notice how many natural opportunities the "light measure" of anapests provides for your voice to choose to pause, expressing your individual interpretation while fully respecting the meter.

From "The Quaker Alumni," John Greenleaf Whittier (1860)

Forgive me, dear friends, if my vagrant thoughts seem
Like a school-boy's who idles and plays with his theme.

Forgive the light measure whose changes display
The sunshine and rain of our brief April day.

To read such a skillfully written metrical passage aloud is almost like performing prewritten music on the instrument of your own voice. The last line, in particular, allows your speaking voice to pause expressively for nearly as long as you like after "rain" and after "brief" while still remaining completely within the meter.

Anapestic meter is still being used for serious contemporary subjects, as shown by this excerpt from a recent narrative poem:

From "Mother's Side," Alfred Nicol

But again follows close behind once for some men.
The hope that his sisters invested in him—
like the little warm flame of a whiskey—grew dim,

but was never snuffed out like the promise he made
which he broke every day for as long as he stayed . . .

Here, the use of this traditional meter along with conventional syntax and diction somehow underscores the poem's wan, rueful bitterness about the wasted potential of a life. The conversational tone of anapestic poetry can extend to pathos or to humor as well:

From "The Boys," Oliver Wendell Holmes (1859)

Yes, we're boys,—always playing with tongue or with pen,—
And I sometimes have asked,—Shall we ever be men?
Shall we always be youthful, and laughing, and gay,
Till the last dear companion drops smiling away?

From "A Fable for Critics," James Russell Lowell (1848)

There comes Poe, with his raven, like Barnaby Rudge,
Three-fifths of him genius and two-fifths sheer fudge,
Who talks like a book of iambs and pentameters,
In a way to make people of common-sense damn metres . . .

In the fourth line quoted, Lowell is taking advantage, for humorous purposes, of one of the great potentials of metrical verse: its ability to goad people to stress syllables they wouldn't ordinarily stress.

Anapests' leisurely pacings are wonderful for creating a light, sensual, romantic tone, whether in long lines, as in the poem by Sara Teasdale, or short lines:

From "Maud," Alfred, Lord Tennyson (1855)

She is coming, my own, my sweet;
Were it ever so airy a tread,
My heart would hear her and beat,
Were it earth in an earthy bed;
My dust would hear her and beat,
Had I lain for a century dead,
Would start and tremble under her feet,
And blossom in purple and red.

Because of the short lines, the iambic substitutions feel even more significant in the poem. But whether this passage is considered iambic with anapestic substitutions, or anapestic with iambic substitutions, the anapests are contributing a delicious sense of pausing, of slowness, of space, of readiness for physical and emotional intensity.

The intensely descriptive potential of anapests can be demonstrated by two passages dwelling on the physical detail of death and of sensuality, respectively:

From "The Destruction of Sennacharib," George Gordon, Lord Byron (1815)

And there lay the rider distorted and pale,
With the dew on his brow, and the rust on his mail:
And the tents were all silent, the banners alone,
The lances unlifted, the trumpet unblown.

The repetition of the "un" prefix makes the meter feel completely necessary, and the anapestic pace is solemn, as if a camera were panning slowly over the smallest details of the battlefield. The details and the meter both have a more chaotic, rumpled feeling in this excerpt describing a follower of the wine god Bacchus:

From Atalanta in Calydon, *Algernon Charles Swinburne (1865)*

The ivy falls with the Bacchanal's hair
Over her eyebrows hiding her eyes;
The wild vine slipping down leaves bare
Her bright breast shortening into sighs;
The wild vine slips with the weight of its leaves,
But the berried ivy catches and cleaves
To the limbs that glitter, the feet that scare
The wolf that follows, the fawn that flies.

In addition to the iambic substitutions, the variations include a trochee in the second line and spondees in the fourth and fifth lines. Swinburne manipulates the combination of iambs and anapests to vary the pace and create sensual suspense, at the same time that the imagery and word-music weave their own texture.

The galloping potential of anapests is put to use in this famous riding poem:

From "How They Brought the Good News from Ghent to Aix," Robert Browning (1845)

Not a word to each other; we kept the great pace
Neck by neck, stride by stride, never changing our place;
I turn'd in my saddle and made its girths tight,
Then shorten'd each stirrup, and set the pique right,
Rebuckled the cheek-strap, chain'd slacker the bit . . .

One of the joys of being skilled in meter is the ability to write effective parodies, and this poem is no exception:

"How I brought the good news from Aix to Ghent (or Vice Versa)," R. J. Yeatman and W. C . Sellar" (1933)

I sprang to the rollocks and Jorrocks and me,
And I galloped, you galloped, he galloped, we galloped all three . . .
Not a word to each other; we kept changing place,
Neck to neck, back to front, ear to ear, face to face;

And we yelled once or twice, as we heard a clock chime,
Would you kindly oblige us, *Is that the right time?*

Perhaps because of the energy that rising meter gives to the end of a line, the rising meters—iambs and anapests—lend themselves more easily than trochees or dactyls to the alternation of three- and four-foot lines, called ballad or folk meter (which is in turn, very uncommon in dactyls or trochees):

From "The Hunting of the Snark," Lewis Carroll (1876)

And the Banker, inspired with courage so new
It was matter for general remark,
Rushed madly ahead and was lost to their view
In his zeal to discover the snark.

But while he was seeking with thimbles and care,
A Bandersnatch swiftly drew nigh
And grabbed at the Banker, who shrieked in despair,
For he knew it was useless to fly.

Iambs can slow the tempo of anapestic lines, just as anapests speed up the tempo of an iambic line. The alternation of line length also adds texture to a poem. "The Hunting of the Snark" alternates lines that end in anapests with lines that end in iambs. Since the poem adheres to the syllable count so exactly (there are no other iambs in the poem), those single syllables make a difference: the lines with iambic endings feel considerably shorter, even though the whole poem is in anapestic tetrameter. The most famous poem in anapestic ballad stanza, indeed one of the most famous poems in English, also uses occasional iambs in an anapestic base:

"Annabel Lee," Edgar Allan Poe (1849)

It was many and many a year ago,
In a kingdom by the sea,
That a maiden there lived whom you may know
By the name of Annabel Lee;
And this maiden she lived with no other thought
Than to love and be loved by me.

Here Poe takes full advantage of the light, dreamy potential of anapestic meter, evoking its kinship to the old oral ballads with the "once upon a time" opening, but adding another two lines to the stanzas, perhaps to make us realize we are in the grip of unreality.

For many of the poets quoted in this section, anapestic meter was mostly used as a diversion from other meters, a "light measure" chosen for popular subjects. As a result, much of its potential remains unexplored. To give a taste of the anapest's possible range, here is a passage of political outrage, from the poet who used anapestic meter most consistently, and therefore had the most opportunity to learn to vary it:

From "A Song in Time of Revolution," Algernon Charles Swinburne (1860)

The wind has the sound of a laugh in the clamour of days and of deeds:
The priests are scattered like chaff, and the rulers broken like reeds.

The high-priest sick from qualms, with his raiment bloodily dashed;
The thief with branded palms, and the liar with cheeks abashed.

They are smitten, they tremble greatly, they are pained for their pleasant things:
For the house of the priests made stately, and the might in the mouth of the kings.

They are grieved and greatly afraid; they are taken, they shall not flee:
For the heart of the nations is made as the strength of the springs of the sea. . .

For the breaking of gold in their hair they halt as a man made lame:
They are utterly naked and bare; their mouths are bitter with shame.

Wilt thou judge thy people now, O king that wast found most wise?
Wilt thou lie any more, O thou whose mouth is emptied of lies?

Swinburne uses a number of different devices to change the mood of the meter at various points in the poem. There is the unexpected skipped syllable in the line, "For the breaking of gold in their hair they halt as a man made lame."

There is the alliteration and assonance in the line, "They are grieved and greatly afraid; they are taken, they shall not flee." In the last couplet, there is the staggering of two parallel phrases so they occur at different places in the line.

In "A Song in Time of Revolution," almost all the feet are anapests or iambs. But other triple feet are an excellent way to add texture, variety, and expressiveness to anapestic rhythm. Such modulations are done skillfully in these varied lines from "The Night Before Christmas":

As dry leaves that before the wild hurricane fly,
When they meet with an obstacle mount to the sky.

The moon on the breast of the new-fallen snow
Gave the luster of midday to objects below

"as DRY LEAVES" and "the WILD HUR-" are bacchics. "with an ob-" is called a tribrach, the three-syllable equivalent to a pyrrhic. "FALLen-SNOW" and "GAVE the LUST-" are cretics. These kinds of variations can be as subtle as the common variations in iambic meter. If you read the passage aloud, or aloud to yourself, slowly, you will have a chance to notice how well they work by feeling the difference in your mouth between these syllables and the regular anapestic rhythm. This passage from a contemporary poem shows how complex the variations in a line of anapestic meter can be:

From "Halo in Decline," Indigo Moor

In your death, it appears as by Providence, bold:
all of gold, a thin halo rides high on your cheek
as you float down the Tiber, a glacial sweet shine—
still warm in the current, enough to cause steam
to rise slow in rivulets on Tiber's smooth skin.

The passage is all anapests until the fourth line, which is varied only by an iamb in the first foot. But the last line consists of an iamb, cretic, fourth paean, and bacchic—and yet, in the anapestic context of the poem, it still sounds like an anapestic line.

This poem gathers great expressiveness from an irregular combination of iambs and anapests:

From "Under the Waterfall," Thomas Hardy (1914)

. . . And when we had drunk from the glass together,
Arched by the oak-copse from the weather,
I held the vessel to rinse in the fall,
Where it slipped, and it sank, and was past recall,
Though we stooped and plumbed the little abyss
With long bared arms. There the glass still is.
And, as said, if I thrust my arm below
Cold water in a basin or bowl, a throe
From the past awakens a sense of that time,
And the glass we used, and the cascade's rhyme.
The basin seems the pool, and its edge
The hard smooth face of the brook-side ledge,
And the leafy pattern of china-ware
The hanging plants that were bathing there . . .

The spondee of "bared arms" and the fourth paean of "-er in a bas-" are skillfully expressive variations, both seeming to convey the feeling of cold water on a bare arm. But perhaps the most surprising variation here is the three iambs in a row: "The basin seems the pool." If you are reading quickly, it's easy to think that the second foot is an anapest, "seems the pool." This reading swallows up the word "seems" entirely, just as the reality of the basin is swallowed up by the overpowering memory of the two lovers' meeting by the pool. But because the poem is tetrameter and that would give the line only three feet, we know that the line really scans as three iambs followed by an anapest. So we need to go back and read the word "seems" excruciatingly slowly to balance "-in seems" with the other feet in the poem, enacting in a different way the power of the approaching memory.

An anapestic rhythm infuses this poem:

From "The Lifeguard," James Dickey

In a stable of boats I lie still,
From all sleeping children hidden.
The leap of a fish from its shadow
Makes the whole lake instantly tremble.

With my foot on the water, I feel
The moon outside . . .

I wash the black mud from my hands.
On a light given off by the grave
I kneel in the quick of the moon
At the heart of a distant forest
And hold in my arms a child
Of water, water, water.

The particular dreamy earnestness of tone is hard to imagine without anapestic meter. This free verse, so regular as to feel almost perfectly anapestic in many passages, gives an indication of the wonderful potential of anapests for a contemporary poetry.

Anapests, perhaps because they are a "rising" meter and more similar to iambs than trochees or dactyls, have been used somewhat more often than the falling meters in English-language poetry. But still, it was only in the late nineteenth century that three-syllable feet were fully accepted into poetry in English—a few decades before metrical poetry began to be largely displaced by free verse. Now that we have all meters available to us, to experiment with anapests and find your own vocabulary for the versatile anapestic meter will certainly add to your options as a poet.

Dactylic Meter (/uu)

The word "dactyl" derives from the Greek word for "finger," and a finger provides an easy way to remember this foot whose pattern in the classical system of prosody was a long syllable followed by two short syllables: hold up your index finger and start counting the phalanges from the bottom up. Though your bottom phalange may not really be longer than the top two, you will probably get the analogy. Dactylic meter is my own favorite noniambic meter, the meter that first inspired my interest in noniambic meters when, immersing myself in iambic pentameter passages for my PhD dissertation, I began to find passages of this magnificently fluid meter lurking in iambic and free verse poetry. I found the dactylic meter so gorgeous, and the emotions it seemed to unlock so powerful, that I felt compelled to begin to use it in my own poems.

It is actually surprising that so little dactylic poetry has been published in English, given the importance of this meter to the entire Western tradition of poetry. The **dactylic hexameter,** or line of six dactyls, was the standard epic meter of classical poetry, including Homer's *Odyssey* and *Iliad,* and, following them, Virgil's *Aeneid.* Another central meter was the **elegiac couplet,** consisting of a dactylic hexameter followed by a dactylic pentameter, with spondees allowed to be substituted for the dactyls in certain places. This was a standard mnemonic used by British students studying classical poetry to help them remember the pattern:

Down in a deep, dark dell sat an old cow munching a beanstalk.
    Out of its mouth came forth yesterday's dinner and tea.

Or, as Ovid put it more succinctly in his *Amores* (1.1.27): "Sex mihi surgat opus numeris, in quinque residat": "Let my work surge in six feet, subside again in five."

Longfellow chose dactylic hexameter for his epic poem of the United States, *Evangeline,* because of the line's epic history, and the dactylic meter gives a strong, rolling quality to Longfellow's story of the exiled woman searching America for her lover. Earlier in this book, you read the opening of *Evangelina.* Here is another passage:

From Evangeline, *Henry Wadsworth Longfellow*

Far asunder, on separate coasts, the Acadians landed;
Scattered were they, like flakes of snow when the wind from the northeast
Strikes aslant through the fogs that darken the Banks of Newfoundland.
Friendless, homeless, hopeless, they wandered from city to city,
From the cold lakes of the North to sultry Southern savannas—
From the bleak shores of the sea to the lands where the Father of Waters
Seizes the hills in his hands, and drags them down to the ocean,
Deep in their sands to bury the scattered bones of the mammoth.
Friends they sought and homes; and many, despairing, heartbroken,
Asked of the earth but a grave, and no longer a friend nor a fireside.
Written their history stands on tablets of stone in the churchyards.
Long among them was seen a maiden who waited and wandered,
Lowly and meek in spirit, and patiently suffering all things . . .

As if a morning of June, with all its music and sunshine,
Suddenly paused in the sky, and, fading, slowly descended
Into the east again, from whence it late had arisen.
Sometimes she lingered in towns, till, urged by the fever within her,
Urged by a restless longing, the hunger and thirst of the spirit,
She would commence again her endless search and endeavor;
Sometimes in churchyards strayed, and gazed on the crosses and
tombstones,
Sat by some nameless grave, and thought that perhaps in its bosom
He was already at rest, and she longed to slumber beside him.
Sometimes a rumor, a hearsay, an inarticulate whisper,
Came with its airy hand to point and beckon her forward.
Sometimes she spake with those who had seen her beloved and known
him,
But it was long ago, in some far-off place or forgotten.
"Gabriel Lajeunesse!" said they; "O, yes! we have seen him.
He was with Basil the blacksmith, and both have gone to the prairies;
Coureurs-des-Bois are they, and famous hunters and trappers,"
"Gabriel Lajeunesse!" said others; "O, yes! we have seen him.
He is a Voyageur in the lowlands of Louisiana."
Then would they say: "Dear child! why dream and wait for him longer?
Are there not other youths as fair as Gabriel? others
Who have hearts as tender and true, and spirits as loyal?
Here is Baptiste Leblanc, the notary's son, who has loved thee
Many a tedious year; come, give him thy hand and be happy!
Thou art too fair to be left to braid St. Catherine's tresses."
Then would Evangeline answer, serenely but sadly—"I cannot!
Whither my heart has gone, there follows my hand, and not elsewhere
For when the heart goes before, like a lamp, and illumines the pathway,
Many things are made clear, that else lie hidden in darkness."

Even the most regular dactylic poetry, of which *Evangeline* is an example, makes frequent use of trochees, often at line endings but throughout the line as well. The trochees add contrast and texture without disrupting the falling rhythm, just as anapests do in an iambic line without disrupting the rising rhythm. The last line of the passage above plays with the expectation of frequent trochees by using the trochaic word "village" directly before a caesura, as part of a dactylic foot. Though the rhythm of the word "village" parallels the final trochee, "farmers," the syllable "the" after it adds an almost melancholy fall, reestablishing the dactylic pattern.

Dactyls have a magnificent pull to them, a sway; they come in waves. This passage uses their mystery well. Each line ends with a trochee, making them technically "adonic" lines (see the section on sapphic stanza) but dactylic sounds. Dactyls sound so distinctive that a relatively small but consistent percentage of them creates a distinct dactylic effect:

"Mushrooms," Sylvia Plath (1957)

Perfectly voiceless,
Widen the crannies,
Shoulder through holes. We

Diet on water

Robert Browning's "The Lost Leader" conveys passionate anger against another poet, who has "sold out," in a gathering rush of regular dactyls:

Just for a handful of silver he left us,
  Just for a ribbon to stick in his coat—

While the trochee is by far the most common variation in dactylic meter, another fairly common variation is that dactylic lines sometimes begin with the running start, an "extra-syllable beginning" (structurally analogous to the "extra-syllable ending" that occurs in iambic lines, and, like them, marked in parentheses). The extra-syllable beginning occurs in lines 2, 5, 7, and 10 in this poem about Arachne, a weaver who was turned into a spider by Athena because she boasted that her weaving was better than the goddess's:

"Arachne Gives Thanks to Athena," A. E. Stallings

It is no punishment. They are mistaken—
The brothers, the father. My prayers were answered.
I was all fingertips. Nothing was perfect:
What I had woven, the moths will have eaten;
At the end of my rope was a noose's knot.

Now it's no longer the thing, but the pattern,
And that will endure, even though webs be broken.
I, if not beautiful, am beauty's maker.
Old age cannot rob me, nor cowardly lovers.
The moon once pulled blood from me. Now I pull silver.
Here are the lines I pulled from my own belly—
Hang them with rainbows, ice, dewdrops, darkness.

Some dactylic lines, as does line 5 above, actually begin with two extra unstressed syllables. Some might prefer to scan "At the end of my rope was a noose's knot" as an anapestic line, but since that would make it the only anapestic line in a dactylic poem, the principle of prosodic consistency makes it preferable to scan it with a two-syllable running start and a final foot missing two unstressed syllables:

(u u) | /   u u | /   u u| /   u| / (u u)
At the end of my rope was a noose's knot

Other variations in dactylic lines include the antibacchic (//u) (as in the first foot of line 9 in Stallings's poem), cretic (/u/) (as in the first foot of line 8 in Stallings's poem), first paean (/uuu), and molossus (///) (as in the third foot of the last line of Stallings's poem). As we have seen, a frequent type of "footless" dactylic line, like the footless trochaic line, skips either one or both final unstressed syllables (a line that skips two final unstressed syllables could be called a "double footless line"). Look for the footless lines in the following passage:

From "Goblin Market," Christina Rossetti (1859)

Apples and quinces,
Lemons and oranges,
Plump unpecked cherries,
Melons and raspberries,
Bloom-down-cheeked peaches,
Swart-headed mulberries,
Wild free-born cranberries,
Crab-apples, dewberries,
Pine-apples, blackberries,
Apricots, strawberries;—

There are three footless lines, including those ending with QUINces" and "CHERries." Can you find the third?

The following poem, a paean to marchers for workers' rights, begins in dactylic hexameter, then switches after two stanzas to dactylic pentameter:

"At Last the Women Are Moving," Genevieve Taggard (1935)

Last, walking with stiff legs as if they carried bundles
Came mothers, housewives, old women who knew why they abhorred
    war.
Their clothes bunched about them, they hobbled with anxious steps
To keep with the stride of the marchers, erect bearing wide banners.

Such women looked odd, marching on American asphalt.
Kitchens they knew, sinks, suds, stew-pots and pennies . . .
Dull hurry and worry, clatter, wet hands and backache.
Here they were out in the glare on the militant march.

How did these timid, the slaves of breakfast and supper
Get out in the line, drop for once dish-rag and broom?
Here they are as work-worn as stitchers and fitters.
Mama have you got some grub, now none of their business.

Oh, but those who know in their growing sons and their husbands
How the exhausted body needs sleep, how often needs food,
These, whose business is keeping the body alive,
These are ready, if you talk their language, to strike.

Kitchen is small, the family story is sad.
Out of the musty flats the women come thinking:
Not for me and mine only. For my class I have come
To walk city miles with many, my will in our work.

Like Longfellow, Taggard chose the dactylic hexameter, meter of the great classical epics, to lend heroic dignity to her story. Taggard's dactylic meter is rougher and more awkward than Longfellow's, perhaps in solidarity with the "stiff legs" of the women she writes about. She intersperses many trochees with the dactyls, and she uses running starts ("came," "there," "Oh, but") antibacchics ("clothes bunched a," "stiff legs as," "line, drop for"), cretics ("housewives, old," "bearing wide"), one-syllable feet followed by a rest ("Last," "(e)rect," "once," "odd," "suds"), and first paeans ("Mama have you," "ready, if you"). The dactylic rhythm is powerful, running over these obstacles and rough places, and uniting the poem with great energy. A more measured and metaphysical use of the meter shapes the following poem:

"The Slip," Rachel Hadas

Empty and trembling, haloed by absences,
whooshings, invisible leave-takings, finishes,
images, closure: departures so gracefully
practice their gestures that when they do happen,
dazzled with sunlight, distracted by darkness,
mercifully often we miss the event.
So many hours, days, weeks, years, and decades
spent—no, slathered and lavished and squandered
ardently, avidly gazing at nothing,
pacing the pavement or peering round corners,
setting the table and sniffing the twilight,
sitting and gazing at edges, horizons,
preparing occasions that leave us exhausted,
recovering, staggering back to a climax.
Dramas of use, inanition, repletion!
And there all along, except not there forever,
was the beloved. The foreground? The background?
Thoughtful, impatient, affectionate, angry,
tired, distracted, preoccupied, human,
part of our lives past quotidian limits,
there all the while and yet not there forever.

As with most dactylic poems, the most common substitutions here are trochees. But Hadas uses many different variations to keep this rhythm from being monotonous. She actually substitutes an anapest for a dactyl (when they DO HAPpen); this is a daring move, but she uses performative utterance to get away with it: since the sense demands extreme stress on DO for rhetorical effect anyway, the extreme stress on DO needed to make the reader notice that this really is an anapest in a dactylic context makes total sense. She also uses a spondee

(HOURS, DAYS), a bacchus (WEEKS, YEARS and), an antispast (PEERing ROUND), two amphibrachs in a row (prePARing ocCASions) followed by an entire line of amphibrachs (reCOVering, STAGger ing BACK to a CLIMax). And the metrical climax fully expresses the climax in the poem's meaning; immediately afterward, the poem regains its balance and the last seven lines are completely regular, reminding us that not only the beloved but also the meter were "there all along."

By contrast, the poem below uses completely regular dactylic trimeter without relying on any metrical substitutions except for trochees and footless lines to keep the reader's interest. Instead, the question and answer format provides a dramatic structure of repetition and variation that builds suspense, and the short lines create a sense of movement:

"The Denouement," *R. S. Gwynn*

Who were those persons who chased us?
They were the last of the others.

Why must we always be running?
We are the last of our own.

Where is the shelter you spoke of?
Between us. All around us.

Shall we be safe until morning?
There is no doorway to enter.

How shall we live in this desert?
Just as we did in the farmlands.

How was it done in the farmlands?
Just as it shall be here.

What is the word for this place?
No one has ever used it.

When shall I hear the word?
Never, until it is spoken.

Who were my father and mother?
Trust me to keep your secret.

What is the mark on your forehead?
What is the mark on your cheek?

Dactylic meter, as a triple, falling meter, is metrically the furthest a poet can move from the double, rising meter of iambic. Perhaps that explains why dactyls seem to carry such surprising and powerful energies. When I began to write in dactyls, I was rewarded immediately by finding a different voice for my poems. That is why I encourage you to explore all the metrical possibilities you can find in your own poems: so you will know how to write all the voices hidden within you.

Mixed Meters

Sometimes you may run across a poem that you know is rising or falling in meter, but the meter is hard to identify as iambs or anapests, or even as trochees or dactyls, since it has about the same amount of double and triple feet. You don't need to choose; these patterns are called mixed meter (the Greek term is *logodaeic*). Often, these poems are easy to read, popular poems, the kind that used to be printed in newspapers back when newspapers printed lots of poetry. They are meant to be read aloud and have an effect similar to accentual poems. Scan the following poem by Georgia Douglas Johnson to notice the anapests and iambs:

Georgia Douglas Johnson, "Your World" (1962)

Your world is as big as you make it
I know, for I used to abide
In the narrowest nest in a corner
My wings pressing close to my side

But I sighted the distant horizon
Where the sky-line encircled the sea
And I throbbed with a burning desire
To travel this immensity.

I battered the cordons around me
And cradled my wings on the breeze
Then soared to the uttermost reaches
with rapture, with power, with ease!

This poem moves fluidly between anapests and iambs; the many extra-syllable endings sometimes give the poem the swing of amphibrachs also. This meter works in quite a different way than the more "literary" poems in this chapter, where a clear base meter persists through various metrical variations and asserts itself again at the end. Johnson's poem is the kind of popular verse that is really meant for the ear, and our ears enjoy the changes of rhythm and tempo, the counterpoint between various triples and a running accentual beat, without needing to focus on the base-meter-and-variation dynamic that is fundamental to the rhythms of most of the other metrical poems we have discussed.

Another kind of mixing of meters is simply to splice together lines of different meters in one poem. This is not done as often as it should be. In the following excerpt, the effect is self-conscious:

From "Mezzo Cammin," Judith Moffett

I mean to mark the Midway Day
With soundings in this verse form. Say,
Muse, how you hate it!
I know your taste for excess. But
These jingly rhymes must undercut,
Counter, deflate it . . .

The short lines consist of a dactyl and a trochee (like the last line of a sapphic stanza), while the longer lines are all iambic tetrameter. The effect is unusual and quite fascinating. In the following poem, a tour de force which imitates the variety of musical instruments, the different meters of each stanza create a palette of different feelings:

From "A Hymn for St. Cecilia's Day," John Dryden (1687)

What passion cannot Music raise and quell?
When Jubal struck the chorded shell,

His listening brethren stood around,
And, wondering, on their faces fell
To worship that celestial sound:
Less than a God they thought there could not dwell
Within the hollow of that shell,
That spoke so sweetly, and so well.
What passion cannot Music raise and quell?

The trumpet's loud clangour
Excites us to arms,
With shrill notes of anger,
And mortal alarms.
The double double double beat
Of the thundering drum
Cries Hark! the foes come;
Charge, charge, 'tis too late to retreat!

The soft complaining flute,
In dying notes, discovers
The woes of hopeless lovers,
Whose dirge is whisper'd by the warbling lute.

Of course, it is not only the meter itself—iambic tetrameters, pentameters, and trimeters, amphibrachic dimeters and trimeters—that creates such palpably different effects, but also Dryden's weaving in of other aspects of the language: word-music, syntax, and syllable weight.

Tips for Writing in Meter

Step 1. Writing Early Drafts
There are two main methods; choose the one that sounds most enjoyable to you.

Method A: Start by feeling the beat strongly and then open yourself to letting the words come. Do not censor yourself. Relax, or allow the meter itself to relax you. Meter can hypnotize your mind so that you may write things you never intended to say. Dance or chant your words. Write nonsense if it's easier.

Method B: Write what you want to say in prose, free verse, or in a meter that is easy for you. Then choose a meter to translate it into. You might listen for a meter that is beginning to emerge by itself, or simply decide which meter you want to use. As you translate it, read it aloud as you go to make sure you are still on track with the beat.

Whichever method you use, *read aloud* to yourself frequently as you write.

Step 2. Check for Meter

Check for metrical consistency by reading your poem aloud and exaggerating your intended meter. When you find a place where the wrong syllable of a word is emphasized, stop. This is your signal to fix the meter. For example, if you intended to write anapestic meter, read your lines aloud like this:

I am WRITing in ANapests NOW, and you KNOW
that it MAKES things sound STRANGE to do THAT, but don't WOR-
ry, just GO on, you KNOW we can SING, happilY

As you are reading and exaggerating, when you get to the word "happilY," your ear will notice that the third syllable sounds unnatural when it is accented. That's a signal that that part of the poem is not following the base meter. Often, a simple change of word order will fix the meter—in this case, "we can HAPpily SING." Until you have the basic pattern down and are quite sure of your ear, it is best to follow the base meter exactly, with no variations at all. (If you are confident you know what you are doing and are ready to try varying the meter on purpose, see step 4.)

Step 3. Check for Language

Check your poem for the following common mistakes and correct them:

- Any unnatural word order (syntax). Example: "my hat so red I put on my head"
- Filler words that don't mean anything. Example: "the sun *so* bright," "when I *did* go outside"

- Archaic or overly literary words that you would never use otherwise, that thought they had a right to sneak in along with the meter. Example: "e'er," "yonder," "lo!"

Step 4. Check for Fluidity

- Once you are sure your meter is right, read your poem aloud and notice places where the rhythm sounds too singsong or mechanical or predictable. Experiment with changing these places. Sometimes a simple word change that doesn't actually change the meter will work. For example, the line "We WALK unDER the SUNny SKY" sounds mechanical, while substituting the word "AMPle" for "SUNny" sounds much more fluid and interesting; although the meter is the same, the consonants and vowels are different, slowing the word in different places and giving the line more rhythmic interest.
- In other cases, you may want to try some of the metrical variations discussed in the chapters that follow. After a little practice, your ear will tell you which variations add fluidity and which ones undermine the meter.
- After adding variations, read your poem aloud again with your meaning or emotional tone in mind, to see if the variation adds meaning to the poem. Be careful that the rhythm works for the mood you are trying to set, not against it.

Step 5. Listen to Your Poem

- Read your poem in a natural voice, with natural intonation, to yourself. Or sing it. See how it sounds. Feel free to dwell on the rhythm, immerse yourself in it. Tinker with it for fun.
- Read it to a friend. Ask your friend to close their eyes and listen not for the meaning of the words, but for the sound. Ask them if they notice any places where the beat sounds off. Ask about boring places, interesting places, and beautiful places.

Step 6. Listen to Your Poem Freshly

Let the poem sit for as long as possible without looking at it, and then read it aloud to yourself one more time.

Amphibrachs, Dipodics, and Hendecasyllabics

The world is so full of a number of things
I'm sure we should all be as happy as kings.

—ROBERT LOUIS STEVENSON

There are numerous other noniambic patterns, and they are all worth writing. Feel free to skip this section if this is your first exposure to this material, but once you have the basics down, you may want to come back to this chapter so you can venture out and try your hand at cretics, amphibrachs, hendecasyllabics, sapphics (which are discussed in the stanza chapter since they are technically a stanza) and other less common metrical patterns.

Amphibrachs (u/u) make a meter with a distinct and compelling rhythm. The central syllable of each foot is stressed, and the meter is not usually varied. While they may be familiar to you as the meter of many limericks ("There was a young poet from Utah, / who found that she liked writing met-ah"—now you finish the poem!), they have a more dignified history as a staple meter of Russian poetry:

"The White Bird," Anna Akhmatova (1914) (trans. Annie Finch with George Kline)

So worried about me, so jealous, so tender—
As steady as God's sun, as warm as Love's breath—
he wanted no songs of the past I remembered.
He took my white bird, and he put it to death.

At sunset, he found me in my own front room.
"Now love me, and laugh, and write poems," he said.
So I dug a grave in the old alder's gloom,
Behind the round well, for my happy, bright bird.

I promised him I wouldn't cry any more;
The heart in my chest is as heavy as stone,
And everywhere, always, it seems that I hear
The tender, sweet voice of the one who is gone.

It's common in amphibrachs to substitute an iamb or spondee for the final foot (as in the second and fourth lines).

Although amphibrachs are not common in English now outside of limericks, at one time they had great appeal. For proof, here is one of the most popular American poems ever written, sold in numerous editions and memorized by generations of children:

From "The Old Oaken Bucket," Samuel Woodworth (1817)

How dear to this heart are the scenes of my childhood,
When fond recollection presents them to view!
The orchard, the meadow, the deep-tangled wild-wood,
And every loved spot which my infancy knew!
The wide-spreading pond, and the mill that stood by it,
The bridge, and the rock where the cataract fell,
The cot of my father, the dairy-house nigh it,
And e'en the rude bucket that hung in the well—
The old oaken bucket, the iron-bound bucket,
The moss-covered bucket which hung in the well.

That moss-covered vessel I hailed as a treasure,
For often at noon, when returned from the field,
I found it the source of an exquisite pleasure,
The purest and sweetest that nature can yield.
How ardent I seized it, with hands that were glowing,
And quick to the white-pebbled bottom it fell;
Then soon, with the emblem of truth overflowing,
And dripping with coolness, it rose from the well
The old oaken bucket, the iron-bound bucket,
The moss-covered bucket arose from the well.

How sweet from the green mossy brim to receive it,
As poised on the curb it inclined to my lips!
Not a full blushing goblet could tempt me to leave it,
The brightest that beauty or revelry sips.
And now, far removed from the loved habitation,
The tear of regret will intrusively swell,
As fancy reverts to my father's plantation,
And sighs for the bucket that hangs in the well
The old oaken bucket, the iron-bound bucket,
The moss-covered bucket that hangs in the well!

Amphibrachs are often overlooked when people write about English meter, and you will sometimes see amphibrachic poems classified as anapests with the first syllable missing. But in fact, the two rhythms sound quite distinct. Read aloud two lines of amphibrachs (for example, the lines by Stevenson quoted at the beginning of this section) and two lines of anapests (for example, the lines quoted from "The Boys" by Oliver Wendell Holmes). If you are unsure of the difference, try forcing the lines into each others' meter. If you read the Stevenson lines as if they were exaggerated anapests, pausing a second after each stress, you may feel a little seasick, as if you are swimming against slapping waves: "The WORLD | is so FULL | of a NUM | ber of THINGS." By contrast, if you read them as exaggerated amphibrachs, pausing for a second after each foot, the syntax and phrasing will feel much more natural: "The WORLD is | so FULL of | a NUMber | of THINGS." Similarly, if you read the Holmes lines as exaggerated amphibrachs, it will feel forced, jerky, and constantly interrupted: "we're BOYS al | ways PLAY ing | with TONGUE or | with PEN." But if you read it as exaggerated anapests, it will feel more smooth, as if a wave is cresting at the end of each foot: "we're BOYS | always PLAY | ing with TONGUE | or with PEN." Skillful writers of every meter work with the meter, using phrasing, word stress, and intonation both to reinforce the expected pattern and to add surprise and interest to it. Sometimes when you are reading a passage whose meter you don't recognize, it can feel forced and disconnected, like an academic exercise. But once you grasp the right pattern, if the poet knew what they were doing, everything clicks into place and comes to life. That's when you know you have found the right pattern.

When you are learning to write amphibrachs, as with any meter, it helps to read aloud frequently and make sure that you are paying attention to the foot breaks. Try pausing for a split second between feet to notice how the foot break accentuates your meaning, and to make sure you are using the meter to convey the feeling you want to express. If you get confused, just put the poem away for a while and go do something else. When you return, look at it freshly. If you get really confused, find another poem that uses the meter consistently and regularly to use as a rhythmic model.

Another distinctively energetic metrical pattern is the **dipodic.** The word means "two feet," and dipodic meter literally means a kind of meter where pairs of feet are meant to be heard together. Generally, one of the feet has a stronger stress than the other; an example you might know is the Gilbert and Sullivan song, "I am the very model of a modern major general," or this well-known poem:

From "Casey at the Bat," Ernest Lawrence Thayer (1888)

The Outlook wasn't brilliant for the Mudville nine that day:
The score stood four to two, with but one inning more to play.
And then when Cooney died at first, and Barrows did the same,
A sickly silence fell upon the patrons of the game.

A straggling few got up to go in deep despair. The rest
Clung to that hope which springs eternal in the human breast;
They thought, if only Casey could get but a whack at that—
We'd put up even money, now, with Casey at the bat.

While "Casey at the Bat" is written in rising dipodic meter (alternating strong and weak iambs), the passage below is in falling dipodic meter (alternating strong and weak trochees). But each of them uses the other kind of foot occasionally for variation, as in "Clung to" in the rising poem, or "The servants" in the falling poem.

From "The Galley-Slave," Rudyard Kipling (1886)

Bear witness, once my comrades, what a hard-bit gang were we—
The servants of the sweep-head, but the masters of the sea!
By the hands that drove her forward as she plunged and yawed and
    sheered,
Woman, Man, or God or Devil, was there anything we feared?

Was it storm? Our fathers faced it and a wilder never blew.
Earth that waited for the wreckage watched the galley struggle through.
Burning noon or choking midnight, Sickness, Sorrow, Parting, Death?
Nay, our very babes would mock you had they time for idle breath.

In a famous footnote to an essay about poetry, A. E. Housman said he thought dipodic meter represents the future of poetry, and it does have a compelling sound, with its alternating strong and weak stresses evoking the rhythm of walking. The following example, by Arielle Greenberg, reminds us that metrical poetry does not have to follow syntactical restraints and can explore language in a nonreferential way, as much as free-verse poetry can do. The meter is so strongly established by line 5 that our ear compensates for the missing syllable and replaces it with a long "rest."

"The Meter of the Night Sky," Arielle Greenberg

I wonder what would happen if the K in knife was said,
if part of all the Hs in the book had rubbed away,
changing up the shapes of our ancestor's good white bones.

I wonder who's been sleeping in this bale of hay before,
how many eyes adore me, how many needles here.
I wonder who is bedded, sharp and low, like any twin,
kindled by the flickering camp lantern of my name.

It doesn't happen suddenly, but with a rolling hush:
some blossom, something citric, and oh so cavalier,
moves without me, moves in chorus with the pulse of the night sky.

It's my velvet artwork, making pleasure of a peephole.
Without me, it can wonder every G-note in the scale,
every Aries made of starlight. It's the whirring of my plum.

Hendecasyllabics literally means "eleven syllables." The meter is based on a classical meter and, though rarely used, can be a source of uncommon beauty. If you find you enjoy the sapphic stanza—which some people find so beautiful as to be almost addictive—the hendecasyllabic offers the opportunity to maintain the basic sapphic rhythm for a long period, building up momentum. Hendecasyllabics may look complicated, but really each line is simply a trochaic pentameter with one dactyl in the second foot. As with sapphics, because the meter itself is a distinctive pattern, and not just a base rhythm, this is not a meter that is usually varied or substituted in any way.

From "Hendecasyllabics," Algernon Charles Swinburne (1866)

In the month of the long decline of roses
I, beholding the summer dead before me,
Set my face to the sea and journeyed silent,
Gazing eagerly where above the sea-mark
Flame as fierce as the fervid eyes of lions
Half divided the eyelids of the sunset;
Till I heard as it were a noise of waters

Moving tremulous under feet of angels
Multitudinous, out of all the heavens;
Knew the fluttering wind, the fluttered foliage,
Shaken fitfully, full of sound and shadow;
And saw, trodden upon by noiseless angels,
Long mysterious reaches fed with moonlight,
Sweet sad straits in a soft subsiding channel,
Blown about by the lips of winds I knew not,
Winds not born in the north nor any quarter,
Winds not warm with the south nor any sunshine. . .

A beautiful poem in hendecasyllabics is Frost's "For Once, Then, Something." To emphasize that there is no mood or style or subject that fits with any meter, here is a contemporary poem in hendecasyllabics by four-time National Poetry Slam champion Patricia Smith:

"The Reemergence of the Noose," Patricia Smith

Some lamp sputters its dusty light across a
desk. Some hand, in a fever, works the fraying
brown hemp, twisting and knifing, weaving, tugging
tight this bellowing circle. Randy Travis
sings, moans, radios steamy twangs and hiccups,
blue notes backing the ritual of drooping
loop. Sweat drips in an awkward hallelujah.
God glares down, but the artist doesn't waver—
wrists click rhythm, and rope becomes a path to
what makes saviors; the loop bemoans its need to
squeeze, its craving for the ghost of Negro neck.

Smith writes about composing this poem, "I've been troubled by the proliferation of nooses being discovered lately—hanging from trees on school campuses, looped around the knob of a professor's office door—and I knew a poem was percolating, but I didn't know how or when. After several false starts with the hendecasyllabics (which I can finally spell without looking it up), the structure suggested a mood, and the mood gave the poem permission to exist. It was the perfect form."

If you enjoy exploring new metrical patterns, you may want to investigate the discussion and examples of such meters as the ionics, galliambics, choriambs, Asclepiadean meter, cretics, and dipodics referenced in the bibliography.

Meter and Meaning

In a good poem, rhythmical pattern (and other patterning devices such as rhyme) are not something extra but truly embody and arise from the energies of idea, emotion, and meaning at every point of the poem. We all know this; that is why the following anonymous poem works:

From "Dr. Seuss Tech Support," Anonymous

If a packet hits a pocket on a socket on a port,
And the bus is interrupted as a very last resort,
and the address of the memory makes your floppy disk abort,
then the socket packet pocket has an error to report.

If your cursor finds a menu item followed by a dash,
And the double-clicking icon puts your window in the trash,
and your data is corrupted 'cause the index doesn't hash,
then your situation's hopeless, and your system's gonna crash.

If the label on your cable on the gable at your house,
says the network is connected to the button on your mouse,
But your packets want to tunnel to another protocol,
That's repeatedly rejected by the printer down the hall . . .

The poem is funny because we recognize the goofy "meaning" of the metrical pattern combined with the rhyme, and know that it makes a ridiculous contrast to the technical seriousness of the subject matter. In fact, the metrical pattern and the rhyme are more powerful than the subject matter. They trump the meaning, letting us know the poem is not serious.

The opposite dynamic can also be true; in this largely dactylic free-verse poem, the meaning is lighthearted enough, but it is lent just a tinge of seriousness and wider implication by a combination of diction, imagery, and especially the dactylic rhythm:

"What Could it Be," Julia Alvarez

Around the kettle of chicken and rice,
the aunts were debating what flavor was missing.
Tía Carmen guessed garlic.
Tía Rosa, some coarsely ground pepper.
Tía Ana, so tidy she wore the apron,
shook her head, plain salt what was needed.
Tía Fofi, afraid to be wrong, echoed salt.
Just a pinch, she apologized, and reached for the shaker.
Tía Gladys said parsley never hurt anything.
Tía Victoria frowned and pronounced,
Tarragon. No one disagreed.

The tarragon dotted the rice in the cauldron.
And now, as if signaled, the spice jars popped open,
unloading their far eastern wonders:
cumin, turmeric, saffron, and endives.
The aunts each put in a shaker of their favorites.
The steam unwrinkled the frowns from their faces.
They cackled like witches, sampled, and nodded.

Around the table the uncles were grunting,
wolfing their food down, gnawing their chicken bones.
And yet the aunts stopped in the middle of swallows,
heads cocked at each other as if they had heard
in some far off room their own baby crying.
It needed a pinch more of . . . saffron? Paprika?
What could it be they had missed putting in?
The uncles ate seconds and rose in a chorus
of chair scrapes and belches,
falling to slumber on living room couches,
empty plates glowed like the eyes of the spellbound.

The language ("wolfing," "gnawing," "spellbound") and some of the distancing, archetypal imagery ("cackled like witches," "rose in a chorus") helps make it seem that more is going on than is being described and dignifies the domestic scene with perhaps a slight aura of danger; but without the mysterious undercurrent of the dactylic rhythm tying everything together, much of that strange aura would dissipate.

The association of meter with meaning does not mean that the meaning of any particular meter is fixed; we have seen that various meters can express all kinds of feelings. But it does mean that a good poem is always aware of the effect rhythm is having and works with rhythm rather than trying to ignore it. Like a horse, sometimes meter knows where you want to go better than you do, and it is a good idea to listen to it as much as you can.

QUESTIONS FOR MEDITATION OR DISCUSSION

Try to invent your own meter. What is the experience like?

Robert Creeley wrote, "Form is never more than an extension of content, and content never more than an extension of form." How does this apply to meter? Imagine a line of poetry, and then imagine it being written in a different meter. What if it used exactly the same words, with just a syllable or two added or removed? To what extent would it still be the same line?

Do you think that some meters do have their own emotional characteristics, or is meter always flexible? Choose a poem from this chapter with a very distinctive mood, such as "The Raven" or Swinburne's "Hendecasyllabics." Try to transfer it to another meter without disturbing the mood. What do you discover?

QUOTES

Since we live in a universe of rhythms, ideas for the meters of poetry might turn up anywhere.

—John Frederick Nims

The meter that's hardest for you is a power source.

—Joshua Davis

I can think of no better training than listening, day by day, for the caesura in a line of dactylic hexameter.

—Louise Bogan

Learning meter will make you a stronger and better poet no matter what you write. Like a dancer who studies ballet you will suddenly have better posture.

—Kazim Ali

I've always been attracted to the spoken word, and that's what starts me on a poem. It always starts with a jingle, and then I fit the poem to it.

—Sandra Cisneros

My ideal reader keeps an eye out for strange metrical fauna such as bacchics and choriambs.

—W. H. Auden

Vary rhythm enough to stir the emotion you want but not so as to lose impetus.

—Basil Bunting

POETRY PRACTICES

Metrical Templates. Copy two trochaic lines, two dactylic lines, two anapestic lines, and two iambic lines from poems in this book. Then write your own eight lines that follow the meter and rhythm of these eight lines exactly.

Metrical Field Trip. Go on a metrical field trip, to the store, a magazine, the movies, your TV set, a prose book, or your friends' or family's conversation. Listen for snatches of metrical language (such as the three dactyls in the beginning of this sentence). Try to find one example from each of the four basic meters. I define a "snatch" as at least three metrical feet in a row.

Metrical Diagnosis. Write four original passages of 10 lines each, in unrhymed trochaic, iambic, anapestic, and dactylic tetrameter. You can write the same passage in four different meters, or write a new passage for each meter. Nonsense or sense is fine. Which meters do you prefer? Which are difficult? Do they bring out different aspects of your poetry, different themes or attitudes? Practice reading and writing the meters you find difficult, until you have facility in all four.

Metrical Translation. Read "Hiawatha," "Iron," or another trochaic poem aloud to yourself until you feel you have entrained your body to the rhythm. Then write at least 20 lines of trochees (be sure to use a trochee in the first foot of each line). Then translate your poem into dactyls or anapests. How does the mood or impact of the poem change?

Blank Noniambic Verse: Completing the Circle. Write a poem of at least 20 lines in whichever of the four basic meters you have not yet written. Take time to read your poems aloud repeatedly and revise each one in accord with its own metrical nature, so that it is fluent, varied in the best way, and takes advantage of the unique expressive capacities of its own meter.

Mix It Up. Explore noniambic variations. Entrain yourself in either anapestic or dactylic meter, by reading until you have the meter firmly in your ear, and then let yourself run with it, writing what sounds good to you. After you have it down, scan it to look for variations. If the meter is too monotonous, make changes to make the rhythm more expressive and interesting. Use the cretic (/u/), bacchic (//u), antibacchic (uu/), and molossus (uuu).

Metrical Explorations. Write at least one original poem, or metrical "translation" of another poem, in one or more of the rarer meters described in this chapter, such as amphibrachs or hendecasyllabics.

CHAPTER 15

Forms of Free Verse

The free-verse line break is the first and often the only formal poetic device that contemporary readers of poetry may know. It's easy to make fun of bad free verse as "just cut-up prose," but in fact, as greeting-card writers know, the process of cutting up prose—any prose—into lines does surround it with an aura of special attention and poetic dignity. Why? Because the line breaks are a repeated device completely independent from the meaning of the language. The line breaks, through their repeating rhythm, lend the prose that sculptural, structured, formal quality that distinguishes poetry from any other kind of writing.

Virtually any element of language can be repeated in order to structure language into a poem, to give it form. Besides the line break, the repeated, structuring element that makes us recognize a "poem" can be a word sound (in which case the poem rhymes); a rhythmic pattern (in which case the poem is metrical); or a number of accents (in which case the poem is accentual). The repeated element can also be a phrase (making the poem a chant), or sentences (giving the poem a refrain, like a blues poem). It can even be an invisible process (like incorporating every fortieth word in the dictionary), making the poem a procedural poem.

In all these cases, it is the structuring capacity of repetition that lends a poem its distinctively poetic power. The word "structure" is the key. Prose may be decorated with the occasional repetition of alliteration, rhyme, or rhythm. As long as the repetition is random and unpredictable, however lyrical the language may be, it remains lyric prose. But when one repeated element, including the line break, becomes predictable and actually structures the language, then the text becomes a poem.

Line break: the break where a line of poetry ends, indicated by a slash (/) when the poem is reproduced in a prose context. In prose paragraphs (including prose poems) line breaks change according to the margins of the printed text, but in poetry line breaks are always intentional and are always respected by the printer.

Free verse is the way many of us came to appreciate the power of repetition in poetry and the importance of the poetic line. At the beginning of the twentieth century, in her preface to an anthology of Imagist poets, Amy Lowell advocated increased respect for free verse, which she defined as "writing whose cadence is more marked, more definite, and closer knit than that of prose, but which is not so violently nor so obviously accented as the so-called 'regular verse.'" A century later, free verse has become so pervasive that it is somewhat invisible: a sonnet or blues is considered to be a form, while free verse is just accepted as "poetry." But in fact, free verse is a form, with certain poetic shapes, and it has been around in English since long before Amy Lowell. The word "verse" comes from the Latin word *versus,* meaning "the turning of a plow at the end of a furrow." This turning back to create lines gives free verse its repeating pattern. If you ever feel that free verse is more modern than traditional forms, consider the following free verse poem:

"The Collar," George Herbert (1585)

I struck the board, and cried, No more.
I will abroad.
What? Shall I ever sigh and pine?
My lines and life are free; free as the road,
Loose as the wind, as large as store.
Shall I be still in suit?
Have I no harvest but a thorn
To let me blood, and not restore
What I have lost with cordial fruit?
Sure there was wine
Before my sighs did dry it: there was corn
Before my tears did drown it.
Is the year only lost to me?
Have I no bays to crown it?

No flowers, no garlands gay? all blasted?
All wasted?
Not so, my heart: but there is fruit,
And thou hast hands.
Recover all thy sigh-blown age
On double pleasures: leave thy cold dispute
Of what is fit, and not. Forsake thy cage,
Thy rope of sands,
Which petty thoughts have made, and made to thee
Good cable, to enforce and draw,
And be thy law,
While thou didst wink and wouldst not see.
Away; take heed:
I will abroad.
Call in thy death's head there: tie up thy fears.
He that forbears
To suit and serve his need,
Deserves his load.
But as I raved and grew more fierce and wild
At every word,
Me thoughts I heard one calling, Child:
And I replied, My Lord.

Composed in 1585, this poem moves unpredictably among varying (albeit mostly iambic) rhythms and line lengths. Some lines have no countable pattern of stresses; others are in more regular rhythmic patterns, such as lines 6 through 9, which also use rhyme. But the overall effect of the poem is uniquely rhythmic, the internal changes of the speaker's voice creating a dialectic between outward movement and drawing inward, rushes of passion and hesitant thought. Each line of the poem is "free" to follow the shape of the speaker's voice at any point, from the weary, brief enervation of "All wasted?" to the long surge of "But as I raved and grew more fierce and wild."

Six Types of Free Verse

While free verse by definition resists classification, with each poem theoretically being free to jump between any sorts of lines, in practice it tends to fall into distinctive kinds of patterns which are often lumped together. When you write free verse, it is helpful to know which of these traditions you are working in, since they each have different histories, different aims, and different methods.

Long-lined, oral-based free verse is the most ancient type. It descends from Old Testament psalms, which inspired such poets as William Blake, Christopher Smart, and eventually Walt Whitman and Allen Ginsberg. Long-lined free verse usually aims to move readers through their ears, or their internal ears (how your brain "hears" words when you read silently). It lends itself to long sentences, waves and surges of sound, public or political situations, rolling rhythms, repeated phrases, especially at the beginnings of lines, where they are called "anaphora" (as in Whitman's "catalogs"), high rhetoric, and grand gestures.

> **Catalog, in poetry, means a list, whether a litany or simply a list of places, body parts, equipment, etc.**

The line breaks in long-lined free verse are determined by rhythmic units or breath patterns, but not by any visual factors. If you read aloud these poems by Walt Whitman, you will notice your voice following out the contrasting lengths and energetic patterns of each line:

From "Crossing Brooklyn Ferry," Walt Whitman (1856)

8

Ah, what can ever be more stately and admirable to me than
    mast-hemm'd Manhattan?
River and sunset and scallop-edg'd waves of flood-tide?
The sea-gulls oscillating their bodies, the hay-boat in the
    twilight, and the belated lighter?

What gods can exceed these that clasp me by the hand, and with
    voices I love call me promptly and loudly by my nighest name as I
    approach?
What is more subtle than this which ties me to the woman or man that
    looks in my face?
Which fuses me into you now, and pours my meaning into you?

We understand then do we not?
What I promis'd without mentioning it, have you not accepted?
What the study could not teach—what the preaching could not
accomplish is accomplish'd, is it not?

9

Flow on, river! flow with the flood-tide, and ebb with the ebb-tide!
Frolic on, crested and scallop-edg'd waves!
Gorgeous clouds of the sunset! drench with your splendor me, or the
men and women generations after me!
Cross from shore to shore, countless crowds of passengers!
Stand up, tall masts of Mannahatta! stand up, beautiful hills of
Brooklyn!
Throb, baffled and curious brain! throw out questions and answers!
Suspend here and everywhere, eternal float of solution!
Gaze, loving and thirsting eyes, in the house or street or public
assembly!
Sound out, voices of young men! loudly and musically call me by my
nighest name!

"Crossing Brooklyn Ferry," like almost all Whitman's poems, cries out to be declaimed, perhaps from the prow of a ship. It doesn't matter whether the audience is the reader, the waves, the passengers, the clouds, the river, the hills; what matters is the voice of the poet speaking. The long lines, often corresponding to sentences, allow a voice to gather force and momentum. This tendency is so ingrained in long-lined free verse that it can be used ironically for the opposite effect. The very long lines of contemporary poet C. K. Williams's intimate confessions add a disconcerting element of universality and nakedness to his personal ruminations.

Short-lined free verse, on the other hand, aims for the eye rather than the ear of the reader. This type of free verse entered the English language in the early twentieth century through the work of such Imagist poets as H.D. and Ezra Pound, influenced by the avant-garde Vorticist movement and by translations of traditional Chinese poetry. They were struck by the power of the Chinese ideogram, at once both a picture and a letter, and wanted to create a similar contemplative, self-contained objectivity in their free verse poems. Imagists, most notably H.D., cultivated a cool, impersonal style of presenting images.

This style of short-lined free verse aims for a hyper-awareness of every word on the part of the reader:

"Nantucket," William Carlos Williams (1934)

Flowers through the window
lavender and yellow

changed by white curtains—
Smell of cleanliness—

Sunshine of late afternoon—
On the glass tray

a glass pitcher, the tumbler
turned down, by which

a key is lying—And the
immaculate white bed

Unlike in long- and medium-lined free verse, these breaks tend to happen at unnatural places, such as in the middle of a phrase. The visual impact of the line breaks is crucial. It is hard to imagine this kind of free verse existing before the invention of the typewriter, since the spacing of letters, and which words end up under which words, is all-important—just as the contemplation of the calligraphy of a traditional painted Chinese poem is a key part of the experience. Simplicity is key in this central twentieth-century tradition. Anything that appears artificial or clumsy can ruin the effect, including rhetoric, any kind of cliché, too much rhyme or word-music, and repeated or insistent rhythms. The ideal audience for this type of poetry is not a listener in a crowd but a solitary reader contemplating the poem on the page. You wrap yourself around these poems; they don't sweep you away.

Literary or medium-lined free verse tends to aim for the mind rather than the ear or eye. This kind of poem often seems closely linked to metered poetry, and sometimes it hovers around meter. The lines tend to follow syntactic units, breaking at natural pauses between phrases. Often, such poems cultivate immediacy of tone and a plain, conversational style; the main goal is to create an emotional persona for the speaker with whom the reader can identify:

"Blood," Naomi Shihab Nye

"A true Arab knows how to catch a fly in his hands,"
my father would say. And he'd prove it,
cupping the buzzer instantly
while the host with the swatter stared.

In the spring our palms peeled like snakes.
True Arabs believed watermelon could heal fifty ways.
I changed these to fit the occasion.

Years before, a girl knocked,
wanted to see the Arab.
I said we didn't have one.
After that, my father told me who he was,
"Shihab"—"shooting star"—
a good name, borrowed from the sky.
Once I said, "When we die, we give it back?"
He said that's what a true Arab would say.

Today the headlines clot in my blood.
A little Palestinian dangles a truck on the front page.
Homeless fig, this tragedy with a terrible root
is too big for us. What flag can we wave?
I wave the flag of stone and seed,
table mat stitched in blue.

I call my father, we talk around the news.
It is too much for him,
neither of his two languages can reach it.
I drive into the country to find sheep, cows,
to plead with the air:
Who calls anyone civilized?

Where can the crying heart graze?
What does a true Arab do now?

Often, as in this poem, medium-lined free verse uses regular rhythm for extra effect, at the climax or in the last line. In "Blood," the last three lines fall into a strong, incantatory three-beat rhythm: WHO calls ANyone CIVilized?/WHERE can the/CRYing heart GRAZE? / What DOES a true A-rab do NOW?" (When listening for beats, remember that stress is relative; you may hear beats on "heart," "true," and "now," but notice that they are lighter than the capitalized beats. They add texture and slow down the line, but they don't cancel out the regularity of the pattern.)

George Herbert's poem above may be called **variable-lined free verse** because of the great variation in the length of the lines. Variable line free verse is sometimes used for a whole poem, and sometimes just for certain passages that make strong expressive use of the contrast between line-lengths, as in the following couplet:

From "Book of Isaiah," Anne Carson

There is a kind of pressure in humans to take whatever is most beloved by
them and smash it.

Some of the most powerful variable-length free verse is strongly influenced by jazz and has a kinetic, musical drive:

From "Boy Breaking Glass," Gwendolyn Brooks

A mistake.
A cliff.
A hymn, a snare, and an exceeding sun.

The best free verse is alert and conscious of the regular rhythm underlying it, and keeps its head above the rhythmical water. This fluent passage by Audre Lorde segues a dactylic rhythm at the opening of the first line into a trochaic rhythm, which continues through the second line and into the third line, which then emerges as a headless iambic pentameter:

From "Coal," Audre Lorde

Some words are open like a diamond
on glass windows
singing out within the crash of sun

This kind of tension against other meters is crucial when using iambic pentameter in a free verse poem; iambic pentameter is so hackneyed and familiar-sounding that, inserted into prosy free verse without strong counterbalancing rhythms, its presence (especially in the final line of a poem, where it is most likely to appear) can add a smug, flaccid, or pedestrian quality to otherwise good free verse.

A fifth common kind of free verse, called **open field** or **projective free verse,** moves away from the line altogether. A subspecies of graphic poetry, this kind of free verse takes the entire blank space of the page for a visual field, as in this poem:

From "The Torso," Robert Duncan

At the axis of his mid hriff

the navel, for in the pit of his stomach the chord from
Which first he was fed has its temple

At the root of the groin

the pubic hair, for the torso is the stem in which the man
Flowers forth and leads to the stamen of flesh in which
His seed rises

A wave of need and desire over taking me

Cried out my name

(This was long ago; It was another life)

and said,

What do you want of me?

I do not know, I said.   I have fallen in love.   He
Has brought me into heights and depths my heart
would fear   without him.   His look

pierces my side   fire eyes

I have been waiting for you, he said:
I know what you desire

you do not know but through me

And I am with you everywhere.

Duncan's use of the page is almost three-dimensional, like a hologram: the visual and auditory elements work so seamlessly together that it is impossible to separate them, and the reader is drawn into entering the page on its own terms. The spacings themselves take on the character of words; for example, in the lines

I do not know, I said.   I have fallen in love.   He
Has brought me into heights and depths my heart
would fear   without him.   His look

the confusion and fear described in the first and third line are reflected in the spacings, contrasted with the confident beautiful surge of the second line, with its regular five-beat rhythm, and in the lines

I have been waiting for you, he said:
I know what you desire

Here the visual indentation makes the second line read subtly, quietly, as if in a visual depiction of an "undertone."

In the last few decades, open-field poetry has influenced all of free verse so that it is now not uncommon for poets such as Adrienne Rich, Jorie Graham, Frank Bidart, and Tim Seibles to use long spaces in the middle of a line, to arrange margins across the page, to move lines or bits of lines away from the rest of the poem, or otherwise to make free use of the full range of the page and the visual impacts of lines across it. Again, these techniques can add a dramatic visual and narrative dimension to a poem, in addition to the effect of the line breaks on the meanings of the words and lines. For example, in this passage, the short lines and staggering margin create multiple layers of meaning:

From "Sold," Linda Gregerson

"The delicious part," he said, is when
            I get her
      to strip the bed. This is my opening

gambit: she's vacuumed the living room carpet
            with whatever
      she's been using till now,

and I've run the Electrolux over it once and come up
            with a fistful
      of dirt, God's truth—we use

white linen filters and she's watched
            me put
      a new one in. The woman is amazed."

The lineation helps highlight certain phrases, creating a comical subtext alongside the vacuum cleaner sales story.

Prose Poems

Prose poems, our sixth type of free verse, are technically not free verse at all, since they don't use a break at the end of a line. Prose poems don't concern themselves with the line:

From "Before the next war," Susan Schultz

The worms make pieces. Washstand or wasteland, his life a loaded one.
      Girls for guns (don't check statistics). Bag slung over his shoulder, he

> runs awkwardly toward the orange or the red slide. Casualties kill war fever. *Watch out for the baby.* The language of Wall Street must more closely approximate ordinary language (if not its philosophy), he says. Builds a tower of legos and a plastic flower…

The lack of deliberate line breaks creates a relentlessness to this rush of prose. Much in these words feels like a lyric poem: the verbal interest, the clash of dictions, the amused attention to idiomatic language, and the high level of imagery. Some prose poems have a more clearly narrative coherence. This one is by Russell Edson, a writer who has referred to himself as "Little Mister Prose Poem" because of his consistent use of the form:

"You," Russell Edson

> Out of nothing there comes a time called childhood, which is simply a path leading through an archway called adolescence. A small town there, past the arch called youth.
>
> Soon, down the road, where one almost misses the life lived beyond the flower, is a small shack labeled, you.
>
> And it is here the future lives in the several postures of arm on windowsill, cheek on this; elbows on knees, face in the hands; sometimes the head thrown back, eyes staring into the ceiling . . . This into nothing down the long day's arc

The last line of this prose poem is in iambic pentameter; like much free verse, many of Edson's prose poems achieve closure through the use of meter.

Unlike Edson's poem, which uses a meditative mood to unite its thoughts and images, this prose poem, originally published simultaneously in Japanese and English, is focused entirely on one image. The steady attention to one scene unites the text with remarkable focus and concentration.

"A field of fried umbrellas," Sawako Nakayasu

> They are arranged so neatly that one wonders if there are small children beneath them, holding hands so as to keep the rows intact and the columns true, in spite of whatever kind of weather may come.

> Enough fresh oil was used in the frying of these umbrellas that theoretically they should repel any sort of fluid which takes a shot at the field, and in fact this is true, but the unfortunate inherent shape of the umbrella encourages the rain to slip inside the crevices between one fried umbrella and another, getting the toes of the children wet, whether they are there or not.

Because of the lack of line breaks, some writers classify prose poems as "lyric prose," not as poetry. Lewis Turco makes such an argument in his *New Book of Forms.* Yet those who write them usually insist they are poetry because of their lyrical use of language. Some prose poems are structured by repeating patterns in the numbers of sentences, a strategy evident in two classics of prose poetry whose sections are too long to excerpt here: Ron Silliman's *Tjantjing,* with numbers of sentences based on the numbers in the Fibonacci series, and Lyn Hejinian's *My Life,* written in 37 sections of 37 sentences each when she was 37, and then revised into 45 sections of 45 lines each eight years later.

One also might see the repetition of the ending of the prose poem as a sort of ultimate line break which happens once at the end of each prose poem and serves as a repeating structural element. After all, some contemporary poetry does not concern itself with endings at all; this is generally true of poems whose written embodiments are considered to be transcripts of performances, such as the poetry of David Antin. So the ending in a prose poem shouldn't be taken for granted, and if you read a number of prose poems in a row, you begin to get a sense for the repeating rhythm of what I call the "terminal hiatus" at the end of each one. In my opinion, brief length, defined by the terminal hiatus, is what distinguishes a "prose poem" from lyric prose.

The Line in Free Verse

As you will know if you are used to writing and/or reading free verse, a free verse poem can slip into random prosiness if the line breaks are not carefully varied and controlled—just as you will see that formal verse can slip into sing-song doggerel if the meter is not carefully varied and controlled. The line breaks in a free verse poem are the primary way that a poet determines pauses, tension, and emphasis.

Notice how the line breaks can change the feeling of a phrase:

"To a Poor Old Woman," William Carlos Williams (1935)

munching a plum on
the street a paper bag
of them in her hand

They taste good to her
They taste good
to her. They taste
good to her

You can see it by
the way she gives herself
to the one half
sucked out in her hand

Comforted
a solace of ripe plums
seeming to fill the air
They taste good to her

On one level, the line breaks change the meaning of the phrase repeated in the second stanza; "they taste good to her" means what we would expect it to mean; "they taste good / to her" brings us more into the experience of the woman and emphasizes the taste; and "they taste / good to her" is almost a pun, as if the plums are being good to her, or doing her good, by tasting good. On another level that is harder to paraphrase, the line breaks also change the physical reaction we have to reading the words. In other words, line breaks create not only different kinds of meaning, but also different kinds of experience.

When you work on line breaks you become aware that, as Roethke is supposed to have said, "Each line in a poem must be a poem." This state of "poemness," this fullness or completeness to each line, can be achieved in innumerable ways in free verse. In this poem, the abrupt line breaks on "practicing," "old," and "Yusef" add a sort of deadpan humor:

"Breakfast with Naomi Ayala," E. Ethelbert Miller

I guess you'll eat your bagel
after I'm gone. Saturday morning
and we meet at Tryst on 18th street.
It's not my favorite place. Something
about it reminds me of South Africa
before Nelson Mandela started practicing
law. Every time I see you I write a poem.
It's like the sun never setting on the old
empire. I kiss you good-bye before the
check arrives. When I get home I'll
read something by Lucille Clifton or Yusef
Komunyakaa. I want to know what the
other poets are doing these days.

Or the line can play against the sentence for expressive or descriptive effect, in a sort of syntax picture, as in this poem:

"Daybreak," Galway Kinnell

On the tidal mud, just before sunset,
dozens of starfishes
were creeping. It was
as though the mud were a sky
and enormous, imperfect stars
moved across it as slowly
as the actual stars cross heaven.
All at once they stopped,
and, as if they had simply
increased their receptivity
to gravity, they sank down
into the mud, faded down
into it and lay still, and by the time
pink of sunset broke across them
they were as invisible
as the true stars at daybreak.

When the starfish begin to sink into the mud in lines 9–13, the lines also begin to sink down through the poem. The heavy enjambment and the midline commas create a palpable effect of resistance and descent, which evens out into horizontal motion as the last three lines describe the streaks of the sunset.

The focus point of a free-verse line can be a returning (though not predictable) rhythm. Half of the lines in this poem have a five-beat rhythm:

"and where thou art I am," Diane DiPrima

astride the wind. or held
by two hoodlums under a starting truck.
crocheting in the attic.
striding forever out of the heart of quartz
immense, unhesitant, monotonous
as galaxies, or rain; or
lost cities of the dinosaurs now sunk
in the unopening rock.

who keeps the bats from flying in your window?
who rolls the words you drop back into seed?
                                        who picks
sorrows like lice from your heart & cracks them
                                        between her teeth?
who else blows down your chimney with the moon
scattering ashes from your dismal hearth to show
the sleeping Bird in the coals, or is it
garnet you lost?

                                  What laughter spins you
Around in the windy street?

Or the focus can be a surprising enjambment. This enjambment focuses not on a word, as in the Miller line breaks, but on a syntactical unit:

From "Homeless at Home," Gloria Frym

You wore half a smile and I
Wore the other.

The focus can be the impact of a word:

From "Our Bodies," Denise Levertov

a line or groove I love
runs down
my body from breastbone
to waist. It speaks of
eagerness, of
distance.

Almost every line here includes a word that anchors the line with vividness or surprise, and the last line *is* such a word.

It can be a punch line, with visual as well as aural impact:

From "The Humming Birds," Lucinda Roy

There.
        It's yours.
                The key to me.

Go on.

Lick it.

Or a revelation:

From "Hardie," Tim Seibles

I was a child. You think I don't remember?!
You think it's easy keeping all this innocence pent up inside?!

Or each line of the poem can center on a new aspect of an image:

"Margaret Fuller," Lorine Niedecker

She carried books
and chrysanthemums

to Boston
into a cold storm.

Or a phrase full of repeating vowel and consonant sounds:

"Waking up in the Swamp," Sue Standing

Like the old blue sleigh
Up to its runners

In moss and hot, soft needles.

Or the repetition of a word in a fresh way:

From "Five Short Shorts," Hayden Carruth

Why speak of the use
of poetry? Poetry
is what uses us.

Or a dramatic role the line needs to play within the poem as a whole, as in the last line of the following poem:

"The Europeans," Robert Creeley

Or me wanting another man's
wife, etc.
        History.

Unable to keep straight
generations.

Telling them all about
myself.

Whether that identity arises on the meaning level, the visual level, or the sound level, every line in a free verse poem needs to have some reason for being a line. Line breaks can play against expectations; they can be used to emphasize a rhyme or repeating sound, or to mute it:

From "A," Heather McHugh

Partly
Fungal outburst, viral
Outburst, burst

Of life (what are
We turning
To? Remember, numbers
Brought to grief

Make greater grief, as surely as they make
Great names . . .

In this passage, the repeating words "burst" and "grief" are muted but present because of their position midline; imagine the difference in effect if they were repeated at the ends of the lines every time.

Line breaks have a strong effect on the way a reader perceives a poem's logic. A line break can enable the *line* to suggest something very different from the *sentence*, or even to contradict it.

From "Aubade," Kevin Young

There is little else
I love; the small

of yr back, yr thick
bottom

lip stuck out.

From "Lullaby," June Jordan

The evening burns a low
red
line occasional with golden glass
across the sky

On the other hand, sometimes the line breaks occur consistently at the end of sentences or phrases. This is particularly true of long-lined free verse, but it can also be an effective strategy for short-lined or variable line-length free verse:

"The Negro Speaks of Rivers," Langston Hughes (1921)

I've known rivers:
I've known rivers ancient as the world and older than the
  flow of human blood in human veins.

My soul has grown deep like the rivers.

I bathed in the Euphrates when dawns were young.
I built my hut near the Congo and it lulled me to sleep.
I looked upon the Nile and raised the pyramids above it.

I heard the singing of the Mississippi when Abe Lincoln
  went down to New Orleans, and I've seen its muddy
  bosom turn all golden in the sunset.

I've known rivers:
Ancient, dusky rivers.

My soul has grown deep like the rivers.

In this stanza, line breaks function instead of all the elements of punctuation: commas, periods, question marks, and quotation marks:

From "Native Trees," W. S. Merwin

Neither my father nor my mother knew
the names of the trees
where I was born
what is that
I asked and my
father and mother did not

hear they did not look where I pointed
surfaces of furniture held
the attention of their fingers
and across the room they could watch
walls they had forgotten
where there were no questions
no voices and no shade

A poem that always breaks in the middle of a sentence or phrase (enjambment) can create a sense of unbroken flow, or a sense of urgency. The excerpt from Auden's poem uses the broken phrase to create a sense of meditative urgency:

From "Musée des Beaux Arts," W. H. Auden (1938)

About suffering they were never wrong,
The Old Masters: how well, they understood
Its human position; how it takes place
While someone else is eating or opening a window or just walking dully
along . . .

The poem below uses the same technique to create a sense of emotional urgency:

From "I Go Back to May 1937," Sharon Olds

I see my father strolling out
under the ochre sandstone arch, the
red tiles glinting like bent
plates of blood behind his head, I
see my mother with a few light books at her hip
standing at the pillar made of tiny bricks with the
wrought-iron gate still open behind her, its
sword-tips black in the May air,
they are about to graduate, they are about to get married . . .

And this excerpt uses the broken phrase to create a sense of narrative urgency:

From "Leda and the Cowboy," Luci Tapahonso

Even then, as they danced, the things he told her
Were fleeting. Leda smiled and a strange desperation
Engulfed him.

In the following poem, the technique of breaking the line in the middle of a phrase is used only once, at the end of the middle stanza, where it creates a poignant sense of resignation and sadness.

From "Isn't It Enough," Farideh Hassanzadeh

Night by night
more and more,
I feel real.

Like the bloody sound of alarms,
Like the roaring anti-aircraft rounds,
Like the falling bombs and rockets,
which turn the ruins and ashes
into eternal reality;
I feel night by night more real
and old,

so old and real that in the mirror
I see nothing anymore
but an aisle of empty chairs.

Especially after the self-contained line, "I feel real," the addition of the phrase "and old" after the line break seems to be happening in the poet's mind at the minute we are reading, giving it great urgency.

Sometimes it's mysterious what makes a line break work. I began writing free-verse poems in the early 1970s, long before personal computers. Each time I wanted to change a line break I would need to type my entire poem over to get the full effect, but I rarely remember feeling it was a waste of time. It can be hard for a poet to explain such choices; we may need to see it, hear it, almost smell it—to weigh it physically—to decide where the line breaks should go. Though you may not know exactly why or how, after some practice you will begin to recognize a satisfying free verse line when you see it. Ideally, as said above, every line in your free verse poem should have some reason for being a line, whether that identity arises on the sound level, the meaning level, the visual level, or in some other way that is harder to pin down.

Rhythm in Free Verse

Some free verse is unabashedly rhythmic. The rhythm is sometimes created by the dynamic between lines, as in this poem:

"Tonight No Poetry Will Serve," Adrienne Rich

Saw you walking barefoot
taking a long look
at the new moon's eyelid
later spread
sleep-fallen, naked in your dark hair
asleep but not oblivious
of the unslept unsleeping
elsewhere

Tonight I think
no poetry
will serve

Syntax of rendition:

verb pilots the plane
adverb modifies action
verb force-feeds noun
submerges the subject
noun is choking
verb disgraced goes on doing

there are adjectives up for sale

now diagram the sentence

The parallelism of syntax and lines knits the poem together as it conveys the poet's grief, fury, and frustration over the context of war, in which she and the person addressed are living their lives.

Some passages of the most admired twentieth-century free verse, including sections of Yeats and of Elizabeth Bishop's wonderful "The Moose," have an even stronger rhythmic unity, with virtually the same number of strong accents in every line. Try reading them aloud and listen for stronger syllables. As you will see in the next chapter, technically these parts of the poems could work as accentual poetry:

From "Easter 1916," W. B. Yeats (1916)

Hearts with one purpose alone
Through summer and winter seem
Enchanted to a stone
To trouble the living stream.
The horse that comes from the road.
The rider, the birds that range
From cloud to tumbling cloud,
Minute by minute they change;
A shadow of cloud on the stream
Changes minute by minute;
A horse-hoof slides on the brim,
And a horse plashes within it;
The long-legged moor-hens dive,
And hens to moor-cocks call;
Minute by minute they live:
The stone's in the midst of all.

This regularity can work well in a particular passage, but generally when writing free verse, it is best to make sure you don't slip into any regular rhythm for very long. Save that for your accentual poetry. The best free verse is constantly aware of its own lack of predictability, discovering a unique rhythmic energy within each line, and never allowing itself to become comfortable with any shape or rhythm. The following passage by H.D. conveys, both in its rhythms and in its imagery, the excitement and the uncertainty, the sense of risk and even danger, of the most effective free verse:

From "The Walls Do Not Fall," H.D. (1944)

through doors twisted on hinges,
and the lintels slant

cross-wise;
we walk continually

on thin air
that thickens to a blind fog,

then step swiftly aside,
for even the air

is independable,
thick where it should be fine

and tenuous
where wings separate and open,

and the ether
is heavier than the floor,

and the floor sags
like a ship floundering;

we know no rule
of procedure,

we are voyagers, discoverers
of the not-known,

the unrecorded;
we have no map;

possibly we will reach haven,
heaven.

Since free verse often relies to an extra extent on imagery, and since it tries to defamiliarize familiar language with the most minimal tools, practicing free verse for a while can strengthen your eye for imagery and your ear for idiomatic diction even if you are committed to metrical poetry. On the other hand, if you are committed to free verse poetry, practicing meter will teach and strengthen your ear so you can create free verse rhythms that are alive and interesting. Many poets go through phases when they only want to write in free verse or periods when they only want to write in meter. Each of these phases can be good for your poetry and can help you write the other way. Writing free verse is an excellent way to understand what goes into writing a strong poetic line, whether that line is in free verse or meter.

QUESTIONS FOR MEDITATION OR DISCUSSION

Paul Lake claims in his essay "The Verse That Print Bred" that free verse is primarily a visual art. Do you agree or disagree? Here is one suggestion to deepen your thought on this question: Listen to a reading of free verse by the poet, or ask someone to read free verse aloud to you in a natural way, the way they would read it at a poetry reading. Mark down on a piece of paper each time you hear a line break (one simple way to do this is to write down the word just before the break). Then look at the text of the poem and compare the line breaks. How many of them did you hear correctly? How did you recognize them? Read some free verse of your own to someone else. Do they recognize your line breaks? Does it matter to you whether they can? Why or why not?

Ever since Ezra Pound talked about "breaking the pentameter," some people have felt that free verse posed a threat to metrical verse, or that metrical verse posed a threat to free verse, even though many poets write in both modes. Do you think there is any reason that one kind of poetry might threaten the other? Do you have an emotional response to the idea of free verse, or to the idea of metrical verse? If so, what experiences of yours do you think contributed to this feeling?

QUOTES

We believe that the individuality of a poet may often be better expressed in free-verse than in conventional forms.

—Amy Lowell

I am not at all clear what free verse is anymore. That's one of the things you learn not to know.
—Howard Nemerov

Free verse is *not* the poetic equivalent of "free parking" or "free beer" . . . [It] is still organized, like all poems, around technical constraints.
—Michelle Boisseau

I could not use the long line because of my nervous nature.
—William Carlos Williams

In sound and sense it is the music of inner relationships that moves me.
—Robert Duncan

No verse is free for the man [*sic*] who wants to do a good job.
—T. S. Eliot

POETRY PRACTICES

Group (Trading Breaks). Divide into pairs and trade free verse poems. Take 15 minutes to change each other's line breaks to be the way you would want them to be if it were your poem. Meet up again and discuss.

Self-Self-Portrait. Copy the following words, the text of a poem by Jane Hirshfield called "Late Self-Portrait by Rembrandt": "The dog, dead for years, keeps coming back in the dream. We look at each other there with the old joy. It was always her gift to bring me into the present—which sleeps, changes, awakens, dresses, leaves. Happiness and unhappiness differ as a bucket hammered from gold differs from one of pressed tin, this painting proposes. Each carries the same water, it says." Lineate the text into a free verse poem. Only after you are finished, look at Hirshfield's version. Write about what you learn from this experience.

Explorations in Free Verse. Take one of your free-verse poems and rewrite it several times, changing only the line breaks. Try it as long-line free verse, short-lined free verse, medium-lined free verse, variable-lined free verse, and open-field verse. Pick your favorite line breaks from each version and combine them into one favorite version. Try to justify each line break to yourself.

Free Verse Waves. Much free verse gains its power from repetition. Take one of your free verse poems and make it three times longer. Don't add any new words; just incorporate as many repetitions as you like of any of the words already in the poem.

Scroll. Write a contemplative poem in short-lined free verse and inscribe it by hand on a scroll. A rolled-up sheet of typing paper will do if you write it very nicely. Feel free to illustrate it if you like. For inspiration, look at haiku, the lyrics of William Carlos Williams, H.D.'s first book *Sea Garden,* and the work of George Oppen. Hang your scroll on your wall or present it to a friend.

End-Stop versus Enjambment. Write a poem with the line breaks at the ends of sentences or phrases, so that each line is completely self-contained. Now rewrite the poem with enjambment at the end of each line, so that it keeps you tumbling from line to line as you read. For ideas, look at some of Sharon Olds's poems with their breathless rush of line breaks. If you want to take it a little further, try using the "hinge" technique of Audre Lorde and Matthea Harvey.

Howl Redux. Write a public poem in long-lined free verse and read it aloud. For inspiration, look at Robinson Jeffers's "Shine, Perishing Republic" in chapter 1 or Whitman's "Crossing Brooklyn Ferry" in this chapter. For examples of free verse poems that have had public impact, you can look at Allen Ginsberg's "Howl," which caused a sensation when it was first read on October 7, 1955, and became a sort of anthem for the Beat generation. For more recent examples of public free verse, look at the longer-lined sections of Amiri Baraka's controversial "Somebody Blew Up America" and Maya Angelou's poem for Bill Clinton's inauguration, "On the Pulse of the Morning."

Embedding Rhyme. Write a poem including some rhymes that coincide with line breaks. Rewrite it so the rhymes are embedded within lines.

Line Break as Punctuation. Write a poem with no punctuation, using line breaks as the only clues to syntax. You might want to look at Merwin's "Native Trees" as a model. Then take one of your existing free verse poems that does use punctuation and simply remove the punctuation. Compare the two poems. Did writing without punctuation change the way you thought of the line?

PART 4

Shaping Poems: Structure and Form

"There is no poetry of distinction without formal invention, for it is in the intimate form that works of art achieve their exact meaning."

—WILLIAM CARLOS WILLIAMS

Shaping Forms, Structures and Politics

CHAPTER 16

Stanzas: A Poem's Breathing Rooms

Poetic form, like rhythm, is at once physical and anything but physical. It is impossible to revise a poem's structure, its shape, without restructuring its meaning, too. And often, by shaping a poem's physical identity, we free the poem to teach us what we didn't know we needed to know about its deeper levels. So be patient with a poem's overall form and shape, just as you have learned to be with its rhythms and lines. While meter is about structuring the poetic line, poetic form is about structuring the poem as a whole. The basic unit of form is the **stanza,** and most poetic forms either consist of—or, like the sonnet, evolved from—stanzas.

The stanza determines how a poem can take a breath, step back and look at itself, hear itself speak. If a student of mine is completely stuck working on a poem and asks for my opinion on what to do next, more often than not they will show me a single block of text. Having learned in my own experience that often the first step toward finding the final shape of a poem I'm revising is to divide it into stanzas, I frequently advise them to break it into units that will reflect the different movements and parts of the poem. After a poem is separated into independent parts, it's much easier to discover its underlying structure and to experiment with different kinds of logical, narrative, or emotional order.

Sometimes these divisions are a temporary part of the revision process, but often they enhance the final version of the poem as well. As a reader, I find that stanzas make it easier for me to approach and fully enjoy a poem. Stanzas guide me through light and shadow, rhythms of words and silences, spaces where I can stop and think without interrupting the poem. The word "stanza" comes from the Italian word for "room" (as if a poem were a house or other building). I also like to think of stanza breaks as veins or channels that bring air and light into a poem and allow us to better experience the terrain.

The Stanza in Free Verse and Shaped Poems

Stanzas work best if the breaks between them are taken seriously: honored, respected, used consciously to strengthen the transitions and meanings of a poem. It's hard to find a good poem that doesn't follow this principle. For example:

"London," William Blake (1794)

I wandered through each chartered street,
Near where the chartered Thames does flow,
And mark in every face I meet,
Marks of weakness, marks of woe.

In every cry of every man,
In every infant's cry of fear,
In every voice, in every ban,
The mind-forged manacles I hear:

How the chimney-sweeper's cry
Every blackening church appals,
And the hapless soldier's sigh
Runs in blood down palace-walls.

But most, through midnight streets I hear
How the youthful harlot's curse
Blasts the new-born infant's tear,
And blights with plagues the marriage-hearse.

Each stanza makes its own logical unit (and each stanza is also one complete sentence). Like paragraphs in a clearly written piece of prose, each stanza has a clear and separate focus and could be paraphrased independently of the others. The first sets the scene; the second moves from sight to sound and further clarifies the problem; the third focuses on the exploited child and the man sacrificed to violence; and the last brings in the prevailing problem of prostitution and associated disease. Try reading the poem without stanza breaks:

I wandered through each chartered street,
Near where the chartered Thames does flow,

And mark in every face I meet,
Marks of weakness, marks of woe.
In every cry of every man,
In every infant's cry of fear,
In every voice, in every ban,
The mind-forged manacles I hear:
How the chimney-sweeper's cry
Every blackening church appals,
And the hapless soldier's sigh
Runs in blood down palace-walls.
But most, through midnight streets I hear
How the youthful harlot's curse
Blasts the new-born infant's tear,
And blights with plagues the marriage-hearse.

Does it help you appreciate even more how essential the stanzas are to the impact of this poem? (For the opposite effect, try reading Robert Frost's "Bereft" [in chapter 8] with a stanza break after each sentence, and notice how much the power of its forward rush is diminished.)

As in everything else involving writing poetry, of course, the choices in how to use stanzas are infinite even within their limitations. Between the ongoing narrative of a poem like *Beowulf* (originally written without any line breaks at all, let alone stanza breaks) and Blake's "London" lies a continuum of ways to use the stanza. For example, if the separate stanza technique is your basic approach, then diverging from it with an occasional enjambment across stanzas will be experienced by the reader as a powerful change—especially without punctuation, as in this poem, where it happens twice:

"To Earthward," Robert Frost (1923)

Love at the lips was touch
As sweet as I could bear;
And once that seemed too much;
I lived on air

That crossed me from sweet things,
The flow of—was it musk

From hidden grapevine springs
Down hill at dusk?

I had the swirl and ache
From sprays of honeysuckle
That when they're gathered shake
Dew on the knuckle.

I craved strong sweets, but those
Seemed strong when I was young;
The petal of the rose
It was that stung.

Now no joy but lacks salt
That is not dashed with pain
And weariness and fault;
I crave the stain

Of tears, the aftermark
Of almost too much love,
The sweet of bitter bark
And burning clove.

When stiff and sore and scarred
I take away my hand
From leaning on it hard
In grass and sand,

The hurt is not enough:
I long for weight and strength
To feel the earth as rough
To all my length.

A poem's stanzas are a powerful part of its first impression, so it is worth choosing them carefully. If your poem is in unrhymed free verse, you can decide stanza breaks purely on the basis of the poem's meaning:

"Last Apple," Malka Heifetz Tussman (trans. Marcia Falk)

"I am like the last apple
that falls from the tree
and no one picks up."

I kneel to the fragrance
of the last apple
and I pick it up.

In my hands—the tree,
in my hands—the leaf,
in my hands—the blossom,
and in my hands—the earth
that kisses the apple
that no-one picks up.

"Last Apple" uses the stanza breaks organically to reflect the poem's logical parts. An alternative approach is to use stanzas to counterpoint the poem's logic. This free-verse poem breaks stanzas to keep momentum going, to build surprise, to move energy through the poem:

From "June 2," Cole Swensen

Rain falls.
It's June.
I'm dressed in red.
I'm falling.

I'm walking down a stair. It's not brick red, like the roofs, but brazened

Open as if onto
the body room after room

Meet me
by the unused stair

that opens onto the river; you open the door and there, on the water
I was raised to a pious life

and cannot live here.

In **shaped poetry** (sometimes called "visual poetry," or *carmina figurata*), the shape of a stanza is a visual aspect of the poem's art, and a key to the poem's meaning. The earliest shaped poems we know were by ancient Greek poets, who called them *technopaegnia.* These could be extremely clever; for example, the fourth-century B.C. poet Simias of Rhodes wrote "The Egg," a poem shaped like an egg which had to be read alternately from the top and bottom, ending at the center, as if the egg were being eaten. During the Renaissance, this idea was revived by Europeans along with so much else from classical culture, and over a hundred shaped poems were written. Here is perhaps the best known:

From "Easter-Wings," George Herbert (1633)

LORD, who createdst man in wealth and store,
    Though foolishly he lost the same,
        Decaying more and more,
            Till he became
              Most poor:
              With thee
            O let me rise
        As larks, harmoniously,
    And sing this day thy victories:
Then shall the fall further the flight in me.

My tender age in sorrow did beginne:
    And still with sicknesses and shame
        Thou didst so punish sinne,
            That I became
                Most thinne.
                With thee
            Let me combine,

And feel this day thy victorie,
For, if I imp my wing on thine,
Affliction shall advance the flight in me.

In the most skillful shaped poems, such as this one, the words don't simply fill up a shape; they do so in such a way that each word falls in a place that makes visual sense. With the invention of the typewriter in the twentieth century, shaped poetry gained a new potential for accuracy, and of course the computer, allowing infinite worry-free rearranging, has made it more popular still. Today shaped poetry is a thriving genre, and the visual qualities of print are used regularly to deepen a poem's impact, as in this poem by one of the most imaginative shape poets:

"Bleeding," May Swenson

Stop bleeding   said the knife
I would if I   could said the cut.
Stop bleeding   you make me messy with the blood.
I'm sorry   said the cut.
Stop or I will   sink in farther said the knife.
Don't said the   cut.
The knife did   not say it couldn't help it but it sank in farther.
If only you   didn't bleed said the knife I wouldn't have to do this.
I know said   the cut I bleed too easily I hate that I can't
help it I   wish I were a knife like you and didn't have to bleed.
Meanwhile   stop bleeding will you said the knife.
Yes you   are a mess and sinking in deeper said the cut I will
have to   stop.
Have you   stopped by now said the knife.
I've almost   stopped I think.
Why must you   bleed in the first place said the knife.
For the reason   maybe that you must do what you
must do said   the cut.
I can't stand   bleeding said the knife and sank in farther.

I hate it too   said the cut I know it isn't you it's me
you're lucky to   be a knife you ought to be glad about that.
Too many cuts   around said the knife they're messy I don't know
how they stand   themselves.
They don't said   the cut.
You're bleeding   again.
No I've stopped   said the cut see you are coming out now the
blood is drying   it will rub off you'll be shiny again and clean.
If only cuts   wouldn't bleed so much said the knife coming out a little.
But then knives   might become dull said the cut.
Aren't you bleeding   a little said the knife.
I hope not said the   cut.
I feel you are just   a little.
Maybe just a little   but I can stop now.
I feel a little   wetness still said the knife sinking in
a little but then   coming out a little.
Just a little maybe   just enough said the cut.
That's enough now   stop now do you feel better now said the knife.
I feel I have to   bleed to feel I think said the cut.
I don't I don't have   to feel said the knife drying now becoming shiny.

The jagged cut does more than illustrate the meaning of the poem; it illuminates it. The very fact that the shape is a nonverbal device underscores that the unhealthy aspect of the relationship between knife and cut (the way they need and encourage each other) is inescapable just *because* it is unacknowledged, unspoken.

Shaped poetry (along with **concrete poetry,** which uses typography and other effects to make the words of a poem works of visual art in themselves) reminds us of the centrality of visual experience to reading poetry. Though visual power is part of the impact of all stanzas, shaped or concrete poetry is the exception; most stanzas are centrally concerned with the musical aspects of poetry. What follows are descriptions of important traditional stanzas, along with a few of my own favorites.

Two- and Three-Line Stanzas

Any two-line stanza is called a **couplet.** By far the most common and well known of couplets is the iambic pentameter rhymed couplet, named the **heroic couplet.** During the eighteenth century, the heroic couplet was considered the perfect poetic form, and it is remarkably capable of capturing thought in a memorable way, as in these couplets:

From "Essay on Man," Alexander Pope (1744)

God loves from whole to parts: but human soul
Must rise from individual to the whole.
Self-love but serves the virtuous mind to wake,
As the small pebble stirs the peaceful lake;
The centre mov'd, a circle straight succeeds,
Another still, and still another spreads;
Friends, parent, neighbour, first it will embrace;
His country next; and next all human race;
Wide and more wide, th' o'erflowings of the mind
Take ev'ry creature in of ev'ry kind:
Earth smiles around, with boundless bounty blest,
And Heav'n beholds its image in his breast.

Heroic couplets are usually printed together, not separated by spaces. However, since they tend to fall into a series of self-contained units and sometimes memorable units, usually ending with a period or comma, it also makes sense to consider them as separate stanzas. And the same criteria of cohesion and integrity apply to them as apply to separate stanzas. Some of these couplets about poetry, excerpted from various places in another long poem by Pope, are likely to be familiar to you:

From "Essay on Criticism," Alexander Pope (1711)

A little Learning is a dang'rous Thing;
Drink deep, or taste not the Pierian Spring:

Words are like Leaves; and where they most abound,
Much Fruit of Sense beneath is rarely found.

True Wit is Nature to Advantage drest,
What oft was Thought, but ne'er so well Exprest

Nay, fly to Altars; there they'll talk you dead;
For Fools rush in where Angels fear to tread.

In Poets as true Genius is but rare,
True Taste as seldom is the Critick's Share.

True Ease in Writing comes from Art, not Chance,
As those move easiest who have learn'd to dance.

Good-Nature and Good-Sense must ever join;
To err is Human; to Forgive, Divine.

Skilled writers of heroic couplets tend to link the pairs of lines together by other means in addition to rhyme. Common techniques include **parallelism** (lines echoing each others' grammatical structure) or a **chiasmus** (x-shaped grammatical structure). In the fifth couplet above, Pope uses a chiasmus to cement the lines together: "Poets" in the first half of the first line corresponds to "Critick's" in the second half of the second line, while "true Genius" in the second half of the first line corresponds grammatically with "true Taste" in the first half of the second line. In the unforgettably gruesome couplets below, Margaret Cavendish uses a chiasmus in the next-to-last couplet, and grammatical parallelism in the second couplet:

"Nature's Cook," Margaret Cavendish (1653)

DEATH is the *Cook* of *Nature;* and we find
Meat drest severall waies to please her *Mind.*
Some *Meates shee* rosts with *Feavers, burning hot,*
And some *shee* boiles with *Dropsies* in a *Pot.*
Some for *Gelly* consuming by degrees,
And some with *Ulcers,* Gravie out to squeese.
Some *Flesh* as *Sage she* stuffs with *Gouts,* and *Paines,*

Others for tender *Meat* hangs up in *Chaines.*
Some in the *Sea she pickles* up to keep,
Others, as *Brawne* is sous'd, those in *Wine steep.*
Some with the *Pox,* chops *Flesh,* and *Bones* so small,
Of which *She* makes a *French Fricasse* withall.
Some on *Gridirons* of *Calenture* is broyl'd,
And some is trodden on, and so quite spoyl'd.
But those are *bak'd,* when smother'd they do dye,
By *Hectick Feavers* some *Meat* She doth *fry.*
In *Sweat* sometimes *she stues* with *savoury smell,*
A *Hodge-Podge* of *Diseases* tasteth well.
Braines drest with *Apoplexy* to *Natures* wish,
Or swimmes with *Sauce* of *Megrimes* in a *Dish.*
And *Tongues* she dries with *Smoak* from *Stomack's* ill,
Which as the second *Course* she sends up still.
Then *Death* cuts *Throats,* for *Blood-puddings* to make,
And puts them in the *Guts,* which *Collicks* rack.
Some hunted are by *Death,* for *Deere* that's red.
Or *Stal-fed Oxen,* knocked on the *Head.*
Some for *Bacon* by *Death* are *Sing'd,* or *scal'd,*
Then powdered up with *Flegme,* and *Rhume* that's salt.

The balance and control that heroic couplets convey can work beautifully not only for uplifting and improving subjects but also for satire, or to create contrasts with chaotic or gruesome subject matter, as Cavendish shows.

A three-line stanza is called a **tercet** no matter what rhyme pattern it has. With all lines rhyming, it is called a **triplet:**

From "A Vision of Poets," Elizabeth Barrett Browning (1844)

He hears a silent gliding coil.
The snakes strain hard against the soil,
His foot slips in their slimy oil,

And toads seem crawling on his hand,
And clinging bats but dimly scanned
Full in his face their wings expand.

Our ears seem used to hearing two rhyming lines; adding a third in a row, as Browning does here to create an intense gothic effect, can feel like an exaggeration. That may be why the best-known three-line stanza is **terza rima,** which never juxtaposes the rhyming lines.

Terza rima is a leapfrogging stanza of interweaving rhymes. Each new stanza takes the rhyme from the middle line of the last stanza, repeats it as the first and last line, and adds a new rhyme in the middle line: aba bcb cdc ded efe fgf, and so on. Because the terza rima pattern is self-generating with its ongoing momentum, and is always refreshed by the addition of the new rhyme, it has a lot of stamina. So it was an inspired choice for Dante's ambitious three-volume medieval epic poem, the *Divine Comedy.* Here is the famous opening of the first book of the poem in the original Italian and in English:

From The Inferno, *Dante Alighieri (1321)* (TRANS. MICHAEL PALMA)

Nel mezzo del cammin di nostra vita
mi ritrovai per una selva oscura
ché la diritta via era smarrita.

Ahi quanto a dir qual era è cosa dura
esta selva selvaggia e aspra e forte
che nel pensier rinova la paura!

Tant'è amara che poco è più morte;
ma per trattar del ben ch'i' vi trovai,
dirò de l'altre cose ch'i' v'ho scorte.

Io non so ben ridir com'i' v'intrai,
tant'era pien di sonno a quel punto
che la verace via abbandonai.

Midway through the journey of our life, I found
myself in a dark wood, for I had strayed
from the straight pathway to this tangled ground.

How hard it is to tell of, overlaid
with harsh and savage growth, so wild and raw
the thought of it still makes me feel afraid.

Death scarce could be more bitter. But to draw
the lessons of the good that came my way,
I will describe the other things I saw.

Terza rima can also create impetus and passion in shorter lyric poems. Here is the first section of one of the most famous terza rima poems:

From "Ode to the West Wind," Percy Bysshe Shelley (1819)

O wild West Wind, thou breath of Autumn's being,
Thou from whose unseen presence the leaves dead
Are driven, like ghosts from an enchanter fleeing,

Yellow, and black, and pale, and hectic red,
Pestilence-stricken multitudes:—O thou
Who chariotest to their dark wintry bed

The wingèd seeds, where they lie cold and low,
Each like a corpse within its grave, until
Thine azure sister of the Spring shall blow

Her clarion o'er the dreaming earth, and fill
(Driving sweet buds like flocks to feed in air)
With living hues and odours plain and hill;

Wild Spirit, which art moving everywhere;
Destroyer and Preserver; hear, O hear!

Shelley uses a couplet to signal the end of the passage, creating the effect of a sonnet.

Terza rima can be varied by following its constraints less exactly, as Derek Walcott does in his epic poem *Omeros* and in this poem:

From "The Bounty," Derek Walcott

The mango trees serenely rust when they are in flower,
nobody knows the name for that voluble cedar
whose bell-flowers fall, the pomme-arac purples its floor.

The blue hills in late afternoon always look sadder.
The country night waiting to come in outside the door;
the firefly keeps striking matches, and the hillside fumes

with a bluish signal of charcoal, then the smoke burns
into a larger question, one that forms and unforms,
then loses itself in a cloud, till the question returns.

Walcott generally follows the pattern of having the middle line of a stanza pick up a rhyme from the preceding stanza, but the first and last lines of the stanza only tend to rhyme in alternate stanzas. The effect can be disconcerting on the level of the stanza, but the sense of terza rima is maintained throughout the poem.

Couplet: two-line stanza
Tercet: three-line stanza
Quatrain: four-line stanza
Cinquain: five-line stanza
Decima: ten-line stanza

Four-Line Stanzas

Just as rooms have four walls, four lines is by far the most common length for a poetic stanza. There are a surprising number of ways to organize these four lines. **Dickinson stanza** (also called **ballad stanza, hymn stanza,** or **folk stanza**) is a four-line stanza whose second and fourth lines always rhyme, but first and third lines may not: abab or xaxa. In poetry, this stanza is excellent for telling long stories (see the chapter 18 on the ballad). It usually has a 4-3-4-3 movement (sometimes 4-4-4-4), in iambic or accentual meter. The pattern of 4-3-4-3 feet or accents is the most common meter in English besides iambic pentameter; you have probably heard it hundreds of times in folk songs, hymns, country music songs, advertisements, TV show theme songs, or nursery rhymes like this nonsense rhyme:

"Three Children," Mother Goose (1719)

Three children sliding on the ice
Upon a summer's day,
As it fell out, they all fell in,
The rest they ran away.

Now had these children been at home,
Or sliding on dry ground,
Ten thousand pounds to one penny
They had not all been drowned.

You parents all that children have,
And you that have got none,
If you would have them safe abroad,
Pray keep them safe at home.

The alternating rhymes give the listener a clear sense of the movement of the poem, counteract monotony, and make it clear where one stanza ends and the next begins—especially useful if you are going to make the kind of associative leaps that are common to ballads. The same kind of effect happens here in a more serious poem:

From "As I Walked Out One Evening," W. H. Auden (1942)

As I walked out one evening,
Walking down Bristol Street,
The crowds upon the pavement
Were fields of harvest wheat.

And down by the brimming river
I heard a lover sing
Under an arch of the railway:
"Love has no ending . . .["]

But all the clocks in the city
Began to whirr and chime:
"O let not Time deceive you,
You cannot conquer Time . . .

"In headaches and in worry
Vaguely life leaks away,
And Time will have his fancy
To-morrow or to-day. . .

"The glacier knocks in the cupboard,
The desert sighs in the bed,
And the crack in the tea-cup opens
A lane to the land of the dead. . . .

"O stand, stand at the window
As the tears scald and start;
You shall love your crooked neighbour
With your crooked heart."

It was late, late in the evening,
The lovers they were gone;
The clocks had ceased their chiming,
And the deep river ran on.

Auden's poem gains much of its uncanny impact from the echoes of folk poetry that are strengthened by his choice of stanza. A famous poem by Countee Cullen uses the same associations to underscore its point:

"Incident," Countee Cullen (1925)

Once riding in old Baltimore,
Heart-filled, head-filled with glee,
I saw a Baltimorean
Keep looking straight at me.

Now I was eight and very small,
And he was no whit bigger,

And so I smiled, but he poked out
His tongue, and called me, "Nigger."

I saw the whole of Baltimore
From May until December;
Of all the things that happened there
That's all that I remember.

The singsong familiarity of the verse form makes the shock at the end of the second stanza feel that much more visceral; the reader's feeling of being punched in the stomach is similar to what we imagine the speaker might have felt. In the same stanza, Cullen exploits, by contradicting it, the principle that the second rhyme sound should be more familiar than the first; the second rhyme is emphasized with a rather nightmarish inevitability that goes along with the rhythmic lulling.

Another four-line stanza pattern rhymes aabb. This stanza is a particular challenge to pull off; the danger is that it will seem to split into two couplets. In this extremely well-known poem, Byron varies the devices that tie the stanzas together to keep them fresh:

From "The Destruction of Sennacherib," George Gordon, Lord Byron (1815)

Like the leaves of the forest when Summer is green,
That host with their banners at sunset were seen;
Like the leaves of the forest when Autumn hath blown,
That host on the morrow lay withered and strown.

For the Angel of Death spread his wings on the blast,
And breathed in the face of the foe as he passed;
And the eyes of the sleepers waxed deadly and chill,
And their hearts but once heaved, and for ever grew still!

And there lay the steed with his nostril all wide,
But through it there rolled not the breath of his pride;
And the foam of his gasping lay white on the turf,
And cold as the spray of the rock-beating surf.

And there lay the rider distorted and pale,
With the dew on his brow, and the rust on his mail;
And the tents were all silent, the banners alone,
The lances unlifted, the trumpet unblown.

The first stanza quoted uses suspense; the second uses a surprisingly unparallel parallelism ("Angel of death," "eyes of the sleepers"); the third uses a single intense image; the last uses a contrast between a closeup and a broad view of the battlefield. Each of these stanzas creates a different kind of link to tie the poem together across its center "seam."

One especially memorable four-line stanza is the **"In Memoriam" stanza,** named after Alfred, Lord Tennyson's celebrated long elegy for Arthur Hallam. The stanza rhymes abba, and the fourth line, coming so far after its rhymemate, has a haunting, lost quality. It is rare for a stanza to be named after a single poem, but Tennyson's tour de force draws on that lost quality so well that it is easy to see why the name has stuck. Once, the best friend of one of the students in a class I was teaching had died suddenly. That day we read the entire poem aloud, each of us reading a stanza until we had gone around the class several times and finished the poem. It was a moving experience, not only because the poem focuses on the incomprehensibility of early death, but also because the structure of the stanzas, each of which ends on a kind of waiting note, linked all of us who read together as if in a chain.

From "In Memoriam," Alfred, Lord Tennyson (1850)

Oh, yet we trust that somehow good
    Will be the final end of ill,
    To pangs of nature, sins of will,
Defects of doubt, and taints of blood;

That nothing walks with aimless feet;
    That not one life shall be destroy'd,
    Or cast as rubbish to the void,
When God hath made the pile complete;

That not a worm is cloven in vain;
    That not a moth with vain desire

Is shrivell'd in a fruitless fire,
Or but subserves another's gain.

Behold, we know not anything;
I can but trust that good shall fall
At last—far off—at last, to all,
And every winter change to spring.

So runs my dream; but what am I?
An infant crying in the night;
An infant crying for the light,
And with no language but a cry.

Here is a more recent poem using the same stanza. Written in 1959 about the danger of nuclear war in the aftermath of Hiroshima, today it resonates equally well as a poem about global climate change:

"Advice to a Prophet," Richard Wilbur

When you come, as you soon must, to the streets of our city,
Mad-eyed from stating the obvious,
Not proclaiming our fall but begging us
In God's name to have self-pity,

Spare us all word of the weapons, their force and range,
The long numbers that rocket the mind;
Our slow, unreckoning hearts will be left behind,
Unable to fear what is too strange.

Nor shall you scare us with talk of the death of the race.
How should we dream of this place without us?—
The sun mere fire, the leaves untroubled about us,
A stone look on the stone's face?

Speak of the world's own change. Though we cannot conceive
Of an undreamt thing, we know to our cost
How the dreamt cloud crumbles, the vines are blackened by frost,
How the view alters. We could believe,

If you told us so, that the white-tailed deer will slip
Into perfect shade, grown perfectly shy,
The lark avoid the reaches of our eye,
The jack-pine lose its knuckled grip

On the cold ledge, and every torrent burn
As Xanthus once, its gliding trout
Stunned in a twinkling. What should we be without
The dolphin's arc, the dove's return,

These things in which we have seen ourselves and spoken?
Ask us, prophet, how we shall call
Our natures forth when that live tongue is all
Dispelled, that glass obscured or broken

In which we have said the rose of our love and the clean
Horse of our courage, in which beheld
The singing locust of the soul unshelled,
And all we mean or wish to mean.

Ask us, ask us whether with the worldless rose
Our hearts shall fail us; come demanding
Whether there shall be lofty or long standing
When the bronze annals of the oak-tree close.

Wilbur is a learned and conscious poet; it seems likely that he was using the "In Memoriam" rhyme scheme purposely for this poem about loss. Since Wilbur's lines vary in length, there is not such a clear sense of anticipation and delay as there is at the end of each stanza of the Tennyson. The more casual, prosaic tone of the longer lines also mutes the effect, but it remains as a sobering undercurrent.

Another haunting four-line stanza form is the unique **sapphic stanza,** whose invention is credited to the great ancient Greek poet Sappho. This stanza is one of very few that always has a particular, exact metrical pattern:

Trochee-trochee-dactyl-trochee-trochee
Trochee-trochee-dactyl-trochee-trochee

Trochee-trochee-dactyl-trochee-trochee
Dactyl-trochee

"Moon and Stars," Sappho (trans. John Myers O'Hara) (1910)

When the moon at full on the sill of heaven
Lights her beacon, flooding the earth with silver,
All the shining stars that about her cluster
Hide their fair faces;

So when Anactoria's beauty dazzles
Sight of mine, grown dim with the joy it gives me,
Gorgo, Atthis, Gyrinno, all the others
Fade from my vision.

If you failed to stress the word "when" in the first line, no doubt you had to read it again until you did so. Here is a contemporary metrical translation of another Sappho poem:

Sappho, "Household of the Muses" (trans. Annie Finch)

It is not appropriate, in a household
Given to the Muses. Those lamentations
Do not belong here.

Again, unlike with other metrical patterns in this book so far, which can be changed through substitutions or expressive variation without destroying the basic meter, this particular pattern of trochees and dactyls *is* the definition of a sapphic stanza. Because the stanza is defined by its exact pattern of metrical feet, if it were altered through variation, it would probably not be "read" as a sapphic stanza by readers. This is why poets who use sapphic stanzas do not usually alter their meter for expressive purposes.

Often, when a new poetic form is first used, poets are self-conscious about writing in such an unusual form—and the self-consciousness shows itself, very literally, in allusions to the form and its history. Because Sappho is known as a great love poet, it is no coincidence that Swinburne, the decadent late-nineteenth-century poet who was one of the first to appreciate the sapphic stanza's unique appeal for poetry in English, dedicated his only sapphic stanzas to Aphrodite, the goddess of love.

"Hymn to Aphrodite," Algernon Charles Swinburne (1868)

All the night sleep came not upon my eyelids,
Shed not dew, nor shook nor unclosed a feather,
Yet with lips shut close and with eyes of iron
Stood and beheld me.

Then to me so lying awake a vision
Came without sleep over the seas and touched me,
Softly touched mine eyelids and lips; and I too,
Full of the vision,

Saw the white implacable Aphrodite,
Saw the hair unbound and the feet unsandalled
Shine as fire of sunset on western waters;
Saw the reluctant

Feet, the straining plumes of the doves that drew her,
Looking always, looking with necks reverted,
Back to Lesbos, back to the hills whereunder
Shone Mitylene;

Heard the flying feet of the Loves behind her
Make a sudden thunder upon the waters,
As the thunder flung from the strong unclosing
Wings of a great wind.

Here is a more contemporary version of the stanza, with just a few variations from the meter:

"Effort at Speech," William Meredith
For Muriel Rukeyser

Climbing the stairway gray with urban midnight,
Cheerful, venial, ruminating pleasure,

Darkness takes me, an arm around my throat and
Give me your wallet.

Fearing cowardice more than other terrors,
Angry I wrestle with my unseen partner,
Caught in a ritual not of our making,
panting like spaniels.

Bold with adrenaline, mindless, shaking,
God damn it, no! I rasp at him behind me,
Wrenching the leather from his grasp. It
breaks like a wishbone,

So that departing (routed by my shouting,
not by my strength or inadvertent courage)
Half the papers lending me a name are
gone with him nameless.

Only now turning, I see a tall boy running,
Fifteen, sixteen, dressed thinly for the weather.
Reaching the streetlight he turns a brown face briefly
phrased like a question.

I like a questioner watch him turn the corner
Taking the answer with him, or his half of it.
Loneliness, not a sensible emotion,
breathes hard on the stairway.

Walking homeward I fraternize with shadows,
Zigzagging with them where they flee the streetlights,
Asking for trouble, asking for the message
trouble had sent me.

All fall down has been scribbled on the street in
Garbage and excrement: so much for the vision
Others taunt me with, my untimely humor,
so much for cheerfulness.

Next time don't wrangle, give the boy the money,
Call across chasms what the world you know is.
Luckless and lied to, how can a child master
human decorum?

Next time a switchblade, somewhere he is thinking,
I should have killed him and took the lousy wallet.
Reading my cards he feels a surge of anger
blind as my shame.

Error from Babel mutters in the places,
Cities apart, where now we word our failures:
Hatred and guilt have left us without language
that might have led to discourse.

We use the word "lesbian" today because Sappho, author of great love poems to women, lived on the island of Lesbos. So the sapphic stanza has naturally been felt an appropriate form for lesbian love poetry:

From "Dusk: July," Marilyn Hacker

I would love my love, but my love is elsewhere.
I would take a walk with her in the evening's
Milky pearl. I'd sleep with my arms around her
Confident body,

Arms and legs asprawl like an adolescent.
We're not adolescents. Our friends are dying
And between us nothing at all is settled
Except our loving.

The beautiful, captivating last line of the sapphic stanza is perhaps its most compelling charm. This shorter last line, consisting of one dactyl and one trochee, is called an **adonic,** named after a poem written in that stanza to mourn the death of the goddess Venus's beautiful young lover, Adonis. Recently, I told a poet-friend that the sapphic strikes me as an erotic stanza, even aside from its history. Challenged to explain why, I told her that it has to do with the tension of opposites: the single dactylic foot hidden inside the trochaic lines, building momentum there until, in the adonic, it emerges into a pairing, a balance, with a single trochee. As this tension and resolution between trochee and dactyl recurs in each stanza, the adonic takes on more and more potential power. A good adonic is hard to forget. If you listen for adonics, you will hear them everywhere: "Tell me you love me"; "Here, let me help you"; "How could you do that?"; "Look, I'm your mother!"; "Wow, I'm exhausted."

A more complicated four-line classical stanza that is still used, though less frequently than the sapphic, is the **alcaic stanza,** attributed to the poet Alcaeus. The first two lines are the same: / / u / / / u u / u / (first and second feet may be changed to amphibrachs [u/u], and the last foot to a pyrrhic [uu]). The third line is / / u / / / u / / (any or all of the feet may be changed—the first and third to amphibrachs [u / u] and the second to /u/). The fourth line is / uu / uu / / (last foot may be changed to a trochee [/u]). Here are some examples:

From "Psalm 120," Mary Sidney (ca. 1590)

Too long, alas, too long have I dwelled here
With friendly peaces furious enemies:
Who when to peace I seeke to call them,
Faster I find to the warre they arm them.

From "Evening," William Blake

Now, while the west-wind slumbereth on the lake,
Silently dost thou with delicate shimmer
O'erbloom the frowning front of awful
Night to a glance of unearthly silver.

From "The Garden at Dawn," Robin Skelton

My morning mind is clouded and blurred with dream.
Dream holds the one great key to the shining whole
We share with whirlpools, gods, and children
Aware realities move like music.

From "Going Back to the River," Marilyn Hacker

Life's not forever, love is precarious.
Wherever I live, let me come home to you
As you are, as I am, where you
Meet me and walk with me to the river.

It is such a subtle meter that it may be hard to hear the pattern, and yet even so, a shimmering complexity keeps moving in rhythm directly under the surface of the poem.

Longer Stanzas

There are no well-known five-line stanzas, though of course poets have invented them for particular poems. Here is one poem that uses a simple five-line stanza rhymed ababa:

"Home is So Sad," Philip Larkin

Home is so sad. It stays as it was left,
Shaped to the comfort of the last to go
As if to win them back. Instead, bereft
Of anyone to please, it withers so,
Having no heart to put aside the theft

And turn again to what it started as,
A joyous shot at how things ought to be,
Long fallen wide. You can see how it was:
Look at the pictures and the cutlery.
The music in the piano stool. That vase.

Typical of Larkin's great formal virtuosity, this poem makes good use of the rather forlorn potential of the "extra" last line in this stanza, which lingers on, unwanted and unsure, after the usual, and probably expected, abab quatrain has finished.

During the Tudor and Stuart periods, arguably the most inventive and exciting time for poetry in English, a six-line stanza, made of a quatrain followed by a couplet, was common:

From "Venus and Adonis," William Shakespeare (1593)

He burns with bashful shame: she with her tears
Doth quench the maiden burning of his cheeks;
Then with her windy sighs and golden hairs
To fan and blow them dry again she seeks:
He saith she is immodest, blames her 'miss;
What follows more she murders with a kiss.

Even as an empty eagle, sharp by fast,
Tires with her beak on feathers, flesh and bone,
Shaking her wings, devouring all in haste,
Till either gorge be stuff'd or prey be gone;
Even so she kissed his brow, his cheek, his chin,
And where she ends she doth anew begin.

This adaptable stanza was used both for very short lyrics of two or three stanzas, and for long narratives such as this 1,194-line poem. The constant restarting, summing up, and restarting again of the action creates an interesting motion through a poem. This stanza is thought to have influenced the development of the English sonnet form.

Closely related to the six-line stanza is the seven-line stanza used by the colonial poet Anne Bradstreet for her "Contemplations." Bradstreet used the stanza ababccc, each stanza ending in a hexameter, to recreate the meandering paths of spiritual reflection:

From "Contemplations" (1678)

Then higher on the glistening Sun I gazed,
Whose beams was shaded by the leavie tree;
The more I looked, the more I grew amazed,
And softly said, "What's glorly like to thee?"
Soul of this world, this universe's Eye,
No wonder some made thee a diety;
Had I not known better, alas, the same had I.

Of the longer stanzas, **rhyme royal** is one of the most well known and versatile. A seven-line stanza rhyming ababbcc, it can be used for long narrative poems and also serves well for short lyrics. Traditionally, it is in iambic pentameter, but it doesn't need to be. Rhyme royal is also called "Troilus stanza" because Chaucer first used it in English, for his beautiful long narrative poem *Troilus and Criseyde:*

From Troilus and Criseyde, *Geoffrey Chaucer (ca. 1386)*

Out of these blake wawes for to sayle,
O wind, O wind, the weder ginneth clere;
For in this see the boot hath swich travayle,
Of my conning, that unnethe I it stere:
This see clepe I the tempestous matere
Of desespeyr that Troilus was inne:
But now of hope the calendes biginne.

The name "rhyme royal" relates to the fact that this stanza was traditional in ceremonies honoring royalty. Two notable long contemporary poems in rhyme royal are Sonia Sanchez's elegy for her brother, and Major Jackson's long tour de force dedicated to Gwendolyn Brooks:

From "Letter to Brooks," Major Jackson

12.
What fevered my wrist was this: you could
    Have amicably thanked me for the ride,
Extending your elbow-length glove, you could
    Have disappeared in that opulent façade,
    Instead you asked if I'd read alongside
That night. I left and bought a pad from Kmart
Then wrote all the poems I knew by heart,

13.
Which numbered two,—one of those, a haiku.
    The evening thickens dense as trees
Except the feel of reading on stage with you.

Truth be told, I've come to believe such deeds
Define as much the black tradition and seed
The garden Clarence Major speaks. If it thrives,
Scores bend on hand and knee keeping it alive.

Here, the metrically irregular lines and occasional slant rhymes create a tension with the regularity of the form.

The eight-lined stanza called **ottava rima,** rhymed abababcc, is only one line longer than rhyme royal, but that one line makes all the difference. It gives the stanza enough space to change direction and bring in a variety of moods. The third repetition of each a and b rhyming word also allows the stanza to gather more force, which gives additional energy to the couplet when it finally happens. Originally Italian, the stanza was tried by several poets in English, including those early experimenters with the sonnet, Wyatt and Sidney. But it was during the Romantic period that *Don Juan,* Byron's satirical narrative poem about a man who can't resist women, established ottava rima as an important stanza in English. Byron's extremely popular poem endowed this stanza with a reputation for wit and satire and a declamatory and public, rather than privately musing, tone:

From Don Juan, *George Gordon, Lord Byron (1819)*

My poem's epic and is meant to be
Divided in twelve books, each book containing,
With love and war, a heavy gale at sea,
A list of ships, and captains, and kings reigning,
New characters; the episodes are three.
A panoramic view of hell's in training,
After the style of Virgil and of Homer,
So that my name of epic's no misnomer.

All these things will be specified in time
With strict regard to Aristotle's rules,
The vade mecum of the true sublime,
Which makes so many poets and some fools.
Prose poets like blank verse, I'm fond of rhyme.
Good workmen never quarrel with their tools.

I've got new mythological machinery,
And very handsome supernatural scenery.

There's only one slight difference between
Me and my epic brethren gone before,
And here the advantage is my own, I ween,
(Not that I have not several merits more,
But this will more peculiarly be seen);
They so embellish, that 'tis quite a bore
Their labyrinth of fables to thread through,
Whereas this story's actually true.

The next poet to be known for his use of ottava rima, William Butler Yeats, built on the Byronic tradition but gave the stanza his own stamp, infusing it with his distinctive tone of meditative high seriousness:

From "Among School Children," W. B. Yeats (1928)

Labour is blossoming or dancing where
The body is not bruised to pleasure soul.
Nor beauty born out of its own despair,
Nor blear-eyed wisdom out of midnight oil.
O chestnut-tree, great-rooted blossomer,
Are you the leaf, the blossom or the bole?
O body swayed to music, O brightening glance,
How can we know the dancer from the dance?

Stanzas longer than eight lines are unusual, but one incomparable nine-line stanza will always hold a special place in poetry in English: the **Spenserian stanza.** Devised by Spenser for use in his magnificent, fanciful epic poem in honor of Queen Elizabeth, the *Faerie Queene,* it is a nine-line stanza with a unique interlocking rhyme scheme (ababbcbcc) and a very beautiful extra-long last line (six feet long, called an "alexandrine"). Though few poets have tried it—Keats's "Eve of St. Agnes" is a famous exception—it is worth trying. When I have written Spenserian stanzas, I've found myself caught up in passages of intricate description, but the stanza also lends itself to drama, as in this passage describing the warlike Britomart, a legendary soldier who here stands for the military strength of England and of Queen Elizabeth I:

From The Faerie Queene, *Edmund Spenser (1590)*

Wherewith enrag'd she fiercely at them flew,
And with her flaming sword about her layd,
That none of them foule mischiefe could eschew,
But with her dreadfull strokes were all dismayd:
Here, there, and euery where about her swayd
Her wrathfull steele, that none mote it abide;
And eke the *Redcrosse* knight gaue her good aid,
Ay ioyning foot to foot, and side to side,
That in short space their foes they haue quite terrifide.

Tho whenas all were put to shamefull flight,
The noble *Britomartis* her arayd,
And her bright armes about her body dight:
For nothing would she lenger there be stayd,
Where so loose life, and so vngentle trade
Was vsd of Knights and Ladies seeming gent:
So earely ere the grosse Earthes gryesy shade
Was all disperst out of the firmament,
They tooke their steeds, & forth upon their iourney went.

These adjacent stanzas from Keats's poem make use of both the potential for drama and for description:

From "The Eve of St. Agnes," John Keats (1819)

Out went the taper as she hurried in;
Its little smoke, in pallid moonshine, died:
She clos'd the door, she panted, all akin
To spirits of the air, and visions wide:
No uttered syllable, or, woe betide!
But to her heart, her heart was voluble,

Paining with eloquence her balmy side;
As though a tongueless nightingale should swell
Her throat in vain, and die, heart-stifled, in her dell.

A casement high and triple-arch'd there was,
All garlanded with carven imag'ries
Of fruits, and flowers, and bunches of knot-grass,
And diamonded with panes of quaint device,
Innumerable of stains and splendid dyes,
As are the tiger-moth's deep-damask'd wings;
And in the midst, 'mong thousand heraldries,
And twilight saints, and dim emblazonings,
A shielded scutcheon blush'd with blood of queens and kings.

A shorter stanza might easily be thrown off balance by the longer line at the end, but Spenser's genius was to balance the long line and the long stanza, a symmetry that his great admirer Keats found a perfect frame for his own skill at intricate description.

When Keats died of consumption at the age of 25, two years after writing this famously lush poem, his close friend Percy Bysshe Shelley added to the significance of the Spenserian stanza by choosing it for his elegy on Keats, "Adonais." The elegy is 495 lines long and offers plenty of time for Shelley's metaphysical meditations:

From "Adonais: An Elegy on the Death of John Keats,"
Percy Bysshe Shelley (1821)

He is made one with Nature: there is heard
His voice in all her music, from the moan
Of thunder, to the song of night's sweet bird;
He is a presence to be felt and known
In darkness and in light, from herb and stone,
Spreading itself where'er that Power may move
Which has withdrawn his being to its own;
Which wields the world with never-wearied love,
Sustains it from beneath, and kindles it above.

He is a portion of the loveliness
Which once he made more lovely: he doth bear
His part, while the one Spirit's plastic stress
Sweeps through the dull dense world, compelling there,
All new successions to the forms they wear;
Torturing th' unwilling dross that checks its flight
To its own likeness, as each mass may bear;
And bursting in its beauty and its might
From trees and beasts and men into the Heaven's light.

The splendours of the firmament of time
May be eclips'd, but are extinguish'd not;
Like stars to their appointed height they climb
And death is a low mist which cannot blot
The brightness it may veil. When lofty thought
Lifts a young heart above its mortal lair,
And love and life contend in it for what,
Shall be its earthly doom, the dead live there
And move like winds of light on dark and stormy air.

It is hard to imagine such ample musings taking place in a more confined space such as rhyme royal or ottava rima. But then, the wonderful thing about a stanza is that once it has been used for a certain kind of poem, it comes to seem as if it has always been that way.

The last stanza we will discuss is a 10-line stanza, the **decima.** The decima is of Hispanic origin and dates back to the fifteenth century. It has been used only rarely in English so far, though it has recently been rediscovered by contemporary Hispanic poets including Pat Mora and Cynthia Gutierrez. There are numerous variations of rhyme scheme, but the stanza always has 10 lines. While Mora uses an unrhymed stanza, the most common rhyme scheme is probably abbaaccddc:

"Decima," George Santayana

Silent daisies out of reach,
Maidens of the starry grass,

Gazing on me as I pass
With a look too wise for speech,
Teach me resignation—teach
Patience to the barren clod,
As, above your happier sod,
Bending to the wind's caress,
You—unplucked, alas!—no less
Sweetly manifest the god.

Santayana, perhaps the first poet to bring this stanza into English, was known for his philosophical meditations. Here, he uses a short line to meditate on the timeless lesson of a simple theme.

The Dynamic Stanza

While most common stanzas can be classified by length, as they are here, it is important to realize that length is not the defining characteristic of a stanza. What really holds a stanza together is the energetic connection among its own lines, and between it and other stanzas in the poem. A case in point is Paul Muldoon's poem "The Outlier" in chapter 8, in which each stanza adds a new line. This form, so appropriate for the poem with its echoes of childhood poems that keep adding parts, such as "The Farmer in the Dell," reminds us that a strong poem makes its form for its own purposes. The following poem, from a young poet's first book, builds stanzas based on the numbers in the Fibonacci sequence:

"Light Warning," Emily Galvin

No.

Wait

for it.

You know how

The air feels after everything

Has been carried out, doors and windows closed?

Deep wintertime—I felt the cold coming through the glass, the old blade
loose

In my left hand. Late at night I used to sit against the window at the far
end of my bed

And hope like hell that something would break through. The intimacy of
drywall, cold air leaking through. I watched the glass sink through
itself inside the window-frame. Sore ribs. I kept on staring through,

As if only waiting. Wheels in the ditch. Body on the wall. Red sky all night
that time of year. Where I live now, it never gets that cold.
Sometimes, though, when the fires get close enough to let a little ash
into the air, I think of windowpanes, and sparks fly out my mouth.

This is an idea that could easily have fallen flat, but in this case, there is an electric engagement with the form that builds a kind of tensile connection within and between the stanzas. A workable stanza is always dynamic. As you choose or devise a stanza for your poem, make sure that you feel the quickening of interest that assures you that this stanza is, indeed, alive for you for the duration of this poem.

Whether you write in free verse or form, your poetry will benefit if you become comfortable with writing stanzas of different lengths. You will find that a poem that doesn't work at all in a long stanza can come to life if you put it into a short stanza, and vice versa. Since stanzas frame the entire context of a poem, a strong vocabulary of stanzas is one of the most useful tools a poet can have.

QUESTIONS FOR MEDITATION OR DISCUSSION

What does a room mean to you? In your notebook, freewrite a description of a room where you would like to be. How big would it be? How wide? How tall? Would it be rectangular or circular or something else? What would the walls be like? Then imagine a poetic stanza that feels the same way. It could be an existing stanza or one you invent yourself. How do you think that stanza functions like a room? Does the metaphor tell you anything more about how poetry works?

T. S. Eliot wrote, "The bad poet is usually unconscious where he [*sic*] ought to be conscious, and conscious where he ought to be unconscious." Where do you think a poet should be conscious, and where unconscious? Is the stanza a place for consciousness or unconsciousness?

QUOTES

Without form, how could words bear the weight of emotions?
—Maya Sharma

To see the world for what it is, one needs the line, and later the larger field of the stanza or whatever you care to call it.
—Charles Simic

I don't feel that writing in traditional forms is giving up power, going over to the enemy. The word belongs to no one, the houses built of words belong to no one. We have to take them back from those who think they own them.
—Julia Alvarez

POETRY PRACTICES

Group (Readabout). Choose a long poem in stanzas and read it aloud, each person taking one stanza. It's fine to repeat the poem a few times. This is a good way to get a sense of the movement of a particular stanza shape.

Stanza Sampler. Take one of your unrhymed poems and break it up into at least four different lengths of stanza. You might try it in couplets, tercets, quatrains, seven-line stanzas, and irregular-length stanzas. Notice the differences it makes to the poem. Are you inspired to make different kinds of revisions for the different poems?

Follow That Tune. Write a poem to be sung to the tune of the *Gilligan's Island* theme song, your favorite country song, or another ballad stanza tune that you know well.

Meditation Rooms. Many stanza forms, including, in this chapter, rhyme royal, ottava rima, the Spenserian stanza, and the decima, have been used for meditative poetry: poetry that meditates on philosophical themes. Choose one of these stanzas and write a poem musing on a theme. Give yourself plenty of room.

Cutting Up Free Verse. Take a free verse poem you want to revise and cut it up with scissors into stanzas or, if you don't have stanzas, into units that seem to belong together. Rearrange the stanzas various ways. When you have something you like, tape it together.

Train of Quatrains. For this exercise, you can use an existing poem of your own in quatrains, or write a new poem in quatrains, or use someone else's poem in quatrains. Whichever you choose, revise at least three stanzas of the poem into three different quatrain rhyme patterns: abab, aabb, and abba. You will need to alter the grammar and the rest of the lines in each stanza somewhat to make it flow smoothly. How does the reorganization of the rhyme pattern affect the poem?

Weaving a Story. Write a narrative poem in terza rima. Optional: base it on an incident from Dante's *Divine Comedy;* on a dream; or on a vision of the afterlife. Or try writing a narrative in Spenserian stanzas, rhyme royal, or ottava rima. You can start a new narrative, or add some stanzas onto an existing narrative poem such as *The Faerie Queene* or *Don Juan.*

Stanza Essences. Write a new poem in three different ways: one version in heroic couplets, one in sapphics or alcaics, and one in rhyme royal.

CHAPTER 17

Worth Repeating: Forms Based on Repetition

You know I'm drifting and I'm drifting just like a ship out on the sea.
Well, I'm drifting and I'm drifting like a ship out on the sea.
Well, you know I ain't got nobody in this world to care for me.

The second line of the blues poem above may look as if it doesn't add anything important, but try reading the stanza without it. Then read the full stanza again. Try to describe what the repeated line adds to the poem.

Is it something about rhythm, pacing? Is it something that happens in your body as you wait for the line to finish? Is it a change in mood or tone of voice? Whatever the repeated line adds, we feel it in our heartbeats, our breathing, the tensing of our muscles. The physicality of poetry is its most untranslatable and unique characteristic, and repeating poems are structured to glory in this physicality.

While all poems have some elements of repetition—rhymes, sounds, rhythms, stanzas, images, even the fact of line breaks (even images and metaphors are based on kinds of repetition) the special kinds of poems in this chapter are structured on repeating phrases or refrains. Numerous poetic patterns from numerous cultures are based on this kind of blatant repetition. Like the blues, repeating structures were often originally songs or oral poems; they are "lyric" poems in the truest sense of the word. The structures of repeating poems provide templates for passion, awe, melancholy, delight, anger, and other emotional experience, reminding us that all emotions, however profound or transcendent, are experienced in our bodies, and connecting us, through our bodies, with the eternal cycles of time.

One of the most simple, powerful literary techniques, the repetition of the beginning words or phrases of lines, or of clauses, is called **anaphora.** It dates back at least to the Hebrew of the Old Testament:

From "Song of Solomon" (ca. 965 B.C.), King James Bible (1611)

His head is as the most fine gold, his locks are bushy, and black as a raven.
His eyes are as the eyes of doves by the rivers of waters, washed with milk,
and fitly set.
His cheeks are as a bed of spices, as sweet flowers: his lips like lilies,
dropping sweet smelling myrrh.
His hands are as gold rings set with the beryl: his belly is as bright ivory
overlaid with sapphires.
His legs are as pillars of marble, set upon sockets of fine gold: his
countenance is as Lebanon, excellent as the cedars.
His mouth is most sweet: yea, he is altogether lovely. This is my beloved,
and this is my friend, O daughters of Jerusalem.

The repetition of the word "his," combined with the repeating grammatical structure, creates the simplest kind of anaphora. A more obvious use of anaphora occurs in the work of Walt Whitman, who was directly influenced by the King James Bible. Whitman is the poet who is best known for using anaphora in English. Here it lends an incantatory impact to the opening of one of his most moving poems:

From "Out of the Cradle, Endlessly Rocking," Walt Whitman (1859)

Out of the cradle endlessly rocking,
Out of the mocking-bird's throat, the musical shuttle,
Out of the Ninth-month midnight,
Over the sterile sands and the fields beyond, where the child leaving his
bed wander'd alone, bare headed, barefoot,
Down from the shower'd halo,
Up from the mystic play of shadows twining and twisting as if they were
alive,
Out from the patches of briers and blackberries,
From the memories of the bird that chanted to me,
From your memories sad brother—from the fitful risings and fallings I
heard,
From under that yellow half-moon late-risen, and swollen as if with tears,
From those beginning notes of yearning and love there in the transparent
mist,

From the thousand responses of my heart never to cease,
From the myriad thence-arous'd words,
From the word stronger and more delicious than any,
From such as now they start the scene revisiting,
As a flock, twittering, rising, or overhead passing,
Borne hither, ere all eludes me, hurriedly,
A man, yet by these tears a little boy again,
Throwing myself on the sand, confronting the waves,
I, chanter of pains and joys, uniter of here and hereafter,
Taking all hints to use them, but swiftly leaping beyond them,
A reminiscence sing.

Anaphora is a decorative technique, not a structural one: it can't be predicted like the rhyme scheme of a sonnet. Like all decorative techniques in poetry, it requires a sure instinct and a light touch to avoid deadening the effect by becoming too predictable. Here, Whitman uses it beautifully, modulating from the repetitions of "out" to "from" with a transition as subtle as a skilled painter blending colors. Here is the end of a poem by a young contemporary poet using anaphora for more startling effects:

From "O Great Slacker," Olena Kalytiak Davis

. . . becaUSE after a while Sorrow is a tasty Meat
beCAUSE we can't see ourselves Gnawing, Chewing
BEcause there is nothing New and nothing not New, Known
beCause we like to call ourselves WE and stand Together
beCaUse that allows ME to separate out from this sown this mown this
    cowering Crowd
and say onto you: i am your Remembrancer, your Requiter
i am Loud in your Sickness
you are Gnashing my Teeth
in Vain

The repeating words function as placeholders and time-markers. Combined with Davis's unorthodox use of capitalization, syntax, and diction, they give a ritualistic quality to the poem, perhaps partially in echo of another heavily anaphoric and idiocynsncratic poem written centuries earlier, Christopher Smart's *Jubilate Agno:*

From Jubilate Agno, *Christopher Smart (1760)*

For I will consider my Cat Jeoffry.
For he is the servant of the Living God, duly and daily serving him.
For at the first glance of the glory of God in the East he worships in his way.
For in this is done by wreathing his body seven times round with elegant quickness.
For then he leaps up to catch the musk, which is the blessing of God upon his prayer.
For he rolls upon prank to work it in.
For having done duty and received blessing he begins to consider himself.
For this he performs in ten degrees.
For first he looks upon his forepaws to see if they are clean.
For secondly he kicks up behind to clear away there.
For thirdly he works it upon stretch with the forepaws extended.
For fourthly he sharpens his paws by wood.
For fifthly he washes himself.
For sixthly he rolls upon wash.
For seventhly he fleas himself, that he may not be interrupted upon the beat.
For eighthly he rubs himself against a post.
For ninthly he looks up for his instructions.
For tenthly he goes in quest of food.
For having consider'd God and himself he will consider his neighbour.
For if he meets another cat he will kiss her in kindness.
For when he takes his prey he plays with it to give it a chance.
For one mouse in seven escapes by his dallying.
For when his day's work is done his business more properly begins.
For he keeps the Lord's watch in the night against the adversary.
For he counteracts the powers of darkness by his electrical skin and glaring eyes.
For he counteracts the Devil, who is death, by brisking about the life.
For in his morning orisons he loves the sun and the sun loves him.
For he is of the tribe of Tiger.
For the Cherub Cat is a term of the Angel Tiger.

For he has the subtlety and hissing of a serpent, which in goodness he suppresses.
For he will not do destruction if he is well-fed, neither will he spit without provocation.
For he purrs in thankfulness, when God tells him he's a good Cat.
For he is an instrument for the children to learn benevolence upon.
For every house is incomplete without him, and a blessing is lacking in the spirit. . .
For the Lord commanded Moses concerning the cats at the departure of the Children of Israel from Egypt.
For every family had one cat at least in the bag.
For the English Cats are the best in Europe.
For he is the cleanest in the use of his forepaws of any quadruped.
For the dexterity of his defence is an instance of the love of God to him exceedingly.
For he is the quickest to his mark of any creature.
For he is tenacious of his point.
For he is a mixture of gravity and waggery.
For he knows that God is his Saviour.
For there is nothing sweeter than his peace when at rest.
For there is nothing brisker than his life when in motion.
For he is of the Lord's poor and so indeed is he called by benevolence perpetually—Poor Jeoffry! poor Jeoffry! the rat has bit thy throat.
For I bless the name of the Lord Jesus that Jeoffry is better.
For the divine spirit comes about his body to sustain it in complete cat.
For his tongue is exceeding pure so that it has in purity what it wants in music.
For he is docile and can learn certain things.
For he can set up with gravity which is patience upon approbation.
For he can fetch and carry, which is patience in employment.
For he can jump over a stick which is patience upon proof positive.
For he can spraggle upon waggle at the word of command.
For he can jump from an eminence into his master's bosom.
For he can catch the cork and toss it again.
For he is hated by the hypocrite and miser.
For the former is afraid of detection.
For the latter refuses the charge.

For he camels his back to bear the first notion of business.
For he is good to think on, if a man would express himself neatly.
For he made a great figure in Egypt for his signal services.
For he killed the Ichneumon-rat very pernicious by land.
For his ears are so acute that they sting again.
For from this proceeds the passing quickness of his attention.
For by stroking of him I have found out electricity.
For I perceived God's light about him both wax and fire.
For the Electrical fire is the spiritual substance, which God sends from
heaven to sustain the bodies both of man and beast.
For God has blessed him in the variety of his movements.
For, tho he cannot fly, he is an excellent clamberer.
For his motions upon the face of the earth are more than any other
quadruped.
For he can tread to all the measures upon the music.
For he can swim for life.
For he can creep.

In the poem below, the repetitions are more formally structured and predictable. They create a sense of import and solemnity, perhaps evoking the kind of Native American ritual traditions about which Harjo often writes:

"Ah, Ah," Joy Harjo

for Lurline McGregor

Ah, ah cries the crow arching toward the heavy sky over the marina.
Lands on the crown of the palm tree.

Ah, ah slaps the urgent cove of ocean swimming through the slips.
We carry canoes to the edge of the salt.

Ah, ah groans the crew with the weight, the winds cutting skin.
We claim our seats. Pelicans perch in the draft for fish.

Ah, ah beats our lungs and we are racing into the waves.
Though there are worlds below us and above us, we are straight ahead.

Ah, ah tattoos the engines of your plane against the sky—away from these
waters.
Each paddle stroke follows the curve from reach to loss.

Ah, ah calls the sun from a fishing boat with a pale, yellow sail. We fly by
on our return, over the net of eternity thrown out for stars.

Ah, ah scrapes the hull of my soul. Ah, ah.

From the first line, with its unexpected period after "marina," it is clear that repetition will be given priority over idiomatic usage in this poem. The exactness of the repetition of the words "ah, ah" has the force of a traditional chant. Such consistent poetic decisions set an appropriately serious stage for the introduction of the phrase "hull of my soul" in the last line, which otherwise might have seemed too intense for the poem.

The following poem also uses repetition in a formal manner, as if the repeated phrases are patiently building a strong, steady place to structure an intense emotional experience:

"Looking at Each Other," Muriel Rukeyser (1913)

Yes, we were looking at each other
Yes, we knew each other very well
Yes, we had made love with each other many times
Yes, we had heard music together
Yes, we had gone to the sea together
Yes, we had cooked and eaten together
Yes, we had laughed often day and night
Yes, we fought violence and knew violence
Yes, we hated the inner and outer oppression
Yes, that day we were looking at each other
Yes, we saw the sunlight pouring down
Yes, the corner of the table was between us
Yes, bread and flowers were on the table
Yes, our eyes saw each other's eyes
Yes, our mouths saw each other's mouth
Yes, our breasts saw each other's breasts
Yes, our bodies entire saw each other

Yes, it was beginning in each
Yes, it threw waves across our lives
Yes, the pulses were becoming very strong
Yes, the beating became very delicate
Yes, the calling the arousal
Yes, the arriving the coming
Yes, there it was for both entire
Yes, we were looking at each other

The word "yes" is used so naturally as part of each clause that it is only as the end of the poem approaches that one realizes the people in the poem are also saying "yes" to each other's love. In order for that meaning of the word "yes" to emerge, a reader has to move outside the formal structure of the poem, which makes us realize how much we have been contained inside the immediacy of the described experience. "Looking at Each Other" is based on syntactical repetition (repeating a sentence structure). Rukeyser establishes the pattern of syntactical repetition just enough with the repeating word "we" so that we can recognize it beginning to break down as the lovers' passion starts to break through. In the box you will find examples of more formal structures of repetition, developed by rhetoricians in Classical times to make their writing more powerful.

Some classical rhetorical strategies involving repetition:

Anaphora:
Repetition of the same word at the beginning of successive lines or clauses
See poem by Oleana Kalytiak Davis, this chapter.

Epistrophe
The opposite of anaphora: repetition of the same word at the ends of successive clauses

Symploce: combination of anaphora and epistrophe

> **The yellow fog that rubs its back upon the window-panes,**
> **The yellow smoke that rubs its muzzle on the window-panes**
> **T. S. Eliot, "The Love Song of J. Alfred Prufrock," 1917**

Anadiplosis:
Repetition of the last word of one clause at the beginning of the following clause:

Here is no question of whiteness,
white as white can be, with a purple mole
at the center of each flower.
Each flower is a hand's span ...
William Carlos Williams, "Queen Anne's Lace," 1921

Polyptoton
Words are repeated as different parts of speech, or as different forms of the same word-stem.

Thou, whose shadow shadows doth make bright—
How would thy shadow's form form happy show . . .
Shakespeare, Sonnet 43

Also see the use of the words "losing," "lost," and "loss" at the end of Elizabeth Bishop's "One Art" in the section on the villanelle.

Antanaclasis
Repetition of a word with a different meaning (pun)

If we don't hang together, we'll hang separately (Benjamin Franklin).

Epizeuxis:
Emphatic repetition of a word with no other words between:

Who lit cigarettes in boxcars boxcars boxcars racketing through snow toward lonesome farms in grandfather night (Allen Ginsberg, *Howl*)

The powerful and pleasurable technique of repetition is central to the very nature of poetry. So it is not surprising that poets over the centuries, and all over the world, have developed poetic forms, simple and elaborate, that structure and channel repeating patterns of poetic lines: forms like the African American blues, the Malaysian pantoum, the French villanelle, sestina, roundel, and triolet, the Italian canzone, and the Indian and Middle Eastern ghazal. To write a poem in one of these repeating forms requires, and helps develop, skills that are important to your writing of poetry generally. To make the repeating lines of a villanelle work effectively, for example, you will need to learn how to use restraint effectively, including the creation of suspense, the management of pacing, and great sensitivity to timing and context. You will also learn a kind of ingenuity: how to do a lot with a little, how to achieve effects with very few additional words, how to achieve subtle differences of tone through placement of the repeating words. And these kinds of skills are key to any poem.

We will now explore some of the best-known and most-loved of these repeating forms. As you learn to write these kinds of poems, keep in mind that though repeating structures can help make poems memorable, moving, and fun to read, there is a danger of monotony. To guard against this danger, keep three principles in mind when writing a repeating poem: 1. A line that will occur twice should be at least twice as good as a regular line. 2. Reading aloud as you revise (always, of course, but especially with repeating poems) will help ensure that you are building dramatic tension as the poem goes on. 3. Shifts in context can keep refrains fresh; usually, refrains work best when they have a different emotional connotation—or even a different meaning—each time they occur.

The Blues

The **blues poem,** a uniquely American poetic form, is based on the pattern of lyrics of blues songs that African American musicians developed in the South after the Civil War, drawing from West African work songs with a call-and-response pattern. For decades an oral tradition, the blues were popularized and recorded by musicians such as Robert Johnson and W. C. Handy in the early twentieth century. Ever since Countee Cullen and Langston Hughes wrote the first blues poems during the Harlem Renaissance, this classic song form has inspired African American poets, and more recently poets of other races.

Hughes's early "The Weary Blues" embeds actual blues lyrics into a different stanza structure:

"The Weary Blues," Langston Hughes (1923)

Droning a drowsy syncopated tune,
Rocking back and forth to a mellow croon,
I heard a Negro play.
Down on Lenox Avenue the other night
By the pale dull pallor of an old gas light
He did a lazy sway . . .
He did a lazy sway . . .
To the tune o' those Weary Blues.
With his ebony hands on each ivory key
He made that poor piano moan with melody.
O Blues!
Swaying to and fro on his rickety stool
He played that sad raggy tune like a musical fool.
Sweet Blues!
Coming from a black man's soul.
O Blues!
In a deep song voice with a melancholy tone
I heard that Negro sing, that old piano moan—
"Ain't got nobody in all this world,
Ain't got nobody but ma self.
I's gwine to quit ma frownin'
And put ma troubles on the shelf."
Thump, thump, thump, went his foot on the floor.
He played a few chords then he sang some more—
"I got the Weary Blues
And I can't be satisfied.
Got the Weary Blues
And can't be satisfied—
I ain't happy no mo'
And I wish that I had died."
And far into the night he crooned that tune.
The stars went out and so did the moon.

The singer stopped playing and went to bed
While the Weary Blues echoed through his head.
He slept like a rock or a man that's dead.

The simplicity of the poem's structure creates a dignified, archaic setting for the deep traditions it evokes, and for the ambiguity of the emotions at the end. Later poets began the tradition of copying the actual structure of blues lyrics. The blues traditionally sing of problems, hardships, "the blues"—but these "literary" blues poems have sung the range of emotions from humor, such as Raymond Patterson's "Computer Blues," which includes the lines, "Hey, you blowed the fuse, / ain't no computer built /that can stand the blues" to righteous anger, as in Sanchez's poem "Song No. 2" below.

The structure of blues is simple. The first line is repeated, sometimes with a slight change, and the stanza ends with a rhyming third line. Since the repeating lines happen right after each other, it is a special challenge to make each line sound fresh, or freshly motivated. In Leadbelly's song "Good Morning Blues," the repetition adds suspense that increases the humor of the final line:

Good mornin' blues, blues, how do you do?
Good mornin' blues, blues, how do you do?
I'm doin' all right, good mornin', how are you?

Like many poems based on song forms, blues poems often complicate the original form by adding new subtleties appropriate to the page. Written blues can add new lines, change the repeating line, or take away the rhyme from the basic pattern.

The most important aspects of writing blues are to keep the imagery vivid, the language direct, and the emotion true. Singing as you go is probably a good idea; if you can't sing it, maybe you don't feel it. Here is Sonia Sanchez's "Song No. 2":

i say. all you young girls waiting to live
i say. I say i say all you young girls waiting to live
i say. all you sisters takin yo pill
i say. all you sisters thinkin you won't, but you will

don't let them kill you with their stare
don't let them closet you with no air
don't let them feed you sex piece-meal
don't let them offer you any old deal.

i say. step back sisters. We're rising from the dead
i say. step back johnnies. we're dancing on our heads
i say. step back man. no mo hangin by a thread
i say. step back world. can't let it all go unsaid.

i say. all you young girls molested at ten
i say. all you young girls giving it up again and again
i say. all you sisters hanging out in every den
i say. all you sisters needing your own oxygen.

don't let them trap you with your coke
don't let them treat you like one fat joke
don't let them bleed you till you broke
don't let them blind you in masculine smoke.

i say. step back sisters. we're rising from the dead
i say. step back johnnies. we're dancing on our heads
i say. step back man. no mo hanging by a thread.
i say. step back world. can't let it all go unsaid.

When writing a poem in blues form, it's important to listen for the differences between your repeating lines, and to bear in mind the emotional weight of the blues tradition. Once when I asked Sanchez to talk about the blues, she made a remark that shows how much the blues is a physically felt poetic form for her: "When I have been expansive and sassy and wanted to flaunt it and to come off the edge of the paper, I have dealt with the blues, sung the blues, lived the blues, tasted the blues—I have made the blues, I've been the blues."

The blues form is so versatile that it has influenced much contemporary poetry and is beginning to develop its own characteristic variations. This blues poem by Natasha Tretheway combines the blues with the couplet of a sonnet at the end:

"Graveyard Blues," Natasha Trethewey

It rained the whole time we were laying her down;
Rained from church to grave when we put her down.
The suck of mud at our feet was a hollow sound.

When the preacher called out I held up my hand;
When he called for a witness I raised my hand—
Death stops the body's work; the soul's a journeyman.

The sun came out when I turned to walk away,
Glared down on me as I turned and walked away—
My back to my mother, leaving her where she lay.

The road going home was pocked with holes,
The home-going road's always full of holes;
Though we slow down, time's wheel still rolls.

I wander now among names of the dead:
My mother's name, stone pillow for my head.

As A. E. Stallings points out about this poem, "The concluding couplet thus does double duty, for it is at the same time a blues tercet missing its final line; the poem ends in an absence, in inconsolable silence."

The Villanelle

Like the blues, the **villanelle** is based on a pattern of repeating lines, and like the blues, it was invented to be heard. This captivating form is based on a traditional dance and accompanying song sung by farmworkers (the name comes from the Italian word *villano,* meaning peasant). In the sixteenth century the villanelle stanza arrived in France, where it was used for poems of any length. Later, English poets standardized the 19-line version that is familiar to us today.

A good villanelle is like a good romantic relationship. It is structured by two lines that are dying to get together; there is a period of suspense before they do get together; and in the meantime, a changing context provides a series of new discoveries about the lines each time they appear. Good villanelles in English are rare, but they are worth the effort because, when they work, they are unforgettable.

The form of a villanelle keeps the two repeating lines close but apart through seven stanzas of mounting tension until, in the last two lines of the poem, they join. The key to a good villanelle is to come up with two lines that are genuinely attracted to each other but also completely independent of each other, so that their final coupling will feel both inevitable and surprising:

I wake to sleep, and take my waking slow.
I learn by going where I have to go
—FROM "THE WAKING," Theodore Roethke (1953)

Or,

Do not go gentle into that good night.
Rage, rage against the dying of the light.
—FROM "DO NOT GO GENTLE INTO THAT GOOD NIGHT," Dylan Thomas (1951)

Or,

the art of losing is not too hard to master,
though it may look like (*Write* it!) like disaster
—FROM "ONE ART," Elizabeth Bishop (1976)

Here is the way this particular magic happens: a villanelle is built of five stanzas of three lines each and a sixth, four-line stanza. The first and third lines of the first stanza take turns being repeated as the last lines of the other three-line stanzas. It's like making a braid with three strands: you alternate one line from the top, one line from the bottom, until you have used them each three times, and then you end with both of them together.

Every line ends in one of two rhyme sounds, which are marked a and b in the poem below. As discussed in the rhyme chapter, the standard way to show repeating lines in a rhymed poem is to capitalize the letters and number them. In the poem below, A1 and A2 are the two repeating lines. It's more complicated to describe than it is to show, so take a look at the poem below. Successful villanelles often deal, as does this one, with obsessive or haunting subject matter:

"The House on the Hill," Edwin Arlington Robinson (1894)

They are all gone away,	A1
The House is shut and still,	b
There is nothing more to say.	A2
Through broken walls and gray	a
The winds blow bleak and shrill:	b
They are all gone away.	A1
Nor is there one to-day	a
To speak them good or ill:	b
There is nothing more to say.	A2
Why is it then we stray	a
Around the sunken sill?	b
They are all gone away,	A1
And our poor fancy-play	a
For them is wasted skill:	b
There is nothing more to say.	A2
There is ruin and decay	a
In the House on the Hill:	b
They are all gone away,	A1
There is nothing more to say.	A2

Don't forget to make sure that all the middle lines rhyme with each other. It's easy to overlook this step in the excitement of figuring out how to make your repeating lines (the technical term is **repetends**) sound natural.

Though Robinson's villanelle is very successful at using end-stopped lines (sentences that end with the end of the line), many of the best villanelles use enjambment to incorporate the repetends in a more natural-sounding way:

"Milk the Mouse," Michael Ryan

He'll pinch my pinky until the mouse starts squeaking.
The floor lamp casts a halo around his big, stuffed chair.
Be strong Be tough! It is my father speaking.

I'm four or five. Was he already drinking?
With its tip and knuckle between his thumb and finger,
he'll pinch my pinky until the mouse starts squeaking

Stop, Daddy, stop (it was more like screeching)
and kneels down before him on the hardwood floor.
Be strong Be tough! It is my father speaking.
What happened to him that he'd do such a thing?
It's only a game, he's doing me a favor
to pinch my pinky until the mouse starts squeaking

because the world will run over a weakling
and we must crush the mouse or be crushed later.
Be strong Be tough! It is my father speaking.

To himself, of course, to the boy inside him weeping,
not to me. But how can I not go when he calls me over
to pinch my pinky until the mouse starts squeaking
Be strong Be tough? It is my father speaking.

Though Ryan alters punctuation and changes the meaning of the repeating lines significantly through context, the discomfiting strength of this villanelle is enhanced by the exactness with which he repeats the actual words of those lines. As with all repeating poetic forms, how much liberty to take with the form is purely a matter of personal style. This famous villanelle takes some liberties:

"One Art," Elizabeth Bishop (1976)

The art of losing isn't hard to master;
so many things seem filled with the intent
to be lost that their loss is no disaster.

Lose something every day. Accept the fluster
of lost door keys, the hour badly spent.
The art of losing isn't hard to master.

Then practice losing farther, losing faster:
places, and names, and where it was you meant
to travel. None of these will bring disaster.

I lost my mother's watch. And look! my last, or
next-to-last, of three loved houses went.
The art of losing isn't hard to master.

I lost two cities, lovely ones. And, vaster,
some realms I owned, two rivers, a continent.
I miss them, but it wasn't a disaster.

—Even losing you (the joking voice, a gesture
I love) I shan't have lied. It's evident
the art of losing's not too hard to master
though it may look like (*Write* it!) like disaster.

With characteristic ingenuity, Bishop chooses to alter the line about "disaster" quite a bit but to keep the other line almost unchanged, like a sort of anchor that makes the changes to the other line more unnerving by contrast. This strategy goes well with the restrained and somewhat ironic tone of her villanelle. At the other end of the spectrum is an equally famous villanelle that uses the form without any changes at all, this time in order to create a rhapsodic sense of certainty.

"Do Not Go Gentle into That Good Night," Dylan Thomas (1951)

Do not go gentle into that good night,
Old age should burn and rave at close of day;
Rage, rage against the dying of the light.

Though wise men at their end know dark is right,
Because their words had forked no lightning they
Do not go gentle into that good night.

Good men, the last wave by, crying how bright
Their frail deeds might have danced in a green bay,
Rage, rage against the dying of the light.

Wild men who caught and sang the sun in flight,
And learn, too late, they grieved it on its way,
Do not go gentle into that good night.

Grave men, near death, who see with blinding sight
Blind eyes could blaze like meteors and be gay,
Rage, rage against the dying of the light.

And you, my father, there on the sad height,
Curse, bless, me now with your fierce tears, I pray.
Do not go gentle into that good night.
Rage, rage against the dying of the light.

Written when Thomas's father was dying, this poem seems to hold on to the exactness of the form as a way of both resisting the knowledge of change and marshaling more energy to address it.

Generally speaking, the lines may have greater impact if they are repeated without changing, and one change can have great impact (as does the change in the last line of "One Art") if it is the only big change in the poem. To have the most options and the most potential power in your villanelle, my advice is to do your best to write your villanelle perfectly with no changes to the repeating lines, and then change them later if you think it will improve the poem. That way, if you decide to vary the repetends, you'll be confident you are doing it for the good of your poem rather than out of laziness.

While the villanelle form has not been changed and varied as much as the sonnet—probably because it hasn't been around in English nearly as long—there are still plenty of examples of creative variations on the form. Here is one with very short lines:

"Contagion," Mendi Obadike

Hearing her cry
from the hallway,

I don't know why

another eye
opens in me.
Hearing her cry—

selfishly, I
try to close it.
I don't know why.

Something inside
burns and chokes my
hearing. Her cry.

I break and hide
from everything.
I don't know. Why?

I don't know why
I can't stomach
hearing her cry.
I don't know why.

While Obadike has omitted the rhyming of the middle lines in each stanza and used vowel rhyme for some of the first lines, she employs the repetends very strictly, with no variations at all except in punctuation. This combination works well with such short lines; to follow the entire rhyme scheme exactly in such a small space might have been overwhelming, but the exact repetition of the repetends carries a sense of the full rigor of the form.

The Sestina and Canzone

The **sestina** and **canzone** were invented by the troubadours, under the poetic influence of Persian (Iranian) poetry by way of Spain. In fact, the sestina, **ballade, kyrielle, rondeau,** canzone, and **triolet** are just a few among the hundreds of poetic forms invented by the troubadours, those ingenious poets of certain regions of France in the twelfth and thirteenth centuries. Both men and women were troubadours, and their main subject was love; these poets felt it was an insult to one's beloved not to invent a brand-new poetic form for your love poem.

The sestina, like the villanelle, has the virtue of a certain simplicity, which may explain why these two forms have become especially popular in English-language verse. A sestina repeats end-words (sometimes called **teleutons,** from the Greek word *telos,* meaning end), not entire lines. It consists of six six-line stanzas and a three-line stanza. The six stanzas repeat the same end-words in a set pattern. The pattern may look confusing at first, but you make the same motions each time as you move from one stanza to the next: like braiding hair, you take the outside strands first, first the bottom and then the top, using the previous stanza's last word, first word, next to last word, second word, and so on in that order until all six words have been used. If you do this, you will end up with this pattern (keeping the original stanza's number for each word): first stanza 123456, second stanza 615243, third 364125, fourth 532614, fifth 451362, sixth 246531. For closure, there is a three-line stanza (called an *envoi* or *tornada*) that includes all six words: 5, 3, 1 as end words, and 2, 4, 6 in the beginnings or middles of the lines. (The double sestina does the same thing over again with the same six words, for a total of 12 six-line stanzas and an envoi.)

Poets began to use the sestina in English during the Renaissance, generally as something of a curiosity. Here are two stanzas of Sidney's double sestina, a conversation about unrequited love between two shepherd-boys:

From "Ye Gote-heard Gods," Sir Philip Sidney (1590)

Strephon:
You Gote-heard Gods, that loue the grassie mountaines,
You Nimphes that haunt the springs in pleasant vallies,
You Satyrs ioyde with free and quiet forests,
Vouchsafe your silent eares to playning musique,
Which to my woes giues still an early morning;
And drawes the dolor on till wery euening.

Klaius:
Mercurie, foregoer to the euening,
heauenlie huntresse of the sauage mountaines,
louelie starre, entitled of the morning,

While that my voice doth fill these wofull vallies,
Vouchsafe your silent eares to plaining musique,
Which oft hath Echo tir'd in secrete forrests . . .

The rhythm of the end-stopped lines, the chorus of different shepherds' voices, and the mythological theme lend a charming and unique ritualistic effect to this poem, establishing an evocative ancestry for the sestina in English.

Though structurally rather easy to write (and thus one of the most common formal poetry assignments in beginning poetry workshops), the sestina is difficult to write successfully. It tends to sag in the middle, so it can be helpful to consider planting a deliberate surprise there. And of course, the end words are crucial. As poet Jim Cummins has remarked, "Two teleutons die, and the air goes out of the ball; the game is over." It can make a sestina more lively to use one or two words that can take on multiple meanings or act as different parts of speech, as with the word "long" in the following sestina, but don't overdo this tactic or your readers will get dizzy.

From "Sestina of the Tramp-Royal," Rudyard Kipling (1896)

But, Gawd, what things are they I 'aven't done?
I've turned my 'and to most, an' turned it good,
In various situations round the world
For 'im that doth not work must surely die;
But that's no reason man should labour all
'Is life on one same shift—life's none so long.

Therefore, from job to job I've moved along.
Pay couldn't 'old me when my time was done,
For something in my 'ead upset it all,
Till I 'ad dropped whatever 'twas for good,
An', out at sea, be'eld the dock-lights die,
An' met my mate—the wind that tramps the world!

It's like a book, I think, this bloomin' world,
Which you can read and care for just so long,
But presently you feel that you will die
Unless you get the page you're readi'n' done,

An' turn another—likely not so good;
But what you're after is to turn 'em all.

There is nothing quite like the feeling of inhabiting the world of a sestina, where the end-words you created yourself become so familiar that they begin to feel oddly natural each time you encounter them again. Ezra Pound evoked this strange energy when he called the sestina "a thin sheet of flame folding and infolding upon itself." Pound's "Sestina: Altaforte" was one of the first powerful modern examples of the form, and it was only with the twentieth century's tolerance for strangeness and defamiliarization that the sestina really began to come into its own and establish a tradition among poets in English. The repetition in a sestina such as Elizabeth Bishop's famous "Sestina," which uses the teleutons "house," "grandmother," "child," "stove," "almanac," and "tears," can lead a reader into a dream world of compulsions and inevitabilities:

"Sestina," Elizabeth Bishop (1965)

September rain falls on the house.
In the failing light, the old grandmother
sits in the kitchen with the child
beside the Little Marvel Stove,
reading the jokes from the almanac,
laughing and talking to hide her tears.

She thinks that her equinoctial tears
and the rain that beats on the roof of the house
were both foretold by the almanac,
but only known to a grandmother.
The iron kettle sings on the stove.
She cuts some bread and says to the child,

It's time for tea now; but the child
is watching the teakettle's small hard tears
dance like mad on the hot black stove,
the way the rain must dance on the house.
Tidying up, the old grandmother
hangs up the clever almanac

on its string. Birdlike, the almanac
hovers half open above the child,
hovers above the old grandmother
and her teacup full of dark brown tears.
She shivers and says she thinks the house
feels chilly, and puts more wood in the stove.

It was to be, says the Marvel Stove.
I know what I know, says the almanac.
With crayons the child draws a rigid house
and a winding pathway. Then the child
puts in a man with buttons like tears
and shows it proudly to the grandmother.

But secretly, while the grandmother
busies herself about the stove,
the little moons fall down like tears
from between the pages of the almanac
into the flower bed the child
has carefully placed in the front of the house.

Time to plant tears, says the almanac.
The grandmother sings to the marvelous stove
and the child draws another inscrutable house.

Bishop's sestina is something of a tour de force; she forgoes the usual tricks of making a word "go farther" by using it in several senses, and she also violates the typical rule of varying parts of speech in the teleutons. They are all nouns, and yet the poem maintains interest and energy.

In a letter to Marianne Moore about another of her sestinas, "A Miracle for Breakfast," Bishop wrote an observation about the issue of end words: "It seems to me that there are two ways possible for a sestina—one is to use unusual words as a termination, in which case they would have to be used differently as often as possible. . . .That would make a very highly seasoned kind of poem. And the other way is to use as colorless words as possible—like Sydney [Sir Philip Sidney], so that it becomes less of a trick and more of a natural theme and variations. I guess I have tried to do both at once."

Another significant twentieth-century sestina uses the self-contained world of the form to cast a different kind of spell, an agonized and reverent response to the Holocaust. Serving in the army in World War II, Anthony Hecht helped liberate a concentration camp, about which he has written, "the place, the suffering, the prisoners' accounts were beyond comprehension. For years afterward I would wake up shrieking." This poem is about a child killed by the Nazis:

"The Book of Yolek," Anthony Hecht

Wir Haben ein Gesetz,
*Und nach dem Gesetz soll er sterben.**

The dowsed coals fume and hiss after your meal
Of grilled brook trout, and you saunter off for a walk
Down the fern trail. It doesn't matter where to,
Just so you're weeks and worlds away from home,
And among midsummer hills have set up camp
In the deep bronze glories of declining day.

You remember, peacefully, an earlier day
In childhood, remember a quite specific meal:
A corn roast and bonfire in summer camp.
That summer you got lost on a Nature Walk;
More than you dared admit, you thought of home:
No one else knows where the mind wanders to.

The fifth of August, 1942.
It was the morning and very hot. It was the day
They came at dawn with rifles to The Home
For Jewish Children, cutting short the meal
Of bread and soup, lining them up to walk
In close formation off to a special camp.

How often you have thought about that camp,
As though in some strange way you were driven to,
And about the children, and how they were made to walk,
Yolek who had bad lungs, who wasn't a day

Over five years old, commanded to leave his meal
And shamble between armed guards to his long home.

We're approaching August again. It will drive home
The regulation torments of that camp
Yolek was sent to, his small, unfinished meal,
The electric fences, the numeral tattoo,
The quite extraordinary heat of the day
They all were forced to take that terrible walk.

Whether on a silent, solitary walk
Or among crowds, far off or safe at home,
You will remember, helplessly, that day,
And the smell of smoke, and the loudspeakers of the camp.
Wherever you are, Yolek will be there, too.
His unuttered name will interrupt your meal.

Prepare to receive him in your home some day.
Though they killed him in the camp they sent him to,
He will walk in as you're sitting down to a meal.

* We have a law, and according to the law he must die.

The forgotten child, abominably killed, is forever memorialized in these stanzas, even if you don't notice the special secret the poem holds. Jeff Balch has recently pointed out that "The Book of Yolek" contains a hidden acrostic, in the style of Jewish liturgical poems of remembrance. Look at the last letters of each of the teleutons. P implies the letter *peh,* which appears in the upper right corner of traditional Jewish gravestones and stands for the word meaning "here."

If Bishop's and Hecht's poems take advantage of the strangeness a sestina can impart, the following poem revels in its potential for realism. The poet zeroes in on the biggest challenge of the form, the repeating of the same words through the potentially sagging middle, and turns it to her dramatic advantage:

"Untoward Occurrence at an Embassy Poetry Reading," Marilyn Hacker

Thank you. Thank you very much. I'm pleased
to be here tonight. I seldom read

to such a varied audience. My poetry
is what it is. Graves, yes, said love, death
and the changing of the seasons
were the unique, the primordial subjects.

I'd like to talk about that. One subjects
oneself to art, not necessarily pleased
to be a colander for myths. It seasons
one to certain subjects. Not all. You can read
or formulate philosophies; your death
is still the kernel of your dawn sweats. Poetry

is interesting to people who write poetry.
Others are involved with other subjects.
Does the Ambassador consider death
on the same scale as you, Corporal? Please
stay seated. I've outreached myself. I read
your discomfort. But tonight the seasons

change. I've watched you, in town for the season,
nod to each other, nod to poetry
represented by me, and my colleagues, who read
to good assemblies; good citizens, good subjects
for gossip. You're the audience. Am I pleased
to frighten you? Yes and no. It scares me to death

to stand up here and talk about real death
while our green guerrillas hurry up the seasons.
They have disarmed the guards by now, I'm pleased
to say. The doors are locked. Great poetry
is not so histrionic, but our subjects
choose us, not otherwise. I will not read

manifestos. Tomorrow, foreigners will read
rumors in newspapers. . . . Oh, sir, your death
would be a tiresome journalistic subject,
so stay still till we're done. This is our season.

The building is surrounded. No more poetry
tonight. We are discussing, you'll be pleased

to know, the terms of your release. Please read
these leaflets. Not poetry. You're bored to death
with politics but that's the season's subject.

Because of the predictability of the end words, the sestina can lend itself well to humor. John Ashbery's "Farm Implements and Rutabagas in a Landscape" presents a surreal picnic where Popeye, Bluto, Wimpy, and Olive Oyl trade non sequiturs in a bizarre setting. Oulipo poet Harry Mathews's "Histoire" treats the teleutons as a kind of ad lib game, forcing terms like "fascism," "sexism," "racism" and "Marxism" to act as food items, places, and parts of the body with very amusing results. Even Bishop's "Sestina" has a whimsical quality.

Generally, you will have the most success with a sestina if you choose at least half concrete nouns; in most poems, abstract words can get extremely dull when they are repeated so often. Earle Birney's sestina based on the words "isthmus," "iguanas," "earthquake," "women," "hotsprings," and "Diaz" is quite a mouthful. Of course, words that are extremely interesting can call a lot of attention to themselves when they are repeated so often. As for the common question of whether it's legitimate to change the end-words by pluralizing or other small alterations: whether to do so is, as we have seen, a matter of personal style. As with the villanelle, my advice would be to stay as close to the pattern as possible before deciding to make any change. The best alterations are the result of aesthetic choice, not evidence of the lack of patience to follow the pattern exactly!

The following sestina is from a young adult novel by Helen Frost, written entirely in sestinas and sonnets:

"my choice . . . KATIE," Helen Frost

I sleep in my sleeping bag in a room
with a lock in the basement of the place
on Jackson Street. And I feel safe.
If Keesha wants to talk to me, she knocks
first, and if I want to let her in, I do.
If I don't, I don't. It's my choice.

There's not too much I really have a choice
about. Mom would say I chose to leave my room
at home, but that's not something anyone would do
without a real good reason. There's no place
for me there since she got married. Like, one time, I knocked
her husband's trophy off his gun safe,

and he twisted my arm—hard. I never feel safe
when he's around. I finally asked my mom to make a choice:
him or me. She went, *Oh, Katie, he'll be fine.* Then she knocked
on our wooden table. I blew up. I stormed out of the room
and started thinking hard. In the first place,
I know he won't be *fine.* I didn't tell her what he tries to do

to me when she works late. In a way, I want to, but even if I do,
she won't believe me. She thinks we're safe
in that so-called nice neighborhood. *Finally, Katie, a place*
of our own. And since she took a vow, she thinks she has no choice
but to see her marriage through. No room
for me, no vow to protect *me* if he comes knocking

on my door late at night. He knocks
and then walks in when I don't answer. Or even when I do
answer: *Stay out! This is my room*
and you can't come in! I could never be safe
there, with him in the house. So, sure, I made a choice.
I left home and found my way to this place,

where I've been these past two weeks. And I found a place
to work, thirty hours a week. Today Mom knocked
on the door here. She wanted to talk. I told her, *You made your choice;*
I made mine. She wondered what she could do
to get me to come home. But when I said, *It's not safe*
for me as long as he's there, she left the room.

My choice is to be safe.
This room is dark and musty, but it's one place
I do know I can answer *no* when someone knocks.

The variations, such as "knock," "knocked," and "knocking," suit the informal tone of this poem; but so much variation would ruin the intense power of some other sestinas. Whatever you do, be consistent; if you are going to change one word in your sestina, it's best to change several, so it will look like a deliberate decision and not an oversight. If you are consistent, you can make just about any variation. I've even heard of a sestina that uses the repeating words at the beginnings of the lines instead of the end. Another modification is rhyme; here are two stanzas of a rhymed sestina:

From "Sestina," Algernon Charles Swinburne (1872)

Yet the soul woke not, sleeping by the way,
. . . Watched as a nursling of the large-eyed night,
And sought no strength nor knowledge of the day,
. . . Nor closer touch conclusive of delight,
Nor mightier joy nor truer than dreamers may,
. . . Nor more of song than they, nor more of light.

For who sleeps once and sees the secret light
. . . Whereby sleep shows the soul a fairer way
Between the rise and rest of day and night,
. . . Shall care no more to fare as all men may,
But be his place of pain or of delight,
. . . There shall he dwell, beholding night as day.

I will close with a few words about the canzone. This form is similar to the sestina, but almost twice as long, one reason it is rarely used. The five teleutons appear in this order (each line represents one 12-line stanza):

ABAACAADDAEE
EAEEBEECCEDD
DEDDADDBBDCC
CDCCECCAACCB
BCBBDBBEEBAA
ABCDE

Probably the most accomplished recent canzone in English is the following elegy:

"Lenox Hill," Agha Shahid Ali

(In Lenox Hill Hospital, after surgery, my mother said the sirens sounded like the elephants of Mihiragula when his men drove them off cliffs in the Pir Panjal Range.)

The Hun so loved the cry, one falling elephant's,
he wished to hear it again. At dawn, my mother
heard, in her hospital-dream of elephants,
sirens wail through Manhattan like elephants
forced off Pir Panjal's rock cliffs in Kashmir:
the soldiers, so ruled, had rushed the elephant,
The greatest of all footprints is the elephant's,
said the Buddha. But not lifted from the universe,
those prints vanished forever into the universe,
though nomads still break news of those elephants
as if it were just yesterday the air spread the dye
("War's annals will fade into night / Ere their story die"),

the punishing khaki whereby the world sees us die
out, mourning you, O massacred elephants!
Months later, in Amherst, she dreamt: She was, with diamonds, being stoned to death. I prayed: If she must die,
let it only be some dream. But there were times, Mother,
while you slept, that I prayed, "Saints, let her die."
Not, I swear to you, that I wished you to die
but to save you as you were, young, in song in Kashmir,
and I, one festival, crowned Krishna by you, Kashmir
listening to my flute. You never let gods die.
Thus I swear, here and now, not to forgive the universe
that would let me get used to a universe

without you. She, she alone, was the universe
as she earned, like a galaxy, her right not to die,
defying the Merciful of the Universe,
Master of Disease, "in the circle of her traverse"
of drug-bound time. And where was the god of elephants,

plump with Fate, when tusk to tusk, the universe,
dyed green, became ivory? Then let the universe,
like Paradise, be considered a tomb. Mother,
they asked me, So how's the writing? I answered My mother
is my poem. What did they expect? For no verse
sufficed except the promise, fading, of Kashmir
and the cries that reached you from the cliffs of Kashmir

(across fifteen centuries) in the hospital. Kashmir,
she's dying! How her breathing drowns out the universe
as she sleeps in Amherst. Windows open on Kashmir:
There, the fragile wood-shrines—so far away—of Kashmir!
O Destroyer, let her return there, if just to die.
Save the right she gave its earth to cover her, Kashmir
has no rights. When the windows close on Kashmir,
I see the blizzard-fall of ghost-elephants.
I hold back—she couldn't bear it—one elephant's
story: his return (in a country far from Kashmir)
to the jungle where each year, on the day his mother
died, he touches with his trunk the bones of his mother.

"As you sit here by me, you're just like my mother,"
she tells me. I imagine her: a bride in Kashmir,
she's watching, at the Regal, her first film with Father.
If only I could gather you in my arms, Mother,
I'd save you—now my daughter—from God. The universe
opens its ledger. I write: How helpless was God's mother!
Each page is turned to enter grief's accounts. Mother,
I see a hand. Tell me it's not God's. Let it die.
I see it. It's filling with diamonds. Please let it die.
Are you somewhere alive, Mother?
Do you hear what I once held back: in one elephant's
cry, by his mother's bones, the cries of those elephants

that stunned the abyss? Ivory blots out the elephants.
I enter this: The Belovéd leaves one behind to die.
For compared to my grief for you, what are those of Kashmir,

and what (I close the ledger) are griefs of the universe
when I remember you—beyond all accounting—O my mother?

The Rondeau, Triolet, Kyrielle, and Tritina

Three shorter forms that also use intense repetition are the rondeau, triolet, and **tritina.** Though the enterprising Sir Thomas Wyatt wrote several rondeaux during the Renaissance, the rondeau and triolet forms really gained their place in English in the late nineteenth century. The tritina was invented in the twentieth century by Marie Ponsot, perhaps as a version of the sestina. The rondeau may be the most versatile of the three, the triolet the most memorable, and the tritina the most haunting. The rondeau's 13 lines use only two rhymes plus a *rentrement* (a partial-line repetition, made of the first word or few words of line 1), in this pattern:

(R)a
a
b
b
a

a
a
b
R

a
a
b
b
a
R

When it was reintroduced centuries later, the rondeau was used mostly for very light verse, as is evident from this first stanza:

From "The Same Imitated," Austin Dobson (1877)

YOU bid me try, *blue-eyes*, to write
A Rondeau. What!—forthwith?—tonight?
Reflect. Some skill I have, 'tis true;
But thirteen lines!—and rimed on two!
"Refrain" as well. Ah, Hapless plight!

Like Hughes, whose "The Weary Blues" may be the first blues poem written in English, Dobson is extremely self-conscious about writing in a new form. This is common with any form new to a poet; you may have written a sonnet about writing a sonnet yourself, or seen a poem like this by a fellow poet new to a form. Twenty years after Dobson's version, the rondeau was so established that not only was it not necessary to be self-conscious; it was possible for Paul Laurence Dunbar to use the form in a dense, wry, agonized, and multilayered way in his signature poem:

"We Wear the Mask," Paul Laurence Dunbar (1896)

We wear the mask that grins and lies,
It hides our cheeks and shades our eyes—
This debt we pay to human guile;
With torn and bleeding hearts we smile
And mouth with myriad subtleties,

Why should the world be over-wise,
In counting all our tears and sighs?
Nay, let them only see us, while
We wear the mask.

We smile, but oh great Christ, our cries
To Thee from tortured souls arise.
We sing, but oh the clay is vile
Beneath our feet, and long the mile,
But let the world dream otherwise,
We wear the mask!

Dunbar is normally known for more lighthearted poems about the African American experience. As happens surprisingly often with poets, his most famous poem is uncharacteristic of his normal style. Perhaps the extreme constraints of the rondeau, by contrast with his usual looser and more popular ballad style, distracted and freed him to express a more painfully honest level of emotion.

This contemporary rondeau by the formally virtuosic Marilyn Hacker, embedded into a longer poem, also explores painful emotion:

From "Love, Death, and the Changing of the Seasons," Marilyn Hacker

Why did Ray leave her pipe tobacco here
in the fridge? Iva asks me while we're
rummaging for mustard and soy sauce
to mix with wine and baste the lamb. "Because
cold keeps it fresh." That isn't what she means,

we both know. I've explained, there were no scenes
or fights, really. We needed time to clear
the air, and think. What she was asking, was,
"Why did Ray leave

her stuff if she's not coming back?" She leans
to extremes, as I might well. String beans
to be sauteed with garlic, then I'll toss
the salad; then we'll eat (Like menopause
it comes in flashes, more or less severe:
why did you leave?)

In the rondeau redouble, repetitions haunt even more, with the form ABAB babA abaB babA' abaB' babaR (the capital letters indicate the repetition of whole lines, and R, the *rentrement,* does not have to rhyme with anything). The kyrielle, a simple form rhyming aabB so the last line of every stanza is a refrain, has been used for religious verses; Thomas Campion's refrain is "O God, be merciful to me."

Like the rondeau, the triolet lends itself well, though not exclusively, to light or semilight verse:

"Triolet," G. K. Chesterton

I wish I were a jelly fish
That cannot fall downstairs:
Of all the things I wish to wish
I wish I were a jelly fish
That hasn't any cares,
And doesn't even have to wish
"I wish I were a jelly fish
That cannot fall downstairs."

Here is one of the best-known recent triolets:

"Triolet on a Line Apocryphally Attributed to Martin Luther," A. E. Stallings

Why should the Devil get all the good tunes,
The booze and the neon and Saturday night,
The swaying in darkness, the lovers like spoons?
Why should the Devil get all the good tunes?
Does he hum them to while away sad afternoons
And the long, lonesome Sundays? Or sing them for spite?
Why should the Devil get all the good tunes,
The booze and the neon and Saturday night?

The amphibrachic swing of the meter, combined with the ironic tone and theme, create a bittersweet quality that brings out hidden depths in a form which has often been thought of as suited only for trifles.

A related, almost brand-new form is the tritina. Each of the tritina's three three-line stanzas ends with the same three words, but in a different order. The poem concludes with a line containing all the end words:

"Roundstone Cove," Marie Ponsot

The wind rises. The sea snarls in the fog
far from the attentive beaches of childhood—
no picnic, no striped chairs, no sand, no sun.

Here even by day cliffs obstruct the sun;
moonlight miles out mocks this abyss of fog.
I walk big-bellied, lost in motherhood,

hunched in a shell of coat, a blindered hood.
Alone a long time, I remember sun—
poor magic effort to undo the fog.

Fog hoods me. But the hood of fog is sun.

The Paradelle

The most amusing, and most recently invented, repeating form in the French tradition is the paradelle, which appeared in the 1980s when poet Billy Collins published a bizarre poem called "Paradelle for Susan" that began with this stanza:

I remember the quick, nervous bird of your love.
I remember the quick, nervous bird of your love.
Always perched on the highest, thinnest branch.
Always perched on the highest, thinnest branch.
Thinnest love, remember the quick branch.
Always nervous, I perched on your highest bird the.

Accompanying the poem was a footnote explaining that the paradelle was an obscure form invented by the medieval French troubadours, akin to the villanelle and sestina. Many people took this footnote as truth. However, when you look carefully at a paradelle, you realize that it is impossible that it could have been invented by the troubadours. The reason is that it's just about impossible to write a poem that makes sense in this form, and the troubadours always made sense. In fact, the paradelle is the perfect postmodern form, at once a historical parody and a challenge to engage in exploratory writing. The paradelle also seems to have been influenced by the blues, marking it as a distinctively American form and giving it an odd familiarity for all its strangeness. This fact may also account for its popularity, which has certainly surprised its inventor.

To write a paradelle, you write a line and repeat it; write another line and repeat it; and then end the stanza with two lines that include all the words from those two lines and no other words. You repeat this for three stanzas. The fourth stanza is the climax of the poem; it includes all the words from the entire poem and no other words.

It can seem impossible to do this and have the poem make (logical) sense. I couldn't imagine how anyone could approach the paradelle other than impressionistically until I encountered Henry Taylor's paradelle, which is the closest I've seen to one that does make sense. As I learned from him later, his secret was to write the last two lines of each stanza first:

"Paradelle: Nocturne de la Ville," Henry Taylor

Somewhat behind, rather than
After, Villiers de l'Isle-Adam

An empty chair inhabits a troubled dream.
An empty chair inhabits a troubled dream.
Hoisted to light from wells of unknown depth,
Hoisted to light from wells of unknown depth.
Hoisted from an unknown chair to dreams of light,
A troubled depth inhabits empty wells.

The lamp says he feels it's slow use his way.
The lamp says he feels it's slow use his way.
"Around the street here I'm no drunk prisoner.
Around the street here I'm no drunk prisoner."
The drunk feels his slow way around the street lamp.
"It's no use," he says. "I'm a prisoner here."

Leaves fall from trees, moths fly to city lights.
Leaves fall from trees, moths fly to city lights.
On thin ice skaters flash across the dark.
On thin ice skaters flash across the dark.
Ice leaves the city to flash on fall trees;
Thin skaters fly from moths across dark lights.

It's fall. The city around feels slow to light.
No thin trees fly, flash a chair from ice;
A hoisted lamp lights moths. Across the street
From here an empty drunk leaves skaters troubled;
His unknown prisoner inhabits depths of dream.
"I'm on the way to use dark wells," he says.

Now there is a whole anthology of paradelles available. It includes other examples of paradelles that do make sense, and that seem to have lost their self-consciousness about being a new form. It is interesting to consider whether the paradelle could ever become so established that it would no longer be considered to have a necessarily playful aspect.

The Ghazal

The **ghazal,** an ancient Arabic form from the seventh century, has been wildly popular in Persia, India, and elsewhere for centuries. Like the pantoum, the ghazal was radically simplified when it first came to America in the 1970s; the first contemporary American "ghazals" were simply poems in two-line free-verse stanzas. The most devoted practitioner of the form in this manifestation is Robert Bly, who has published three volumes of ghazals. Bly seems most interested in how the juxtapositions of the ghazal can urge us into spiritual and social awareness:

"Call and Answer," Robert Bly

Tell me why it is we don't lift our voices these days
And cry over what is happening. Have you noticed
The plans are made for Iraq and the ice cap is melting?

I say to myself: "Go on, cry. What's the sense
Of being an adult and having no voice? Cry out!
See who will answer! This is Call and Answer!"

We will have to call especially loud to reach
Our angels, who are hard of hearing; they are hiding
In the jugs of silence filled during our wars.

Have we agreed to so many wars that we can't
Escape from silence? If we don't lift our voices, we allow
Others (who are ourselves) to rob the house.

How come we've listened to the great criers—Neruda,
Akhmatova, Thoreau, Frederick Douglas—and now
We're silent as sparrows in the little bushes?

Some masters say our life lasts only seven days.
Where are we in the week? Is it Thursday yet?
Hurry, cry now! Soon Sunday night will come.

In recent years, the ghazal in English has developed a closer formal relation to its actual roots thanks to the work of the poet Agha Shahid Ali. During his tragically brief life, the delightful and charismatic Ali educated a generation of poets in the traditional requirements and beauties of the ghazal. As a result, we now know much more about the complexities of the form in its original incarnations.

The ghazal uses repetition in a daring and interactive way. Each stanza is a self-contained couplet. The second line of each stanza ends with a rhyme word (the *quafia*) followed by a repeating phrase (the *radif*). In Tamam Khan's "Ghazal About Marakesh," for example, two-line stanzas end with the phrases "hued in Marakesh," "allude in Marakesh," and "interlude in Marakesh." It is customary for a poet to embed their own name in the ghazal's last stanza.

Traditionally, and nowadays as well, the ghazal is sung by poets who have the status of rock stars, to an audience that chants back the refrain at the end of each stanza (the rhyme word is the clue that the refrain is coming). The subjects of the stanzas can range from philosophy to history to love to politics; each stanza can be completely self-contained in meaning, with only the form and the repeating words linking the stanzas together. The excitement and pleasure of the ghazal lies in the metaphysical capaciousness of the form and the poet's and reader's pleasure in its ingenuity and linguistic challenges.

Obviously, when you are writing a ghazal the choice of the radif will be your most important decision. The choice of the rhyme sound for the quafia is almost as important; be sure you choose a sound that has plenty of interesting rhymes, since you may be having so much fun you will find it hard to stop adding couplets to your ghazal, and you won't want to run out. I always remember Agha Shahid Ali's valuable piece of advice: use a rhyming dictionary to find very fresh, unusual rhyming words for the quafia.

"Ghazal of the Lagoon," John Drury

Morning, on the promenade, there's a break in the light
rain here in the serene republic. I take in the light.

Every walker gets lucky at this gaming table,
where the gondoliers, like croupiers, rake in the light.

Through the glare of a restaurant's window, I see
fish glinting, like spear points that shake in the light.

I could sit on the edge and get wet forever,
all to consider a speed boat's wake in the light.

Furnaces burn. We sweat until we shine, fired up
by the wavy vases glassblowers make in the light.

Row me out, friars, in your *sandolo* on the waves
that glitter like ducats, for God's sake, in the light.

The harshness of the repeating "-ake" sound gives Drury's poem additional interest, and perhaps adds to the impression of sharply shimmering water. The same sound has a very different feeling in another ghazal, where it acquires a melancholy, depressive force through being repeated exactly, a few syllables after the rhyming sound. Khalvati uses her name in the last couplet, as tradition dictates.

"Ghazal," Mimi Khalvati

When you wake to jitters every day, it's heartache.
Ignore it, explore it, either way, it's heartache.

Youth's a map you can never refold,
from Yokohama to Hudson Bay, it's heartache.

The moon in a swoon, you're in his arms,
the fandango starts, the palm trees sway, it's heartache.

Oh love, love, who are centuries old.
It's not time or absence I can't weigh, it's heartache.

Heartache with women, heartache with men.
Call myself straight or call myself gay, it's heartache.

Stop at the wayside, name each flower,
the loveliness that will always stay: it's heartache.

Wherever I am, I'm elsewhere too
in a cloud you'd think, but isn't, grey. It's heartache.

Why do nightingales sing in the dark?
What the eye can't see, the soul will say, it's heartache.

Who would dare to call their pain despair?
As long as faith holds true, men can pray, it's heartache.

Let the Sufi meaning of my name,
"a quiet retreat," heal as it may its heartache.

Pantoum

The **pantoum** form known in English is a simplified version of a traditional Malaysian form. Because of the ingenuity and profound simplicity of its structural principle—the same principle as leapfrog—the pantoum is perhaps one of the easiest repeating forms to write successfully in English. Like sewing, like weaving, like day and night, the pantoum gains power through repeated alternations: the first and third lines in the first stanza become the second and fourth lines in the next stanza, then the first and third lines of the second stanza become the second and fourth lines in the third stanza, and so on for as long as you want your poem to last. The last stanza usually repeats lines 1 and 3 of the first stanza but in reverse order, making a perfectly closed circle. Sometimes the stanzas can rhyme, as they do in the original Malaysian form and in Nellie Wong's "Grandmother's Pantoum" below, but they don't have to rhyme, and some poets even use the form with only end words repeated instead of entire lines.

Vince Gotera advises his poetry students to choose a subject for the pantoum that they feel obsessive about, so that the repetitions will seem more natural. He says, "The pantoum can give the poet a formula in which things can be said again and again credibly and plausibly. In addition, I am attracted to the pantoum because it is originally a Malay form; I am a Filipino American and thus part of a people descended from Malays. The pantoum, to me, is a way of coming home." One of Gotera's pantoums, "Chain Letter Pantoum," is on the obsessive subject of chain letters. Anne Waldman's "Baby's Pantoum" uses the form to show the diffuse, perpetually present-time perspective of a newborn. The form can create a dizzying spiral effect that lends itself to almost any lyrical, passionate theme; I've seen good pantoums about subjects from dancing to thunderstorms. On the other hand, in the words of poet Stephen Cramer, "If you're writing a pantoum and not paying strong enough attention to the line, you can feel like you're walking the wrong way on a conveyor belt."

At its best, like all repeating forms, the pantoum repeats lines in such a way that they sound new each time they occur. In "Grandmother's Song," for example, first the grandmothers are blinded by the sun's rays, then those looking at the bracelets and rings are blinded.

"Grandmother's Song," Nellie Wong

Grandmothers sing their song
Blinded by the sun's rays
Grandchildren for whom they long
For pomelo-golden days

Blinded by the sun's rays
Gold bracelets, opal rings
For pomelo-golden days
Tiny fingers, ancient things

Gold bracelets, opal rings
Sprinkled with Peking dust
Tiny fingers, ancient things
So young they'll never rust

Sprinkled with Peking dust
To dance in fields of mud
So young they'll never rust
Proud as if of royal blood

To dance in fields of mud
Or peel shrimp for pennies a day
Proud as if of royal blood
Coins and jade to put away

Or peel shrimp for pennies a day
Seaweed washes up the shore
Coins and jade to put away
A camphor chest is home no more

Seaweed washes up the shore
Bound feet struggle to loosen free
A camphor chest is home no more
A foreign tongue is learned at three

Bound feet struggle to loosen free
Grandchildren for whom they long
A foreign tongue is learned at three
Grandmothers sing their song

The cycling, recurring shape of the pantoum seems a perfect choice for this poem about the cycles of generations, the persistence of the present within the past, and the recurring pull of tradition on a child.

The pantoum is used in a very different and equally effective way in the following poem:

From "A Date With Robbe-Grillet," Elaine Equi

What I remember didn't happen.
Birds stuttering.
Torches huddled together.
The café empty, with no place to sit.

Birds stuttering.
On our ride in the country
the café empty, with no place to sit.
Your hair was like a doll's . . .

By using lines very similar to each other ("birds stuttering" and "birds strutted," for example), varying line-lengths, and striking a delicate balance of syntax and imagery between lulling coherence and jarring incoherence, Equi intensifies the disorienting quality of the pantoum's repetitions and creates a dreamworld where it's hard to see the forest for the trees. Her use of the pantoum is suited to a poem devoted to Robbe-Grillet, whose novels and films dissolve time and character with dreamlike and compelling repetitions.

The following pantoum uses the same disorienting quality to delve, through circumlocutions and repetition, into a painful subject.

"The Mountain Is Holding Out," Paul Muldoon

The mountain is holding out
for news from the sea
and the raid on the redoubt.
The plain won't level with me

for news from the sea
is harder and harder to find.
The plain won't level with me
now it's non-aligned

and harder and harder to find.
The forest won't fill me in
now it, too, is non-aligned
and its patience wearing thin.

The forest won't fill me in
nor the lake confess
to its patience wearing thin.
I'd no more try to second guess

why the lake would confess

to its regard for its own sheen,
no more try to second guess
why the river won't come clean

on its regard for its own sheen
than why you and I've faced off across a ditch.
For the river not coming clean
is only one of the issues on which

you and I've faced off across a ditch
and the raid on the redoubt
only one of the issues on which
the mountain is holding out.

By reserving the crucial mention of "you and I" until late in the poem, the poem creates the effect of holding out. As the repeating phrases circle around to the beginning again just after this moment, the frustrating sense of defensiveness is complete, self-enclosed like the small military fortification known as a "redoubt."

Refrain in Free Verse and Form

Like the chorus of a song, a **refrain** links together different parts of a poem by repeating the same words over and over between them. Refrains are part of the structure of many poetic forms, including the rondeau, ballade, and triolet, and some ballads. But refrains can be added to any poem, to bring in beauty and variety and a kind of resonance. This is as true of poems in free verse as of poems in meter. Lucia Trent's "Breed, Women, Breed" uses a regular refrain at the beginning of each free verse stanza:

"Breed, Women, Breed," Lucia Trent (1929)

Breed, little mothers,
With tired backs and tired hands,
Breed for the owners of mills and the owners of mines,
Breed a race of danger-haunted men,
A race of toiling, sweating, miserable men,

Breed, little mothers,
Breed for the owners of mills and the owners of mines,
Breed, breed, breed!

Breed, little mothers,
With the sunken eyes and the sagging cheeks,
Breed for the bankers, the crafty and terrible masters of men,
Breed a race of machines,
A race of anemic, round-shouldered, subway-herded machines!

Breed, little mothers,
With a faith patient and stupid as cattle,
Breed for the war lords,
Offer your woman flesh for incredible torment,
Wrack your frail bodies with the pangs of birth
For the war lords who slaughter your sons!

Breed, little mothers,
Breed for the owners of mills and the owners of mines,
Breed for the bankers, the crafty and terrible masters of men,
Breed for the war lords, the devouring war lords,
Breed, women, breed!

Jane Kenyon's best-known poem, "Otherwise," uses a more irregular refrain, the phrase "It might have been otherwise," repeated after various sentences describing her activities during one day. The refrain gives a dignity and importance to the mundane activities she describes:

"Otherwise," Jane Kenyon

I got out of bed
on two strong legs.
It might have been
otherwise. I ate
cereal, sweet
milk, ripe, flawless
peach. It might

have been otherwise.
I took the dog uphill
to the birch wood.
All morning I did
the work I love.

At noon I lay down
with my mate. It might
have been otherwise.
We ate dinner together
at a table with silver
candlesticks. It might
have been otherwise.
I slept in a bed
in a room with paintings
on the walls, and
planned another day
just like this day.
But one day, I know,
it will be otherwise.

Refrains in free verse, as in the Trent and Kenyon poems, often tie together a variety of aspects of the poem. In formal verse, on the other hand, a refrain can add a paradoxical element of difference. This can be most evident in a poem in strict form, where the content is controlled:

From "A Boy's Will," Henry Wadsworth Longfellow (1858)

Often I think of the beautiful town
That is seated by the sea;
Often in thought go up and down
The pleasant streets of that dear old town,
And my youth comes back to me.
And a verse of a Lapland song
Is haunting my memory still:
"A boy's will is the wind's will,
And the thoughts of youth are long, long thoughts."

I can see the shadowy lines of its trees,
And catch, in sudden gleams,
The sheen of the far-surrounding seas,
And islands that were the Hesperides
Of all my boyish dreams.
And the burden of that old song,
It murmurs and whispers still:
"A boy's will is the wind's will,
And the thoughts of youth are long, long thoughts."

I remember the black wharves and the ships,
And the sea-tides tossing free;
And Spanish sailors with bearded lips,
And the beauty and mystery of the ships,
And the magic of the sea.
And the voice of that wayward song
Is singing and saying still:
"A boy's will is the wind's will,
And the thoughts of youth are long, long thoughts."

I remember the bulwarks by the shore,
And the fort upon the hill;
The sunrise gun, with its hollow roar,
The drum-beat repeated o'er and o'er,
And the bugle wild and shrill.
And the music of that old song
Throbs in my memory still:
"A boy's will is the wind's will,
And the thoughts of youth are long, long thoughts."

I remember the sea-fight far away,
How it thundered o'er the tide!
And the dead captains, as they lay
In their graves, o'erlooking the tranquil bay
Where they in battle died.
And the sound of that mournful song
Goes through me with a thrill:

"A boy's will is the wind's will,
And the thoughts of youth are long, long thoughts" . . .

I once read this poem to an audience, at Longfellow's two-hundredth birthday party in the museum that was his childhood home. Since it is a poem of 10 stanzas with a long refrain, I was anxious the refrain might be tedious for the listeners, but that was not at all the case; in every stanza, the refrain conveyed a different mood and called for a different kind of delivery. If you try reading this excerpt from it aloud, you may have the same experience. Edgar Allen Poe, in his discussion of the composition of "The Raven" in the questions at the end of this chapter, that the same refrain, if skillfully handled, can have many different meanings in different contexts.

Sometimes the words of a refrain are varied for a specific effect. For example, Thom Gunn's "Carnal Knowledge," a poem about making love with a woman even though they both know he is gay, ends every stanza until the last one with the alternating refrains, "I know you know I know you know I know" and "You know I know you know I know you know." In the last of the six stanzas, as the speaker grows impatient with the pretense and tells the woman to leave, the refrain sheds its layers of complexity, and the last stanza ends simply, "I know you know." The change is effective precisely because of the conscientiousness with which the refrains have been repeated up until that point.

QUESTIONS FOR MEDITATION OR DISCUSSION

How do you feel about the kinds of extreme constraints that the forms introduced in this chapter impose on a poem? How do they change the experience of writing a poem at each stage: inspiration, initial writing, revision, completion? Are there certain themes that feel right to address in repeating forms?

One of the most common points made by the 60 contributors to the anthology *A Formal Feeling Comes: Poems in Form by Contemporary Women*, including Judith Barrington and Honor Moore, whose remarks are excerpted below, was that strict form helped them express painful feelings and describe painful experiences they had not been able to address before in poetry. Does this surprise you? Have other kinds of formal shapes (besides the poetic) ever been helpful to you after painful experiences?

What have the poems in this chapter gained by the use of repetition? What have they lost?

It is a truism that subtlety is the key to using a repeating form successfully. The following poem, a tour-de-force written by the anagrammatic alter ego of form guru Lewis Turco, takes on this assumption head-on:

"Sestina," Wesli Court

It drives you crazy to write a sestina.
First off, in order to write a sestina
you need six end-words that don't shout, "Sestina!"
One should hide the fact that it's a sestina
you're writing. I mean, why holler "Sestina!"
if you don't have to? Why give the sestina

game away right away? For a sestina
needs to be a subtle thing. A sestina
should lead readers away from the sestina,
make them think, "This is no kind of sestina,
it's a sixteener, maybe, no sestina
sustaining itself on sestets. Sestina

indeed! I don't believe it. A sestina
doesn't announce itself, "I'm a sestina,
no less! I live on end-words, a sestina
to end sestinas! I'm a sustainer
of sounds, echoes of a choral Sistiner
bouncing off Michaelangelo sixteen or

so ways from Rome to Nome." A fine sestina
that would be. Thirty-nine lines of sestina
mumbling into the reader's ear, "Sestina,
sestina, sestina." Who could sustain a
poem like that for so long? A sestina
ought perhaps to read more like a sonetto

rispetto than like what it is. Sestina
end-words are *teleutons,* and a sestina
should tell you tons about what a sestina
is all about. Certainly, a sestina
is about disguise, subtlety, sestina
reticence, reluctance to be sestina-

like. Rather, it ought to be a soul-stainer,
nuanced, a mind-mellower. A sestina
ought not to be the thing, just the sustainer
of thingness in the memory. Sestina
is teleutonals, not end-words. Sestina
is an earful of sense, not a sestina

ending in a coda that says *sestina,*
repeating end-words, *sestina, sestina,*
sestina, and a final time, *sestina!*

What is the serious point of this poem? Do you find it convincing?

Assuming you've written at least one of the forms covered in this chapter, how was the experience different for you than writing other kinds of poems in free verse or form? How did you approach the challenge of creating a sense of movement or plot? How different do your repeating lines or phrases feel from each other? Do you feel that the poem is still in your own "voice" or does the form seem to have taken over?

QUOTES

It was only after the University, when I started reading traditional narratives and listening to oral technique, that it began to click in my mind that I had been doing the same thing unconsciously and that other Native writers had been doing it too. . . . It has given my work more validity, to know that I am using an ancient technique. But I try not to overdo it. I use repetition just enough to create a nice tension. The skill comes in recognizing when not to overdo it.

—Lenore Keeshig-Tobias

I make reference to Keats, Donne, and Shakespeare every time I write a sonnet, but the blues is a homegrown form with a rich history that is equally alive to me. If I bow to Keats and Wang Wei, I must also bow to Langston Hughes. To be true to the selves that I am, I must keep my muse versatile and diverse.

—Marilyn Chin

One of the striking things about the blues tradition is the way the instrument becomes that other, alternative voice . . . the realm of conventionally articulate speech is not sufficient for saying what needs to be said. We are often making that same assertion in poetry.

—Nathaniel Mackey

[The sestina's] restraint became the walls of the room, the recurrence of end words a verbal equivalent for the relentlessness of the molester's intentions. Embraced in its sure architecture, the violated child, silent for thirty years, is free to tell her story.

—Honor Moore

A few years ago, I wrote a sequence of six villanelles dealing with my mother's death by drowning. I do not think I could have written that particular piece without a strict form . . . I also think that the villanelle itself was important to the subject—I couldn't have used just any tight form. I had always thought that the shape of the villanelle, with its repeating lines that come together at the end, suggested both tides and circles.

—Judith Barrington

There are so many sounds! A poem having one rhyme?
A good life with a sad, minor crime at the end.

Each new couplet's a different ascent: no great peak
but a low hill quite easy to climb at the end . . .

—John Hollander, "Ghazal"

In carefully thinking over all the usual artistic effects—or more properly *points*, in the theatrical sense—I did not fail to perceive immediately that no one had been so universally employed as that of the *refrain.* The universality of its employment sufficed to assure me of its intrinsic value, and spared me the necessity of submitting it to analysis. I considered it, however, with regard to its susceptibility of improvement, and soon saw it to be in a primitive condition. As commonly used, the refrain, or burden, not only is limited to lyric verse, but depends for its impression upon the force of monotone—both in sound and thought. The pleasure is deduced solely from the sense of identity—of repetition. I resolved to diversify, and so heighten the effect, by adhering in general to the monotone of sound, while I continually varied that of thought: that is to say, I determined to produce continuously novel effects, by the variation of the *application* of the refrain—the refrain itself remaining, for the most part, unvaried.

—Edgar Allan Poe, on the composition of "The Raven"

POETRY PRACTICES

Learning to Repeat. Write a poem in any of the forms in this section.

Repeat Translation. Write the same poem five times, in all the five forms covered in this chapter, so you will see what each shape can do with the same impetus and theme.

Blues Riff. Listen to some classic blues songs. Then write a poem in blues stanza using one of the lines from a song combined with lines of your own.

Ghazal Performance. Write a ghazal. Perform it to a group of people in the traditional manner, with the audience reciting the *radif.*

Dramatic Sestina. Write a sestina addressed to an audience, based on the model of "Untoward Occurrence at an Embassy Poetry Reading." Pay extra attention to the middle, so it doesn't sag.

Villanelle Permutations. Write a villanelle with no variation in the repetends (check to see how much use you've made of enjambment, and whether you've varied the meanings of the repeating lines through context). Save this version as Version 1. Then alter it to vary only the first repetend, first slightly (save as Version 2) and then more dramatically (Version 3). Then vary only the second repetend, first slightly (Version 4), then dramatically (Version 5). Compare your five versions. Which is the stronger poem?

Pioneer Repetition. Write a poem in a repeating form that has rarely been used, such as the elegantly simple **quatern.** The quatern is a poem of 16 lines, in any meter, divided into four stanzas. The same line appears as the first line of the first stanza, the second line of the second stanza, the third line of the third stanza, and the last line of the poem.

Nonce Repetition. Invent your own form making use of repeating lines or refrains.

Rhetorical Quilt. Write a poem using four or more of the rhetorical figures that involve repetition.

CHAPTER 18

Chaos in Fourteen Lines: The Sonnet

Sociologists have discovered a surprising fact. When a group of people are in an unfenced space, no matter how large, they gravitate toward the outskirts and leave the middle empty. On the other hand, in a fenced space, they will spread out and enjoy the use of the whole area. Maybe this truth helps explain the charm of courtyards, and the fact that the word "paradise" meant, originally, "a walled enclosure." It may also help explain the lasting appeal of the **sonnet,** the form that Rita Dove has called a "little world."

Did I say lasting appeal? Doesn't everyone know that the sonnet should be dead by now? As the poet Tim Yu put it in his blog, " The real issue, to my mind, in using a form like the sonnet is *belatedness.*" Doesn't it go without saying that the sonnet is a form too late for itself, too old-fashioned to really exist? Somehow, though, the sonnet has not cooperated with the reports of its death. People keep writing them. This chapter will explore why, and how, and along the way, investigate a new model of how poetry works through time that might modify somewhat the twentieth-century doctrine of poetic "progress."

"A sonnet is a moment's monument, / memorial to one dead deathless hour," wrote Dante Gabriel Rossetti in one of the most famous sonnets on the sonnet (as you might expect, no other form has inspired nearly as many tributes to itself). Rossetti expresses one of the most useful powers of the sonnet: the ability to keep a moment, to hold a feeling or experience and turn it around in the light of our awareness until many facets are evident. This multifaceted quality gives the sonnet a paradoxical feeling of freedom and expanse within confines:

"Nuns Fret Not," William Wordsworth (1807)

Nuns fret not at their convents' narrow room;
And hermits are contented with their cells;

And students with their pensive citadels;
Maids at the wheel, the weaver at his loom,
Sit blithe and happy; bees that soar for bloom,
High as the highest Peak of Furness-fells,
Will murmur by the hour in foxglove bells:
In truth the prison, into which we doom
Ourselves, no prison is: and hence for me,
In sundry moods, 'twas pastime to be bound
Within the Sonnet's scanty plot of ground;
Pleased if some Souls (for such there needs must be)
Who have felt the weight of too much liberty,
should find brief solace there, as I have found.

This sonnet is in iambic pentameter, as are all the sonnets in this chapter unless specified otherwise. Wordsworth uses both the meter and the form with grace to illustrate the paradox of what Emerson called the "restraints that make us free." I recently saw the deep, embracing blossoms of purple foxgloves for the first time in a friend's garden; I now understand even better the sensual pleasure, wonder, and calmness that Wordsworth, who wrote 500 sonnets, was describing here. For me also, the feeling of starting a sonnet can carry a sense of mingled freedom, comfort and curious excitement that is different from starting any other kind of poem.

The quality of exploring all facets of a subject does not mean sonnets are always calm; it also means they are able to carry the full force of a lyric outburst with complete conviction. Claude McKay's sonnet "If We Must Die," written in 1919 in response to a wave of white attacks on African Americans, is such a sonnet. This poem's urgency carried so clearly that it was recited decades later by Winston Churchill to exhort Britain to fight the Nazis, and entered into the U.S. *Congressional Record:*

"If We Must Die," Claude McKay (1919)

If we must die—let it not be like hogs
Hunted and penned in an inglorious spot,
While round us bark the mad and hungry dogs,
Making their mock at our accursed lot.
If we must die—oh, let us nobly die,

So that our precious blood may not be shed
In vain; then even the monsters we defy
Shall be constrained to honor us though dead!
Oh, Kinsmen! We must meet the common foe;
Though far outnumbered, let us show us brave,
And for their thousand blows deal one deathblow!
What though before us lies the open grave?
Like men we'll face the murderous, cowardly pack,
Pressed to the wall, dying, but fighting back!

While the sentiments are powerful, the imagery strong, and the art skillful, I don't think these qualities account fully for the impact that McKay's sonnet had on so many people. Though all these aspects play a part in the poem's effect, I give the most credit to how well McKay understood and worked with the sonnet form itself. The first two quatrains have a somber tone, a heaviness emphasized by the repeating phrase "if we must die," with its sonorous spondee. But at the beginning of line 9, with the phrase "Oh, Kinsmen!," McKay's sonnet seems to stop, take a deep breath, and regather its energies for a big push to the finish.

The ninth line of either the Italian or the English sonnet form is called the **volta,** the Italian word for "turn." At this point, the sonnet form is designed to change from one idea, tone, or approach in the octave to a different idea, tone or approach in the sestet. And, just as the secret of success in poetry may be to make full use of what you find most unique and distinctive about poetry, the secret to success with any poetic form may be making full use of whatever is most unique and distinctive about the form. Skillful sonnets usually take good advantage of the volta, the most unique and distinctive aspect of a sonnet.

In McKay's volta, many factors, including syntax, meter, trope, word-music, and connotation as well as meaning, conspire to make the turn as effective as it is. Let's start with the word "must," for example. If you read aloud the lines containing this word at the beginnings of the first two quatrains, you will hear something between resigned bitterness and sad determination conveyed by the spondaic stress on the first "must," and a firmer, mounting determination in the second "must." But after the volta, the same word has changed its intensity entirely, the spondee conveying an unstoppable force that floods over the expected unstressed syllable in irresistible exhortation.

Word-music plays a part as well, as the three "m"s in "men," "must," and "meet" gather together to surpass and overwhelm the previous "m"s in "making their mock" and "monsters." It is also significant that one of these "m" sounds happens in the syllable "men," contrasting "men" with the simile of "hogs" that opened the poem, and setting the stage for the transformation that will happen by the end of the poem, where the African American prisoners will have become "men" while their oppressors still remain a "pack" of dogs. The phrase "Oh, Kinsmen!" right at the volta is the heart of the sonnet not only because it brings in the word "men," but also because it does so through the word "kinsmen," emphasizing that it is only in their sense of brotherhood that the prisoners will find the strength they need to prevail.

When you read the poem aloud, you may notice that your energy level and pulse rate rise after line 9. I think the most significant reason for this change is metrical. With the word "kinsmen," the poem begins to take on a more trochaic feel. The caesura after "kinsmen" sets the stage for the rest of the line to sound strongly trochaic: "We must meet the common foe" sounds exactly like a footless trochaic line, and phrases such as "far outnumbered" continue the powerful rocking trochaic rhythm, in contrast to the doggedly iambic feeling of the octave, where the only trochaic words ("hunted" and "making") are dutifully combined to their traditional and most impotent place in the first foot of the line. The trochaic undercurrent of this poem is no surprise in the context of African American poetics; as discussed previously , the trochaic meter has been used by African American poets as a powerful alternative to iambic meter in such poems as Cullen's "Heritage" and Brooks's *The Anniad.*

It's hard to imagine "If We Must Die" in another kind of poetic form—a ballad, or quatrains, or free verse. Who would have thought the sonnet, known so well as the vehicle for plaintive or poignant poems of love, would also prove the perfect vehicle for McKay's revolutionary call: at once big and loose enough for the pacing and circling of authentic power, and small and structured enough for the channeling and building of directed force? How can a poetic form be so versatile? We might as well ask, though, how can a human voice be so versatile? Something in the shape of the sonnet seems so well suited to convey human feeling that it can feel almost like a throat, a hand, a voice—and yes, also like a stanza or room that is especially well proportioned to suit the human form.

And, as it turns out, there is truth behind this idea of the connection between the sonnet and the human body. Almost all traditionally formed sonnets have 14 lines and consist of an **octave** (8 lines) and a **sestet** (6 lines) with the significant shift in emphasis of the volta between them. The critic Paul Oppenheimer has observed that since the last two lines of a sonnet are often separated off from the rest in a couplet or an implied couplet that closes the poem, the proportions of the form are 6:8:12. And this proportion, in fact, represents the special mathematical ratio which the Greeks called the Golden Mean.

Quatrain: a group of four lines linked by rhyme

Octave: First eight lines of a sonnet

Sestet: last six lines of a sonnet

Volta: the "turn" after line 8 of a sonnet, often signaled by a word such as "but" or "yet," where the poem takes on a new perspective or attitude

The Golden Mean: the ratio in which the distance of the two extremes from the middle number is the same fraction of their own quantity (b a over a = c b over c)

Italian sonnet: Sonnet rhyming abbaabbacdecde (Italian sestet) or cdccdcd (Sicilian sestet)

English sonnet: Sonnet rhyming ababcdcdefefgg

A ratio found throughout nature, the Golden Mean is apparent in the proportions by which flower petals grow, twigs sprout from stems, and the shapes of snowflakes crystallize. It is also a ratio evident in the proportions of the human body. Oppenheimer feels that this compelling ratio is one of the reasons for the sonnet's lasting power, which has brought it into numerous languages and made it part of the vocabulary of virtually every major poet in Italian, German, French, Spanish, and English over seven centuries.

In fact, the sonnet is the ultimate stanza, an enclosed place of words alive with currents of energy and places to rest. It has provided a place for some of the most intense and memorable lines in English-language poetry to come into being: How do I love thee? Let me count the ways . . . Getting and spending, we lay waste our powers . . . That time of year thou mayst in me behold . . . Euclid alone has looked on Beauty bare . . . Oh mother, mother, where is happiness . . . one day

I wrote her name upon the strand . . . A sudden blow, the great wings beating still . . . When I have fears that I may cease to be . . . Fool, said my muse to me, look in thy heart and write.

The Italian and English Sonnet

The **Italian** or **Petrarchan** sonnet is the strictest form, with only two rhyming sounds in the octave and three in the sestet. This economy of rhyme sounds can bring great beauty, so the form sounds like the inhale and exhale of a breath. This two-part structure lends power to the volta, which we have seen can structure the thought process in ways from the obvious ("In truth, the prison . . .") to the more subtle:

"Unholy Sonnet," Mark Jarman

After the praying, after the hymn-singing,
After the sermon's trenchant commentary
On the world's ills, which make ours secondary,
After communion, after the hand wringing,
And after peace descends upon us, bringing
Our eyes up to regard the sanctuary
And how the light swords through it, and how, scary
In their sheer numbers, motes of dust ride, clinging-
There is, as doctors say about some pain,
Discomfort knowing that despite your prayers,
Your listening and rejoicing, your small part
In this communal stab at coming clean,
There is one stubborn remnant of your cares
Intact. There is still murder in your heart.

This poem, where the worshiper tries to integrate repressed feelings into a pious character, serves as a good illustration for Oppenheimer's idea of the sonnet as the container for the personality's complexity (see below). The smooth and almost imperceptible transition of the volta perhaps underscores the difficulty the speaker has at first in consciously accepting the hidden thoughts.

This caustic narrative sonnet uses the volta to create a change of scene:

Sonnet 115, John Berryman (1947)

All we were going strong last night this time,
the mosts were flying & the frozen daiquiris
were downing, supine on the floor lay Lise
listening to Schubert grievous & sublime,
my head was frantic with a following rime:
it was a good evening, and evening to please,
I kissed her in the kitchen—ecstasies—
among so much good we tamped down the crime.

The weather's changing. This morning was cold,
as I made for the grove, without expectation,
some hundred Sonnets in my pocket, old,
to read her if she came. Presently the sun
yellowed the pines & my lady came not
in blue jeans & a sweater. I sat down & wrote.

Edna St. Vincent Millay, one of the most noted writers of sonnets in the twentieth century and called by Edmund Wilson the successor to Shakespeare, frequently favored the Italian form. Some say the Italian form is harder to write in English than the English form, since it needs more rhymes for each sound; but in Millay's hands the rhymes rarely sound forced. Here is her contribution to the genre of the sonnet about writing a sonnet:

"I will put Chaos into fourteen lines," Edna St. Vincent Millay (1941)

I will put Chaos into fourteen lines
And keep him there; and let him thence escape
If he be lucky; let him twist, and ape
Flood, fire, and demon—his adroit designs
Will strain to nothing in the strict confines
Of this sweet Order, where, in pious rape,
I hold his essence and amorphous shape,
Till he with Order mingles and combines.
Past are the hours, the years, of our duress,
His arrogance, our awful servitude:
I have him. He is nothing more nor less

Than something simple yet not understood;
I shall not even force him to confess;
Or answer. I will only make him good.

The Italian sonnet's lack of a closing couplet and greater balance between octave and sestet doesn't mean it can't be used to great rhetorical force. The combination of energy and containment, development and resting, that structures "If We Must Die" is part of the quality that helped make Emma Lazarus's sonnet for the Statue of Liberty so durable and beloved:

"The New Colossus," Emma Lazarus (1883)

Not like the brazen giant of Greek fame
With conquering limbs astride from land to land;
Here at our sea-washed, sunset gates shall stand
A mighty woman with a torch, whose flame
Is the imprisoned lightning, and her name
Mother of Exiles. From her beacon-hand
Glows world-wide welcome; her mild eyes command
The air-bridged harbor that twin cities frame,
"Keep, ancient lands, your storied pomp!" cries she
With silent lips. "Give me your tired, your poor,
Your huddled masses yearning to breathe free,
The wretched refuse of your teeming shore,
Send these, the homeless, tempest-tost to me,
I lift my lamp beside the golden door!"

While the first line and a half after the volta is somewhat thrown away, Lazarus more than makes up for it in the last four lines of the sestet, which can stand as a quatrain on their own, and which carry in four lines all the accumulated force that McKay disperses throughout his sestet. So, while "The New Colossus" may not fully embody the potential of the sonnet as a sonnet, it is still a reflection of the rhetorical power of the form.

The **English** or **Shakespearean** sonnet, adapted from the Petrarchan model by Sir Henry Howard, Earl of Surrey, and Sir Thomas Wyatt, and perfected by Shakespeare, has a more logically complex shape than the Italian, with a pattern of 4-4-4-2 lines:

Sonnet 12, William Shakespeare (1609)

When I do count the clock that tells the time,
And see the brave day sunk in hideous night;
When I behold the violet past prime,
And sable curls all silvered o'er with white;
When lofty trees I see barren of leaves,
Which erst from heat did canopy the herd
And summer's green all girded up in sheaves
Borne on the bier with white and bristly beard:
Then of thy beauty do I question make
That thou among the wastes of time must go,
Since sweets and beauties do themselves forsake,
And die as fast as they see others grow;
And nothing 'gainst Time's scythe can make defence
Save breed to brave him, when he takes thee hence.

Like Mckay's English sonnet, this one uses the first quatrain to establish an idea and the second to build on it in a different but related way. Where as McKay's volta introduced a new emotional tone, in this sonnet, as in most of Shakespeare's line 9, the volta brings in a new idea or logical approach: the idea of the lover—and a new attitude of questioning insecurity. The final couplet, like the final couplet of "If We Must Die," sums up the problem and offers a solution—in this case to produce "breed," creative or actual progeny.

The English sonnet's closing couplet, and the great logical potential of its structure, doesn't mean it can't be used for a poem with a delicate balance between octave and sestet. This remarkable sonnet about balance has always seemed to me not only like a love poem but also like a tribute to the sonnet form itself:

"The Silken Tent," Robert Frost (1942)

She is as in a field of a silken tent
At midday when a sunny summer breeze
Has dried the dew and all its ropes relent,
So that in guys it gently sways at ease,
And its supporting central cedar pole,
That is its pinnacle to heavenward

And signifies the sureness of the soul,
Seems to owe naught to any single cord,
But strictly held by none, is loosely bound
By countless silken ties of love and thought
To every thing on earth the compass round,
And only by one's going slightly taut
In the capriciousness of summer air
Is of the slightest bondage made aware.

There is very unusual secret in this sonnet. Read it through carefully and see if you can find what it is (hint: it has something to do with punctuation).

Whether in the Italian or English form, the sonnet allows for dialectical opposition, tension and resolution within one stanza; it can unite opposing attitudes within one identity. Paul Oppenheimer makes a convincing argument that because the sonnet allowed room to struggle with oneself, it marks not only the beginning of modern poetry but the beginning of the modern idea of our "self" as having a complex internal life. If this is so, then the sonnet form is likely to continue to be useful at least as long as we encourage such feelings of interiority; and the current resurgence of sonnets suggests that the form can help express the decentered contemporary "self" as well.

Writing Sonnets

Louise Bogan, a famously careful poet, only allowed herself to write one sonnet, which she called "Single Sonnet":

"Single Sonnet," Louise Bogan (1937)

Now, you great stanza, you heroic mould,
Bend to my will, for I must give you love:
The weight in the heart that breathes, but cannot move,
Which to endure flesh only makes so bold.

Take up, take up, as it were lead or gold
The burden; test the dreadful mass thereof.
No stone, slate, metal under or above
Earth, is so ponderous, so dull, so cold.

Too long as ocean bed bears up the ocean,
As earth's core bears the earth, have I borne this;
Too long have lovers, bending to their kiss,
Felt bitter force cohering without motion.

Staunch meter, great song, it is yours, at length,
To prove how stronger you are than my strength.

With all the intimidating drama and power that this form has inspired, embodied by Bogan in images of heavy ancient minerals, it can take some daring to attempt one of your own. Some poets are awed at the thought of trying to join the company of the fabulous sonnets they have read. Others feel anger and hatred at a poetic shape they equate with constraint and tradition. And perhaps others are threatened by the very power that Oppenheimer describes, the power to create a sense of internal "self" from two opposing forces.

However, not every poem in the sonnet form is centered on the conventional idea of the self or its moods. Claude McKay's sonnet, for example, takes on a public and very external voice; John Berryman's is a narrative; and the following sonnet is a kind of charm, impersonal in voice though deeply felt. (Please note that it is not iambic pentameter, unlike the other sonnets discussed so far.)

"Tiger Drinking at Forest Pool," Ruth Padel

Water, moonlight, danger, dream.
Bronze urn, angled on a tree root: one
Slash of light, then gone. A red moon
Seen through clouds, or almost seen.
Treasure found but lost, flirting between
The worlds of lost and found. An unjust law
Repealed, a wish come true, a lifelong
Sadness healed. Haven, in the mind,
To anyone hurt by littleness. A prayer
For the moment, saved; treachery forgiven.
Flame of the crackle-glaze tangle, amber
Reflected in grey milk-jade. An old song
Remembered, long debt paid.
A painting on silk, which may fade.

This more recent sonnet, while unyieldingly classical in form, communicates a disjunctive, postmodern sense of (un)self:

"Sonnet," Karen Volkman

Say sad. Say sun's a semblance of a bled
blanched intransigence, collecting rue
in ray-stains. Smirching pages. Takes its cue
from sateless stamens, flanging. Florid head

got no worries, waitless. Say you do. Say
photosynthesis. Light, water, airy bread.
What eats its source, its orbit? Something bad:
some plural petal that will not root or ray.

Sow stray. Salt night for saving, dreaming clay
for heap, for hefting. Originary ash
for stall and stilling. Say it *will,* it said.

Corolla corona, bliss-bane—delay
surge and sediment. Say instrument and gash
and ruminant remnant. Rex the ruse. Be dead.

In fact, the sonnet form is extremely versatile, which is probably the real secret of its longevity. When you write one, you may be surprised. Once you get the hang of it, the pleasure of freedom within confines can become intoxicating, and can draw depths out of your poetry that you didn't know existed. In the effort to make your sonnet work right, because of its many constraints, you may need to revise more courageously than you have ever revised before and may find new images, themes, and rhymes being summoned to enrich your poems. But be prepared for the first few sonnets to be throwaways, especially if you haven't written one before. As a young poet, Ezra Pound wrote a sonnet every day for a year. I doubt that he kept many of them.

Sonnets have most often been written in iambic pentameter, but it is the rhyme scheme that defines a sonnet; there can be sonnets in any meter or in free verse. Mona van Duyn's "Sonnet for Minimalists" is in iambic dimeter. Ruth Padel's sonnet, above, opens in trochees and wavers between iambic pentameter and tetrameter lines; while heavily rhythmical, it is so irregular that it should probably be called free verse. June Jordan's "Something Like a Sonnet for Phillis Miracle Wheatley," in honor of the eighteenth-century poet who was brought to the United States as a slave, is written in dactylic meter:

"Something Like a Sonnet for Phillis Miracle Wheatley," June Jordan

Girl from the realm of birds florid and fleet
flying full feather in far or near weather
Who fell to a dollar lust coffled like meat
Captured by avarice and hate spit together
Trembling asthmatic alone on the slave block
built by a savagery travelling by carriage
viewed like a species of flaw in the livestock
A child without safety of mother or marriage

Chosen by whimsy but born to surprise
They taught you to read but you learned how to write
Begging the universe into your eyes:
They dressed you in light but you dreamed with the night.
From Africa singing of justice and grace,
Your early verse sweetens the fame of our Race.

When writing a sonnet, I tend to stop frequently and "listen" internally for what should come next, with the form as a guide. I try not to write down anything unless it comes from an internal voice, because I know that with a sonnet the original shape will probably stick around a long time as I revise (unlike with other poems, where I tend to switch the order of stanzas). Once the rhyme words are in place I keep them in their original spots as much as possible, revising around them but keeping them as a scaffolding. One point to keep in mind is that the sonnet form is so embedded in the subliminal memories of English speakers that sometimes, a poem wants to be a sonnet without our conscious knowledge. If you keep this option in mind, it may help you to finish a poem more easily than you expected.

Like many powerful things, a sonnet is a two-edged sword. It can work for you if you understand its strengths, but against you if you treat them too lightly or ignore their power. The main thing to remember is to be sensitive to the divisions of the quatrains and the volta: make sure each quatrain has its own idea, and that the powerful transition of the volta corresponds with a transition in your mood or meaning.

Sonnets and Sequences

The most common mistake I see in beginning sonnets is that the poet tries to squeeze too much into the poem: too many thoughts, too many images, too many characters, too many plots. It is as if a sonnet's unique structure, with its two symmetrical yet asymmetrical parts and the torque-like energy that both blends and opposes them with each other, has its own size and weight which must be taken into account. Although of course there are always exceptions, at first it is a good idea to assume that you can't fit the same number of different things into a sonnet that you might expect to fit into, say, a fourteen-line poem in free verse. The very aspect of the sonnet that gives it its extra purport, its momentum and influence, means that it can become too easily crowded and confused, with the subject matter distracting from and obfuscating the form, rather than making good use of the form. It's better to keep it simple, to focus on one idea or aspect of an idea for each sonnet. Rossetti called the poem "a moment's monument" for good reason.

What should you do if you have already written one of these jam-packed sonnets? Consider unfolding it into a **sequence** of two or three or six sonnets, or more, each sonnet treating one aspect of your story or idea. You will be better able to develop your poems with vivid imagery if you allow plenty of space to stretch out in each sonnet-room. From their very beginning, sonnets have been composed in long sequences, from Petrarch and Shakespeare themselves (the sonnet sequences that earned the names Petrarchan and Shakespearean for the Italian and English sonnets were 227 sonnets long and 154 sonnets long, respectively) up through Elizabeth Barrett Browning's sequence of 44 *Sonnets from the Portuguese* (of which her famous "How do I love thee? Let me count the ways" is only the best known), to later narratives-in-sonnets such as George Meredith's *Modern Love* and Edna St. Vincent Millay's *Fatal Interview.*

If this idea appeals to you, one particular kind of sonnet sequence you might enjoy trying is a **crown of sonnets,** a sequence in which the last line of each sonnet doubles as the first line of the next. A recent example is Marilyn Nelson's "A Wreath for Emmett Till." When the crown is complete, you will have seven sonnets (unless you want to write a double crown, which is twice as long). The last sonnet takes the last line of sonnet six as its first line, and the first line of the first sonnet as its last line. While your crown may look like a circle, the best crowns, like all the best sonnet sequences, work more like a spiral than a circle, taking the reader through a sequence of different and deepening aspects of the central concern, rather than circling through the same places. Generally, to avoid monotony you will want to aim for a lot of variety in sound and meaning among the repeating lines that link together your crown, just as it is generally best to aim for variety in the rhyme sounds within each sonnet.

Reclaiming the Sonnet

Some contemporary poets trying to write sonnets find themselves oppressed, not only by the form's traditional creation of a certain kind of self, but also by the stereotype that a sonnet sequence is written by a man about a voiceless woman. In this case, you might reflect that, almost as soon as that custom started, women were overturning it. For example, the sixteenth-century French poet Louise Labe wrote a wonderful book of sonnets on male beauty and her own passion; her sonnet on impotence is a classic, as is her best-known poem, "Kiss Me Again":

Sonnet 18, Louise Labé (1555) (trans. Annie Finch)

Kiss me again, rekiss me, and then kiss
me again, with your richest, most succulent
kiss; then adore me with another kiss, meant
to steam out fourfold the very hottest hiss
from my love-hot coals. Do I hear you moaning? This
is my plan to soothe you: ten more kisses, sent
just for your pleasure. Then, both sweetly bent
on love, we'll enter joy through doubleness,
and we'll each have two loving lives to tend:
one in our single self, one in our friend.
I'll tell you something honest now, my Love:
it's very bad for me to live apart.
There's no way I can have a happy heart
without some place outside myself to move.

Written before Shakespeare's sonnets, this sonnet sequence brings a female voice into the love-sonnet tradition from the beginning. The tradition can remain a hard one to enter, especially if you are conscious of its history, its power, and the intimidating genius of some of the poets who have used it before. Many contemporary poets are irresistibly attracted to the sonnet, but at the same time feel a strong need to distance themselves from it lest they be overwhelmed by the form. They have created this distance in three main ways: through subject matter, through form, and through syntax.

Among contemporary poets in the United States, gay poets have been particularly interested in working within the long tradition of the love sonnet, perhaps because their subject matter inherently provides a position of distance. Marilyn Hacker's very fine crown of sonnets "Eight Days in April" celebrates love between women. The line of accomplished gay male sonnetteers stretches back from the contemporary poet Rafael Campo through Owen Dodson:

"Midnight Bell," Owen Dodson (1947)

This cannot be the hour for oral speech:
Words vying with the wind, with private sounds
Of other lovers striving on the beach,
With waves: the sand sniffers, the hounds.
No, this is quiet in between the long
Sentences, the lengths of speech at will.
Let the eyes remember, the ears catch the songs
We sing deep in the bone, in the still
Unoutward parts, that have their resurrection
In themselves. Cancel the mouth of poetry and prose;
Be eager now to seek the dark confection
In the flesh and feed until desire goes,
Until we sleep, until we cannot tell
Why midnight walked and did not ring her bell.

The traditional sonnet remains an excellent place to contest, undermine and reconfigure romantic stereotypes. Poets have also innovated by introducing subject matter earlier thought inappropriate for sonnets. John Donne's sonnets on religion were revolutionary in the seventeenth century:

"Batter My Heart," John Donne (1633)

Batter my heart, three person'd God; for, you
As yet but knocke, breathe, shine, and seeke to mend;
That I may rise, and stand, o'erthrow mee, and bend
Your force, to breake, blowe, burn and make me new.
I, like an usurpt towne, to another due,
Labour to'admit you, but Oh, to no end,
Reason your viceroy in mee, mee should defend,
But is captiv'd, and proves weake or untrue.
Yet dearely I love you, and would be loved faine,
But am betroth'd unto your enemie:
Divorce mee,untie, or breake that knot againe;
Take mee to you, imprison mee, for I
Except you'enthrall mee, never shall be free,
Nor ever chast, except you ravish mee.

In the early nineteenth century, Wordsworth's introduction of topical and political subject matter also broke taboos. It may be hard to imagine many subjects outside of gay love that would be considered subversive for a sonnet now; perhaps that is why, until recently, contemporary heterosexual American poets have been tending to distance themselves from the sonnet's form instead of from its themes.

Variations and Deformations of the Sonnet

Never static, the form of the sonnet has mutated numerous times since its invention by a lawyer in twelfth-century Italy, based on an old folk song stanza. Milton and Spenser each invented new sonnets that are named after them, and Shakespeare and Petrarch each built such durable versions of the form in their respective languages that the two major forms of sonnet took their names.

Until the twentieth century, the major variations in the sonnet were "formal" variations that preserved the basic qualities of the form. The **Miltonic sonnet** is a Petrarchan sonnet without the volta. The **Spenserian sonnet** has an innovative overlapping rhyme scheme but still keeps the couplet separate:

Some variations on the sonnet:

Caudated (tail) sonnet: a sonnet of any type, followed by an extra couplet (or sometimes an extra trimeter, followed by a heroic couplet, followed by a trimeter rhymed with the first, followed by another heroic couplet). For examples, see Milton's "On the New Forcers of Conscience" and Hopkins's "Tom's Garland."
Chained or linked sonnet: each line starts with last word of previous line
Continuous or reiterating sonnet: uses only one or two rhymes in the entire sonnet
Crown of sonnets: a sequence of sonnets, each of which begins with the last line of the previous sonnet
Curtal sonnet: a shortened sonnet, a form invented by Gerard Manley Hopkins
French sonnet: starts like the Italian sonnet, then adds a couplet at the volta, followed by an alternating quatrain: abbaabbaccdede
Heroic sonnet: an 18-line sonnet. English version: add a fourth quatrain, before the couplet. Italian version: two "heroic octaves" of abababcc plus a couplet
Interwoven sonnet: includes both medial and end rhyme
Miltonic sonnet: an Italian sonnet with no break in sense at the volta, creating a gradual culmination of the idea
Retrograde sonnet: reads the same backward as forward
Sonnet sequence: a group of sonnets on the same theme (most sonnets in Rennaissance were written in long sequences of up to 50 sonnets)

ababbcbccdcdee. Gerard Manly Hopkins's **curtal sonnet** uses the same proportions but makes them smaller, so instead of 8 and 6 lines, the two parts are 6 and 4½ lines in length:

"Pied Beauty," Gerard Manly Hopkins (1877)

Glory be to God for dappled things
For skies of couple color as a brindled cow;
For rosemoles all in stipple upon trout that swim
Fresh firecoal chestnut falls; finches' wings;

Landscape plotted and pieced
Fold, fallow and trim.
Glory be to God for dappled things
All things counter, original, spare, strange;
Whatever is fickle, freckled (who knows how?)
With swift, slow; sweet, sour; adazzle, dim
He fathers forth whose beauty is past change;
Praise him.

Gwendolyn Brooks's mid-twentieth-century experiment maintained the sonnet's formal structure, but changed the feeling of the form:

"the sonnet-ballad," Gwendolyn Brooks (1949)

Oh mother, mother, where is happiness?
They took my lover's tallness off to war,
Left me lamenting. Now I cannot guess
What I can use an empty heart-cup for.
He won't be coming back here any more.
Some day the war will end, but, oh, I knew
When he went walking grandly out that door
That my sweet love would have to be untrue.
Would have to be untrue. Would have to court
Coquettish death, whose impudent and strange
Possessive arms and beauty (of a sort)
Can make a hard man hesitate—and change.
And he will be the one to stammer, "Yes."
Oh mother, mother, where is happiness?

While Brooks maintains the form of an English sonnet, the dialogue, the directly emotional voice of the girl, the simple and universal narrative, and the repetition of the first line, like a refrain, add the immediacy and narrative urgency of a ballad.

When I was in my twenties, partly out of poetic curiosity, partly for feminist reasons, and partly out of a desire to help reestablish form with a difference in the postmodern age, I set out to invent my own sonnet. Based on many such experiments, here are my personal minimum criteria for a variation to feel closely related enough to the sonnet so that I still feel the connection to the form's roots: the poem keeps some kind of consistent meter, though not necessarily iambic pentameter; the poem's length and proportions, like the sonnet's, feel similar to the palm of my hand; the poem has some kind of meaning-dynamic between different parts, analogous to the volta; and every line in the poem has at least one rhyming partner, to keep the vital propulsive force of the form. Nearly twenty years later, I was finally given the form of my sonnet by a figure from a dream. It's a much more radical departure than I could have imagined in my twenties: a nine-line poem in dactylic tetrameter with the form abcbcbaca, which I call the "nonnet." It's taken me yet another decade of organic, tentative, tactful experiment, pushing at my own boundaries, to begin to feel familiar with writing nonnets, and I am just beginning to suspect that my form may be workable and useful. If it turns out that it is, my variation would be honored to be in the company of numerous others, famous and obscure, from all centuries.

Contemporary formal variations of the sonnet include such permutations as unrhymed metrical sonnets of 14 lines with a volta; rhymed nonmetrical (free verse) sonnets; sonnets that are metrically variable (avoiding a consistent meter); and sonnets of various lengths (including 16, 18, and 12 lines) that keep rhyme and meter. When the influential poet Robert Lowell published three books of unrhymed sonnets in the 1960s and 1970s, most were dense iambic pentameter:

"History," Robert Lowell

History has to live with what was here,
clutching and close to fumbling all we had—
it is so dull and gruesome how we die,
unlike writing, life never finishes.
Abel was finished; death is not remote,
a flash-in-the-pan electrifies the skeptic,
his cows crowding like skulls against high-voltage wire,
his baby crying all night like a new machine.
As in our Bibles, white-faced, predatory,
the beautiful, mist-drunken hunter's moon ascends—
a child could give it a face: two holes, two holes,
my eyes, my mouth, between them a skull's no-nose—

O there's a terrifying innocence in my face
drenched with the silver salvage of the mornfrost.

Lowell's unrhymed sonnet follows strictly the rhetorical shape of the English sonnet, with each quatrain having its own subject, a dramatic change of mood at the volta, and a concluding couplet that steps back from the poem to take a wider view.

Informal sonnet variations (or "deformations," as Michael Boughn has proposed calling them in recognition of their subversive attitude toward the form) jettison meter as well, basically keeping nothing but the name "sonnet," though they may be 14 lines and/or may have a volta. The most central writers of this kind of sonnet are Ted Berrigan and Bernadette Mayer. Here is a poem from Berrigan's first book, *Sonnets* (1964), for which he took fragments of poems written earlier and collaged them into an approximate sonnet shape:

In Joe Brainard's collage its white arrow
he is not in it, the hungry dead doctor.
Or Marilyn Monroe, her white teeth white—
I am truly horribly upset because Marilyn
and ate King Korn popcorn," he wrote in his
of glass in Joe Brainard's collage
Doctor, but they say "I LOVE YOU"
and the sonnet is not dead.
takes the eyes away from the gray words,
Diary. The black heart beside the fifteen pieces
Monroe died, so I went to a matinee B-movie
washed by Joe's throbbing hands. "Today
What is in it is sixteen ripped pictures
does not point to William Carlos Williams.

While there is no regular meter or rhyme, the poem has 14 lines and, significantly, the line "and the sonnet is not dead" is not only in regular meter (trochaic tetrameter, or headless iambic tetrameter, depending how much one privileges the iambic meter), but appears resoundingly at the end of the octave, constituting a volta. This tradition of playful or subversive deformation of the form has continued, largely through the influence of Mayer's book *Sonnets,* consisting of free-verse poems of different lengths that usually preserve a volta or turn about halfway through. Some more recent examples that preserve only one formal aspect of the traditional sonnet are Lee Ann Brown's "Quantum Sonnet," consisting of disjointed phrases of free verse rhymed according to the Shakespearean pattern, and Terrance Hayes's poem "Sonnet," consisting of the same iambic pentameter line ("We sliced the watermelon into smiles") repeated 14 times. Other deformations take the form more loosely still, sometimes treating it as a conceptual framework only. Jen Bervin's book *Nets,* for example, uses tracing paper to cross out certain words in sonnets by Shakespeare to create a palimpsest series of "sonnets." A remarkable range of other experiments with the idea and the body of the sonnet are collected in the British anthology *The Reality Street Book of Sonnets.*

Poet David Cappella has applied the terms "endoskeleton" and "exoskeleton" to the two basic approaches to varying the sonnet. I find Cappella's categories extremely useful because they are descriptive rather than judging in one direction or the other. As he has explained, "Some sonnets use the sonnet form as an endoskeleton—those are the poems that are actually written according to the sonnet form. But my poems use the form as an exoskeleton. I think of the sonnet form as a hard skeleton that exists outside and beyond my poems. My poems assume that the sonnet exoskeleton exists and play off of it, inhabit it, even though they are not structured internally according to the form."

One of the most interesting aspects of the sonnet's recent history, however, is that there seems to be a trend now away from informal deformations or exoskeletons, and back, as if in backlash, to the strictest and most conservative form of the sonnet, as in the case of Karen Volkman, whose sonnet appears earlier in this chapter. Volkman's collection of extremely experimental iambic pentameter sonnets does not experiment at all with the most traditional aspects of the form—not even with meter. Such poets are radically questioning the hundred-year-old idea that form is old-fashioned and free verse is new.

The sonnet has already risen from the dead once. It suffered over a hundred years of silence during the reign of the heroic couplet. Only a short few decades before the sonnets of Wordsworth and Keats, Samuel Johnson wrote in his authoritative *Dictionary,* "[The sonnet] is not very suited to the English Language, and has not been used by anyone of eminence since Milton"—thus giving eternal hope to any poet who feels drawn to an unpopular form or style of writing.

Now, the sonnet may be rising from the dead again. Could it be that further great changes for the sonnet are in store? Or could be that Western poetry is finally building a sustainable tradition, a vocabulary of kinds of formal and free poetry that will last, as the ghazal has lasted for millennia in India and the Arabic world? The very familiarity of the sonnet expands a poet's possibilities for working with and changing it, and when you begin to explore this stubbornly persisting form, you may find that its apparently confining poetic structure is, in fact, one of the most accommodating.

QUESTIONS FOR MEDITATION OR DISCUSSION

Look through the sonnets in this chapter and elsewhere in the book. Notice the many different ways that the volta structures the thought processes of these sonnets. What general trends and categories of volta do you see?

Read as many English and Italian sonnets as you can find, in this book and elsewhere. Looking at theme, mood, and movement, how would you characterize the differences between the traditions of these two central forms of the sonnet?

Keats invented the form for this sonnet in an attempt to improve on the English and Italian sonnet forms. How is his form different from the others? Do you think it succeeds as a new sonnet form? Why or why not? You may need to write at least one to understand how it works.

"If By Dull Rhymes Our English Must Be Chain'd," John Keats (1848)

If by dull rhymes our English must be chain'd
And, like Andromeda, the sonnet sweet
Fetter'd, in spite of pained loveliness;
Let us find out, if we must be constrain'd,
Sandals more interwoven and complete
To fit the naked foot of Poesy;
Let us inspect the lyre and weigh the stress
Of every chord and see what may be gain'd
By ear industrious and attention meet:
Misers of sound and syllable, no less
Than Midas of his coinage, let us be
Jealous of dead leaves in the bay wreath crown;
So if we may not let the Muse be free,
She will be bound with garlands of her own.

William Carlos Williams, a founder of twentieth-century free verse, wrote, "You cannot write a sonnet without making gestures of loyalty to the court of Elizabeth I." What do you think of this statement?

QUOTES

I feel the initial choice, the conscious choice, of one verse form over another is not always the choice to match the feeling, but rather a choice to contain, to control, to otherwise make the feeling safe to explore . . . the verse form almost becomes the arms of comfort in which to express the enormity of emotion.

—Molly Peacock

There's the sonnet shape, fair enough, but it's not just a matter of rhyming the eight lines and the other six; they happen to be set on top of one another like two boxes, but they're more like a torso and pelvis.

—Seamus Heaney

I am a poet who has from the very beginning written in free verse, but there have been times in my life when I have retreated to form. When I have had to deal with formal pain, I have retreated to the sonnet.

—Sonia Sanchez

I like the sonnet form because it gives you the chance to develop some thought, and then come to a conclusion. It's all totally false—that's not how you really think, but in a way, it is how you think, so that's why sonnets are interesting. Sonnets pretend to reflect the way you think. That's always been my theory. . . . A good way to write a sonnet is to walk fourteen blocks. Write one line for each block . . . You can do it easily in a city, because there are all these words around.

—Bernadette Mayer

POETRY PRACTICES

(Group) Bouts-Rime. This is a traditional poetry game. Agree on a set of end words (you can borrow them from an existing sonnet if you like). Each person will write a sonnet using the same end words.

(Group) Group Sonnet. Agree on a meter, rhyme scheme, and number of lines for your sonnet. Mark a piece of paper with one letter of the rhyme scheme accompanied by a number (a-1 for the first a-rhyme, etc.) on each line. Pass the paper around a group of 14 people, or the right size group so there is one person per line. As soon as one person writes a line marked by a 1, they write the letter and *only* the rhyme sound (not the word) on the board. For example, if you have line a-1 and you end it with "boat," you would write "a = ote" to signify the sound *only* without giving away your word. Each person writes one line with the agreed-on meter and rhyme and folds the paper so the next person can't see the previous line, then passes it along. Option: the first person can leave a grammatical clue (verb, plural noun, etc.) for the next line. Share the finished product.

Basic Sonnet Exericise. Write an English sonnet or an Italian sonnet. Optional: recast the sonnet in the other form. How does this change the poem?

Sonnet Sprints. Write three English or Italian sonnets, as quickly as you like. Then choose one of them to work on slowly. Feel free to steal from the others.

(Advanced Exercise) Garlands of Your Own. Invent a sonnet form of your own. I would suggest that if you want your form perceptibly to evoke the sonnet tradition, and the harmonious and concentrated power that distinguishes that tradition, you follow or at least recognize these guidelines:

a. Use meter—any meter, as long as you keep to the same meter throughout.

b. Keep the length at 14 lines, or within one or two lines of it.

c. If you invent a new rhyme scheme, make sure that it is a symmetrical one: each word should rhyme with something, with no loose ends.

d. Either use a volta, or otherwise keep in mind an energy pattern like the in-and-out breath of the Italian sonnet, or the logical argument of the English sonnet.

CHAPTER 19

Deep Story: The Ballad

When you choose to write a **ballad,** you are hooking into one of the oldest living forms of poetry in English, a form that is almost purely narrative and yet carries strong dramatic and lyric intensity. You may find that your poems gain depth and power by the mere fact of participating in such a mysterious, sometimes funny, sometimes violent, sometimes heart-wrenching tradition—a tradition that preserved for centuries, alongside the traditions of written poetry, the influences and moods of the vibrant oral culture that once permeated English-language poetry.

Ballads are story-poems (or, more accurately, song-poems, since this kind of poem was traditionally sung) that focus on crucial moments of action, with little interpretation or introspection. The doggedly "anonymous" nature of the ballads, their focus on love and gore, and the fact that the scholars who collected and published them in the eighteenth and nineteenth centuries—Bishop Percy, Walter Scott, and James Francis Child—traced most of them to women, during the same period that Grimm and Anderson were collecting fairy tales from the illiterate women who had them passed them down through generations, have led to the speculation that the ballads were largely the work of female poets. And at this point it does seem likely that, to quote Virginia Woolf, "Anonymous was a woman." While we may never know for sure, perhaps this association of the ballad with a marginal counterculture has to do with the fact that some of the twentieth-century and contemporary poets who have done the most brilliant work with the form have been women or African American poets.

The ballad is one of the most ancient, flexible, and enduring kinds of narrative poems. Traditionally, the action in a ballad is compressed and can span great leaps in time, in part because the action—passion, murder, betrayal—is attention-getting even from a distance. But to counterbalance this large scale, ballads traditionally also focus in on a few small details—the eels that Lord

Randal ate for lunch, the shoe in the rubble of the bombed Birmingham church—that add memorability and telegraph the strength of their emotion. A refrain frequently holds the ballad together and adds continuity and drama; since ballads, like sonnets, have a history in musical performance, the refrain also makes them work better as songs. Some scholars believe that, traditionally, a lead singer sang the narrative lines and a chorus sang the refrains.

Folklorists who record material from oral culture use the term "type" for the basic skeleton of a common story or song, and "variants" for the different versions developed by various performers. Traditional ballads exist in multiple variants, altered over time by many singers; for example, the well-known ballad "Lord Randal," about a young man poisoned by his sweetheart, is one of 15 variants of the same basic story and format collected by Child. Several of these variants are addressed to "Lord Randal," but others use "Lord Donald," "King Henry," "Billy," or other names. In the "Billy" variant, the young man is poisoned by his grandmother instead of his sweetheart. Child prefaces the ballad with the list of people from whom he had collected this version: "Note: a. Communicated by Mrs. L. F. Wesseihoeft, of Boston, as sung to her when a child by her grandmother, Elizabeth Foster, born in Maine, who appears to have learned the ballad of her mother about 1800. b. By a daughter of Elizabeth Foster, as learned about 1820. c. By Miss Ellen Marston of New Bedford, as learned from her mother, born 1778. ? d. By Mrs. Cushing, of Cambridge, Mass., as learned in 1838 from a schoolmate, who is thought to have derived it from an old nurse. e. By Mrs. Augustus Lowell, of Boston. f. By Mrs. Edward Atkinson, of Boston, learned of Mrs. A. Lowell, in girlhood. g. By Mrs. A. Lowell, as derived from a friend.":

"Tiranti, My Son" (Child Ballad #12, Variant I), Anonymous (eighteenth century)

"O WHERE have you been, Tiranti, my son?
O where have you been, my sweet little one?"
"I have been to my grandmother's; mother make my bed soon,
For I'm sick to my heart, and I'm faint to lie down."

"What did you have for your supper, Tiranti, my son?
What did you have for your supper, my sweet little one?"
"I had eels fried in butter; mother, make my bed soon,
For I'm sick to my heart, and I'm faint to lie down."

"Where did the eels come from, Tiranti, my son?
Where did the eels come from, my sweet little one?"
"From the corner of the haystack; mother, make my bed soon,
For I'm sick to my heart, and I'm faint to lie down."

"What color were the eels, Tiranti, my son?
What color were the eels, my sweet little one?"
"They were streaked and striped; mother, make my bed soon,
For I'm sick to my heart, and I'm faint to lie down."

"What'll you give to your, father, Tiranti, my son,
What'll you give to your father, my sweet little one?"
"All my gold and my sllver; mother, make my bed soon,
For I'm sick to my heart, and I'm faint to lie down."

"What'll you give to your mother, Tiranti, my son?
What'll you give to your mother, my sweet little one?"
"A coach and six horses; mother, make my bed soon,
For I'm sick to my heart, and I'm faint to lie down."

"What'll you give to your grandmother, Tiranti, my son?
What'll you give to your grandmother, my sweet little one?"
"A halter to hang her; mother, make my bed soon,
For I'm sick to my heart, and I'm faint to lie down."

"Where'll you have your bed made, Tiranti, my son?
Where'll you have your bed made, my sweet little one?"
"In the corner of the churchyard; mother, make my bed soon,
For I'm sick to my heart, and I'm faint to lie down."

Like a strictly observed meter that conveys strong feeling when the poet alters it slightly (think of Millay's "Love is Not All"), the restricted form of the ballad can convey great emotion when the personal is finally allowed to seep through the objective outlines of the story and the relentless repetition of the refrain. When Tiranti answers, "a halter to hang her, mother," those words can convey as much emotion as many a long lyric poem. In the ballad "Clerk Saunders," Lady Margaret spends the night with her lover Saunders, only to have her brothers discover them and murder her lover. It is hard to imagine a more pitiful cry than her plea at his grave:

Is there any room at your head, Saunders?
Is there any room at your feet?
Or any room at your side, Saunders,
Where fain, fain I would sleep?

Ballads are usually written in a four-line stanza, called the "folk stanza" or "ballad stanza," in which at least the second and fourth lines rhyme. The unrhymed first and third lines typically add action and new information, while the rhymed lines build emotion through sound and repetition. The first and third lines of a stanza have four beats, and the second and fourth typically have three, resulting in a pattern of 4-3-4-3 beats per line. There has been much discussion over whether ballad meter is an accentual or an accentual-syllabic meter; the best explanation seems to be that it is a dipodic meter (see chapter 14), with stronger stresses on the first and third syllables, and weaker stresses on the second and fourth. Because of the dipodic pattern, it can sound as if there is an omitted unstressed syllable (sometimes called "a metrical rest") at the end of lines 2 and 4. This American version of an old Scottish ballad uses the standard 4-3-4-3 stanza:

"The Willow Tree," Anonymous (American version, collected eighteenth century)

There was a youth, a cruel youth,
Who lived beside the sea,
Six little maidens he drowned there
By the lonely willow tree.

As he walked o'er with Sally Brown,
As he walked o'er with she,
And evil thought came to him there,
By the lonely willow tree.

O turn you back to the water's side,
And face the willow tree,

Six little maidens I've drowned here,
And you the seventh shall be.

Take off, take off, your golden crown,
Take off your gown, cried he.
For though I am going to murder you
I would not spoil your finery.

Oh, turn around, you false young man,
Oh turn around, cried she,
For 'tis not meet that such a youth
A naked woman should you see.

He turned around, that false young man,
And faced the willow tree,
And seizing him boldly in both her arms,
She threw him into the sea.

Lie there, lie there, you false young man,
Lie there, lie there, cried she,
Six little maidens you've drowned here,
Now keep them company!

He sank beneath the icy waves,
He sank down into the sea,
And no living thing wept a tear for him,
Save the lonely willow tree.

If you are writing a ballad and want to get the hang of this form, try singing your poem to the tune of "Amazing Grace," "The Yellow Rose of Texas," or the *Gilligan's Island* theme song. The tunes of many of Bob Dylan's songs would also work. Folk meter or ballad meter is also the meter of hymns and country music, and some children's songs. By singing, you'll probably be able to tell quite easily whether your poem is in the right rhythm.

While the 4-3-4-3 form is the most typical kind of ballad and the easiest to use, there are many versions of the stanza. One common variation is the 4-4-4-4 pattern of "Tiranti, My Son." Any narrative poem in quatrains with a refrain, especially one with gory or creepy subject matter, is likely to be classified as a ballad. The remarkable overlooked poet Helen Adam, known for her association with poets such as Robert Duncan during the San Francisco Renaissance of the 1960s, was born in Scotland at a time when the ballad tradition was still a living oral tradition. She absorbed the ballad thoroughly, and used numerous variations of it in crafting uniquely uncanny poems. In this one, the dipodic swing of the meter is almost dizzying:

"I Love My Love, " Helen Adam (1960)

In the dark of the moon the hair rules.—Robert Duncan

There was a man who married a maid. She laughed as he led her home.
The living fleece of her long bright hair she combed with a golden comb.
He led her home through his barley fields, where the saffron poppies grew.
She combed, and whispered, "I love my love." Her voice like a plaintive
coo.
Ha! Ha!
Her voice like a plaintive coo.

He lived alone with his chosen bride. At first their life was sweet.
Sweet was the touch of her playful hair binding his hands and feet.
When first she murmured adoring words, her words did not appall.
"I love my love with a Capital A. To my love I give my All.
Ah! Ha!
To my love I give my All."

She circled him with the secret web she wove as her strong hair grew.
Like a golden spider she wove and sang, "My love is tender and true."
She combed her hair with a golden comb, and shackled him to a tree.
She shackled him fast to the Tree of Life. "My love I'll never set free.
No. No.
My love I'll never set free."

Whenever he broke her golden bonds he was held with bonds of gold.
"Oh! cannot a man escape from love, from Love's hot smothering hold?"
He roared with fury. He broke her bonds. He ran in the light of the sun.

Her soft hair rippled and trapped his feet, as fast as his feet could run,
Ha! Ha!
As fast as his feet could run.

He dug a grave, and he dug it wide. He strangled her in her sleep.
He strangled his love with a strand of hair, and then he buried her deep.
He buried her deep when the sun was hid by a purple thunder cloud.
Her helpless hair sprawled over the corpse in a pale resplendent shroud.
Ha! Ha!
A pale resplendent shroud.

Morning and night of thunder rain, and then it came to pass
That the hair sprang up through the earth of the grave, and it grew like
golden grass.
It grew and glittered along her grave alive in the light of the sun.
Every hair had a plaintive voice, the voice of his lovely one.

"I love my love with a capital T. My love is Tender and True.
I'll love my love in the barley fields when the thunder cloud is blue.
My body crumbles beneath the ground but the hairs of my head will grow.
I'll love my love with the hairs of my head. I'll never, never let go.
Ha! Ha!
I'll never, never let go."

The hair sang soft, and the hair sang high, singing of loves that drown,
Till he took his scythe by the light of the moon, and he scythed that
singing hair down.
Every hair laughed a lilting laugh, and shrilled as his scythe swept
through.
"I love my love with a capital T. My love is Tender and True.
Ha! Ha!
Tender, Tender, and True."

All through the night he wept and prayed, but before the first bird woke
Around the house in the barley fields blew the hair like billowing smoke.
Her hair blew over the barley fields where the slothful poppies gape.
All day long all its voices cooed, "My love can never escape,

No, No!
My love can never escape."

"Be still, be still, you devilish hair. Glide back to the grave and sleep.
Glide back to the grave and wrap her bones down where I buried her deep.
I am the man who escaped from love, though love was my fate and doom.
Can no man ever escape from love who breaks from a woman's womb?"

Over his house, when the sun stood high, her hair was a dazzling storm,
Rolling, lashing o'er walls and roof, heavy, and soft, and warm.
It thumped on the roof, it hissed and glowed over every window pane.
The smell of the hair was in the house. It smelled like a lion's mane,
Ha! Ha!
It smelled like a lion's mane.

Three times round the bed of their love, and his heart lurched with despair.
In through the keyhole, elvish bright, came creeping a single hair.
Softly, softly, it stroked his lips, on his eyelids traced a sign.
"I love my love with a capital Z. I mark him Zero and mine.
Ha! Ha!
I mark him Zero and mine."

The hair rushed in. He struggled and tore, but wherever he tore a tress,
"I love my love with a capital Z," sang the hair of the sorceress.
It swarmed upon him, it swaddled him fast, it muffled his every groan.
Like a golden monster it seized his flesh, and then it sought the bone,
Ha! Ha!
And then it sought the bone.

It smothered his flesh and sought the bones. Until his bones were bare
There was no sound but the joyful hiss of the sweet insatiable hair.
"I love my love," it laughed as it ran back to the grave, its home.
Then the living fleece of her long bright hair, she combed with a golden comb.

Because the ballad tradition is so familiar, so engrained in our literature, it is easy to play off of it for various effects, as Langston Hughes does in "Madam and the Census Man." Hughes uses a short-lined version of the ballad form, as Adam used a long-lined version:

"Madam and the Census Man," Langston Hughes (1949)

The census man,
The day he came round,
Wanted my name
To put it down.

I said, JOHNSON,
ALBERTA K.
But he hated to write
The K that way.

He said, What
Does K stand for?
I said, K—
And nothing more.

He said, I'm gonna put it
K—A—Y.
I said, If you do,
You lie.

My mother christened me
ALBERTA K.
You leave my name
Just that way!

He said, Mrs.,
(With a snort)
Just a K
Makes your name too short.

I said, I don't
Give a damn!
Leave me and my name
Just like I am!

Furthermore, rub out
That MRS., too—
I'll have you know
I'm *Madam* to you!

As it gently mocks Madam K, this poem connects to the tradition of comic ballads, which often take place in domestic settings and pit a woman against a man. On another level, the ancient form elevates Madam K's dignity, giving her resistance to being disrespected the dramatic poetic form of a historic event. Speaking in the form strengthened by the tradition of centuries of anonymous ballad-makers before her, she gains authority and authenticity.

As long as ballads have been composed (I don't say "written," because of the oral roots of the form), some of them have told stories of historical and political events. This tradition works well for more serious contemporary ballads, from Robert Pinsky's "The Shirt" to Dudley Randall's "The Ballad of Birmingham." Although "The Ballad of Birmingham" involves dialogue, the frame of the poem is narrative. It is composed in four "balances," a common structure of pairs of stanzas that correspond to or answer each other:

"Ballad of Birmingham: On the Bombing of a Church in Alabama, 1963,"
Dudley Randall (1969)

"Mother, dear, may I go downtown
Instead of out to play,
And march the streets of Birmingham
In a Freedom March today?"

"No, baby, no, you may not go
For the dogs are fierce and wild;
And clubs and hoses, guns and jails
Aren't good for a little child."

"But, mother, I won't be alone.
Other children will go with me,
And march the streets of Birmingham
To make our country free."

"No, baby, no, you may not go
For I fear those guns will fire.
But you may go to church instead
And sing in the children's choir."

She has combed and brushed her night-dark hair,
And bathed rose petal sweet,
And drawn white gloves on her small brown hands,
And white shoes on her feet.

The mother smiled to know her child
Was in the sacred place,
But that smile was the last smile
To come upon her face.

For when she heard the explosion,
Her eyes grew wet and wild.
She raced through the streets of Birmingham
Calling for her child.

She clawed through bits of glass and brick,
Then lifted out a shoe.
"O, here's the shoe my baby wore,
But, baby, where are you?"

If your ballad feels awkward or the language unnatural, don't give up right away. It takes a little practice to be able to use the stanza naturally. Because a ballad's lines are so short and the audience's attention needs to be riveted to the plot, it is even more important to keep your language conversational. The main things to avoid, as with all metered poetry, are unnatural word order and extra "filler" words. A light touch is key to a good ballad. If you find yourself struggling with a stanza, rather than trying to force it, consider letting it go and starting that stanza again from scratch.

Child wrote that "the true popular ballads are the spontaneous products of nature." While this remark does not do justice to the artistry of those who composed them, it is true that the most effective ballads do have a quality of inevitableness and ease. One tactic that may help you achieve a more natural effect is to tap literally into the form's oral roots. Try singing your stanzas, instead of writing them down, as you compose them. If you find yourself repeating a lot, you will have learned firsthand the source of one of the form's conventions. William Motherwell, an early collector of Scottish ballads, described in 1827 how the "uniformity of phraseology . . . not only assisted the memory in an eminent degree, but served as a kind of groundwork, on which the poem could be raised. . . . Indeed the original production of these common-places betokens no slender ingenuity on the part of these song inditers." The technique of using repeating phrases to compose poetry orally is also, of course, key to the epic tradition (see chapter 5).

Poets since the eighteenth century have been writing "literary" poems that, like "The Ballad of Birmingham," take advantage of the evocative power of ballad tradition. Some well-known examples from the Romantic period are Keats's "La Belle Dame Sans Merci" and Coleridge's long "Rime of the Ancient Mariner." An excerpt from Coleridge's poem shows that it has many differences from the traditional ballad, and yet it evokes them to good advantage:

From "The Rime of the Ancient Mariner," Samuel Taylor Coleridge (1798)

I look'd upon the rotting sea,
And drew my eyes away;
I look'd upon the rotting deck,
And there the dead men lay.

I looked to heaven, and tried to pray;
But or ever a prayer had gusht,
A wicked whisper came, and made
My heart as dry as dust.

I closed my lids, and kept them close,
And the balls like pulses beat;
For the sky and the sea, and the sea and the sky
Lay like a load on my weary eye,
And the dead were at my feet.

But the curse liveth for him in the eye of the dead men.

The cold sweat melted from their limbs,
Nor rot nor reek did they:
The look with which they look'd on me
Had never pass'd away.

An orphan's curse would drag to hell
A spirit from on high;
But oh! more horrible than that
Is the curse in a dead man's eye!
Seven days, seven nights, I saw that curse,
And yet I could not die.

The action moves much, much more slowly than the action of a traditional ballad, and repetition is not used as a consistent part of the poem's structure but only occasionally, for effect, as in the last stanza quoted; Coleridge also adds sophisticated structural variations such as the italicized refrain and the six-line stanza. Still, it is probable that this poem's distinct links to the ballad tradition are a major factor in its lasting appeal.

The opening of the following poem also uses echoes of traditional ballads, but in a sophisticated literary way:

From "The Burglar of Babylon," Elizabeth Bishop (1965)

On the fair green hills of Rio
There grows a fearful stain:
The poor who come to Rio
And can't go home again.

On the hills a million people,
A million sparrows, nest,
Like a confused migration
That's had to light and rest,

Building its nests, or houses,
Out of nothing at all, or air.

You'd think a breath would end them,
They perch so lightly there.

But they cling and spread like lichen,
And the people come and come.
There's one hill called the Chicken,
And one called Catacomb;

There's the hill of Kerosene,
And the hill of Skeleton,
The hill of Astonishment,
And the hill of Babylon.

The formulaic opening "fair green hills," and the repetition of the names of the hills, give the poem the quality of an authentic tale. The poem goes on to tell the story of Micucu, who was "a burglar and killer /An enemy of society." Micucu goes to his aunt who tells him to hide in the hills:

Below him was the ocean.
It reached far up the sky,
Flat as a wall, and on it
Were freighters passing by,

Or climbing the wall, and climbing
Till each looked like a fly,
And then fell over and vanished;
And he knew he was going to die.

He could hear the goats baa-baa-ing.
He could hear the babies cry;
Fluttering kites strained upward;
And he knew he was going to die.

Micucu is killed, and the long poem ends with another poignant repetition:

On the fair green hills of Rio
There grows a fearful stain:

The poor who come to Rio
And can't go home again.

There's the hill of Kerosene,
And the hill of the Skeleton,
The hill of Astonishment,
And the hill of Babylon.

Like Bishop's poem, contemporary poet Lee Ann Brown's "The Ballad of Susan Smith" makes use of the uncanny familiarity and ancient power of the ballad form. To tell the story of the white woman who killed her children in 1999 and blamed an imaginary black man for the crime, Brown uses a pattern of 4-4-4-4 accents and faithfully follows a repeating refrain just as in a ballad written centuries ago.

From "Ballad of Susan Smith," Lee Ann Brown

I put my car into reverse
        On a lee and lonely
This will be my Babies' hearse
        Down by the green lake side-ee-o

I am a daughter of the Mills
        On a lee and lonely
Young I am but doomed to kill
        Down by the green lake side-ee-o . . .

The action in all these ballads shifts focus from the long term—the Civil Rights movement, a pattern of six murders, Susan Smith's lying legal strategy—to the small, precise detail: the exact words someone said, the golden crown, the bloody hands, the fluttering kite, the baby shoes. Such details lend the stories their vividness.

QUESTIONS FOR MEDITATION OR DISCUSSION

Imagine taking one of the most traumatic or difficult events in your memory—either a personal tragedy or a community tragedy—and turning it into a ballad. If you don't like the idea, why not? Does it feel too public, or too simple, or too disrespectful? If you do like the idea, why? Do you feel relief? Amusement? Exhilaration? A sense of connection? What do you imagine it was like to live in the kind of community that routinely turned difficult or tragic stories into ballads?

Arguably, popular songs have taken some of the place of ballads in our culture today, putting difficult events into artistic form. One example is the song "Abraham, Martin, and John," popular in the wake of the assassinations of John F. Kennedy and Martin Luther King. I remember listening to this song as a very young teenager and finding it a cathartic experience. My son may feel the same way about a contemporary song, "September Sky," written after the September 11, 2001, attack on New York. Can you think of other songs that have the same effect?

Sing one or more ballads, either traditional or contemporary. Try solo singing and group singing with the group singing the refrains. How does this change your experience of the poems?

Psychologists and historians (most notably the philosopher of history Hayden White) claim that the act of telling a story about a difficult event is an important way for a person or a culture to come to terms with it. Is this true in your experience? Can you think of times when you were bursting to tell a story about something that had happened to you? What do those stories have in common? Would any of them be an appropriate story for a ballad, or does a ballad lend itself to a different kind of story? Do you think that rhyme and meter are more suitable for certain kinds of stories, and prose for other stories?

QUOTES

I'm no singing it exactly the way my mother sang it and I'm no singing the way that my uncle taught it to me. Because I have taken it played with the words and put my own identity into it.

—Sheila Stewart, ballad singer

What I do remember is the way he sang it, standing easily and using not much more than a speaking rather than a singing voice. . . . Far from intruding itself, his personality vanished altogether; there was only a voice rhythmically telling a story to a tune.

—Willa Muir

The diction of a ballad may be conversational but the rhythm is not.
—Susan Tichy

POETRY PRACTICES

Ballad Comparison. Here is one of the six Scottish versions, collected by Child, of the ballad that became "The Willow Tree" in the United States (printed in this chapter). Compare the two versions; notice how the story both changes and stays the same.

"Lady Isabel and the Elf-Knight" (Child Ballad #4), Version D, Anonymous (eighteenth century)

O heard ye of a bloody knight,
Lived in the south country?
For he has betrayed eight ladies fair
And drowned them in the sea.

Then next he went to May Collin,
She was her father's heir,
The greatest beauty in the land,
I solemnly declare.

"I am a knight of wealth and might,
Of townlands twenty-three;
And you'll be lady of them all,
If you will go with me."

"Excuse me, then, Sir John," she says;
"To wed I am too young;
Without I have my parents' leae,
With you I dare na gang."

"Your parents' leave you soon shall have,
In that they will agree;
For I have made a solemn vow
This night you'll go with me."

From below his arm he pulled a charm,
And stuck it in her sleeve,
And he has made her go with him,
Without her parents' leave.

Of gold and silver she has got
With her twelve hundred pound,
And the swiftest steed her father had
She has taen to ride upon.

So privily they went along,
They made no stop or stay,
Till they came to the fatal place
That they call Bunion Bay.

It being in a lonely place,
And no house there was night,
The fatal rocks were long and step,
And none could hear her cry.

"Light down, he said, "fair May Collin,
Light down and speak with me,
For here I've drowned eight ladies fair,
And the ninth one you shall be."

"Is this your bowers and lofty towers,
So beautiful and gay?
Or is it for my gold," she said,
"You take my life away?"

"Strip off," he says, "thy jewels fine,
So costly and so brave
For they are too costly and too fine
To throw in the sea wave."

"Take all I have my life to save,
O good Sir John, I pray;

Let it ne'er be said you killed a maid
Upon her wedding day."

"Strip off," he says, "thy Holland smock,
That's bordered with the lawn,
For it's too costly and too finde
To rot in the sea sand."

"O turn about, Sir John," she said,
"Your back about to me,
For it never was comely for a man
A naked woman to see."

But as she turned him round about,
She threw him in the sea,
Saying, "Lie you there, you false Sir John,
Where you thought to lay me.

"O lie you there, you traitor false,
Where you thought to lay me,
For though you stripped me to the skin,
Your clothes you've got with thee."

Her jewels fine she did put on,
So costly, rich and brave,
And then with speed she mounts his steed,
So well she did behave.

That lady fair being void of fear,
Her steed being swift and free,
And she has reached her father's gate
Before the clock struck three.

Then first she called the stable groom,
He was her waiting man;
Soon as he heard his lady's voice
He stood with cap in hand.

"Where have you been, fair May Collin?
Who owns this dapple grey?"
"It is found one," she replied,
"That I got on the way."

Then out bespoke the wily parrot
Unto fair May Collin:
"What have you done with false Sir John,
that went with you yestreen?"

"O hold your tongue, my pretty parrot,
And talk no more to me,
And where you had a meal a day
O now you shall have three."

Then up bespoke her father dear.
From his chamber where he lay:
"What aileth thee, my pretty Poll,
That you chat so long or day?"

"The cat she came to my cage-door,
The thief I could not see,
And I called to fair May Collin,
To take the cat from me."

Then first she told her father dear
The deed that she had done,
And next she told her mother dear
Concerning false Sir John.

"If this be true, fair May Collin,
That you have told to me,
Before I either eat or drink
This false Sir John I'll see."

Away they went with one consent,
At dawning of the day,

Until they came to Carline Sands,
And there his body lay.

His body tall, by that great fall,
By the waves tossed to and fro,
The diamond ring that he had on
Was broke in pieces two.

And they have taken up his corpse
To yonder pleasant green,
And there they have buried false Sir John
For fear he should be seen.

Now that you know how different two versions of the same ballad can be from each other, write your own version of one of Child's ballads, of another ballad in this chapter, or of a ballad written by another student. Keep a few key elements, but make lots of significant changes in the poem to suit your own politics, gender, class, personal history, or other agenda (thanks to Susan Tichy for this assignment).

A Ballad for Now. Write a ballad on a political, social, or environmental theme.

Tabloid Ballad. Write a ballad based on a wild story from a tabloid newspaper (thanks to R. S. Gwynn for this assignment).

Personal Ballad. Write a ballad based on a story that happened to a friend or family member.

Ballad of a Secret. Write a ballad based on a secret (thanks to Susan Tichy for this assignment).

PART 5

Sharing Poems: Publishing and Performing

"Poets' food is love and fame."

—PERCY BYSSHE SHELLEY

CHAPTER 20

Revisioning Revision

> Metrical composition is always very difficult to me, nothing is done upon the first day, not one rhyme is in its place; and when at last the rhymes begin to come, the first rough draft of a six-line stanza takes the whole day. At that [early] time I had not formed a style, and sometimes a six-line stanza would take several days, and not seem finished even then; and I had not learnt, as I have now, to put it all out of my head before night, and so the last night was generally sleepless . . .
>
> —W. B. YEATS

> If poetry comes not as easily as leaves to a tree, it had better not come at all.
>
> —JOHN KEATS

Some poems come to us fully formed; the French word for such poems is *données.* Others can absorb years and years of revision before, to use Yeats's phrase for a finished poem, they "click shut like a box." As a veteran of both kinds of poems, I offer the advice in this chapter for those poems that are not spoken perfectly into your ear by the Muse at first.

Revision Tactics and Strategies

To do a good job of revision, you must be willing to, in Theodore Roethke's words, "murder your darlings." That means to value the whole effect of the poem before any one particular part of it. If the parts you are the most fond of, proud of, or attached to are the parts that are interfering with the poem as a whole, you have to be willing to let them go for the sake of the whole. On the other hand, don't feel you need to get rid of things just because you can. Lately it seems that the free verse principle of concision has become, perhaps by default, the bottom line principle of revision. We tend to approach any poem with the attitude, "Which unnecessary words can I remove?" At this point I remind my students to savor the poem and consider its purpose. Removal is not necessarily a goal in itself; if you have something that's working, you should probably make sure you have a good reason to remove words before you go ahead and do so. I've found that poets who enjoy writing in form may be especially prone to over-purging; without the solid resistance of a form they can keep weeding out parts of a poem until there is hardly anything left. If you recognize yourself in this scenario, be gentle with yourself, allow yourself to enjoy and linger over your words, and take a hard look at your poem's structure to make sure it is strong enough to stand up to the rigors of your revision process.

Perhaps for the same reason that "time heals all wounds," time is the best reviser. If you are not happy with a poem, just put it away. It's amazing what a day, a month, a year, or 10 years can do to make it easier to revise a poem. You will find yourself easily discarding passages that may have required your blood, sweat, or tears to perfect.

In an essay, Baron Wormser collates a variety of tried-and-true advice on revision: "One can offer fairly sane approaches as in first expand, then contract or begin another draft at another place in the poem from where you originally began or don't be wedded to the first impulse or—the most basic advice—don't think at the outset that you know what you are writing about." All these tactics depend on a certain amount of objectivity, and time is the best provider of objectivity that I know.

Print out and keep all your drafts. For one thing, it makes it a lot easier to murder your darlings if you know they'll have a chance to rise from the dead. For another, you never know what you will want to use down the road. I spent 10 years revising one of my poems, saving every draft. Ultimately, I decided to keep only the last line of my revised version. For the rest of the poem, I went back to a very early draft. It was worth 10 years to have arrived at the new last line—but if I hadn't had the old version to return to, it would all have been wasted.

Even if you think a poem is absolutely perfect, always be willing to experiment with revising it. It can't hurt, it might be a huge help, and you can always go back to the original.

Print out clean copies as often as you can during the revision process. Seeing a poem in a final-looking, neatly printed version provides some of the same objectivity as seeing it in print. Not only will this help prevent losing valuable drafts; it will help you make the best revision decisions, providing the distance to judge most accurately whether your current set of revisions is going to work.

Let the poem be a living piece of language. Read aloud or under your breath over and over again as you revise. Imagine yourself as the ideal speaker of the poem and act it out in that speaker's voice. Roll on the floor, dance your lines. Put it on tape and listen to it over and over while you do the dishes. Put it on paper and tape it to your bathroom mirror. Bring it to bed. Put it into two voices and let the voices argue and fight with each other while you inhabit their bodies. Don't worry about looking silly! I've heard it on good authority that the Muses prefer silliness to dullness.

Big Changes, Small Changes: Opening Doors

Be willing to make huge changes, not just small ones. Generally, in my own work and in teaching, I aim for the big things first. There's no sense in tinkering with word choice if the whole stanza containing the word has to go. The most common initial "fixes" I see called for by student poems are these: cutting out unnecessary information at the beginning; dividing into stanzas; and rearranging sections, especially turning the beginning into the end. These steps can make a poem find its own life and direction so that revision will take on a life of its own.

When a poem isn't working right, I look for the most powerful part of it—the stanza, or line, or even phrase where the poem comes to life and starts to leap off the page. Then I see what it would take for the entire poem to rise to that level. Often, that means opening with the powerful part and either reordering or discarding what had come before it in the poem. Sometimes it means paying attention to the form or the rhythm or the tone of the most powerful part and looking at the rest of the poem with that rhythm or attitude in mind.

Sometimes it's not so clear what is the most powerful part. In that case, there are many large-scale tactics that may shake the poem awake so you can get a better look at where it really wants to go. Try interspersing the first and last stanzas, cutting out the middle two-thirds of the poem, or writing the whole poem backward. Cut off the beginning, cut off the end, rewrite the whole thing with different pronouns or no pronouns at all. If it is unrhymed, try rhyming it; if it is in rhymed couplets, put it into terza rima.

It's important not to fetishize any particular aspect of the poem. To emphasize my point, I'll say it with three levels of diction: everything should be up for grabs, possible to question, available for inspection. A poem is more important than any of its parts, including even its meaning. If an over-attachment to meaning is holding you back, try a few small transgressions of meaning and see how they feel. If the poem uses the word "yes" in several crucial places, try replacing each "yes" with the word "no." That wasn't so bad, was it? It's still your poem. I am convinced that breaking the taboo against changing meaning is one of the most important challenges that beginning poets face in revision. Imagine if Sylvia Plath had stuck with the original meaning of the last line of "Lady Lazarus," which has now become the poem she is best known for—her signature poem. If Plath had felt she needed to stay wedded to the meaning of her original ending, "I eat fire," or the first revised version, "I eat the air," she would never have made the courageous alteration in meaning that created the ending which makes the poem famous:

> Out of the ash
> I rise with my red hair
> and I eat men like air.

When I am having trouble "murdering my darlings," especially the darlings of meaning, it helps for me to remember that the words I first wrote down are not necessarily those I *meant* to write. Sometimes I feel as if the words I actually wrote may be shorthand, or stand-ins, for my real, hidden, meaning. Thinking about "Lady Lazarus" in this way, perhaps Plath really meant to write "I eat men" on an unconscious level, but was consciously afraid or unable to write that down at first. The phrase "I eat fire" could have been a temporary stand-in for her *real* meaning, which she only discovered later in revision. Whether or not this is true of any particular poem, to allow this possibility may open up a brave new world of meaning for you as you revise.

Meaning, accuracy to reality, diction, style, form: every part of a poem is a potential door that can be reopened. Like Alice in Wonderland down the rabbit hole with her magic key, you simply need to locate the right door, the aspect of the poem that is not as alive as it could be. Methods of revisions are as individual as poets—and poems—but I think most poets would agree that playfulness is a healthy component of a living revision process. If something seems wrong but you don't know what it is, try changing some things around just for fun, and you may find that you uncover important clues in the process. If the poem is in an informal tone, rewrite it in high rhetorical style. If it uses long words, rewrite it in monosyllables. If it is in iambs rewrite it in dactyls; if it is in free verse rewrite it in iambs; if it is in dactyls rewrite it in free verse. If the lines are four feet long rewrite them into five feet; if they are five feet long rewrite them into three. If it makes a lot of logical sense, rewrite it in an elliptical style; if it is in an elliptical style, spell out all the meanings. Do anything and everything to open up your unfinished poem to the powerful energies that are hovering around it, anxious to get in. If you know you are keeping all your drafts, you'll feel safe experimenting with radical changes.

Once you begin to have a sense of your poem's best overall shape, it's time to pay attention to the micro-level also. In one of his famously eloquent letters, John Keats described his composition process with a metaphor that captures the richness of poetry that is developed to its utmost, full of treasures waiting for anyone who cares to dig deeply enough to discover them: he said he aimed "to load every rift with ore." In lines such as these, from the poem that has been found to be the most anthologized poem in English, every rift does seem loaded:

From "To Autumn," John Keats (1819)

And fill all fruit with ripeness to the core;
To swell the gourd, and plump the hazel shells
With a sweet kernel; to set budding more,
And still more, later flowers for the bees,
Until they think warm days will never cease,
For Summer has o'er-brimm'd their clammy cells.

The combination of word-music (look at the "l's" and "m's"), phrasing (look at the counterpoint between where the caesura falls in the different lines), imagery and diction (notice the contrast between the different verbs) does seem to be brimming over with the same kind of richness described in these lines. These are the kinds of lines that invite rereading and rerereading. Even punctuation marks in poetry can be breathtakingly beautiful; here is another memorable semicolon from T.S. Eliot's *Four Quartets* (1943):

Where is there an end to it, the soundless wailing,
The silent withering of autumn flowers
Dropping their petals and remaining motionless;
Where is there an end to the drifting wreckage . . .

Allow yourself to enjoy such things; having a reason to do so is one of the great benefits of writing poetry. In free verse, a line break can make all the difference; in metrical verse, one extra accent in a line can give the entire poem a completely different attitude. As you read aloud, or quietly, or internally, savor small differences in consonants, vowels, syllable length, the weight of accents, diction, connotation, and tone. Small revisions to lines can create the kind of linguistic richness that will make a poem get off the page and sing.

Focus

What about the narrative level of a poem? Sometimes as I revise, I feel like a painter or sculptor, working not by thinking or reading, but only by instinct, by "feel." When the poem feels finished, I sometimes discover that the meaning has changed in ways I never anticipated. At some point in the revision process, it is essential to take the long view and think about what your poem is saying to readers, and what you want it to say. Gray Jacobik's "Adding Ideas to the Major Idea," described in the "Poetry Practices" section at the end of this chapter, is an excellent example of this level of revision.

Still, don't forget to distinguish between meaning inside the poem and meaning outside it. Information is not always a good thing; one of the most common mistakes I see is that beginning poets are too attached to how the situation that inspired the poem really happened. They want the poem to be an accurate record of their experience, and they feel they are cheating if they don't orient the reader to all the facts as they happened. If the poem is about visiting someone in the hospital, they feel forced to include, for example, a whole first stanza describing the car accident that landed the person there, and how it happened. But in fact, now that the real-life incident is over, your allegiance as a poet is to the poem and your readers, not to a full reporting of the situation. And readers may get more out of your poem if you leave some of the background specifics up to their own imagination; for instance, if they have had a similar experience visiting a person sick with cancer, too much detail about the accident might prevent them from identifying with the poem. The key is to figure out what your poem is *really* about underneath. If it is about the vagaries of fate, then include the accident. If it is about empathy with someone in pain, then focus on the hospital room.

A related problem I see in beginning poets' work is that the poem either starts too early or ends too late. Tolstoy is said to have written 150 pages as a warm-up before starting each novel, and then discarded them. Consider following his example and cutting out the "running start" that may have helped you get going but which you no longer need, or leaving off an ending that trails on after the poem has reached its true ending. Again, the key is to identify the core focus of your poem, in order to discover where it really begins or ends. One way to find the core is to put yourself in the position of a bored reader who is wondering why they should be reading your poem. Imagine them asking, "So what?" The answer to this question is your core point. You will find more on this topic in the "Questions for Meditation or Discussion" section at the end of this chapter.

Re-formations

If you are having trouble locating the point or core of your poem, you may find that putting your poem into a form, or a different form, even temporarily, is an excellent way to make yourself focus on its most important aspects. In writing as in life, when you need to focus on what matters most, other things can become surprisingly superfluous. When you turn your poem, even temporarily, into a sonnet and have only 14 lines to work with, you may better be able to decide what you consider truly essential in your material. This does not mean you should exclude vivid sensual imagery or exact details that are relevant to the heart of your poem, but it does mean that your poem has a right to its own existence; it doesn't have to be true to anything but itself.

Changing the form or stanza can make a remarkable difference to a poem. Look at the difference between these two versions of the beginning of a poem by Yeats:

From "Cap and Bell" (draft of "The Cap and Bells")

A Queen was loved by a jester,
and once, when the owls grew still,
He made his soul go upward
and stand on her window sill.
In a long and straight blue garment
It talked, ere the morn grew white,

It had grown most wise with thinking
On a foot-fall hushed and light.

From "The Cap and Bells," W.B. Yeats (1894)

The jester walked in the garden:
The garden had fallen still;
He bade his soul rise upward
And stand on her window-sill.

It rose in a straight blue garment,
When owls began to call:
It had grown wise-tongued by thinking
Of a quiet and light footfall.

The full version of the draft, included in Wallenstein and Barr's excellent book of revisions, makes it even clearer how the separated quatrains come into sharper focus and clearer alignment with themselves, how their grammar becomes simpler and their imagery more vivid. The division into stanzas gives the poem clarity of focus and immediacy; it also allows space for the mystery in the poem to settle between the cracks of the story.

Audience and Feedback

Writing for an audience, whether real or imagined, can help you do your best work. It keeps you on your toes. I always keep a pen handy on three kinds of occasions that I have found provide some of my own most startlingly effective insights for revision: when reading a poem aloud to an audience for the first, second, or third time; when opening an envelope of rejected poems from a magazine; and—yes—when opening a journal to see one of my poems in print for the first time.

What about making use of an actual audience when you revise? Feedback from others, poets or nonpoets, can be an irreplaceable part of the revision process—but be careful not to show others work that is so raw you may end up feeling invaded, distracted, or confused. I've found that the best time to show someone else a poem is when you feel it is almost finished, but something just doesn't seem quite right, and you have been spending so much time with it that you can no longer think about it clearly. When possible, I prefer to give people two different versions to compare or to choose from, so their comments can be channeled in a positive direction; it can be a lot easier to hear, "I prefer your first version of line 6 because . . ." than to hear, "I really don't like line 6." Even in a workshop, it is sometimes possible to provide alternate versions, and there's no need to be embarrassed; even Emily Dickinson sometimes wrote two alternatives for a word in a poem.

The most valuable feedback from others is often of the "reader response" variety. When you are so familiar with a poem of yours that everything in it seems perfectly normal, it can be extremely useful to hear, "Wow, I really don't understand that part," or, "She refers to the mother here, right, and not the daughter," when you meant it to be the daughter. I usually take this kind of feedback very seriously, unless these are poems that I consciously intend to be mysterious and fragmented. And this is feedback that any educated person can provide, even people who aren't poets and don't consider themselves expert in poetry. In fact, this may be a kind of feedback you will find especially valuable if you would like your poems to appeal to an audience outside of the world of poets.

The most important thing I can say about others' opinions is probably something you know already: take all feedback with a grain of salt. Nobody cares about your poem the way you do. Even misguided feedback can prove valuable by creating a kind of Rorschach test effect: not telling you anything new but instead helping you clarify what you really want. When someone says, "Why don't you just cut out the telephone poles in stanza 3," it can make you know with more certainty than ever that you love the telephone poles and want to add more about them. This kind of suggestion is very helpful, even if you don't take it. And if you show the poem to more than one person and notice how you feel about their responses, and one says something you agree with and the other doesn't, that's even better.

When you do get feedback from others that feels helpful, it's important to give yourself time on the other end to absorb and digest their opinions. You are the one who has to live with your poems, and even a suggestion that sounds good at first can end up not wearing well in the end. I'd say that about half of the suggestions I've liked at first from others (poets and nonpoets equally) have become part of my poems; I have rejected the other half eventually, sometimes soon, and sometimes years later.

Tone

With practice, you can become your own best critical audience. Perhaps the most useful method I have found is to listen to the TONE of your own poems. Tone is a poem's overall attitude or mood—like a tone of voice. Reading your poem aloud to yourself as you revise is one of the best ways to apprehend its tone. This works especially well with lyric poems. Try reading aloud next time you are revising. How would you describe the tone? Whiny? Shy? Arrogant? Conflicted? Ironic? Passionate? There are thousands of possible combinations of moods. Next, ask yourself honestly if this is exactly the tone you want your poem to have. If not, then what tone would you want it to have instead? Concentrate on your desired tone until you can hear it in your mind's ear, and it will function as an unerring guide so you can easily and surely make all kinds of changes, whether in diction, syntax, image, meaning, or form. Take a look at this poem written in 1912 by Robert Frost. It's an early version of his 1936 poem "Design," which you can read on page 145. What is the difference in tone between the two versions? How is the tone created in each version?

Robert Frost, "In White" (1912)

A dented spider like a snow drop white
On a white Heal-all, holding up a moth
Like a white piece of lifeless satin cloth -
Saw ever curious eye so strange a sight? -
Portent in little, assorted death and blight
Like the ingredients of a witches' broth? -
The beady spider, the flower like a froth,
And the moth carried like a paper kite.

What had that flower to do with being white,
The blue prunella every child's delight.
What brought the kindred spider to that height?
(Make we no thesis of the miller's plight.)
What but design of darkness and of night?
Design, design! Do I use the word aright?

Titles

When you are revising a poem, don't forget to think about the title. Poem titles seem even more important than most titles of paintings or of music; not just a label, a poem's title seems to send a wave-frequency into the text that changes the quality and experience of the work itself. Imagine what it would be like to read William Carlos Williams's poem "This is Just to Say" if it were called "Note on the Icebox," or Sylvia Plath's "Lady Lazarus" if it were called "Another Suicide Attempt."

Recently I took a course in intuition skills, where I learned a trick to help remember your dreams: give the dream a title the minute you wake up. It's as if the title builds a door leading from your consciousness into your unconscious mind, which you can find again and open when you need it. Like a dream's title, a poem's title also seems to provide a door into the poem for the reader, and it can affect the way a reader approaches a poem.

Sometimes the title of a poem comes to me first, and it reminds me that I want to go back and write the poem later. Certain titles have dogged me for years until I finally wrote a poem to go with them. And sometimes, a title can literally make a poem. These two witty poems would not make sense without their titles:

"Reflection on a Wicked World," Ogden Nash

Purity
Is obscurity.

"On Hearing a Lover Not Seen for Twenty Years Has Attempted Suicide," Agha Shahid Ali

I suspect it was over me.

As far as revision is concerned, my final piece of advice is this: don't worry too much about writing for those who give you feedback, since your poem may have many more readers whose responses are bound to be different. Instead, whenever you write, write for the best audience you can imagine. If you need to imagine an audience composed only of your Muse and your favorite poets, alive or dead, you will be in fabulous company. If you need to imagine an audience composed of family and friends at your cousin's wedding next month, you will also be in fabulous company. Don't feel you need to worry about what is being published by other poets in journals (today's hot trend will look hackneyed in a few years anyway). There is no such thing as writing for the wrong audience, but it can help you be true to yourself and do your best work if you keep in mind who you *really* want your audience to be.

A Checklist for Revision

Read it aloud!

What is the purpose, the focus of the poem—what is the "So what?" Is it an ambiguity, a mystery, a discovery? Let the focus of the poem emerge. Feel free to cut away extraneous material that distracts from it, even if you cut away the bulk of the poem. You will free your poem, as Michelangelo cut away the marble from his sculptures of people emerging from stone.

Read it aloud again!

Does the form of the poem perfectly embody, explore, enhance, and express its meaning at every point? If the poem is in free verse, are there any distracting metrical passages you should get rid of? Is every line of your free-verse poem a poem? Are the line breaks strong and worthwhile? Are the stanza breaks? If the poem is in a form, is the form and meter accurate? If you are using rhyme, are the rhymes consistently either perfect rhymes or slant rhymes, with any exceptions contributing to the whole meaning and effect of the poem? Otherwise, one slant rhyme may look like a mistake in a poem full of perfect rhyme, and one perfect rhyme can make a group of slant rhymes seem dim in comparison.

Read it aloud again!

Is the language exciting? Does it sound good? Are the words the best words? There is no shame in using a thesaurus and a rhyming dictionary to look for more interesting words.

Read it aloud again!

What is the tone of the poem? If a speaker is implied, is the diction consistent? Is the grammar natural, unless it is supposed to be unnatural on purpose? Are the speaker's moods moving and true?

Read it aloud again!

What about punctuation and grammar? To paraphrase Ezra Pound, who said poetry should be at least as well-written as prose, here's another motto: "Poetry should be at least as well-punctuated as prose." Even though the sentences are in a poem, they are still sentences and need to function as sentences. If you are writing an impressionistic poem that doesn't use punctuation, make sure that you are being consistent even in this. Inconsistencies will look like mistakes.

Read it aloud again!

Are the hidden connotations of the words working for your poem? Use an etymological dictionary and make sure you know the root meaning of all the key words in your poem.

Read it aloud again!

Look for redundancies and repeated words. As a general rule, if something happens twice it looks like an oversight; if it happens three or more times, it looks like a conscious pattern. Get rid of the former and make sure the latter really are conscious.

And, finally —read it aloud!

QUESTIONS FOR MEDITATION OR DISCUSSION

Some beginning poets are afraid to revise. Others find it the best part of writing. Where do you fall along this spectrum? What are your reasons?

Choose a dozen poems from this book that you enjoy. For each one, identify the place where it finally answers the question "So what?" For example, imagine Countee Cullen's poem "Incident" without the second stanza, and you will see that the question "So what?" is answered in the last line.

Think of some of your most memorable poem titles. How did they come to you? Do you enjoy titling poems? The poet Baron Wormser has said, "If the poem is really finished, the title's a piece of cake." This doesn't seem to be true in my experience. Is it in yours? Can you imagine never writing a single poem with a title, like Emily Dickinson?

Choose six poems in this book that you think are especially well titled. What, if anything, do they have in common? Why do you think you chose them? Find six titles you really don't like, and think about them in a group as well. What do you they have in common? Based on this data, come up with a set of criteria that you like for poem titles. Now look at the titles of a group of your own poems. How well do they fit your criteria?

How much do you generally revise your poems? If it's not much, why is this? Have you been unsure of how to proceed? Are you afraid of hurting the poem?

What process did my poem "Revelry" go through in the drafts below? What relation do you see between the first draft shown and the final version? Are these the same choices you would have made in revising the poem? (If you have a copy of the essay about these revisions, "Revising Revelry," you can compare your thoughts with the account in the essay.)

Sample Set of Drafts of "Revelry" by Annie Finch

These are sample drafts chosen from dozens made over a period of months. Discussion of the revision process for this poem can be found in the essay "Revising Revelry," published online and in the book *Poem, Revised,* listed in Chapter 2.

Version 1: Untitled

This is the war that wills aloud,
in voices hushed or caved or wrung
out of the rack that sweetness hung
here for the measure of this crowd.
Profiles rock poised air. The proud
lips listen, voices feel. Eyes thrill
alive with words that blend their fill
seasoned through table, rung, or cloud.
Words pour and parry, spiral, among
the single and paired and multiple,
into the cups that will not spill.
Drink in the warmth that marks the tongue
that has been spoken here, and sung.

Version 2: Untitled

This is the hour that breathes aloud
over the mouths that slip and sing

where a new culture galloping
bends alive around cup and cloud.
Deep in this landscape that the dark
warms, and the morning light lets go,
chairs root and rung their hearts with snow,
curtains are velvet thick, like bark.
Blood warms the lips and moves the skin;
voices find hours to revel in.
In words all hushed or caved or wrung,
here for the measure of this crowd,
I drink in the warmth that marks the tongue
that has been spoken here, and sung.

Version 3: A Prayer for Sitwells Café

Voices believe words and move free;
lust fills our lips; blood moves our skin.
Open our mouths to sip and sing.
Chairs root. Their hearts are runged with snow,
the curtains grow velvet thick, like bark.
Bend us alive around cup and cloud
through a new culture, galloping.
Passion is only revelry;
these are the hours to revel in.
Deep in this landscape ringed with dark,
warm us with the morning we let go.
This is the hour to breathe aloud,
to drink like the warmth of a learning tongue,
spoken and speaking, singing, sung.

Version 4: A Prayer for Sitwells Café

Voices believe words and move free;
lust fills our lips; blood moves our skin.
Passion is only revelry;
these are the hours to revel in.

Chairs root. Their hearts are runged with snow,
the curtains grow velvet thick, like bark.
Bend us alive around cup and cloud
through a new culture, galloping.
Passion is only revelry;
these are the hours to revel in.

Deep in this landscape ringed with dark,
warm us with the morning we let go.
This is the hour to breathe aloud.
Passion is only revelry;
these are the hours to revel in.

Open our mouths to sip and sing.
Drink like the warmth of a learning tongue,
spoken and speaking, singing, sung.

Final Version: "Revelry"

Chairs root. Their hearts are runged with snow.
Curtains grow velvet thick, like bark,
in this warm landscape ringed with dark.
Is passion only revelry?

Voices believe words and move free;
lust fills our lips; blood moves our skin.
We bend alive around cup and cloud.
These are the hours to revel in.

QUOTES

The correction of prose, because it has no fixed laws, is endless, [but] a poem comes right with a click like a closing box.
—W. B. Yeats

I don't write poems, I rewrite them.
—Robert Lowell

I washed thy face, but more defects I saw,
And rubbing off a spot still made a flaw.
—Anne Bradstreet, "The Author to Her Book"

Writing is revision.
—Ernest Hemingway

Never revise.
—Jack Kerouac

The willingness, the ardent desire even, to revise, separates the poet from the person who uses poetry as therapy or self-expression.
—Richard Tillinghast

Of all the Causes which conspire to blind
Man's erring Judgment, and misguide the Mind,
What the weak Head with strongest Byass rules,
Is Pride, the never-failing Vice of Fools.
Whatever Nature has in Worth deny'd,
She gives in large Recruits of needful Pride;
For as in Bodies, thus in Souls, we find
What wants in Blood and Spirits, swell'd with Wind;
Pride, where Wit fails, steps in to our Defence,
And fills up all the mighty Void of Sense!
If once right Reason drives that Cloud away,
Truth breaks upon us with resistless Day;
Trust not your self; but your Defects to know,
Make use of ev'ry Friend—and ev'ry Foe.
—Alexander Pope, "Essay on Criticism, Part II, 1711"

My own experience is that the work on a poem "surfaces" several times, with new submergence after each rising.
—Muriel Rukeyser

A poem is finished only when it is abandoned in despair.
—Paul Valéry

We ascribe beauty to that which has no superfluous parts; which exactly answers its end; which stands related to all things.
—Ralph Waldo Emerson

When I revise, I am always trying to give voice to whoever in the story doesn't have one.

—Patricia Smith

Nothing so difficult as a beginning
In poesy, except perhaps the end;
For oftentimes when Pegasus seems winning
The race, he sprains a wing, and down we tend.
—George Gordon, Lord Byron

Poetry, like schoolboys [*sic*], by too frequent and severe correction, may be cowed into dullness!

—Samuel Taylor Coleridge

The friends that have it I do wrong
Whenever I remake a song
Should know what issue is at stake,
It is myself that I remake.
—W. B. Yeats

Easy reading is damn hard writing.

—Nathaniel Hawthorne

POETRY PRACTICES

Casting a Cold Eye. Take a poem of yours you had thought was finished, completed at least a month ago or preferably longer—as long as possible. Pretend it is someone else's poem and revise it with complete ruthlessness.

Hearing Your Own Voice. Tape yourself reading one of your poems. Listen to the tape with a pen and a copy in hand, revising as you listen.

Adding Ideas to the Major Idea. Identify your poem's major idea. Write it out as a prose statement. Develop two associated ideas (in the form of statements) not now in the poem. See where those ideas might fit in, or how the poem might grow longer to accommodate them. Ask if there's some way at least one of those two new ideas can be represented imagistically. Invent that image (perhaps in the form of a metaphor, simile, or other figure of speech) and work it into the poem. Ask if this new image can be extended (a more elaborate metaphor, additional associations, etc.). Work these extended ideas into the poem. (Thanks to Gray Jacobik.)

The Soul of Wit. Take a long poem and cut it into a poem one-tenth of its original length.

Hook-up. Take two short poems of yours and combine them into one longer poem. Take them apart and rearrange them as much as you like. Add or subtract more words if you need to.

Trading Voices. Switch poems with a friend or partner. Revise the other person's poem as if it were your own work and then return your revision to them. Explain why you made the changes you did.

Who, Me? Take a poem with at least two characters (it's fine if one of them is an implied character who is only being addressed, a nonhuman character, etc.). Rewrite it from a different character's point of view.

Free Verse / Form Swap. Take a free verse poem, put it into a form, and back into free verse again. Or, take a formal poem, put it into free verse, and back into a form again—either the original form or another one.

CHAPTER 21

Bearing the Gift: Sharing Your Poetry through Publication and Readings

This ocean, humiliating in its disguises
Tougher than anything.
No one listens to poetry. The ocean
Does not mean to be listened to. A drop
Or crash of water. It means
Nothing.
It
Is bread and butter
Pepper and salt. The death
That young men hope for. Aimlessly
It pounds the shore. White and aimless signals. No
One listens to poetry.

—JACK SPICER

It's likely that all serious poets nowadays have felt the kind of despair Spicer is expressing—and also the defiance. The poetry that no one listens to is "tougher than anything," as necessary as bread or salt. So, as with any worthwhile pursuit, to write poetry must be, in the end, its own reward. Given this situation, not everyone wants to put time and effort into going public as a poet.

If you do decide to go public, you may find that sharing your poetry must also sometimes be its own reward. Even nationally known poets have stories of showing up to give a reading and finding one, or three, or eleven people in the audience. In such situations, the pleasure of sharing must come mostly from within: to give a reading of your words to others, or to experience your poetry in print, is satisfying in itself and helps improve your poems. It can provide a needed jolt of objectivity, and it can challenge and motivate you to work at writing your best. And of course, the morale-boosting that comes simply from daring to share your work can ultimately help you to persevere in writing poetry.

It can be terrifying to contemplate the world of publications and readings when you are just starting out, but with persistence that world will open to you, one step at a time. Readings may come first, or publishing may come first, or the two may develop together. Some poets get the most satisfaction out of sharing their work in person and interacting with an audience; others think of readings primarily as a way to publicize their published work. Whichever you prefer, you may find it most helpful to think of this work as the giving of a gift.

Where and How to Send out Your Poems

Before publishing a book, it is customary to publish poems in a number of magazines first. The usual rule is to start small. Use one of the directories listed in "A Poet's Bookshelf" in chapter 2 to locate likely magazines, or browse through literary journals in a bookstore, library, or online. It's an important habit to read at least a few issues of a magazine, and preferably to subscribe, before sending them your poems. You will save yourself and the editors a lot of wasted time by ruling out places that are not a good fit, and the only way to know for sure is to read the magazine. Editors usually work hard for little or no pay and, understandably, they hate getting submissions from people who have no idea what kind of work their journal publishes. If the editor is a poet, you can also look up samples of the editor's own work, which is likely to give you an idea of their editorial taste.

Include from three to five poems in your offering (this is a term of my own invention, which you are welcome to use if you like; the most common term is "submission," but I find "offering" more fun and more dignified). Only include more poems than this if you have seen guidelines written by the magazine that specify another number. Include a simple cover letter that says you are sending your poems for consideration and list your previous publications. If you feel you need to send to more than one magazine simultaneously, check in the directory to make sure that this will be in keeping with the magazine's policy, and mention in your letter that you are doing so.

If you haven't published before, it's okay to mention where you have studied poetry or given readings and other professional-sounding facts. In the interest of staying professional, you will probably want to avoid information about your personal life or your own thoughts about your poems. Use your best judgment, however, and write a letter that feels good to you. Sometimes editors do appreciate a more personal slant. And saying something about the magazine or about the editor's own work can't hurt.

Use a regular letter-sized envelope (*not* a big manila envelope) and always include a stamped, self-addressed, letter-sized envelope, folded into thirds and tucked inside your folded sheaf of poems. Some commercially slanted writing guides advise putting a copyright notice on your work or adding a word count, but don't do it; it will look amateurish. Many journals take online submissions on their websites and sometimes by email.

When trying to decide where to offer your poems, you might think of a stock portfolio as an analogy. If your goal is to be ambitious while keeping your ego relatively sound, a balance between a couple of "high risk," very competitive journals and several smaller, more approachable publications tends to work well. Small Internet journals can be accessible places to publish your first poems. Usually you can read the archived back issues for free, and often they will accept emailed submissions. But keep in mind that, while some Internet journals are happy to publish work that has previously appeared in print journals, few print journals are willing to publish work that has appeared online.

Occasionally, a small journal is willing to take previously published work that has appeared in another small print journal whose circulation is unlikely to overlap with theirs. If you make such an arrangement, be sure to be honest about it from the beginning, and ask them to include a line worded something like, "This poem was first published in . . . ," to give credit to the previous publication. But be aware that the larger and more prestigious publications can afford to be, and usually are, extremely scrupulous about avoiding *any* sort of previous publication.

For those who have trouble bringing themselves to send out poems, here is advice left as part of the legacy of Reetika Vazirani, a sweet and talented poet who died tragically at a young age. Reetika advised poets to set aside a regular time to send out, and to make the event festive by burning incense or candles and playing music. Poet Julie Enzer advises deciding in advance which poems to send where, and listing the magazines in order in advance, so that when the time comes you simply have to print them, write a letter, fill the envelopes, and mail. And of course, the more issues of a journal you read before offering them your poems, the more comfortable you will feel sending them your own work, and the more likely you will be to send something they can use.

Rejections

Even form rejection notes can be regarded as a badge of honor. Some poets keep theirs neatly on file, some discard them calmly, some paper their walls with them. Years ago, my sister offered to take me out to a fancy dinner after I had collected 100 rejection slips. Her plan worked: not only did it get me in the habit of collecting rejections—in other words, sending my poems out—but it started me thinking of them as a positive thing. I amassed almost four hundred and had a wonderful dinner with my sister before I threw the rejections out in one big satisfying ritual and stopped saving them. Ever since, I have seen rejections as the valuable trophy of a brave effort. Anything handwritten on a rejection note is an encouraging sign, and if you get a personal note, you may want to send again to that journal within a few months.

Internet journals are sometimes quite quick to respond. You may need to wait several months or more for an answer from a print journal. If you don't hear back in about six months, feel free to email or write, including another SASE, and ask politely if they have finished considering your work. If you don't get a reply within a month, write and tell them you are withdrawing your offering, and that if you don't hear back from them, you will consider yourself free to send it elsewhere.

While you are waiting for that dinner, here are a couple of poems to read if you find yourself getting fed up with rejections:

"We are Sorry to Say," Rachel Loden

that the decision has gone against
these poems. It just up and went

against them, like an enormous rearing
horse, a careening locomotive, and we

tried to get out of the way. We still
wake up screaming. Frankly

the decision scares us
more than a little. We think it wears

a muscle shirt and is named Bluto,
but who really knows? All we want

is peace and quiet, maybe a cottage
in the Hamptons, some sort of tonic

for our splintered nerves. That's what
we want, but there are sparrows

on the roof. And white roiling seas
of manuscripts that curse

and shriek, and tender envelopes
that bleed hysterically when opened.

From "Dear Editor," Kim Addonizio

Thank you for your form rejection letter
which I discovered on a small scrap of paper
at the bottom of my SASE.

Editor, I am sorry to inform you
that I cannot use your rejection at this time.
Perhaps another time will be better.

But somehow I doubt it will get better . . .
you are a retromingent crap weasel
who is possibly only a graduate student

and not a real editor at all.
Therefore I am returning your rejection to you
along with some of my new work

which I think you will agree is my strongest yet,
and whose universal themes you will recognize
from my many previous submissions.

Addonizio's poem turns the tables in a way that must fulfill many a poet's unconscious dream. Loden's title and first stanza will be familiar to anyone who has ever been rejected by *The New Yorker,* since it quotes the form rejection used by that magazine for many decades. I have gotten it myself, more than once, as I was reminded the other day when I received an email from a very young poet asking how to get published in the most prestigious magazines. She reminded me of myself at sixteen, sending my poems off proudly, over and over, to *The New Yorker,* in blissful ignorance of the reality of the situation. And yet those rejections thickened my skin, and every time the poems came back, I learned more about how to have faith in their strength and how to make them stronger.

Taking Things into Your Own Hands

Rejections hurt, and it takes courage to persist in publishing your poetry in spite of the inevitable mass of them. Is all the bitterness you may find yourself swallowing really just sour grapes? Well, yes and no. If it seems to you that the best poetry is not always what is published in the best places, you may actually be on to something true. After all, the literary world is full of cliques and groups, like any other field. Many of the people who are published where you want to be have been paying their dues for years, allowing editors to become familiar with them and their work. Even if you don't feel you are lucky, if you are persistent and believe in your work, and are willing to start with small publications if necessary, it is likely that you will find your niche and that your turn will come in due time.

Meanwhile, if you find yourself frustrated with the kind of poetry that *is* being published and recognized, or feel that your kind of poetry is not getting the attention it deserves, or want to shake up the current establishment, or simply want more chances to be part of the literary world, you have the option of taking things into your own hands. After all, this is how change usually happens: someone turns frustration into action. Enterprising poets have been reshaping the power structures of the literary world for centuries, from Marlowe to Wordsworth to Whitman to Pound to Brooks. Consider starting your own reading series or editing your own magazine or anthology. As June Jordan realized, such literary projects have real impact, especially for marginalized groups such as women poets and poets of color; her book *Poetry for the People* is a practical and inspiring guide. To run a reading series or edit an anthology is a great way to learn more about the poetry world, begin to develop your own aesthetic, and make your mark on current taste. Through undertaking such projects, you will become far too busy to feel bitter, and before you know it, your career as a publishing poet will be under way.

Arranging and Planning a Poetry Reading

At some point, even if you don't go as far as starting a reading series, you may find yourself wanting to give a poetry reading. If you haven't been invited yet, feel free to offer your services as a reader to bars, cafes, bookstores, or libraries. At bars and cafes, a payment is not uncommon, even if the poets just get a portion of whatever is collected at the door. At benefits, bookstore readings, and even some writers' conferences and community events, there may not be any payment. There's nothing wrong or humiliating with reading for free if necessary. Even some of the most famous poets are glad to read for free to the right audience. As Lewis Hyde's wonderful book about art and economics, *The Gift,* explains, all art is a gift to our culture and thrives best when shared freely. If you want to be paid, be sure to ask; you never know. And whether or not you are being paid, as the giver of a gift, be sure to claim all due respect. Do not hesitate to ask for a podium, a microphone, a glass of water, and someone to introduce you.

Once you have the reading lined up, it's a good idea to rehearse. Though good readings can be spontaneous or planned, planning makes sense especially when you are starting out. Look at the overall shape of your reading, and study how other poets organize their readings. Tracie Morris, a brilliant performer of her own poems, introduced a fabulous reading simply by saying, "I'm going to read some political poems and then some woman poems." This was just enough information to orient the audience and give the reading a memorable overall shape. I've noticed that a lot of practiced readers claim attention with a sure-fire audience-pleaser at the beginning, then add variety by alternating long and short or serious and humorous poems. Another possibility is what I call the "circus" model, based on a great performance I once saw: start slow, with low-key material, and build to your most powerful work just before the end.

Some poets follow the generous custom of always reading at least one poem by another poet at every reading. Some poets have a "signature" poem that they use to begin or end all their readings; Anne Sexton used to begin with the poem

"Her Kind." When giving readings after each of my books has come out, I've found that one poem from each book has felt like a natural beginning for a reading, and one a natural ending for a reading. Though I don't always open and close with these poems, I have done so often enough that I enjoy the ritual feeling of starting and ending with them, linking different readings I've done together in my mind.

Performing Your Work

Rehearse first, if possible, preferably with a tape recorder or with a friend who is ready to give honest feedback. Either way, be sure to become familiar with your poems so you can either recite them from memory or at least look around briefly at the audience as you are reading. For a **poetry slam,** a competitive recitation, you will need to memorize them all. Like most "performance poets," Terri Ford knows all her poems by heart. During her readings she stands calmly with her hands behind her back. It is disarming to be addressed so directly, and the audiences are blown away. Even if you are reading your work from the page, though, don't be afraid of dramatic pacing and pauses. The audience deserves something more from you than they could get simply from reading your book.

So here you are at the podium. You've been introduced, and you've thanked your hosts and greeted your audience. You may choose to introduce your first poem with an informal comment or two, or you may just want to launch into it. Either way, be sure to read as slowly and clearly as you can. Rushing and mumbling are by far the most common mistakes that readers make.

If you are reading metrical poems, practice the delicate art of making the meter clear while avoiding singsong delivery, and of pausing just long enough at the line break so the audience can orient themselves to the end of the line, but not long enough to actually interrupt the natural movements of the sentences. If you are reading free verse, the technique is similar: pause just long enough at the line break to register that it is there—but please try to avoid the monotonous habit of ending each line with a rising intonation that has become such a stultifying cliché of contemporary readings.

Perhaps the best single piece of advice I've ever gotten about giving readings was to think of each poem as focusing on one dramatic center, one climax, and to keep that structure in mind as you read. It makes it easier for an audience to grasp a poem when it is delivered with dramatic focus. Remember that your reading is, at least for most people in the audience, a substitute for the experience of reading your work in print. Sometimes I read a short, dense poem twice in a row; a short poem just goes by too quickly for me to appreciate, and as an audience member, I have always wished that other poets would do this. Since I have begun to do it myself, a few people in the audience always thank me and say they got much more out of the poem.

Most poets space their poems with a small amount of "patter": interesting facts, backgrounds, and anecdotes that make it easier for your audience to move their attention from one poem to another. While some poets read wonderfully with very few comments between poems, the odds are that you will make at least a few remarks. In your patter, it's not necessary to predict what the poem is going to say, or give away any surprises. Appropriate remarks include definitions of unusual words, some background about the theme or shape of the poem (villanelle, love poem to a parakeet, poem made only of phrases you heard spoken as a child, etc.). If you are a gregarious person by nature, don't be afraid to address the audience directly, make jokes, or ask for responses. But if they are solemn and quiet anyway, take it as a compliment: it means they are really focusing on your work.

When I was just starting to perform my poetry, I shared the stage one evening with Molly Peacock, an experienced reader who gave a riveting reading. Later I asked her how she managed to maintain such a level of energy and suspense after many years of readings. I've never forgotten her response. "How many poems did you read tonight?" she asked me. "About twelve, I think." "Well, I only read six during my reading, which was the same length of time." She explained to me that she thinks of each poem as a jewel, an experience so intense that the audience shouldn't be forced to listen too quickly or take in too much at once. She thinks of her own presence between poems as a frame for these jewels. She takes her time with the poems and doesn't squeeze too much in.

It is important to stick to the allotted time, especially if you are reading with others. Even if you are reading alone, less is usually more. Unless you are well known and being paid handsomely so you don't want to cheat people out of their money's worth, it's far better to read for too short than too long a time. Though it may be hard to choose which poems to share, a handful of well-delivered poems will be most memorable. Remember the old adage, "Leave them wanting more." You may find it easier to stop comfortably if you have scheduled an outing with friends or colleagues afterward, so that you can recover gradually from the excitement without a letdown.

Finally, the most important advice I can offer about giving a reading is simply to enjoy it. If there is ever a time to be fully engaged in the present moment, it's when you are sharing your poems with others. Just dismiss any doubts or anxiety and let yourself take pleasure in embodying the words you have worked so hard to craft. If it is a pleasure for you, the joy is likely to come through to the audience as well. I will never forget the beautiful sight of Stanley Kunitz at the age of eighty, rocking back and forth in self-evident delight at the rhythms of his own words as he gave a fantastically successful reading to a huge, packed house. The scientist Charles Hartshorn wrote a book to answer the question, "Do birds enjoy singing?" The answer, he had discovered, was yes. As poets, we can enjoy our singing too.

Collaboration

This chapter would not be complete without mention of the joys and opportunities that artistic collaboration offers a poet. Poetry is by nature a gift, and gifts should be given freely. If the world doesn't seem to want to publish or read your poems, it could be that you would do better to give the gift in a different way—perhaps a way that will give you additional enjoyment as well.

The section on dramatic poetry in chapter 3 includes a discussion of collaborating with actors and directors when producing performances of your poetry. In addition to artists who work in theater, poetry also lends itself well to collaboration with painters, sculptors, architects, composers, singers, filmmakers, landscape designers, choreographers, and dancers—not to mention other poets.

Poetry's roots are collaborative. The most ancient poets accompanied their lyrics with stringed instruments and their narrative poems with drumming. Poetic drama was staged by actors and dancers from ancient Greece to the Renaissance. Numerous poets have illustrated their own poems with drawings or had them illustrated by others, or carved into buildings or sculptures.

If you are feeling stuck or stale, look around at the other artists around you and think about ways that you could share your poetry in connection with another artist's work, whether working with a choreographer to stage dances based on your poems, mounting a gallery exhibition or publishing a book of visual/poetry collaborations, or adapting your work to film or music. Not only will you gain a new and wider audience; you may find your poems themselves drawn in inspiring new directions.

QUESTIONS FOR MEDITATION OR DISCUSSION

How important is publication for you as a poet? Would you be as good a poet if no one ever read your poems? The following poem by John Keats was discovered written inside the cover of one of his books after his death.

"This Living Hand," John Keats (1821)

This living hand, now warm and capable
Of earnest grasping, would, if it were cold
And in the icy silence of the tomb,
So haunt thy days and chill thy dreaming nights
That thou wouldst wish thine own heart dry of blood
So in my veins red life might stream again,
And thou be conscience-calmed—see here it is—
I hold it towards you.

The powerful immediacy of this poem reaches beyond the grave. Would the poem be as moving if he had published it before he died?

Is it possible to publish one's work too early? What could be the negative consequences of doing so?

What do you think should be the goal of a poetry reading? Is it to increase understanding of the poet's work, to entertain, to move the audience in an aesthetic or spiritual way, to raise awareness about poetry in general, to communicate about a social, personal, or political issues? Think about all the poetry readings you have been to. Which do you think were the best ones and why? What kind of poetry reading do you want to give? What kind of impression or feeling do you want to project?

QUOTES

Humility is an indispensable ally, enabling concentration to heighten gusto. There are always objectors, but we must not be too sensitive about not being liked or not being printed.

—Marianne Moore

I feel assured I should write from the mere yearning and fondness I have for the Beautiful even if my night's labours should be burnt every morning and no eye ever shine upon them.

—John Keats

To have great poets there must be great audiences too.

—Harriet Monroe

If fame belonged to me, I could not escape her; if she did not, the longest day would pass me on the chase . . . My barefoot rank is better.

—Emily Dickinson

Chameleons feed on light and air:
Poets' food is love and fame.

—Percy Bysshe Shelley

For the kids, spoken word is a reconnection with the oral tradition, a return to the origin of language, its sound, its music.

—Tim McLaughlin, coach of slam poetry team, Santa Fe Indian School

Performance is implicit in the role of the poet. I work on the page; I work off the page. It's not a problem of choosing one over another.

—Anne Waldman

Do not commit your poems to pages alone. Sing them, I pray you.

—Virgil

Poetry is a graveyard of talent destroyed by ambition, yet ambition is rarely ruined by talent.

—William Logan

The fruitfulness of a gift is the only gratitude for the gift.

—Meister Eckhart

"The Coat," W. B. Yeats (1914)

I made my song a coat
Covered with embroideries

Out of old mythologies
From heel to throat;
But the fools caught it,
Wore it in the world's eyes
As though they'd wrought it.
Song, let them take it,
For there's more enterprise
In walking naked.

Publication—is the Auction
Of the Mind of Man—
Poverty—be justifying
For so foul a thing
Possibly—but We—would rather
From Our Garret go
White—Unto the White Creator—
Than invest—Our Snow . . .
—Emily Dickinson

CHAPTER 22

Getting It Together: Creating a Chapbook or Book

At some point, you may feel you want to collect some poems into a publication. You don't have to involve many poems. Emily Dickinson sewed her poems into small "fascicles." The brief **chapbook,** sometimes containing only 8 to 12 poems, has long been a respected poetic creation. You don't even have to have a publisher, either; a long list of respectable poets have produced at least one self-published book, including Whitman and William Carlos Williams. Self-publishing a book can be extremely rewarding. I feel more intimacy with my own self-designed, self-published first poetry book than I do with any of my other books.

You may be thinking about making a book because you are tired of making photocopies for friends. You may want the feeling of reading your work from a bound book (in the months before each of my books has been published, I've had the desperate feeling that I couldn't stand another hour of shuffling through those particular manuscripts during readings). You may want a book to help you attract reading opportunities, or to sell at readings. You may feel a creative need to push your work in this direction. As poet Marcella Durand has said, "Self-publishing is a wonderful way to truly 'conceptualize' your work by fusing mediums and to carry something through from start to finish."

If you do self-publish a chapbook, at some point you'll have to think about typeface, layout, paper quality, art, and other elements of design; the cover (color or black and white?); the binding (hand-sewn books are beautiful; copy shops have quick binding options; and there are numerous other creative and amazing ways to assemble a book, from an envelope to a box to a necklace), and distribution (whether to look for a distributor such as Small Press Distribution, peddle copies to bookstores on consignment, sell on your own website, on a commercial website, or as an e-book, or simply sell your books at readings). Dan Poynter's *The Self-Publishing Manual* (Para Publishing) is the classic resource for such questions.

If, instead, you are ready to look for a "real" publisher, you will find that the so-called small presses are the most accessible place to start publishing poetry. Some of the country's most respected poets have had their careers with small presses. When you start to investigate small presses, easily done online since most of them have websites, you will find that many sponsor poetry contests. While some of these contests have been "outed" for unfair practices (especially on the website foetry.com), most are run in a fair and aboveboard way, and often these contests are the only way the publisher will consider first books. If you do enter a contest, be sure to follow any contest guidelines, even the tiniest details, exactly, or you may forfeit your chance to be considered.

Another excellent way to begin to find the right press is to look at a selection of their books and imagine where yours would fit in. Browsing through independent literary bookstores that carry a good selection of small-press books, and also through libraries, is a great way to start narrowing down the huge number of publishers. You can also attend bookfairs and conferences where publishers display their books, such as the annual Poetry Showcase at Poets' House in New York, or the annual Association of Writing Programs (AWP) Conference, held in a different city each year. At such events, you may even have a chance to meet some of the publishers in person.

After you have narrowed down the publishers to a handful that publish poetry you admire and that seem realistic possibilities, you can either enter their first-book contest or send a direct inquiry, if you find they are open to first-book submissions. When you approach a publisher, keep in mind that, even with well known presses and certainly with small presses, poets are now normally expected to do much of their own marketing and promotion. This means arranging and giving readings, compiling mailing lists to send out postcards or emails alerting people to your book, and perhaps traveling to poetry events and conferences. If you can let a potential publisher know that you are aware of this and willing to do your part to promote the book, the publisher is more likely to consider you a "publishable" poet. Of course, self-publishers need answer only to themselves about these issues—and can keep all the sales income as well.

Arranging Your Book of Poems

Whether you are publishing a book yourself, already have a publisher, or are planning to go through the process of sending out your manuscript until you find one, the poems first need to be arranged in some order. If you wrote your poems as part of a book in the first place, organizing your book will probably be quite straightforward. There is an implicit coherence to books conceived of as books, whether book-length poems—from Spenser's *Faerie Queene* to Longfellow's *Evangeline* to Sharon Doubiago's *South America Mi Hija*—or a series of poems that tell one story—from the Finnish *Kalevala* to George Meredith's *Modern Love* to Rita Dove's *Thomas and Beulah*—or poems that relate to one theme or subject—from George Herbert's *The Temple* to Jean Toomer's *Cane* to Davis McCombs's *Ultima Thule.* If your book is going to be a collection of poems in the true sense of the word, however, you will face a paradoxical challenge as you begin to arrange your volume. Each of your poems is a full entity in itself; when you finished it, you felt a sense of closure and completeness. Yet you now need to reconceptualize your poems as mere parts of a larger whole. This process can be dizzying and/or excruciating, particularly with first or second books of poetry, when the poems may have been written under many and changing influences.

You will probably find it useful to look at how other books have been organized (see the second item under "Poetry Practices" at the end of the chapter). For example, Jenny Factor's *Unraveling at the Name* unfolds in chronological order. C. S. Giscombe's *Giscombe Road* is centered around the identity of a place. Lucinda Roy's T*he Humming Birds* is organized into a section of narratives and two thematic sections. Patricia Smith's *Blood Dazzler* is focused on one incident, Hurricane Katrina. My own first book *Eve* is structured around nine different goddesses. Though you will discover that there are pretty much as many structures to books of poems as there are books of poems, some generalizations are possible.

Basically, there are two approaches to organizing a book: associative and metaphorical. The associative approach relies on the threads created as a reader moves from one poem to another, often using overlapping images, themes, or even phrases to link adjacent poems. For Renee Ashley, the logic is one of developmental coherence: "I like to think of a book ms. as a single poem: poems in the front that pique curiosity, poems at the end that somehow resolve or move towards resolution." The metaphorical approach, on the other hand, treats the book, or its sections, as part of an overarching larger structure, which may never be apparent to the reader all at once but which nevertheless gives the book form, a solidity. W. B. Yeats organized his books according to elaborate structures, with poems in certain spots corresponding to poems in other sections. For Allison Joseph, the rationale of a book is that it creates a persona for the poet: "The poems work together as a whole to reveal something about the poet's ambitions and desires."

Some poets are very logical about the book-arranging process, arranging the poems in piles by theme or imagery and then linking the piles. Others spread all the poems out, sit among them more or less blindly, and try different arrangements by instinct. I recommend a large surface such as the floor or a bed, though some people use desks or tables. I would not recommend a computer screen; I can't imagine not being able to hold piles of poems in my hand and physically shuffle them while assembling a book. As you go, you may find yourself spotting all kinds of connections between poems that you've never noticed before. You will probably make last-minute revisions. And you may well find yourself throwing out poems you had planned to include because they just don't seem to fit. Probably not all your finished poems will go in one book; some will be more appropriate for a future collection. Some of my poems waited over 20 years to find the right book.

However you start, the necessary and best approach is, simply, to start. You might end up spending a lot of time rearranging and reshuffling the order of the poems, so it makes sense to begin by simply putting together something you will be able to improve on. You might think about what connects poems, or you might think about contrasts between them. You might arrange the poems into a big group, or divide them into several subsections, with numbers or with titles. If you have trouble arriving at an initial arrangement, you can start with an alphabetical order (Harryette Mullen's award-winning book *Sleeping With the Dictionary* uses alphabetical order, which is not only appropriate to the book's dictionary and wordplay theme, but makes it very easy to find the poems!) or the order in which you wrote the poems, or a purely random order. There will likely be a lot of false starts before you find the right order. When I hit on a table of contents I really like, I always write it down, even though I know I am likely to change the order a hundred times. The process of writing it down makes me feel freer to abandon it and move on.

Here is an approach to ordering a book that is an interesting combination of the random and the planned. I have seen it credited to Bruce Weigl. First choose the poem you want to open your book, a very strong poem that sets the mood for your collection. Then choose the poem you want to end the book, the final effect you want to leave in readers' minds. Now divide your remaining poems into stacks based on their subject matter: politics, love, your dog, travel, etc. Go through the stacks in order, pulling one poem from each stack and adding them to the manuscript until you have used them all up. Use this provisional arrangement as a basis to work from, rearranging according to the principles discussed elsewhere.

Once you have arrived at an initial order—any order—the next step is to *read* your book. Or let it read you. Read it over and over, just as you would read a poem you are revising. As you go through the pages, you will probably find juxtapositions that you like and others that seem jarring or dull and that you feel moved to change. You may see a pattern or a plot emerging: some poems will feel as if they belong near the beginning, others near the end. As always, go with your instincts. If you are comfortable with using your intuition, I would encourage you to trust the movements of your hands, even if sometimes they seem to be shuffling pages without your being aware of what they are doing.

After you have finally settled on an order, you may want to show the book to a trusted friend or another poet to get their input (some of my friends have left the arrangements of their books entirely up to other people, who they feel have a more objective view of the poems than they do). If you are afraid of losing track of an arrangement you liked, just write down the new order each time you arrive at one that feels "finished." This collection of draft tables of contents might be, at the very least, interesting to look at in the future.

An eminent poet once described to me his habit when presented with a strange young poet's manuscript: he reads the first three poems and the last three poems, then decides if he wants to bother with the rest. This focus on beginnings and endings is probably not an uncommon approach to reading a book or manuscript—no wonder people sometimes worry how to start or end! The first poem can set the tone for a book, draw the reader in, define the poetic self, pay tribute to predecessors, or act as a sort of invocation. The last poem can serve as an ars poetica, a summation, a coda, a flashback, a farewell. Whatever poems you put in these crucial spots, remember that they are likely to be read as if they were doing initial or terminal things whether or not you intended them to do so—so it's best to choose your beginning and ending consciously, if not carefully.

Assembling a collection can be intimidating. It forces you to create, at least to some extent, a narrative out of poems that may have been written simply as lyrics. And by bringing the poems into a narrative, you are required to commit, at least to some extent, to a rationale for your book, an attitude, a public role for your poetry: in short, a "poetics." These are intense responsibilities, so don't be surprised if you find the first experience harrowing, and if it takes you a long time—years, maybe, with many poems added or omitted—to truly complete your arrangement. Whether you settle on an implied narrative arc (common arcs nowadays seem to be "sorrow to acceptance," "idealism to realism," and "despair to hope"), or on carefully paced random juxtapositions, a series of thematically coherent groupings, or any other kind of pattern, in the process of putting your poems into a book you will learn a lot about yourself as a poet.

As you go about assembling your book, one reason to make sure to do your very best with it is that you may find yourself continuing to live with it and "work on it" for a long time after it is published. In the contemporary publishing world, as mentioned above, even the very best publishers, let alone the valiant smallest presses, rely heavily on poets to get the word out about their own books. So even if you didn't self-publish your book, most likely you will actively need to create a readership for yourself if you want your book to find its audience. You are more than likely to end up learning the skills of a marketer, publicist, distributor, press agent, booking agent, and travel agent all in one, urging bookstores to carry your book, giving readings, sending out press releases to newspapers, and putting the book into the hands of reviewers. It's a never-ending process, but it can be a satisfying one, especially if you truly believe in your book.

QUESTIONS FOR MEDITATION OR DISCUSSION

If you do want to publish a book, what is your motive? What is your true goal? Do you want readers? How many? What kind? How hard are you willing to work to get them? It's important to be honest with yourself.

While many people assume there is no money in poetry, I've known poets who found ingenious ways to make money with their poems, from the poet in a park in Boston who wrote me a poem on the spot, on a topic of my choice, for five dollars, to poets who sell T-shirts and coffee mugs with lines from their poetry on their websites. True, most well-known poets at the moment make their money almost entirely from teaching and giving readings, but there's no reason that it has to stay that way. Do you think poets should make money with their poetry? Why? How? When? How much?

QUOTES

Books live almost entirely because of their style, and the men of action who inspire movements after they are dead are those whose hold upon impersonal emotion and law lifts them out of immediate circumstance.

—W. B. Yeats

Publishing a book of poetry is like dropping a rose petal down the Grand Canyon and waiting for the echo.

—Don Marquis, *The Sun Dial*

[Robert Frost's] *Complete Poems* have the air of being able to educate any faithful reader into tearing out a third of the pages, reading a third, and practically wearing out the rest.

—Randall Jarrell

If there's no money in poetry, neither is there poetry in money.

—Robert Graves

O God, O Venus, O Mercury, patron of thieves,
Lend me a little tobacco-shop,
or install me in any profession
Save this damn'd profession of writing
where one needs one's brains all the time.

—Ezra Pound

POETRY PRACTICES

Minibook. Take three of your poems and arrange them in various orders. How does the experience of reading them differ, depending on the order?

T.O.C. Spy. Examine the tables of contents of nine books of poetry. What do you learn about the poet simply from this, without looking at the rest of the book?

Stylistic Analysis of a Book of Poetry. Write an essay four to five pages long consisting of detailed observations (generalizations backed up with quotes) about the styles and techniques used in a book of contemporary poetry. What are the poet's usual themes? How does the poet write about them using line length, form (meter, forms, accentual verse, free verse), stanza, refrain, repetition, expressive variation if the poet writes in meter, line breaks, enjambment, word-music, diction, type of rhyme if any, voice, point of view, imagery, allusions, echoes of other poets' styles, etc.?

Chapbook. Make a chapbook: a small, simple self-"published" book (originally it meant "cheap-book") designed to take your poems into the literary realm. Choose your favorite and/or most polished 5 to 10 pages of poetry and arrange them into your chapbook. Think about the order of the poems carefully. Then design a format, typeface, cover, illustrations, etc. to suit your poems and yourself. One simple way to do this is to fold typing paper in half and put staples down the middle, but there are many other possibilities.

Web Book. If you have a website or networking page, you can make poems available there through a downloadable PDF file designed much like your chapbook, or simply by posting them online.

Afterword: *A Blessing on the Poets*

by Annie Finch

Patient earth-digger, impatient fire-maker,
Hungry word-taker and roving sound-lover,
Sharer and saver, muser and acher,
You who are open to hide or uncover,
Time-keeper and -hater, wake-sleeper, sleep-waker:
May language's language, the silence that lies
Under each word, move you over and over,
Turning you, wondering, back to surprise.

Appendix: Scansions

This section includes representative excerpts from poems in regular meter, and longer excerpts from poems with more irregular meters. There are also links to online scansion resources at the author's website, www.anniefinch.com. *If you get really stuck, you may email the author with scansion questions through the website's contact page.*

Chapter 11: Accent

"Jeans," Roseanne Roseannadanna (Gilda Radner)

 '   '   '   '
Jeans jeans the magical pants (seven syllables)

       '   '   '   '
the more they itch the more you dance (eight syllables)

      '   '   '   \   '
the more you dance the more people watch (nine syllables)

    '   '   '   '
to see how you scratch that itch in your crotch. (ten syllables)

"The Seafarer" (ninth century)

  '   '   '   '
maeg ic be me sylfum   soðgied wrecan

 '   '   '   '
siþas secgan   hu ic geswincdagum

 '   '   '   '
earfoðwile   oft þrowade

bitre breostceare   gebidan hæbbe
gecunnad in ceole   cearselda fela

From "The Seafarer" (A.D. 950) (trans. Annie Finch)

I keep the track   of a song true of me,
to tell of trials,   struggling times,
hard days,   how I endured.
I have carried   bitter cares,
had on ships   a house of cares;

From "Respiration," Mos Def

This ain't no time where the usual is suitable
Tonight alive, let's describe the inscrutable
The indisputable, we New York the narcotic
Strength in metal and fiber optics
where mercenaries is paid to trade hot stock tips
for profits, thirsty criminals take pockets

"The Moose," Elizabeth Bishop
For Grace Bulmer Bowers

From narrow provinces
of fish and bread and tea,
home of the long tides
where the bay leaves the sea
twice a day and takes
the herrings long rides,

where if the river
enters or retreats
in a wall of brown foam
depends on if it meets
the bay coming in,
the bay not at home . . .

"Famine," Landis Everson

In the middle of the night at least twenty deer
Came out upon my pillow to graze,
Gazing down at me with sad, round eyes,

Their pointed hooves quilting my pillow.
And I thrashed gently in sleeplessness,
Moving not to disturb them, wondering
At the famine this year that forces so many
To roam to poor, unfamiliar pastures.
The moon through the window throws cold light
Upon their curved backs, making a forest
Of crossed antler shadows on sheets
That until now have been flawless and starved.

From "The Girlfriends," Elizabeth Woody

Filled with old lovers, in the clutch of the chair,
you are a bloom of uncombed hair.

Scanning Exercises

From "Easter 1916," W. B. Yeats (1919)

Hearts with one purpose alone
Through summer and winter seem
Enchanted to a stone

To trouble the living stream.
The horse that comes from the road,
The rider, the birds that range
From cloud to tumbling cloud,
Minute by minute they change;
A shadow of cloud on the stream
Changes minute by minute;
A horse-hoof slides on the brim,
And a horse plashes within it;
The long-legged moor-hens dive,
And hens to moor-cocks call;
Minute by minute they live:
The stone's in the midst of all.

"From a Railway Carriage," Robert Louis Stevenson (1913)

Faster than fairies, faster than witches,
Bridges and houses, hedges and ditches;
And charging along like troops in a battle
All through the meadows the horses and cattle:

All of the sights of the hill and the plain
Fly as thick as driving rain;
And ever again, in the wink of an eye,
Painted stations whistle by.
Here is a child who clambers and scrambles,
All by himself and gathering brambles;
Here is a tramp who stands and gazes;
And here is the green for stringing the daisies!
Here is a cart runaway in the road
Lumping along with man and load;
And here is a mill, and there is a river:
Each a glimpse and gone forever!

If wishes were horses, beggars would ride.
If turnips were watches, I would wear one by my side.
And if "ifs" and "ands" were pots and pans,
There'd be no work for tinkers!

Chapter 12: Meter

From "Sir Gawain and the Green Knight," The Gawain Poet fourteenth century)

4-beat accentual meter

From Þe lorde ful lowde with lote and laȝter myry,
When he seȝe Sir Gawayn, with solace he spekez;
Þe goude ladyez were geten, and gedered þe meyny,
He schewez hem þe scheldez, and schapes hem þe tale

From "Sir Gawain and the Green Knight" (trans. Marie Borroff)

4-beat accentual meter

The lord laughed aloud, with many a light word.
When he greeted Sir Gawain—with good cheer he speaks.
They fetch the fair dames and the folk of the house;
He brings forth the brawn, and begins the tale
Of the great length and girth, the grim rage as well,
Of the battle of the boar they beset in the wood.

From "The Wife of Bath's Tale," Geoffrey Chaucer (ca. 1390)

iambic pentameter

˘ ´ | ˘ ´ |˘ ´ |˘ ´ |˘ ´ |(˘)
My fifthe housbonde, God his soule blesse,

˘ ´ |˘ ´ |˘ ´ | ˘ ´| ˘ ´|(˘)
Which that I took for love and no richesse,

˘ ´ | ˘ ´ |˘ ´ |˘ ´|˘ ´
He somtyme was a clerk of Oxenford,

˘ ´ | ˘ ´ | ˘ ´ |˘ ´ |˘ ´
And hadde left scole, and wente at hom to bord

˘ ´ | ˘ ´ | ´ ˘ |˘ ´|˘ ´
With my gossib, dwellynge in oure toun,

From "The Wife of Bath's Tale" (trans. Sinan Kökbugur)

Iambic pentameter

˘ ´ | ˘ ´ | ˘ ´ | ˘ ´|˘ ´
My fifth husband, may God his spirit bless!

˘ ´|˘ ´|˘ ´ | ˘ ´ | ´ ˘
Whom I took all for love, and not riches,

˘ ´ | ˘ ´ |˘ ´| ˘ ´| ´ ˘
Had been sometime a student at Oxford,

˘ ´ |˘ ´ |˘ ´ | ˘ ´ |˘ ´
And had left school and had come home to board

˘ ´ | ˘ ´ |˘ ´ |˘ ´ | ˘ ´
With my best gossip, dwelling in our town,

´ ´ | ˘ ´ | ˘ ´ | ˘ ´|˘ ´
God save her soul! Her name was Alison.

˘ ´ | ˘ ´ | ˘ ´ |˘ ´|˘ ´
She knew my heart and all my privity

´ ˘ | ˘ ´ | ˘ ´|˘ ´ | ` ´
Better than did our parish priest, s'help me!

From *Hiawatha,* Henry Wadsworth Longfellow (1855)

Trochaic tetrameter

´ ˘ | ´ ˘ | ´ ˘ | ´ ˘
Ye who love the haunts of Nature,

´ ˘ | ´ ˘ | ´ ˘ | ´ ˘
Love the sunshine of the meadow,

´ ˘ | ´ ˘ | ´ ˘ | ´ ˘
Love the shadow of the forest,

´ ˘ | ´ ˘ | ´ ˘ | ´ ˘
Love the wind among the branches,

´ ˘ | ´ ´ ˘ | ˘ ˘ | ´ ˘
And the rain-shower and the snow-storm,

´ ˘ | ´ ˘ | ˘ ´ | ´ ˘
And the rushing of great rivers

´ ˘ | ´ ˘ | ´ ˘ | ´ ˘
Through their palisades of pine-trees,

´ ˘ | ´ ˘ | ´ ˘ | ´ ˘
And the thunder in the mountains

. . .

From "To My Dearest and Loving Husband," Anne Bradstreet (1678)

˘ ´ | ˘ ´ | ˘ ´ | ˘ ´ | ˘ ´
If ever two were one, then surely we.

˘ ´ | ˘ ´ | ˘ ´ | ˘ ´ | ˘ ´
If ever man were loved by wife, then thee;

˘ ´ | ˘ ´ | ˘ ´ | ˘ ´ | ˘ ´
If ever wife was happy in a man,

˘ ´ | ˘ ´ | ˘ ´ | ˘ ´ | ˘ ´
Compare with me ye women if you can.

˘ ´ | ˘ ´ | ˘ ´ | ˘ ´ | ˘ ´
I prize thy love more than whole mines of gold . . .

The heavens reward thee manifold, I pray.
Then while we live, in love let's so persever,
That when we live no more we may live ever.

From "The Night Before Christmas," Henry Livingston Jr. (ca. 1822)

'Twas the night before Christmas, and all through the house,
not a creature was stirring, not even a mouse.
The stockings were hung by the chimney with care,
in hopes that St. Nicholas soon would be there.
The children were nestled all snug in their beds,
while visions of sugarplums danced in their heads,
and mamma in her 'kerchief, and I in my cap,
had just settled down for a long winter's nap,
when out on the lawn there arose such a clatter . . .

From Evangeline, Henry Wadsworth Longfellow (1850)

This is the forest primeval. The murmuring pines and the hemlocks,
Bearded with moss, and in garments green, indistinct in the twilight,
Stand like Druids of eld, with voices sad and prophetic,

Stand like harpers hoar, with beards that rest on their bosoms.
Loud from its rocky caverns, the deep-voiced neighboring ocean
Speaks, and in accents disconsolate answers the wail of the forest.

This is the forest primeval; but where are the hearts that beneath it
Leaped like the roe, when he hears in the woodland the voice of the
  huntsman?
Where is the thatch-roofed village, the home of Acadian farmers?
Men whose lives glided on like rivers that water the woodlands,

"Hound Pastoral," Lisa Jarnot

Of the hay in the barn
and the hound in the field

of the bay in the sound, of the
sound of the hound in the field

From "Parable," Allison Joseph

Sweep the walk and cook the dinner,
have his babies but stay thinner.

´ ˘| ´ ˘ | ´ ˘ | ´ ˘
Raise his children, feed them knowledge,
´ ˘| ´ ˘ | ´ ˘ | ´˘
clean the house with spit and polish.

´ ˘ | ´ ˘ | ´ ˘ | ´ ˘
Wipe their noses, scrub their fingers,
´ ˘ | ´ ˘| ´ ˘ | ´ ˘
do their laundry, tweeze their splinters,

´ ˘ | ´ ˘ ˘ | ´ ˘ | ´ ˘
buy the groceries, sew on patches,
´ ˘ | ´ \ | ´ ˘| ´ ˘
while your hair falls out in thatches.

"Nineveh Fallen," Rachel Loden
Kuyunjik, palace mound

´ ˘ ˘ | ´ ˘ \
Nineveh fallen. My
´ ˘ ˘| ´ ˘˘
Ghostly battalion
´ ˘ \ | ´ ˘ \
Silver-bell ankle rings
´ ˘ ˘| ´ ˘˘
Tatterdemalion

´ ˘ ˘ | ´ ˘ ˘ | ´ (˘˘)
Babylon Cadillac. Black
´ ˘ | ´ ˘ ˘
Candle guttering . . .

Chapter 13: The Many Voices of Iambic Meter

"Approaching a Significant Birthday, He Peruses *The Norton Anthology of Poetry,*" R. S. Gwynn

All human things are subject to decay.
Beauty is momentary in the mind.
The curfew tolls the knell of parting day.
If Winter comes, can Spring be far behind?
Forlorn! the very word is like a bell . . .

"Ulysses," Alfred Lord Tennyson (1842)

It little profits that an idle king,
By this still hearth, among these barren crags,
Match'd with an aged wife, I mete and dole
Unequal laws unto a savage race,
That hoard, and sleep, and feed, and know not me.
I cannot rest from travel; I will drink
Life to the lees. All times I have enjoy'd
Greatly, have suffer'd greatly, both with those
That loved me, and alone; on shore, and when
Thro' scudding drifts the rainy Hyades

Vext the dim sea. I am become a name;
For always roaming with a hungry heart
Much have I seen and known,—cities of men
And manners, climates, councils, governments,
Myself not least, but honor'd of them all,—
And drunk delight of battle with my peers,
Far on the ringing plains of windy Troy.
I am a part of all that I have met;
Yet all experience is an arch wherethro'
Gleams that untravell'd world whose margin fades
For ever and for ever when I move.
How dull it is to pause, to make an end,
To rust unburnish'd, not to shine in use!

From "Breaking Old Grounds," by Charles Martin

It really seems to want to be our friend,
Returning, is it, out of sympathy
Or just to see how everything will end?
Waiting, in either case, for one like me
To show up some morning at the backyard fence.

"I Shall Go Back," Edna St. Vincent Millay (1923)

I shall go back again to the bleak shore,
And build a little shanty on the sand
In such a way that the extremest band
Of brittle seaweed will escape my door
But by a yard or two. And nevermore
Shall I return to take you by the hand.
I shall be gone to what I understand,
And happier than I ever was before.
The love that stood a moment in your eyes,
The words that lay a moment on your tongue,
Are one with all that in a moment dies,
A little undersaid and oversung.
But I shall find the sullen rocks and skies
Unchang'd from what they were when I was young.

"The Illiterate," William Meredith (1958)

Touching your goodness, I am like a man
Who turns a letter over in his hand
And you might think this was because the hand

Was unfamiliar but, truth is, the man
Has never had a letter from anyone;
And now he is both afraid of what it means
And ashamed because he has no other means
To find out what it says than to ask someone.

His uncle could have left the farm to him,
Or his parents died before he sent them word,
Or the dark girl changed and want him for beloved.
Afraid and letter-proud, he keeps it with him.
What would you call his feeling for the words
That keep him rich and orphaned and beloved?

Trochees as Variations

From "Among School Children," W. B. Yeats (1928)

Labour is blossoming or dancing where
The body is not bruised to pleasure soul,
Nor beauty born out of its own despair.

From "I Wandered Lonely as a Cloud," William Wordsworth (1804)

I wandered lonely as a cloud
That floats on high o'er vales and hills,
When all at once I saw a cloud,
A host of golden daffodils,
Beside the lake, beneath the trees,
Fluttering and dancing in the breeze.

Spondees and Pyrrhics as Variations

Do not go gentle into that good night,
Rage, rage against the dying of the light.

How many dawns, chill from his rippling rest
The seagull's wings shall dip and pivot him,
Shedding white rings of tumult, building high
Over the chained bay waters Liberty—

I summon up remembrance of things past

And beauty making beautiful old rhyme

If this be error and upon me proved
That I in your sweet thought would be forgot

From "Some Girls," Suzanne Doyle
for Andrea Vargas

The risk is moral death each time we act,
And every act is whittled by the blade
Of history, pared down to brutal fact . . .
We are a different kind of tough; we hawk
Our epic violence in bleak bars, in bed, in art.

We crept in the tall grass and slept till noon

With his damned hoobla-hoobla-hoobla-how

There is a wide, wide wonder in it all

Slowly the poison the whole blood stream fills

From "Essay on Criticism," Alexander Pope (1711)

But when loud surges lash the sounding shore,
The hoarse, rough verse should like the torrent roar;
When Ajax strives some rock's vast weight to throw,
The line too labors, and the words move slow;
Not so, when swift Camilla scours the plain,
Flies o'er the unbending corn, and skims along the main.

Headless and Extra-syllable Lines

From "Those Winter Sundays," Robert Hayden

(˘) ´ | ˘ ´ | ˘ ´ | ˘ ´ | ˘ ´ (˘)
Sundays too my father got up early

From "Prologue" to The Canterbury Tales, Geoffrey Chaucer

(˘) ´ | ˘ ´ | ˘ ´ | ˘ ´ | ˘ ´ (˘)
When that Aprille with his showres soote

From *Hamlet*, William Shakespeare (1602)

˘ ´ | ˘ ´ | ˘ ´ || ` ˘ | ˘ ´ (˘)
To be, or not to be: that is the question:

´ ˘ | ˘ ´ | ˘ ˘ | ˘ ´ | ˘ ´ (˘)
Whether 'tis nobler in the mind to suffer

˘ ´ | ˘ ´ | ˘ ˘ | ` ´ | ˘ ´ | (˘)
The slings and arrows of outrageous fortune,

˘ ˘ | ´ ´ | ˘ ´ | ˘ ´ | ˘ ´ (˘)
Or to take arms against a sea of troubles,

˘ ´ | ˘ ´ | ˘ ´ | ` || ˘ ´ | ˘ ´
And by opposing end them? To die: to sleep;

˘ ´ || ˘ ˘ | ˘ ´ | ˘ ´ | ˘ ´
No more; and by a sleep to say we end

˘ ´ | ` ˘ | ˘ ´ | ˘ ´ | ˘ ˘ ´
The heart-ache and the thousand natural shocks

˘ ´ | ˘ ´ | ˘ || ´ | ˘ ´ | ˘ ´ | (˘)
That flesh is heir to, 'tis a consummation

˘ ´ | ˘ ˘ | ` ´ | ˘ ´ | ˘ ´
Devoutly to be wish'd. To die, to sleep;

˘ ´ | ˘ ´ | ˘ ´ | ˘ ´ | ˘ ´
To sleep: perchance to dream: ay, there's the rub;

˘ ˘ | ` ´ | ˘ ´ | ˘ ´ | ` ´
For in that sleep of death what dreams may come

˘ ´ | ˘ ´ | ˘ ´ | ˘ ´ | ˘ ´
When we have shuffled off this mortal coil,

Must give us pause: there's the respect
That makes calamity of so long life;
For who would bear the whips and scorns of time,
The oppressor's wrong, the proud man's contumely,
The pangs of despised love, the law's delay,
The insolence of office and the spurns
That patient merit of the unworthy takes,
When he himself might his quietus make
With a bare bodkin? who would fardels bear,
To grunt and sweat under a weary life,
But that the dread of something after death,
The undiscover'd country from whose bourn
No traveller returns, puzzles the will
And makes us rather bear those ills we have

Than fly to others that we know not of?
Thus conscience does make cowards of us all;
And thus the native hue of resolution
Is sicklied o'er with the pale cast of thought,

Sonnet 30, Edna St. Vincent Millay (1931)

´ ˘| ˘ ´ |˘ ˘| ˘ ´ |˘ ´
Love is not all: it is not meat nor drink

˘ ´ |˘ ´ |˘ ´ |˘ ´ |˘ ´
Nor slumber nor a roof against the rain;

˘ ´ |˘ ´ |˘ ´ |˘ ´ | ˘ ´
Nor yet a floating spar to men that sink

˘ ´ | ˘ ´ | ˘ ´ | ˘ ´ |˘ ´
And rise and sink and rise and sink again;

´ ´ | ˘ ´ | ˘ ´ | ˘ ´ | ˘ ´
Love can not fill the thickened lung with breath,

˘ ´ | ˘ ´ | ˘ ´ | ˘ ´ | ˘ ´
Nor clean the blood, nor set the fractured bone;

˘ ´ |˘ ˘ ´ |˘ ´ | ˘ ´ | ˘ ´
Yet many a man is making friends with death

˘ ˘ ´ |˘ ´ | ˘ ´ |˘ ´ |˘ ´
Even as I speak, for lack of love alone.

˘ ´ | ˘ ´ | ` ´ |˘ ´| ˘ ˘ ´
It well may be that in a difficult hour,

´ ´ |˘ ´ |˘ ´ |˘ ˘ |˘ ´
Pinned down by pain and moaning for release,

˘ ´ |˘ ´ | ` ´| ˘ ´ |˘ ´(˘)
Or nagged by want past resolution's power,

˘ ´ |˘ ´ |˘ ˘ ´ | ˘ ´ |˘ ´
I might be driven to sell your love for peace,

˘ ´ |˘ ´ |˘ ˘ ´ | ˘ ´ |˘ ´
Or trade the memory of this night for food.

˘ ´ | ` ´ |˘ ´ | ˘ ´ |˘ ´
It well may be. I do not think I would.

"Chosen," Marilyn Nelson

˘ ´ | ´ ˘ |˘ ´ | ˘ ´ | ˘ ´
Diverne wanted to die, that August night.

˘ ´ | ` ´ |˘ ´ |˘ ´ |˘ ´
His face hung over hers, a sweating moon.

˘ ´ |˘ ´ |˘ ´ | ` ˘ |˘ ´
She wished so hard, she killed part of her heart.

If she had died, her one begotten son,
her life's one light, would never have been born.
Pomp Atwood might have been another man:

born with a single race, another name.
Diverne might not have known the starburst joy
her son would give her. And the man who came

out of a twelve-room house and ran to her
close shack across three yards that night, to leap
onto her cornshuck pallet. Pomp was their
share of the future. And it wasn't rape.
In spite of her raw terror. And his whip.

From "Birches," Robert Frost (1915)

When I see birches bend to left and right
Across the lines of straighter darker trees,
I like to think some boy's been swinging them.
But swinging doesn't bend them down to stay
As ice-storms do. Often you must have seen them

Loaded with ice a sunny winter morning
After a rain. They click upon themselves
As the breeze rises, and turn many-colored
As the stir cracks and crazes their enamel.
Soon the sun's warmth makes them shed crystal shells
Shattering and avalanching on the snow-crust—
Such heaps of broken glass to sweep away
You'd think the inner dome of heaven had fallen.
They are dragged to the withered bracken by the load
And they seem not to break; though once they are bowed
So low for long they never right themselves:
You may see their trunks arching in the woods
Years afterwards, trailing their leaves on the ground . .

Expressive Variation and Keeping Your Balance

"Batter My Heart," John Donne (1610)

Batter my heart, three-person'd God, for you
As yet but knock, breathe, shine, and seek to mend;
That I may rise and stand, o'erthrow me, and bend
Your force to break, blow, burn, and make me new.

I, like an usurp'd town to'another due,

Labor to'admit you, but oh, to no end;

Reason, your viceroy in me, me should defend,

But is captiv'd, and proves weak or untrue.

Yet dearly I love you, and would be lov'd fain,

But am betroth'd unto your enemy;

Divorce me, untie or break that knot again,

Take me to you, imprison me, for I,

Except you'enthrall me, never shall be free,

Nor ever chaste, except you ravish me.

Sonnet 116, William Shakespeare (1609)

Let me not to the marriage of true minds

Admit impediments. Love is not love

Which alters when it alteration finds,

Or bends with the remover to remove:

O no! it is an ever-fixed mark

That looks on tempests and is never shaken;

It is the star to every wandering bark,

˘ ´ | ˘ ´ | ˘ ´ | ˘ ´ | ˘ ´ (˘)
Whose worth's unknown, although his height be taken.

´ ` | ´ ´ | ˘ ´ | ˘ ´ | ˘ ´
Love's not Time's fool, though rosy lips and cheeks

˘ ´ | ˘ ´ | ˘ ´ | ˘ ´ | ˘ ´
Within his bending sickle's compass come:

´ ´ | ˘ ´ | ˘ ˘ | ´ ´ | ˘ ´
Love alters not with his brief hours and weeks,

˘ ´ | ˘ ´ | ` ˘ | ˘ ˘ | ˘ ´ | ˘ ´
But bears it out even to the edge of doom.

˘ ´ | ˘ ´ | ˘ ˘ | ˘ ´ | ` ´
If this be error and upon me proved

` ´ | ˘ ´ | ˘ ´ | ´ ´ | ˘ ´
I never writ, nor no man ever loved.

Iambic Dimeter, Trimeter, Tetrameter, and Fourteeners

From "Open House," Theodore Roethke (1941)

˘ ´ | ˘ ´ | ˘ ´
My secrets cry aloud.

˘ ´ | ˘ ´ | ˘ ´
I have no need for tongue.

˘ ´ | ` ´ | ˘ ´
My heart keeps open house,

˘ ´ | ˘ ´ | ˘ ´
My doors are widely swung.

"I Had a Dove," John Keats

˘ ´ | ˘ ´ | ˘ ˘ ´ | ` ´
I had a dove and the sweet dove died;

˘ ´ | ´ ´ | ˘ ´ | ˘ ´ | (˘)
And I have thought it died of grieving:

˘ ´ | ˘ ˘ ´ | ˘ ˘ ´ | ˘ ´
O, what could it grieve for? Its feet were tied,

˘ ˘ ´ | ˘ ´ | ˘ ˘ ´ | ` ´ | (˘)
With a silken thread of my own hand's weaving;

(˘) ´ | ` ˘ ´ | ` ´ | ˘ ˘ ´
Sweet little red feet! why should you die—
(˘) ´ | ´ ˘ ´ |˘ ´ | ´ ´
Why should you leave me, sweet bird! why?
˘ ´ |˘ ´ |˘ ˘ ´ |˘ ´
You liv'd alone in the forest-tree,
(˘) ´ | ` ˘ ´ | ˘ ˘ ´ | ` ˘ ´
Why, pretty thing! would you not live with me?
˘ ´ | ˘ ´ |˘ ´ | ˘ ´ ´
I kiss'd you oft and gave you white peas;
(˘) ´ | ˘ ` ´ |˘ ˘ ´ |˘ ´ ´
Why not live sweetly, as in the green trees?

"My Papa's Waltz," Theodore Roethke (1942)

˘ ´| ˘ ´ | ˘ ´
The whiskey on your breath
˘ ´ |˘ ´ | ` ´ (˘)
Could make a small boy dizzy;
˘ ´| ˘ ´ | ˘ ´
But I hung on like death:
˘ ´ |˘ ˘ |˘ ´(˘)
Such waltzing was not easy . . .

From "Under the Rose," Christina Rossetti (1866)

˘ ´ | ˘ ´ |˘ ´
I think my mind is fixed
˘ ´ | ` ˘ | ´ ´
On one point and made up:
˘ ˘ ´ |˘ ´ |˘ ´
To accept my lot unmixed;
´ ˘|˘ ´ | ˘ ´
Never to drug the cup . . .

"Justice," Langston Hughes (c. 1931)

That Justice is a blind goddess
Is a thing to which we black are wise:
Her bandage hides two festering sores
That once perhaps were eyes.

"Love (III)," George Herbert (1633)

Love bade me welcome; yet my soul drew back,
Guilty of dust and sin.
But quick-eyed Love, observing me grow slack
From my first entrance in,
Drew nearer to me, sweetly questioning
If I lacked anything. . .

From "Metamorphoses," Ovid, trans. Arthur Golding (1567)

Howebeit he that did pursue of both the swifter went,
As furthred by the feathred wings that Cupid had him lent,
So that he would not let hir rest, but preased at hir heele
So neere that through hir scattred haire she might his breathing feele . . .
This piteous prayer scarsly sed: hir sinewes waxed starke,
And therewithall about hir breast did grow a tender barke.

Hir haire was turned into leaves, hir armes in boughes did growe,
Hir feete that were ere while so swift, now rooted were as slowe.
Hir crowne became the toppe, and thus of that she earst had beene,
Remayned nothing in the worlde, but beautie fresh and greene.
Which when that Phoebus did beholde (affection did so move)

Note: At this time in the history of the language, "remained" was pronounced with three syllables.

Chapter 14 : The Metrical Palette:

"Metrical Feet: A Lesson for a Boy" (1803)

Trochee trips from long to short.
From long to long in solemn sort,
Slow Spondee stalks, strong foot!, yet ill-able.
Ever to keep up with Dactyl's trisyllable.
Iambics march from short to long,.
With a leap and a bound the swift Anapests throng.

Trochaic Meter (/ u)

Double, double, toil and trouble,
Fire burn, and cauldron bubble . . .
Eye of newt, and toe of frog,

´ ˘ | ´ ˘ | ´ ˘ | ´ (˘)
Wool of bat, and tongue of dog,

´ ˘ | ´ ˘ | ´ ` | ´ (˘)
Adder's fork, and blind-worm's sting,

´ ˘ | ´ ˘ | ´ ˘ | ´ (˘)
Lizard's leg, and howlet's wing,

´ ˘ | ´ ˘ | ´ ˘ ˘ | ´ ˘
For a charm of powerful trouble,

´ ˘ | ´ ` | ´ ˘ | ´ ˘
Like a hell-broth boil and bubble.

"Tyger ! Tyger !" William Blake (1794)

´ ˘ | ´ ˘ | ´ ˘ | ´ (˘)
Tyger! Tyger! burning bright

´ ˘ | ´ ˘ | ´ ˘ | ´ (˘)
In the forests of the night,

´ ˘ | ´ ˘ | ´ ˘ | ´ (˘)
What immortal hand or eye

(˘) | ´ ˘ | ´ ˘ | ´ ˘ | ´ (˘)
Could frame thy fearful symmetry?

´ ` | ´ ˘ | ´ ˘ | ´ (˘)
In what distant deeps or skies

´ ˘ | ´ ˘ | ` ` | ´ (˘)
Burnt the fire of thine eyes?

´ ˘ | ´ ` | ´ ˘ | ´ (˘)
On what wings dare he aspire?

´ ˘ | ´ ` | ´ ˘ | ´ ˘
What the hand dare sieze the fire?

From *The Song of Hiawatha,* Henry Wadsworth Longfellow (1860)

´ ˘ | ´ ˘ | ´ ˘ | ´ ˘
By the shores of Gitche Gumee,
´ ˘ | ´ ˘ | ´ ` | ´ ˘
By the shining Big-Sea-Water,
´ ˘ | ´ ˘ |´ ˘| ´ ˘
Stood the wigwam of Nokomis,
´ ˘ |´ ˘ | ´ ´|´ ˘
Daughter of the Moon, Nokomis.
´ ˘|´ ˘| ´ ˘ | ´ ˘
Dark behind it rose the forest,
´ ˘ | ´ ˘ | ´ ˘ | ´ `
Rose the black and gloomy pine-trees,
´ ˘ |´ ˘ | ´ ˘|´ ˘
Rose the firs with cones upon them;
´ ˘|´ ˘| ´ ˘ | ´ ˘
Bright before it beat the water.
´ ˘ | ´ ˘ | ´ ˘ | ´ ˘
Beat the clear and sunny water,
´ ˘ | ´ ˘ | ´ ` | ´ ˘
Beat the shining Big-Sea-Water.

From "Iron," Sarah Josepha Hale (1823)

´ ˘| ´ ˘ | ´ ˘ | ´ ˘
. . .Then a voice, from out the mountains,
´ ˘ | ´ ´ | ´ ˘ | ´ (˘)
As an earthquake shook the ground,
˘ ´ | ´ ˘ | ´ ˘ | ´ ˘
And like frightened fawns the fountains,
´ ˘ | ´ ˘|´ ˘ | ´ (˘)
Leaping, fled before the sound;
` ˘ |´ ˘ | ´ ´ | ´ ˘
And the Anak oaks bowed lowly,
´ ˘˘ |´ ˘ | ´ ˘ | ´. (˘)
Quivering, aspen-like, with fear-

´ ˘ | ´ ˘ | ´ ` | ´ ˘
While the deep response came slowly,

´ ˘ | ´ ˘ | ´ ` | ´
Or it must have crushed mine ear!

From *The Anniad*, Gwendolyn Brooks (1949)

´ ˘ | ´ ˘ | ´ ˘ | ´ (˘)
Think of sweet and chocolate,

´ ˘ | ´ ˘ | ´ ˘ | ´ (˘)
Left to folly or to fate,

´ ˘ | ´ ˘ | ´ ˘ | ´ (˘)
Whom the higher gods forgot,

´ ˘ | ´ ˘ | ´ ˘ | ´ (˘)
Whom the lower gods berate;

´ ˘ | ´ ˘ | ´ ˘ | ´ (˘)
Physical and underfed

´ ˘ ˘ | ´ ˘ | ´ ˘ | ´ (˘)
Fancying on the featherbed

´ ˘ | ´ ˘ | ´ ˘ | ´ (˘)
What was never and is not . . .

"Lullaby," W. H. Auden (1940)

´ ˘ | ´ ˘ | ´ ˘ | ´ (˘)
Lay your sleeping head, my love,

´ ˘ | ´ ` | ´ ˘ | ´ (˘)
Human on my faithless arm;

´ ˘ | ´ ˘ | ´ ˘ | ´ (˘)
Time and fevers burn away

´ ˘ | ´ ˘ ˘ | ´ ˘ | ´ (˘)
Individual beauty from

´ ˘ | ´ ˘ | ´ ˘ | ´ (˘)
Thoughtful children, and the grave

Proves the child ephemeral:
But in my arms till break of day
Let the living creature lie,
Mortal, guilty, but to me
The entirely beautiful.

Anapestic Meter (˘˘)

"I Would Live in Your Love," Sara Teasdale (1911)

I would live in your love as the sea-grasses live in the sea,
Borne up by each wave as it passes, drawn down by each wave
that recedes;
I would empty my soul of the dreams that have gathered in me,
I would beat with your heart as it beats, I would follow your soul
as it leads.

From "Paul Revere's Ride," Henry Wadsworth Longfellow (1860)

. . . Then he climbed the tower of the Old North Church,
By the wooden stairs, with stealthy tread,
To the belfry chamber overhead,
And startled the pigeons from their perch

On the sombre rafters, that round him made
Masses and moving shapes of shade,—
By the trembling ladder, steep and tall,
To the highest window in the wall,
Where he paused to listen and look down
A moment on the roofs of the town
And the moonlight flowing over all.

From"A Fable for Critics," James Russell Lowell (1848)

There comes Poe, with his raven, like Barnaby Rudge,
Three-fifths of him genius and two-fifths sheer fudge,
Who talks like a book of iambs and pentameters,
In a way to make people of common-sense damn metres . . .

From "Maud," Alfred, Lord Tennyson (1855)

She is coming, my own, my sweet;
Were it ever so airy a tread,
My heart would hear her and beat . . .

Would start and tremble under her feet,
And blossom in purple and red.

From "The Destruction of Sennacharib," Lord Byron (1815)

And there lay the rider distorted and pale,
With the dew on his brow, and the rust on his mail:
And the tents were all silent, the banners alone,
The lances unlifted, the trumpet unblown.

From *Atalanta in Calydon,* Algernon Charles Swinburne (1865)

The ivy falls with the Bacchanal's hair
Over her eyebrows hiding her eyes;
The wild vine slipping down leaves bare
Her bright breast shortening into sighs;
The wild vine slips with the weight of its leaves,
But the berried ivy catches and cleaves
To the limbs that glitter, the feet that scare
The wolf that follows, the fawn that flies.

From Robert Browning, "How They Brought the Good News from Ghent to Aix" (1845)

I sprang to the stirrup, and Joris, and he;
I gallop'd, Dirck gallop'd, we gallop'd all three;
"Good speed!" cried the watch, as the gate-bolts undrew;
"Speed!" echoed the wall to us galloping through;
Behind shut the postern, the lights sank to rest,
And into the midnight we gallop'd abreast.

Not a word to each other; we kept the great pace
Neck by neck, stride by stride, never changing our place

From "The Hunting of the Snark," Lewis Carroll (1876)

And the Banker, inspired with courage so new
It was matter for general remark,
Rushed madly ahead and was lost to their view
In his zeal to discover the snark.

"Annabel Lee," Edgar Allan Poe (1849)

It was many and many a year ago,
In a kingdom by the sea,
That a maiden there lived whom you may know

By the name of Annabel Lee;
And this maiden she lived with no other thought
Than to love and be loved by me.

From "A Song in Time of Revolution," Algernon Charles Swinburne (1860)

The wind has the sound of a laugh in the clamour of days and of deeds:
The priests are scattered like chaff, and the rulers broken like reeds.

The high-priest sick from qualms, with his raiment bloodily dashed;
The thief with branded palms, and the liar with cheeks abashed.

They are smitten, they tremble greatly, they are pained for their
    pleasant things:
For the house of the priests made stately, and the might in the mouth
    of the kings.

They are grieved and greatly afraid; they are taken, they shall not flee:
For the heart of the nations is made as the strength of the springs
    of the sea . . .

For the breaking of gold in their hair they halt as a man made lame:
They are utterly naked and bare; their mouths are bitter with shame.

Wilt thou judge thy people now, O king that wast found most wise?
Wilt thou lie any more, O thou whose mouth is emptied of lies?

From"The Night Before Christmas," Henry Livingston, Jr. (c. 1822)

As dry leaves that before the wild hurricane fly,
When they meet with an obstacle mount to the sky.

The moon on the breast of the new-fallen snow
Gave the luster of midday to objects below

From "Under The Waterfall," Thomas Hardy (1914)

. . . And when we had drunk from the glass together,
Arched by the oak-copse from the weather,
I held the vessel to rinse in the fall,
Where it slipped, and it sank, and was past recall,
Though we stooped and plumbed the little abyss
With long bared arms. There the glass still is.
And, as said, if I thrust my arm below

Cold water in a basin or bowl, a throe
From the past awakens a sense of that time,
And the glass we used, and the cascade's rhyme.
The basin seems the pool, and its edge
The hard smooth face of the brook-side ledge,
And the leafy pattern of china-ware
The hanging plants that were bathing there...

From "The Lifeguard," James Dickey

I wash the black mud from my hands.
On a light given off by the grave
I kneel in the quick of the moon
At the heart of a distant forest
And hold in my arms a child
Of water, water, water.

Dactylic Meter (/ ˘˘)

This is the forest primeval. The murmuring pines and the hemlocks,
Bearded with moss, and in garments green, indistinct in the twilight,
Stand like Druids of eld, with voices sad and prophetic,
Stand like harpers hoar, with beards that rest on their bosoms.

Loud from its rocky caverns, the deep-voiced neighboring ocean
Speaks, and in accents disconsolate answers the wail of the forest.

This is the forest primeval; but where are the hearts that beneath it
Leaped like the roe, when he hears in the woodland the voice of
the huntsman?
Where is the thatch-roofed village, the home of Acadian farmers? . . .

"Mushrooms," Sylvia Plath (1957)

Perfectly voiceless,
Widen the crannies,
Shoulder through holes. We

Diet on water

"Arachne Gives Thanks to Athena," A.E. Stallings

It is no punishment. They are mistaken—
The brothers, the father. My prayers were answered.
I was all fingertips. Nothing was perfect:
What I had woven, the moths will have eaten;
At the end of my rope was a noose's knot.

Now it's no longer the thing, but the pattern,
And that will endure, even though webs be broken.
I, if not beautiful, am beauty's maker.
Old age cannot rob me, nor cowardly lovers.
The moon once pulled blood from me. Now I pull silver.
Here are the lines I pulled from my own belly—
Hang them with rainbows, ice, dewdrops, darkness.

From "Goblin Market," Christina Rossetti (1859)

Apples and quinces,
Lemons and oranges,
Plump unpecked cherries,
Melons and raspberries,
Bloom-down-cheeked peaches,
Swart-headed mulberries,
Wild free-born cranberries,
Crab-apples, dewberries,

′ ˘ ˘ | ′ ˘ ˘
Pine-apples, blackberries,
′ ˘ ˘ | ′ ˘ ˘
Apricots, strawberries;—

"At Last the Women Are Moving," Genevieve Taggard (1935)

(˘) ′ ˘ ˘ | ′ ′ ˘|′ ˘ | ′ ˘ | ′ ˘ (˘)
Last, walking with stiff legs as if they carried bundles
(˘) ′ ˘ | ′ ` ` | ′ ˘ ˘ | ′ ˘ `
Came mothers, housewives, old women who knew why they
˘ | ′ ˘ (˘)
abhorred war.
(˘) ′ ′ ˘| ′ ˘ ˘ | ′ ˘ ˘ | ′ ˘ | ′ |(˘˘)
Their clothes bunched about them, they hobbled with anxious steps
(˘) ′ ˘ ˘ | ′ ˘ ˘ | ′ ˘ ˘ | ′ | ′ ˘ ` | ′ ˘ (˘)
To keep with the stride of the marchers, erect bearing wide banners.

(˘) ′ ˘ ` | ′ | ′ ˘ ˘ ˘| ′ ˘ ˘ |′ ˘ (˘)
Such women looked odd, marching on American asphalt.
′ ˘ ˘ | ′ ′ | ′ | ′ ` ˘ | ′ ˘ (˘)
Kitchens they knew, sinks, suds, stew-pots and pennies . . .
′ ˘ ˘ ˘| ′ ˘ | ′ ˘| ′ ′ ˘ | ′ ˘ (˘)
Dull hurry and worry, clatter, wet hands and backache.
′ ˘ ˘ | ′ ˘ ˘ | ′ ˘ ˘ | ′ ˘ ˘ | ′ (˘˘)
Here they were out in the glare on the militant march.

′ ˘ ˘ | ′ ˘ ˘ | ′ ˘| ′ ˘ ˘ | ′ ˘ (˘)
How did these timid, the slaves of breakfast and supper
′ ˘ ˘ ˘| ′ ` ˘ | ′ | ′ ` ˘ | ′ (˘˘)
Get out in the line, drop for once dish-rag and broom?
′ | ′ ˘ ˘| ′ ` ˘ | ′ ˘ ˘ | ′ ˘ (˘)
Here they are as work-worn as stitchers and fitters.
′ ˘ ˘ ˘ | ′ ˘ | ′ ˘ | ′ ˘ ˘ | ′ ˘
Mama have you got some grub, now none of their business.

(´ ˘) | ´ ˘| ´ ˘ ˘ | ´ ˘ | ´ ˘ ˘ | ´ ˘
Oh, but those who know in their growing sons and their husbands

´ ˘ ˘ | ´ ˘ | ´ ˘ ` | ´ ˘ | ´ ˘ ˘ | ´ (˘˘)
How the exhausted body needs sleep, how often needs food,

´ ˘ | ´ ˘ ˘ | ´ ˘ ˘ | ´ ˘ ˘| ´ (˘˘)
These, whose business is keeping the body alive,

´ ˘ | ´ ˘ ˘ ˘ | ´ ˘ | ´ ˘ | ´ (˘˘)
These are ready, if you talk their language, to strike.

´ ˘ ˘ | ´ ˘ | ´ ˘ | ´ ˘ | ´ (˘˘)
Kitchen is small, the family story is sad.

´ ˘ ˘ | ´ ˘ | ´ ˘ | ´ ˘ ` | ´ ˘
Out of the musty flats the women come thinking:

(˘ ˘) | ´ ˘ ˘ | ´ ˘ | ´ ˘ | ´ ˘ ˘ | ´ (˘˘)
Not for me and mine only. For my class I have come

(˘)| ´ ´ ˘ | ´ ˘ | ´ ˘ ˘ | ´ ˘ ˘ | ´ (˘˘)
To walk city miles with many, my will in our work.

"The Slip," Rachel Hadas

´ ˘ ˘ | ´ ˘ | ´ ˘ ˘| ´ ˘ ˘
Empty and trembling, haloed by absences,

´ ˘ ˘| ´ ˘ ˘ | ´ ´ ˘ | ´ ˘ ˘
whooshings, invisible leave-takings, finishes,

´ ˘ ˘ | ´ ˘ ˘| ´ ˘ ˘| ´ ˘ ˘
images, closure: departures so gracefully

´ ˘ ˘ | ´ ˘ ˘ | ˘ ˘ ´| ´ ˘
practice their gestures that when they do happen,

´ ˘ ˘ | ´ ` ˘| ´ ˘ ˘ | ´ ˘
dazzled with sunlight, distracted by darkness,

´ ˘ ˘ |´ ˘ ˘ | ´ ˘ ˘| ´ (˘˘)
mercifully often we miss the event.

"The Denouement," R. S. Gwynn

' ˘ ˘ | ' ˘ ˘ | ' (˘)
Who were those persons who chased us?

' ˘ ˘ | ' ˘ ˘ | ' ˘ (˘)
They were the last of the others.

' ˘ ˘ | ' ˘ ˘ | ' ˘ (˘)
Why must we always be running?

' ˘ ˘ | ' ˘ ˘ | ' (˘˘)
We are the last of our own.

' ˘ ˘ | ' ˘ ˘ | ' ˘ (˘)
Where is the shelter you spoke of?

(˘) ' ˘ | ' ˘ | ' ˘ (˘)
Between us. All around us.

' ˘ ˘ | ' ˘ ˘ | ' ˘ (˘)
Shall we be safe until morning?

' ˘ ˘ | ' ˘ ˘ | ' ˘ (˘)
There is no doorway to enter.

Mixed Meters

"Your World," Georgia Douglas Johnson (19–)

˘ ' | ˘ ˘ ' | ˘ ˘ ' (˘)
Your world is as big as you make it

' ˘ | ˘ ˘ ' | ˘ '
I know, for I used to abide

˘ ˘ ' | ˘ ˘ ' | ˘ ˘ ' (˘)
In the narrowest nest in a corner

˘ ' | ˘ ˘ ' | ˘ ˘ '
My wings pressing close to my side

˘ ˘ ' | ˘ ˘ ' | ˘ ˘ ' | ˘
But I sighted the distant horizon

˘ ˘ ' | ` ˘ ' | ˘ ˘ '
Where the sky-line encircled the sea

˘ ˘ ´ | ˘ ˘ ´ | ˘ ˘ ´
And I throbbed with a burning desire
˘ ´ |˘ ˘ ´| ˘ ˘ ´
To travel this immensity.

˘ ´ ˘ | ˘ ´ | ˘ ˘ ´ (˘)
I battered the cordons around me
˘ ´ |˘ ˘ ´ |˘ ˘ ´
And cradled my wings on the breeze
˘ ´ |˘ ˘ ´|˘ ˘ ´ | ˘
Then soared to the uttermost reaches
˘ ´ |˘ ˘ ´|˘ ˘ ´
with rapture, with power, with ease!

From "Mezzo Cammin," Judith Moffett
˘ ´ |˘ ´ | ˘ ´ |˘ ´
I mean to mark the Midway Day
˘ ´ |˘ ˘| ˘ ´ | ` ´
With soundings in this verse form. Say,
´ ˘ ˘ | ´ ˘
Muse, how you hate it!
˘ ´ | ˘ ´ | ˘ ´|˘ ´
I know your taste for excess. But
˘ ´ |˘ ´ | ˘ ´ |˘ ´
These jingly rhymes must undercut,
´ ˘ ˘|´ ˘
Counter, deflate it. . .

From "A Hymn For St. Cecilia's Day," John Dryden (1687)
˘ ´ | ˘ ´ |˘ ´|˘ ´ | ˘ ´
What passion cannot Music raise and quell?
˘ ´|˘ ´ | ˘ ´ | ˘ ´
When Jubal struck the chorded shell,
˘ ´ |˘ ˘ ´ | ˘ ´ |˘ ´
His listening brethren stood around,

˘ ´ | ˘ ˘ | ˘ ´ | ˘ ´
And, wondering, on their faces fell

˘ ´ | ˘ ´ | ˘ ´ | ˘ ´
To worship that celestial sound:

´ ˘ | ˘ ´ | ˘ ´ | ˘ ´ | ˘ ´
Less than a God they thought there could not dwell

˘ ´ | ˘ ´ | ˘ ´ | ˘ ´
Within the hollow of that shell,

˘ ´ | ˘ ´ | ˘ ´ | ˘ ´
That spoke so sweetly, and so well.

˘ ´ | ˘ ´ | ˘ ´ | ˘ ´ | ˘ ´
What passion cannot Music raise and quell?

˘ ´ ˘ | ` ´ ˘
The trumpet's loud clangour

˘ ´ ˘ | ˘ ´ (˘)
Excites us to arms,

˘ ´ ˘ | ˘ ´ ˘
With shrill notes of anger,

˘ ´ ˘ | ˘ ´ (˘)
And mortal alarms.

˘ ´ | ˘ ´ | ˘ ´ | ˘ ´
The double double double beat

˘ ˘ ´ | ˘ ˘ ´
Of the thundering drum

` ´ | ˘ ` ´
Cries Hark! the foes come;

´ ´ | ˘ ˘ ´ | ˘ ˘ ´
Charge, charge, 'tis too late to retreat!

Amphibrachs, Dipodics, and Hendecasyllabics

˘ ´ ˘ | ˘ ´ ˘ | ˘ ´ ˘ | ˘ ´
The world is so full of a number of things

˘ ´ ˘ | ˘ ´ ˘ | ˘ ´ ˘ | ˘ ´ (˘)
I'm sure we should all be as happy as kings.
—Robert Louis Stevenson

"The White Bird," Anna Akhmatova (1914)

So worried about me, so jealous, so tender—
As steady as God's sun, as warm as Love's breath—
he wanted no songs of the past I remembered.
He took my white bird, and he put it to death.

From Samuel Woodworth, "The Old Oaken Bucket" (1817)

How dear to this heart are the scenes of my childhood,
When fond recollection presents them to view!
The orchard, the meadow, the deep-tangled wild-wood,
And every loved spot which my infancy knew!

Ernest Lawrence Thayer, from "Casey at the bat" (1888)

The Outloook wasn't brilliant for the Mudville nine that day;
The score stood four to two, with but one inning more to play
And then when Cooney died at first, and Barrows did the same,
A sickly silence fell upon the patrons of the game.

Rudyard Kipling, From "The Galley-Slave" (1886)

By the hands that drove her forward as she plunged and yawed and sheered,
Woman, Man, or God or Devil, was there anything we feared?

"The Meter of the Night Sky," Arielle Greenberg

˘ ´ | ˘ ` | ˘ ´ | ˘ ` | ˘ ´ | ˘ ` | ˘ ´
I wonder what would happen if the K in knife was said,

˘ ´ | ˘ ` | ˘ ´ | ˘ ` | ˘ ´ | ˘ ´ | ˘ ´
if part of all the Hs in the book had rubbed away,

(˘) ´ | ˘ ` | ˘ ´ | ˘ ` | ˘ ´ | ˘ ` | ` ´
changing up the shapes of our ancestor's good white bones.

From "Hendecasyllabics," Algernon Charles Swinburne (1866)

´ ˘ | ´ ˘ ˘ | ´ ˘ | ´ ˘ | ´ ˘
In the month of the long decline of roses

´ ˘ | ´ ˘ ˘ | ´ ˘ | ´ ˘ | ´ ˘
I, beholding the summer dead before me,

´ ˘ | ´ ˘ ˘ | ´ ˘ | ´ ˘ | ´ ˘
Set my face to the sea and journeyed silent,

´ ˘ | ´ ˘ ˘ | ´ ˘ | ˘ ˘ | ´ ˘
Gazing eagerly where above the sea-mark

´ ˘ | ´ ˘ ˘ | ´ ˘ | ˘ ˘ | ´ ˘
Flame as fierce as the fervid eyes of lions

´ ˘ | ´ ˘ ˘ | ´ ˘ | ´ ˘ | ´ ˘
Half divided the eyelids of the sunset;

´ ˘ | ´ ˘ ˘ | ´ ˘ | ´ ˘ | ´ ˘
Till I heard as it were a noise of waters

´ ˘ | ´ ˘ ˘ | ´ ˘ | ´ ˘ | ´ ˘
Moving tremulous under feet of angels . . .

"The Reemergence of the Noose," Patricia Smith

´ ` | ´ ˘ ˘ | ´ ˘ | ´ ˘ | ´ ˘
Some lamp sputters its dusty light across a

´ ˘ | ´ ˘ ˘ | ´ ˘ | ´ ˘ | ´ ˘
desk. Some hand, in a fever, works the fraying

´ ` | ´ ˘ ˘ | ´ ˘ | ´ ˘ | ´ ˘
brown hemp, twisting and knifing, weaving, tugging

´ ˘ | ´ ˘ ˘ | ´ ˘ | ´ ˘ | ´ ˘
tight this bellowing circle. Randy Travis

sings, moans, radios steamy twangs and hiccups,
blue notes backing the ritual of drooping
loop. Sweat drips in an awkward hallelujah.
God glares down, but the artist doesn't waver—
wrists click rhythm, and rope becomes a path to
what makes saviors; the loop bemoans its need to
squeeze, its craving for the ghost of Negro neck.

"What Could it Be," Julia Alvarez

Around the kettle of chicken and rice,
the aunts were debating what flavor was missing.
Tía Carmen guessed garlic.
Tía Rosa, some coarsely ground pepper.
Tía Ana, so tidy she wore the apron,
shook her head, plain salt what was needed.

Credits

The Publishers gratefully acknowledge the following for permission to reproduce copyright material:

A

Helen Adam, "I Love my Love." Used by permission of the Estate of Helen Adam, The Poetry Collection, State University of New York at Buffalo. Kim Addonizio, "Dear Editor." Kim Addonizio, "Blues for Dante Alighieri" from *What Is This Thing Called Love* by Kim Addonizio. Copyright © 2004 by Kim Addonizio. Used by permission of W.W. Norton & Company, Inc. Anna Akhmatova, "Solitude" from *The Complete Poems of Anna Akhmatova, Volume II,* translated by Judith Hemschemeyer (Somerville, Mass.: Zephyr Press, 1989). [14 lines]. Agha Shahid Ali, "Lenox Hill," "On Hearing A Lover Not Seen For Twenty Years Has Attempted Suicide", from *Rooms Are Never Furnished* by Agha Shahid Ali. Copyright © 2002 by Agha Shahid Ali. Used by permission of W.W. Norton & Company, Inc. Dante Alighieri, excerpt [9 lines] from "The Inferno," translated by Michael Palma. Copyright © 2002 by Michael Palma. Used by permission of W.W. Norton & Company, Inc. Anonymous, excerpt [9 lines[from *Sir Gawain and the Green Knight: A New Translation,* translated by Marie Borroff. Copyright © 1967 by W.W Norton & Company, Inc. Used by permission of W.W. Norton & Company, Inc. Julia Alvarez, "What Could It Be?" from *Homecoming, Revised Edition* (New York: Plume, 1996).

B

Joe Balaz, "Da History of Pigeon" from *Ola* (Kaneohe, Hawai'i: Tinfish Net/Work Chapbooks). Judith Barrington, "The Poem" from *Horses and the Human Soul* (Story Line, 2004). Margo Berdeshevsky, from "Special Tales in Ten Lines" from *But a Passage in Wilderness* (Bronx: Sheep Meadow Press, 2007). Ted Berrigan, "Sonhets XV" from *The Sonnets* by Ted Berrigan, copyright © 2000 by Alice Notley, Literary Executrix of the Estate of Ted Berrigan. Used by permission of Viking Penguin, a division of Penguin Group (USA) Inc. Wendell Berry, "The Peace of Wild Things" from *Selected Poems of Wendell Berry* (New York: Counterpoint, 1998). John Berryman, Sonnet 115 ["All we were going strong last night"] from *Collected Poems 1937–1971* (New York: Farrar, Straus & Giroux, 1989). Jen Bervin, "Shakespeare's Sonnet 15" from *Nets* (Ugly Duckling Press,

2004). Elizabeth Bishop, "The Moose," "One Art," "Sestina," and excerpts [40 lines] from "The Burglar of Babylon" from *The Complete Poems 1926–1979* (New York: Farrar, Straus & Girouz, 1983). Robert Bly, "The Old Woman Frying Perch" from *Morning Poems* (HarperCollins, 1997). Robert Bly, "Call and Answer" from *My Sentence was a Thousand Years of Joy* (HarperCollins, 2005). Louise Bogan, "Single Sonnet" from *The Blue Estuaries: Poems 1923–1968* (New York: The Noonday Press, 1968). Christian Bök, "Chapter I for Dick Higgins" [prose poems, 82 words] and "Chapter O for Yoko Ono" [prose poem, 103 words] from *Eunoia*, by Christian Bök (Coach House Books, 2001). Catherine Bowman, "Wedding Invitation III" from *The Plath Cabinet* (New York: Four Way Books, 2009). Gwendolyn Brooks, "Speech to the Young: Speech to the Progress-Toward," excerpt [7 lines] from "To the Diaspora," "We Real Cool," excerpt [7 lines] from "The Anniad" from *Annie Allen* (New York: Harper, 1949), excerpt [7 lines] from "Beverly Hills, Chicago" and "The Sonnet-Ballad." Lee Ann Brown, excerpt from "Ballad of Susan Smith, A Modern Cruel Mother Ballad" from *The Sleep That Changed Everything*, copyright © 2003 by Lee Ann Brown and reprinted by permission of Wesleyan University Press.

C

Nina Cassian, "Licentiousness," translated by Brenda Walker and Andrea Deletant, from *Life Sentence: Selected Poems*, edited by William Jay Smith. Copyright © by Nina Cassian. Used by permission of W.W. Norton & Company, Inc. Anne Carson "God's List of Liquids," from *Glass, Irony and God*, copyright © 1995 by Anne Carson. Reprinted by permission of New Directions Publishing Corp. Lorna Dee Cervantes, "Freeway 280" from *Emplumada* (Pittsburgh: University of Pittsburg Press, 1982). Originally published in *The Latin American Literary Review* 5, no. 10 (1977). Lucille Clifton, excerpt [4 lines] from "I am accused of tending to the past" from *Quilling: Poems 1987–1990* (Rochester: BOA Editions, 1991). Billy Collins, "Paradelle for Susan" from *Picnic, Lightning*, by Billy Collins, © copyright 1998. Reprinted by permission of the University of Pittsburgh Press. Billy Collins "Introduction to Poetry" from *The Apple that Astonished Paris* (Fayetteville: University of Arkansas Press, 1988). Eduardo C. Corral, "Acquired Immune Deficiency Syndrome" from *Indiana Review* (Spring 2002). Hart Crane, "Voyages IV," from *Complete Poems of Hart Crane* by Hart Crane, edited by Marc Simon. Copyright © 1933, 1958, 1966 by Liveright Publishing Corporation. Copyright © 1986 by Marc Simon. Used by permission of Liveright Publishing Company. Countee Cullen, "Incident" from *Color* (New York: Harper & Brothers, 1925), p. 15. e.e Cummings, "O sweet spontaneous." Copyright © 1923, 1951, 1991 by the Trustees for the e.e Cummings Trust. Copyright © 1976 by George James Firmage, "pity this busy monster, maunkind." Copyright © 1944, 1972, 1991 by the Trustees for the e.e. Cummings Trust, from *Complete Poems: 1904–1962* by e.e Cummings, edited by George J. Firmage. Used by permission of Liveright Publishing Corporation.

D

Emily Dickinson, "I started early—Took my Dog—," "The Bustle in a House," and "Tell all the Truth but tell it slant," from *The Poems of Emily Dickinson*, Thomas H. Johnson, ed., Cambridge, Mass.: The Belknap Press of Harvard University Press, Copyright © 1951, 1955, 1979, 1983 by the President and Fellows of Harvard College. Owen Dodson, "Midnight Bell" from *Powerful Long Ladder* (New York: Farrar, Straus & Giroux, 1946). Hilda Doolittle, "The Walls Do Not Fall" excerpt, from *Collected Poems, 1912–1944,* copyright © 1982 by The Estate of Hilda Doolittle. Reprinted by permission of New Directions Publishing Corp. John Drury, "Ghazal of the Lagoon" from *The Disappearing Town* (Oxford, OH: Miami University Press, 2000). Robert Duncan, excerpt [8 lines] from "Often I Am Permitted to Return to a Meadow" from *The Opening of the Field,* copyright © 1960 by Robert Duncan. Reprinted by permission of New Directions Publishing Corp.

E

Russell Edson, "You" from *The Wounded Breakfast* copyright © 1985 by Russell Edson and reprinted by permission of Weleyan University Press. Odysseus Elytis, excerpt [4 lines] from "Maria Nefele's Song." Translated by Olga Broumas, from *Eros, Eros, Eros* (Port Townsend, Wash.: Copper Canyon Press, 1998). Louise Erdrich "The Butcher's Wife" from *Jacklight* (New York: Holt, Rinehart and Winston, 1984). Copyright © 1984 by Louise Erdrich, reprinted with permission of The Wylie Agency LLC. Elaine Equi, excerpt [8 lines] from "A Date with Robbe-Grillet" from *Ripple Effect: New and Selected Poems* (Minneapolis: Coffee House Press, 2007). Originally collected in *Surface Tension* (Minneapolis: Coffee House Press, 1989). Landis Everson, "Famine" from *Everything Preserved: Poems 1955–2005* (St. Paul: Graywolf Press, 2005).

F

Ruth Forman, "Sometime," from *Renaissance* (Boston: Beacon Press, 1997). Helen Frost, "My Choice (KATIE)" from *Keesha's House* (New York: Farrar, Straus & Giroux, 2003).

G

Emily Galvin, "Light Warning" from *Do the Math* (Tupel Press). Ray Gonzalez, "It was a Turtle" from *The Hawk Temple at Tierra Grande* (Rochester: BOA Editions, 2002). Veronica Golos, "From the Visit—South Carolina" from *The Drunken Boat* (Winter 2000). Arielle Greenberg, "The Meter of the Night Sky" from *Salt* (Metrical Poetry Feature, edited by Annie Finch), 2005. Thom Gunn, "The Night Piece" from *Collected Poems* (New York: Noonday Press, 1994). R.S. Gwynn, "The Denouement" from *No Word of Farewell: Poems 1970–2000* (Ashland, Ore.: Story Line Press, 2001). By permission of the author.

H

Marilyn Hacker, excerpt [first 15 lines] from ["Why did Ray leave her pipe tobacco here"] from *Love, Death and the Changing of the Seasons* (W.W. Norton & Company, 1986) Copyright © 1986 Marilyn Hacker. Marilyn Hacker, "Rune of the Finland Woman." Copyright © 1985 by Marilyn Hacker, from *Selected Poems: 1965–1990* by Marilyn Hacker. Used by permission of W.W. Norton & Company, Inc. Marilyn Hacker, excerpt [8 lines] from "Dusk: July" from *Winter Numbers* by Marilyn Hacker. Copyright © 1994 by Marilyn Hacker. Used by permission of the author and W.W. Norton & Company, Inc. Marilyn Hacker, "Untoward Occurrence at an Embassy Poetry Reading" from *First Cities: Collected Early Poems 1960–1979* (New York: W.W. Norton & Company, 2003). Rachel Hadas, "The Slip" in *Halfway Down the Hall* © 1988 by Rachel Hadas and reprinted with permission of Wesleyan University Press. Joy Harjo, "Ah, Ah" from *How We Became Human: New and Selected Poems: 1975–2001* by Joy Harjo. Copyright © 2002 by Joy Harjo. Used by permission of W.W. Norton & Company, Inc. Farideh Hassanzadeh-Mostafavi, "Isn't It Enough?" (Washington, DC: Foreign Policy In Focus, June 12, 2007). Yona Harvey, "Going to Hear My Child's Heartbeat for the First Time Part 2" (Spring 2002). Robert Hayden, "Those Winter Sundays." Copyright © by 1966 by Robert Hayden, from *Angle of Ascent: New and Selected Poems by Robert Hayden.* Used by permission of Liveright Publishing Corporation. Seamus Heaney, "Digging" from *Death of a Naturalist* (London: Faber & Faber, 1969). Anthony Hecht, "The Book of Yolek," copyright © 1990 by Anthony Hecht, from *The Transparent Man* by Anthony Hecht. Used by permission of Alfred A. Knopf, a division of Random House, Inc. Brenda Hillman, "Before My Pencil" in *Cascadia* © 2001 by Brenda Hillman and reprinted by permission of Wesleyan University Press. Brenda Hillman, "Male Nipples," from *Loose Sugar* copyright © 1997 by Brenda Hillman and reprinted by permission of Wesleyan University Press. Jane Hirshfield, "Late Self-Portrait by Rembrandt" from *After* (New York: HarperCollins, 2006). Copyright © 2006 by Jane Hirshfield. Reprinted by permission of HarperCollins Publishers, Inc. L. E Hogan "Ravelings" from *Log Cabin Chronicles* (November 1996). John Hollander, "Adam's Task," copyright © 1993 by John Hollander, from *Selected Poetry* by John Hollander. Used by permission of Alfred A. Knopf, a division of Random House, Inc. Andrew Hudgins, "Threat and Lamentations" from *The Glass Hammer: A Southern Childhood, Poems by Andrew Hudgins.* Copyright © 1994 by Andrew Hudgins. Reprinted by permission of Houghton Mifflin Harcourt Publishing Company. All Rights Reserved. Langston Hughes, "Island," "Nightmare Boogie," "Casualty," "Justice," "The Negro Speaks of Rivers," "The Weary Blues," and "Madam and the Census Man" from *The Collected Poems of Langston Hughes* by Langston Hughes, edited by Arnold Rampersad and David Roessel, Associate Editor, copyright © 1994 by the Estate of Langston Hughes. Used by permission of Alfred A. Knopf, a division of Random House, Inc.

J

Major Jackson, "Letter to Brooks," from *Hoops* by Major Jackson. Copyright © 2006 by Major Jackson. Used by permission of W.W. Norton & Company, Inc. Michael Jarman, "Unholy Sonnet" ["After the praying, after the hymn-singing"] from *Questions for Ecclesiastes* (Archland, Ore.: Story Line Press, 1997). Allison Joseph, "Parable" Reprinted by permission of Allison Joseph.

K

Olena Kalytiak Davis, excerpt [10 lines] from "O Great Slacker" from *Shattered Sonnets Love Cards and Other Off and Back Handed Importunities* (New York: Bloomsbury Publishing, 2003). Reprinted with the permission of Bloomsbury USA. Bob Kaufman, "Oregon," from *The Ancient Rain: Poems 1956–1978,* copyright © 1981 by Bob Kaufman. Reprinted by permission of New Directions Publishing Corp. Mimi Khalvati, "Ghazal: it's heartache" from *The Meanest Flower* (Manchester: Carcanet Press, 2007). Venus Khoury-Ghata, ["Autumn preceded summer by one day"] from *She Says,* translated by Marilyn Hacker (St. Paul, Minn.: Graywolf Press, 2003) [10 lines]. Galway Kinnell, "Hide and Seek, 1933" from *Strong is Your Hold: Poems by Galway Kinnell* Copyright © 2006 by Galway Kinnell. Reprinted by permission of Houghton Mifflin Harcourt Publishing Company. All rights reserved. Maxine Kumin, "Morning Swim." Copyright © 1965 by Maxine Kumin, from *Selected Poems 1960–1990* by Maxine Kumin. Used by permission of W.W. Norton & Company, Inc. Stanley Kunitz, "Touch Me" from *Passing Through: The Later Poems, New and Selected* by Stanley Kunitz. Copyright © 1995 by Stanley Kunitz. Used by permission of W.W. Norton & Company, Inc.

L

Philip Larkin, "Home Is So Sad" from *Collected Poems* (New York: Farrar, Straus & Giroux, 1994). Denis Lee, "history" from *UN* (House of Anansi Press). Vachel Lindsay, "The Flower-Fed Buffaloes" from *Going-to-the-Sun* (New York: D. Appleton & Company, 1923). Rachel Loden, "Ninevah Fallen" from *The Richard Nixon Snow Globe* (Wicklow, Ireland: Wild Honey Press, 2005). Later in *Dick of the Dead* (Boise: Ahsahta Press, 2009). Rachel Loden, "We Are Sorry to Say" from *Hotel Imperium* (Athens: The University of Georgia Press, 1999). Audre Lorde, "Coal" from *Collected Poems* (New York: Norton, 1997). Copyright © 1968, 1970, 1973 by Audre Lorde, from *The Collected Poems of Audre Lorde* by Audre Lorde. Used by permission of W.W. Norton & Company, Inc. Robert Lowell, "History" from *History* (New York: Farrar, Straus & Giroux, 2001). Li-Young Lee, "Eating Together" from *Rose* (Rochester: BOA Editions, 2000), p. 49.

M

Archibald MacLeish, "Ars Poetica" from *Collected Poems 1917–1982* by Archibald MacLeish. Copyright © 1985 by The Estate of Archibald MacLeish. Reproduced by permission of Houghton Mifflin Harcourt Publishing Company. All rights reserved. Jackson Mac Low, "Call Me Ishmael" from *Stanzas for Iris Lezak* (Something Else Press, 1971). Excerpt [44 words] from email to Jena Osman. Reprinted with the permission of Anne Tardos and the Estate of Jackson Mac Low. Michael Magee, "Pledge 1" from *Morning Constitutional* (Handwritten Press, 1999). Lisa Suhair Majaj, "Jerusalem Song," first published in *The Poetry of Arab Women: A Contemporary Anthology,* ed. Nathalie Handal (Interlink Publishing, 2001). Randall Mann, "At the Heron" from *Complaint in the Garden* (Omaha: Zoo Press, 2004). Heather McHugh, excerpt from "A" in *Hinge and Sign: poems, 1968–1993,* copyright © 1994 by Heather McHugh and reprinted by permission of Wesleyan University Press. Peter Meinke, "Zinc Fingers" from *Zinc Fingers: Poems A to Z* by Peter Meinke, copyright © 2000. Reprinted by permission of the University of Pittsburgh Press. William Meredith, "The Illiterate" and "Effort at Speech" from *Effort at*

Speech: New and Selected Poems (Evanston, Ill.: TriQuarterly Books, 1977). W. S. Merwin "Some Last Questions" from *The Second Four Books of Poems* (Port Townsend, Washington: Copper Canyon Press, 1993). Copyright © 1967 by W .S. Merwin, reprinted with permission of The Wylie Agency LLC. Edna St. Vincent Millay, Sonnet 30 ["Love is not all; it is not meat nor drink."], "I Shall Go Back," and "I will Chaos in fourteen lines" from *Collected Poems* (New York: HarperCollins Publishers). Edna St. Vincent Millay, "My Candle Burns at Both Ends" from *Collected Poems* (New York: HarperCollins Publishers). Copyright © 1922, 1950 by Edna St. Vincent Millay. Lisel Mueller, "Love Like Salt," from *Alive Together* (Baton Rouge: Louisiana State University Press, 1995). Paul Muldoon, excerpt [9 lines] from "The Old Country" from *Horse Latitudes* (New York: Farrar, Straus & Giroux, 2006). Paul Muldoon, "The Outlier" and "The Mountain Is Holding Out" from *Horse Latitudes* (New York: Farrar, Straus & Giroux, 1998).

N

Sawako Nakayasu, "A Field of Fried Umbrellas" from *Texture Notes* by Sawako Nakayasu (Letter Machine Editions, November, 2009). Ogden Nash, "Reflection on a Wicked World" (Little Brown & Company, 1940). Marilyn Nelson, "Chosen" from *The Homeplace* (Baton Rouge: Louisiana State University Press, 1990). Pablo Neruda, "Ode to the Onion," translated by Ken Norris. Naomi Shihab Nye, "Blood" from *Words Under the Words: Selected Poems* (Portland Oregon: Far Corner Books, 1995). By permission of the author, Naomi Shihab Nye, 2009.

O

Mendi [Lewis] Obadike, "Contagion" from *Armor and Flesh* (Detroit: The Lotus Press, 2004). Adrian Oktenberg, poem ["Darling, your face is turning white/becoming featureless an untracked field of snow"] from *The Bosnian Elegies* [11 lines] (Ashfield, MA: Paris Press, 1997). Sharon Olds, excerpt [9 lines] from "I Go Back to May 1937" from *The Gold Cell* by Sharon Olds, copyright © 1987 by Sharon Olds. Used by permission of Alfred A. Knopf, a division of Random House, Inc.

P

Dorothy Parker, "Verse for a Certain Dog," "Fighting Words," from *The Portable Dorothy Parker* by Dorothy Parker, edited by Marion Meade, copyright © 1928, renewed copyright © 1956 by Dorothy Parker. Used by permission of Viking Penguin, a division of Penguin Group (USA) Inc.

R

Joan Retallack, "AIDS/DI/SAPPEARANCE" from *How To Do Things With Words* (Los Angeles: Sun & Moon Press, 1998). Adrienne Rich, "Tonight no Poetry Will Serve" from *The Nation* (May 28, 2008). Adrienne Rich, "In Those Years." Copyright © 2002, 1995 by Adrienne Rich, from *The Fact of A Doorframe: Selected Poems 1950–2001* by Adrienne Rich. Used by permission of the author and W.W. Norton & Company, Inc. I. A

Richards, "Dismission" from *New & Selected Poems* (Manchester, Carcanet Press, 1978). Rainer Maria Rilke, "I Praise." Translated by Denise Levertov, from *Light Up The Cave,* copyright © 1981 by New Directions Publishing Corp. Reprinted with permission of New Directions Publishing Corp. Theodore Roethke, "Open House," copyright © 1941 by Theodore Roethke, "My Papa's Waltz," copyright © 1942 by Hearst Magazines, Inc., "Four for Sir John Davies," copyright 1953 by Theodore Roethke, from *Collected Poems of Theodore Roethke* by Theodore Roethke. Used by permission of Doubleday, a division of Random House, Inc. Michael Ryan, "Milk and Mouse" from *New and Selected Poems by Michael Ryan.* Copyright © Michael Ryan. Reprinted by permission of Houghton Mifflin Harcourt Publishing Company. All rights reserved.

S

Sonia Sanchez, "Song No. 2" from *Under a Soprano Sky* (Trenton: Africa World Press, 1987). Aram Saroyan, three-word poem ["cat/book/city"] from *Complete Minimal Poems* (Brooklyn: Ugly Duckling, 2007). Aaron Shurin, ["If the judgement's cruel"] from *Involuntary Lyrics* (Omnidawn, 2005). Maura del Serra, "Emily Dickinson," translated by Michael Palma, from *Infinite Present: Selected Poems.* Emanuel Di Pasquale and Michael Palma, trans. (Boca Raton, Fla.: Bordighera Press, 2002). Patricia Smith, "The Reemergence of the Noose" from *Ashville Poetry Review* (2008): 159. Kate Sontage, excerpt (23 lines) from "Making Step Beautiful in Maine" from *Are You Experienced?: Baby Boom Poets at Midlife,* Ed. Pamela Gemin (University of Iowa Press, 2003). Gary Soto, "A Red Palm" from *New and Selected Poems* (San Francisco: Chronicle Books, 1995). A. E. Stallings, "Arachne Gives Thanks to Athena" from *Beloit Poetry Journal 46,* no. 2 (Winter 1995–1996). A. E. Stallings, "Triolet on a Line Apocraphally Attributed to Martin Luther" from *Poetry* (April 2005). Sue Standing, excerpt [3 lines] from "Waking Up in the Swamp" from *Gravida* (Marshfield, Mass.: Four Way Books, 1995). George Starbuck, "Fable for Blackboard" from *Bone Thoughts* (Yale University Press, 1960). Wallace Stevens, "The Comedian as the Letter C: from *The Collected Poems of Wallace Stevens* (New York: Alfred A. Knopf, 1982). Cole Swensen, excerpt [12 lines] from "June 2" from *Such Rich Hour* (Iowa City: University of Iowa Press, 2001). May Swenson, "Bleeding." Reprinted with the permission of the Literary Estate of May Swenson. May Swenson, "Motherhood." Reprinted with the permission of The Literary Estate of May Swenson.

T

Genevieve Taggard, "At Last the Women are Moving" from *Collected Poems 1918–1938* (New York: Harper & Row, 1938). Reprinted with the permission of Judith Benét Richardson. Henry Taylor, "Paradelle: nocturne de la Ville." Jean Toomer, "Portrait in Georgia," from *Cane* by Jane Toomer. Copyright © 1923 by Boni & Liveright, copyright © renewed 1951 by Jean Toomer. Used by permission of Liveright Publishing Corporation. Quincy Troupe, excerpt [35 lines] from "Poem for Friends" from *Transcircularities: New and Selected Poems* (Minneapolis: Coffee House Press). Natasha Trethewey, "Graveyard Blues" from *Native Guard: Poems by Natasha Trethewey.* Copyright © 2006 by

Natasha Trethewey. Reprinted by permission of Houghton Mifflin Harcourt Publishing Company. Marina Tsvetaeva, excerpt [11 lines] from "Desk," translated by Elaine Feinstein, from *Selected Poems* (New York: Penguin, 1993). Malka Heifetz Tussman, "Last Apple" from *The Penguin Book of Modern Yiddish Verse* by Irving Howe, Ruth R. Wisse, and Khone Shmeruk, copyright © 1987 by Irving Howe, Ruth Wisse, and Khone Shmeruk. Used by permission of Viking Penguin, a division of Penguin Group (USA) Inc.

V

Karen Volkman, "Say Sad" (ms title: "Sonnet") from *Nomina* (Rochester: BOA Editions, 2008).

W

Dan Waber, "Ars Poetica" [two-line poem]. Derek Walcott, excerpt [9 lines] from "The Bounty" from *The Bounty* (New York: Farrar, Straus & Giroux, 2006). Derek Walcott, excerpt "Love After Love" from *Collected Poems 1948–1984* (New York: Farrar, Straus & Giroux, 1986). Rosemarie Waldrop, "Signatures of Doctrine" from *Pom2* (Brooklyn: PomPomPress, 2002). Barrett Watten, excerpt (10 lines) from "Plasma" from *Frame (1971–1990)* (Los Angeles: Sun & Moon, 1997). Williams Carlos Williams, "Nantucket" and "To a Poor Old Woman" from *The Collected Poems of William Carlos Williams, Volume 1, 1909–1939,* edited by Christopher MacGowan (New York: New Directions Publishing Corporation, 1988).

Y

W. B. Yeats, excerpt [24 lines] from "The Death of Cuchulain" (verse play) (1939) from *Selected Poems and Four Plays,* edited by M. L. Rosenthal (New York: Scribner, 1996).

Z

Dan Zimmerman, excerpt [18 lines] from "Isotopes" (Frame Publications).

Index